MW00345455

REASON AND THE
REASONS OF FAITH

THEOLOGY FOR THE TWENTY-FIRST CENTURY
CENTER OF THEOLOGICAL INQUIRY

Theology for the Twenty-first Century is a series sponsored by the Center of Theological Inquiry (CTI), an institute, located in Princeton, New Jersey, dedicated to the advanced study of theology. This series is one of its many initiatives and projects.

The goal of the series is to publish inquiries of contemporary scholars into the nature of the Christian faith and its witness and practice in the church, society, and culture. The series will include investigations into the uniqueness of the Christian faith. But it will also offer studies that relate the Christian faith to the major cultural, social, and practical issues of our time.

Monographs and symposia will result from research by scholars in residence at the Center of Theological Inquiry or otherwise associated with it. In some cases, publications will come from group research projects sponsored by CTI. It is our intention that the books selected for this series will constitute a major contribution to renewing theology in its service to church and society.

WALLACE M. ALSTON, JR., ROBERT JENSON, AND DON S. BROWNING
SERIES EDITORS

What Dare We Hope?
by Gerhard Sauter

The End of the World and the Ends of God
edited by John Polkinghorne and Michael Welker

God and Globalization, Volume 1:
Religion and the Powers of the Common Life
edited by Max L. Stackhouse with Peter J. Paris

God and Globalization, Volume 2:
The Spirit and the Modern Authorities
edited by Max L. Stackhouse with Don S. Browning

God and Globalization, Volume 3:
Christ and the Dominions of Civilization
edited by Max L. Stackhouse with Diane B. Obenchain

Redemptive Change:
Atonement and the Christian Cure of the Soul
by R. R. Reno

King, Priest, and Prophet:
A Trinitarian Theology of Atonement
by Robert Sherman

In Search of the Common Good
edited by Patrick D. Miller, Jr., and Dennis McCann

Reason and the Reasons of Faith
edited by Paul J. Griffiths and Reinhard Hütter

REASON AND THE REASONS OF FAITH

Edited by
Paul J. Griffiths and Reinhard Hütter

t&t clark

NEW YORK • LONDON

T & T Clark International
Madison Square Park, 15 East 26th Street, New York, NY 10010

T & T Clark International
The Tower Building, 11 York Road, London SE1 7NX

T & T Clark International is a Continuum imprint.

Unless otherwise indicated, biblical quotations are from the New Revised Standard Version of the Bible, copyright 1989, Division of Christian Education of the National Council of the Churches of Christ in the United States of America. Used by permission. All rights reserved.

Cover art: Benozzo Gozzoli (1420–1497). The Triumph of Saint Thomas Aquinas. Painted for the cathedral of Pisa. Louvre, Paris, France. Copyright Erich Lessing/Art Resource, NY

Cover design: Wesley Hoke

Library of Congress Cataloging-in-Publication Data

Reason and the reasons of faith / edited by Paul J. Griffiths and Reinhard Hütter.
    p. cm. — (Theology for the twenty-first century)
 Includes bibliographical references and indexes.
 ISBN 0-567-02830-5 (hardcover)
 1. Faith and reason—History of doctrines—21st century. I. Griffiths, Paul J. II. Hütter, Reinhard, 1958- III. Series.
 BT50.R43 2005
 231'.042—dc22
                                                2004021993

Printed in the United States of America

05 06 07 08 09 10   10 9 8 7 6 5 4 3 2 1

To Colin Gunton:
requiescat in pace

CONTENTS

PART THREE
Situating Reason Theologically: Reason in the Passage of Modernity

PART FOUR
Readings of Reason after *Fides et Ratio*: Why Philosophy Matters for Theology

ACKNOWLEDGMENTS

The essays that make up this book are the product of six three-day meetings held between December 2000 and May 2003 at the Center of Theological Inquiry in Princeton, New Jersey. Our first and most fundamental debts are to that institution, whose director, Wallace Alston, and staff, especially Kathi Morley and Marion Gibson, made our meetings materially possible and deeply pleasurable. Robert W. Jenson, the Center's theologian-in-residence, provided intellectual leadership and sound advice from beginning to end, and was also a full participant in our discussions.

We have also had essential help, financial and practical, from our home institutions. At Duke University we gratefully acknowledge the support provided by the Divinity School, and especially by Anne Weston, without whose editorial skills the book would be much worse than it is. And at the University of Illinois in Chicago we are pleased to thank the College of Liberal Arts and Sciences, the Program in Catholic Studies, and especially Cherrie Gottsleben for her help in checking references and preparing the index.

We must also thank our contributors, whose work can be read in these pages. Their patience, energy, and willingness to take theological and philosophical differences seriously within the context of Christian faith have instructed us, and we are grateful for it. Their time, energy, thoughts, and words are an act of service to the body of Christ.

Paul J. Griffiths
Reinhard Hütter
Feast of the Annunciation 2004

Introduction

— Paul J. Griffiths and Reinhard Hütter —

The Project

Faith and reason are presently in crisis. This judgment, albeit controversial, constitutes the inner motor of this project. The central danger of this crisis does not so much consist in the denial as in the banalization of God, whether as a fundamentally irrational claim of faith or at best as a purely regulative idea of reason. However, offering an account of the hope that is in us (1 Pet 3:15), and hence of the faith that gives rise to hope, requires on the part of Christian theology a rigorous intellectual effort, in short, the unfettered use of reason for the sake of faith in the God who is always greater than anything that can be thought. The point of such rigorous intellectual effort is not to offer a theological legitimization of reason as such, but rather to put reason to work theologically so that it comes genuinely to itself in realizing that God is and remains greater than anything that can be thought. Moreover, recognizing the limits and weaknesses of reason is possible only from a vantage point that deepens, broadens, and at the same time questions reason's horizon. Such a deepening, broadening, and questioning, however, always and only occurs reasonably, that is, through reason's own action.

Reasoning as the way by which reality is comprehensively disclosed and the reasons of faith are accounted for, however, has fallen onto hard times in church and theology. This is the crisis of reason in faith. The rigor of sustained inquiry and argumentation and the art of *quaestio* and dialectic have been replaced with primarily rhetorical strategies and the overall concern for practical applicability. While questions of attractiveness and persuasiveness are good and important, and play a significant role in the work of Augustine and the Cappadocian Fathers, they have come to be seen as alternatives to rigorous inquiry and argumentation. This is not a choice that would have made sense to the Fathers. In the contemporary context, in which the unity

1

of the transcendentals is no longer acknowledged, attractiveness and truth become exclusive alternatives and, in consequence, everything becomes reducible to incommensurable and hence conflicting interests such that the question of truth is transformed into the question of power. Having forsaken the power of truth, much contemporary theology has fallen under the spell of the truth of power.

Philosophy has not fared any better. With the significant exception of analytic philosophy, skeptical, relativist, and reductionist trends dominate wide sections of the contemporary philosophical discourse. This is the crisis of faith in reason. Much of philosophy has abandoned reason's capacity to disclose reality, and the hard sciences and technology have succeeded in subjugating much of our reality to the instrumental logic of technocratic reasoning. One result is that virtuality and reality are becoming harder to differentiate. The advances of technocratic reason in neurology, artificial intelligence, and cybernetics support the idea that reason is an epiphenomenon of extremely complex neural processes, fully explicable and fully controllable in light of these processes.

In the middle of these crises of faith in reason and reason in faith, Pope John Paul II issued the encyclical *Fides et Ratio* in 1998.[1] This document encourages reconsideration and reclamation of reason's capacity to apprehend reality, to judge and delineate its own limits, and to make an essential contribution to theology's task. The pope argues that in order to perform their task of interpreting, clarifying, and ordering the data of the tradition, theologians need not only conceptual precision and analytic skill but also a reliably realist philosophy. *Fides et Ratio* also depicts a deep intimacy between faith and reason, so deep that a crisis of reason is inevitably also a crisis of faith, and an encouragement of reason always also an encouragement of faith. And it engages some of the currents of thought in late modernity and early postmodernity that have cast suspicion upon reason's capacities to arrive at knowledge.

Prompted in part by the encyclical's promulgation, and in part by a more general sense that the question of faith and reason was ripe for reconsideration, a group of systematic theologians from Europe, the United States, and Asia met regularly twice a year over a period of three years at the Center of Theological Inquiry in Princeton, New Jersey, to discuss the state of the question. At the last meeting, we invited an internationally renowned philosopher in order to engage our findings and theses. The group represented Eastern Orthodox, Roman Catholic, Anglican, Lutheran, and Reformed voices. It

---

1. The encyclical letter was promulgated at Rome on 14 September 1998. The text may be found in its official Latin and in eight other languages (including English) through the Vatican's Web site: http://www.vatican.va. See also Laurence Paul Hemming and Susan Frank Parsons, ed., *Restoring Faith in Reason: A New Translation of the Encyclical Letter 'Faith and Reason' of Pope John Paul II* (Notre Dame, IN: University of Notre Dame Press, 2003). There is by now a considerable interpretive literature on the encyclical, among which we note: David Ruel Foster and Joseph W. Koterski, ed., *The Two Wings of Catholic Thought: Essays on* Fides et Ratio (Washington, DC: Catholic University of America Press, 2003); Timothy L. Smith, ed., *Faith and Reason: The Notre Dame Symposium 1999* (Chicago: St. Augustine's Press, 2001); Kevin Hart, "Fides et Ratio et . . . ," *American Catholic Philosophical Quarterly* 76, no. 2 (2002): 199–220.

was by no means homogeneous in its convictions about theological method and in its philosophical preferences, though the differences on these matters did not always follow denominational lines. This denominational and theoretical diversity provided an ideal starting point for a rigorous ecumenical inquiry into the challenge that the contemporary crisis of faith and reason poses and, more importantly, into the resources that the reasons of faith offer for constructively addressing the crisis of faith and reason.

In short, the program of the present volume is to inquire into the reasons of faith in order to offer theological resources to constructively address the double crisis of faith in reason and reason in faith. We inquire, first, into the theological constitution of reason; second, into reason as one specific faculty of the human being; third, into the significance of the philosophical shifts of modernity for theology; and fourth, into the importance of philosophy for theological inquiry.

However, being broadly in agreement with the encyclical *Fides et Ratio* about the crisis in which reason finds itself in late modernity does not entail that all contributors to this volume agree with the descriptive and prescriptive claims of the encyclical. What is more, this project does not claim to overcome this double crisis in one single collective effort. While some academics might think or wish it, the world cannot be saved in one sabbatical. Instead of any premature gestures of saving faith and reason, our intention is—after *Fides et Ratio*—to bring to the fore reason's distinct theological contours. For this it is necessary to remember intensively central aspects of the theological tradition as well as the philosophical past, to discern carefully the contemporary challenges for faith and reason in philosophy and science, and to articulate and address actively some of the substantial theological divergences between Catholics and Protestants in addressing these questions and consequently in (mis)understanding each other. The desert fathers, Gregory of Nyssa, Augustine, Aquinas, Scotus, Luther, Calvin, Kierkegaard, and Barth, are the theological voices drawn upon most often by contributors to the volume. Modern philosophical voices such as Hume, Locke, Kant, Nietzsche, Wittgenstein, Heidegger, as well as contemporary analytic philosophy, are also engaged in various ways and to varying degrees. What came as a surprise to the group as a whole is the important role that Thomas Aquinas takes in the essays of quite a number of contributors, two of whom are not Roman Catholic—again a surprising and hopeful ecumenical phenomenon.

Faith and Reason Related and Distinguished

"Faith" and "reason" are English nouns with roots in Latin (*fides, ratio*), and, through Latin, also in Greek (*pistis, logos*, and other terms). They became part of the English lexicon largely because of Christianity, and as a result users of English have most often taken the Christian senses of these terms as primary. This is true even when Christianity is not understood or is rejected. As with so many other words, ordinary English usage of these terms can hardly avoid being explicitly Christian, and even when it manages this it remains implicitly so. Christian thought and talk crouches always at the door for speakers of European languages; it waits to spring upon the unwary and to conform secular semantics and syntax to its own.

Christian use and understanding of these terms, separately and in conjunction, is however far from clear or uncontested. To say that ordinary English usage is fundamentally Christian is therefore not yet to say much. Saying more awaits an account of at least the lineaments of a properly and fully Christian semantics and syntax of faith and reason. This is what we offer in the brief lexical account that follows, by way of prolegomenon to the detailed arguments of each essay. We intend to sketch a specifically Christian mode of thinking and talking about faith and reason. We do not, however, claim that every element in this sketch is uniquely Christian. Many inform Jewish and Islamic thought and talk about faith and reason; some, too, are evident in patterns of discourse developed by those without historical connection to Christian thought, and by those whose only relation to Christianity is one of explicit, root-and-branch rejection. But these matters are not our concern. We want, to begin with, only to indicate the most basic structural features of Christian thought and talk about faith and reason and to suggest points of divergence and dispute within the Christian account. What we provide will necessarily be stipulative, ahistorical, and highly schematic. It will receive historical and conceptual nuance in the essays that make up the body of the volume.

To begin, reason is a property or quality possessed by human beings. It is, however, not only we human beings who have reason and who as a result are (at least sometimes) rational. It is fundamental to Christian orthodoxy to say that God, too, is rational—the second person of the Holy Trinity is the *logos*, the very principle of all reason—and that we are rational (to the extent that we are) only because we have been created in the image of the Holy Trinity and thus participate in God's *ratio*. Talk of human reason and reasonability cannot, therefore, be finally divorced from talk of God as principle of all reason—this is a basic syntactic rule the violation of which rejects orthodoxy. Within obedience to this rule, there are many different ways to speak of the relation between God's reason and ours, and there is no broad agreement among Christians about the best language for this purpose. The rule, though, remains constant.

God gives reason to those who have it, and God has not chosen to give it only to us. There is also a rational angelic order, witnessed to in Scripture and much discussed by tradition. Angelic reason is not in every way like human reason; it too is what it is by participation in divine reason, but its mode of participation (to choose one among the disputed vocabularies for analyzing the relation between divine and nondivine reason) differs from the human mode of participation. The nature of the difference will not further concern us here.

Christians have mostly thought that only angels and humans among created things are possessors of reason. There are scriptural and Aristotelian reasons for this restriction: The creation accounts in Genesis are sometimes read to entail it, and Aristotle's specification of the possession of reason as the differentiating characteristic of the species "human" entered so deeply into the soul of the Latin Christian West (matters are a little different in the Greek Christian East) that the restriction was often assumed as obvious. It is not, however, quite as obvious as it may seem, and while the question of whether there are rational creatures other than angels and humans is an interesting one, we shall assume no answer to it in the remarks that follow.

Reason, then, is a property given by God and possessed by us in virtue of our status as creatures of and participants in God. It is not, however, possessed by all of us identically, nor by any one of us always in the same way and to the same intensity. The child in the womb, the forty-five-year-old, and the centenarian are not all equally reasonable. The person with severe brain damage or the sufferer from a degenerative disorder such as Alzheimer's are not as reasonable (do not possess reason) with the same intensity as is the mathematician constructing a proof of a difficult theorem or the quarterback coordinating a difficult play under pressure. There are—it seems at first blush right to say—human beings who live their lives without ever using reason; such might be exceedingly short-lived people, those who die before birth or live only a very short time after it. And there are people who live much of their lives being reasonable at high intensity. And, of course, there are people at every point between these two extremes. Therefore, although Christians are constrained to say that it is proper (definitional of or essential) to humans to be reasonable, to have reason, we must also say that we are not all reasonable to the same extent or in the same way.

This creates some difficulties. A traditional and attractive solution is to say that what all humans have is a disposition or capacity to be reasonable in the right circumstances. But since none of us is always in the circumstances that make reason's use possible (we are all sometimes unconscious or dazed by desire or paralyzed by fear), and some of us never are in this life (we may not have bodies such as to permit it, perhaps, or our environment might completely prevent our disposition from becoming active), it follows that none of us is always reasonable and some of us never are. At least this follows if by "being reasonable" we mean actualizing a disposition, bringing it from potency to act. But saying this is perfectly compatible with saying that all human beings are created with a disposition to be reasonable. It is a disputed question whether the disposition to reason is given identically in each case, but this we shall not pursue.

The Christian syntax of reason suggested so far, then, is that reason is a dispositional property given by God to all of us, though not necessarily given identically to each of us. Other creatures also have this disposition, and all creatures who have it to any degree possess it only by way of participation in God and as a creative gift of God—though, again, the mode of participation need not be identical, either within or across species. This syntax prevents thought or talk of human reason being thought or talk about humans only.

The idea that human reason is self-creating, or self-founding,[2] and the quest for radical autonomy in matters of reason are ruled out by the syntax of Christian thought about reason.

What does this dispositional property dispose us to do? So far, we have spoken syntactically and so also mostly formally. Now we must turn to a Christian semantics of reason, and in offering that we will have to descend some way from the heights of abstraction required by syntactic analysis. Speaking semantically then, reason disposes those who have it to engage in particular kinds of activity when circumstance permits and encourages. These activities are operations of thought, which is to say at least that they are not constitutively or exhaustively physical operations. Most typically, the reasoner constructs arguments and forms judgments, both of which are activities aimed at understanding. The judgment (*Peter is a good man; Jerusalem is in Israel; genocide is an unacceptable instrument of foreign policy*) makes a claim about the order of things. When the judgment is true, or adequate, what is claimed by it conforms the mind to that God-given order; when the judgment is false, or inadequate, it turns the mind from reality and toward a fabricated simulacrum of the real. The act of judgment as just described may be encapsulated by the Augustinian (and also Thomist) slogan *cum assentione cogitare*, 'to think with assent.' Argument is an additional and different mental operation; it may provide justification for or elucidation of a judgment. Whichever of these it does, however, it too is aimed at understanding (and sometimes also at depicting) the order of things.

The vocabulary used in the preceding paragraph is not the only one available to or properly usable by a Christian semantics of reason. But the central elements in what is said in that vocabulary are proper to such a semantics. The judgments and arguments offered by reasoners are, in Christian understanding, always responsive to something given from without; what they elucidate and claim is never only themselves (as it would be in most forms of idealism), and so a Christian semantics of reason must always provide for a relation between the products of reasoning's work (the judgment and the argument) and what it is that these products are about. The relation of "aboutness" may be specified in a variety of vocabularies (adequation, intentionality, and so forth); the Christian tradition has been fecund in such vocabularies, as well as in lively theoretical debate about which of them is to be preferred. This is another area, then, in which creative disagreement among Christians is evident (some of it present in this volume). We note only that the absence of interest in and specification of the aboutness relation intrinsic to reasoning's proper products carries with it the absence of a characteristically Christian semantics of reason. The capacity to reason is a gift from without, rooted in creation; reasoning's characteristic interest is in understanding the character of that creation, and thus in coming to know how to respond rightly to it.

---

2. We have in mind here René Descartes's ambition "à reformer mes propres pensées et de bâtir dans un fonds qui est tout à moi," *Discours de la méthode* §2.3, ed. George Heffernan (Notre Dame, IN: University of Notre Dame Press, 1994), 30. From a Christian viewpoint, this is profoundly malformed talk.

Reasoners, then, offer judgments and arguments as truth-aimed and truth-conducive instruments of understanding. It is natural to human beings to do this, at least in the sense that our disposition to do it in the right circumstances is given to us by God in our very creation, and as a result belongs to our nature. A Christian semantics of reason, however, must go on to say that it is not natural to us to succeed in reasoning well in the same way that it is natural to us to reason at all. It is not merely that we are finite and fallible and that our reasoning disposition needs to be properly trained and exercised in order that we become able to reason well about many of the more complex aspects of the created order. (Consider probability theory or metaethics as examples of such complexities.) It is also that something has gone wrong with our reason: It is not what God intended it to be, and this means that we can unambiguously and straightforwardly trust our judgments neither about the order of things nor about the validity of the arguments we offer in support of those judgments. The reason that belonged to our first, prelapsarian nature is not the reason that belongs to our second nature, the one with which each of us is born after Adam and Eve's ejection from Eden.

A Christian description of reason, then, must begin by affirming that our reasoning acts can bring us to knowledge of the order of things as well as to a position from which we can argumentatively justify that knowledge. These are the principal properties of the gift of reason. But the confident assertion just made is not yet fully Christian; it must be placed under erasure by the assertion of reason's corruption by sin. "Erasure" here does not mean obliteration, removal without remainder; what is erased remains visible and active even though under erasure, much as sedimented limestone may be metamorphosed and turned on edge by the heat of volcanic eruption and yet still preserve visible traces of the regular layers of its original formation. Or it is like the writing erased from a piece of parchment when it is washed in preparation for reuse; such erased writing is nonetheless visible to the trained eye even when it has been overwritten by something new. Christian confidence in reason is always in these ways confidence-under-erasure; anything less (confidence alone, erasure alone) is not and cannot be fully Christian. Christian reasoning about reason (such as that undertaken in this volume) can appropriately be likened to the trace left upon a palimpsest attempting to discern its own track.

Saying this does not, of course, yield a single position on the vexed question of how much confidence in reason remains or should remain. Christian opinion is arranged along a broad spectrum on this question, with some expressing a deep suspicion of almost all reason's assertions, and others claiming that reason's capacity to know the order of things and to argue for that knowledge has been impaired only in minor and insignificant ways and that suspicion should not, therefore, go very far. But all agree that our capacities to know without error and to argue without fallacy are not what they might have been, not what we would like them to be, and not what we are likely to think them. The possibilities for self-delusion on this matter are many.

Reason and reasoning, as so far sketched, are capacious categories. Judgments and arguments may be made about many different things (carpentry, navigation, mathematics, politics, aesthetics, metaphysics), and reasoning in these varied spheres proceeds from different (and sometimes incompatible) assumptions about how good judgments and arguments are to be distinguished from bad, and about which sources may properly be appealed to as authoritative. This is neither surprising nor problematic; it accounts for the fact that reason has often been sorted into subkinds: practical reason, theoretical reason, and so on. The disposition to reason is best understood as a class-category, a genus with many species, just as is the disposition to use language: There are no speakers of language but only speakers of French, German, English, Japanese, and so on; similarly, there are no reasoners, but only philosophers, mathematicians, carpenters, political theorists, and so on. This is too often forgotten, and we shall have to return to the point below when we come to consider the relations between faith and reason.

Reasoners who do not share the chastened confidence in reason required of Christians will typically misunderstand their own capacity to reason and will be either overconfident in the judgments and arguments they make, or they will despair of reasoning and abandon themselves without remainder to the sirens of *libido* and *superbia*, permitting these to proliferate unchecked. When reason does not misprize itself in these ways, it will come to argue dispassionately and lucidly for the inevitability of its own failures, though not for their universality. The extent to which a reasoner's view of reason diverges from a properly Christian view of reason can be discerned by the extent to which it approaches overconfidence or despair. Christian thought about reason occupies a middle ground between these two extremes, which is to say that Christians can be neither rationalist nor fideist.

So much for reason. About the semantics and syntax of faith we can be briefer, for many of the same fundamental points must be made about it as were made about reason. Faith too is a human property, shared (if at all) only with angels among creatures (but it is probably better to say that angels do not need faith because they have direct awareness of God, and not, as we do, awareness *per speculum in aenigmate*). It too is a gift freely given, having God as both its origin and its point of proper return. But here matters begin to diverge.

Reason, we have said, is in some sense natural to us. The disposition to come to make true judgments about the nature of things and to offer valid arguments in support of those judgments is inscribed upon us, much as is the disposition to become a user of language or a walker upon two legs. But, some Christians have wanted to say, faith is not like that. Its absence does not call our nature as human into question, and its presence or absence, as a result, should not be attributed to nature but rather to grace, an unmerited gift inscrutably given to some and withheld from others. It is a pattern of thought like this that leads to talk of reason as natural and faith as supernatural, or to faith as one among the theological virtues. This understanding of faith presupposes the view that God has created some without the disposition or capacity for faith. Some Christians do accept this view, and only they can say that the disposition for faith is not natural to each of us, not given to each of us with our human nature as human beings.

For others, the syntax of Christian talk about faith does not distinguish it from reason by saying that the latter is natural to us and the former is not. It distinguishes them, instead, at the semantic level, by addressing the question of the conditions under which each can become active. Faith and reason, as dispositions, are equally natural, equally universal; but they are substantively different and, for reasons that will become apparent, there are fewer people of faith than there are reasonable people.

But faith, whether as disposition or action, is never for Christians merely a matter of assent to truths. It is also a disposition to trust and the activity of trusting. The object of this trust is paradigmatically a person (God, as Father, Son, and Spirit), but derivatively also a testimony (Scripture and its authoritative interpretation), an institution (the church, which is Christ's body), and individual members of that body (other Christians). Faith understood in this way is not principally cognitive, but rather constitutive of a relation that could not otherwise be entered into. This aspect of faith became constitutive of the Reformation tradition such that faith has an intellectual as well as an affective component: assent to truth and trust in God's promises.

Semantically, then, Christians say that faith is like reason in that it is a disposition that, when active, produces assent to claims or judgments about the order of things. (This is not all it does, but for the purpose of differentiation from reason it is what we will begin with.) But faith comes to make the acts of assent it makes by accepting as authoritative a testimony that comes from outside itself. The testimony in question is quite specific: It is the testimony of Scripture and the authoritative tradition of its interpretation by the church. To understand faith in this way, of course, is to limit it to Christians. Jews and Muslims may also have faith to the extent that they take as authoritative the same scriptural witness (to what extent that is so is a question on which we offer here no opinion); but others cannot have it because they do not treat as authoritative the particular testimony that Christians do. It is, then, we suggest, characteristic of Christian talk about faith to speak of it as a virtue peculiar to Christians—which of course says nothing about the possible salvation of non-Christians, nor about other virtues they may have. If faith is a universal disposition that becomes active only in response to a particular testimony, then those who possess it will of necessity be related explicitly and knowingly to just that testimony and to no other.

Christians differ among themselves, of course, as to the relative weight that ought to be given to the two variables mentioned—to Scripture and to the authoritative tradition of its interpretation by the church—as also about the boundaries to be drawn around each. But all Christians do and must give some weight to each. It is, then, by coming to take just this testimony as authoritative and only by so coming that Christians are able to make some of the most characteristically and distinctively Christian claims: that God is triune, that Jesus Christ was God incarnate who died to redeem us from sin, that he was born of a virginal woman, and so on. This is faith's cognitive aspect: It is a disposition to take as authoritative a particular testimony, and to come to knowledge about the order of things (including especially knowledge of God) that could not otherwise be known by human beings.

This account provides one way of distinguishing faith from reason. Faith does something that reason does not do, and as a result it comes to know things that reason cannot, by itself, know. It is also true that reason permits us to know things that faith cannot bring us to know: Taking as authoritative the testimony of Scripture and its interpretation by the church will not help you much with Fermat's last theorem or with the four-color problem; it will also not help you to figure out how to fix your car. And, it would appear, there are many things that can be known both by faith and by reason. Arguably, the truth that there is a nature possessed by human beings is one among these; perhaps too the truth that there is one God, maker of heaven and earth, is of the same sort.

There have always been and will no doubt continue to be disputes among Christians as to whether some particular truths belong to the set of those knowable only by faith, those knowable only by reason, or those knowable by both. The syntax of Christian talk inevitably generates such difficulties (a nice case is provided by the claim *Scripture under the tradition of its interpretation by the church is cognitively authoritative*—is this known by faith, by reason, or potentially by either?), and there is no algorithm for their resolution that does not deploy commitments on other, equally controversial topics. We have intended so far to emphasize only one of the constraints upon explicitly Christian talk of faith in relation to reason: that the former brings those who have it to knowledge they could not have gained by way of the latter only—and, typically, to knowledge that can only be elucidated, not justified, by argumentative reason.

The Christian syntax of faith has been influenced by a contingent but interesting fact about the Greek and Latin languages: Greek has both noun (*pistis*) and verb (*pisteuō*) forms derived from the same stem, which makes it natural enough in Greek to think of faith both as something possessed (*pistis*)—a dispositional or occurrent property—and as something done (*pisteuō*), an action undertaken. But in Latin this is not so. The noun *fides*, the standard translation of *pistis* in Scripture and in ordinary Christian writing, has no corresponding verb. The ordinary solution is to use *credo* for the verbal forms; so, typically, the church's symbols of faith (creeds) begin in Greek with *pisteuō* (or *pisteuomen*), thus showing even in the form of the word that what follows is the content or object of an act of *pistis*. But this is obscured in Latin, in which the symbols begin with *credo* (or *credimus*). The same is true in English, where there is the noun "faith" but no active verb (except those formed with auxiliaries, such as "to have faith").[3] The first words of an English confession of faith then become "I (or 'We') believe . . ." rather than

---

3. German, however, functions in this matter like Greek, having both noun (*der Glaube*) and verb (*glauben*) forms derived from the same stem, so that in German faith is also thought of as something possessed (*der Glaube*) and something done (*glauben*).

"I/We have faith . . ." This has led to a fairly deep distinction in ordinary English usage between an act of faith and an act of belief, one not directly or obviously warranted by the syntax of Christian talk itself. A properly Christian syntax and semantics of faith recognizes that faith enacted is, in its cognitive dimensions, an act of assent not to be formally distinguished from belief. The central function of the church's symbols is then to provide authoritative summations of what, cognitively speaking, faith provides the possibility (or, perhaps better, inevitability) of assent to. This explains, too, the common English locution, "the faith," as periphrasis for the content of what is assented to.

These are the lineaments of a fundamental Christian syntax and semantics of faith. Its nonnegotiable points are: that faith as disposition and action is sheer unmerited gift from God (which is also to be said of reason); that the disposition for faith becomes active more rarely and less reliably than many other human dispositions; that when it does become active, when a man or woman becomes a person of active rather than dispositional faith (explicit rather than implicit faith, if you prefer), knowledge is gained that could not otherwise be had; that such knowledge is derived in the first instance from trust in Scripture and the authoritative tradition of its interpretation; and that active faith involves (or is largely defined by) loving trust in God on the part of those who have it.

"Faith and reason" is a phrase that comes trippingly off the tongue in English, much as do "love and marriage" or "bread and butter." This has not always been so; the thought that properly relating faith to reason is a key task of Christian thought itself has a very peculiar (and relatively short) history, but it is so now. And like those of any fixed and half-frozen trope, the associations of and meanings suggested by the faith-and-reason pair are many and not always compatible one with another. Consider the love-and-marriage pair: Is it that marriage is love's proper culmination, that in which the love between a man and a woman find their proper end? Or is it that when love issues in marriage it vanishes beyond recall, suffocated by the strictures of convention and social form? Or is it that love and marriage have not much, really, to do with one another, and that the task of the thinker (and perhaps also the lover) is simply to disentangle the one from the other? All these connotations are abroad, no doubt, and a similar range is evident in the faith-and-reason pair. Our task here is only to provide the lineaments of Christian thought about these matters.

According to the sketch already given, faith is a kind or species of reason. This may seem counterintuitive, but if "reason" is a generic term for the disposition to make judgments and offer arguments about the order of things, and "faith" a term for the disposition to make such judgments in response to a particular testimony, then it follows at once that faith is a kind of reason. This is, moreover, an important point for Christians to make, for it immediately checks a tendency (on the part of Christians and non-Christians alike) to think of faith and reason as in some way opposed to one another. If faith is a kind of reason, this cannot be right.

But more can be said. We have suggested that reason is a genus with many species, which is to say that there are many ways to come to make judgments and offer arguments about the order of things. Each species of reason has its characteristic modes of procedure and its characteristic canonical authorities. Judicial reasoning in the United States, for example, has the U.S. Constitution as a canonical authority, together with the authoritative tradition of its interpretation. Mathematical reasoning, it might be said, deploys among its canonical authorities the proofs that a majority of mathematicians judge valid; mathematical reasoning then typically proceeds by assuming the validity of these proofs. Reasoning about such things as whether a particular painting is beautiful or a particular piece of music euphonious has its canons and methods too. Faith then takes its place as a species of reasoning among many others. Faith is to reason, we might say, as speaking English is to speaking a language or being a husky is to being a dog.

This is perhaps too obvious to need emphasis. But much writing about faith and reason (by Christians as well as non-Christians) ignores it and treats reason as one monolith and faith as another—and, moreover, as monoliths at the same level of abstraction. This, it seems to us, is a bad tactical move and one deeply inadequate to the facts of the matter. It leads often to futile and bad-tempered efforts to justify faith by contrasting it with something that does not exist—namely, reason, considered monolithically as a practice leading to the formation of beliefs on a level with faith. This can lead to all sorts of oddities: to the view, for example, that what distinguishes faith from reason is that (considered in its cognitive aspect) the former generates beliefs in response to testimony considered authoritative while the latter does not. This is not the case; many kinds of reasoning (perhaps most, perhaps even all, though this is not a question to be further explored here) generate beliefs in response to testimony considered authoritative. The testimony considered authoritative by faith is a different testimony than that considered authoritative by other forms of reasoning.

If this view of the relation between faith and reason is accepted, a number of Gordian knots are cut and a properly Christian view of the relations between faith and other kinds of reasoning follows quite straightforwardly.

The first element of such a view is that faith will never become the only kind of reasoning that Christians use or need; this should be sufficiently obvious from what has already been said. Christians do and should use many forms of theoretical and practical reasoning that do not proceed by way of explicit response to the testimony of Scripture and its authoritative interpretation.

The second element is that the deliverances of faith have, for Christians, certitude; they are irrefragably correct. This is among their defining characteristics. And this means that when a particular deliverance of faith conflicts with a belief generated by some other species of reason, Christians have only two options. The first is to reject the conflicting belief in favor of the deliverance of faith; the second is to judge that what seemed to be a deliverance of faith in fact was not, and thereby to make it possible to accept the conflicting belief. Christian history provides many examples of both responses, and that both are possible shows at least that it is not always easy for Christians to discern just what the deliverances of faith are, and that it is possible for decisions about this to be wrongly made. But none of this alters the fundamental procedural rule: When a deliverance of faith (a belief generated by the peculiar form of reasoning that is faith) conflicts with a belief generated by some other form of reasoning, the former trumps the latter.

The third element is that once the disposition for faith becomes active, it transfigures and reframes every other form of reasoning. Faith's deliverances have something to say about the deliverances of these other forms of reasoning that, first, they cannot say by or about themselves, and, second, they cannot say about faith's deliverances. To fully explore this would require an exercise in systematic theology quite beyond our scope here. It will have to suffice to say, telegraphically (elaboration of many of these points is found in most of the essays that constitute the body of this volume), that faith's deliverances include the following truths about all forms of reasoning, including itself: first, that none of them is self-founding but, rather, that each is a gift; second, that none of them is closed or self-sufficient or axiomatically complete, but, rather, that each generates paradox when it attempts to complete itself, and, thus, indicates the necessity of its completion by faith; third, that each and every exercise of reason is, when properly understood, itself an act of praise and worship to the fact of its own givenness, an act of joyful submission to its giver. This last is an essential part of what John Paul II meant in *Fides et Ratio* by saying that when philosophy responds to the gospel as Mary did to the angel Gabriel's announcement to her—by saying "May it be to me according to your word"—it finds its inquiries rising *ad summam perfectionem* (§108). This is true of all forms of reasoning.

We turn now, in light of this schematic analysis, to some particular comment on the essays provided by our contributors.

Approaching Reason Theologically

One result of approaching reason in a consistently theological way, which is to say by explicitly assuming and deploying the truth of the doctrinal content of the Christian faith, is that tacit and normative assumptions about reason that suggest faith to be inherently arational or even antirational can be unmasked. Approaching reason in this way also permits theology to become fully articulate in conceiving, understanding, and responding to the gift of reason. Every understanding and depiction of reason and reason's capacities is normatively configured by convictions that remain concealed until they are directly engaged. This is as true (but no more true) of a Christian understanding and depiction of reason as of any other. Approaching reason theologically, then, reveals by making explicit the normative horizon from within which reason is approached by Christians. This normative horizon is constituted doctrinally, which is to say by the reasons of faith, and the first five essays in this volume approach reason through the lens of particular Christian doctrines: revelation, the Trinity, Christ, and the cross.

Reason approached via a full account of revelation unmasks one central tenet of modern secular reason: criterial immanentism. This tenet becomes immediately evident when one maintains, as Alan J. Torrance does, "that it is a fundamental claim of Christian orthodoxy that the conditions for the recognition and affirmation of Christian truth are intrinsic to the event of revelation," for the question "Where and how does God speak?" is first and foremost a question about criteria. These criteria are not given, extrinsically, to the Christian faith; rather, they are intrinsic to God's self-communication and can only be accounted for by *logikon latreian* (Rom 12:2), the "rational and reverent participation in the mind of Christ, in the Son's epistemic and, indeed, semantic . . . communion with the Father." However, this understanding of how the criteria of revelation are themselves given by revelation—a consensus reaching from Ignatius and Athanasius to Kierkegaard and Barth—is challenged most fundamentally by the assumption that these criteria are inherent in human reason and only need to be tapped by turning to oneself in such a way that revelation collapses into a form of self-knowledge. Torrance notes that this is a timeless challenge with roots at least as old as Socrates, but his first detailed engagement is with a modern paradigmatic instantiation in the work of David Strauss. He shows how in the case of Strauss the notion of criterial immanentism, of submitting the Christian faith rigorously to the prior but unexamined givens of an Enlightenment rationality, preempts the normativity of the gospel and simultaneously renders the interpretive criteria applied and the self-understanding sustained via these criteria universal and absolute, that is, quasi-divine.

In a second step, Torrance demonstrates how Kierkegaard offers a most rigorous account of the intrinsic incoherence of the Socratic project, that is, criterial immanentism. As Kierkegaard shows, understanding the criteria of revelation entails a *metanoia*, "a re-creation for 'authentic existence' involving passionate, subjective commitment to a particular way of viewing and understanding the world." In order to show constructively what this *metanoia* entails, Torrance turns to Bonhoeffer and Barth as his primary interlocutors to establish theologically how the divine self-communication constitutes its own vestibule: christologically, by pointing to its substantive center in the concrete person of Christ; ecclesiologically, by identifying its specific location; pneumatologically, by accounting for its concrete occurrence; eschatologically, by acknowledging the provisional and time-bound nature of the forms of expression through which it is received.

In a final step, Torrance draws upon Alvin Plantinga's notion of "properly basic beliefs" (beliefs that do not require to be justified or accounted for with reference to other more basic beliefs or suppositions) in order to elucidate the common strand in Kierkegaard's, Bonhoeffer's, and Barth's lines of argument. This move allows him to return to the beginning by way of a double critique. First, he revisits criterial immanentism, this time in the form of Locke's highly influential evidentialism, that is, the notion of epistemic duty, the maxim that all beliefs must be based on evidence and that the firmness with which beliefs are held must be proportionate to the quality of the evidence for them. Second, he criticizes the assumption that there exist two separate sources of justified or warranted belief, one being faith, the other reason. As Torrance maintains, "Faith and reason and philosophy only operate in truth when they operate within an ecclesial context."

Bruce D. Marshall approaches the question of faith and reason by exploring the epistemic significance of faith in the Trinity. This approach is highly relevant for contemporary Christian theology because two conflicting claims are frequently put forth in recent discussions of faith and reason. One suggests that an adequate theological approach to the question of faith and reason has to be in a fundamental way Trinitarian, while a broad stream of traditional Christian reflection on faith and reason is opposed to this claim. Contemporary Christian thought on the Trinity seems to be caught between two apparently incompatible theses: (1) Reason cannot know the world aright unless the reasoner knows the Trinity; (2) whether reason knows the world aright has nothing to do with whether the reasoner knows the Trinity.

Drawing on Thomas Aquinas as his main interlocutor, but also on Duns Scotus and Johann Gerhard, and engaging Karl Rahner and Hans Urs von Balthasar, Marshall argues that these two claims do not pose a genuine dilemma, because both are false. At the same time, each of them departs from an important underlying Christian conviction that Marshall wants to affirm. In the course of his essay, he shows how the basic Christian claims behind each of these fallacies can be upheld without having to face the alleged dilemma between the claim that reason cannot know the world aright unless the reasoner knows the Trinity, and the claim that whether reason knows the world aright has nothing to do with whether the reasoner knows the Trinity. According to Marshall, belief in the Trinity has a precise negative epistemic significance in that it excludes as false all beliefs inconsistent with it. However, the epistemic significance of such belief is not limited to this function. Rather, by believing in the Trinity persons will come to hold many beliefs they would not otherwise reach; they may, for example, gradually come to see signs of the Trinity everywhere. Hence, Marshall concludes that the Christian conviction that this world bears the stamp of the Trinity all the way down should not be confused with the claim that the triune God can be known from his worldly vestiges, or that only the Trinity can account for the world we actually have.

Colin Gunton and Robert W. Jenson approach reason theologically by exploring a christological question rarely considered: "What follows for our understanding of reason from the fact that the universal Logos is the singular human person Jesus of Nazareth?" They proceed to argue that given the Christian grammar determined by the rules "Jesus is the eternal Logos" and "It is 'one and the same' who is born of Mary and born eternally in God," every reliable tracing of the Logos in things in general must conform to the story of Jesus' life, death, and resurrection. This is claimed in a conscious opposition to the abstract, disembodied notion of Logos in Greek philosophy and in German idealism. For Christians, God's wisdom is understood primarily as Jesus, the man on the cross, a mode of address from God to us. God's wisdom is, therefore, not truth abstracted from life but truth as and in life.

Hence, the proper reading of the Chalcedonian Christology leads to the insight that being rational—seeking and following the Logos in all things—is determined by the fact that the Father creates and upholds the world through a particular person, Jesus, who is his intelligible word of address. Consequently, theology must claim to be a universal discourse in the sense that any discourse must be irrational that cannot be interpreted to be rational by the church's discourse about Jesus the Christ. Moreover, it is the theological rationality inherent in the humanity of Christ, Gunton and Jenson aver, that led eventually to a belief that the structures of created being are imbued with meaning given it by its Creator, a belief that eventually gives rise to the natural sciences.

As Gunton and Jenson press the point, God's eternal Word is identical with the crucified Christ, and hence the wisdom of the cross is none other than God's eternal wisdom. For this reason, any theological inquiry into faith and reason would be seriously deficient if it were not to attend explicitly and extensively to the wisdom of the cross. Lois Malcolm and Mark McIntosh address this topic in their respective essays in different but complementary and mutually enriching ways.

By drawing constructively on the most recent exegetical literature, Malcolm first offers a close and comprehensive reading of 1 Cor 1–3, analyzing the kind of cognitive arguments Paul uses to show what the cross discloses about true wisdom and power, the very fecundity of God's wisdom present in the kenosis of the cross; hence her key notion of kenotic abundance. In a second step, she expounds the implications of her exegesis for an epistemology of the cross. Participating in Christ's life and death, Christ's kenotic abundance, entails a dying and rising with Christ, communally embodied and contextually enacted in the complex circumstances of discerning what is "good and acceptable and perfect" (Rom 12:2). The mode of perception enacted by the epistemology of the cross is fundamentally corporate and relational; it gives rise to a genuine hermeneutics of suspicion that undercuts egoistic and factional interests. In order to illustrate the contemporary relevance of Paul's epistemology of the cross, Malcolm enters into dialogue with Charles Taylor and Pierre Hadot, two philosophers who are equally critical of Cartesian epistemology and equally insistent upon the linguistic, existential, and communal constituents of human knowing and reasoning. The purpose of this dialogue is to help Christians, as they consider the relationship between faith and reason, not to get trapped into the lures of Cartesian epistemology but to remain faithful to the wisdom of the cross in its cognitive rationality and the kenotic abundance it enacts.

While Malcolm focuses on the Pauline corpus and draws from it immediate inferences for the contemporary theological discussion, Mark McIntosh mines the wisdom of the cross by asking how—as readers of Paul's letters— early Christian thinkers answered the question, "What does it mean to have the 'mind of Christ,' and how does the notion of 'having the mind of Christ' inform the dynamic of faith and reason?" By way of an exegesis of Evagrius Pontus, Diadochus, and Maximus Confessor, McIntosh explores a milieu in which faith and reason are considered in terms of the mind's healing from sin and partaking in Christ's mind. He argues that for these early Christian thinkers, the word of the cross functions as the authentic measure of discernment and gives rise to a twofold dynamic in faith. First, there is the ascetical dynamic of faith, setting reason free from self-serving and self-indulging illusions about others. Second, there is the mystical activity of faith, a disposing of the mind to understand all things by sharing the mind of Christ, sharing in the divine fullness from which all things come. The fulcrum of this twofold dynamic of faith is the word of the cross initiating and sustaining the painful as well as powerful transition to a new pattern of mind. By drawing on the wealth of Eastern Christian spirituality, McIntosh argues that "the 'mind of Christ' is not some kind of alien rationality that displaces native human reason, but is rather a pattern of rationality that is constantly held open by faith to the wideness of God's mercy," so that faith must ultimately be understood as human reason paying attention to God.

Assessing Reason Theologically—Reason's Proper Glories

Paul J. Griffiths, Reinhard Hütter, and Ernstpeter Maurer thematize reason's proper glories by assessing reason theologically. This approach frees them to identify reason's weakness in three respects: its errancy, its directedness, and its perplexity. Each pursues one of these respects by way of a theological interlocutor, one of the towering and tradition-forming voices of Western Christianity: Augustine, Aquinas, and Luther.

By way of an exegesis of Augustine, Griffiths offers a normative Christian account of how and why reasoning goes wrong. However, Griffiths is not just interested in addressing the question of reason's errors as a way of accounting for reasoning. Rather, he is primarily interested in critically addressing the contemporary problem of many Christians in overestimating the persuasive possibilities of reasoning with respect to theoretical questions. Griffiths regards and attacks as most problematic the "dream of appealing to natural law in order to provide a broadly persuasive ordering of common life in a late-modern democracy, for there, if anywhere, we move in the sphere of theory." This dream is dangerous because it not only seduces Christians into pretending that what they know is known by reason alone, but because this dream is just a dream insofar as it belies what makes it impossible to happen— namely, the puzzling and frequently occurring inability to recognize a true judgment as true and a valid argument as valid. By drawing upon Augustine, Griffiths argues that the occurrence of these kinds of errors in theoretical reason is due to catechetical inadequacy and volitional depravity. According to Griffiths, theoretical error is caused either by a lack of proper instruction in a particular area of complex theoretical discourse, or by the will being ruled by covetous desire, or both. If this explanation were indeed to obtain, any appeal by Christians in complex theoretical matters to "pure reason" or "reason alone" would only encourage and invite erroneous outcomes of such a debate. In short, Christians should never "speak a language from which explicitly Christian talk has been expunged . . . with the vain hope of increasing agreement about theoretical matters." Only a moderately pessimist and as such properly Christian account of reason's errors can prevent Christians from committing this optimist fallacy, deeply entrenched in modernity, of appealing to "reason alone" in matters of public dispute.

Hütter argues that Aquinas's account of the relationship between intellect and will offers a pertinent medicine for the late-modern vacillation between self-asserting instrumental reason on the one hand and epistemological skepticism and ontological nihilism on the other. Drawing upon Aquinas's analysis of the virtue of studiousness and the vice of curiosity, he argues that reasoning's directedness under the condition of sin yields a profound insight into the necessity of a redeemed judgment that in turn gives rise to a metaphysics of creation, for only the latter offers the necessary horizon to understand why curiosity is a vice and to direct the intellect's gaze to its proper object, the ultimate truth. He avers,

> The drama of misdirected reasoning is not that it simply fails and knows nothing. On the contrary, misdirected reasoning is distressingly and shockingly successful in its reductive focus on the creature. Here a metaphysics of creation offers a discursive witness and argumentative pressure by creating a coherently argued difference in judgment and thus provoking the kind of intellectual conflict and crisis that is necessary in order fully to appreciate what only grace followed by catechesis can give.

Maurer inquires into the distinction between sinful and redeemed reason. He does so by following a fundamental insight from Martin Luther's anthropology: Reason is unable to define itself and at the same time is always tempted to define itself. This deep perplexity about itself leads reason to repress those features about itself that point to fundamental antinomies in the structure of reason itself. By drawing on insights in recent mathematics and logic and in conversation with thinkers such as Cantor, Davidson, Putnam, Russell, Quine, and Wittgenstein, Maurer analyzes some of the most striking and puzzling structural problems of reason that went largely undiscovered until the twentieth century. Under the condition of sin, reason operates perfectly well but is distorted in its self-perception that expresses itself in the attempt at ultimate self-constitution. This self-constitution must repress any acknowledgment of its most surprising features, features that point to an irreducible and uncontrollable complexity in reason. Faith liberates reason not to new and unknown epistemic or discursive capacities but to a relaxed attitude (*Gelassenheit*) that allows reason to receive its complexity as an unfathomable unity instead of producing this unity via reduction. In short, according to Maurer, redeemed reason will appreciate and even enjoy its own complexity and unfathomableness as a created reality instead of claiming a false ultimacy and thus attempting to deny its dependence upon the Creator.

Situating Reason Theologically in the Passage of Modernity

The discussion of faith and reason becomes especially urgent in the passage of modernity, a passage greatly imperiled by three cliffs: immanence, univocity, and nihilism. Carver T. Yu, Janet Martin Soskice, and David Bentley Hart each take on the challenge of one of these cliffs by addressing the peril it constitutes and by identifying a course around it.

According to Yu, modern philosophy is haunted by the problem of immanence, for reason within a self-absorbing immanence is reason estranged from its true nature. However, Yu avers, estranged from its true nature, reason takes revenge by pointing out the groundlessness of autonomous reason and thus taking it to nihilism as its logical conclusion. At the center of Yu's argument stands a sustained critique of the metaphysics of immanence as expressed in Hume's immanence of consciousness and in Kant's lawmaking a priori structure of consciousness. Yu's sustained questioning of Hume's logic of immanence leads to the radical suggestion of turning Kant's Copernican revolution around: "Instead of consciousness constituting the world, it is the world that makes consciousness real and concrete." Yu's engagement of Kant takes the form of nature interrogating reason such that reason may take the guiding hand of nature in order to have the knowledge that is its due.

Yu shows that the self-critique of reason issues in the covenantal nature of reason: Because reason is for knowledge and knowledge is inherently relational, reason itself must be understood as inherently relational. In short, according to Yu, the pursuit of knowledge must be understood as a pursuit of communion such that to know something is to actuate communion with it. Hence, reason becomes real in functioning in the act of knowing as an act of covenantal response. Genuine understanding is dialogical, as the Chinese Dao expresses it—a thought that plays a central role in Martin Bieler's essay as well.

In what looks at first glance like a straightforward comparison of Thomas Aquinas and John Locke on naming God versus identifying divine attributes, Soskice undertakes a paradigmatic case study of how reasoned God-talk betrays reason's own pretensions—or not. Her case study demonstrates how a metaphysics operative under the condition of the univocity of being has to become a perfect-being metaphysics. Locke's God is like us in his qualities, only infinitely, or perfectly so—that is, God's qualities turn out to be infinitely more perfect than ours. Such a perfect-being metaphysics as Locke entertained in his strategy of divine attribution ends in a double termination—on the one side in Hume's radical skepticism and on the other in the self-referential cage of Kant's transcendental dialectic of pure reason.

Having thus situated the modern cul-de-sac of univocitism in reason's attempt to name God, Soskice returns to Aquinas's fundamental theological and metaphysical distinction between Creator and creature, a distinction hinging upon the doctrine of creation *ex nihilo* and correlatively upon the doctrine of divine simplicity. With this move, Soskice pushes open the door to the analogy of being, since yes, God "exists," yet the Creator cannot even be said to "exist" in the same way as the creature exists. Thus, by displaying Aquinas's theological strategy of naming God rather than predicating attributes of him, Soskice demonstrates how reason comes into its own only with faith: Creation *ex nihilo* as irreducible datum of faith introduces the crucial difference that draws reason into the practice of analogical naming instead of univocal attributing.

Hart's essay elaborates Soskice's central concern by arguing that the forgetfulness of the difference between naming God and describing his attributes is identical with the forgetfulness of the "ontico-ontological difference." However, instead of simply drawing upon Heidegger's reading of Western metaphysics's forgetfulness, Hart offers a sustained engagement and critique of Heidegger's reading that culminates, according to Hart, in a willful misreading, if not occlusion, of Christian metaphysics, and in an ontology on Heidegger's side that itself is nihilistic. For "however much Heidegger may have succeeded at producing the appearance of a new kind of ontology, he never succeeded in understanding being as truly *ontologically* different from beings. Even his tortuous meditations upon the *Ereignis* serve only to confirm the event of the world in its own immanence, its ontic process, and all the while the question of being fails to be posed." Contrary to Heidegger, Hart insists on Christian metaphysics as the most radical Christian interruption of Western metaphysics, an interruption that gives rise to a fundamentally revised genealogy of nihilism, or better, a situating of nihilism by the Christian interruption of metaphysics as such. Hart demonstrates how this interruption climaxes in the doctrine of creation and its concomitant analogy of being that asserts that "all things live, move, and are in God not because they add to God or in any way determine his essence, but because they are gracious manifestations of his fullness."

Why Philosophy Matters for Theology

Martin Bieler and Romanus Cessario take up a crucial concern of the encyclical *Fides et Ratio* by addressing the question why philosophy matters, and why indeed a specific philosophy is necessary for theology. For both Bieler and Cessario, Thomas Aquinas is the lodestar toward which all argument is attracted.

Bieler argues that *Fides et Ratio*, while not canonizing any particular philosophy, clearly outlines the future tasks of philosophical investigation along the lines of Aquinas's metaphysics. Bieler makes this concern his own by showing first why this approach makes sense precisely in addressing questions of the modern world and why it is precisely Aquinas's philosophy of being that is best suited for this task. Bieler offers an account of Aquinas's intricate interrelationship of faith and reason, theology and philosophy, an account in which theology and the metaphysics of *esse* are equi-primordial while theology holds a distinct form-primacy. In an important concluding section, Bieler draws out the immediate relevance of Aquinas's account for contemporary psychology.

Bieler's comprehensive interpretation of Aquinas's account of being, *esse*, offers a most ideal way of critically engaging Heidegger's philosophy of being while, at the same time, appreciating the force of Heidegger's challenge as well as his failure to grasp and account for Aquinas's superior account. In this way, the essays by Bieler and Hart complement each other splendidly.

Cessario shares the encyclical's concern about the present crisis of philosophical training for theological formation. He forcefully argues that a realist philosophy and metaphysics is the indispensable foundation for the intellectual appropriation of the truth to which faith assents. Certain basic principles, structures, and the transcendent origin of created being constitute philosophical truths that are presupposed by the message of the gospel and hence essential to its intelligibility and communicability. If these presuppositions remain unintelligible, the revelation of God must be perfectly unintelligible. Disregarding the *duplex ordo cognitionis*, the twofold order of cognition, which rests on the twofold order of nature and grace, issues in blocking the role of natural judgment within theology such that serious errors dislodge the mind from revelation and as a result considerably complicate the task of the theologian.

Cessario's essay brings to the fore a central question seriously marginalized in contemporary Roman Catholic theological training and utterly eclipsed in Protestant theological training: the general place and, more importantly, the programmatic role of philosophical training in theological formation. Arguably, the marginalizing and eclipsing of this question has contributed considerably to the present crisis of reason in faith and the overall decline of a thoroughly conceptual rigor and a genuine intellectual yearning for truth among pastors and priests. Instead, the uncritical adoption of syncretistic and agnostic assumptions has led to the amorphous but widespread conviction among many Christians, theologically trained or not, that truth, including the truth of the gospel, is a matter of personal preference, a preference one ultimately cannot account for besides a primordial act of will.

Engaging the Citadel of Secular Reason

Charles Taylor's essay constitutes a philosopher's postscript to a conversation of theologians. While in some important ways closing the volume, his essay also opens it to a different perspective. It is the perspective of what a discourse about faith and reason might look like from the unexamined but normative assumptions held within the citadel of secular reason and what obstacles a successful engagement of these assumptions must overcome. The fundamental problem in fragmented late-modern cultures is the high diversity of places of conviction people occupy and hence where they come from in joining difficult inquiries about reason and even more intricate inquiries about faith and reason.

In a first step, Taylor lays out a kind of meta-argument about the nature of argument. Here he shows the difference between an ordinary understanding of an argument, belonging to the culture of mediational epistemology, and "supersession arguments," which show the superiority of one kind of argument over another and always involve a superseding transition from a position A to a more satisfying position B. Acquiring or deepening of faith, Taylor maintains, involves such superseding transitions from A to B.

In a second step, Taylor situates historically the received distinctions between faith and reason or reason versus revelation. Here, in the very heart of his essay, drawing upon the metaphor of light, he offers a pencil sketch of the constitutive convictions of Enlightenment ideology about reason. While previously light was ambient, surrounding us, and cast by some source, the Enlightenment understands the human submitting everything to procedural reason as the source of a focused light. "Enlightenment," Taylor avers, "understood against the background of these images, constitutes what Wittgenstein called a 'Bild,' a picture that can 'hold us captive,' because we are unaware of the way in which this construal, which is after all one among other possible ones, has become for us the only conceivable meaning of the term. We can see also how, on this reading, normative revelation must be intrinsically counter-Enlightenment." Only by expanding the articulative dimension of rationality and its requisite openness to what is outside and beyond us will a Christian discourse successfully engage the secular citadel held hostage by Enlightenment ideology.

In a final step, Taylor suggests that such a recalibration of our notion of reason requires an in-depth knowledge of those places from which people today have difficulty emerging into faith. In order to facilitate such an engagement, he offers an abbreviated account of the narrative that constitutes the modern secularist worldview, a narrative that involves familiar tropes such as charitable service to humanity via technological progress; growing up from childlike myths about an ordered, meaningful world to the disillusioned but courageous adult perspective of raw materialism; liberating oneself from an authoritarian, misanthropic religion to the freedom of unencumbered scientific inquiry. Engaging this materialist citadel successfully, Taylor maintains, entails understanding aspects of what is good in this citadel—for example, strong convictions about human dignity and philanthropy, aspects that "can meet something fuller and deeper in the same genre, an appeal to go beyond in the same direction, inviting a transition to a better place."

The essays in this volume disagree with one another about some fundamental issues, including most especially how reason's legitimate autonomy should be understood. These disagreements take place, however, in the context of a still more fundamental agreement about what the most significant issues are. This is characteristic of Christian theological discourse. Necessary for its being Christian is that it occur in self-conscious response to God's self-gift in Jesus Christ, and thereby also in self-conscious response to God's gift of creation. Necessary for its being theological is that it be explicitly concerned with God and the things of God as these have been received in the normative witness of Scripture and interpreted, declared, and elucidated by the Christian tradition, which is to say by the church, broadly understood. Meeting these necessities, however, does not yield agreement on all questions. Nor should it; if it did, theology would lose its character as a speculative science and become instead a catechetical activity *simpliciter*.

The disagreements among the contributors—evident in the essays and certainly in the lively discussions during our meetings—take place, then, within the framework of agreement given by the fact that each essay is an exercise in Christian theology. The vocabulary and syntax of the Christian account of things is shared, and the richness of the disagreements possible within this account serves not only to develop that account but also, we hope, to stand as a beautiful lure for those unconvinced of theology's value as a tool for the investigation of reason. In this book the question of reason is asked by faith, but in being asked in this way, reason's contours are illuminated and thrown into relief even for those without faith, which is to say for those who have no direct stake in theology's work.

Theology is not solipsistic or autistic. It is not the church's private language, muttered by Christians to one another in the same way that Freemasons exchange secret handshakes. No, theological talk about faith and reason also addresses the world, the citadel of secular reason, as Charles Taylor puts it. Since that is so, it must (and does) also learn from what inhabitants of that city have done with their reason, and from how they have understood their reasoning acts. *Fides et Ratio*, with which our work began, emphasizes this; Charles Taylor, with whom it came to an end, also does so. Among the tasks for the future, then, is faith's fuller appropriation of secular reason's achievements and self-understandings, a task that can properly proceed only together with faith's effort to understand what may and may not be said about reason from within the contours of a Christian account of things.

PART ONE

Approaching Reason Theologically: Reason and Christian Doctrines— Connections and Disconnections

CHAPTER ONE

Auditus Fidei: Where and How Does God Speak?

Faith, Reason, and the Question of Criteria

— ALAN J. TORRANCE —

The recognition of where and how God speaks is intrinsic to the self-communication of God. Although this belongs to the very heart of the Christian gospel, the history of theology has too often failed to appreciate this. Indeed, the very suggestion is regarded in some quarters as having exclusivist and isolationist, if not dangerously sectarian, implications. The contention of this essay is that, first, confusion on this matter places in question the very integrity and viability of the theological enterprise, and second, clarity on this matter requires us to redress fundamental matters of confusion in how the relationship between faith and reason has been treated. Although space does not allow sufficient discussion of the matter, it is only when the intrinsic relation of the criteria to God's self-disclosure is fully appreciated that we can appreciate the radically *inclusive* nature of the gospel.

Where and how does God speak? is a question about criteria—that is, if it is not merely an invitation to list subjectively those places and ways in which one happens to think that God is speaking. To suggest that God speaks here or there and in this or that way is to adopt criteria. The suggestion that critical criteria are presupposed in such claims, however, is a seductive one. Their logical priority too often suggests some kind of historical priority—that they come first, that they are *pre*suppositions of the recognition of revelation and thus that their recognition must necessarily be *temporally* prior to the revelation event. If they are given in advance of the self-communication of God, then we can assume that these criteria (with their truth-claims) are "prior givens," which are valid in advance of God's self-disclosure and thus foundational to it. But the inescapable question that emerges from any reference to "given" criteria is "Given by what or by whom?" In other words, the question we have set before ourselves immediately becomes a question relating to the origin and grounds of these criteria, namely, "Where and how are these criteria 'given'?" Does "given" mean "given by our culture," for example? Or does it mean "given by the language games that constitute and condition our thinking," that is, given by the way we interpret, divide up, and construct our world? Or does it mean "given in our natures as rational and/or linguistic[1] and/or moral beings?" The critical question which then emerges here is whether what is "given" can be false, can distort and mislead, or whether our "given" systems of processing, prioritizing, and assessing can be assumed to be veridical—whether, that is, they are given *by God*. If this is something we are entitled to assume, *from where does this entitlement derive*?

It might appear that I am simply playing an infinite regress game of a kind that can never be resolved and therefore ought to be ignored. However, to assume that there is no resolution while continuing to make theological statements is, as a matter of fact, to assume a resolution, to stop the buck by making a fideistic commitment to some particular set of presuppositions. Christian revelation, I suggest, commits us unambiguously to the recognition that the buck does stop and must stop and that the question of criteria and suppositions begins in the irreducibly *ecclesial* event of God's self-communication in and through the incarnate Logos recognized and affirmed by the reconciling presence of the Spirit. If this is not affirmed as the ground of theology, Christian thought can only undergo what Aristotle (and Lessing) termed a *metabasis eis allo genos*, a transformation into something of a radically different kind. No other alternative is available to us. *Tertium non datur*.[2]

These comments suggest that it is a fundamental claim of Christian orthodoxy that *the conditions for the recognition and affirmation of Christian truth are intrinsic to the event of revelation*. In other words, to the extent that the Holy Spirit is the means of the perception of the revelation of God in Christ, the event of revelation includes within itself the essential grounds for

---

1. Cf. Noam Chomsky and Jerry Fodor's innatist concept of language—what Richard Rorty refers to as a "wired-in language (and metalanguage) of thought." The easy development from this to a rationalist, Cartesian epistemology is illustrated in Zeno Vendler's *Res Cogitans* (Ithaca, NY: Cornell University Press, 1972), in which he writes of our "native ideas": "As for the content of this native stock of concepts, we can at the present time do no more than make educated guesses. Yet, I think, the task of spelling it out in detail is not an impossible one: Aristotle, Descartes, Kant, and recently Chomsky have succeeded in marking out domains that must belong to this framework. . . . There are, then, the 'clear and distinct' ideas which lend intelligibility to the rest. They are 'a priori' in origin and self-contained in their development: experience cannot change their content. No experience is relevant to one's idea of . . . what it is to believe . . . what is truth . . . what is a person. . . . If these ideas need clarification, the way to obtain it is to reflect on what we all implicitly know and show forth in the correct use of language." Cited in Richard Rorty, *Philosophy and the Mirror of Nature* (Oxford: Blackwell, 1980), 251–52. The theological ramifications of such a position are clear.

2. A common tactic by which to take the edge off the challenge here is to reduce theological statement to amorphous abstraction such that it ceases to offend a wide variety of different criteria of assessment. The "discipline" of theology tolerates here what no other academic institution or "discipline" would. The reason why this is allowed to happen is not only that its subject matter is itself deemed to be inherently and essentially amorphous but, worse, that it *requires* to be regarded as such in the name of the inclusivity of its object. In other words, the epistemological implication of inclusivity becomes indiscriminate access! The political correctness that disallows one from questioning the authenticity of another's spirituality involves the refusal to question the theological claims of others vis-à-vis God— unless, of course, they are deemed to be "exclusivist." What should become clear is that intrinsic to these suppositions is a host of complex truth-claims and criteria—that the inclusive answer to the question "Where and how does God speak?" is "Here, there, and everywhere" or, "In whatever ways you determine to be affirmative of your identity, spiritual insights, convictions, orientations, etc." But how "inclusive" is an approach whose truth-claims involve, for example, the de facto rejection that God is the *Ens concretissimum* and where God's being is inseparable from God's "being-in-act" and "being-as-word." Is it really "inclusive" of the faith of Christians to evacuate God's concrete and ergo *eph'hapax* presence from all that the church determines to be the foundation of its existence and its raison d'être?

the recognition of Christian truth. Its essential criterion, therefore, includes that specific self-authenticating perception that *is* the presence of the Spirit. It is thus inherent within the very nature of Christian revelation that it is neither anticipatable nor endorsable from any prior or independent set of conditions or foundations. It can neither be demonstrated nor affirmed, therefore, from any external Archimedean point.[3] The condition of the perception of the person of Christ, as God's inclusive and affirmative Word to humanity, is none other than the free and creative presence of God as the Holy Spirit.

This means that the recognition and perception of God's presence in Christ is the consequence of an event of paradigmatic *metanoia*, of transformation (metamorphosis[4]), and of reconciliation of mind—and not, indeed, one that can be generated by the knowing subject "off her own bat." For the same reasons, the new paradigm is not one that can be appreciated from within the frame of reference of the Greek mind for which its affirmations are folly. As to the goal of this, it is summed up in the expression *logikon latreian—* rational and reverent participation in the mind of Christ, in the Son's epistemic and, indeed, semantic (*rhematic[5]*) communion with the Father.

As the hackneyed fable of the traveler to Connemara suggests, the body of Christ and the kingdom of God are not places to which we can plot a continuous journey from some secular or foreign point of reference.[6] Providing reasons for the faith that is in one (and which, of course, is integral to the theological task) does not and cannot mean providing rationalistic demonstrations that plot any such direct route. The supposition of so much Christian apologetics, as also of Christianity's critics, that "reason" offers occupancy of some Archimedean country—and whose occupants can rest confident in the inherent reliability of immanent truth criteria—stands at odds with the gospel's witness to a transformed and all-transforming event of recognition that is given in and through nothing less than the free and creative presence of God.

These preliminary comments mark out the territory I wish to explore. The position sketched could be supported by biblical exegesis[7] and by analysis of

---

3. Cf. Fergus Kerr's critique of Karl Rahner in which he draws on Wittgenstein and Heidegger in exposing the "megalomania" inherent in the theological desire to find an "Archimedean point." Kerr, "Rahner Retrospective III: Transcendence or Finitude," *New Blackfriars* 62 (1981): 378–79.

4. Cf. Rom 12:2. Given that we are not to be schematized by this world, our thinking requires to be reschematized in and through our being brought to be *en Christo*. See the concluding paragraph of Mark McIntosh's essay in this volume, "Faith, Reason, and the Mind of Christ," p. 142.

5. Cf. John 17:8. The Son gives us the *rhemata* (words/participative speech-acts) that the Father gave him.

6. A local inhabitant was once asked the way to Connemara. The reply ran, "If I were going to Connemara, I wouldn't be going from here!"

7. One could consider the account of Peter's recognition of Jesus that "flesh and blood" could not deliver and the fact that that recognition involved the reconstitution of Simon as Peter. One could consider the extensive eye/sight and ear/hearing metaphors in the Synoptic, Johannine, and Pauline corpora implying that the conditions of acknowledgment require to be given and are not innate. There is the Pauline emphasis on the fact that the discernment of truth requires a transformation of minds, which cannot be "schematized" by the secular order (Rom 12:2). Finally, there is the extensive utilization of the regeneration or "born from above" metaphors in the Johannine corpus. In sum, central to and, indeed, held in common by the New Testament writings is the fundamental emphasis that revelation involves and includes the provision by God ("from above") of the conditions for the recognition of God through God's free and creative presence. They are not innate or immanent in our flesh and blood but the result of the creative reconciliation of our minds and paradigms.

patristic debate about the meaning of *metanoia* in the New Testament.[8] But that is a task for another essay. Here I shall pursue the question first through conversation with David Strauss as representative of a particular kind of modern response to the question of the relation between the Socratic demand for self-knowledge and the Christian demand for response to God's self-gift in revelation.

The Timeless Challenge of the Socratic: Criterial Immanentism and the Pursuit of the "Given"

I should now like to consider one paradigmatic case that has not only been highly influential in its impact on the shape and direction of contemporary theology but that illustrates the inevitability with which criterial immanentism translates theological statements into anthropological statements or, indeed, autobiographical statements.

The developments leading to David Strauss's hermeneutics and introduction of "myth theory" are well documented and do not require extensive analysis here.[9] Suffice it to say that behind Strauss's theological approach stand two key elements. First, there is the epistemology of Leibniz with its dichotomization between necessary truths supplied by reason (to which epistemic access is a priori) and contingent truths mediated by sense perception. Second, there is Spinoza's emphasis that the truth of a historical narrative cannot provide knowledge of God—the latter deriving solely from general ideas possessing epistemic certainty. These provide, in turn, the background to Lessing's famous insistence that events and truths belong to radically different and logically unconnected categories. This outcome was the devaluation of the significance of the historical and the "contingent" in favor of necessary truths of reason. Theology thus came to be perceived as belonging to the domain of the a priori determinations of "reason" together with all that "reason" counted as its dictates.[10] The inevitable consequence was a concern to reformulate Christian doctrine in the light of the immanent predeterminations and confident prescriptions of the sphere of subjective reasoning.[11] That the influence of idealism in the theological sphere

8. I have in mind here, for example, Athanasius's emphasis upon the epistemic significance of the Holy Spirit in the *Letters to Serapion*, trans. C. R. B. Shapland (London: Epworth, 1951). This emphasis strongly supports the view that only God can reveal God to those (all humanity) in a state of alienation from him in such a way as to provide the epistemic conditions sufficient for assent to the central claims of Christianity.

9. For a recent scholarly analysis, see Timothy J. Lawson, "The Influence of Benedict D. Spinoza's Philosophy on the Theology of David Friedrich Strauss" (PhD diss., King's College, London, 1994).

10. Cf. *Über den Beweis des Geistes und der Kraft* (1777) in which we find Lessing's famous affirmation that "accidental truths of history can never become the proof of necessary truths of reason." Henry Chadwick, ed., *Lessing's Theological Writings* (London: A&C Black, 1956), 53.

11. This can be seen in Lessing's early essay (c. 1753) "The Christianity of Reason" ("Das Christentum der Vernunft"), which foreshadowed the speculative restatements of the doctrine of the Trinity using Leibnizian ideas in *The Education of the Human Race (Die Erziehung des Menschengeschlechts)*, 1780. See Henry Chadwick, *Lessing's Theological Writings* (Palo Alto, CA: Stanford University Press, 1956), and also his article "Lessing, Gotthold Ephraim" in *Encyclopaedia of Philosophy*, ed. Paul Edwards, vol. 4 (New York: Collier and Macmillan, 1967), 443ff.

thrived in this climate is evidenced by the natural synthesis in Strauss's methodology of the influences of Leibniz and Spinoza, on the one hand, and Hegelian idealism on the other.[12] These influences led him to interpret the primary interest of the gospels as lying in the evidence they provided of the workings of consciousness in the sphere of religious experience.[13] Utilizing Hegel's concept of "unconscious invention," the gospels were interpreted as poetic evidence of the "purely human desire to realize the immanent goal of Spirit in its journey toward the Hegelian Being-in-and-for-itself."[14] The gospels came to be interpreted in terms of an assumed synthesis or coincidence of the *human* idea, reason, and spirit with *God* who, in turn, was identified as the absolute Idea, as absolute Reason and Spirit. What resulted was the historically ominous transfer of christological and theological attributes onto the human race, as advocated in the famous dogmatic conclusions of Strauss's critical examination of the life of Jesus. That this follows naturally from the immanentism that characterizes (and sustains) idealist approaches is plain.[15]

> Thus by a higher mode of argumentation, from the *idea* of God and man in their reciprocal relation, the truth of the conception which the church forms of Christ appears to be confirmed. . . . [H]ere, the veracity of the history is deduced from the truth of those conceptions. That which is rational is also real. . . . Proved to be an idea of reason, the unity of the divine and human nature must also have an historical existence.

But does this mean, Strauss asks, that we must attach exclusive value to that particular piece of history associated with the life of Jesus?

> This is indeed *not* the mode in which Idea realizes itself; it is not wont to lavish all its fullness on one *exemplar,* and be niggardly towards all others—to express itself perfectly in that one individual, and imperfectly in all the rest: it rather loves to distribute its riches among a multiplicity of exemplars which reciprocally complete each other—in the alternate appearance and suppression of a series of individuals. And is this no true realization of the idea? Is not the idea of the unity of the divine and human natures a real one in a far higher sense, when I regard the whole race of mankind as its realization, than when I single out one man as such a realization? Is not incarnation of God from eternity, a truer one than an incarnation limited to a particular point of time?

---

12. Strauss was, of course, a student of the Hegelian F. C. Baur and went on to study under Hegel himself.

13. Hayden V. White, "David Friedrick Strauss" in *Encyclopaedia of Philosophy,* ed. Paul Edwards, vol. 8 (New York: Macmillan, 1972), 25.

14. Ibid., 26.

15. The following quotations are taken from the section entitled "Dogmatic Import of the Life of Jesus" in Strauss, *The Life of Jesus Critically Examined (Das Leben Jesu kritisch bearbeitet),* trans. George Eliot (London: Chapman, Brothers, 1848), 779–80 (italics mine).

He then summarizes as follows:

This is the key to the whole of Christology, that, as subject of the predicate which the church assigns to Christ, we place, instead of an individual, an idea. . . . In an individual, a God-man, the properties and functions which the church ascribes to Christ contradict themselves; in the idea of the race, they perfectly agree. Humanity is the union of the two natures—god become man, the infinite manifesting itself in the finite, and the finite spirit *remembering* its infinitude; it is the child of the visible Mother and the invisible Father, Nature and Spirit; it is the worker of miracles, in so far as in the course of human history the spirit more and more completely subjugates nature, both within and around man, until it lies before him as the inert matter on which he exercises his active power; it is the sinless existence, for the course of its development is a blameless one, pollution cleaves to the individual only, and does not touch the race or its history. It is Humanity that dies, rises and ascends to heaven, for from the negation of its phenomenal life there ever proceeds a higher spiritual life. . . . This alone is the absolute sense of Christology. . . . The phenomenal history of the individual, says Hegel, is only a starting point for the mind.[16]

The affirmation of the veridical status of "rational" criteria immanent within the mind can do no other than interpret the history of Jesus, together with all other history, as exemplifying these prior suppositions. It is these suppositions that constitute the absolute. The result is a selective process of value transfer from Jesus (or whoever else is perceived to exemplify the criteria one applies) to humanity as it is unfolding. What is then affirmed is the ascension and deification of the universal (humanity as a whole) and the denigration of the particular, the material, and the "phenomenal" (the spatio-temporal). What drives this is *anamnesis*—our remembering our infinitude, the transcendent within. The sole criteria throughout are those eternal ideas immanent within the human spirit.

Strauss's approach exemplifies how the supposition of criterial immanence inevitably leads to the material identification of God's self-communication with the universalization and absolutization of our own interpretative criteria and self-understandings.[17] The theological ratification of our criteria identifies self-knowledge with knowledge of the divine, that is, the universal, the "rational," the timeless, the immaterial. Given that the historical (the spatio-temporal) can do no more than exemplify, only one response to the Where question is possible. "Where" God speaks is answered in terms of that which is assumed to be universally and timelessly immanent. In short, the sole and full answer is that supplied by the Delphic oracle.

---

16. Whether Hegel would have been happy with Strauss's interpretation of his thought is a matter for debate. There is clearly, however, more than sufficient continuity to illustrate the point I wish to make here.

This story—the story of the reduction of a properly Christian epistemology to a Delphic one—could be pursued through the byways of neo-Kantian idealism and into the thought of Rudolf Bultmann, which is best understood as a transfiguration of Christian theology into precisely a form of that kind of idealism.[18] Both Bultmann and Strauss, with all their differences, offer an answer to the How and Where of divine self-communication conditioned by an immanentist epistemology intimately intertwined with idealist assumptions. Such positions effectively evacuate the divine self-communication of its content. What should also be plain is that all forms of criterial immanentism must ultimately lead to one of the following: (1) a monist fusion and identification of the divine and the human; or (2) an irresolvable dualism rendering God irrelevant to human knowing and understanding; or, worst of all, (3) the confused adoption of supposed or postulated "middle axioms."[19]

The Givenness of God and Criterial Immanentism: "Better Well Hanged Than Ill Wed"

No theologian has explored the underlying issues here and anticipated their outworkings with greater clarity and profundity than Søren Kierkegaard. In his pseudonymous *Philosophical Fragments*,[20] he distills the essence of the debate with idealism as one concerning the question of the nature and status of the criteria in terms of which we determine what is true.[21] Accordingly, he opens by asking the question with which Plato wrestled in the *Meno,* namely, "Can the truth be learned?" Here he addresses the "pugnacious proposition" that underlies the appeal of idealism: "a person cannot possibly seek what he knows, and, just as impossibly, he cannot seek what he does not know, for what he knows he cannot seek, since he knows it, and what he does not know he cannot seek, because, after all, he does not even know what he is supposed

---

17. It is not surprising that Strauss's *Das Leben Jesu kritisch bearbeitet* would so influence Feuerbach in his concern to explore further human consciousness and the psychological mechanisms underlying mythmaking.

18. The most lucid statement of Bultmann's own self-understanding is to be found in his late *Jesus Christ and Mythology* (London: SCM Press, 1960), esp. 45ff. On neo-Kantianism in general and Bultmann's relation thereto, see Roger Johnson, *The Origins of Demythologizing: Philosophy and Historiography in the Theology of Rudolf Bultmann* (Leiden: E. J. Brill, 1974); A. C. Thiselton, *The Two Horizons: New Testament Hermeneutics and Philosophical Description with Special Reference to Heidegger, Bultmann, Gadamer, and Wittgenstein* (Exeter: Paternoster, 1980). There is an excellent discussion of neo-Kantianism by Lewis White Beck in *Encyclopedia of Philosophy*, ed. Paul Edwards, vol. 5 (New York: Macmillan, 1972), 468ff.

19. It is not insignificant that John Baillie, the "Christian Platonist" who has had such an influence on the moderate tradition advocating "middle axioms," studied under Cohen and Natorp. In his "Confessions of a Transplanted Scot," in *Contemporary American Theology: Theological Autobiographies* (New York: Round Table, 1933), 33–59, he comments on having attended the lectures of Eucken, Cohen, and Natorp and adds that "the course of my reflections was notably affected by them" (43). This influence was combined with that of the British idealists Bradley, Bosanquet, Pringle-Pattison, and Sorley.

20. Significantly, he chose to do so under the pseudonym of an agnostic (Johannes Climacus), who occupies a position outside the faith and makes no Christian assumptions.

21. That his discussion relates to Hegel in particular does not make it any less relevant to the neo-Kantian school of thought that would come later.

to seek."[22] In short, if we do not already possess within us the necessary criteria for the recognition of the truth (criteria, that is, which must ultimately contain the truth), we can neither search for the truth nor, indeed, recognize it when we come across it. The seductive appeal of idealism is that it solves the problem of discovery by affirming that the truth and thus the criteria for the recognition of truth are already immanent within us. To the extent that the truth is within it cannot be introduced to us; it can only be discovered as something we have known from eternity. For this reason, Socrates interprets all learning and seeking to be forms of recollecting. All teaching becomes, therefore, a form of midwifery whereby learners (*mathetai*[23]) are enabled to give birth to the knowledge already immanent within them.[24] Consequently, Socrates would pose questions to slaves (relating to geometry, for example) that the slaves would answer as they were helped to become aware of what they already knew. He would then, recognizing his own insignificance as a mere midwife, quietly disappear from view and move on, concerned to do nothing that might attract attention to himself and thus distract the learner from that highest relation, namely, his relation to the truth that is within. "In the Socratic view, every human being is himself the midpoint, and the whole world focuses only on him because his self-knowledge is God-knowledge."[25] Thus, the teacher can and must never be anything other than a mere facilitator: "If I were to imagine myself meeting Socrates, Prodicus, or the maidservant in another life, there again none of them would be more than an occasion, as Socrates intrepidly expresses it by saying that even in the underworld he would only ask questions, for the ultimate idea in all questioning is that the person asked must himself possess the truth."[26]

Integral to this is the consequence that if Socrates were to allow himself to become associated *in any way whatsoever* in the mind of the learner with his relation to the truth, that would be to distort his relation to the truth. For the teacher to undermine that relation would signify that, far from being the friend of the learner, he would have become the learner's enemy. That is, he would be eclipsing or distorting the highest relation that a human being can possess, namely, the learner's relation to the truth. It is necessarily the case, therefore, that the identity of the teacher be seen to be ultimately and absolutely insignificant, whomever that teacher might be. Moreover, the learner's temporal "point of departure" in remembering the truth (like the teacher and the occasion) would similarly require to be viewed as "a nothing." In short, the moment I discover the truth I recognize that the temporal point of departure and also the teacher are and can be of no decisive

---

22. Johannes Climacus (Søren Kierkegaard), *Philosophical Fragments*, trans. Howard V. Hong and Edna H. Hong (Princeton, NJ: Princeton University Press, 1985), 9.

23. "Learner" translates the term *mathetes* that we normally translate as "disciple." Kierkegaard is contrasting two different kinds of discipleship.

24. This was the divine commission to Socrates that constrained him to be a midwife but forbade him to give birth "because between one human being and another *maieuesthai* (to deliver) is the highest, giving birth indeed belongs to the god." Climacus, *Philosophical Fragments*, 10–11.

25. Ibid., 11.

26. Ibid., 12–13.

significance. They are lost to the eternal, having no bearing on my relation-ship to the truth that is a timeless and eternal one. Indeed, I could not find the temporal moment of discovery again "even if I were to look for it, because there is no Here and no There, but only an *ubique et nusquam* (everywhere and nowhere)."[27]

In sum, if the source of knowledge, discovery, and the recognition of the truth is immanent within the inquirer, then the teacher and the temporal occa-sion have and can have absolutely no significance. Whether it is Jesus, Gandhi, the Dalai Lama, or a dead dog who facilitates the birthing of my immanent understanding of God and reality, this is and can be of no relevance whatso-ever because there can and must be no association or confusion of the Truth and my relation to the Truth with any particular individuals or spatio-temporal histories and any relation I might have to either. They can be noth-ing more than accidental (or incidental) exemplars, as Strauss saw so clearly.

"If the Situation Is to Be Different . . ."

"If the situation is to be different, then the moment in time must have such decisive significance that for no moment will I be able to forget it, neither in time nor in eternity, because the eternal, previously non-existent, came into existence in that moment."[28] That is, if the theological scenario is to differ epistemically from the idealist one, then there must be an *intrinsic* relation-ship between the truth, our relation to the truth, and the specific "moment in time" or "occasion." Given this alternative presupposition, the pseudony-mous Johannes Climacus[29] goes on to reconsider the relations involved in the question "Can the truth be learned?"

Clearly, if the moment possesses decisive significance in the learner's rela-tion to the truth, "then the seeker up until that moment must not have pos-sessed the truth, not even in the form of ignorance. . . . Consequently, he has to be defined as being outside the truth. . . . He is, then, untruth."[30] But this brings us back again to the question of the *Meno.* How then is the learner to recognize the truth? If he is in untruth he clearly cannot be "reminded" of it.

Since the teacher cannot remind the learner who is "outside the truth" of what the truth is, if the learner is to obtain the truth, "the teacher must bring it to him, but not only that."

Along with it, he must provide him with the condition for understand-ing it, for if the learner were himself the condition for understanding the truth, then he merely needs to recollect, because the condition for under-standing the truth is like being able to ask about it—the condition and

27. Ibid., 13.
28. Ibid.
29. It is significant to Kierkegaard's argument that his pseudonym is an agnostic. In short, you do not have to be a Christian to perceive the radical and irreducible incompatibility between idealism and Christianity.
30. Climacus, *Philosophical Fragments,* 13.

the question contain the conditioned and the answer. (If this is not the case, then the moment is to be understood only Socratically.)[31]

Here Kierkegaard presents the single most pertinent challenge to dogmatic, hermeneutic, and theological method, the fundamental question to which the question set as our topic directs us. The criteria for the recognition and appropriation of the self-communication of God as Truth cannot be extrinsic to that event of self-communication without our committing ourselves to the Socratic position in toto.

As Kierkegaard goes on to establish, if we are not to return to the Socratic, then the teacher is not a midwife but a "deliverer" who delivers us from error and the unfreedom integral to it by constituting *in himself* the condition of our being in relation to the truth. Such a teacher, Kierkegaard suggests, would require to be understood not only as deliverer but also as reconciler eternally inseparable from the learner's relation to the Truth. As for the "moment," it is short and temporal and therefore passes, yet it is "filled with the eternal"— that is, it is intrinsically linked to the eternal. Consequently, he suggests, we might call it the "fullness of time"![32]

If the moment is to be of "decisive significance" and if we are not to return to the Socratic, then the change that takes place denotes a transition from nonbeing to being. Something radically new takes place or is created—a being-in-relation that was not there previously, even in embryonic form. There is a reconstitution, a rebirth, a conversion: "In as much as [the learner] was untruth, he was continually in the process of departing from the truth; as a result of receiving the condition in the moment, his course took the opposite direction, or he was turned around. Let us call this change *conversion*."[33] The effect of this is to expose the profound contrast between *metanoia* as the condition of our relation to the truth, and the Socratic *anamnesis*. Whereas *anamnesis* denotes the confirmation and ratification of the epistemic criteria immanent within us, *metanoia* denotes, by contrast, a profound transformation of the epistemic orientation of the whole person. As New Testament scholars J. Behm and E. Würthwein explain, *metanoia* as conceived in the proclamation of Jesus "affects the whole man, first and basically the center of personal life, then logically his conduct at all times and in all situations, his thoughts, words and acts."[34]

It is imperative to appreciate here, however, that this kind of epistemic reorientation does not assume an irrational "leap in the dark." As Murray Rae observes, "It involves neither the abandonment of reason (it is not *contra rationem*) nor an addition to reason (it is not *supra rationem*) but rather reason's redemption." He continues:

---

31. Ibid., 14.
32. Ibid., 18.
33. Ibid.
34. J. Behm and E. Würthwein, "*Metanoeo* and *metanoi* or *metanoia*" in *Theological Dictionary of the New Testament*, ed. Gerhard Kittel, vol. 4 (Grand Rapids: Eerdmans, 1967), 1002. I owe this reference and the thrust of the following discussion of Kierkegaard's interpretation of "conversion" to Murray Rae, *Kierkegaard's Vision of the Incarnation: By Faith Transformed* (Oxford: Clarendon Press, 1997), ch. 6.

The canons of reason are not as neutral as is often supposed but are themselves the product of a particular world view, typically a dualist one, whether it be the cosmological dualism between the *cosmos noetos* and the *cosmos aisthetos* of Plato, the Cartesian dualism between *res cogitans* and *res extensa* or the Kantian dualism between *phenomena* and *noumena*. However much Hegel, with his phenomenology of spirit, attempted to escape such dualisms his philosophy does not attain the hoped for reconciliation of the eternal and the temporal but is simply the sublation of the latter by the former. Hegel thus retains the prejudice of his above mentioned forbears against the Biblical notion that history is the locus of divine self-disclosure. Kierkegaard, on the other, considers that those who have eyes to see and ears to hear are those who by God's grace have been able to let go of such limited frameworks and to perceive the world anew under the condition which is called faith.[35]

Kierkegaard's concept of conversion as a radically discontinuous transition (involving a transformation of apperception, orientation, and understanding) is thus considerably more than a mere "Gestalt switch" (a suggestion that M. J. Ferreira considers at length[36]), by which we can switch between one way of looking at the world and another, and assume each "seeing as" to be as valid as the other. Rather, Rae argues, it shares more in common with a "paradigm shift" which recognizes that progress in knowledge (as in scientific knowledge) is not a matter of continuous evolutionary advancement or some kind of deductive progression. There is a radical discontinuity between the old and new paradigms, and there is nothing that can be done from within the old paradigm that may constitute a propaedeutic for the new. To quote Rae again, "By the standard of the new paradigm those who continue to operate within the old exist in untruth and employ structures of understanding which compel them to dismiss the claims of those who have undergone a paradigmatic transition."[37] It is important to appreciate here that "reason cannot itself be regarded as a framework or paradigm, much less an absolute or neutral one, but must rather be understood as a tool, very likely among others, which makes possible the heuristic functioning of a particular paradigm. . . . Reason is constrained by the paradigm within which it operates and cannot be the means by which that same paradigm is undermined and replaced."[38] This is precisely what is implied by Kierkegaard's comment concerning Hegelianism, that "it is impossible to attack the System from a point within the System."[39]

This is not to suggest, however, that that *metanoia* on which our being in relation to the Truth—and thus to God's self-communication—depends can

---

35. Rae, *Kierkegaard's Vision of the Incarnation*, 113.
36. M. J. Ferreira, *Transforming Vision: Imagination and Will in Kierkegaardian Faith* (Oxford: Clarendon, 1991), 33ff.
37. Rae, *Kierkegaard's Vision of the Incarnation*, 119.
38. Ibid., 120.
39. Søren Kierkegaard, *The Point of View for My Work as an Author: A Report to History*, trans. Walter Lowrie (London: Oxford University Pess, 1939), 131 n. Sikes comments, "The System is invulnerable if one grants it the two essential elements of any system—its methodology and its presuppositions. It

be subsumed within some wider category of "paradigm shifts." As Eberhard Jüngel argues, "Theology has to do with a paradigm change *sui generis*: the existential change in human understanding conveyed by the phrases *ta tes sarkos phronein* and *ta tou pneumatos phronein* (Rom 8:5)."[40]

As Kierkegaard appreciates, a "system of existence cannot be given." To the extent that the gospel bears witness to our deliverance to a new form of existing, we do not have a system given to be thought or appropriated or even appreciated. Rather, the *metanoia* at its heart speaks of a re-creation for an "authentic existence" involving passionate, subjective commitment to a particular way of viewing and understanding the world.[41]

How Does God Speak? Moving beyond Vestibules

Kierkegaard's argumentation places in question approaches to theology that begin by establishing a priori, foundational prolegomena to theological perception or understanding. This can take the form of a propaedeutic, endorsing *pre*suppositions, *pre*conditions, *pre*understandings,[42] *pre*apprehensions,[43] and so on. These address the How of God's speaking by reference to the a priori determinations of human capacities (or, indeed, incapacities) and prior orientations. The very acknowledgment of transcendence, however, involves the displacing or critical suspension of questions that assume that the relevant criteria of judgment are internal. If the recognition of transcendence is not to reduce to *apophasis*—arguably the most seductive form of human self-assertion—it is the recognition that questions posed from a ground within the self must themselves be questioned. It was the reconstituted Peter, not Simon, that was the ground of the recognition of Jesus as the Messiah.[44] To the extent that Peter, however, then sought to interpret what was and was not to be expected of Jesus in the light of his preunderstandings of messiahship, the "Counter-Logos" (Bonhoeffer) reprimanded him for an approach that was nothing less than demonic. Why? Because it involved an approach

---

was then the task of Climacus to refute it on these two grounds." Walter Sikes, *On Becoming the Truth* (St. Louis: Bethany Press, 1968), 64 (cited in Rae, *Kierkegaard's Vision of the Incarnation*, 125n50).

40. Eberhard Jüngel, "Response to Josef Blank," in *Paradigm Change in Theology*, ed. Hans Küng and David Tracy (New York: Crossroad, 1989), 297–98.

41. As such, it may be seen to involve commitment to what Evans describes as a particular "plausibility structure." See C. Stephen Evans, *Kierkegaard's "Fragments" and "Postscript"* (Atlantic Highlands, NJ: Humanities Press, 1983), 264ff.

42. That is, the Heideggerean concept of the *Vorverständnis*, which has influenced modern theological debates, together with some of the other preparatory conceptualities (the *vorontologisch*, the *vorphänomenal*, the *vorphilosophisch*—the *Präparat*) that characterize the phenomenological method of *Sein und Zeit* and that we have seen to have been taken over in Bultmann's exposition of hermeneutical method.

43. Cf. Karl Rahner's concept of the human subject's *Vorgriff* as discussed in *Foundations of Christian Faith: An Introduction to the Idea of Christianity*, trans. William Dych (London: Darton, Longman & Todd, 1978), 33ff., and also in chs. 5 and 12 of *Hearers of the Word* (New York: Seabury, 1969).

44. No one expresses the fundamental issues here more clearly than Hans Urs von Balthasar, who comments on this text: "Simon the fisherman, before his meeting with Christ, however thoroughly he might have searched within himself, could not possibly have found a trace of Peter. . . . In the form 'Peter' Simon was capable of understanding the word of Christ, because the form itself issued from the word and was conjoined with it." Hans Urs von Balthasar, *Prayer* (London: SPCK, 1973), 48–49.

wherein the pressure of interpretation was *from* his preunderstanding *to* God's self-presentation and not the other way around.[45]

It is precisely this insight that characterizes Bonhoeffer's reference to Kierkegaard in addressing the "christological question" in his lectures on Christology.[46] Opening with the assertion "Teaching about Christ begins in silence," he cites Kierkegaard's insistence that we be silent before the Absolute. This silence, Bonhoeffer comments, "has nothing to do with mystical silence which, in its absence of words, is, nevertheless, the soul secretly chattering away to itself. The church's silence is silence before the Word."[47] In short, Christology demands a *methodological* silence. The Logos qua divine Logos cannot be subsumed ("crucified") by the requirements of our prior, predetermined, and predetermining *logoi*. To this extent, the Logos requires that we interpret it as the Anti-Logos/Counter-Logos—the one who stands to judge, question, and revise all our presuppositions (methodological, epistemological, and otherwise) vis-à-vis God and God's purposes for humanity. There can thus be no Hegelian assimilation of the Counter-Logos within the human Logos,[48] and there can be no assimilation of the one Christ either within a general interpretation of the human race or within the general categories of interpretation characteristic of the human race.

In sum, the "How" question in my title is addressed in and through asking the "Who" question. As Bonhoeffer puts it, "The question 'Who?' is the question of transcendence. The question 'How?' is the question of immanence."[49] This excludes from christological thought, therefore, the question as to "how the fact of the revelation can be conceived. This question is tantamount to going behind Christ's claim and providing an independent vindication of it. Here the human Logos presumes to be the beginning and the Father of Jesus Christ."[50]

---

45. A similar danger can be found in the fondness in much contemporary theology for grounding theological exposition in a philosophy of "Being." Apart from the very real questions (logical and otherwise) that must be raised vis-à-vis all attempts to hypostatize the existential quantifier, it can be extremely difficult to know what precisely is being said when God is identified as "Being." The risk is that this constitutes warrant for reformulating God's self-presentation in the light of a prior metaphysic. It is not least for these reasons that Colin Gunton and Robert W. Jenson's critique of the notion of the *Logos asarkos* is so significant (see their essay "The *Logos Ensarkos* and Reason" in this volume). Attempts to interpret the *Logos ensarkos* in the light of a prior conceptuality of the *Logos asarkos* can all too easily replace the Logos revealed in Christ with our own *logoi*, that is, with our own metaphysical and philosophical allegiances to which we have, thereby, attached theological status. In this regard, I have some concerns here with the direction of certain parts of David Bentley Hart's stimulating essay in this volume, "The Offering of Names: Metaphysics, Nihilism, and Analogy."

The failure of certain forms of "natural" theology and metaphysics of being to offer a critique of developments in Nazi Germany and in South Africa during the apartheid years make all too plain the profound importance of ensuring that at every point the direction of the pressure of interpretation is from the gospel of the incarnate Word to our present situations and *not* from our own interpretations of the world to the interpretation of God and his purposes for our contemporary world. The reversal of the direction of interpretation constitutes nothing less than a repudiation of revelation and its purpose.

46. It is not insignificant that these were given in 1933, the year in which Bonhoeffer set out courageously to oppose anti-Semitism and the assimilation of Christianity within the prior demands and agendas of German culture.

47. Dietrich Bonhoeffer, *Christology*, trans. John Bowden (London: Collins, 1966), 27.

48. Ibid., 29–30.

49. Ibid., 30.

50. Ibid., 33. It is interesting to note Athanasius's parallel suspicion of the "How" question. "Having learned these things, they ought not to be so bold as to ask doubting, how these things could be." *Letters to Serapion*, 106.

What this suggests is that there is ultimately no distinction to be drawn between idealist approaches that interpret objective knowledge as objectification, that is, the construction or generation (*Erzeugung*) of its objects and those that uphold prior subjective criteria (for example, in the name of "fundamental theology") that *merely* operate censorship and discrimination in and through the process of discernment. The selective predetermination of what does and does not count in determining the content of God-talk and revelation is equally invalid in both cases with regard to the Substance, or *Fundamentum*, of theology. In the final analysis, both construct the *Sache* (material) in question and dictate the terms of its "speech" by identifying themselves and their claims with the How and Where of God's self-communication. This is not, of course, to deny that any considerations offered could ever be pertinent or appropriate; to make any such denial would itself constitute an illegitimate a priori predetermination for precisely the same reasons. It is emphatically not my concern, therefore, to advocate a priori that we rule out as invalid any a priori determination of criteria.[51] My concerns here are irreducibly a posteriori ones: (1) that we recognize that the very nature of Christian revelation or divine self-disclosure implies that the propriety and impropriety of critical criteria are to be determined *out of the event of God's self-communication itself* and (2) that consideration of the nature of this event suggests that the determination to "rule in" independent, immanent criteria of assessment in advance of the revelation event is incompatible with the nature and content of that event's self-referential claims. To interpret God's self-disclosure in the light of predeterminations as to its nature and shape constitutes a de facto denial of that self-disclosure.

The Divine Self-Communication as Constituting Its Own Vestibule

If Kierkegaard's utilization of the agnostic Climacus to undermine what I am calling "criterial immanentism" (together with the methodological and epistemological vestibules associated with it) takes the form of a *via negativa*,[52] Karl Barth's critique, like Dietrich Bonhoeffer's, takes the form of a *via positiva*. It operates out of Christian affirmation and not by way of any general demonstration of mutual incompatibilities. In offering a "church dogmatics," he seeks to establish the nature of theological knowledge by way of a *Nachdenken* or a "backward look"—outlining the methodological, criterial, and epistemological conditions of God's self-communication to human creatures, where these are conceived as "postsuppositions" carried and established in, through, and with the event of the divine address itself.

---

51. My concern here is not a philosophical one, like that of Derrida.

52. It is imperative to realize that Kierkegaard is not seeking to offer a demonstration of the truth of Christianity. If he were, his approach would, of course, be guilty of internal inconsistency. It is for this reason that Kierkegaard uses the agnostic pseudonym and opens with a one-sentence preamble: "The question is asked by one who in his ignorance does not even know what provided the occasion for his questioning in this way" (Climacus, *Philosophical Fragments*, 9).

Seven interrelated facets of Barth's discussion are pertinent to this.[53]

The Ecclesia as Constituting the "Where" of Divine Self-Communication

Barth categorically refuses to begin with the question "How is human knowledge of revelation possible?" For the theologian to ask such a question would imply either (a) that there is, or can be, doubt as to whether revelation is known, or (b) that "insight into the possibility of knowledge of divine revelation" can be expected from the "investigation of human knowledge" in abstraction. The former involves a de facto repudiation of revelation's having taken place. The latter constitutes, at best, a form of disobedience in the face of revelation. Why? Because it seeks to validate the particularity of the revelation event with recourse to universal structures that are deemed to be *more* foundational. It is thus to see these universal, timeless structures as the primary self-disclosure of God. It is they, and not Christ, that are perceived to be the incarnate Logos.

If the body of Christ is the place of the discernment of God, we do not stand outside it either to confirm or to test this revelation. When we speak of or acknowledge revelation, we are using what J. L. Austin would term a "success word." To acknowledge Christian revelation is to speak of something *that has taken place*. It is to speak in the light of that reality. To cite Bonhoeffer again, "In the church in which Christ has revealed himself as the Word of God, the human Logos puts the question: Who are you, Jesus Christ, Word of God, Logos of God? The answer is given, the church receives it new every day."[54]

The Holy Spirit as the "Point of Connection" between God and Human Hearing

Barth writes, "According to Holy Scripture God's revelation occurs in our enlightenment by the Holy Spirit of God to a knowledge of His Word. The outpouring of the Holy Spirit is God's revelation. In the reality of this event consists our freedom to be the children of God and to know and love and praise Him in His revelation."[55] The condition for the appropriation and thus realization of God's self-communication is the Holy Spirit alone. It is the Spirit, the *Ens concretissimum*, who constitutes the point of connection (*Anknüpfungspunkt*) between God and the human hearer and who is the condition of our having the ears to hear. The "revealedness" of revelation is to be understood in terms of the creative presence of the Spirit alone, and not

---

53. This brief discussion of Barth is largely a précis of part of the first chapter of my book *Persons in Communion: An Essay on Trinitarian Description and Human Participation* (Edinburgh: T&T Clark, 1996).
54. Dietrich Bonhoeffer, *Christology*, trans. Edwin Robertson (London: Collins, 1978), 32.
55. Karl Barth, *Church Dogmatics*, ed. G. W. Bromiley and T. F. Torrance, vol. 1.2 (Edinburgh: T&T Clark, 1956), 203.

some innate, immanent, and static intersection between the divine and the human conceived as some self-selected and self-endorsed human capacity.

The Nonneutrality of the Christian Theologian

To be "absolutely neutral" in relation to God is to be "absolutely hostile" to God.[56] Noncommitment before the revelation event or the prioritizing of other criteria or grounds as foundational to the reality of the self-giving disclosure of God is not an appropriate theological option. In short, the very facticity of revelation involves a correlation between theological truthfulness and obedience. To acknowledge the event of Christian revelation is to acknowledge that we begin there. If we refuse not only to interpret God but also to allow our interpretation of God to be "informed" out of revelation, we deny revelation. In the language of Kierkegaard, we are endorsing as foundational or fundamental a form of existence that is outside truth and must be understood, therefore, as "error."

The Inseparability of the Formal and the Material

It is radically inappropriate, therefore, to separate formal and material considerations and to introduce prior or "foundational" philosophical prescriptions at the methodological, epistemological, or ontological levels.[57]

As Eberhard Jüngel summarizes Barth here, "[T]he Being of God proceeds, and thus precedes all human questioning."[58] Christian theology is, therefore, a reflecting (*Nachdenken*, lit., "after-thinking") on the proceeding of God toward the contingent, created order as the Logos and in the Spirit. God's being-as-such or God's being-in-this-way *precedes* and thus both initiates and determines all truly theological questioning (the "Who" question addressed to God) *ab initio*. The significance of this for theology is that it "realizes that all its knowledge, even its knowledge of the correctness of its knowledge, can only be an event, and cannot therefore be guaranteed as correct knowledge from any place apart from or above this event."[59] Theological prolegomena must invariably be postlegomena.

Semantic *Metanoia*

Intrinsic to the event of God's self-communication is the a posteriori revision of the meaning of the terms we use and the provisionality of the suppositions

---

56. Ibid., 1.1, 47–48. "(I)f the eternal presence of Christ is to be revealed to us in time, there is a constant need of that continuing work of the Holy Spirit in the Church and to its members which is always taking place in new acts." Ibid., 513.

57. It is this feature to which Jüngel refers when he argues that "Barth's doctrine of the Trinity as dogmatic interpretation of God's self-interpretation possesses an anti-metaphysical and anti-mythological significance." Jüngel, *The Doctrine of the Trinity: God's Being Is in Becoming*, trans. Horton Harris (Edinburgh: Scottish Academic Press, 1976), 29.

58. Ibid., xx. ("[D]as Sein Gottes geht und eben so allem menschlichen Fragen zuvorkommt," Eberhard Jüngel, *Gottes Sein Ist im Werden: Verantwortliche Rede vom Sein Gottes bei Karl Barth: Eine Paraphrase* [Tübingen: J. C. B. Mohr, 1976], 10.)

59. Barth, *Church Dogmatics*, 1.1, 42.

that accompany them. The impropriety of an a priori foundationalism relates no more to our interpretation of method and our ways of knowing than to the functioning of the terminology we use. Whenever we make theological statements or ask theological questions, we make suppositions with respect to the meanings of the terms we use. These suppositions, which are inevitable and potentially innocent, become less than innocent if we fail to appreciate their provisionality or "sketchlike" quality.[60] Hence, semantic reformation or reconciliation is thus *intrinsic* to revelation, not least because thought and language are irreducibly interrelated.

The Identity in God between Word and Act and the Irreducibly Personal Nature of God's Word

Barth also stresses the identity (rather than mere correspondence) in God between God's Word and God's act: "God's Word is itself God's act."[61] God's Word is "enacted Divine event."[62] Consequently, whenever God speaks to humanity, the content is a *concretissimum*.[63] It is an act, and an act, moreover, that includes its hearing. There can be no dichotomy, therefore, between God's act of communication as Word and God's being communicated as Word. When revelation takes place, the church has come into being. Neither can there be any dichotomy between God's *work* and God's *being*. Consequently, when we are talking about the perception of God's Word, we are not engaging in an anthropological discussion about human capacity; we are talking about *God*. And to the extent that we are doing this, we are the church in communion with the *Being* of God. As Barth comments, when we speak of the Holy Spirit, "We are always speaking of the event in which God's Word is not only revealed to man but also believed by him."[64]

This brings us to the essentially *personal* nature of God's self-communication. There can be no conceptual reduction of God's Word. It is the truth precisely by virtue of its being God's speaking person—"*Dei loquentis persona.*"[65] This

---

60. Suppositions here can too easily become, in R. G. Collingwood's language, "relative presuppositions" or, more sinisterly, "absolute presuppositions," which are so fundamental to one's frame of reference that one is not even aware of what one is presupposing. Collingwood, *Essay on Metaphysics* (Oxford: Clarendon, 1940).

61. Barth, *Church Dogmatics*, 1.1, 147. It is this that gives rise to Horst Pöhlmann's comment that Barth is committed to an "actualistic ontology." Pöhlmann, *Analogia entis oder Analogia fidei? Die Frage der Analogie bei Karl Barth* (Göttingen: Vandenhoeck & Ruprecht, 1965), 119. He suggests also, "Man kann deshalb ohne Übertreibung von einem Panaktualismus Barths sprechen" (117). As I argue in ch. 4 of *Persons in Communion*, it is certainly not Barth's intention to seek to universalize an actualistic concept of being. His emphasis on the a posteriori nature of theological articulation precludes this kind of ontological agenda. For his criticism to work, Pöhlmann must show that Barth's grounds for refusing to operate theologically with a dualism between God's being and act are foreign to an a posteriori theological description of the New Testament notions of the divine Presence, Glory, Word, and the identification of the Redeemer as "Immanuel."

62. Barth, *Church Dogmatics*, 1.1, 59.

63. Ibid., 1.1, 140.

64. Barth, *Church Dogmatics*, 1.1, 182. Again we see that to attempt to speak about God on the basis of some predetermined set of epistemological criteria or independent grounds is simply not to speak about the same God. Why? Because without the divine proceeding that is the Holy Spirit and the incarnate Logos, God is not God—God is not the God whose being is in this becoming. The point here is not the affirmation of any *logical* necessity of the divine utterance being heard but simply a theological one concerning the coinherence of the person of the Word in Jesus Christ and the Holy Spirit.

65. Barth, *Church Dogmatics*, 1.1, 136. Barth uses the same Latin phrase later on (p. 304) where he again stresses the irreducibly concrete particularity of the divine address in revelation as this is to be

implies again that revelation in Christ is not *an* objective reality, where ultimate reality is thereby attached to *oneself* as subject. It is *the* objective reality in that the subjective agent in the event is God. God's Word is thus as unanticipatable and unrepeatable by human beings as God's Being is unanticipatable or unrepeatable. We can no more anticipate the Word than we can be its authors. This means, moreover, that what God speaks can never be known or true anywhere in abstraction from God himself. "It is known and true in and through the fact that He Himself says it" and "that He is present in person in and with what is said by Him."[66]

Eschatological Provisionality

To the extent that the eschatological qualification "not yet fully realized" relates to the human act of God-talk, we must also recognize the time-governed and provisional nature of our terminology and forms of expression. One implication of this is that there is no place, therefore, for any conceptuality that constitutes a "natural" bridge between the times, between the *regnum gloriae* and the *regnum gratiae*. If a concept is provided that possesses a realized eschatological function, then this must be affirmed *subsequent* to the event of revelation by grace and must not be presupposed by it. Moreover, its meaning and rules of use will always need to be reformed; it is a conceptuality that is "on the way," that is, undergoing a process of semantic reconciliation.

God's Self-Communication and "Properly Basic" Beliefs

The implication of Kierkegaard's, Bonhoeffer's, and Barth's arguments is that the event of God's self-communication in the Word perceived by the Spirit conditions and establishes "properly basic" beliefs, to borrow Alvin Plantinga's terminology.[67] These are beliefs that do not need to be justified or accounted for with reference to other more basic beliefs or suppositions. That is because they are basic and warranted—warrant that neither is nor must be demonstrable by making recourse to universally accessible evidence. This is not unrelated to Bonhoeffer's statement that "Jesus' testimony to himself stands by itself as self-authenticating. . . . The fact of the revelation of God in Christ cannot be either established or disputed scientifically."[68] To deny that

---

identified with the being of God: "According to Scripture God's revelation is God's own direct speech which is not to be distinguished from the act of speaking and therefore is not to be distinguished from God Himself, from the divine I which confronts man in this act in which it says Thou to him. Revelation is *Dei loquentis persona*."

66. Barth, *Church Dogmatics*, 1.1, 137. "The personalizing of the concept of the Word of God, which we cannot avoid when we remember that Jesus Christ is the Word of God, does not mean its deverbalizing." Barth, *Church Dogmatics*, 1.1, 138. It is its personal nature that underscores its verbal quality. To emphasize the former serves to strengthen, rather than to detract from, the latter.

67. For his most recent discussions of "proper basicality," see his *Warrant the Current Debate* (Oxford: Oxford University Press, 1993), ch. 4, and *Warrant and Proper Function* (Oxford: Oxford University Press, 1993), ch. 10. In *Warrant the Current Debate*, he suggests that for Calvin "certain beliefs about God are . . . properly basic" and mentions his doctrine of the *sensus divinitatis* in this regard (86). This is ambiguous since, for Calvin, our *sensus divinitatis* does not remain properly functional as it would have done *si integer stetisset Adam* (if Adam had remained whole).

68. Bonhoeffer, *Christology*, trans. John Bowden (London: Collins, 1966), 32–33.

this is the case is to rule out the validity of God's self-communication in Christ *tout court.* Moreover, any denial of this on theological grounds will require one to make recourse to basic beliefs of some other kind—which will themselves be ascribed to divine action of some kind.

This is emphatically not to say that *everyone* is justified in claiming his or her particular religious beliefs to be "properly basic." Neither is it to say that one cannot articulate why one regards it appropriate to claim one's beliefs to be properly basic; the function of the above arguments is to do precisely that. However, it is also the case that one may not be able to demonstrate one's reasons to be valid or properly basic to people operating on the basis of other incompatible basic beliefs. To expect this to be possible would itself be a contradiction of the perception that God's self-disclosure includes his self-identification. It would be to deny that not only the propriety but also the perception of that propriety derive from and are carried by the divine self-communication itself. In other words, the very nature of our "properly basic" beliefs is that they do not acknowledge the assumption that other suppositions constitute a more basic Archimedean point from which we can assess the proper basicality of the beliefs communicated in and through God's self-communication. To insist that any "information" communicated must be ratifiable, confirmable, *and hence discernible* with recourse to basic beliefs quite independent of the divine address constitutes, of course, a return to the Socratic!

Unfortunately, the desire to do precisely this is deeply rooted within the European tradition. This is apparent in Descartes' concern in his *Meditations* to establish the roots of the tree of knowledge—roots that are to be found, not surprisingly, within the self conceived as a self-affirming *res cogitans.*[69] However, the most significant influence here is not Cartesian foundationalism so much as that form of classical foundationalism we find in Locke, for whom a belief is justified when I have "done my best" to fulfill my intellectual duties.[70] In *An Essay Concerning Human Understanding* (1690), John Locke established classical evidentialism by asserting that "all beliefs need to be based on evidence" and that we have duties not to believe anything for which we do not have evidence.[71] In short, "[B]elief cannot be afforded to anything, but upon good reason," or, as W. K. Clifford would famously argue, "It is wrong, always, everywhere, and for anyone to believe anything upon insufficient evidence."[72] As Stephen Evans adds, concerning the resulting epistemic duties, "Not only must we base our beliefs on evidence; we must also proportion the 'firmness' of our belief to the quality of the evidence."[73]

Three obvious problems result from this widely influential assumption. First, any assessment of any belief must itself presuppose other beliefs.

---

69. Descartes was, of course, influenced by the Platonist dimension of the thought of Augustine, to whom he owes the *cogito ergo sum* argument. Epistemic certainty is to be found within the self.

70. C. Stephen Evans, *The Historical Christ and the Jesus of Faith* (New York: Oxford University Press, 1996), 213.

71. Ibid., 208ff.

72. W. K. Clifford, *Lectures and Essays* (London: Macmillan, 1901), 183. Cf. Alvin Plantinga, *Warranted Christian Belief* (New York: Oxford University Press, 2000), 89, and Evans, *Historical Christ and the Jesus of Faith*, 298 n. 12.

73. Evans, *Historical Christ and the Jesus of Faith*, 209.

Second, it is entirely unclear how we might begin to determine the evidential support for our beliefs. Are we, for example, supposed to step outside them in order to occupy some beliefless Archimedean point? Clearly, the very advocacy of such a position is belief contingent. There is, in short, a serious problem of internal consistency attending any such advocacy. Third, this whole approach assumes that we have some kind of voluntary control or sovereignty over our beliefs—so that I can decide to believe something less firmly by a direct act of self upon self. The most basic human psychology suggests that this is quite impossible.

Such a position would mean, for example, that I have an epistemic duty to determine how much evidence I have to believe that I am not a brain in a vat on Alpha Centauri. Once I have carried out my duties by working this out (one wonders how!), I then have a duty not to believe that I am not a brain in a vat to a degree greater than my evidence warrants.

Endless further issues emerge relating, for example, to the status and justifiability of moral beliefs—that malformed babies should not be given a lethal injection at birth, for example, as a colleague of mine once advocated. How is it possible to determine that such a belief is sufficiently evidenced to be justified? The conclusion we are forced to draw is that, as Alston, Wolterstorff, and Plantinga have argued, "being justified in believing something is not identical with being able to justify a belief."[74]

To know something is to hold beliefs that are both true and warranted. Contemporary externalist epistemology argues, convincingly in my view, that warrant or justification involves a concept of proper epistemic function.[75] Given that one's individual thought processes are irreducibly bound up with the semantic functionality of the community of which one is part and which, therefore, conditions the way one interprets and understands reality, there can be no dichotomy between the proper functionality of the knowing subject and the proper functionality of the semantic community in which one participates. Here again, one perceives the significance of the dogmatic insistence on the inseparability of the perception of God's self-communication from participation not in the old, noetically ("dianoetically"[76]) dysfunctional humanity, but in the new humanity, in the reschematized body of the *eschatos Adam*. Properly basic, justified true belief must be seen emerging in and through reconciled participation in the community of the redeemed. The questions "where" and "how" God speaks must be answered ecclesially.[77]

So what are the implications of the above for a theological account of the relationship between faith and reason? It should be clear from what I have argued thus far that I would question approaches that appeal to natural

---

74. Ibid., 216.

75. I do not share Bruce Marshall's suspicion of externalist epistemology since I have no problem in suggesting that if a true belief is generated within us by God that this is relevant to the belief's epistemic status. See Bruce D. Marshall, "Putting Shadows to Flight: The Trinity, Faith, and Reason," in this volume.

76. The reference here is to Paul's statement that we are *echthroi te dianoia* (Col 1:21).

77. This would not be considered new by those Greek fathers who emphasized the self-authenticating nature of the Word (the *Autologos*) manifest to the *ekklesiastikon phronema* (the ecclesial mind) in a context of worship (*eusebeia*).

"reason" as providing the conditions or context for the recognition of God's self-disclosure.[78] It has often been held, however, in both Reformed[79] and Catholic circles, that there are "two separate sources of justified or warranted belief."[80] What is variously referred to as either "reason" or "philosophy" is held to constitute one source of knowledge, and faith another. Something of this is reflected in the papal encyclical *Fides et Ratio*, which reiterates the affirmation of the First Vatican Council that "there exists a knowledge which is proper to faith surpassing the knowledge proper to human reason, which nevertheless by its nature can discover the Creator." Pope John Paul II continues, "There exists a twofold order of knowledge, distinct not only as regards their source, but also as regards their object" (9). The deliverances of both reason and faith are assumed to be in harmony and lead to "truth in all its fullness." The truth, he argues, "which God reveals to us in Jesus Christ, is not opposed to the truths which philosophy perceives"(34). This may at first appear to establish more than it does. As Alvin Plantinga comments, "That much is truistic, no truth of any kind can contradict any truth of any kind. What is not truistic is the pope's further claim: since God is the author both of faith and of our reason, God would not bring it about or permit it to be that faith and reason were in conflict."[81]

So is it the case that the dictates of both faith and reason will inevitably be in harmony and can always be assumed to be so? The answer depends in part on our definitions of "faith" and "reason." If we define "faith" and "reason" in such a way that they become "success words" (J. L. Austin) and constitute veridical relations to their proper objects, then it may indeed be appropriate to suggest that they will not be in conflict. But if reason refers to human processes of reasoning and what human reasoning actually delivers, then it is not at all clear that God would not permit them to be in conflict. And clearly the likelihood of conflict is doubled if it is allowed that faith can also be confused as to its object.

All this raises problems. First, is it the case, as the pope seems to think, that God would not allow human reason to go astray such that it always delivers a body of knowledge in harmony with the deliverances of faith? What grounds might lead us to think so? Would the basis of such a supposition lie with reason? If so, then this suggests a circularity: To argue that reason confirms that reason can be trusted to generate a true and non–a priori body of knowledge seems suspect. If, however, this claim is made on the basis of faith, then we have in fact affirmed the priority of the insights of faith and, indeed,

---

78. Karl Barth defines Christian faith as "the illumination of the reason in which men become free to live in the truth of Jesus Christ and thereby to become sure also of the meaning of their own existence and of the ground and goal of all that happens." Barth, *Dogmatics in Outline*, trans. G. T. Thomson (London: SCM Press, 1966), 22.

79. See, for example, Charles Hodge's *Systematic Theology*, vol. 1 (London: Thomas Nelson and Sons, 1873). Hodge operates with a high doctrine of the place of reason in theology: "It is the prerogative of reason to judge the credibility of a revelation" (50). He also argues for the importance of "Innate Knowledge": "It cannot be doubted that there is such knowledge, i.e., that the soul is so constituted that it sees certain things to be true immediately in their own light" (191).

80. Here I am citing Alvin Plantinga's review of *Fides et Ratio*, in *Books and Culture*, July/August 1999, to which I am extensively indebted in my critique of the papal encyclical.

81. Plantinga, review of *Fides et Ratio*.

its foundational role in informing the way we interpret reason and its dictates! This in turn would seem to undermine the pope's advocacy of a "truly propaedeutic path" (90), not to mention the foundational role of so-called fundamental theology.

Second, suppose we argue (as seems to be implied) that reason really can establish the validity of its function on its own terms; then this raises a further problem. Bertrand Russell's set theory and property paradoxes illustrate how reason applied in its most rigorous form can find itself demonstrating logically incompatible conclusions from innocent premises.[82] In short, the most rigorous applications of human reason may be seen to generate deductive conclusions that are in tension with themselves and that must be seen as such by the law of the excluded middle. In short, reason itself seems to suggest that reason, left to its own resources, does *not* constitute an indubitable ground of certain knowledge.[83]

Third, it is not possible to ignore the fact that reason invariably operates from an epistemic base, that is, a series of affiliations, allegiances, or "canons" on the basis of which its deductive processes do their work. These generally cannot be demonstrated by virtue of reason's rationally contemplating its own products or operating *ab initio* on its own grounds. Even in the most exact sciences, reason necessarily assumes a series of suppositions and assumptions taken on faith, as these include memory, testimony, the collective testimony of the scientific community—and we might also include nondemonstrable heuristic intuitions, the stuff of our "tacit dimension," subliminal awareness, and the like. Indeed, it is hard to conceive of anything other than the most trivial operations of reason that do not operate from an epistemic base—that is, which do not assume affiliations grounded in "faith" of one kind or another. As Charles Taylor comments in his contribution to this volume (343), "Indeed, totally unaided reason probably doesn't get you farther than your nose." This is not to undermine or undercut the operations of reason; it is simply to point out that this is how reason functions. Confusion here is not unrelated to that which underpins Lockean evidentialism—that is, it results from the refusal to appreciate the fact that *every* sphere of understanding assumes suppositions taken on faith.

One of the purposes of this essay has been to emphasize the importance of what the pope refers to as the *auditus fidei* and that, I have suggested,

---

82. "Russell's paradox represents either of two interrelated logical antinomies. The most commonly discussed form is a contradiction arising in the logic of sets or classes. Some classes (or sets) seem to be members of themselves, while some do not. The class of *all* classes is itself a class, and so it seems to be in itself. The null or empty class, however, must *not* be a member of itself. However, suppose that we can form a class of *all* classes (or sets) that, like the null class, are *not* included in themselves. The paradox arises from asking the question of whether *this* class is in itself. It is if and only if it is not. The other form is a contradiction involving properties. Some properties seem to apply to themselves, while others do not. The property of *being a property* is itself a property, while the property of *being a cat* is not itself a cat. Consider the property that something has just in case it is a property (like that of *being a cat*) that does *not* apply to itself. Does this property apply to itself? Once again, from either assumption, the opposite follows. The paradox was named after Bertrand Russell, who discovered it in 1901." *Internet Encyclopaedia of Philosophy*, ed. James Fieser, http://www.utm.edu/research/iep/p/par-russ.htm.

83. Cf. Ernstpeter Maurer's discussion of Russell's set theory antinomies in the section on "Perplexity" in his admirable essay in this volume, "The Perplexity and Complexity of Sinful and Redeemed Reason."

involves our being given the ears to hear. Is it not clearly the case that the *auditus fidei* does indeed have something to say vis-à-vis our engagement with philosophy and the assumptions of philosophers, as well as those of ethicists and political scientists, not to mention the philosophical assumptions of so many other disciplines—such as gender studies or evolutionary psychology, for example? The question with which the age-old concern with the relationship of faith and reason is confronted boils down to this: Under what circumstances is it ever appropriate, let alone rational, for us as Christians to seek to put the *auditus fidei* and its deliverances to one side and appeal to some supposed faculty of autonomous reason that is conceived as operating in a manner entirely free from nondemonstrable beliefs?

This raises three additional questions: (1) Would it be possible, in the name of an appeal to "reason" and philosophy, to separate from my thinking those beliefs constitutive of my epistemic base and that relate to God's purposes vis-à-vis all that is, the meaning of life, who God is, and so on? (2) Even if this were possible, why would I want to do this if I believed that faith offered me insight into the nature of ultimate questions and the meaning of life? (3) Even if it were possible and if I were to desire to do this, would it be an appropriate response to the creating and reconciling God who (one might deduce from the very facticity of revelation) desires that I operate from beliefs generated by the Holy Spirit and intrinsic to the recognition of who Christ is when it comes to interpreting God, the world, and humanity? Indeed, would such an approach not constitute, as I have suggested above, a de facto denial of revelation (to the extent that the fact of revelation would seem to suggest divine endorsement that our understanding *requires* him to disclose himself and his purposes) if the implication of revelation is that we are not able to know as we should, that we are not able to understand the meaning of life aright, that philosophy and its deliverances may not be reliable? Finally, if the Light of the World is presented to the Body of Christ, as the incarnate Word, *homoousios to patri*, why would we and why should we wish to find our way by what, by comparison, can only be regarded as the created light of the stars? Why should we wish to circumscribe the incarnation in this way, or relocate it to some exclusive sphere of "salvation"? Moreover, why should we wish to ground our understanding of it in a fundamental theology, or predetermine its interpretation by way of a *praeparatio* or propaedeutic path?[84]

As a violinist, I use all four fingers of my left hand.[85] It is conceivable that I could choose to use only three fingers or possibly two.[86] But what good reason could there possibly be for choosing not to use all the resources at hand

---

84. The extent of my profound agreement with Paul Griffiths's admirable analysis of how reasoning goes wrong should be entirely clear. The implications of (a) his rejection of "the dream of appealing to natural law in order to provide a broadly persuasive ordering of common life in a late-modern democracy," as also (b) his insistence that we should speak from "the full depth of our knowledge" and avoid pretending "that what we know is known by the exercise of reason alone," are immense. If appreciated universally, these two points would have a profound impact on the whole shape of contemporary theological debates. See Paul J. Griffiths, "How Reasoning Goes Wrong: A Quasi-Augustinian Account of Error and Its Implications," in this volume, p. 159.

85. This example is adapted from a climbing analogy used by Alvin Plantinga.

86. Paganini sought to impress audiences by performing compositions using only one string of his violin, but the concern of his playing ceased, thereby, to be performing with maximal musical profundity.

when performing a Brahms sonata? Is it and can it be rational, let alone an appropriate response to revelation, for Christians to choose not to bring all their best epistemic resources to bear on the interpretation of reality, the meaning of human life, and so on right from the start? What conceivable grounds could there be, therefore, for bracketing out God's self-disclosure in considering *all* the fundamental methodological and epistemological questions of theology? This disclosure, after all, presents itself as involving the reconciliation and reschematization of our minds in such a way that we are given eyes to see and ears to hear what, otherwise, we would not see or hear aright, if at all—not least, any limitations in our seeing and hearing!

True Faith and True Reason

I have argued at some length that the knowledge that lies at the heart of the Christian faith places in question all our prior epistemic allegiances. For that reason, it challenges all forms of what I have called "criterial immanentism"— the dogma that our criteria for assessing theological truth-claims are pregiven within our innate preunderstandings and, as such, are veridically predetermined. I have suggested, moreover, that the failure of theologians to appreciate this has generated the profoundly destructive challenges to the Christian faith that have emerged from within the discipline of theology over the last two hundred years.

I have also discussed related points of confusion associated with Cliffordian evidentialism on the one hand and with the suppositions of the papal encyclical *Fides et Ratio* on the other. I have argued for an integrated understanding of the roles of faith and reason where we recognize that reason always operates from an epistemic base that is not *itself* delivered by reason, that it thus requires faith to function, and that it is profoundly confused, therefore, (a) to identify reason with the very diverse and often inimical (both to each other as also to the Christian faith) deliverances of "philosophy," and (b) to think that it is cogent, let alone appropriate, for Christians to put faith to one side in the name of utilizing reason in the context of theology.

God's self-disclosure has been presented as including that acknowledgment that is faith and that constitutes the liberation of reason for proper epistemic function, that is, for the fulfillment of its divinely intended purpose. What now must be considered is the locus of that proper epistemic function. Where and in whom might such "proper epistemic function" be found? Enlightenment thought confidently assumed that it could be found within oneself to the extent that one had confirmed—by internal (properly functional?) means— that one was fulfilling one's epistemic duties. In radical contrast, however, the thrust of the gospel is that that which is desired and required of humanity— the "righteous requirements" (*dikaiomata*) definitive of its proper function— are to be found nowhere else than in that one true human who is both the incarnate Logos and the *eschatos Adam*. These are fulfilled in him and are fulfilled as such *in our place* and *on our behalf*. It is in him that both the Father and creation are known in truth—and this is a knowing in which we are given to participate. What this means is that righteousness and right relatedness in all its forms are found first and foremost objectively *en Christo*. What this means is that every facet of human existence, to the extent that it fulfills God's purposes for us, must be interpreted as the gift of participating by the Spirit in the incarnate Son's communion with the Father. Thus, not only must Christian worship and Christian ethics be defined in these terms,[87] but precisely the same may be said of faith and the proper operations of our reason.[88] Proper epistemic function vis-à-vis God must be interpreted in the light of an all-embracing conception of participation *en Christo*[89]—that is, it is to be interpreted as the gift of participating by the Spirit in the incarnate Son's epistemic, noetic, and semantic communion with the Father.[90] No one knows the Father save the Son and those to whom the Son gives him to be known. This epistemic participation is irreducibly bound up with what I have described elsewhere as "semantic participation"—participation in Christ's *rhemata*, as John articulates it.[91]

This suggests that the proper theological function of both faith and reason must be interpreted christologically. There is only one in whom we find true faith in the Father, just as there is only one who knows the Father in truth. There is only one human, therefore, whose reasoning operates from a reconciled epistemic base—a base that was not *echthros te dianoia*, which was not alienated in its capacity for noetic penetration through (*dia*) to God's purposes, that is, Jesus Christ. The creation of the body of Christ was the creation by the Spirit of a communion of persons set free for participation in the sole priest of our confessing, our believing, and our rational thinking (*noein/logein*).

This suggests that faith and reason and philosophy only operate in truth when they operate within an ecclesial context—a context that opens up knowledge which, in a profound sense, constitutes precisely the beginnings of that knowledge of *ta panta* after which the pope was seeking in *Fides et Ratio*. This is because knowledge of the incarnate Logos is not a localizable or circumscribable body of knowledge; it concerns, as Jüngel argues, correspondence to the Truth—*adaequatio intellectus et rei*.[92] This is not correspondence to a truth but to the Truth, the ground and grammar of the contingent order.

There are few places where this is more clearly articulated than in a lecture that Karl Barth gave in the ruins of Bonn University in 1946. Here he spoke

---

87. These must be interpreted in terms of the sole priesthood of Christ—as the gift of participating by the Spirit in the incarnate Son's communion with the Father, with his imaging, as the true *imago Patris*, of God's faithfulness to humanity.

88. This is to offer emphatic endorsement of Reinhard Hütter's insistence that the question of the relationship between faith and reason, theology and philosophy, is a genuinely *theological* question. See Hütter's essay, "The Directedness of Reasoning and the Metaphysics of Creation," in this volume.

89. See the particularly insightful theological analysis of our communal sharing in the mind of Christ offered by Mark McIntosh in his essay in this volume, "Faith, Reason, and the Mind of Christ."

90. Cf. Hütter's statement in his contribution to this volume that "reason's directedness now participates through faith, inchoately, in the directedness of the Logos to the Father that *is* the Spirit, the triune identity that is the eternal law of triune love."

91. John 17:8. Here we see the close connection between sharing in the Son's knowing of the Father and receiving the *rhemata* that the Son receives from the Father. See my discussion of this in Torrance, *Persons in Communion*, 325ff.

92. Eberhard Jüngel, *Theological Essays II*, trans. A. Neufeldt-Fast and J. B. Webster (Edinburgh: T&T Clark, 1995), 191–95.

in the context of the most tragic failure of human faith and reason and of the almost inconceivable consequences of the church's confused compartmentalization of two supposedly distinct bodies of knowledge. This dichotomization amounted to the failure to recognize that the incarnate Son is none other than the one Logos through which all things were made (*ta panta*). To recognize this means that all our thinking—not least our thinking about faith and reason—must be reschematized from that center to the extent that it constitutes the locus (or *topos*, to use Athanasius's word) of God's self-disclosure in space and time through the reconciliation of our minds to the Truth.

> The truth of Jesus Christ is not one truth among others; it is *the* truth, the universal truth, that creates all truth as surely as it is the truth of God, the *prima veritas* which is also the *ultima veritas*. For in Jesus Christ God has created all things, He has created all of us. We exist not apart from Him, but in Him, whether we are aware of it or not; and the whole cosmos exists not apart from Him, but in Him, borne by Him, the Almighty Word.[93]

---

93. Barth, *Dogmatics in Outline*, 26.

CHAPTER TWO

Putting Shadows to Flight:
The Trinity, Faith, and Reason

— BRUCE D. MARSHALL —

Theologians these days often suggest that an adequate theological approach to the problem of faith and reason has to be, in some fundamental sense, Trinitarian. At the same time, a broad stream of traditional Christian reflection on faith and reason seems, at least to some of its modern advocates, thoroughly opposed to this suggestion. Attempts to say what the Trinity has to do with faith and reason tend, in other words, toward two apparently incompatible theses.

(1) Reason cannot know the world aright unless the reasoner knows the Trinity.

(2) Whether reason knows the world aright has nothing to do with whether the reasoner knows the Trinity.

To its defenders, (1) follows from a basic Christian conviction. The created world, as the work precisely of the triune God, bears the stamp of the Trinity all the way down. As a result, the world as we have it makes sense only if God is the Trinity. In the end, a reasoner who fails to believe in the Trinity cannot consistently fail to be a skeptic or a nihilist. If she's true to her own convictions, she will be a reasoner for whom the world finally makes no sense. That non-Trinitarians do regularly fail to be skeptics or nihilists is not a result of reason's triumph, but of happy inconsistency. From this point of view, defenders of (2) are worse than Rahner's "mere monotheists," for whom the God who redeemed the world in Christ, to say nothing of the God who created the world *ex nihilo*, might just as well not have been triune.[1] They've failed to learn an even more basic lesson of Christian faith in the Trinity: It's impossible to be a "mere monotheist." The choice is between Trinitarian faith and nihilism.

---

1. Karl Rahner, *The Trinity*, trans. Joseph Donceel, 2nd ed. (New York: Crossroad, 1997), 10.

Advocates of (2) find their thesis equally rooted in nonnegotiable Christian convictions. The triune God made the world to be known by rational creatures, but is himself, in his triunity, inherently beyond the reach of created reason. As a result, any reasonable person is capable of making sense of the world, regardless of whether she knows anything about the Trinity. Even for Christians, figuring out what it is right to believe about nature or history has nothing to do with what we believe about the Trinity; these matters belong to two different cognitive or epistemic orders. From this point of view, (1) is a lapse into fideism and irrationalism. By allowing no rational certainties available to all human beings, regardless of whether they believe in (or have even heard of) the Trinity, defenders of (1) invite ridicule of the Trinitarian faith—what Aquinas calls the "derision of infidels" (I, 32, 1, c).[2] They imply (whether or not they admit it openly) that only Christians can be competent scientists or historians, and that failure to believe in the Trinity is somehow deeply irrational.

Here I will argue that (1) and (2) pose no genuine dilemma for us. They are both false, and we should avoid the temptation of supposing that we need to choose between them. The specter of the irrational haunts them both, though in different ways, and both let the imagined difficulty of keeping irrationality at bay control their view of what Christian faith in the Trinity has to do with right reason. But the shadow of nihilism needn't tempt us to think that making rational sense of the world requires faith in the Trinity. Nor need the shadow of fideism tempt us to think that belief in the Trinity leaves untouched the rational sense we make of the world.

At the same time, each thesis takes off from an important Christian conviction that should be maintained. I'll try to show here how we can uphold the basic Christian claims on both sides of the argument without ending up faced by a choice between the two. Differently put: my aim is to understand the relationship between faith and reason in robustly Trinitarian terms, without giving grounds for the *irrisio infidelium*.

In order to do this, I will look at two much-debated theological questions: whether creation is an act of the three divine persons in their distinctness from one another, and whether the Trinity can be known by natural reason. My main interlocutor will be Thomas Aquinas, not necessarily because I think we need to follow him at any particular point (and especially not to prejudice the argument in favor of [2]), but because discussion of the issues with which we are here concerned comes back to him—whether in praise or in blame—as much as to any figure in Christian theology. The hope is that reflecting on these questions will help us sort out issues of being and belief when it comes to the Trinity—will help us see what God's triunity has to do with an epistemic outlook at once faithful and reasonable.

---

2. References to the *Summa theologiae* of Thomas Aquinas will be made by part number only, as here: I, 32, 1, c = *Summa theologiae*, part I, question 32, article 1, body of the article. Here and throughout the essay, all translations are my own; where reference is made to existing English translations, I have freely modified these in light of the original.

Trinity and Creation

Like many others before and since, Aquinas thinks that the product or term of the divine creative act always has a triune structure. Having intellect and will, rational creatures (humans and angels) are made in the image of the Trinity (in them "the representation of the Trinity is found in the form of an image"; I, 45, 7, c; cf. 93, 5). But in every creature "the representation of the Trinity is found in the form of a vestige": Insofar as each thing exists, "it points to the person of the Father (*demonstrat Personam Patris*)"; insofar as it is one sort of thing rather than another, "it represents the Word"; insofar as it is ordered to an end, "it represents the Holy Spirit, in that he is love" (I, 45, 7, c). At least at first glance, Aquinas apparently thinks that all creatures represent the Trinity in a way accessible to us. An image or vestige of the Trinity can be "found" in creatures, or as Augustine says, the vestige "appears" (I, 45, 7, sc; quoting *De trinitate* VI, x, 12).

In fact, the world is saturated with the Trinity. Everything about which we human beings might come to have true beliefs, regardless of whether we mark those beliefs as belonging to "faith" or to "reason," is either created to resemble the triune God, or is the triune God himself. Not only are the objects and states of affairs we might know Trinitarian across the board, but we the knowers bear the stamp of the Trinity. Indeed, we have the capacity to know—to produce an internal word and love that to which our word corresponds—just because we are made in the image of the Trinity. Moreover it's not in knowing ourselves or any creature, but precisely in knowing God (or at least being ineluctably ordered toward knowing God) that we actually exist in the image of the Trinity. "The divine image . . . is found in the human being by noticing the word conceived in knowing God, and the love that flows out of this knowledge. Thus the image of God is found in the soul in that the soul is borne—or is capable of being borne—into God" (I, 93, 8, c).

All these claims are more or less commonplace. Regardless of what it makes of the *vestigia Trinitatis*, however, contemporary Trinitarian theology is apt to be more concerned about whether the divine creative *act* itself has an irreducibly Trinitarian structure. To this warmly debated question Aquinas gives a flamboyantly affirmative answer.

Of course the act of creation, "to produce the being (*esse*) of things," is, like all divine acts involving creatures, single. There are not three divine creative acts, one for each person of the Trinity. In *this* sense, "to create is not unique (*proprium*) to one person, but is common to the whole Trinity" (I, 45, 6, c). This does not mean, however, that the three persons undertake the act of creation in an undifferentiated way, let alone that creation is somehow an act of the essence and not of the persons (since essences don't do anything; Aquinas hews consistently to the axiom that "it is individual subjects who act (*actus sunt suppositorum*)"; I, 39, 5, ad 1). On the contrary, "the divine persons have causality with respect to creation according to the distinctive character of their processions (*secundum rationem suae processionis*)"; each person undertakes the act of creation in a way unique to him (I,

45, 6, c; cf. ad 2).[3] More than that: the processions of the Son as *Verbum* from the Father, and of the Spirit as *Amor* from both "are the reasons for the coming forth of creatures (*sunt rationes productionis creaturarum*)" (I, 45, 6, c).[4]

Aquinas insists that the processions of the divine persons are the *ratio* not only for the coming forth of all creatures from God but also for the return of creation to God; not only for the gift of creation but for the gifts of grace and glory. These latter gifts outstrip creation in that they join us to God more intimately than does the first gift. Yet creation is not action at a distance, any more than are the grace of salvation and the bestowal of the beatific vision. All involve a "coming forth of the divine persons into creation" (*processio divinarum personarum in creaturas*), for which the Trinitarian *processio personarum* is in each case the one sufficient *ratio*.

> We have to see that the return of creatures to their goal takes place by way of the very realities through which creatures issue from their source. Just as we have earlier said that the coming forth of the divine persons themselves is the reason (*ratio*) for the production of creatures by the first principle, so also the same procession is the reason for their return to the final goal: just as we have been created by the Son and the Holy Spirit, so also we are joined by them to the ultimate goal. . . . Against this background the coming forth of the divine persons into creation can be considered in two ways. On the one hand, insofar as it is the reason that creatures issue from their source. Understood in this way, the coming of the divine persons into creation is located in the natural gifts, by which we exist at all. . . . The coming of the divine persons into creation can also be looked at insofar as it is the reason for the return of creatures to their final goal. Understood in this way, the coming of the divine persons into creation takes place only with respect to those gifts which join us in the closest possible way to our final end, namely to God. These are justifying grace and glory.[5]

Thus, every act of God has the processions of the divine persons as its final *ratio*, regardless of whether the outcome of the act be thought of as pertaining

---

3. This is Aquinas's position from the beginning. In the prologue to his commentary on the *Sentences*, he observes that "just as a little stream flows out of a river, so the temporal coming forth *(processus)* of creatures flows out of the eternal coming forth of the persons." *Scriptum super libros Sententiarum* (hereafter *In Sent.*), vol. 1, ed. R. P. Mandonnet (Paris: Lethielleux, 1929), 2.

4. To be sure, problems lurk here that there is no room to pursue at present. Like many others, Aquinas wants to say that all divine actions whose effect is a creature are numerically one, and at the same time that all such acts are carried out by each of the divine persons in a different way. But this means that, for example, "to create," as an act carried out by the Father, must have at least one feature or characteristic different from "to create" as an act carried out by the Son and the Spirit, and "to create" as an act carried out by the Son must have at least one feature or characteristic different from "to create" as an act carried out by the Spirit. Creation is thus an act that differs in at least one of its features as carried out by Father, Son, and Spirit, respectively. And this appears to make it not one action, but three: One person's action *x* is apparently discernible from any action *x* of both other persons. This leaves the numerical unity of *x* a bit of a puzzle. For some thoughts on how this problem might be handled, see Bruce D. Marshall, "What Does the Spirit Have to Do?" in *Reading John with St. Thomas Aquinas*, ed. Michael Dauphinas and Matthew Levering (Washington, DC: Catholic University of America Press, 2005).

5. *In* I *Sent.* 14, 2, 2, c. For one of the "earlier" texts to which Aquinas refers here, see note 7; see also *In* I *Sent.* 32, 1, 3, c: "The procession of the divine persons is in a way the origin (*quaedam origo*) of the procession of creatures."

to "nature" or to "grace." In fact, this applies *a fortiori* to those acts that lead creatures back to God, since the saving deeds that join us to God as our ultimate end depend on actual missions of the divine persons, while creation does not. The coming of the Son and the Spirit for the salvation of the world therefore yields an apprehension of God as the Trinity that exceeds any we might otherwise have; their missions give us what Aquinas calls a *cognitio quasi experimentalis*.[6] Indeed, you can't know about the divine acts that accomplish the world's salvation without knowing how to distinguish the persons of the Trinity from one another, and that requires some grasp, provided by the missions, of each in his personal uniqueness. That the divine acts and created outcomes that go beyond the "natural gifts" (and so, if you like, may be labeled "supernatural") are triune all the way down is thus relatively uncontested. Since you can't even know about these acts and outcomes without knowing the Trinity, they must be well saturated with the Trinity. In trying to understand the extent to which the distinctions among the divine persons make an impression on God's acts and works, we can therefore confine ourselves to the harder case: the coming forth of creatures from God, prescinding from all that's involved in their return to God.

In what sense are the coming forth of the Son and that of the Spirit together the *ratio* for the coming forth of creatures? The following text may shed some light on this:

> Let us assume, in accordance with our faith, the procession of the divine persons in unity of essence, although no argument may be found which is sufficient to prove this (*ad cuius probationem ratio sufficiens non invenitur*). This coming forth of the divine persons, which is perfect, must be the reason and the cause for the coming forth of creatures. Therefore we trace back the coming forth of creatures, which represent the perfection of the divine nature only imperfectly, to a perfect image which contains the divine perfection with absolute fullness, namely the Son. He is the natural principle, as it were, of the coming forth of creatures from God, insofar as they imitate his nature, who is their exemplar and reason for existing. At the same time, the coming forth of creatures stems from the generosity of the divine will. So in the same way we have to trace the coming forth of creatures back once again to a single principle, which is, as it were, the reason for this whole generous outpouring. This is love, which is the reason for all the gifts which

---

6. This "experimental"—or we could say "experiential"—knowledge of the divine persons results from our being joined to each divine person by grace in a way unique to that person, and thus rooted in his *propria*, viz., in his own personal uniqueness. "In virtue of the reception of these two [i.e., the Holy Spirit and the Son] there is effected in us a likeness of that which is unique to each person (*similitudo ad propria personarum*)" (*In* I *Sent.* 15, 4, 1, c). This applies precisely to those gifts of grace that belong to the persons by what Aquinas calls "appropriation." Thus, with regard to the Spirit in particular: "[B]y a gift appropriated to a person . . . there is effected in us a union with God (*conjunctio ad Deum*) in the manner which is unique to that person (*secundum modum proprium illius personae*). When the Holy Spirit is given, this happens through the gift of love. Hence this knowledge is, as it were, experiential" (*In* I *Sent.* 14, 2, 2, ad 3). On this passage, cf. Albert Patfoort, "Cognitio ista est quasi experimentalis," *Angelicum* 63 (1986): 3–13. On appropriations in Aquinas, see Bruce D. Marshall, *Trinity and Truth* (Cambridge: Cambridge University Press, 2000), 254–56.

the will gives. Therefore it is necessary that there be a person in God who comes forth by way of love, and this is the Holy Spirit.[7]

This passage is perhaps as elusive as it is suggestive.[8] Aquinas seems at least to argue, however, that no divine *productio* of creatures could fail to have a distinctively Trinitarian shape. And since the act of creation necessarily follows the unalterable pattern of *processiones* among the three who undertake it in common, no result—no creature the three might produce—could fail to embody, albeit imperfectly, the Trinitarian shape of the act that makes it. The Father might make creatures of any sort, but whatever creatures he makes will represent or resemble him, just because they are made through the perfect image he generates, and they will be ordered to him as their end, just because they are made by the perfect love who proceeds from him. There might not be any creatures at all, but if there are, the eternal coming forth of the Son is the *ratio*—the reason—why they cannot help being like him, and the coming forth of the Spirit is the reason why they cannot help desiring him.[9] That there are creatures at all stems from God's generosity; it is a "generous outpouring." But that creatures are at least a vestige of the Trinity is the natural result of the fact that it's the Trinity who makes them.

Aquinas finds still further specificity in the triune shape of God's creative act. The Holy Spirit, as love in person, is not simply the reason why there can be creatures who desire (and at least to that extent love) God. He is in a sense the reason (*quasi ratio*) why there is any creation in the first place. Creation is a voluntary act of the triune God, initiated by the Father. Like any voluntary act, creation takes place on account of love, since it's love that incites the will to do something, rather than simply contemplate the possibilities. By creating, the triune God gives the radical gift of a share in his own perfection to that which is not God. But the love on which this act of giving depends can't be elicited by the recipient exactly, since the very existence of the recipient—the creature—is part of the gift. Presumably it can't be elicited by the mere *idea* of the creature, since the love that gives of one's own plentitude, unlike the love that desires to make good a lack, isn't directed toward what might be, but toward what is.

But the Father never lacks an existent adequate to his love, since he always has a Son. It's precisely his love for the Son, Aquinas suggests, that gives the Father a good enough motive (not a necessary cause) to make a world. The world can be a gift of the triune God to that which is not (cf. Rom 4:17) because it is, first of all, a gift of the Father, in love, to the Son: "[T]he love of the Father reaching out to the Son (*tendens in Filium*) as its object is the reason why God bestows every gift (*omnem effectum*) of love on creatures"

---

7. *In* I *Sent.* 10, 1, c.

8. For an extensive analysis of it, see Gilles Emery, *La Trinité créatrice* (Paris: J. Vrin, 1995), 368–83, 537–40. On this topic in Aquinas, see also Max Seckler, *Das Heil in der Geschichte: Geschichtstheologisches Denken bei Thomas von Aquin* (Munich: Kösel Verlag, 1964), 81–108.

9. On this see Marshall, *Trinity and Truth*, 112–15. Regarding the Spirit as exemplar, and not simply causal agent, of the desire of creatures for the life of God, recall the text (I, 45, 7, c) cited in the first paragraph of this section: Every creature "*represents* the Holy Spirit, insofar as he is love" (italics mine).

(*In* I *Sent.* 14, 1, 1, c). In fact, as Aquinas later argues, the Father sees to the creation of the world in order to present that world as a gift in love precisely to the *incarnate* Son, to Jesus Christ "just insofar as he is a human being (*secundum quod homo*)."[10] For Aquinas, this is the way to read John 3:35: "The Father loves the Son, and has given all things into his hand," as the text reads in the Vulgate upon which Aquinas comments. The Father's love for the Son *secundum quod homo*, the love that abounds on account of the Son's being human, is the ultimate reason (*principium*) why "it is said that the Father has given all things into the hand of the Son, both in heaven and on earth. . . . [T]he reason for this gift is that he loves him . . . for the love of the Father is the reason for creating any creature at all."[11]

For Aquinas, the Father's love for the Son does, however, have a natural (as distinguished from voluntary) product—not the world, but a divine person, the Holy Spirit. Of course for Aquinas, the Spirit proceeds *from* the Son, as well as from the Father. But it is precisely the love of the Father for the Son, fully returned by the Son's love for the Father, that ultimately accounts for the Spirit's coming forth. In Aquinas's hands, that is, the *Filioque* finds its root not in the reduction of Father and Son to an undifferentiated single principle of the Spirit, but in the ordered mutual love of Father and Son, and so in their complete personal distinction: "Love itself comes forth from the Father delighting in the Son, and the Son delighting in the Father (*Ipse Amor procedit a Patre diligente Filium, et a Filio diligente Patrem*)."[12] Since the Spirit proceeds from the Father specifically on account of the Father's love for the Son, coming forth *to* the Son is apparently as basic to the Spirit's procession as coming forth *from* the Son.[13] And this brings us back to the Spirit himself as a reason for creation. Precisely as proceeding to the Son (*tendens in Filium*) and not only from him, the Spirit just is the "love by which the Father loves the Son," and as such the "love by which [the Father] loves the creature, when he imparts his own perfection to it" (*In* I *Sent.* 14, 1, 1, c).

For Aquinas, then, it seems that the act of creation has a quite specific triune shape. In particular, there can be a world at all not just because there is a Holy Spirit whose procession belongs to the "cause and reason for the whole production of creatures" (*In* I *Sent.* 14, 1, 1, c), but because the Holy Spirit is the *amor Patris tendens in Filium*. In *this* sense the Spirit himself is

---

10. On the interpretation of *"secundum quod . . ."* ("in virtue of . . . ," "on account of . . . ," or "insofar as . . .") locutions in Aquinas's Christology, see Bruce D. Marshall, *Christology in Conflict* (Oxford: Blackwell, 1987), 184–85.

11. Thomas Aquinas, *Super Evangelium S. Ioannis Lectura*, ed. R. Cai, 5th ed. (Turin and Rome: Marietti, 1952), 3, 3, no. 545 (hereafter, *In Ioannem*).

12. Thomas Aquinas, *Super Evangelium S. Matthaei Lectura*, ed. R. Cai, 5th ed. (Turin and Rome: Marietti, 1951), 17, 1, no. 1436.

13. On the Spirit proceeding to as well as from the Son, see also I, 36, 2, ad 4. On the Father's love for the Son eliciting the procession of the Spirit, cf. I, 27, 4, ad 2: "[L]ove is [not] begotten, but what is begotten is the reason for love (*amor [non] sit genitus, sed quod genitus sit principium amoris*)." At the same time, Aquinas consistently rejects the thought that the Father's love for the Son, whether taken essentially (as the Father's act simply in virtue of his possession of the one divine essence) or notionally (as the Holy Spirit), elicits the generation of the Son himself. Cf. I, 41, 2 ad 2; *In Ioannem* 3, 3, no. 545; 5, 3, no. 753; 15, 2, no. 1999; Thomas Aquinas, *Super Epistolam ad Romanos Lectura*, 1, 3, no. 27, in *Super Epistolas S. Pauli Lectura*, vol. 1, ed. R. Cai, 8th ed. (Turin and Rome: Marietti, 1953).

quasi ratio totius liberalis collationis, "the reason for this whole generous outpouring" (*In* I *Sent.* 10, 1, c).

What goes for God's creative action generally goes in particular for the act by which God brings it about that we know. That we actually attain any knowledge, that we apprehend any truth, depends not only on the capacity for knowledge that goes with being the *imago Trinitatis*, but also on the action of the Trinity. This applies to any knowledge whatever, and not only to the apprehension of those truths that we might classify as belonging to "faith." Here Aquinas does not hesitate to take his epistemic cues from the Apostle Paul: "Just as the air remains in darkness without a light to illuminate it, so also our intellect by itself, unless it is illuminated by the first truth, remains in mendacity (*de se in mendacio remanet*). Hence, insofar as it depends on him, every human being is a liar when it comes to his intellect, and only has truth to the extent that he participates in divine truth."[14] The "first truth" (*prima veritas*), who illuminates our minds to know whatever they know, is not simply "the one God" without distinction of persons, still less the divine nature, but the Son or Word—indeed, as Aquinas does not hesitate to say, the incarnate Word: "This human being is divine truth itself. In other human beings there are many participated truths, insofar as the first truth shines in their minds through many likenesses, but Christ is this truth."[15] The Spirit also has his own role in bringing it about that we know: "Every truth, by whomever it is uttered, is from the Holy Spirit. He is the one who infuses the natural light, and moves us to understand and to speak the truth" (I–II, 109, 1, ad 1).[16] The roles of the Son and the Spirit in this action are not to be equated: "The Son hands on his teaching to us, since he is the Word, but the Holy Spirit makes us capable of learning what he teaches" (*In Ioannem* 14, 6, no. 1958).

We may well have good cause to divide up true utterances and beliefs between those that belong to "faith" and those that belong to "reason." But whatever we make of the distinction between faith and reason, it seems that for a theologian like Aquinas (as for many contemporary Trinitarian theologians, regardless of whether they recognize their kinship with him) matters epistemic are Trinitarian all the way down. Prior to any distinction between faith and reason, the action of the triune God impresses upon the known, the knowers, and the knowledge alike an irreducibly Trinitarian shape.

Can We Prove the Trinity? Part I

So far we have been exploring, by way of a prominent example, the kinds of arguments one might make for the following claim: Any world the triune

---

14. Aquinas, *Super Epistolam ad Romanos Lectura*, 3, 1, no. 255. Cf. *In Ioannem* 8, 6, no. 1250.

15. *In Ioannem* 1, 8, no. 188. Cf. *In Ioannem* 1, 10, no. 207: "All created truths have been brought about by [Christ]. They are in a way participations and reflections of the first truth." Christ is the *lumen* who guides the way to the truths of reason as well as those of faith. "Illumination, or being illuminated by the Word, is understood in two ways: as pertaining to the light of natural knowledge (*cognitionis*) . . . and as pertaining to the light of grace" (*In Ioannem* 1, 5, no. 128; cf. 8, 2, no. 1142).

16. Aquinas attributes this remark to Ambrose, via the *Glossa ordinaria* on 1 Cor 12:3, and he cites it often. Cf. *In Ioannem* 1, 3, no. 103; 14, 4, no. 1916.

God might create will resemble and desire him as a whole and in all of its parts. That is:

(3) If God is triune, then all possible worlds are at least a vestige of the Trinity.

Given the epistemic bearing we have just assigned to this claim—that our knowing is Trinitarian all the way down—it might seem as though (1) has carried the day. We might be tempted, in other words, to find in (3) warrant for a further and stronger claim:

(4) Only if God is the Trinity can this world be, and be known.[17]

If this thesis is correct, then we have warrant for the claim that we can know the Trinity from the created world (*per creaturas*, as it was traditionally put)—that is, you can't think (4) is right unless you think it's possible to give a rational demonstration of the Trinity.

This requires a bit of explanation, since on the surface (4) is not an epistemic claim, but simply an assertion about the relation between God and the world. We need to be clear, though, about the epistemic implications of (4), and, equally, about what follows epistemically if (4) is false.

According to (4), the world as we have it is linked by logical necessity to the triunity of God. This statement does not simply assert that the existence of this world and our knowledge of it depend upon a God who is in fact triune. It makes a much stronger claim: No one but the triune God *could* bring about the world that we have and the knowledge we have of it. From this it follows that an adequate account of this world, of its nature, structure, and origin, must trace the world back to the triune God; it must conclude that God is the Trinity. Of course, it may be that our grasp of the world has not yet led us to a demonstration of the Trinity. Various contingencies (lassitude, logical blunders, ignorance of the needed data) may have prevented us so far from constructing a successful argument for the Trinity. But if (4) is true, it must be possible to construct such an argument; the Trinity must be knowable by natural reason. Or, more precisely, if (4) is true and yet we deny that natural reason is able to know the Trinity, then we deny not that the Trinity can be inferred from the world, but that we could ever succeed in doing it— that human beings could ever give, by cognitive means they might conceivably have at their disposal, an adequate account of the world they inhabit.[18]

---

17. This can be generalized: Only if God is the Trinity can any possible world be, and be known. From this, (4) evidently follows, so for present purposes we can let the two stand or fall together.

18. It may seem pointless simply to talk about whether the Trinity can be proven, since the concept of proof or demonstration is context-dependent. What will count as proven, so the suggestion goes, depends upon the context of belief and practice in which an argument is made, and so naturally varies with time and place.

This is surely right when it comes to the *persuasiveness* of a proof—its capacity to convince people. Conviction obviously depends on shared acceptance of premises and on shared background beliefs (perhaps regarding the epistemic status of the premises—that, e.g., they are truths accessible to any reasonable person). So whether an argument is likely to get counted as a proof no doubt varies by context. But

Thus, if (4) is true, there must be general features of the world that resemble or point to the Trinity in such a way that they are, by themselves, enough to yield the knowledge that God is triune.[19] (4) implies, in other words, not simply that the world includes features that Christian faith knows to be vestiges of the triune Creator, but that these features are *sufficient* to lead us to knowledge of the Trinity, and thus to knowledge of their own vestigial status. And conversely: if (4) is false, then there will be no general feature of the world that is sufficient of itself to lead us to knowledge of the Trinity. In this case it will be impossible to prove that God is the Trinity—not because we lack the wit to do it, but because the world can have no general feature that could not be explained or accounted for in some other way than by appeal to the Trinity.

Contemporary theologians seldom avow that they're out to *prove* that God is the Trinity. Yet the insinuation that it's finally irrational not to believe in the Trinity regularly infiltrates current Trinitarian theology. Acknowledging some general feature of the world (for example, that there's meaning, value, or purpose in it that we didn't put there) commits you to believing in the Trinity, even if you haven't yet reached the point of recognizing this. To think otherwise is inconsistent, and in that normative sense irrational. That theologians who make this assumption seldom venture a rigorous proof of the Trinity might not signal so much a failure of nerve as remarkable confidence. To them the assumption apparently seems obvious enough that it doesn't take much of an argument, nothing so elaborate as a proof, to make it plain.

Current arguments for claims like (4) proceed in a number of different ways. Sometimes it's suggested that only the triune God (or perhaps *a* triune God) can account for the possibility of a world that is genuinely distinct from God, yet wholly dependent on, reflective of, and ordered to God. Only a creator (the Father) who already has an other entirely adequate to himself (the Son) and loves this other in an entirely adequate way (the Holy Spirit) can account for the possibility of a world that is truly other to him, yet does not float free of him—a secular universe suspended over the void, in which God could only appear as an intruder. Without the Trinity, so the argument goes, we are left with the alternatives of pantheism and nihilism. We may not

---

whether it *is* a proof doesn't depend on anyone being persuaded by it, but only on whether a true conclusion is soundly inferred from true premises. So there can be proofs that don't widely persuade (think, for an obvious case, of certain rigorous demonstrations in higher mathematics, which don't persuade most of us because we don't understand them), and of course persuasions which aren't proofs. (I'm grateful to Paul Griffiths for his insistence on this point.)

As we will see, some of the chief parties to the high medieval debate over whether the Trinity can be demonstrated agreed pretty much entirely about which premises were true, and to a large extent about the epistemic status of the premises as well. The argument between, say, Bonaventure and Aquinas on this point was not a dialogue of the deaf between two people who failed to realize that they inhabited different cultural contexts and took different things for granted. It was a disagreement about what followed from what—about what could be inferred from beliefs they both shared.

19. By "general" features I mean those that just come with the sort of world this is (to use Aquinas's example, that every single thing has being, kind, and end), as distinguished from those features that depend on some particular divine action within the world. Surely features of the latter sort—the incarnation of the Word, the resurrection of Jesus—depend on the triunity of God in the fashion specified by (4). But that's not germane to the present question, which is whether the Trinitarian shape of the world as such (3) requires that God be the Trinity (4).

be able to *refute* pantheism and nihilism, but we can show that these unhappy possibilities are all that remain for those who decline to believe in the Trinity.

Hans Urs von Balthasar sometimes suggests this sort of argument, though he does not work it out in detail.

> A creation other than God yet positively related to him cannot be imagined by any non-Christian religion (including Judaism and Islam). For where God (even as Yahweh or Allah) can only be the One, no satisfying explanation for the Other can be found. Where this is thought through philosophically (which doesn't really happen in Judaism and Islam), the world as the Other and the Many can only be conceived as a falling away (*Herausfall*) from the One, which enjoys blessedness alone, and in itself.[20]

In fact, a God who was other than triune would have to lack the property most necessary for him to appear in the world as other than a threat to the creature: "A God without the difference of hypostases cannot be the God whom revelation knows: the God of love."[21]

Karl Rahner aims at the same conclusion—only the Trinity can account for the world we actually have—though he takes an anthropological route. Human experience is an inextricable mixture of light and darkness, joy and despair, and it is the "experience of darkness" that is "the real argument against Christianity." Just this darkness, in fact, confronts us with an all or nothing choice. Shall we accept that despite the darkness, the light and joy of existence "can be explained only by an absolute light, an absolute joy, an absolute love and glory, an absolute being"? If we do, we have already experienced and embraced the triune God: the final mystery of absolute love (the Father), who fully gives himself to us in the depths of our existence (the Holy Spirit), and can be expected to have given himself with equal fullness in the historical and publicly tangible dimension of our existence (Jesus Christ, the Son). Or shall we give in to despair, and despite the light we experience find as the final mystery of our existence only "an empty nothingness, which explains nothing"? Experience and reason cannot compel me to embrace Christianity

---

20. Hans Urs von Balthasar, *Theologik II: Wahrheit Gottes* (Einsiedeln: Johannes Verlag, 1985), 166. Cf. 169: "From a God who dispenses with every difference a world distinct from himself can originate only as that which has been left behind (*ein Abgefallenes*)." Balthasar here makes explicit, and does not scruple to endorse, a disquieting implication of the claim that our effort to know the world aright must lead either to knowledge of the Trinity on the one hand, or to pantheism or nihilism on the other. If we think that (a) Trinitarian faith and (b) pantheism or nihilism are exhaustive epistemic alternatives, then we've already decided that Jews and Christians do not worship the same God, since the Jews, failing to worship the Trinity, *eo ipso* invoke a sub-Christian deity, which Trinitarian faith defines itself by rejecting. But on this score the burden of proof, precisely for Christian theology, is, I think, the other way around: not on showing that Jews worship the same God as Christians, but on showing that we Christians succeed in worshiping the God of Israel. See Bruce D. Marshall, "Do Christians Worship the God of Israel?" *Knowing the Triune God*, ed. James J. Buckley and David S. Yeago (Grand Rapids: Eerdmans, 2001), 231–64.

21. Balthasar, *Theologik* II, 76; see also Hans Urs von Balthasar, *Theodramatik* IV (Einsiedeln: Johannes Verlag, 1983), 72 (Eng. trans. *Theo-Drama*, vol. 5, trans. Graham Harrison [San Francisco: Ignatius Press, 1998], 82). Seckler attributes a similar position to Aquinas (see *Das Heil in der Geschichte*, 97–98); with what justice we will see at the end of this section.

over nihilism. But they at least enable me to see that the only thing I could "exchange for Christianity" is "emptiness, despair, night, and death."[22]

Arguments like Rahner's regularly migrate toward an even stronger claim. Not only is Trinitarian faith the only alternative to nihilism, but nihilism turns out to be self-refuting. Surely, Rahner suggests, the nihilist thinks it's honorable, even glorious, to face up to the meaninglessness of existence. But how can there be anything honorable and glorious at all "in the abyss of absolute emptiness and absurdity?"[23] While Rahner sometimes holds that we're faced with a genuine choice between all and nothing, Christianity and nihilism, he also seems to say that the would-be nihilist simply hasn't realized that the position he's trying to stake out is self-contradictory. Theological attempts to force a choice between nihilism and the Trinity often betray this sort of ambivalence about whether nihilism is really possible—whether it constitutes a coherent (and therefore genuinely threatening) alternative to Christianity.

The argument can also take a more directly epistemic twist. Upon the Trinity, and specifically upon the action of the Son and the Spirit, depends the very possibility of knowledge, and with that the very intelligibility of the world for us. That the world is finally unintelligible, and so meaningless, is once again a nihilistic conclusion. But the nihilist presupposes intelligibility in the very act of claiming that the world is unintelligible. If nihilism thus refutes itself, then it's not just irrational to believe that we can make sense of the world while denying that the world is the work of the triune God. Unbelief simply isn't a rational alternative to Trinitarian faith.

Aquinas may sometimes give the impression that he is also persuaded of (4). As we have seen, for example, it's specifically the procession of the Holy Spirit which is the *ratio* that accounts for the possibility of creation: no Holy Spirit, no creation. But he announces his position on the matter in the same breath. There can be no demonstration of the Trinity, for "no argument may be found which is sufficient to prove this" (*In I Sent.* 10, 1, c).[24] Aquinas accepts (3), but he declines any attempt to infer (4) from it, or from anything else.

Aquinas's technical reason for this, in his celebrated discussion of the point in the *Summa theologiae*, is that creation can't give us an adequate basis upon which to infer the Trinity, since the capacity to create and the act of creation are shared by the three persons of the Trinity ("the creative power of God . . . belongs to the unity of essence, not to the distinction of persons"; I, 32, 1, c). But we shouldn't be misled by this. Since the world bears the mark of the Trinity all the way down, if we don't believe in the Trinity, we will be liable to misunderstand the world in quite basic ways: "[T]he knowledge of the

22. Karl Rahner, "Über die Möglichkeit des Glaubens heute," *Schriften zur Theologie*, vol. 5 (Einsiedeln: Benziger Verlag, 1964), 11-32; the quoted passages are from pp. 14–17 (Eng. trans. "Thoughts on the Possibility of Belief Today," *Theological Investigations*, vol. 5 (New York: Seabury, 1966), 6–8.

23. Ibid., 16 (ET, 7).

24. Cf. the text cited in note 7 for the context of this statement. Remarkably, Balthasar's citation *in extenso* of this Aquinas text (*Theodramatik* IV, 54–55; *Theo-Drama*, vol. 5, 62–63) omits this crucial passage on the epistemic status of belief in the Trinity. Reading in this selective way, Balthasar introduces a number of the Aquinas passages I've discussed here in support of a position that Aquinas explicitly rejects: "A non-trinitarian God could not be the creator" (*Theodramatile*, 53; ET 61).

divine persons was necessary for us . . . in order to think rightly (*ad recte sentiendum*) about the creation of things." Ignorant of the Son, we might suppose that creation is necessary rather than contingent, "that God has produced things by natural necessity." Ignorant of the Spirit, we might suppose that God creates out of need rather than out of love: "on account of some poverty which creatures make good (*propter aliquam indigentiam*) . . . and [not] on account of the love of his own goodness" (I, 32, 1, ad 3). We might, indeed, be pantheists or nihilists. But it's one thing to say that ignorance of the Trinity leads to deficiencies in our knowledge of the world and inclines us to outright mistakes; that's implied in (3). It's quite another thing to say that the knowledge we have of the world requires us to believe in the Trinity, and so can itself surmount ignorance of the Trinity.

The world is saturated with the Trinity, but we can only recognize this basic truth about the world, Aquinas argues, if we already believe in the Trinity (somewhat, for example, as we can only recognize a portrait as the likeness of a real person if we have some acquaintance with the individual who sat for it). Given the Trinity (*Trinitate posita*, as Aquinas says), we can recognize all manner of arrangements in the world—the order and goodness we find to some degree in everything around us, the triune structure of our own minds—as genuine vestiges or images of the Trinity. "Given the Trinity, there is a certain fitting character to arguments of this kind (*Trinitate posita, congruunt huiusmodi rationes*)" (I, 32, 1, ad 2)—these are the sorts of effects we rightly expect from this source. But these same states of affairs could be explained quite plausibly in other ways. Aquinas's argument to this point, as is well known, sounds strikingly modern: "It is similar to astronomy, where the system of eccentric orbits and epicycles is posited because by assuming this position, we can save the way things appear to the senses (*hac positione facta, possunt salvari apparentia sensibilia*). . . . [N]evertheless this does not suffice to prove that the system is true, since it is possible that appearances could also be saved by assuming some other position" (I, 32, 1, ad 2). It will always be possible to account for the triunity about in the world without taking it as the vestige of a triune creator.[25]

---

25. In the widespread manner of Trinitarian theology at the time, Aquinas argues, to be sure, that there can only be two processions and three persons in God (cf. I, 27, 5; 30, 2; 41, 6; somewhat in this vein the text cited in note 7, especially the last sentence). But these arguments shouldn't be taken as surreptitious attempts to demonstrate that God is triune. Proceeding *Trinitate posita*, they're attempts to understand what the faith teaches, not to prove its truth.

Aquinas is quite explicit about this, especially regarding his own effort to understand the Trinitarian faith by way of the two immanent acts of the created intellect, knowing and willing, and the "processions" that attend these acts (the so-called psychological analogy; cf. I, 27, 1). Since "intellect is not found univocally in God and in us" (I, 32, 1, ad 2), and the validity of demonstrative arguments depends on all the terms having the same sense in the premises and in the conclusion, no reflection on the dynamics of created knowledge and love can warrant the conclusion that God is the Trinity. If we didn't already know that God is the Trinity, no psychological analogy could make good the lack. This sort of reasoning about the Trinity thus falls under Aquinas's general stricture: "Given the Trinity, there is a certain fitting character to arguments of this kind, but not in such a way that these arguments suffice to prove the Trinity of persons" (I, 32, 1, ad 2). For misreadings of Aquinas on this score, see John Milbank and Catherine Pickstock, *Truth in Aquinas* (New York: Routledge, 2001), 52–56 (cf. my comments in *The Thomist* 66, no. 4 [2002]: 632–37), and Wolfhart Pannenberg, *Systematische Theologie*, vol. 1 (Göttingen: Vandenhoeck & Ruprecht, 1988), 313–14 (Eng. trans. *Systematic Theology*, vol. 1, trans. Geoffrey W. Bromily [Grand Rapids: Eerdmans, 1991], 287–89).

In this way Aquinas defends (3): If God is the Trinity, then any possible world has to resemble his triunity, at least as vestige. But we can't infer (4) from this: that since there's triunity about in the world, and the world is God's creation, God has to be the Trinity. So far as we can tell in this life, that God is the Trinity is a sufficient but not a necessary condition for the world to be a vestige saturated with triunity. This helps explain why Aquinas readily makes two claims that may seem at first glance to be incompatible. The processions of the Son and the Spirit from the Father are the ultimate reason why there can be creatures at all, yet the created world as we have it would be possible even if God were not triune. Creation both is and is not impossible unless God is the Trinity, but in different senses. Since God is the Trinity—*Trinitate posita*—a world whose *ratio* fails to lie in the processions of the Son and the Spirit is in fact impossible, as is a world that fails to be a vestige of the Trinity. But it will always be possible to conceive of this world as having been created by a God without these processions—by a God who was not triune.[26]

The upshot of Aquinas's argument is that (3) should not be confused with the following biconditional, which we can get by combining (3) and (4), but can never get from (3) alone:

(5) If, and only if, God is triune are all possible worlds at least a vestige of the Trinity.[27]

Differently put: the world can't teach us about the Trinity, and so can't teach us the deepest truths about itself. But creation's epistemic limits cut both ways. They mean that the world can't teach us conclusively *not* to be pantheists or nihilists. Only the triune God who made it can do that, by teaching us about himself. And this means that we needn't fly for refuge to belief in the Trinity in order to avoid the misery of pantheism or nihilism. We might simply see that the world *requires* neither that we be Trinitarians nor that we be nihilists, but simply leaves such questions open.[28]

---

26. The distinction between real and logical possibility may be of some use here. What's really possible is what's compatible with the states of affairs that actually obtain; what's logically possible is what may be conceived without contradiction. A creation whose source was not the Trinitarian processions is really impossible, but logically possible. Aquinas makes a related distinction, between what's possible "given some assumption" (*ex suppositione*), and what's possible "simply and absolutely" (III, 46, 2, c; cf. I, 25, 3). On the assumption that God is the Trinity, a world without a triune creator whose vestige it is belongs in the class of what's impossible *ex suppositione*, but the general features of this world can be thought without contradiction to stem from a nontriune source.

27. As before, this is not an epistemically neutral claim, since it allows us to infer that God is the Trinity from the uncontested assumption that there is an actual world.

28. Anthropological or existential arguments for (4) have an additional problem. They take off from the premise that experience and reason drive us to embrace absolute joy or nihilistic despair, absolute being or absolute nothingness. The apologetic motive for this premise is not hard to see: If nihilism is the only alternative, whatever reservations we may have about Christianity pale into insignificance. But in this case (unlike some other arguments for [4]), the premise is surely implausible. Christian theologians have been strikingly reluctant to reckon with the obvious fact that lots of perfectly reasonable people think the material world is pretty much all there is, the origins and destiny of the universe and the human race are obscure and probably not very noble, and the likelihood of personal survival beyond the bounds of this bodily life is slim indeed. Yet the presumed absence of a transcendent truth doesn't prevent these people from searching for the many truths still to be found—why should it? The lack of an ultimate good doesn't prevent the recognition that some human acts are much better than others; that there is no eternal happiness doesn't mean that life has to be one long howl of loneliness and despair. Karl Barth deserves credit for being one of the few recent theologians to have explicitly acknowledged and come to grips with this

Can We Prove the Trinity? Part II

After the thirteenth century Aquinas's position became increasingly standard in Roman Catholic theology, though not until recent times primarily out of deference to him (Scotus, for example, influentially holds that the Trinity cannot be known by natural reason, but not because he finds Aquinas's arguments on the point convincing).[29] In Vatican I's "twofold order of knowledge" (*duplex ordo cognitionis*), the Trinity presumably falls among those "mysteries hidden in God which cannot be known unless they are divinely revealed,"[30] though *Dei Filius* declines, no doubt wisely, to specify any *mysteria* in particular.

Protestant theology has tended to be even more vigorous in its rejection of (4) and, thereby, of (5). To take one example: The seventeenth-century Lutheran Johann Gerhard insists, as one might expect from a post-Reformation Protestant, that the Trinity is a wholly scriptural doctrine, but at the same time a teaching that can safely be derived only from Scripture: "The mystery of the Trinity should, and can, be gleaned not from the little brooks of the Fathers, nor from the murky depths of the scholastics, but from the entirely clear source which is sacred scripture."[31] And when it comes to the impossibility of

---

state of affairs: "Between unconditional surrender and defiance, between atheism and faith . . . is there not a definite and very fatal middle path . . . namely the way of resignation, the perhaps unworthy but in its way quite realistic possibility of indifference?" (*Die kirchliche Dogmatik* III/2 [Zollikon-Zürich: Evangelischer Verlag, 1948], 138; Eng. trans. Barth, *Church Dogmatics* III/2, trans. Geoffrey Bromily et al. [Edinburgh: T&T Clark, 1960], 117).

29. Scotus's characteristically complex argument on this point is most fully developed in *Quaestiones Quodlibetales* 14, ed. Felix Alluntis (Madrid: Biblioteca de Autores Cristianos, 1968), translated into English by Allan B. Wolter as *God and Creatures: The Quodlibetal Questions* (Princeton, NJ: Princeton University Press, 1975). It's an especially interesting discussion, because Scotus there suggests, though he doesn't develop explicitly, a much more radical way of blocking (4) than Aquinas proposes: Deny (3). Scotus suggests, in other words, that God's triunity does *not* require, as (3) supposes, that any world God might create must be at least vestigially triune. In the divinity proper to him, Scotus argues, "God . . . is only present to a created intellect purely voluntarily" (*Quod.* 14, 10 [36], ed. Alluntis, 510). More generally, any divine "motion *ad extra* . . . is entirely contingent, and consequently belongs immediately to the [divine] will, as its principle" (*Quod.* 14, 16 [63], ed. Alluntis, 520). Richard Cross glosses the latter remark as follows: "[A]ny relationship between a creature and the divine essence is contingent, dependent upon the divine will" (*Duns Scotus* [Oxford: Oxford University Press, 1999], 7). Being the Trinity is that which is most proper to God (cf. *Quod.* 14, 9 [35], ed. Alluntis, 508). So being a vestige of the Trinity, even more than any relationship a creature might have to the divine essence, is contingent. That the world God has actually made is vestigially Trinitarian is not in dispute. But the triune God could perfectly well have made a world that bore no trace of his triunity.

Whether this is actually Scotus's position on (3) I won't try to decide here. In his express discussions of the Trinitarian *vestigia* he doesn't explicitly consider this line of thought (e.g., *Lectura* I, 3, 2, 1 [*Ioannis Duns Scoti Opera Omnia*, ed. C. Balic et al. (Vatican City: Typis Polyglottis Vaticanis, 1950–), 16:311–24]), though there are some passages that might be read in this direction (cf. 323.22–324.2). In any case, for reasons cognate to those developed in the last section of this essay, the rejection of (3) just suggested would make relatively little difference to the overall epistemic picture, and so to the way one understands the basic relationship between faith and reason. It's at least worth observing, though, that Scotus, sometimes charged with fatally obscuring "the ontological difference," here seems to suggest a considerably more radical difference between divine and created being than Aquinas (in line with his argument, on many fronts, that there's too much necessity in Aquinas's conception of the relationship between God and creatures). That God, and so, if you like, "being itself," can only be triune doesn't mean that created being has to be triune. God is not bound to share anything of himself with creatures, even supposing that he freely wills to make some. Being a vestige of the Trinity doesn't just go with being a creature. It's a gift beyond being.

30. Heinrich Denzinger and Adolf Schönmetzer, eds, *Enchiridion Symbolorum Definitionum et Delarationum* 36th ed. (Barcelona: Herder, 1976).

31. Johann Gerhard, *Loci theologici: exegesin sive uberiorem explicationem*, Locus III: *De Sanctissimo Trinitatis Mysterio*, caput 1, §15 (1625), ed. Johann Friedrich Cotta, vol. 3 (Tübingen: Georg Cotta, 1764), 214b.

proving that God is the Trinity by natural reason, Gerhard thinks Aquinas doesn't go far enough. While Gerhard appreciates Aquinas's firm rejection of attempts to prove the Trinity, he thinks Aquinas still expects too much of fallen reason.[32] Aquinas suggests that by natural reason Christians will at least be able to meet objections brought against faith in the Trinity, from any quarter— to show, without appeal to the authorities upon which faith relies, that what Christians believe about God is not impossible.[33] But without the docility introduced by Christian faith's reformation of reason, Gerhard argues, we cannot grasp even the rational possibility of the Trinity. To unbelievers, the modest replies to objections that Aquinas wants to offer will appear as risible as the demonstrations he rightly repudiates.

> Among Christians, who are instructed in the word of God and by faith embrace the mystery of the Trinity, this can be shown by natural reason [viz., that what the Christian faith proclaims concerning the Trinity is not impossible]. But among the heathen, who are ignorant of the Trinity, and among the heretics, who stubbornly deny it, this can hardly be shown. For they, having cast aside the light of the heavenly word, presume to make judgments about this mystery by the principles of reason. This is why they pronounce it absurd and impossible.[34]

It's all the more striking to observe, therefore, how persistent have been the efforts of theologians, both before and after Aquinas, to show that the Trinity is rationally unavoidable. Here we will consider only one further argument to this effect, though it's one of the most durable. The argument stems from the thought that God is the highest good. Aquinas's contemporary Bonaventure gives a lucid and unrestrained version of it. God, he assumes, is that which is best (*optimum*). But that which is best, he argues,

> exists in such a way that it cannot be rightly thought of unless it is thought of as three and one. For "the good is said to be self-diffusive." Therefore the highest good is most highly self-diffusive. . . . Therefore unless in the highest good there is eternally a real and consubstantial production, and a hypostasis equal in nobility to the one who produces it, both in the mode of generation and of spiration (so that there is with the eternal principle an eternal co-principle)—unless, that is, there is in the highest good a beloved and a co-beloved, one begotten and another spirated, that is, the Father, and the Son, and the Holy Spirit—it would

---

32. For the appreciation, see Gerhard, *Loci theologici: exegesin*, Locus III, caput 1, §26 (Cotta, vol. 3, 223a).

33. Thus, for example, the conclusion of I, 32, 1, c: "We should not try to prove matters of faith except from authorities, to those who accept the authorities. With others it suffices to defend the claim that what the faith proclaims is not impossible." Gerhard paraphrases this text as follows: "By natural reason we can defend the claim that what the Christian faith proclaims about the Trinity is not impossible" (citation in the next note). Here, as often, Gerhard's citations of Aquinas's don't exactly follow the latter's text, though Gerhard's addition of "by natural reason" (*ex naturali ratione*) seems like a fair gloss on what Aquinas is doing.

34. Gerhard, *Loci theologici: exegesin*, Locus III, caput 1, §31 (Cotta, vol. 3, 228a).

not be the highest good, because it would not pour itself out in the highest possible way. For the temporal diffusion in creation is focused and punctiliar when compared with the immensity of eternal goodness. Hence a greater diffusion than that can be thought, namely one in which the diffusive one shares with another his whole substance and nature. Therefore he would not be the highest good if he could lack these things, either in reality or in thought.[35]

To analyze briefly: It belongs to the notion of "good" that whatever has this characteristic (and that's everything, in some degree) is self-giving or "self-diffusive." This characteristic of good things requires that the highest good be most highly—most perfectly—self-diffusive. Quite apart from the fact that creation has to be seen as a free act of God and not an inevitable self-diffusion, the production of creatures cannot satisfy the requirement that the highest good be perfectly self-diffusive. The finite goodness of creatures, however great it may be, is related to the infinite goodness of God as point is related to line; the goodness of creatures thus infinitely fails to match the infinite self-diffusion of the highest good. Since God is the highest good, therefore, he cannot fail to pour forth a person equal to himself, to whom he imparts "his whole substance and nature," and these two persons cannot fail to produce a third, as adequate object of the infinite love that they must share.[36]

Thus, Bonaventure implements the scholastic axiom adapted from Pseudo-Dionysius, "bonum dicitur diffusivum sui," in order to make an argument for the following proposition:

(6) If, and only if, God is the Trinity is God the highest good.

This claim shares with (5) a genuinely biconditional structure. If (6) is true, then to deny that God is the Trinity requires denying that God is the highest good; similarly, if (5) is true, then denying that God is the Trinity requires denying that all possible worlds are at least vestigially triune. For just this reason, both claims readily lend themselves to attempted proofs that God is the Trinity. If we can get our interlocutor to grant that there must be a highest good, or that there's triunity about in the world, then we can show her that she has to believe in the Trinity.[37]

---

35. Bonaventure, *Itinerarium mentis in Deum*, VI, 2 (*S. Bonaventurae Opera Omnia* [Quaracchi: Ex Typographia Collegii S. Bonaventurae, 1882–1902], 5:310b–311a). Among the several English versions, see *The Journey of the Mind to God*, trans. Philotheus Boehner, ed. Stephen F. Brown (Indianapolis: Hackett, 1993), 33.

36. Accounting for the procession of a third person in God without opening the door to an infinite number of processions and persons is a persistent problem for this argument, though not one its defenders have failed to address. For our purposes we can leave this problem aside.

37. It should be observed that the *status* of this argument in Bonaventure is remarkably unclear. In his early commentary on the *Sentences*, Bonaventure seems firmly to repudiate any access to the triunity of God by rational reflection on creation alone: "[I]n no way (*nullo modo*) is the Trinity of persons knowable from creatures, by ascending rationally from the creature into God" (*In I Sent.* 3, 1, 4, c [*Opera Omnia* 1, 76b]). This is generally cited as his official position. But a bit earlier in the same commentary he had said, regarding the plurality of persons in God, not only that "faith says it (*fides dicit*)," but also that "reasoning . . . shows it (*rationes . . . ostendunt*), if anyone considers the matter without contradiction." The *rationes* in question all seem to be matters that Bonaventure regards as accessible from creatures: the

The big difference between (6) and (5), of course, is the proposition to which the triunity of God is related as necessary condition. For (5), following (4), it's a claim about the created world. This prompts the thought that a person who fails to believe in the Trinity has to be profoundly deluded about the world (has to be a pantheist or a nihilist, for example). Whatever the merits of this claim (none, if you agree with Aquinas), it doesn't, as we've seen, follow from a Trinitarian proposition like (3). It's arguably a considerable advantage of (6) that the proposition to which it relates the Trinity as a necessary condition is not a claim about creation, but itself a claim about God. This allows for an attempted proof of God's triunity that needn't leave deniers of the Trinity deluded about creation, but simply—if more significantly—about God. One of its drawbacks, probably more compelling to us than to Bonaventure and his contemporaries, is that the existence of a supreme good may itself seem even less rationally obvious, and so a less promising basis for an argument, than the triunity of whatever lies to hand in the world.

Theologians for whom the Trinity is beyond the reach of rational demonstration have long been aware of arguments built around (6), and naturally have given reasons why they don't think such proposals are convincing. For Aquinas this is just the sort of argument that will seem wonderfully fitting or congruent *Trinitate posita*, but that won't suffice to prove the Trinity. The term or product of an infinitely good act, he argues, need not itself be infinite.

---

supreme blessedness, perfection, simplicity, and primacy of God (*In I Sent.* 2, 2, c [*Opera Omnia* 1, 54a]). Later on, *Breviloquium* I, 2 displays a similar ambiguity. It's faith which dictates that God is to be thought of "in the highest and most reverent way *(altissime et piissime)*," yet "not only does sacred scripture attest that God is to be thought of *altissime*, but truly every creature does as well" (citing Augustine, *De trinitate* XV, iv, 6). Whether grasped from Scripture or from creatures, this dictate requires that we think of God at least as capable of "communicating himself in the highest way . . . by having eternally a beloved and a co-beloved" (*Opera Omnia* 5, 211a; Eng. trans. *The Breviloquium* [*The Works of Bonaventure*, vol. 2], trans. José de Vinck [Paterson, NJ: St. Anthony Guild, 1963], 35–36).

　　As far as I can tell, the closest Bonaventure comes to clarity on this point is in his *Quaestiones disputatae de mysterio Trinitatis* 1, 2, c (*Opera Omnia* 5, 55b–56a; Eng. trans. *Disputed Questions on the Mystery of the Trinity* [*Works of St. Bonaventure*, vol. 3], trans. Zachary Hayes [St. Bonaventure, NY: Franciscan Institute, 1979], 131; I am grateful to Martin Bieler for his observations regarding the interpretation of this passage). Bonaventure there claims, once again, that "by the light with which the human being is naturally endowed, and sealed as by the light of the divine countenance, everyone's own reason dictates to him that the first principle is to be thought of in the highest and most reverent way. . . . In this Christians, Jews, and Muslims, and even heretics, agree." The naturally given light, however, falls short of informing us that to think of God *altissime et piissime* means precisely to think of him as "able and willing to produce an eternal beloved and co-beloved, equal to and consubstantial with himself; that to think *this* of God is to think in the highest and most reverent way . . . [T]he naturally endowed light does not dictate by itself, but the infused light" (italics mine). By the natural light we know *that* God is to be thought of *altissime et piissime*, but we don't know exactly *how* to do it. We lack, it appears, some premise (that the one we think of in this way must be supremely self-diffusive good?) necessary to infer the Trinity from the contents of our highest and most pious thoughts. Scriptural revelation, it seems, supplies the missing premise, but once we have it, a compelling argument for the triunity of God falls into place. In this way one might clarify Bonaventure's position, though when the argument returns in *Itinerarium* VI, 2, these qualifications are absent. So whether he would accept the suggested clarification remains a bit hard to say. For a version of the argument from God's perfect goodness to the Trinity from a theologian who seems to have made up his mind about its status, see Jonathan Edwards, "The Miscellanies," no. 96, in *The Works of Jonathan Edwards*, vol. 13, ed. Thomas A. Schafer (New Haven, CT: Yale University Press, 1994), 263–64. This is not Edwards's only argument for the Trinity, nor, apparently, the one he regards as most compelling. He remarks in general, "I think it is within the reach of naked reason to perceive certainly that there are three distinct in God . . . and that there are not nor can be any more distinct" (257). Richard Swinburne has lately claimed persuasive (though probable rather than demonstrative) force for what is essentially Richard of St. Victor's version of this argument. See Swinburne, *The Christian God* (Oxford: Clarendon, 1994), 177–80, 190–91.

The humblest piece of creation can therefore display God's infinitely self-giving goodness without requiring that we posit person-constituting processions in God. "For infinite goodness to share itself it is not necessary that something infinite proceed from God, but only that [what proceeds from God] receive divine goodness in the manner appropriate to it" (I, 32, 1, ad 2).

Here too the debate between Bonaventure (for example) and Aquinas concerns not what can be assumed, but what really follows from assumptions that neither doubts. One can grant Bonaventure's premises that God is the best, and the best must be maximally self-diffusive. Aquinas happily endorses both claims. It doesn't matter, moreover, whether we know these truths by nature, by grace, or by some combination of the two (a point on which, as we have seen, Bonaventure is not entirely clear). The argument still doesn't go through. As long as an infinite act need not have an infinite term, we can quite consistently account for God's supremely self-diffusive nature without recourse to God's triunity. Still less does God's self-diffusive goodness have to produce a finite term. Both sides in the medieval debate assume that creation cannot be necessary for God, but must be contingent on God's will to make a world, since the acts of one who is supremely self-diffusive good must also be supremely voluntary.[38] So not only truths about creatures but even truths about God's own nature fail to require that God be the Trinity.

The counterargument here can also take different forms. Thus, Matthias Joseph Scheeben gives a sympathetic account of (6) and its advocates in the midst of an extended and vigorous argument against the demonstrability of the Trinity. When Richard of St. Victor and Bonaventure try to prove the Trinity on the basis of God's infinite goodness (or, *mutatis mutandis*, of his infinite power or blessedness), they inevitably introduce as premises beliefs that are beyond the reach of reason. Reason can indeed know, Scheeben argues, that God is infinitely self-communicating goodness. But reason "can only extend this striving for self-communication with surety to such cases as it knows to be possible. But this is not the case with regard to a *substantial* self-communication. Therefore reason may not posit that the infinite goodness of God extends precisely to this sort of self-communication."[39] Instead,

---

38. On this last point note Aquinas's take on "bonum diffusivum sui," *In De Divinis Nominibus* IV, 1 (no. 271), ed. Ceslaus Pera (Turin: Marietti, 1950); cf. also I, 5, 4, ad 2.

39. *Die Mysterien des Christentums*, §7.3 (my emphasis). Matthias Joseph Scheeben, *Gesammelte Schriften*, vol. 2, ed. Joseph Höfer (3rd ed., Freiburg: Herder, 1958; first published 1865), 33. Eng. trans. *The Mysteries of Christianity*, trans. Cyril Vollert (St. Louis: Herder, 1946), 39 (italics mine). Scheeben here develops a line of thought already well established in nineteenth-century German Catholic theology, especially following the conflict over Anton Günther's speculative theology (for which an apprehension of the Trinity is an essential element in human self-consciousness). Thus, Johannes Evangelist von Kuhn argues that "if God is triune, there must be traces of this, his inner being, in his works." But only "after something has been revealed to us of the inner relationships of the divine being . . . do we look once again at the world, and especially at our own spirit, created after the image of God, in order to see whether we can find traces of the triune God in it." It's like recognizing another person's facial features at a distance; we can't do it unless "we have previously become acquainted with the person. Then we know what to look for" (Kuhn, *Katholische Dogmatik*, vol. 2, *Die christliche Lehre von der göttlichen Dreieinigkeit* [Tübingen, 1857; reprint Frankfurt, 1968], 501). As Kuhn observes (503), none less than Dante took a position on whether the Trinity can be known by natural reason, and got it right:

> Madness! that reason lodged in human heads
> Should hope to traverse backward and unweave
> The infinite path Three-personed substance treads.

Purgatorio III, 34–36 (in the translation of Dorothy Sayers) "we only know the Trinity in God as possible and admissible . . . from the fact that revelation displays it to us as real."[40] Thus, instead of being rational proofs, arguments like those of Richard and Bonaventure become "supra-rational, by assuming truths of faith."[41] There's nothing wrong with this, but it ought to be recognized for what it is: a reflective unfolding of the radiant content of the mystery, and not a rational proof of it.[42]

We can readily break off the argument at this point. In the long dispute over whether the Trinity can be known by natural reason, those who say it can't seem well able to cast doubt on every effort to say it can.

Being and Belief

It may seem as though two contradictory views of faith and reason, embodied in (1) and (2), have come to blows at just this point, and that the defeat of (1) entails the triumph of (2). It's quite possible to know all sorts of truths about the world without knowing the Trinity, so knowing the Trinity must not, it appears, have anything important to do with knowing the world aright. But the story actually has a different moral.

If the argument so far is right, the triune God wouldn't have to be in order for us to have the world we do. The case seems not to have been made, and in that nature of the case perhaps can't be made, that the statement "God is the Father, the Son, and the Holy Spirit" is linked by logical necessity to any statements that propose general truths about the world (even if there's no dispute about the truth of these general statements). From this it follows that we can consistently have all sorts of true beliefs about the world we have without believing in the Trinity.

But (2) makes a much stronger claim. Its defenders suppose that the faith of Christians in the triune God, while perhaps soteriologically indispensable, is irrelevant to anyone's overall picture of what we ought to believe. This is to hold that whether we can *prove* God is the Trinity is decisive for the epistemic role of belief in the Trinity. If it can't be linked by logical necessity to beliefs that aren't unique to Christians, then on this view it plays no role, except for some limited Christian purposes, in decisions about what ought to be regarded as true. If it falls in principle outside the class of the provable, then while true and important, it has no epistemic bearing on the countless matters where reason rightly seeks proof or demonstration.

That it's reasonable not to believe in the Trinity does not, however, imply that belief in the Trinity is epistemically insignificant. In fact, whether we follow Aquinas in rejecting such proof—in rejecting (5) and (6)—or whether we follow Bonaventure (some of the time) in accepting, it will actually make little

---

40. *Mysterien*, §7.3 (35; ET, 41).
41. Ibid., §7.3 (36; ET, 43); cf. §6 (25; ET, 30): "[W]hether unintentionally or by sleight of hand, one has recourse to an article of faith, and thereby breaks the thread of the proof."
42. Thus Scheeben excuses Richard and Bonaventure: "In the flight of their ecstatic spirits they transport themselves to the heights to which faith points them, and when they look around there with their reason, everything seems to be as near and accessible as what reason can really penetrate on its own" (*Mysterien*, §7.3 [33, n. 5; ET, 39]).

epistemic difference. The overall epistemic picture for a person who believes in the Trinity will be pretty much the same, regardless of whether she acknowledges that a reasonable person can decline to hold this belief, or supposes that it's finally irrational not to believe in the Trinity. In both cases it will be, against (2), a picture in which belief in the Trinity is entirely central to the total worldview of someone who holds that belief true.

This needs to be spelled out a bit. That acquiring any true belief at all depends on the Trinity at every point, as advocates of (1) rightly insist, doesn't by itself decide the precise epistemic arrangement among the beliefs themselves.[43] This remains the case for the most part even if we think we can prove that God is the Trinity. Even someone who thinks the Trinity is demonstrable need not, in other words, ask the pilot to display his baptismal certificate—or *a fortiori*, to recite a proof from "bonum diffusivum sui"—before she next gets on an airplane. She can be quite confident of the pilot's capacity for aeronautical reasoning in any case.

This isn't, as defenders of (2) mistakenly suppose, because faith in the Trinity is epistemically irrelevant to the rest of what we believe. It's simply because having a true belief about the Trinity isn't sufficient to establish the truth of most other beliefs. Still less is believing in the Trinity necessary for having most other true beliefs. If the Trinity can be proven—if it is necessary that God be the Trinity in order for a world to have the general features that ours in fact does—then the number of beliefs whose truth will depend upon the truth of Christian claims about the Trinity will be slightly larger than otherwise. But the truth or falsity of the vast majority of our beliefs will still not depend on whether belief in the Trinity is true. On the contrary, it will always be the case that relatively few other beliefs are true because our belief in the Trinity is true. Therefore, regarding the Trinity as the center of our total belief system doesn't commit us to the absurd suggestion that unbelieving scientists and historians are thoroughly ignorant about nature and history. It doesn't even commit us to the claim that disputed questions quite close to the heart of Christian faith can always be resolved by appeal to Trinitarian convictions.

---

43. Confusion on this score sometimes stems from the supposition, common among defenders of (1) (though hardly unique to them), that where a belief comes from, its onto- or psychogenesis, is decisive for its epistemic status. In order for me to believe in God, God himself has to give me the belief, and with that a whole new epistemic paradigm. This donation apparently *warrants* the belief; if the belief comes from me and not from God, it's unwarranted, though (presumably) not on that account necessarily untrue. But as Alan J. Torrance concludes his essay in this volume by observing, *all* true beliefs come from God, who in Christ "creates all truth" (here Torrance cites Barth, who in this follows Thomas Aquinas; cf. above, notes 14–15). Epistemically, the beliefs in question can be trivial or exalted; they can either have or lack warrant for the people who hold them. Whatever the epistemic case, they can't be true unless they're a gift from God. When put to theological use, epistemologies that depend on notions like reliability and proper function (such as Plantinga's) regularly miss this point and assume that divine action brings about, and so warrants, only a relatively narrow range of beliefs, namely those which are centrally or distinctively Christian. If, however, "every truth . . . is from the Holy Spirit" (cf. note 16), then the fact that a belief comes from God doesn't help us decide whether it has warrant at all (since some true beliefs aren't warranted), still less whether it has epistemic priority or requires a revision of our epistemic paradigm. So we'll have to figure out which beliefs come from God by arranging the contents of our beliefs in such a way that we can figure out which ones are true, and letting this order among our beliefs—our epistemic priorities—tell us where warrant lies. We won't figure out which beliefs are warranted (still less which of these require a revision of our epistemic priorities) by first deciding which ones God brings about—and couldn't even if we had a list of all the beliefs that have, or ever will, come from God.

Consider, for example, the long debate in Christian ethics about whether it is sometimes permissible to lie for a good end. Jerome and Augustine disagreed sharply over this, prompted by the theologically freighted question about what to make of the New Testament's indications (Acts 16:3; 21:26) that even after the death and resurrection of Christ the apostles continued to observe the cultic regulations of the Mosaic law. Jerome held that this was a kind of pious fakery on the part of the apostles, inspired by their desire not to scandalize the Jews whom they laudably sought to convert. Augustine would have none of this. Precisely because they served a good end, the apostles (of whose virtue we cannot doubt) could not have lied to bring it about. This required him to grant, as he clearly realized, that even after the passion of Christ the observance of the ceremonial law is legitimate, at least for a time.[44]

How would the belief that God is the Trinity enable one to resolve this important dispute? It's not clear what sort of considerations might succeed in establishing the truth of propositions like the following:

(7) If God is the Trinity, then it is sometimes permissible to lie for a good end,

or its contradictory,

(8) If God is the Trinity, then it is never permissible to lie for a good end.

In defense of either of these claims one might appeal to what the triune God has done—for example, reward Abraham's use of Sarah to deceive Pharaoh (Gen 12:10–20), or, conversely, command us not to bear false witness. Obviously, this just poses anew the question of how the narrative or commandment is to be interpreted. But in any case all the deeds of the triune God with respect to creatures are contingent. Thus, no action with respect to creatures can be derived from God's triune identity. That God is the Trinity will, in other words, never be sufficient to establish that some contingent state of affairs obtains. Some further determination—that, for example, God has decided to act in this or that way—will have to be added in order to justify such a conclusion. Consequently, we could never hope to establish the truth of a proposition like (7) or (8) by reference to what God has done.

Alternatively, one might try to defend either of these claims by appeal to noncontingent properties of the triune God. It's surely not contingent, for example, that the triune God is truthful (or faithful). That he proves himself to be such in all his works and ways simply goes with being the God he is. Here too, however, it's not entirely clear that God's triunity is logically *sufficient* to establish that God has the attribute of truthfulness. Does God's truthfulness follow logically, for example, from the person-constituting relations or characteristics of the Father, the Son, and the Spirit? Or do we have to

---

44. Aquinas gives a detailed account of this dispute in I–II, 103, 4, ad 1, and sides with Augustine, despite having a somewhat less rigorous attitude toward mendacity than his predecessor.

learn about God's faithfulness a posteriori from the persistent fidelity of the divine persons to one another and to us in time? But even if God's truthfulness is a logically necessary consequence of his triunity, it doesn't follow that (8) is right and (7) is wrong. Here too the contingency of divine action in time seems to block the needed inference. That God himself never lies doesn't rule out that he might permit creatures to lie under certain circumstances.

That claims about the Trinity will rarely suffice to settle disputes about what to believe doesn't mean that faith in the Trinity is epistemically impotent or peripheral, as defenders of (2) suppose. On the contrary, it just goes with the nature of belief and of a belief system. Our convictions about the Trinity have more wide-reaching epistemic implications than anything else we believe. But in the nature of the case, the truth of belief in the Trinity is not, to put the point in traditional terms, the *conditio per quam* for the truth of all the rest of our beliefs. Its truth is not the reason they are true. But then the truth of no other belief is either. And *holding* this belief is surely not a *conditio per quam* for holding any other true beliefs. A person can hold countless other true beliefs without holding this one. But the same goes for any other true belief. A reasoner doesn't need to know the Trinity in order to have lots of true beliefs. But the same goes for any other item of knowledge we might have. That the Trinity is the *ratio* of all creatures doesn't require that *beliefs* about the Trinity be the *rationes* of all our beliefs about creatures.

In none of these ways does faith in the Trinity appear to suffer from any epistemic disability in comparison with the rest of the items that might belong to our belief system. Still less is belief in the Trinity irrelevant, as (2) proposes, to deciding what other beliefs we're entitled to hold. Rather, the Trinity is entirely central to a Christian system of belief in its totality, including whatever orders of cognition we think such a system of belief rightly contains. That is to say, in whatever area and on whatever grounds, we cannot decide which beliefs we're entitled to hold without testing them for their fit—at minimum, their consistency—with the convictions that make up the church's Trinitarian faith. Whether we know the world aright thus fails to float entirely free of whether we believe in the Trinity. Regardless of how well justified we think we are in holding it, we can count no belief as true, and *a fortiori* as an item of knowledge, that fails to fit with faith in the Trinity.[45]

This holds no less if we deny that we can prove the Trinity than it does if we think our proof works. At this point it makes no significant difference whether we accept or reject (5) and (6). Granted belief in a triune God who creates all things to conform to him in their own way—*Trinitate posita,* whether by faith or by reason—we cannot segregate beliefs about the Trinity into an epistemic order of their own, where we regard them as doubtless true but irrelevant to the epistemic order ruled by reason (however defined) that

---

45. Janet Martin Soskice makes a similar claim about the epistemic significance of belief in creation *ex nihilo*. It can't be demonstrated, but everything else we believe about the world has to fit with it, and it makes an enormous difference to the way we understand the spatio-temporal universe we inhabit. See Soskice, "Naming God: A Study in Faith and Reason," in this volume.

can get along quite well without them.[46] Agreement with the convictions that constitute Christian faith in the Trinity is the *conditio sine qua non* for counting any belief as true, including scientific and historical ones. It doesn't matter whether we assign a belief to the order of "faith" or that of "reason." Either way, no true belief can fail at least to be consistent with these Trinitarian convictions; their epistemic reach, while mainly critical rather than constitutive (*sine qua non* rather than *per quam*), is unlimited.[47]

The epistemic significance of faith in the Trinity is not limited to this precise but purely negative role of excluding as false all beliefs inconsistent with it. Believing in the Trinity, and participating in the triune life by the Spirit's gift, I will naturally come to hold many beliefs I would not otherwise reach, indeed that would very likely never occur to me. I will, for example, gradually learn to see signs of the Trinity everywhere, to find in the turning of every leaf a reflection of the eternal coming forth of the Son from the Father. I could not see the world this way unless I believed that the source of all things is the triune God, who makes all things in such a way that they show forth his threefold glory in some vestigial fashion or another. Did I not see the world this way my knowledge of it would be impoverished, even if not, so far as it went, erroneous. Knowledge of the world as reflecting the glory of the Trinity goes well beyond merely satisfying the condition of consistency with Trinitarian faith that any claim to truth must meet. Yet it is not deduced or inferred, and in that sense directly warranted, by belief in the Trinity. Claims about where the Trinitarian *vestigia* lie vary and sometimes conflict; they can't all be right. But if the world shows forth the glory of the triune God, these claims are sure to be a good deal more right than wrong. The epistemic significance of faith in the Trinity thus does not lie only in decisions about what to believe, in matters of justification or warrant. Trinitarian faith serves as an incitement to knowledge we would otherwise never attain.[48]

That (1) is wrong doesn't, therefore, mean that (2) is right. It's not necessary to believe in the Trinity to have a largely true, and largely warranted, view of the world. But granting this—denying (4) through (6)—doesn't make the Trinity epistemically peripheral. We can't regard as true any belief that conflicts with faith in the triune God. It's as important epistemically as a belief could possibly be.

---

46. At this point I disagree with the sort of Thomism that takes Vatican I's *duplex ordo cognitionis* to license such an epistemic segregation. On this view, a right understanding of the relationship between nature and grace requires that whether one believes in the Trinity (or holds any other belief distinctive to Christian faith) simply has nothing to do with decisions about what *else* we can take as true. But epistemizing the tangled disputes about nature and supernature only darkens already murky waters. We can make as much as we like of the ontological independence and priority of nature to grace. It remains quite impossible to suppose that one could believe in the Trinity with the certainty of supernatural faith, and coherently regard as true any belief, however "natural," that is inconsistent with faith in the Trinity.

47. On the ideas briefly sketched in the last two paragraphs—especially on why it is Trinitarian convictions in particular that enjoy this privileged epistemic status—see Marshall, *Trinity and Truth*, ch. 5. That this is also Aquinas's epistemic position I argue in "Faith and Reason Reconsidered: Aquinas and Luther on Deciding What Is True," *The Thomist* 63, no. 1 (1999): 1–48, and "*Quod Scit Una Uetula*: Aquinas on the Nature of Theology," in *The Theology of Thomas Aquinas*, ed. Rik Van Nieuwenhove and Joseph Wawrykow (Notre Dame, IN: University of Notre Dame Press, 2005).

48. I'm grateful to Mark McIntosh for pressing this point upon me.

Still less does rejecting (4) through (6) deny the impress of the Trinity on all creatures and on the divine act of creation itself. Nor does it deny that this Trinitarian stamp on all things is (*Trinitate posita*, to be sure) ready to be *found* by us, as defenders of (1) rightly worry and defenders of (2) too easily suggest. Believing that God, and so God's world, are triune all the way down doesn't require us to suppose, on pain of making the Trinity epistemically irrelevant, that it's irrational not to believe in the Trinity. It simply urges us to avoid equating the order of being with the order of belief. The Christian conviction that this world bears the stamp of the Trinity all the way down shouldn't be mixed up with the claim that the triune God can be known from his worldly vestiges, or that only the Trinity can account for the world we actually have.

Here too, that the Trinity is the *causa et ratio totius productionis creaturarum* (*In* I *Sent.* 14, 1, 1, c) doesn't mean that *beliefs* about the Trinity are either the causes or the reasons for most of the rest of what we believe. But they don't need to be. Making rational sense of the world doesn't require faith in the Trinity. But faith in the Trinity yields an immeasurable difference in the rational sense we make.

CHAPTER THREE

The *Logos Ensarkos* and Reason

— Colin Gunton and Robert W. Jenson[1] —

We hope with this essay to make an initial assault on a relatively unconsidered question[2]: What follows for our understanding of reason from the fact that the universal Logos is the singular human person Jesus of Nazareth? Of some of the propositions we will put forward, we are as certain as it is reasonable to be in such matters; we advance others much more tentatively.

I

It is a dogmatically ascertained item of Christian grammar: "Jesus is the eternal Logos" is an identity statement; in the language of the dogma as defined at Chalcedon, there is but one *hypostasis* of the Logos and the man Jesus.[3] This must minimally mean—even if the point is not always fully appreciated—that there can be no successful reference to the eternal Logos that does not in fact refer to Jesus in his historical actuality, whether this is known to the referrer or not (just as there can be no accurate identifying description of "the historical" Jesus that leaves his reality as the eternal Logos out of account, though this provocative side of the matter is not here our assignment). It is "one and the same" who is born of Mary and born eternally in God.[4] Since the Logos, whatever might have been,[5] is in fact the incarnate Logos, there can be no reliable tracing of the logos of things in general that does not in fact conform—

---

1. Since Colin Gunton, to the bereavement of his friend, one-time teacher, and coauthor of this essay, died just before the final session of our group, this version of the essay was changed from the version presented to that session only in minor matters.
2. Or perhaps we should say that it is relatively unconsidered in later theology. Maximus Confessor, for one, is surely untouched by our stricture.
3. Norman P. Tanner, ed, *Decrees of the Ecumenical Councils* (Washington, DC: Georgetown University Press, 1990), 1:86.14–87.2.
4. Ibid.
5. We will come in the following to the problematic signaled here by this clause.

again whether this is known to the thinker or not—to the story of Jesus' life, death, and resurrection.

We must admit that the negations of the previous paragraph imply a critique of certain developments in the tradition, a critique that has been variously received in the group. Some ways of speaking of an "unincarnate Logos" (*Logos asarkos*) contaminate the theological concept with associations inimical to at least two essential implications of an orthodox Christology; as we will see, an orthodox Christology is central to our project. First, they generate a dualism of intelligible and sensible worlds, since the sensible revelation and the intelligibility of things are now separately referenced. This dualism finally impedes the very notion of incarnation, along with much else vital to Christian theology. Second, they have indeed sometimes tempted theologians to do what we have just ruled out for theology, that is, to identify the Logos merely cosmologically, apart from reference to the Incarnate One.

Our systematic concept of "the Word" should not in our judgment be primarily determined by Hellenistic religious speculation about a divine entity, the Logos, cosmologically intermediate between eternity and time, but by Israel's hearing of torah[6]—which is not to say anything against "the Greeks" as such or to decry their place in the history of Christian theology. Just how powerfully Hellenistic usage was present to John the Evangelist's mind when he wrote of the Logos (John 1) will perhaps continue to be disputed until we can ask him, since it does not seem that argument about the matter, which has occurred throughout the tradition, is strictly exegetical or historical.

Two hermeneutical points seem to us decisive in the meantime.[7] First, the text John actually produced—whatever associations may or may not have been present in his thinking—plays on Gen 1, where the world is brought into being and given its form and value by God's torah-like utterance. We should read it in that connection, as every text should be understood in its full context of the whole of Scripture and not necessarily in context of a reconstructed whole mind of the author or the author's community. Second, Jesus is the Word only in that he is the Messiah of Israel; therefore, the Word that he is must be continuous with the Word identified in Israel's creation and covenantal narratives. This torah is first guidance and only thereupon rationale; therefore, the Word in Genesis and then in John's gospel—again, whatever the historical John the Evangelist (if indeed there was such a person) may have had to the front or back of his mind—is guiding address, *sermo*, first and just and only so reason, *ratio*. Luther was right when he explicitly corrected a tradition dominant in the exegesis of Gen 1, which interpreted "said" as "thought:" "Moses uses the word *amar*, which simply denotes the spoken word. . . . By a mere word that he speaks God makes heaven and earth from nothing." Then he interprets John from Genesis: also the Word "that is in the divine being" is "an uttered word by which something is ordered and enjoined."[8]

---

6. In the Old Testament and in Judaism, torah is God's guiding and mandating address to his people.

7. At some points in our group's discussions they did not prove so. David Bentley Hart, in this matter, as in matters where he and we agree, is a champion of the Greek determinants of the Christian tradition.

8. Martin Luther, *Werke* (Weimar: Böhlau, 1883), 42:13.13.

Nor should we separate God's Word from his Wisdom. The Kantian divorce of pure and practical reason is one of the more baneful legacies with which modern theology has struggled. It may be that greater attention to the character of wisdom in Scripture can here be salvific. If it is indeed the case that John's prologue and other so-called cosmic Christologies in the New Testament draw on the conceptuality with which Israel construed wisdom, this must remind us that the rationality we seek in the world and try to practice in ourselves is not to be separated as "pure" reason from the practical reason involved in the living of life, for Hebrew wisdom is not truth abstracted from life but truth as and in life. Insofar as this wisdom is immanent in creation, this means that the creation does not make merely mathematical or descriptive sense, but primally makes teleological sense; in Prov 8, the Wisdom who was God's architect at creation parades this status to enforce her offer to teach the good life. Paul's only affirmative and explicitly theological use of *sophia*, in 1 Cor 1–2, is not of an unincarnate Logos but of the crucified Christ, who just as such is said to be the power and wisdom of God in action. Both parts of this observation are important: God's wisdom is not disembodied but is the man on the cross, and the wisdom that appears on the cross is more than information or theory.

It is no doubt true that if we abstract from the identity of the Logos as Jesus the Christ, we should not say that *sermo* in God is prior to *ratio*; developments from this proposition have proven unfortunate.[9] But neither should one then make *ratio* prior to *sermo* in deity, since this could well lead back to Aristotle unbaptized.[10] One should make neither of these moves, since one should not perform the original abstraction.

The objection that will be made to some assertions in the previous paragraphs is, of course, that John's prologue propounds the universal—"In the beginning was the Logos. . . . All things were made through him"—thirteen verses before it records the particular—"The Logos became flesh." Does not John here do what we have decried, namely, refer to the eternal Logos as the not yet incarnate? We think, however, that the role of the prologue as indeed *prologue* to a gospel in which an aggressively incarnate protagonist discourses with the Father and with us as himself one of the Trinity,[11] and declares—note the tenses—"Before Abraham was I am," forbids a crudely serial-chronological interpretation of the prologue. If Scripture is to interpret Scripture, we may note that in the great passage of Colossians, the one in whom "all things in heaven and earth were created" is the "beloved Son" of Jesus' baptism and the transfiguration, the agent of redemption and forgiveness (Col 1:13–15).

Of course, a question remains: Just what may then be said or not said about the Logos as he is in whatever sort of "time" those thirteen verses of John's prologue span? The authors are not sure whether we agree in answering that

---

9. Warnings from our group, lest we veer in that direction, have pointed above all to developments in German idealism.

10. Notoriously, Aristotle's God is pure thought and wholly silent.

11. The most blatant instances are, of course, chs. 13 and 17.

question, or if we disagree exactly where the disagreement is located,[12] or indeed exactly what the disagreement would be about. We both can begin with the arresting logic of a passage in Irenaeus: "[God's] only-begotten Word, who is always present with the human race, united to and mingled with his own creation . . . and who became flesh, is himself Jesus Christ."[13] One of us will go so far with such logic as to deny that what eternally precedes[14] "became flesh" is any actual unincarnate state of the Logos; the other would stress more the historical newness marked by the birth to Mary, and so speak somewhat more definitely of a preincarnate Logos. It is anyway clear that the temporal references of John's gospel, and indeed of much of the New Testament, equally defeat all efforts to construe them on an infinite time line or by reference to an eternity conceived as a point somehow perpendicular to a time line.[15]

The authors are, in any case, agreed that great ascesis must be exercised in saying anything about a Logos not incarnate as Jesus. We agree: there is not and never has been (whatever "has been" can mean in this context) a Logos not eternally shaped to the flesh he bears, or who could or can be reliably referenced or evoked apart from reference to that flesh in its historical concreteness.[16] God is certainly not otherwise God for the creation than he is God in the gospel, and God in the gospel is who he is in the relation between the Father and that Son who—again whatever might have been—is Jesus of Nazareth. These agreements seem to us sufficient to be going on with our investigation.[17]

II

What it means to be rational, to seek and follow the logos at work in all things, is thus determined by the fact that the Father creates and upholds the world through a particular person, his intelligible Word of address who is Jesus. The Greek thinkers were right to discern in the world a universal rationality. What they could not know, and indeed found offensive when it was proposed to a late generation among them, was its identity as a particular embodied person. Thus, they were defenseless against the temptation to seek epistemic security by locating universal rationality in an ideal world abstracted from particularity and matter. Their modern successors, such as

---

12. The footnote originally at this point read, "We suppose that if it exists it is located within the ancient Reformed/Lutheran christological quarrel. Perhaps someday we will return to the question and see if the old division can be transcended, at least in our case." Sadly, as things now are, this project will not be undertaken.

13. Irenaeus, *Against Heresies*, 3.16.6. This way of identifying the one who "became" Jesus Christ as "himself" Jesus Christ can, of course, be found throughout the patristic tradition.

14. The oddity of the phrase "eternally precedes" signals the reason why a merely linear construal of time will not accommodate the incarnation.

15. That is, neither Aristotle nor Plato is any use here.

16. The actuality of a *logos asarkos* is undoubtedly one occasion of division in our group, also among those who on other matters seem agreed. It will, in any case, not do simply to say that the privative attached to "flesh" simply represents the before of "became incarnate," since it is the meaningfulness of "before" in the case of God the Son's birth that is the problem.

17. We are not sure if these agreements are shared by all members of our group. If and where they are not shared, there is serious theological disagreement.

Descartes or Kant, have inherited the tendency. And too much modern theology has acquiesced in thus idealizing the Logos, thus creating a repeatedly disastrous incoherence at the heart of theology, since particularity and materiality are the very point of incarnation. That grotesque abstraction, "the Christ," who can be reimaged in various genders or races or classes, is the pitiful dead end of Christology that conforms to this tendency.

Theology must therefore claim to be a universal discourse, in the sense that any discourse must be irrational that cannot be interpreted by the church's discourse about Jesus the Christ. It need not actually be so interpreted to be rational, but it must be capable of it. Perhaps, for example, a biology that eschews teleology may have an interesting proposal or two left to it, but only a very determined ideologue can fail to see its increasing alienation from the phenomena it purports to illumine. Indeed, the discipline seems to be approaching the point where only a Trinitarian and so teleological interpretation of its observations and fragments of theory can make an intellectually respectable construct.[18] As for physics, its recent development constantly makes theologians out of the physicists; it would be good if their efforts on that line were less naive or transparently motivated by antitheistic bias.[19]

There are thus two aspects of our position, both of which are important to us. First, a discourse need not actually be interpreted by the gospel to be rational. We do not think that only a believer can be a scientist or technician or good person—and indeed, providing a christological ground precisely for natural reason is one of our objectives. Second, we do think that the rationality of a discourse that abstracts from the reality of the world, as this is determined by the story of Christ and its eschatological teleology, must hang in the air, and that in the history of such a discourse this precarious situation will manifest itself.

To be sure, there can be wrongly imperialist versions of theology's claim to universality, an error into which some medieval conceptions or that of such thinkers as Wolfhart Pannenberg or the authors of this essay may possibly fall. The error will be avoided in a conception determined by an orthodox Christology. Such Christology, with its affirmation of one person who is unmixed and unadulterated creature and Creator, will so shape the claim as to allow the relative independence of other discourses, while holding that claims to entire autonomy from theology are idolatrous. This is a direct implication of the christologically determined doctrine of creation also, which holds to the real and contingent existence of what is not God, while denying that it came into being or perdures apart from God's agency in his Word.

Vice versa, all truth, however discovered, must be seen by theology as in one or another way christological. It is a Barthian conviction shared by the authors: We are to discern the Light itself in every "little light" throughout creation, however bright or dim. The incarnation is God's affirmation of the

---

18. Which is not to say that various enterprises conducted within biology departments, such as the study of cells at the molecular level, cannot flourish.
19. Thus, "many-world" construals of quantum cosmology have no warrant at all, apart from unwillingness to give any comfort to the notion of creation.

whole created world, of matter and spirit alike; this is particularly relevant to the affirmation basic to the modern sciences that rationality inheres in perceptible things. We do not confront an ideal world related only to our minds, but an embodied Word who speaks to us likewise-embodied persons.

The historical thesis often advanced is indeed credible, that the modern sciences are finally the child of the biblical doctrine of creation. In view of the fact that we have so far made only disparaging references to some assumptions and practices of contemporary scientists, we stress this point. The theological rationality inherent in the humanity of Christ led over time to a belief that the structures of created being, as well in its material as in its ideal dimensions, are imbued with meaning given it by its Creator. Nature is in this sense the product of grace because God is gracious in all his doings.[20] The natural sciences can, in such a light, be conceived as a right human response to the cultural mandate of Gen 1:26–28. The right dominion of the material creation is the calling of the natural scientist, even though his works, like those of all humans, are in various ways corrupted by sin.[21] It does not, therefore, follow that everything scientists suppose or do is underwritten by a theologically determined conception of universal rationality; the incarnation affirms our quest for truth only by first judging our human corruption of truth and world alike,[22] a connection explored in depth by several of our colleagues in this project.

III

We must now attend to the God-world relation in its fully theological reality. What is the universal logos that takes its being from the actual, embodied Logos of the Father? What are the characteristics of reality to which reason must attend in order to be reason, if Jesus is the Logos? (We cannot in this essay—and indeed we could not do it in any number of essays—provide a complete list of such characteristics.) The first we instance is *availability*.

The Word eternally spoken by the Father is the perfect self-utterance of the Father. Therefore, this Word must be itself a speaker—and so not properly an "itself" but a "himself." It follows that the discourse of Father and Son is intrinsically *embodied*, that is, it is an address between mutually *available* someones, who can pick each other out and so respond to each other. In fact, whatever might have been, the someone available to the Father is Jesus, available by his human embodiment, and the someone available to the Son is the Father, available to the Son as the creator, through the Spirit, of the Son's own specific humanity. Thus, the Logos who grounds all rational proceedings in the world and in responses to the world does so as the available partner in a conversation that God is.

---

20. We realize that this is to operate with a rather different conception of nature than do some of our fellow essayists.

21. Early and definitive arguments for this position are by Michael B. Foster, "The Christian Doctrine of Creation and the Rise of Modern Natural Science," *Mind* 43 (1934): 446–68, reprinted in C. A. Russel, ed., *Science and Religious Belief* (London: University of London Press, 1973), 294–315. See also R. Hooykaas, *Religion and the Rise of Modern Science* (Edinburgh: Scottish Academic Press, 1972), and the many relevant works of T. F. Torrance.

22. This point is important over against the constructs of some "science and religion" professionals.

Since this availability is grounded in the incarnation, it is at once an ideal and a material availability, or rather, one in which these two aspects may be distinguished but not construed as separately actual. Since the Word is mandate before it is explanation, the rational, the moral, and the aesthetic realms may not be divorced from one another. The created order is available as mandated by the Word, and so not just as the occasion for the ascertaining of facts or the formulating of theories. The created order is available in its rationality for understanding, use, and enjoyment, variously according to the kind of entity that confronts us, according to the Word's mandate that it shall be.

We may instance the human body. A rational knowledge of it includes knowledge of its right use, including, for example, the discrimination of appropriate and inappropriate forms of sexual activity, or eschewing the culturally asserted right to sovereignty over "one's own body" (as it is, of course, fundamental to current American abortion law). A knowledge of the body that abstracts from these things is not just incomplete, its rationality is always threatened. We may instance music as having its own logos, including the possibility of discriminating between music that blesses and music that degrades. Or we may, continuing at this randomly, instance food and drink, which are known precisely when their bane and blessing are both known. In all such matters, the modern ethic of choice divorces behavior in and to the material world from the logos intrinsic to the creation.

A second key notion is *relationality*. The being of the triune God is constituted in the relations of the in-fact embodied Son to his Father in the Spirit. Must not then the creation have a relational structure that is appropriate to its being created by such a God? This is a more general consideration than the previous one because availability is itself a kind of relation. But the generality assists in making an essential point. If the kind of analogy just suggested is proper, created things are in such fashion relationally structured that their being and so their *logoi* are functions of what they are to one another.

The working out and so the understanding of this relationality, as it bears on the relation between faith and reason, begins in a particular form of human being-together. For the Fourth Gospel, knowledge of God becomes actual as the Spirit of truth relates to the Father, through Jesus, those whom the Father has chosen. The Spirit of truth is the Spirit of Jesus, who is the truth. To know the truth is therefore to know the Father through Jesus, and this is not the knowledge of mere individuals but of members of a community of worship and confession. There is thus no private knowledge of belief, but only that formed by the community in its articulation of the content of its faith.[23]

Thus, what is learned in the *koinonia* of the church becomes a model for all human rationality. It is not that there is no rationality outside the thought of those who acknowledge this truth, but that all truth and rationality take this kind of shape, whether it is acknowledged or not. (We might suggest that Wittgenstein's arguments against the possibility of a private language reflect some appreciation of this central truth.) Our words are not private,

---

23. This concern is developed in the essay by Carver T. Yu, "Covenantal Rationality and the Healing of Reason," in this volume.

but arise out of our relations with one another and with the world in which our lives are set.

Different identifications are proposed of the relations within which finite beings are reasonable, whether as objects or subjects. The Greeks held that the divine world and the intelligible world are the same, so that the divine world's relation to the human mind constitutes the human mind's rationality. The mind finds truth by recollecting the divine world with which it is in some way continuous. Christian theology must say instead that we are continuous not with the divine but with the material world, the dust from which we are made. Yet—and here the Greeks were right—there must be something about our minds that is able to engage the logos of the reality that reaches our minds by the senses.

The incarnation enables this relation and shows us how it holds, in that it broadens the scope of the relations that enable rationality to include the particular and material. Indeed, it enables us to think of a spectrum of activities we may call rational. Thus, animals are in a way rational; dogs recognize their master's voice, and rats learn their way around the levers. It also broadens our understanding of the scope of human rationality, encouraging developments of the kind to be found in Ernstpeter Maurer's essay, "The Perplexity and Complexity of Sinful and Redeemed Reason," in this volume. The dualism of sensible and intelligible worlds encourages the view that only concepts strictly so-called are able to encompass the truth of being. An incarnational view opens us to the broader possibilities to be found in the variety of human linguistic responses to the world, especially the metaphorical, and prevents us from a too-restrictive view of what can express the truth of being. It opens us to the sheer profundity and inexhaustibility of things, and it displays the difficulties of devising a satisfactory account of the relation between synthetic and analytic propositions. This last point moves us to treat one particular sort of rationality, which at one point occupied the group's concern.

Despite all convincing attacks on the notion of analyticity,[24] we do persist in feeling (and that is perhaps here the right word) that some propositions could not be false. Even if repeated experience of putting one billiard ball in an empty sack, and then another, and then opening it to find three, convinced us that one plus one was, with billiard balls in this sack, three, if asked what two plus two would then be, we would either be at a loss for any answer at all or would construe our answer on the tacit supposition that one plus one was two in every other case than our experiment. Why is this? Because we are determined by a particular linguistic tradition? We think not. We think there is a christological-Trinitarian ground for our intuition.

It is our conviction that all truth is indeed contingent, on God. But a (contingent!) distinction can be made between synthetic and analytic truth, because God is the triune God and not a monotheos.

---

24. In the last session of our group, we were intrigued to find Quine's attack on the notion of analyticity dismissed by our guest philosopher, Charles Taylor. For our own purposes, however, we do not need to refute Quine. Perhaps it is so that no secure *concept* of analyticity is possible; what we seek to justify christologically is the ineluctable conviction that the concept attempts to cover.

CHAPTER FOUR

The Wisdom of the Cross

— Lois Malcolm —

> So let no one boast about human leaders. For all things are yours, whether Paul or Apollos or Cephas or the world or life or death or the present or the future—all belong to you, and you belong to Christ, and Christ belongs to God.
>
> (1 Cor 3:21–23)

What is an essay on the wisdom of the cross doing in a volume on faith and reason? Does not reflection on the cross belong to devotional literature, handbooks on preaching, or, at best, dogmatic reflection on the atonement? Is not the cross, in the words of the Apostle Paul, a "stumbling block" for Greeks, who "desire wisdom"—the ultimate sign of "foolishness" to the "wise" and "weakness" to the "strong" (1 Cor 1:18–2:5)? Does it not serve for Christians to signify the ultimate limit of reason?

Theologians who have emphasized the centrality of the cross—since the Reformation, for example, Martin Luther, and later Søren Kierkegaard and Karl Barth—have tended to be highly skeptical of what human reason can achieve. By contrast, theologians interested in apologetics, philosophical theology, or natural theology have tended to avoid reference to the crucifixion of Jesus.[1]

This essay addresses the following questions in light of these observations: What kind of logic does Paul use in the classical locus for his understanding of the "wisdom of the cross"? What might this tell us about his epistemology

---

1. Even the speech attributed to Paul at the Areopagus (Acts 17:22–31), an important biblical precedent appealed to by apologists, does not mention the cross. Only Greek poetic statements, Jewish polemic against idolatry, and the resurrection are used in his argument. The quotation in 17:28 ("In him we live and move and have our own being") may come from the sixth-century B.C.E. philosopher-poet Epimenides. The second quotation ("For we too are his offspring") is from Aratus (*Phaenomena* 5), a third-century B.C.E. poet.

of the cross, that is, his mode of perceiving the world by way of the cross?[2] Further, what might such an epistemology have to say about the relationship between faith and reason?

After a brief description of the context that gives rise to these questions, I offer a close reading of 1 Cor 1–3, focusing on the kind of arguments Paul uses to depict what the cross tells us about true wisdom and power. I conclude by drawing out the implications of this analysis for an epistemology of the cross and our understanding of the relationship between faith and reason. At the heart of my argument will be the theme of kenotic abundance, a theme that is central, I will argue, to Paul's understanding of the message of the cross and the way it enacts "the wisdom and power of God."[3]

The Cross, Faith, and Reason

Since the Reformation at least, the cross within Christian theology has often been identified with the critique of any kind of rapprochement between faith and reason. This stems partly from a misreading of the contrast Luther makes in *The Heidelberg Disputation* (1518) between a "theologian of glory" and a "theologian of the cross." As he makes clear in that treatise, Luther's intent is *not* to declare that "wisdom itself is evil" or that "the law is to be evaded." His point, rather, is to demonstrate how "human beings misuse the best in the worst manner." A "theologian of glory" claims to see the "invisible things of God" by seeing through earthly things (events and works). A "theologian of the cross," by contrast, comprehends what is "visible of God" through "suffering and the cross." The latter "says what a thing is," whereas the former pretends that what is evil is good and what is good is evil. At the heart of this contrast is whether one is willing simply to trust in God's love, which always—unconditionally—"creates what is pleasing to it," or whether one seeks to trust in human love, which always—conditionally—is pleased only by what it finds attractive.

Luther's influence is apparent in later major thinkers who criticize the Enlightenment's focus on reason's prowess. For Kierkegaard, the paradox of the cross is the offense and "impossibility" of direct communication that forces one to rely on faith alone.[4] For Barth, the *theologia crucis* (theology of the cross) is the "temptation" and "comfort" that alone can counter the idolatry he contends is inherent in the *analogia entis* (analogy of being).[5] Even Friedrich Nietzsche's suspicion of morality as a guise for the will to power can be seen as a secularized version of Luther's suspicion of the way human beings misuse the best in the worst of manners.[6]

---

2. J. Louis Martyn refers to Paul's "epistemology of the cross"; see, e.g., his "Epistemology at the Turn of the Ages," in *Theological Issues in the Letters of Paul* (Nashville: Abingdon, 1977), 89–110.

3. See also Mark McIntosh's eloquent analysis of discernment and the wisdom of the cross, "Faith, Reason, and the Mind of Christ," in this volume.

4. See Søren Kierkegaard, *Practice of Christianity*, ed. and trans. Howard V. Hong and Edna H. Hong (Princeton, NJ: Princeton University Press, 1991).

5. See Karl Barth, *Church Dogmatics* (Edinburgh: T&T Clark, 1936–1969), vol. I, part 1.

6. Compare, e.g., the logic Luther uses in the *Heidelberg Disputation* (1518) to criticize the pretensions of false wisdom and moralism with that Nietzsche uses in *On the Genealogy of Morals*, trans. Walter Kaufman and R. J. Hollingdale (New York: Vintage Books, 1989).

As we have pointed out, Luther's critique of wisdom and the law in the *Heidelberg Disputation* was of the way they can become another form of idolatry—that is, another means of justifying oneself instead of trusting in God. Luther himself had a place for a robust doctrine of creation (which undergirds a theological understanding of wisdom and the law). Kierkegaard presupposed a complex understanding of reason. And Barth had a place for the natural theology of the "lights of creation."[7]

Nonetheless, a casual and often popular understanding of Luther's "theology of the cross"—and its influence on later theology—might lead one to presuppose that it negates any account of the relationship between faith and reason, and, we might add, wisdom and law on the one hand, and the power of God to create and destroy on the other. A liberal version stresses a suffering God who is impotent in the face of evil. A conservative version stresses a capricious God whose chief characteristic is that he "kills, curses, accuses, judges, and demands," with little focus on our participation in God's power, goodness, and life. In both cases, the cross is identified with an epistemology that perceives a world where the connection between goodness and power is not immediately apparent—and where faith is primarily linked with the presence or absence of power, and not also with goodness or, for that matter, wisdom.[8]

Given this casual conception of the cross and its theological import, it is somewhat surprising to find much recent Pauline scholarship stressing the cognitive character of Paul's arguments, especially since Luther's theology of the cross finds its ultimate roots in Paul. Starting with Schweitzer's *The Mysticism of Paul the Apostle*,[9] the historical account of New Testament scholarship in the past two centuries has largely been an attempt to rethink Paul "behind" the line of theological interpreters from Augustine to the three thinkers mentioned above (Luther, Kierkegaard, and Barth). In recent decades, studies have emphasized Paul's relationship to Judaism and the law,[10] his relationship to the Stoics,[11] and the social and political setting for his various letters.[12] Even those who work within a broadly Reformation reading of

---

7. See Barth, *Church Dogmatics*, IV/3.

8. Michael Gillespie's observation may be relevant at this point. The figure of a dark, "hidden" God emerges with the rise of nominalist philosophy and its critique of Aristotelian metaphysics, along with the devastation of the Black Death and the papal schism that brought the medieval world and the coherence of its worldview to an end. What emerges is a new (nominalist) idea of God as a God who overturns all eternal stands of truth and justice and puts the will in place of reason and freedom in place of necessity and order. This God's *potentia absoluta*, or absolute power, is greater than his *potentia ordinata*, or ordained power. Indeed, Gillespie argues, one might trace contemporary nihilism's intellectual and spiritual origins not to Nietzsche's assertion of the death of God but to the new idea of God that emerged in the late medieval period. See Michael Gillespie, *Nihilism before Nietzsche* (Chicago: University of Chicago Press, 1996), 24.

9. Albert Schweitzer, *The Mysticism of Paul the Apostle*, trans. William Montgomery (New York: Henry Holt, 1931); see esp. 101–40.

10. See, as exemplars of this argument, Krister Stendahl, "The Apostle Paul and the Introspective Conscience of the West," *Harvard Theological Review* 56 (1963): 199–215, and *Paul among Jews and Gentiles* (Philadelphia: Fortress, 1976); and E. P. Sanders, *Paul and Palestinian Judaism: A Comparison of Patterns of Religion* (Philadelphia: Fortress, 1977).

11. See, most recently, Troels Engberg-Pedersen, *Paul and the Stoics* (Edinburgh: T&T Clark, 2000).

12. Frequently quoted studies include Abraham Malherbe, *Social Aspects of Early Christianity* (Philadelphia: Fortress, 1983); Wayne Meeks, *The First Urban Christians: The Social World of the Apostle Paul* (New Haven, CT: Yale University Press, 1983); and Gerd Theissen, *The Social Setting of Pauline Christianity: Essays on Corinth*, trans. John H. Schütz (Philadelphia: Fortress, 1982).

Paul have nonetheless radically rethought that interpretation—from Rudolf Bultmann's existentialist reading to the more apocalyptic readings of Ernst Käsemann[13] and, more recently, J. Louis Martyn and J. Christiaan Beker.[14]

In turn, given the way philosophical theology within both Protestantism and Catholicism has tended to shy away from discourse about the cross, it is surprising to find the cross at the heart of Pope John Paul II's argument in defense of reason in *Fides et Ratio*, a defense grounded in christological and Trinitarian claims. This contrasts sharply with Vatican I's *Dei Filius*, which buttressed its defense of religious belief with rational arguments and the premise of a sharp distinction between two orders of knowing (*duplex ordo cognitionis*), by faith and by reason.[15] The centrality of the cross—and the overall mode of argument used in *Fides et Ratio*—reflect both the retrieval of patristic and medieval sources that characterized much Roman Catholic theology during the early and middle part of the twentieth century and the embrace of historical-critical studies of the Bible after Vatican II. Further, the theology of the cross has played an important role in the pope's own life and work. Both his doctoral thesis, *The Problem of Faith in the Works of St. John of the Cross* (1948), and his own phenomenological and personalist account of human agency are compatible with his depiction in *Fides et Ratio* of how the cross "purifies" reason.[16]

The focus of recent scholarship on Paul and the prominent role of the cross in *Fides et Ratio* open up a space for examining the cognitive arguments Paul uses to depict how the cross redefines the relationship between power and wisdom and, by implication, the relationship between faith and reason.

Introduction to 1 Corinthians

General Comments

Following Alexandra Brown, we can observe that Paul makes an epistemological argument in 1 Cor 1–3.[17] He uses perceptual words throughout—

---

13. See, e.g., Ernst Käsemann, "On the Subject of Primitive Christian Apocalyptic," in *New Testament Questions Today*, trans. W. J. Montague (Philadelphia: Fortress, 1969); "The Saving Significance of the Death of Jesus," in *Perspectives on Paul*, trans. Margaret Kohl (Philadelphia: Fortress, 1971).

14. See, e.g., J. Louis Martyn, "Apocalyptic Antinomies in Paul's Letters to the Galatians" and "Epistemology at the Turn of the Ages: 2 Corinthians 5:16," in *Theological Issues in the Letters of Paul* (Nashville: Abingdon, 1997). See also J. Christiaan Beker, *Paul the Apostle: The Triumph of God in Life and Thought* (Philadelphia: Fortress, 1980), and *Paul's Apocalyptic Gospel: The Coming Triumph of God* (Philadelphia: Fortress, 1982).

15. *Fides et Ratio* also presupposes the two orders of knowing, but embeds them within its christological and Trinitarian presuppositions.

16. See Pope John Paul II, *The Acting Person*, trans. Andrzej Potocki (Dordrecht, Holland: D. Reidel, 1979).

17. See Alexandra Brown, *The Cross and Human Transformation: Paul's Apocalyptic Word in 1 Corinthians* (Minneapolis: Fortress, 1995). For additional studies that discuss Paul's epistemology, see Robin Scroggs, "New Being: Renewed Mind: New Perception: Paul's View of the Source of Ethical Insight," in *The Texts and the Times: New Testament Essays for Today* (Minneapolis: Fortress, 1993); Stanley K. Stowers, "Paul on the Use and Abuse of Reason," in *Greeks, Romans, and Christians: Essays in Honor of Abraham J. Malherbe*, ed. David L. Balch et al. (Minneapolis: Fortress, 1990); and Stephen M. Pogoloff, *Logos and Sophia: The Rhetorical Situation of 1 Corinthians* (Atlanta: Scholars Press, 1992). See also Paul W. Gooch, *Partial Knowledge: Philosophical Studies in Paul* (Notre Dame, IN: University of Notre Dame Press, 1987).

apokalypsis (unveil, reveal), *eidon* (see, perceive), *ginōskō* (know), *gnōmē* (intention, mind), *gnōsis* (knowledge), *nous* (mind), *oida* (know), *sophia* (wisdom), to name some of the most prominent.[18] He seeks to enact a perceptual shift in his readers "performatively"—that is, by *doing* what he is *saying* in the saying of it (e.g., by announcing the message of the cross) or by seeking to bring about an effect in his hearers (e.g., by persuading and appealing to them to be reconciled). This perceptual shift is enacted in his appeal that his readers shift their standpoint from one that is egoistic, factional, and hierarchical to one that is shared, in which his readers seek the same mind and purpose.[19]

He does so by way of a two-stage argument. First, he announces the new age and the new mode of perception that the cross ushers in, an announcement that disrupts the normal way of seeing and experiencing things. Second, he describes what it might mean to view things from the vantage point of that new age, a perspective identified not only with a corporate rationality but with the presumption of abundance, that, as Paul tells his readers at the end of the section, "all things are yours"—life and death, and past, present, and future.[20] What we will trace is how he appropriates both Jewish apocalyptic themes and Stoic rhetorical strategies in order to enact this shift, even as he transforms them by way of his understanding of the cross.

Paul's First Letter to the Corinthians was written in 54 C.E., several years after the founding of the congregation.[21] Corinth was a bustling urban center of cultural and ethnic diversity. There is little question that the problems in the Corinthian congregation dealt largely with matters of political status and distinctions. Wayne Meeks suggests that the early Christians were status inconsistent, that is, they were economically prosperous but not of high status and that this created social instability.[22]

Paul writes the letter in response to conflicts about which he has heard in reports from Chloe's people. Chloe was a woman of some prominence, and her people were probably slaves and other associates. From what can be gathered from Paul's references in the letter, the reports have concerned sexual immorality (5:1–8; 6:12–20), legal disputes (6:1–11), and conflicts over the celebration of the Lord's Supper (11:17–34) and beliefs about the resurrection of the dead (15:1–58). In addition, the Corinthians themselves have written

---

18. Brown lists at least twenty-six verbs in her "operative vocabulary of perception in this text" in *Cross and Human Transformation*, 24, 25.

19. Brown draws on J. L. Austin's analysis of "performative utterance" in *How to Do Things with Words* (Cambridge, MA: Harvard University Press, 1962), 103–9. See her discussion of Austin in *Cross and Human Transformation*, 16–19.

20. Brown describes these two stages in *Cross and Human Transformation*.

21. Commentaries on 1 Corinthians include: Anthony C. Thiselton, *The First Epistle to the Corinthians: A Commentary on the Greek Text* (Grand Rapids: Eerdmans, 2000); Richard Hays, *First Corinthians* (Louisville, KY: John Knox, 1997); C. K. Barrett, *A Commentary on the First Epistle to the Corinthians* (New York: Harper & Row, 1968); William Beardslee, *First Corinthians: A Commentary for Today* (St. Louis: Chalice, 1994); Hans Dieter Betz and Margaret M. Mitchell, "Corinthians, First Epistle to the," *Anchor Bible Dictionary* 1:1139–48; Hans Conzelmann, *1 Corinthians*, trans. James W. Leitch (Philadelphia: Fortress, 1975); Gordon Fee, *The First Epistle to the Corinthians* (Grand Rapids: Eerdmans, 1987); Victor Furnish, *The Theology of the First Letter to the Corinthians* (Cambridge: Cambridge University Press, 1999); Jerome Murphy-O'Connor, *1 Corinthians* (Wilmington, DE: Michael Glazier, 1979). For an analysis of the social conflicts within the Corinthian community, see Dale B. Martin, *The Corinthian Body* (New Haven, CT: Yale University Press, 1995).

22. See Meeks, *First Urban Christians*.

to Paul (7:1a) asking his advice about such things as sex and marriage (7:1b–40), the eating of meat that has been offered to idols (8:1–11:1), and the use of spiritual gifts in the community's worship (12:1–14:40).

As Margaret Mitchell points out, Paul's rhetorical style in responding to these problems is more pastoral counsel and exhortation about specific matters and incidents than general moral exhortation with universal application.[23] Indeed, the fact that there are so many disparate matters discussed in the letter has led many scholars to argue that it represents a collection of letters rather than a single one.[24]

But Mitchell argues that there is a singular purpose that unifies the letter: Paul's call for reconciliation. Paul's argument about the "wisdom of the cross" (1:18–25) is part of the first major proof in the letter (1:10–4:21), a proof in which Paul marshals the antitheses—or what I will call, following Martyn, the "antinomies"—pertaining to the "foolishness of the cross" and "wisdom of the world." He does this to criticize the factionalism he perceives in the Corinthian congregation, a factionalism that divides persons into high and low status and that prefers division to unity, superiority to cooperation. In a similar vein, Richard Hays's commentary on 1 Corinthians highlights how Paul's goal in the letter is that of "community formation," a goal he seeks to enact by "converting the imagination" of his audience. He does this by way of, in Hays's words, an "apocalyptic eschatology" that enacts a "transformation of power and status through the cross." At the heart of this transformation is a knowing that stresses the "primacy of love" even as it takes place within the context of "embodied existence"—that is, in relation to the treatment of actual problems associated with things bodies *do*, such as eat, have sex, worship, use money, and so on.[25]

In sum, the central theme throughout the letter is a call for reconciliation (1:10–17), a call rooted in the understanding of love Paul sets out in 8:1–3, ch. 13, and in his closing appeal to let love govern the community (16:14). But this call for reconciliation is not, as I have pointed out, an abstract argument. It is a diagnosis of how the very specific rivalries and jealousies at the heart of the community's disputes and dysfunctions have their roots in the "boasts" of some persons to have special wisdom and knowledge (1:17, 18–25; 2:6, 11; 3:18–23, 8:1–3).

Apocalyptic and Stoic Resources

In our reading of 1 Cor 1–3, we will trace two resources Paul appropriates and redefines—Jewish apocalyptic motifs and Stoic rhetorical strategies—in depicting how the cross enacts a shift in his readers' perceptions.

First, as Martyn contends, Paul establishes an intrinsic connection between eschatology and epistemology. His argument rests on the turn of the ages, the

---

23. Margaret M. Mitchell, *Paul and the Rhetoric of Reconciliation: An Exegetical Investigation of the Language and Composition of 1 Corinthians* (Louisville, KY: Westminster/John Knox, 1992), 121–57.
24. Ibid., 186–92.
25. Hays, *First Corinthians*, 12ff.

juncture between the old age and the new, at which one is granted a new
means of perception for distinguishing truth from falsehood.[26] Second
Corinthians 5:16–17 depicts this vividly: "From now on, therefore, we
regard no one from a human point of view. . . . So if anyone is in Christ,
there is a new creation: everything old has passed away; see, everything has
become new!"

Paul's two most obvious uses of apocalyptic imagery in 1 Cor 1–3 are
found in 1:18 and 2:8.[27] In 1:18 he depicts how the "message about the cross"
divides humanity into those who are "perishing" and those who are "being
saved." In 2:8 he describes how the "rulers of this age . . . crucified the Lord
of glory." And, as my analysis will make explicit, these themes are found
throughout Paul's discourse on the cross in 1 Corinthians.

The connection Paul makes between the cross and the new age (or new
creation) that it ushers in has roots in the apocalyptic thinking that characterized Second Temple Judaism. The Greek word group *apokalypsis/apoka-
lyptō* can be translated as "unveiling"/"unveil" (rendering *apo* as "out from"
and *kalypso* as "veil") or, more commonly, "revelation"/"reveal." Exemplified
by the book of Daniel (and related literature, e.g., *1 Enoch*), apocalyptic
thinking presupposes deep theological assumptions about the revelation of an
imminent eschaton in which God's embattled sovereignty over time and history is enacted in the passing away of one eon and the ushering in of a new
age.[28] Martyn stresses the epistemological nature of this discourse, highlight-
ing how Paul uses it to demonstrate how the cross has brought about the
turning of the ages for those who can see it—a new way of "knowing according to the cross." At the heart of this logic is the sense that human history is
hopeless, that God has given the elect a true perception of things (a new way
of thinking both of the present and the future), and that only God's judging
and saving activity can bring about a future transformation and perception
of it in the present.[29]

Especially relevant for our reading of 1 Cor 1–3 is Martyn's insight into
the way that the cross ushers in a new age in which old antinomies—
fundamental opposites that were essential in the ancient world for distinguishing people and placing them in hierarchies—disappear.[30] Drawing on Paul's use
of an early baptismal tradition in Gal 3:27–28, Martyn observes how "putting
on Christ" has made basic antinomies (e.g., between Jew and Greek, slave and
free, male and female) disappear because all are now "one in Christ Jesus."
The new Christians in fact have suffered a loss of their familiar cosmos—
"as though a fissure had opened up under their feet, hurling them into an

---

26. Martyn, "Epistemology at the Turn of the Ages."
27. See Brown, *Cross and Human Transformation*, 23–24.
28. See Richard E. Sturm, "Defining the Word 'Apocalyptic,'" in *Apocalyptic and the New
Testament: Essays in Honor of J. L. Martyn*, ed. Joel Marcus and Marion Soards (Sheffield: JSOT Press,
1989).
29. Martyn, "Epistemology at the Turn of the Ages."
30. Note how Martyn uses the word "antinomies": "I use the term 'antinomy' in an idiosyncratic
way, namely to render the numerous expressions by which the ancients referred (in many languages) to a
pair of opposites so fundamental to the cosmos, being one of its elements, as to make the cosmos what it
is." Martyn, "Antinomies," 424 n. 28.

abyss."[31] At the heart of this fissure is the disappearance, made especially clear in Galatians, between law and not-law—between sinning and keeping the law (2:17–19), being wrong and being set right by keeping the law (2:16; 3:12), and being dead and being made alive by the law (3:21). Indeed, Gal 6:15 asserts pointedly that in Christ all is a new creation—beyond circumcision and uncircumcision.

Further, if these old antinomies have disappeared, then they have been replaced by a new set, a new framework or paradigm of opposites—that of the contrast between spirit and flesh. The spirit/flesh contrast is given birth in God's creative act of sending his Son and the Spirit of his Son into this present evil age. Christ is the new creation—the new cosmos—who ushers in this new age. Those baptized into him have put him on as clothing and have his Spirit in their hearts. They now live in this new age—this new way of being in the world—and are guided by the Spirit who enables them to live out of this new life "in Christ."

Nonetheless, there are recurring patterns in 1 Cor 1–3 that are not fully accounted for by apocalyptic themes. Paul appeals to the Corinthians to be in agreement—to have no divisions, to be united in the same mind and purpose (1:10)—at the beginning of this section and at its end (3:1–4), where he chides them for their jealousy and quarreling. In these introductory and concluding sections he contrasts two kinds of "belonging": a belonging to Paul, Apollos, Cephas (a factional "belonging"), and a belonging to Christ, who belongs to God (a belonging in which "all belong to you"). Yet another theme is the contrast he draws with "boasting": the false boasting that comes with belonging to human leaders or deciding who is superior or inferior, and the true boasting that comes from knowing that one already has everything. There is a warrant in this appeal that the apocalyptic themes do not make fully explicit. You do not need to boast falsely or align yourself with factions led by strong personalities, Paul argues, because all is already yours. This wealth—the sheer abundance that is yours by belonging to Christ—makes it unnecessary to find security in an egoistic or factional viewpoint.

Stoic rhetorical strategies offer intriguing insight at this point.[32] Stoicism essentially deals with the question of personal identity—who one is and where one belongs. At the heart of Stoic self-understanding and formation (*oikeiōsis*) is the question of understanding what one considers oneself to be and, consequently, what belongs to one among the things outside oneself. The basic activity here is "cognitive"—having to do with self-awareness.[33] It is precisely this profoundly cognitive (or self-aware) understanding of identity that perhaps constitutes an important framework for Paul's thought about what happens when people become "new creatures" whose identities are now "in Christ." What Stoic writers seek to achieve in ethical argumentation is a shift in their readers' standpoint, from strictly subjective to objective. In this shift, a change occurs from relating everything to one's own subjectivity

---

31. Martyn, "Antinomies," 111–23.
32. I am drawing here primarily from Engberg-Pedersen, *Paul and the Stoics*.
33. See, e.g., Cicero, *De Finibus Bonorum et Malorum*, which is analyzed in *Paul and the Stoics*.

(one's own empirical or prudential concerns) to relating everything to the objective perspective of rationality itself, a view above the individual that the individual may come to occupy (that of reason, or logos). That change from an egoistic standpoint to an objective rational one results in a grasp of the single, unified concept of the good and the true: reason, or the logos. "Wisdom" in this shift essentially means viewing the world from the standpoint of that objective good and the magnanimity of perspective contained within it.

But there is a second shift mediated by this encounter with the good or reason and that is the shift to a social perspective—a shift that parallels the apocalyptic understanding of what it means to live by the Spirit instead of the flesh. Although one may perceive objectively the good for all, it is still possible to remain self-centered and to grasp *cognitively* the transcendental standpoint of reason, but to remain *existentially* at an egoistic level. Thus, a secondary task in ethical formation involves the activity of learning to actually see and perhaps even to feel things from the standpoint of the common good—for example, to see things from another's perspective or to see how one's natural regard for one's kin might be extended to all people.

Something similar is going on in Paul's argument as he seeks to describe not only what incorporation into Christ is about—what happens, say, in the proclamation of the cross—but also how Christ's life might actually be embodied within a community. The overarching task in this section is a call for unity, for a shared mind and a common purpose precisely in the face of jealousy and wrangling. Paul is trying to bring about a shift in his readers from a standpoint rooted merely in a "psychic" or "carnal" mind—an egoistic and factional one—to a standpoint rooted in Christ and the Spirit, one that (like reason, or the logos) enables them to see things from the perspective of a shared good and purpose. Instead of belonging to specific leaders and their agendas, they now belong to Christ, which, as 1 Cor 1–3 makes clear, entails such things as having access to the depths of God and the freedom of being above scrutiny. At the heart of the appeal for a shift in perspective is the presumption that from Christ's perspective—from the standpoint of participating in Christ and ultimately in God—one can afford to be generous with others.

A Reading of 1 Corinthians 1–3

"The Message about the Cross"

We turn now to the actual analysis of Paul's argument. Paul introduces his argument in 1:10 by appealing to his Corinthian brothers and sisters to be "in agreement"—to have "no divisions" but to be "united in the same mind and the same purpose." The issue dividing the Corinthians has to do with baptism, although it is not clear exactly what the problem is (1:14–17). Paul is thankful to God that he did not baptize any of them but simply "proclaimed the gospel" to them—and not, he adds, with "eloquent wisdom," so that the cross might not be "emptied [*kenōthē*] of its power" (1:17). This reference to the cross not being emptied of its power is our first clue that he is dealing with a different understanding of power than the one his readers are accustomed to thinking about. The same word for "empty" (*kenōsis*) is used in Phil 2:5–8, where it is used to describe how Christ Jesus,

> who, though he was in the form of God,
>   did not regard equality with God
>   as something to be exploited,
> but emptied himself [*ekénōsen*],
>   taking the form of a slave,
>   being born in human likeness.
>   . . . .
>   and became obedient to the point of death—
>   even death on a cross.

The apparently paradoxical relationship between "power" and "emptying" will be at the heart of Paul's appeal. In the hymn from Phil 2:6–11, Christ is able to empty himself precisely because he "shares equality" with God. Both the Philippian hymn and this Corinthian appeal to the cross are embedded in appeals for unity and for being of the same "mind." In both instances, Paul appeals to the cross—or Christ's *kenōsis*—as the ground for his appeal for reconciliation and unity. What is often not emphasized in interpretations of either of these texts is the fact that this appeal is based not simply on Christ's *kenōsis* but on the fact that a radically different kind of power is being enacted in that *kenōsis*. This understanding of power is very different from typical human uses of power, but it is a form of power nonetheless.

The new age that the message of the cross ushers in is rooted in a very different understanding of power and wisdom than that which the Corinthians presupposed. Verse 18 introduces an antinomy that makes this point: "For the message about the cross is foolishness to those who are perishing, but to us who are being saved it is the power of God." The apocalyptic announcement of the message of the cross is perceived differently by two different groups. For those "being saved" (*sōzoménois*) it is the "power of God" (*dúnamis theoû*), but for those who are "perishing" (*apolluménois*) it is sheer "foolishness" (*mōría*; v. 18). Note that the contrast here is an odd one. *Foolishness* is usually contrasted with *wisdom* and *weakness* with *power*. As we will see in the next few verses, the message of the cross—precisely in its foolishness and weakness—undoes the usual antinomies that separate Jew from Greek, the wise from the foolish, the weak from the strong, and still later on, those of noble birth from those who are low and despised, things that are from things that are not, and so forth. A "double reversal" or "double negation" is at work in the ushering in of this new age.[34] The wisdom and power that the cross will usher in is neither wise nor foolish in a human sense, but is

---

34. For an analysis of this pattern in Anselm, Søren Kierkegaard, Emmanuel Lévinas, and Jacques Derrida, among others, see Mark C. Taylor, *Nots* (Chicago: University of Chicago Press, 1993).

much wiser than human wisdom; it is neither strong nor weak in a human
sense, but is much stronger than human strength (see, especially, v. 25).

Paul introduces the actual content of this message of the cross in vv. 19–25:

> For it is written,
> a   "I will destroy the wisdom of the wise,
>   and the discernment of the discerning I will thwart."
> b   Where is the one who is wise?
>   Where is the scribe?
>   Where is the debater of this age?
>   Has not God made foolish the wisdom of the world?
> A   For since, in the wisdom of God, the world did not know God
>   through wisdom,
> B   God decided, through the foolishness of our proclamation, to
>   save those who believe.
> A'   For Jews demand signs and Greeks desire wisdom,
> B'   but we proclaim Christ crucified,
> C1   a stumbling block to Jews and foolishness to Gentiles
> C2–D   but to those who are the called, both Jews and Greeks,
>   *Christ* the power of God and the wisdom of God.
> b'   For God's foolishness is wiser than human wisdom,
> a'   and God's weakness is stronger than human strength.

Paul begins by quoting a judgment oracle against Judah's political reliance
on human wisdom and power (Isa 29:14; see also Ps 33:10). He continues
with references to the "wise" (*sophós*), "scribe" (*grammateús*), and "debater"
(*suzētētēs*)—Greek, Jewish, and Roman paragons of human wisdom. This sets
the stage for his use of antitheses, or antinomies, for bringing about a perceptual shift in his hearers so that they can begin to catch a glimpse of what the
foolishness and weakness that the cross enacts might look like.

In doing so, Paul draws on apocalyptic themes. First, (A) an *unmet expectation* is described. The "wisdom of God" is such that the "world did not
know God through wisdom." Instead, what happens is (B) an *unexpected
reversal*: God decides, "through the foolishness of our proclamation, to save
those who believe." Instead of being able to know God by way of wisdom—
what was anticipated—God saves by way of foolishness. In the next verse the
pattern is repeated but specified more clearly. (A') The expectations are stated:
The Jews want signs; the Greeks desire wisdom. Instead, something else happens: (B') Christ crucified is proclaimed. The content of the proclamation—
"Christ crucified"—elicits (C) *two different perceptual responses.* (C1) For
Jews, it is a stumbling block; for the Gentiles, it is foolishness. But (C2) to
those who are called, among both Jews and Greeks, Christ is the power and
wisdom of God. Among this latter group, among the ones who perceive
rightly, we find not only a new perception but (D) *the power of God creating
something new.* In this case, it is a people who are called from among the Jews
and Greeks (who are able to perceive Christ as the power and wisdom of God).

"Consider Your Own Call"

The next section deals explicitly with the new people who are called from among Jews and Gentiles (vv. 26–31):

A	Consider your own call, brothers and sisters:
	not many of you were wise by human standards,
	not many were powerful,
	not many were of noble birth.
B–C	But God chose what is foolish in the world
	to shame the wise;
B–C	God chose what is weak in the world
	to shame the strong;
B–C	God chose what is low and despised in the world, things that are not,
	to reduce to nothing things that are,
D	so that no one might boast in the presence of God.
	He is the source of your life in Christ Jesus,
	who became for us wisdom from God,
	and righteousness
	and sanctification
	and redemption,
D	in order that, as it is written, "Let the one who boasts, boast in the Lord."

This section simply reinforces the fact that this new humanity of Jews and Greeks is created by God's call, a call that reverses the usual conceptions of foolishness/wisdom and weakness/strength. Paul now shifts from a depiction of the *kērygma* itself to an appeal to the Corinthians' own experience. The Corinthian community itself consisted of people of diverse rank and background. Not many among them were wise, powerful, or of noble birth, by human standards (v. 26). But in a fashion that imitates the pattern of Jesus' own ministry and message, in which the "tax collectors and sinners" were often the most eager to drop everything in order to follow him, so within the Corinthian community, "God chose what is foolish in the world to shame the wise; God chose what is weak in the world to shame the strong; God chose what is low and despised in the world, things that are not, to reduce to nothing things that are."

Again, Paul begins with an unmet expectation: (A) God does not choose the wise, the powerful, and those of noble birth. Instead, (B) God chooses the foolish, the weak, and the low and despised, indeed, "things that are not," in order to shame the wise, the strong, and "things that are." The reason? Precisely to shame the wise and strong, and to "reduce to nothing things that are." God reverses precisely what was expected. What should bring approbation (wisdom, strength, noble birth) now brings only shame. This action of God creates two perceptual responses. On the one side are (C) those who are shamed: the wise, the strong, and "things that are." On the other side are (B) those who are chosen: the foolish, the weak, the low, and the despised— "things that are not." What is the purpose of this mode of creating a new community? (D) So that it is clear to all that Christ Jesus is the source of life for the people in this new community—that he, the one who became wisdom for this community, is now its source of righteousness, sanctification, and redemption. And the purpose for this? So that no one can boast of having achieved membership on the basis of his or her own wisdom—so that even those who are chosen are continually reminded that their only reason for boasting lies "in the Lord." Paul concludes the section with yet another quotation. This reference (from Jer 9:23–24; 9:22–23 LXX) is part of a judgment against Israel for pursuing false gods:

> Do not let the wise boast in their wisdom, do not let the mighty boast in their might, do not let the wealthy boast in their wealth; but let those who boast boast in this, that they understand and know me, that I am the LORD; I act with steadfast love, justice, and righteousness in the earth, for in these things I delight, says the LORD.

The contrast here is between might, wealth, and wisdom, on the one hand, and God's steadfast love, justice, and righteousness, on the other.

The same power that could "destroy" the "wisdom of the wise" and "thwart" the "discernment of the discerning" can now choose "things that are not" (the low and despised) to "reduce to nothing things that are." What is being depicted here is a bringing forth of new creation *ex nihilo* ("out of nothing" v. 28). We should note, of course, that this shift is not merely a perceptual shift. A new creation is entailed here, one in which, to use Paul's language in Gal 6:15, "neither circumcision nor uncircumcision is anything"— drawing the law/not-law contrast of Galatians—but "a new creation is everything!" The image of this new cosmos in Christ echoes the image of the new heavens and new earth depicted in Isa 65:17–25, where wolf and lamb feed together, and lion and ox both eat straw. For Paul, salvation is always linked with this remaking—this re-creation—of the world (see also Rom 8:19–23 and 2 Cor 5:17–19).[35]

We clearly have a picture here of eschatological reversal, one that resonates with Mary's song of praise (Luke 1:46–55).[36] In Mary's hymn (traditionally called the Magnificat), God shows "strength with his arm" (Luke 1:51), a phrase that echoes Exod 6:6, which describes how the Lord frees the Israelites from the "burdens of the Egyptians" (i.e., the forced labor they made the Israelites endure) and delivers them out of slavery. This only underlines and deepens the political and economic character of the redemption depicted in the Magnificat, where Mary describes how the Lord scatters the proud,

---

35. Later, Irenaeus would use the term "recapitulation."
36. See also Hannah's prayer (1 Sam 2:1–10), in which God is praised for saving the lowly and oppressed.

brings down the powerful, fills the hungry with good things, and sends the rich away empty. For Luke, we might add, this theme is at the heart of Jesus' ministry, which (quoting Isa 61:1–2) brought good news to the poor, release to captives, recovery of sight to the blind, and freedom to the oppressed (Luke 4:18–19). It is also at the heart of the church's first Pentecost, where (quoting Joel 2:28–32) God's Spirit is poured out on "all flesh"—sons and daughters who prophesy, young men who see visions, old men who dream dreams, and even slaves, both men and women (Acts 2:17–18). Finally, for the gospel writers in general, this kind of reversal is at the heart of Jesus' preaching about the reign of God, a preaching that was welcomed by "tax collectors and sinners" but was resisted by those with religious and political power.

Nonetheless, although this new creation entails political and economic redemption, it is not ushered in by human means. Paul's point here—like Mary's—is that it is God's activity that brings about the reversal, not humans'. Why? So that no one can boast in God's presence (v. 29). At the heart of this reversal is a very real "interchange" in which the new humanity that comes about is linked not with any particular faction but with "your life in Christ Jesus." Christ, Paul avers, "became for us" not only the "wisdom of God" but "righteousness, sanctification, and redemption." Later theological traditions will describe the interchange in this way (in Irenaeus's words): "Christ became like us in order that we might become like him."[37]

This interchange is especially interesting when understood in relation to the political reversals we have just described. This new humanity is defined by Christ's life and not by human conceptions of what is wise, powerful, noble ("things that are"), or for that matter, what is foolish, weak, or low and despised ("things that are not"). A profound paradox is being asserted here. Using Paul's language in Galatians, "new creation" is "everything" here, and the distinction between circumcision and uncircumcision (and we might add foolish and wise, weak and strong, etc.) is "nothing" (Gal 6:15).

"When I Came to You"

Paul now shifts to speak about himself, the one who brought the message of the cross (2:1–5):

A   When I came to you, brothers and sisters,
        I did not come proclaiming the mystery of God to you
        in lofty words or wisdom
B   For I decided to know nothing among you except Jesus Christ,
        and him crucified.
        And I came to you in weakness and in fear and in much trembling.
C1   My speech and my proclamation were not with plausible words
        of wisdom,

---

37. Irenaeus, *Adv. Haer.* 5, preface. ("*Factus est quod sumus nos, uti nos perficeret esse quod est ipse*"). I have drawn the term "interchange" from Morna Hooker, *From Adam to Christ: Essays on Paul* (Cambridge: Cambridge University Press, 1990).

C2   but with a demonstration of the Spirit and of power,
D   so that your faith might rest not on human wisdom but on the
        power of God.

Again, we find (A) that an expectation is unmet. Paul does not come as one
proclaiming "the mystery of God" with "lofty words and wisdom."
Instead, (B) he comes as one who knows nothing else but "Jesus Christ, and
him crucified." He comes, therefore, not with eloquence but, indeed, in
weakness, fear, and trembling. Although we do not have an explicit reference to two modes of perception, we do have (C1) a reference to perception: that in spite of the fact that his proclamation was not done "with
plausible words of wisdom," it is still the case that they communicated a
reality: "Jesus Christ, and him crucified." The very fact that they communicated this—in spite of the fact that Paul's own speech was not "with plausible words"—demonstrates that the creation of this perception is an act of
"the Spirit and of power" (v. 4). Again, the result (D) is that it is clear to all
that the faith of this community rests not on human wisdom—as demonstrated by Paul's capacity to speak or their capacity to interpret—but simply on the power of God.

A profound paradox is being asserted here. In the same way that new life
in Christ undoes distinctions among wise and foolish, weak and strong,
"things that are" and "things that are not" within the community at large, so
on an individual level, the apostle speaks with a "Spirit and power" that
reflexively undoes any attempt on his part to boast of individual distinction.
Further, the point of the paradox is for his hearers' welfare.

Paul appears to be drawing both on prophetic themes—the prophet who
is unworthy but speaks nonetheless (Moses and Isaiah are two exemplars)[38]—
and on lists of hardships that depict the ideal sages' response to adversity.[39]
He consistently modifies the latter to demonstrate that (in the words of
2 Cor 4:7) "the extraordinary power" enacted in this adversity "belongs to
God and does not come from us"(see 1 Cor 4:9–13). Further, the purpose of
the extraordinary power is not for his own self-sufficiency but for another
person's welfare. In the next chapter (1 Cor 4:10–13), for example, he contrasts the apostles and members of the Corinthian community in this way:
"We are fools for the sake of Christ, but you are wise in Christ. We are
weak, but you are strong. You are held in honor, but we in disrepute." He
then describes the apostles in dramatic terms as hungry, thirsty, poorly
clothed, beaten, homeless, and weary from the work of their own hands—
and finally as becoming "like the rubbish of the world, the dregs of all
things." Note the stress here on the connection between the apostles' sufferings and the Corinthians' welfare.

The following chart summarizes the observations we have made so far:

---

38. For Moses' experience, see, e.g., Exod 4:10–11; for Isaiah, see Isa 6.
39. Paul's lists of hardships can be found in 1 Cor 4:9–13; 2 Cor 6:4–10; 2 Cor 11:23–28; Phil
4:11–12; and Rom 8:35–39.

	CONTENT "The message about the cross"	AUDIENCE "Consider your own call"	SPEAKER "When I came to you"
(A) Unmet Expectation	A The world will (or can?) know God through wisdom. A' Jews demand signs. A' Greeks desire wisdom.	Those who are wise, powerful, and of noble birth should be chosen.	The mystery of God should be proclaimed in lofty words or wisdom.
(B) Reversal	B God decided to save the world through the foolishness of our proclamation. B' We proclaim Christ crucified.	God chose what is foolish, weak, low, and despised (things that are not).	Paul knows only Christ crucified and comes in weakness, fear, and trembling.
(C1) Perception of Those "Who are Perishing"	Because they demand signs and wisdom (Jews and Gentiles, respectively), the message of the cross is a stumbling block and foolishness.	As the wise, strong, and powerful (things that are), they are shamed.	His implausible words truly are implausible.
(C2) Perception of Those "Who are Called"	Because they are called (Jews and Greeks), Christ is the power and wisdom of God.	As the foolish, weak, and low and despised (things that are not), they are chosen.	His implausible words are a demonstration of the Spirit and of power.
(D) Outcome (for the "ones being saved")	A new people are called out of Jews and Greeks who perceive that Christ is the power and wisdom of God.	No one can boast since God is the source of life; Christ becomes for us the wisdom of God, and is our righteousness, sanctification, and redemption.	Your faith rests not on human wisdom but on the power of God.

"Yet among the Mature"

Paul's introduction to the next section is intriguing. He has just been criticizing any knowledge of God based on wisdom. Yet he introduces this section with a reference to the "mature" or "perfect" (*teleíois*), who have access to a special kind of "wisdom." Does this not reinforce the very concept that he has been attacking: that there is a higher level of spirituality to be attained based on some special "wisdom"? See 2:6–8:

> Yet among the mature we do speak wisdom, though it is not a wisdom of this age or of the rulers of this age, who are doomed to perish. But we speak God's wisdom, secret and hidden, which God decreed before the ages for our glory. None of the rulers of this age understood this; for if they had, they would not have crucified the Lord of glory.

Many scholars have thought that this section is a gnostic interpolation. But there are enough points of continuity, especially in terms of apocalyptic themes, to suggest that Paul is simply adding another twist to his argument. The "mature" is a reference to those who participate in the perception of the new age, a perception not defined by the "wisdom [*sophían*] of this age" or of the "rulers [*tōn arxóntōn*] of this age," who are, in bold apocalyptic language, "doomed to perish." A central tenet of apocalyptic epistemology is that it is "secret and hidden" to those of "this age" (*toû aiōnos*) but not to God's elect, whose capacity to understand was "decreed before the ages." Indeed, if the rulers of this age had understood this secret and hidden wisdom, they would not have "crucified" the Messiah. Finally, the parallels between this passage and other exemplars of Jewish apocalyptic are strong. Note, for example, its resonance with Dan 2:27–28: "No wise men, enchanters, magicians, or diviners can show to the king the mystery that the king is asking, but there is a God in heaven who reveals mysteries, and he has disclosed [through Daniel] to King Nebuchadnezzar what will happen at the end of days." Paul is no longer dealing with the double reversals he used in depicting how the cross, as well as the wisdom and power it enacts, inaugurates a new age that disrupts human notions of wisdom and strength. His task now is to establish a clearing for describing how the epistemology of this new age actually works.

If his earlier argument established the point that his hearers are no longer defined by the human distinctions that separate people or place them in hierarchies but are now solely defined by their new life in Christ, then his present argument is to describe what it means to operate with this new perception. Drawing on an important apocalyptic theme, he makes clear that only the Spirit can enable one to have this new perception (2:9–10):

> But, as it is written,
>
> > "What no eye has seen, nor ear heard,
> >   nor the human heart conceived,
> > what God has prepared for those who love him"—
>
> these things God has revealed to us through the Spirit; for the Spirit searches everything, even the depths of God. For what human being

knows what is truly human except the human spirit that is within? So also no one comprehends what is truly God's except the Spirit of God.

Only the Spirit is the agent of knowing in apocalyptic traditions (see, e.g., *1 Enoch*).[40] Only the Spirit facilitates a new and true perception of things. When the Spirit possesses a person, that person is enabled to be moved beyond the limits of her own worldly consciousness—her own spirit—and perceive a strange new creation. This Spirit is a foe of the falsehood of "this age" and enables one to see, even now, the future reign of God over against the present apparent reign of evil. The Spirit, then, does not merely disclose the wisdom that is the creative principle that permeates the cosmos (as depicted, e.g., in Prov 7:22–31 or Wis 8:22a–30). Rather, in apocalyptic thought, it announces a new creation and empowers human beings to live eschatologically—that is, out of the power of that future hope—even in the present circumstances of their lives, which may seem to contradict that hope.

This new mode of perception does not rest on human achievement. Paul is an "enthusiast," using that term in its ancient Greek sense.[41] Throughout his corpus, the experience of the Spirit and miracles—and more importantly of speaking and acting with the "Spirit and power"—are at the heart of his understanding of personal and communal life.[42] It is the Spirit who creates the new corporate rationality he is calling for (i.e., "being united in the same mind and same purpose," 1 Cor 1:10)—not ethical or political effort.

And if the Spirit's activity is not merely ethical or political, it is also not merely empirical. It is not related to what one can see, hear, touch, or even experience in feelings. It is, rather—in anticipation of the great love hymn in 1 Cor 13—something God prepares for those who love God. As 1 Cor 13 will make explicit, this love even undoes spiritual pretensions and cannot be identified with the spiritual gifts and practices that could give one cause to "boast" (e.g., tongues, prophetic powers, knowledge, faith to move mountains or give away one's possessions). Prophecies, tongues, and knowledge pass away; all that counts is what counts eschatologically—faith, hope, and love—and the greatest of these is love. And such love is not defined as an ethereal, abstract concept. It is defined, rather, by such mundane manifestations as being patient, kind, not envious (a theme Paul stresses throughout his letters),[43] not boastful or arrogant, not insisting on its own way, nor being irritable or resentful. Such love does not rejoice in wrongdoing but rejoices in truth; finally, it bears, believes, hopes, and endures "all things."

---

40. See the comparison of the role of the Spirit in wisdom and apocalyptic traditions in Brown, *Cross and Human Transformation*, 59–63.

41. "Enthusiasm" goes back to the Greek word *enthousiasmos*, which ultimately comes from the adjective *entheos*, "having the god within," formed from *en-*, "in, within," and *theos*, "god."

42. See, e.g., Gal 3:5; see also 1 Cor 12:4–11; 14:26–33a; 2 Cor 12:12. On the centrality of acting and speaking with the "Spirit and power," see esp. 1 Cor 2:1–5 and Rom 14:18, 19, where Paul speaks of "what Christ has accomplished through me to win obedience from the Gentiles," not only "by word and deed," but "by the power of signs and wonders, by the power of the Spirit of God."

43. This theme is also stressed in Mark McIntosh's essay in this volume. Note, e.g., that for Irenaeus, envy is the primary sin identified with the fall and therefore with idolatry (in contrast, e.g., to Augustine's focus on concupiscence or Luther's focus on despair).

Paul is very clear that this perception comes only from the Spirit, who searches and comprehends the depths of God. In a manner that echoes Dan 2:20–23, Paul presupposes that wisdom and power can come only from God and therefore it is only God who "gives wisdom to the wise and knowledge to those who have understanding" and, more importantly, that only God can reveal "deep and hidden things." Only God's Spirit can comprehend these things—and this Spirit does so "searching everything," even the depths of God. The Spirit gives us access to God's very depths, enabling us to "comprehend" what is truly God's.

Related themes are echoed in Paul's great hymn in Rom 8, where he speaks of our adoption as children of God, an adoption that enables us to have the same intimacy with God that Christ had. Like Christ, we too can now address God with intimacy—"Abba, Father!"—and in so doing claim our inheritance as God's children. Of course, that inheritance is paradoxically linked not only with "glory" but with "suffering," a theme we will explore later (Rom 8:14–17; Gal 4:5–7). In a fashion that echoes this passage in 1 Corinthians, Paul speaks of the profound, if ineffable, intimacy that believers have with God through his Spirit—the very Spirit "who intercedes with sighs too deep for words" (Rom 8:26). In this intercession, it appears that human beings participate in God's interaction with God's own Spirit: God knows the Spirit's mind, and the Spirit intercedes on our behalf according to God's will (8:27).[44]

The *Pneumatikos* and *Psychikos*

This way of knowing through the Spirit, although it is not empirical, is not merely ephemeral or alien to human knowing and experience. Paul uses explicitly epistemological verbs in the next section, such as "receive," "understand," "teach," "interpret," "discern" (2:12–15):

C1	a	Now we have received not the spirit of the world, but the Spirit that is from God,
	b	so that we may understand the gifts bestowed on us by God.
	c	And we speak of these things in words not taught by human wisdom but taught by the Spirit, interpreting spiritual things to those who are spiritual.
C2	a'	Those who live by the mind [*psychikòs*][45] do not receive the gifts of God's Spirit, for they are foolishness to them,
	b'	and they are unable to understand them
	c'	because they are spiritually discerned.
C1	c	Those who are spiritual [*pneumatikòs*] discern all things, and they are themselves subject to no one else's scrutiny.

44. Although Paul does not presuppose a full-blown Trinitarian theology, these references to God's and the Spirit's activity—and our participation in it—do suggest some kind of participation of human beings within the eternal conversation that takes place within God's very being.

45. My translation. The NRSV reads, "Those who are unspiritual do not receive. . . ."

The distinction between these modes of perception is defined by the contrast between the *psychikòs* (those who live by the empirical or prudential mind, a mind that seeks only its egoistic and factional interests) and the *pneumatikòs* (those who live by the Spirit, which has access to everything, even the depths of God). Unfortunately, these *psychikòs* and *pneumatikòs* are translated (e.g., in the NRSV) as "unspiritual" and "spiritual" respectively (in 1 Cor 2), and in relation to the contrast between the "physical" and "spiritual" (in 1 Cor 15:42–49).[46] *Psychikòs* is better translated as having to do with living according to the dictates of what one can see, hear, or touch ("empirical"), on the one hand, or with what appears to be good judgment or common sense—which can include both being wise in handling practical matters and being careful in regard to one's own interests ("prudential")—on the other. The contrast Paul seems to be making here—especially if we interpret his use of these terms in light of the entire context of 1 Cor 1–3—is a contrast between an egoistic or factional viewpoint (which merely seeks one's own or one's group's interests) and a corporate rationality (which seeks the "common good"; cf. 1 Cor 12). The *pneumatikòs* live by the power of the Spirit—a power that gives them access to the very depths of God. They can afford not to be egoistic or factional because they have access to an infinite source of wisdom and power.

This translation is reinforced when we examine how Paul uses the contrast in 1 Cor 15:42–49. There it is used to describe the new resurrected body and to contrast the *sōma psychikòn* (the empirical body) with the *sōma pneumatikòn* (the spiritual body). The *sōma psychikòn* is identified with the first Adam and the "image of the man of dust" (who became merely a "living being"), and the *sōma pneumatikòn* is identified with the last Adam and the "image of the man of heaven" (who became a "life-giving spirit").

A similar parallel is drawn in Rom 5:12–21, where the Christ, as the last Adam, is identified with the "free gift," in contrast to Adam's "trespass." The latter resulted in the "exercise" of death's "dominion," but the former—and the "abundance of grace" associated with it—is identified with the "exercise" of the "free gift of righteousness." At issue here is the contrast between domains of power—whether what "exercises dominion" in a life is death or the "abundance of grace" (death, grace, sin, etc., are for Paul domains of power). Furthermore, note that Paul only introduces the contrast between Adam's disobedience and Christ's obedience after he has discussed the contrast between the "trespass" and the "free gift."[47] In Paul's interpretation of Gen 3, Adam's fall is identified with his attempt to grasp at being godlike—at making judgments, at knowing good and evil—even though he was already

---

46. For a discussion of the relationship between these two modes of perception—a "psychic" or "carnal" one (*psychikòs/sarkikos*) over against a "spiritual" one (*pneumatikòs*)—see Henrik Tronier, "The Corinthian Correspondence between Philosophical Idealism and Apocalypticism," in *Paul beyond the Judaism/Hellenism Divide*, ed. Troels Engberg-Pedersen (Louisville, KY: Westminster John Knox, 2001), 165–96. See also Richard Horsley, "*Pneumatikos* vs. *Psychikos*: Distinctions of Spirit Status among the Corinthians," *Harvard Theological Review* 69 (1976): 269–88; and Birger A. Pearson, *The Pneumatikos-Psychikos Terminology in 1 Corinthians* (Missoula, MT: Scholars Press, 1973).

47. Hooker makes this point in *From Adam to Christ*.

made in the "image of God."[48] This contrasts with Christ, who (as depicted in Phil 2:6–8) did not count "equality with God" as something to be exploited, grasped, or seized (*harpagmòn*) but emptied himself (*ekénōsen*) even to the point of death on a cross.

At issue in these contrasts is a difference in (to use the language of Rom 5) the "domain" of power exercised in a life—whether that power is linked with grasping, which results from a perceived need or lack (Adam sought godlike powers instead of being content with the kind of stewardship over creation he was given) or whether it is linked with emptying, which results only from the presumption of the "abundance of grace" (Christ was content with the "equality with God" he already had).

"Mind of Christ"

Paul's words in the next verse (1 Cor 2:15) border on the dangerous, especially if they are interpreted in empirical terms—that is, from the standpoint of a human hierarchy in which one finite ego or faction has power over another. He actually states that those who are spiritual "discern all things" (*anakrínei [tà] pánta*) and are themselves "subject to no one else's scrutiny [*anakrínetai*]" (v. 15). This, and statements like it, are the source of all later conceptions of Christian freedom—the complete liberty one has (in Christ) not only over death and sin but over the law itself (Paul's argument in Galatians and Romans), and with that other people's judgments.[49]

He goes on to intensify his point (in v. 16) by asking, "For who has known the mind of the Lord [*noûn kuríou*] so as to instruct him?"—a question that in its original context presupposed that no one could possibly know the mind of the Lord (see Isa 40:13, also cited in Wis 9:13, where the LXX translates the Hebrew phrase "spirit [*ruach*] of the Lord" as "mind [*noûn*]"). Paul, however, surprises his readers with the conclusion that "we have the mind of Christ [*noûn christoû*]"—implying perhaps that we do have the mind of the Lord, and therefore can engage in a conversation in which we do actually "instruct him."

What is this mind (*noûs*) that we share with Christ?[50] The closest parallel is Phil 2:5, where Paul exhorts his reader to "let the same mind [*phroneîte*] be in you that was in Christ Jesus." In a manner similar to Stoic appeals to see things from the standpoint of a new, more magnanimous point of reference, Paul appeals to the Philippians to look not to their own interests but to see things from the standpoint of others' interests—to have the "same mind [*phronête*], having the same love, being in full accord and of one mind [*phronoûntes*]" (v. 2). His appeal, however, is not merely to an act of the will. It is about a shift in perception. The Philippians can look to one another's

---

48. This interpretation is similar to those found in Wis 2:24; 2 Esd 3:21, 26; and 2 *Bar* 54:15.

49. See Rom 14 for a classic account of this conception of liberty. See also Martin Luther's "Freedom of a Christian" (1520).

50. See also R. T. Wallis, "*Nous* as Experience," in *The Significance of Neoplatonism*, ed. R. B. Harris (Norfolk, VA: International Society for Neoplatonic Studies, Old Dominion University, 1976; distributed by State University of New York Press, 1976).

interests only if they share Christ's mind, a mind that is so secure—so drenched in the "abundance of grace" (to use the language of Rom 5)—that it can empty itself. This is not, as it is frequently interpreted, an appeal to follow the example of Christ as a mere moral example. This is about a shift in perception—an appeal to the imagination—to see things from the standpoint of the largesse Christ shares with God, a largesse that gives him the freedom not to grasp at or exploit what he has but to empty himself for the sake of another.

Romans 8:5–8 uses the same word where Paul draws a contrast between "those who live according to the flesh [*sárka*]" and "those who live according to the Spirit [*pneûma*]." The former "set their minds [*phronoûsin*] on the things of the flesh," while the latter "set their minds on the things of the Spirit." At issue in this contrast—much like the contrast between the *psychikòs* and *pneumatikòs*—is the difference between domains of power and the modes of perception that those domains enact, between the domain of the flesh (which, because of its grasping, limited standpoint, only ends in death) and the domain of the Spirit (which, because of its infinite abundance, exudes life and peace).

Romans 12 makes a similar argument. Paul urges his readers not to be "conformed to this age [*tō aiōni toútō*]" (my translation) but to be "transformed [*metamorphoûsthe*] by the renewing of your minds [*noós*] so that you may discern [*dokimázein*] what is the will of God—what is good and acceptable and perfect" (v. 2). His appeal here is to allow the mind to be transformed and renewed so that it can shift from the perspective of this age and see things from an eschatological vantage point. It is only from the standpoint of such a renewed mind—that is, from the standpoint of this shift in perspective, this conversion of the imagination—that one can discern God's will, indeed, discern what is good, acceptable, and perfect.

In chapter 3, Paul sharply changes his tone. He refers to his readers now not as the mature or perfect (*toîs teleìois*) but as infants (*nēpíois*)—people of the flesh (*sarkínois*) rather than the Spirit (*pneumatikoîs*). They are not yet ready for solid food and can only be fed with milk. They will remain as infants as long as jealousy and quarreling remain among them—note that "jealousy" (*zēlos*) can also mean "zealous"—and as long as they still can define their identity in relation to the factions and strong leaders they have rallied around. Paul urges them to see these leaders differently. Each one is part of a much larger whole. Each one contributes to a "common purpose." In making this point, Paul draws on the metaphors of a garden and a building. In God's garden, Paul may plant, Apollos may water, but only God gives the growth. In God's building, Paul may lay the foundation, but someone else builds on it. At the heart of all this is his appeal to the Corinthians to shift away from "boasting" and "belonging to," or aligning themselves, with various leaders and factions (e.g., Paul, Apollos, Cephas). His reasoning? You do not need to secure yourself with these alignments. "All is yours," which includes not only these leaders but—here Paul lists fundamental categories—the world, life and death, and present and future. You "belong to Christ," he avers, and "Christ belongs to God" (vv. 21–23).

The closest passage to this section is found in Rom 8, which Paul concludes with the powerful affirmation that nothing "will be able to separate us from the love of God" (v. 39). In saying this, he mentions a longer list of categories of things that cannot separate us from God: death and life, angels and rulers, things present and things to come, powers, height and depth, and "anything else in all creation" (vv. 38–39). This, of course, is not a guarantee that one will escape adversity. What precedes this is a list similar to those Paul mentions elsewhere in his writing: hardships, distress, persecution, famine, nakedness, peril, the sword. He even includes a reference to a lament psalm about being slaughtered as sheep (Ps 44:22). The point here is that the power of God's love, a power that embraces all that exists, is a power that is eschatologically present precisely in the midst of adversity. With this power, one can, to quote one of Paul's most Stoic-sounding expressions, "do all things through [Christ] who strengthens me," whether "being well-fed" or "hungry," "having plenty" or "being in need," and so on (Phil 4:11–14).

Apocalyptic motifs govern Paul's depiction of the message of the cross and how it ushers in a new mode of perception that undoes the antinomies characteristic of the old age (wise or foolish, strong or weak) and creates a new mode of perception in Christ—and a new humanity—among its hearers and speaker (1 Cor 1:8–2:5). These motifs continue to govern his depiction of how the Spirit creates for these hearers a clearing for a new way of perceiving and responding to the world, a new way of understanding and discerning the significance of all things (1 Cor 2:6–16), now that they see things from the perspective of the *pneumatikòs* and not the *psychikòs*.

But there appears to be another pattern at work when we situate this depiction of the cross and the Spirit's activity within his overall appeal for reconciliation at the beginning of 1 Corinthians (chs. 1–3). His appeal (which begins in 1:10–17) is that his readers shift from saying they "belong" to individual leaders to being "in agreement," that there be "no divisions" among them, that they be "united in the same mind and the same purpose." He returns to this appeal (3:1), urging his readers, once again, to shift from jealousy and quarrelling—and saying they "belong" to individual leaders—to sharing a "common purpose" (vv. 1–9). This appeal for reconciliation is not simply an ethical appeal to the will. The logic of his argument aims to get his readers to perceive the world differently—to transform their minds, to convert their imaginations, to shift their perspective. This new perception entails seeing things from the standpoint of the abundance, or plenitude, that inheres in the "mind of Christ," which means having access (through the Spirit, "who searches everything") to the "depths of God," being able not only to "discern all things" but to be "subject to no one else's scrutiny" in that discernment. The clincher to his argument is found in 3:21–34, where he reminds his readers that they need not boast of individual leaders and factions because all is already theirs in Christ—the world, life and death, present and future.[51]

---

51. Note Engberg-Pedersen's comment: "Practical thought: is this not something 'done' by the deliberator 'him- or herself' in a manner that removes it radically from Paul, where everything is a gift from God? Is it not just another form of 'works righteousness'? Answer: Definitely not! It certainly is a 'gift of

What is being called for is a shift from an egoistic, prudential way of viewing things (signified by "I") to one that seeks the "common good" (signified
by "C")—a shift from I to C.[52] As an appeal to the imagination, this shift is
mediated by a new reference point. One cannot suddenly seek the common
good (C) if one still sees things from the standpoint of the *psychikòs* (I). The
new reference point is defined by the "mind of Christ" (X). Apocalyptic
motifs depict how the cross ushers in this new perception and creates a new
set of hearers, but Paul also simply tells his readers that they participate in
Christ's mind: "we have the mind of Christ" or "you belong to Christ, and
Christ belongs to God." We could say that the shift is one from the I to X
(I→X). This parallels the way Stoic arguments make an initial appeal for the
reader to become aligned with the "logos" of reality, to move from I to L
(I→L). The (I→X) is the warrant Paul draws on to make his appeal that his
readers shift from I to C. Because they are in Christ—and see things from his
"abundant" perspective—they are able to shift from a limited egoistic, or factional, focus to the unlimited standpoint of Christ's mind, a standpoint that
will enable them to live "kenotically" and seek not merely their own interests
but those of others.

What is also implied here is that Christ's mind intrinsically seeks the common good (X=C). Indeed, Christ is the source of this new humanity's life, in
spite of their being Jew or Greek, wise or foolish, strong or weak, noble or
low and despised. So being in Christ automatically gives them a communal
standpoint. But since they live between the two ages (the new perspective is
eschatological), the appeal is made to live out of the new identity they have
already been given. Of course, as the apocalyptic understanding of the Spirit
makes clear (1 Cor 2:6–16), only the Spirit can bring about this outlook. Just
as once they are in Christ they can only live out of that life, so their new life
is wholly defined by the source of that life (Gal 2:20). Nonetheless, the appeal
is being made to see things now from the standpoint of Christ's mind (which
they already have) and to set their minds on the things of the Spirit (which
they have already received and which is already teaching them what no eye
has seen, ear heard, etc.). We could say that the appeal now is simply to flesh
out more fully the identity they already have. Given that you are already in
Christ (I→X), Paul is saying, you should live out of the full implications of
that life. Since X=C, flesh that out in your own life (X→C)—live out of the
abundance that is already yours.

Finally, we should note once again that this shift from I to C is not merely
abstract or ethereal. It has to do with the prosaic activities, emotions, and
behaviors that occur in our daily interactions with one another. In 1 Cor 12,
that common good will be linked with the mundane task of figuring out how

---

God' in Paul. But it equally certainly is something 'done' by Christ-believers 'themselves' (cf., most strikingly, Phil 2:12–13). The idea of an *opposition* here is a far later thought. Nor, on their side, did the
philosophers conceive of practical thought as something engaged in by a person ' *him-* or *herself* ' in the
later, radically heightened sense of something to be *contrasted* with what may come 'from the outside.' In
fact, both the 'active *nous*' (in Aristotle, compare his *De Anima* 3.5) and *logos* (in Stoicism) were conceived as phenomena that distinctly transcend human individuals." *Paul and the Stoics*, 310 n. 10.

52. I am modifying here the kinds of argument and symbolism that Engberg-Pedersen uses in *Paul
and the Stoics*.

people with different gifts—and varieties of services and activities—might still work for the common good, since it is the same God who activates these gifts in all of us. This common good is also linked with very specific emotions and behaviors. Galatians 5 offers the most prominent list—the "fruit of the Spirit" ("love, joy, peace, patience, kindness, generosity, faithfulness, gentleness, and self-control" in v. 22)—along with the most prominent list of its contrasts—the "works of the flesh" (including, given Paul's thrust in 1 Cor 1–3, "enmities, strife, jealousy, anger, quarrels, dissensions, factions, envy" in vv. 20–21).

Implications

Paul's "Epistemology of the Cross"

This argument has far-reaching implications for what lies at the heart of any theology of the cross that claims to work within a Pauline understanding of the cross. I simply want to make two sets of observations.

The first set of observations is substantive.[53] The *kenotic* wisdom and power of the cross (the crucified Christ)—precisely in its weakness and foolishness— is paradoxically related to an *abundance* of wisdom and power (the wisdom and power of God).[54] As I have reiterated throughout the essay, at the heart of Paul's argument about the cross, which is the warrant in his appeal for reconciliation, is the abundance of its power—"all things are yours." This does not mitigate Christ's suffering and death, or the shame connected with his crucifixion. Rather, it acknowledges the fact that for Paul it is precisely the shame and suffering of the cross that ushers in a new age, with its far more abundant and generous way of "discerning all things." Much more could be said about the link between suffering and joy and suffering and glory in Paul's writing.[55]

My point is simply to recognize that Paul's understanding of the relationship between the cross and power is much richer than accounts that stress either *kenōsis* (at the expense of divine power) or divine power and agency (at

---

53. Within the Lutheran orthodoxy, the Giessen theologians (following Martin Chemnitz), contended that Christ's humiliation entailed not merely a veiling or concealing of his divine attributes (as their Tübingen opponents had argued) but an actual *kenōsis*—that is, a retraction and suspension—of those powers. Chemnitz always made clear, however, that the self-limitation of the incarnate Christ had to do with the specific way in which divine powers were used in and through human nature. His position was intensified in the nineteenth century by Gottfried Thomasius, who stressed the way in which *kenōsis* was a divine self-limitation but did not stress the relationship of that *kenōsis* to the use of divine power within human nature. Since Thomasius, individual advocates of kenotic thought, especially in Lutheran and Anglican theology, have varied greatly on the question of the extent to which the Logos is said to have "emptied" himself. My reading of Paul is closer to Chemnitz's intention than Thomasius's, since it stresses the intrinsic connection between the *kenōsis* of the cross and its abundant power—Christ's *kenōsis* is possible only because he shared equality with God (Phil 2)!—but I need to develop this point more fully in future work. See Martin Chemnitz, *De Duabus Naturis in Christo* (1580) and Gottfried Thomasius, *Christi Person und Werk* (Erlangen: T Bläsing, 1853–1861).

54. See David Bentley Hart's essay in this volume, "The Offering of Names: Metaphysics, Nihilism, and Analogy," for an extended theological meditation on the character of divine power and wisdom.

55. See, e.g., L. Ann Jervis's discussion of suffering in Paul, "Accepting Affliction: Paul's Preaching on Suffering," in *Character and Scripture: Moral Formation, Community, and Biblical Interpretation*, ed. W. P. Brown (Grand Rapids: Eerdmans, 2002).

the expense of Christ's profound humanity).[56] The cross is not simply about a wrathful God who kills, curses, and judges (as some more conservative Lutheran theologies might presuppose); it also has to do with our participation in this God's wisdom and power.[57] Moreover, it is also not simply about a suffering God who is impotent in the face of evil and pain (as some more liberal Lutheran theologies might presuppose); it also has to do with a profound affirmation of God's wisdom and power in the face of all evil and pain.[58]

This leads to my second set of observations, which relates to the kind of cognitive argument, or epistemology, enacted by Paul's meditation on the cross. At the heart of our participation in Christ's life and the new age that the cross ushers in is a baptism into his suffering and death, a baptism in which we die to our false, egoistic self in order to live in newness of his life (Rom 6). That baptism entails a crucifixion with Christ: I am crucified with Christ nevertheless I live, yet not I but Christ lives in me, and the power I live by is through faith in his life (Gal 2:20). The dying and rising take place precisely within the complex circumstances of discerning "what is good and acceptable and perfect" (Rom 12:2) in actual communities (e.g., as the Corinthian letters make clear, in actual conflicts over sex, money, the use and abuse of power, worship, beliefs about the resurrection, etc.). In those circumstances, Christ's wisdom and power are not an escape from hardship but are there—in the midst of affliction—precisely in the enactment of a life that is, to quote one of Paul's lists, afflicted in every way but not crushed, perplexed but not driven to despair, persecuted but not forsaken, struck down but not destroyed. Indeed, Paul himself carries "in the body the death of Jesus" so that "the life of Jesus may be made visible in our bodies" (2 Cor 4:8–12).

Moreover, this dying and rising is not merely a personal affair but a profoundly corporate—we might say *political*—phenomenon, since baptism

---

56. Two of the most astute "theologians of the cross" of the past couple of decades, Jürgen Moltmann and Gerhard Forde (both deeply influenced by the Lutheran-Barthian Hans Iwand), avoid these pitfalls; see Moltmann, *The Crucified God: The Cross of Christ as the Foundation and Criticism of Christian Theology* (New York: Harper & Row, 1974); and Forde, *On Being a Theologian of the Cross: Reflections on Luther's Heidelberg Disputation, 1518* (Grand Rapids: Eerdmans, 1997). Although the former stresses the "kenotic" character of the "crucified God" and the latter stresses the cross's profound judgment of any idolatry, their positions are nuanced. This is especially the case if one takes into account the larger corpus of their work. See, e.g., Moltmann, *The Spirit of Life: A Universal Affirmation*, esp. ch. 6, where he discusses atonement (Minneapolis: Fortress, 1992). Note also Forde's observation about the connection between atonement—which he understands in relation to a theology of the cross—and *theopoiesis*: "Atonement understood as dying and rising in Christ in faith can also approach and be assimilated to the older patristic language of theopoiesis—of being 'divinized' or 'immortalized' through participation in the victorious and eternal divine life of Christ. . . . If one is quite clear that the 'divine life' we are participating in is that of the triune God who has gone through death in his Son, and that our participation means going through death, by faith, then one can indeed speak of and celebrate such theopoiesis. That would be the point and conclusion of Luther's language of the 'happy exchange.' He takes our life, our place, in order to give us his." Gerhard Forde, "The Work of Christ," in *Christian Dogmatics*, vol. 2, ed. Carl Braaten and Robert Jenson (Philadelphia: Fortress, 1984), 97–98.

57. Compare Martin Bieler's discussion of atonement, "The Theological Importance of a Philosophy of Being," in this volume.

58. The most recent articulation of a "kenotic ontology" can be found in Gianni Vattimo, *After Christianity*, trans. Luca D'Isanto (New York: Columbia University Press, 2002), and *The End of Modernity: Nihilism and Hermeneutics in Popular Culture* (Baltimore: Johns Hopkins University Press, 1988). Although Vattimo offers an intriguing account of the relationship between classic Christian theological themes and contemporary philosophical thought, he interprets *kenōsis* in relation to nihilism, which I would contend is not compatible with Paul's more robust understanding of the "new creation" (Gal 6:15).

entails death not only to the ego but also to the distinctions among people that the ego creates in order to distinguish itself from others. As the passage just quoted makes explicit, "death is at work in us" precisely to give "life in you" (v. 12). This dying and rising does not have to do with the perfection of self-sufficiency but with being able to live freely for others (Gal 5). Further, baptism is always a baptism in the life of Christ in which there is no male or female, Jew or Greek, slave or free, and in which the wise and foolish, strong and weak—and even the lawful and unlawful—are taken in. The new identity given in this baptism is Christ's life—a source of life that undoes the need for these distinctions.

The mode of perception enacted by an "epistemology of the cross," then, is fundamentally corporate and relational, having to do with the common good, with being of the same mind and purpose, looking to one another's interests—and not merely from the standpoint of dispassionate self-sufficiency (the Greek and Roman ideal) but from the standpoint of truly sharing in the sufferings and joys of others.[59] Christ's humanity is one that encompasses male and female, Jew and Greek, slave and free; we participate now in a perspective that encompasses even the most fundamental distinctions that divide humanity.

This corporate rationality is profoundly critical of all egoistic or factional interests; it truly enacts a hermeneutics of suspicion.[60] It "says what a thing is" and brings to light the ways people pretend that what is good is evil and what is evil good—whether in their personal or political affairs as families, communities, institutions, nations, or global economies. But it does so not simply by substituting one side of an antinomy for another—the wise for the foolish (or the foolish for the wise), the strong for the weak (or the weak for the strong), males for females (or females for males), Jews for Greeks (or Greeks for Jews), free persons for slaves (or slaves for free persons), even the lawful for the unlawful (or the unlawful for the lawful). Rather, it does so by creating a new mode of perceiving the world and discerning all things.

What is most interesting about Paul's meditation on the cross is that his critique is embedded within—and paradoxically related to—a tremendous generosity of spirit characterized by an indifference toward one's own interests and compassion for others, one that comes not from willful effort but from the profound realization that, indeed, "all [does] belong to you"—life and death, time, space, powers, and all major categories for perceiving and responding to one's experience in the world (1 Cor 3:27–28; Rom 8:38–39). The critique that breaks a cycle of personal or corporate violence does not simply replace one position for another. Rather, the whole paradigm or way of seeing things from the standpoint of egoistic or factional interests is undone. There is now no need to "boast" of human leaders. To draw on Paul's argument in Galatians and Romans, even the demands of the law cannot be met

---

59. See, e.g., "If one member suffers, all suffer together with it; if one member is honored, all rejoice together with it" (1 Cor 12:26; see also Rom 12:15; 15:1; Gal 6:2; on "sufferings," see 2 Cor 1:17; 11:28–39; and on "joys," see 2 Cor 2:3; 7:13).

60. Paul Ricoeur refers to the great "masters of suspicion"—Freud, Marx, Nietzsche, Kierkegaard, Heidegger—throughout his work.

by substituting the law for sin. Only the "abundance of grace" can enable one not to grasp but instead to be emptied for another.

Epistemology, Faith, and Reason

Of course, I am using "epistemology" here in a somewhat different sense from the way it has been used in the philosophical enterprise from René Descartes, through John Locke and Immanuel Kant, and pursued by various nineteenth- and twentieth-century movements. These individuals and movements have identified epistemology with the task of coming to grips with the problem of knowledge—how we know things—and then only afterward with the task of determining what we can say legitimately about other things, such as God, the world, and human beings. For Descartes, one need first be clear about what the nature of knowledge is before one can make definitive claims about anything, because what one might say about God or the world is first and foremost a knowledge claim.[61]

Because of the contrast between this sense of "epistemology" and the sense we have been using to describe Paul's work,[62] I would like to clarify how what we have been tracing in Paul might be relevant to contemporary philosophical discussions about the relationship between faith and reason.[63]

To do this, I would first like to draw on Charles Taylor,[64] who, like many other contemporary philosophers, has criticized the Cartesian understanding of epistemology.[65] What is most relevant for our purposes, however, is that he offers an alternative that may help explain in more contemporary terms what is taking place in Paul's "epistemology"—understood now in the first sense mentioned above as a way of perceiving the world from a specific vantage point.[66] Descartes, of course, was criticized by many for his "foundationalism," his attempt to find an Archimedean point of certainty from which to base all knowledge claims.[67]

---

61. In addition to Mark McIntosh's essay, my argument here has strong resonances with Reinhard Hütter's analysis of the "directedness of reason" in "The Directedness of Reasoning and the Metaphysics of Creation," and Janet Martin Soskice's comparison of Lockean epistemology with ancient wisdom in "Naming God: A Study in Faith and Reason." Note also related themes in essays by Paul J. Griffiths, "How Reasoning Goes Wrong: A Quasi-Augustinian Account of Error and Its Implications"; Ernstpeter Maurer, "The Perplexity and Complexity of Sinful and Redeemed Reason"; and Carver T. Yu, "Covenantal Rationality and the Healing of Reason," all in this volume.

62. For a use of the word "epistemology" similar to the one I have been using here, see Sarah Coakley, "The Resurrection and the 'Spiritual Senses': On Wittgenstein, Epistemology, and the Risen Christ," in *Powers and Submissions* (Oxford: Blackwell, 2002), 130–52.

63. See also the essay by Soskice, which discusses a similar contrast.

64. In this essay, I am drawing on Charles Taylor's essays in *Philosophical Arguments* (Cambridge, MA: Harvard University Press, 1995). See also his *The Sources of the Self: The Making of Modern Identity* (Cambridge, MA: Harvard University Press, 1992).

65. See, from a range of different perspectives, Hilary Putnam, *The Collapse of the Fact/Value Dichotomy and Other Essays* (Cambridge, MA: Harvard University Press, 2002); Alasdair MacIntyre, *After Virtue: A Study in Moral Theory*, 2nd ed. (Notre Dame, IN: University of Notre Dame Press, 1984); Iris Murdoch, *Metaphysics as a Guide to Morals* (New York: Penguin, 1993); and Richard Rorty, *Philosophy and the Mirror of Nature* (Princeton, NJ: Princeton University Press, 1979).

66. Note that the Greek word *epistēmē*, which means "knowledge" or "understanding," is composed of *epi* (upon) and *histanai* (to stand or place).

67. See, e.g., Richard Bernstein's frequently cited *Beyond Objectivism and Relativism: Science, Hermeneutics, and Praxis* (Philadelphia: University of Pennsylvania Press, 1983).

But Taylor is critical not only of Descartes but of his critics—from W. V. Quine to Jacques Derrida—for not going far enough in rethinking the kind of idealism identified with the post-Cartesian epistemological age. Even though their doctrines of knowledge are very different from Descartes', they still, in Taylor's view, define their ontologies—their views of what is—in terms of a prior doctrine of what one can know. They do not get at the heart of what Taylor is especially critical of in the epistemological tradition inherited from Descartes: the notion that knowledge can serve as a correct representation of an independent reality. At the heart of this view of knowledge, Taylor observes, are a "disengaged subject" (who is wholly separate from the objects she analyzes), an "instrumental" understanding of reason (defined simply as a tool for accomplishing things), and an "atomistic" understanding of human persons (perceiving them primarily to be individuals first before they are social entities).

Taylor offers an alternative to this understanding of epistemology, drawing on a range of modern philosophers from Kant and G. W. Hegel to Heidegger, Ludwig Wittgenstein, and Maurice Merleau-Ponty. What these thinkers share, Taylor contends, is a form of argument (which finds its origins in Kant) that starts from transcendental conditions, indispensable conditions for there being experience or awareness in the world in the first place. Heidegger speaks of the *Lichtung* ("clearing") as a condition for what we call experience; it enables us to perceive that anything can appear or come to light at all. Wittgenstein speaks of the *Lebensform* ("form of life"), which places the meanings of words in a context within specific forms of life. And Merleau-Ponty speaks of the way our embodied agency is the locus of action and desire. Each of these thinkers, in different ways, offers an alternative to the Cartesian epistemological picture.

Especially interesting is the way Taylor draws on Johann Gottfried Herder's conception of language, which anticipates many of these insights, in order to develop an alternative to the epistemological view of language I have described, an alternative that nonetheless invokes reflection as essential to language.[68] For Herder, expression in language has a constitutive role; it arises among and is not entirely disconnected from our earlier stances toward objects of fear or desire, things that figure as obstacles, supports, and the like. This means, on the one hand, that language is a pattern of activity by which we express or realize·a certain way of being in the world. But it also means, on the other hand, that this pattern can only be deployed against a backdrop we can never fully dominate.

Thinking is embodied; subjectivity can never be wholly disengaged from the larger background that informs its reflection. Thus, we are reshaped by language but not dominated by it. We are "makers" of language as well as those who are "made" by it. What this means is that language not only makes possible a new awareness of things, it also opens up new ways of responding

---

68. See Johann Gottfried von Herder, *Philosophical Writings* (Cambridge: Cambridge University Press, 2002).

to them, and those new modes of expression enable us, in turn, to have new feelings that are perhaps even more powerful and refined, and certainly more self-aware. As we express our feelings, we give them a reflective dimension that transforms them. Through language, for example, we can feel not only anger but also indignation, not only love but admiration. From this standpoint, language has more than strictly instrumental functions; indeed, it is not simply prose in the narrow sense, that is, discourse that says something about things, but it can include, in Ernst Cassirer's words, the whole range of "symbolic forms"—from prose to poetry, music, art, and dance.[69] Further, if language is seen primarily as an activity, then it is important to locate that activity within the context of not simply the individual (as atomistic conceptions of the self might), but in conversation, and more broadly, the life of the speech community.

This alternative to Enlightenment accounts of epistemology is not irrelevant, I should note, to Paul's use of apocalyptic and Stoic modes of argument to speak about the "wisdom of the cross" (instead of an "instrumental understanding of reason"). Paul's argument is for a new creation and new humanity in Christ in lieu of hierarchy or factionalism (instead of "atomistic subjectivity"), and reflexively makes its case from the standpoint of a corporate rationality shared in Christ (instead of a "disengaged subjectivity" abstracted from its object of cognition).

Analogous to Taylor's argument for the reflexive character of embodied thinking is Pierre Hadot's thesis about ancient philosophical schools—that they were first and foremost theoretical activities embodied in a way of life.[70] If Taylor contrasted a reflexive understanding of language with Cartesian epistemology, then Hadot contrasts a sapiential understanding of the philosophical task with scholastic approaches, whether medieval or modern, which tend to emphasize the theoretical, abstract, and conceptual side of philosophy at the expense of the existential. Hadot makes his argument primarily in relation to the kind of ancient Greek philosophical schools with which Paul might have been familiar (those of Socrates, Pyrrho, Epicurus, the Stoics, the Cynics, and the Skeptics). He speaks as well of resonances with wisdom traditions from India and China and offers—in view of his reading of ancient philosophy—a different reading of Michel de Montaigne and even of Descartes and Kant, thinkers usually identified with the epistemological tradition. He also mentions other modern thinkers whose approaches are compatible (Rousseau, Shaftsbury, Schopenhauer, Emerson, Thoreau, Kierkegaard, Marx, Nietzsche, William James, Bergson, Wittgenstein, Merleau-Ponty, and still others).

Hadot argues for a reading of ancient philosophy that enables us to conceive of philosophical reflection not only as a concrete, practical activity but also as a transformation of our way of inhabiting and perceiving the world. What philosophy from such a standpoint enacts is a complex interrelation of

---

69. Ernst Cassirer, *The Philosophy of Symbolic Forms* (New Haven, CT: Yale University Press, 1953).
70. Pierre Hadot, *What Is Ancient Philosophy?* trans. Michael Chase (Cambridge, MA: Harvard University Press, 2002).

critical reflection on one's existential attitudes, on the one hand, and the cultivation of a certain way of living and seeing the world, which constitutes for the philosopher a live existential option, on the other. Moreover, this choice is never made in isolation but is set against the background of a community, a philosophical "school" which, in turn, corresponds to the choice of a way of life that entails a desire to be and live in a certain way—indeed, what one could call a conversion of one's being.[71]

Theoretical philosophical discourse has its locus in such an existential option and leads reflexively back to it in the way—via its logical and persuasive force—it incites disciples to live in genuine conformity with their initial choices. This is why spiritual exercises were such an important part of the ancient philosophers' way of life. Especially important were exercises and practices linked with "indifference," the shift from the "egoistic, partial, and limited viewpoint of the individual" to a state of "quiet and peace." This state stands prior to the affirmation of our individual identity against the world and against other people. It stands prior to the egotism and egocentricity that "separate us from the universe, and which sweep us inexorably into the worried pursuit of pleasure and the perpetual fear of pain."[72]

Beyond these arguments proposed by Taylor and Hadot, there are other reasons for redefining what we mean by "epistemology." Even the wisdom tradition, which is appealed to as the precedent for all later natural, fundamental, and philosophical theologies, is not primarily a defense of the intelligibility of religious claims but rather the wooing of people away from the folly of corrupt practices and toward the "fear of the Lord" and the righteousness, justice, and equity that accompany it. Indeed, the speech attributed to Paul at the Areopagus (Acts 17)—in which he draws on Greek poets—deals with the call for a shift away from idolatry. And when the wisdom tradition of the Hebrew Scriptures draws on Greek philosophy, it does so precisely to describe what the person is like who "lives with wisdom"—how this wisdom makes such persons "friends of God, and prophets" (Wis 7:27–28). The attributes of wisdom that it appropriates from Greek thought have to do not with scholastic distinctions or clarity about what one can truly know beyond doubt, but with ways this wisdom "pervades and penetrates all things" and "while remaining in herself . . . renews all things" (Wis 7:24, 27).[73]

Moreover, it is not only the ancients who are interested in these matters. Contemporary psychologists and philosophers, for example, have been paying increasing attention to the intelligibility of emotions and their important connection with rational thought in the empirical structure of the brain. An important thread in these discussions is the critique of the mind/body dualism of the epistemological tradition identified with Descartes and the search

---

71. Note that in *Fides et Ratio*, trust and friendship play an important role in the formation of wisdom, since all human inquiry takes place within the context of some human community, however fragmented.

72. Hadot, *What Is Ancient Philosophy?* 279. Compare Reinhard Hütter's discussion in this volume of *Gelassenheit* and the way it embodies redeemed reason.

73. In Wis 7:22–23, wisdom is described as a spirit that is "intelligent, holy, unique, manifold, subtle, mobile, clear, unpolluted, distinct, invulnerable, loving the good, keen, irresistible, beneficent, humane, steadfast, sure, free from anxiety, all-powerful, overseeing all, and penetrating through all spirits that are intelligent, pure, and altogether subtle."

for a more embodied understanding of cognition (whether that embodiment is in nature or in culture).[74]

Sociologists, for their part, have turned our attention to the fact that the massive secularization that they and the theologians predicted would occur at the turn of the twenty-first century has not occurred.[75] The social changes wrought by global capitalism and the proliferation of mass media systems entail the weakening of traditional, localized beliefs and customs, but the response to this weakening is not always a secularized one. Indeed, the past few decades have seen the rise of movements within major religions (Christianity, Islam, Judaism, and Hinduism) that seek to retrieve traditional religious orthodoxies and forms of practice. Christianity is increasingly identified as a "global Christianity," and not merely as a European or North American phenomenon.[76]

It is interesting in this regard that John Paul II locates his argument in *Fides et Ratio* not in the program of an academic enterprise, but in the Second Vatican Council's call for "evangelization" and the concrete tasks of proclaiming the gospel and catechesis. If, he argues, Jesus, the paschal mystery, heals divisions and creates unity in "new and unsurpassed ways," then we are "no longer strangers and sojourners, but . . . saints and members of . . . God" (Eph 2:19). Moreover, if the universality of Christianity's claims are to be maintained, then those claims need to be linked with all of life, including the complex questions of how we as individuals and societies are to appropriate the technological power to which we have access. And that entails entering into public dialogue over ethical questions with secularists and those of other faiths. For both tasks, the pope seeks to recover a disciplined form of sapiential reflection that draws not only on the philosophical heritage that has already influenced Christianity (e.g., Plato and Aristotle) but on such thinkers as Confucius and Lao-Tze, Tirthankara and Buddha, and even Homer, Euripides, and Sophocles. Of course, Paul's conception of wisdom is defined by the cross, but precisely as the crucified humanity of Christ, this wisdom is not an escape from human experience and the commonsense judgments we make as we discern what is best for ourselves, the people around us, and the communities we participate in. This cruciform wisdom—wisdom shaped by the cross—enables us to discern things in their full creaturely depths. Further, the perspective this wisdom gives is not sectarian, even though its full grasp of the unity of all things in Christ can only be understood eschatologically.[77] Later

---

74. See, among others, Martha Nussbaum, *Upheavals of Thought: The Intelligence of Emotions* (Cambridge: Cambridge University Press, 2001). See also Owen Flanagan, *The Problem of the Soul: Two Visions of Mind and How to Reconcile Them* (New York: Basic Books, 2003).

75. Note that sociologists are rethinking the "secularization" hypothesis. See Peter Berger, ed., *The Desecularization of the World: Resurgent Religion and World Politics* (Grand Rapids: Eerdmans, 1999). Contrast this with his earlier works, *The Noise of Solemn Assemblies: Christian Commitment and the Religious Establishment in America* (Garden City, NY: Doubleday, 1961), and *The Sacred Canopy* (Garden City, NY: Doubleday, 1969).

76. Philip Jenkins, *The Next Christendom: The Coming of Global Christianity* (New York: Oxford University Press, 2002). We have also seen the rise of interest in spirituality, whether that be the appropriation of classical spiritualities or the creation of new forms of spiritual expression. See Wade Clark Roof, *Spiritual Marketplace: Baby Boomers and the Remaking of American Religion* (Princeton, NJ: Princeton University Press, 1999).

77. See, again, McIntosh's essay.

christological traditions would speak of the "enhypostatic union" and how human nature reaches its full completion in Christ's humanity, an important conceptual link for understanding how our own creatureliness—precisely in its creatureliness—participates in Christ's identity. Other essays in this volume discuss in more detail the relationship between Christology and a doctrine or "metaphysics" of creation.[78] My purpose here has simply been to elucidate the distinct epistemology of the cross and the perspective it offers for interpreting and responding to life. Far from being an affront to human reason, this epistemology is rooted in a corporate rationality whose source is Christ's humanity and the new age his death and resurrection usher in. This epistemology offers a radical critique of all empirical or prudential reason, but it does so from the standpoint of the fecundity of God's own wisdom and power. Its critique of egoistic and factional pretensions is rooted in an appeal to an abundance that Paul's readers share because of the cross—an appeal that "all things are yours" because you "belong" to Christ. Further, this appeal is not merely a figment of the human imagination; its perception is rooted in the character of reality understood eschatologically. At the heart of Christ's *kenōsis* is not only judgment and suffering—although it is also profoundly that—but a judgment and suffering that is truly meaningful and potent (that is, it has the capacity to transform and renew things) because it is rooted in God's very depths. But if Paul helps us rethink what lies at the heart of the cross, then he also offers some perspective on the relationship between faith and reason. At issue in Paul's cognitive appeal for reconciliation is not the defense of the intelligibility of the Christian faith, but a call for a shift in perspective.[79] At issue perhaps for theologians and philosophers interested in Christianity is not the "crisis of cognitive claims" (the defense of traditional beliefs in the face of a modern worldview), but the discernment of powers (i.e., how wisdom and power are to be used).[80] Indeed, one could argue that the major conflicts in this century will be conflicts among competing spiritual, religious, and moral visions of the world—whether international or national, or even within the church. At issue will not be yet another defense of the cognitive intelligibility of one's claims—or defense of one's interests—but will be a discernment of the truth within and beyond competing interests. For that task, Christian theologians and philosophers bring their claims about the wisdom of the cross. As they do so, the truth and justice of their contribution rests not only on the substance of its eschatological hope but on whether they are faithful to its cognitive rationality—and the *kenotic abundance* it enacts.

---

78. See esp. the essays in this volume by Martin Bieler, Reinhard Hütter, and Janet Martin Soskice, which discuss a "metaphysics of creation." See also the essay by Colin Gunton and Robert W. Jenson on the Logos and reason, "The *Logos Ensarkos* and Reason."

79. Much more needs to be developed with regard to the character of this "corporate rationality." Especially relevant are attempts at "dialogical philosophy" in the work of Martin Buber, Franz Rosenzweig, and Mikhail Bakhtin, among others. See, e.g., Janet Martin Soskice, "Friendship: Cicero, Buber, and Bakhtin on the Self as More than One," in *Intersubjectivité et theologie philosophique*, ed. Marco M. Olivetti (Padova: CEDAM, 2001). See also, in addition to the work of Charles Taylor discussed above, Paul Ricoeur's *Oneself as Another*, trans. Kathleen Blamey (Chicago: University of Chicago Press, 1994).

80. I am modifying here something I heard David Tracy say in a public lecture at the University of Chicago. He was drawing on Gustavo Gutierrez's reference to a shift from a focus on "cognitive claims" to a focus on the use of "power." I am using "powers" here to refer to the kind of "powers" Paul discusses in Rom 8:38–39; in his list he includes not only "angels" and "rulers" (i.e., human rulers) but also "powers" (which could refer to either human or supernatural powers). Cf. 1 Cor 15:24; Gal 4:8–11; Col 2:15. Note that Tracy refers to the "crisis of cognitive claims" in *Blessed Rage for Order* (New York: Seabury, 1975).

CHAPTER FIVE

Faith, Reason, and the Mind of Christ

— MARK MCINTOSH —

Those who are unspiritual [*psychikos*] do not receive the gifts of God's Spirit, for they are foolishness to them, and they are unable to understand them because they are spiritually discerned [*pneumatikōs anakrinetai*]. Those who are spiritual discern [*anakrinei*] all things, and they are themselves subject to no one else's scrutiny [*anakrinetai*].
"For who has known the mind of the Lord
    so as to instruct him?"
But we have the mind of Christ.

(1 Cor 2:14–16)

Faith and reason are both patterns of human rationality. They are both ways in which human beings exercise their understanding and judgment about whatever is knowable in itself—even when that is so supremely true as to be beyond the grasp of conceptual thought. Is there a way of understanding the differences between faith and reason that does not wash out the basic facts of their mutual relationship—a way, therefore, that can make the nature of each perspicuous to the other? This essay explores a milieu in which faith and reason might be considered afresh. It examines some early Christian diagnoses of human perception and the transformation of human rationality that was prescribed.

The general category I am speaking of here is often called discernment, and I am proposing that we consider this not only in its negative aspect—a capacity to discriminate between healthy and unhealthy dispositions—but also in its more positive aspect as a capacity to appreciate and contemplate the real. Indeed, I will be seeking to develop the following proposal: that a chief debility of the human mind is its painful tendency to fall into fearful and envious patterns of thought, and that it finds healing in the contemplation of that

119

endless resource of self-sharing life that is the Trinitarian life of God.[1] We can in fact find a milieu in which faith and reason *are* considered for the most part in these terms of the mind's healing from sin and its partaking, to quote Paul, in "the mind of Christ" (1 Cor 2:16).

My goal will be to explore this frame of thought as it unfolds in Paul, develops among the hermits and elders of the Egyptian and Palestinian deserts (third century and following), and comes to more analytic expression in the two greatest theorists of that desert spirituality: Evagrius Ponticus (346–399) and Diadochus of Photike (mid-400s). These writers, taken together, suggest what it might mean to share in the mind of Christ, to heal and awaken human rationality from grasping and jealous habits of mind by flooding the whole person with the light of the limitless divine abundance that is in fact the very ground of the mind's activity. Persons whose entire existence has become attuned to this abundance no longer understand anything "according to the flesh," as Paul puts it; that is, they no longer understand reality in terms of a fundamental lack compelling all to anxious self-seeking, but are instead awake to the endless mercy of God's giving life.

Just by way of setting the scene, consider the following observation from Evagrius: "Spiritual fat is the obtuseness with which evil cloaks the intelligence."[2] Here we notice immediately the indissoluble link that this tradition sees between knowledge and spirituality, between vision and the moral life. Behind this conviction, I believe, lies the thought that reality is in fact inaccessible to minds that have fallen into certain debilitating conditions. In our own time, we would likely grant the analogous claim, for example, that prejudice or bias can blind one to the true merits of another person. Racism is an obvious example. To draw an initial implication, this might mean that faith would have an ascetical function, setting the reason free from ugly yet hypnotically self-gratifying illusions about others.

From roughly two centuries after Evagrius, we can see the later development of this perspective in the early Byzantine Maximus the Confessor (580–662). He interprets our passage from 1 Cor 2:16 on the "mind of Christ" by declaring a mystical participation in Christ to be the basis for discerning reality:

> The mind of Christ which the saints receive according to the saying, "We have the mind of Christ," comes along not by any loss of our mental power, nor as a supplementary mind to ours, nor as essentially and personally passing over into our mind, but rather as illuminating the power of our mind with its own quality and bringing the same energy

---

1. Complementary analyses of the mind's self-defeating tendencies are found in the essays of Ernstpeter Maurer and Carver T. Yu in this collection: Maurer, "The Perplexity and Complexity of Sinful and Redeemed Reason"; Yu, "Covenantal Rationality and the Healing of Reason." Further on the Trinitarian framework for thinking about faith and reason, see the large scene painted for us in the essay of Colin Gunton and Robert W. Jenson, also in this volume: Gunton and Jenson, "The *Logos Ensarkos* and Reason."

2. Evagrius Pontikus, *The Centuries*, IV, 36. Quoted in Olivier Clément, *The Roots of Christian Mysticism* (New York: New City Press, 1995), 131.

to it. For to have the mind of Christ is, in my opinion, to think in his way and of him in all situations.[3]

This learning to think as Christ thinks is obviously a central theme I will be exploring carefully. But for the moment simply note again the fact that this tradition clearly sees the transformed disposition of the knower as crucial to the functioning of reason. Moreover, Maximus implies that such a transformation is not a replacement of the human mind with something else; it is an illuminating and energizing of the human mind in all its human rationality, an exercising of it according to a certain "way" (*tropos*) of thinking that makes the discernment of truth possible. So along with the ascetical function of faith, I want to highlight also this mystical activity of faith—a disposing of the mind to understand all things by sharing in the mind of Christ, sharing in that divine fullness from which all things come.

I hasten to add that while one might conceivably make a genealogical claim about the historical links in the development of this tradition of thought, I shall not attempt to do so. My concern is merely to explore this unfolding teaching about discernment as a way of thinking about what it means to think. So I examine first what our authors have to say about the ascetical aspects of discernment, then consider their awareness of a painful transition to a new pattern of mind, and finally turn to the mystical aspects of discernment as a form of intelligence grounded in the abundance of divine life.

Discernment of False-Mindedness

Clearing Away Incorrect Diagnostic Schemes

The texts we are considering call for an important preliminary: In order to discriminate in a healthy way between what is true and what is false, or to understand what is good or right, one has first to become suspicious about one's own critical instincts. The very faculty of judgment one brings to bear on a given situation may itself have become mesmerized by an incorrect diagnostic scheme.

The desert fathers were particularly acute observers of this problem. They placard before us the tendency to slide into comfortably measurable criteria of judgment and the numbing ineptitude that results, as in the following story:

> Abba Lot went to see Abba Joseph and said to him, "Abba, as far as I can I say my little office, I fast a little, I pray and meditate, I live in peace and as far as I can I purify my thoughts. What else can I do?" Then the old man stood up and stretched his hands toward heaven. His fingers became like ten lamps of fire and he said to him, "If you will, you can become all flame."[4]

---

3. Maximus the Confessor, *Chapters on Knowledge*, II, 83 in *Maximus Confessor: Selected Writings*, trans. George C. Berthold (New York: Paulist Press, 1985), 165.

4. Joseph of Panephysis 7, in *The Sayings of the Desert Fathers: The Alphabetical Collection*, rev. ed., trans. Benedicta Ward (Kalamazoo, MI: Cistercian Studies, 1984), 103. This is a translation of the Greek Alphabetical Series of the *Apophthegmata Patrum*, PG, lxv. 72–440.

In this little encounter we can see the tidy conventional appraisal of a spiritual adept exposed as a self-satisfying and yet ultimately frustrating norm. Abba Lot's seemingly moderate, prudent, and wise scheme for discerning his progress has left him feeling curiously restless, never quite accomplishing as much as he feels he perhaps ought to, or else covertly pleased with himself and yet oddly in need of another's approbation. Abba Joseph will surely have an improving refinement to make to the scheme, an exquisitely appropriate modification that will set Abba Lot up perfectly. But Abba Joseph in fact will have nothing to do with Abba Lot's criteria for discernment. Instead, his radical availability to the fire of the Spirit opens before us the unfathomable promise of divine grace that cannot even be conceived within the categories of the conventional scheme of spiritual improvement.

In a similar way, Paul confronts Corinthians who are busy judging, evaluating, discerning, and comparing themselves according to a variety of apparently satisfying criterial schemes. There is the measure of one's baptismal lineage ("Each of you says, 'I belong to Paul,' or 'I belong to Apollos,' or 'I belong to Cephas'" [1 Cor 1:12]). There is the measure of class status and cultural sophistication ("Consider your own call, brothers and sisters: not many of you were wise by human standards, not many were powerful, not many were of noble birth" [1 Cor 1:26]). There is the (probably) proto-gnostic measure of spiritual elitism (the *psychikos/pneumatikos* distinction Paul subverts in 1 Cor 2:14).[5] But in Paul's view, all these discernment schemes are only binding the Corinthians ever more inexorably within a constricted measure of what is truly important. They cannot "receive the gifts of God's Spirit, for they are foolishness to them"; indeed, the gifts of divine outpouring are utterly unapparent and ungraspable within such categories (1 Cor 2:14).

It would be easy enough to blame such cognitive distortion on the fallenness of reason per se, or the sheer incapacity of the unaided human mind to appreciate the divine activity in its midst.[6] But I want to suggest that Paul is not so much attacking human criteria of discernment as pointing out how inadequate are the ones in use currently in Corinth. Paul is proposing another criterion that requires just as much deployment of human rationality, intelligence, and skill to apply it and use it as a noetic norm. As we know, the criterion Paul holds up is God's rescuing action in Christ, the message or word of the cross. Paul, however, is not holding it up as a pristine norm of faith as against all merely rational human norms; he is holding up the cross as a criterion provided by the loving action of God as compared with criteria provided by the envious rivalry of factions. Indeed, J. Louis Martyn has even made a strong case that one of the factions Paul is most concerned to undo is precisely the spiritual elite and culturally sophisticated group who feel that

---

5. The literature on the potential identities of the various factional parties in the Corinthian congregation is quite extensive. For a good introduction and survey to the range of critical views, see the massive commentary by Anthony C. Thiselton, *The First Epistle to the Corinthians: A Commentary on the Greek Text* (Grand Rapids: Eerdmans, 2000). And for a highly nuanced consideration of the letter's noetic import, see the essay of Lois Malcolm, "The Wisdom of the Cross," in the present volume.

6. Cf. Richard B. Gaffin, Jr., "Some Epistemological Reflections on 1 Cor 2:6–16," *Westminster Theological Journal* 57 (1995): 103–24. Though tending in this direction, Gaffin qualifies his attack on reason at 117ff.

they have a far more spiritual, more faith-based, and divinely inspired criterion of discernment than do the ordinary members of the church in Corinth.[7]
Against such a false criterion of discernment, Paul (like Abba Joseph with his
fiery witness to the power of God) points to a divine act of generous love and
away from the more conventional religious tests of spiritual progress.

The fifth-century bishop Diadochus of Photike picks out exactly this kind
of distinction between divine generosity and factional envy. The former provides the right mind for proper discernment, he says, because when the
mind focuses on God's generosity "it no longer needs the praise of men";
furthermore, focusing on the deeds and words of God "keeps the mind free
from fantasy [aphantaston], transfusing it completely with the love of
God."[8] By contrast, principles and conversation grounded in the "wisdom
of this world always provokes self-esteem; because it is incapable of granting us the experience of spiritual perception, it inspires its adepts with a
longing for praise, being nothing but the fabrication of conceited men."[9]
Here, suggests Diadochus, is an authentic diagnostic question: Is your life
truly attentive to what God is doing, or is it unconsciously driven by concern with your own status and how others perceive you? It is intriguing and
important that Diadochus links this latter compulsion for worldly regard
with a tendency toward fantasy, an ego-gratifying fabulation to cocoon the
self or social group in an illusory world more reassuring than real. This is
the kind of cognitive blindness that true discernment heals and false discernment breeds and legitimates.

Specifying the Problem in Corinth

Soon we shall want to analyze the noetic dangers that true discernment
unmasks. But to make sure I do not lead us down the wrong path about all
this, it will be useful to verify my characterization of Paul's targets in Corinth.
For a good part of the twentieth century, the dominant view among New
Testament scholars pointed to a putative theological argument between Paul
and a range of misguided religious tendencies—usually Jewish, or
Hellenizing, or gnostic, and sometimes all three at once. In these interpretations the tendency was then to see Paul as arming himself with a defiant assertion of divine revelation against all human rationality, or with a kind of
existentialist faith against all secular reason.

More recently, scholars have engaged in a good deal of head scratching and
embarrassing pauses whenever someone asks them for detailed proof of the

---

7. Martyn shows how Paul adopts the *psychikos/pneumatikos* distinction of the spiritual elites in
Corinth precisely in order to undo it from within and transfer its cognitive discernment function from criteria of human spiritual progress and ascent to the criterion of God's descent in Christ, especially in the
crucifixion. J. Louis Martyn, "Epistemology at the Turn of the Ages," in *Theological Issues in the Letters
of Paul* (Edinburgh: T&T Clark, 1997); see esp. 98ff.

8. Diadochus of Photiki, *On Spiritual Knowledge and Discrimination*, §11 in *The Philokalia*, vol.
1, trans. G. E. H. Palmer, Philip Sherrard, Kallistos Ware (London: Faber & Faber, 1983), 255. The best
introduction is by Édouard des Places, SJ, in the introduction he gives to his edition: Diadoque de Photicé,
Oeuvres Spirituelles, Sources Chrétiennes 5 (Paris: Editions du Cerf, 1955).

9. Diadochus, *On Spiritual Knowledge and Discrimination*, 255.

actual existence of one or another of these religious tendencies in the church at Corinth. They have also begun to notice that Paul's argument here, as contrasted with that in the Letter to the Galatians, does not really focus on particular, erroneous theological views but rather seems more concerned with the mutual antagonism and painful disunity of the local church. Thus, 1 Cor 1:10 is seen as the real theme of the letter: "Now I appeal to you, brothers and sisters, by the name of our Lord Jesus Christ, that all of you be in agreement and that there be no divisions among you, but that you be united in the same mind and the same purpose." Correlate with this is the emphasis throughout the letter on love and edification for the sake of the body, climaxing with the great praise of love as the ultimate basis of understanding and wisdom in 1 Cor 13.

So what about Paul's rejection of human wisdom and his taunting questions: "Where is the one who is wise? Where is the scribe? Where is the debater of this age? Has not God made foolish the wisdom of the world?" (1 Cor 1:20)? Part of the emerging consensus, says Robin Scroggs, is that in such passages (even including the yet more searing indictment of human noetic malfeasance in Rom 1:18ff.) "the issue is not noetic fallibility or weakness but human rebellion against the creator God. . . . What humankind has denied is the basic reality of God. . . . The rebellion against the true God has created a false world within which false gods play their role as securing and validating the very falsity itself."[10] The result of this alienation from God is that the validating criteria of wisdom are given not by the beneficent Creator but by needy, compulsive idols that require full adherence in order to grant validation of one's status, worth, and position. A number of scholars now identify the driving force in all this as the social and cultural divisiveness that simultaneously validates and enslaves the various social strata of the church.[11]

What Paul is trying to pry the Corinthians loose from, then, is the structure of their relations with one another. The letter reveals a climate "of intense rivalry involving a cross-section of people from different socio-economic and cultural backgrounds."[12] How do these cultural divisions figure into Paul's concern about noetic functioning? Recall Diadochus on the suspicious links between worldly "wisdom" or talk, the persistent need felt by such mental dispositions for the applause of others, and the tendency of such persons to fall into fantasizing. A whole range of epistemological vices begins to spring up in such a climate. Conceit, bragging, boasting, envious comparisons, arrogant attachment to one's own positions, prudish disdain for the new ideas of others all "create conditions in the community that make difficult the pursuit

---

10. Robin Scroggs, "New Being: Renewed Mind: New Perception," in *The Texts and the Times: New Testament Essays for Today* (Minneapolis: Fortress, 1993), 177.

11. See Paul W. Gooch, *Partial Knowledge: Philosophical Studies in Paul* (Notre Dame, IN: University of Notre Dame Press, 1987); Dale B. Martin, *The Corinthian Body* (New Haven, CT: Yale University Press, 1995); Raymond Pickett, *The Cross in Corinth: The Social Significance of the Death of Jesus* (Sheffield: Sheffield Academic Press, 1997); Stephen M. Pogoloff, *Logos and Sophia: The Rhetorical Situation of 1 Corinthians* (Atlanta: Scholars Press, 1992); Stanley K. Stowers, "Paul on the Use and Abuse of Reason," in *Greeks, Romans, and Christians: Essays in Honor of Abraham J. Malherbe*, ed. David L. Balch et al. (Minneapolis: Fortress, 1990).

12. Pickett, *Cross in Corinth*, 37.

of knowledge and the exercise of practical reason."[13] In such an atmosphere of noetic self-importance and rivalry, it is not surprising to hear Paul say, "God chose what is foolish in the world to shame the wise . . . so that no one might boast in the presence of God" (1 Cor 1:27–28).

If one then also factors in the particular high-culture avoidance of anything that might be sniffed at as servile, slavish, or weak, and the corresponding attachment to power and beauty, rhetoric and sophistry, as markers of one's social status, cleverness, and supposed refinement (all things eagerly pursued in the social-climbing atmosphere of Corinth), it becomes urgent for Paul to point out that his teaching absolutely refuses any contest in this arena:[14]

> When I came to you, brothers and sisters, I did not come proclaiming the mystery of God to you in lofty words or wisdom. For I decided to know nothing among you except Jesus Christ, and him crucified. And I came to you in weakness and in fear and in much trembling. My speech and my proclamation were not with plausible words of wisdom, but with a demonstration of the Spirit and of power, so that your faith might rest not on human wisdom but on the power of God. (1 Cor 2:1–5)

As Paul admits later (1 Cor 4:6ff.), he has spoken about himself in passages like this as though the real issue were a rivalrous contest about which of the various apostles to Corinth (Paul, Apollos, Cephas) is the greatest. In fact, he has been speaking this way as a mirror to the whole church, as a lesson against the rivalry and self-important envy that afflicts them: ". . . so that none of you will be puffed up in favor of one against another. For who sees anything different in you? What do you have that you did not receive? And if you received it, why do you boast as if it were not a gift?" (1 Cor 4:6–7). So I want to suggest, following this reading of the conflict in Corinth, that the problem is not with human reason per se as opposed to faith; rather, the problem is the Corinthians' prideful self-deception, as Paul Gooch describes: "They exaggerate their true status and abilities, glorying in themselves. And that is why the concept of boasting is central to the understanding of Paul's critique."[15]

If we are correct in identifying the problem this way, then two important points follow. The first regards the faith and reason question as we have just seen. To quote Gooch again, "Worldly wisdom, though opposed to the true knowledge of God, is opposed not as philosophy against faith but as human conceit that shuts itself up against truth. Paul's critique of such wisdom requires the opposite of an irrationally extreme fideism; it asks for right reasoning and for the cognitive modesty appropriate to all human intellectual activity."[16] The second point concerns the precise pathology of this temptation

---

13. Stowers, "Paul on the Use and Abuse of Reason," 261.
14. Pogoloff, *Rhetorical Situation*, see esp. ch. 5, "Rhetoric and Status."
15. Gooch, *Partial Knowledge*, 26. As Gooch goes on to say rather nicely, such boasters have in Paul's view "succumbed to the primal temptation to become as God without really being able to bring it off."
16. Ibid., 42.

toward noetic error (perhaps we could even call it the "logic" of distorted reason) and the possibility of discerning what is really at work there. To this we now turn.

Envy's Aversion to Truth

What we want to see now is how the word of the cross might be the authentic measure of discernment, how it might permit a liberating recognition of the compulsive idols that drive one away from truth and deeper into fearful and arrogant fantasies. In his Second Letter to the Corinthians, Paul continues his critique of the church's ceaseless sizing-up of one another: "We do not dare to classify [*ankrinai*] or compare [*synkrinai*] ourselves with some of those who commend themselves. But when they measure [*metrountes*] themselves by one another and compare [*synkrinontes*] themselves with one another, they do not show good sense" (2 Cor 10:12). Here Paul uses the same terminological field we saw him employ in 1 Cor 2:14 to talk about proper spiritual discernment. And, as I have just argued, it is exactly Paul's point that this measuring and comparing of one another is a dangerously false principle of discernment. In Paul's view, envious rivalry in cultural and spiritual advancement only renders the parties to the scheme blind and without understanding, stuck in that conflictual and rapacious mentality that he calls thinking according to the flesh: "As long as there is jealousy and quarreling among you, are you not of the flesh, and behaving according to human inclinations?" (1 Cor 3:3).

The desert fathers provide a number of probing analyses of this mentality. What they uncover there is a toxic seepage between envy, anger, fearfulness about the frustration or loss of one's own desires, and a grimly deepening need to best others in order to restore one's own self-esteem. In one classic statement reported by Evagrius, an abba remarks, "I have this reason for putting aside pleasure—that I might cut off the pretext for growing angry. For I know that anger constantly fights for pleasures and clouds the mind with passion that drives away contemplative knowledge."[17] In intensely compact form, this saying captures the abyss we are trying to fathom: First, there is the anxiously possessive pursuit of pleasure, the power to gratify one's drives and thus manifest one's status; second, there is the fear and anger that floods in whenever the success of others dims our splendor; and throughout all this the mind is increasingly clouded and rendered insensible to truth.[18]

Evagrius developed a diagnosis of minds debilitated by fearful envy (an analysis later adapted by John Cassian and Gregory the Great). Out of many years of practice among the desert hermit colonies and conversations with them, Evagrius formulated perhaps his most characteristic insight: that one could, with time, begin to recognize the various illusions that the mind

---

17. Quoted by Evagrius Pontikus in *The Praktikos*, §99, in *The Praktikos* and *Chapters on Prayer*, trans. John Eudes Bamberger. Cistercian Studies Series 4 (Kalamazoo, MI: Cistercian Publications, 1981), 41.
18. Further on the problems of anger, judgment, and wisdom, see the very fine study of Graham Gould, *The Desert Fathers on Monastic Community* (Oxford: Clarendon, 1993).

ceaselessly throws up around us.[19] Evagrius's interest was not simply in exposing the prevaricating self but in freeing it to appreciate the infinitely greater joy of real life. In the more juridical atmosphere of the West, what came to be called the "seven deadly sins," were in Evagrius's formulation merely eight kinds of powerful *logismoi*—thoughts, picturings, considerings: "It is not in our power to determine whether we are disturbed by these thoughts, but it is up to us to decide if they are to linger within us or not and whether or not they are to stir up our passions."[20] Evagrius's concern is not so much that we might tend to overeat or have sex too much or be terribly listless, but rather that each of these is a symptom of a deep and repetitive mental fidget that, unless overcome, is going to distort and cloud the mind.

Each of these fantasies is going to play on a particular aspect of the personality so that one is unable to get beyond the clamor of the will at all; everything and everyone else comes to be apprehended now, if at all, only in terms of the most atavistic needs and fears. So the thought of gluttony afflicts the monk with fears that he might undergo a long illness and a lack of caring physicians ("these things are depicted vividly before his eyes"[21]), or the *logismos*, the mental itch, of sadness drives one to a terrible homesickness, or tantalizes with memories of lost joys:

> Now when these thoughts find that the soul offers no resistance but rather follows after them and pours itself out in pleasures that are still only mental in nature, they then seize her and drench her in sadness, with the result that these ideas she was just indulging no longer remain. . . . So the miserable soul is now shriveled up in her humiliation to the degree that she poured herself out upon these thoughts of hers.[22]

Evagrius consistently spies out this subtle power of these obsessive thoughts, whether gratifying or catastrophic, to disable and stunt the mind. It is significant that in every case there is a fundamental anxiety about scarcity, a fear of somehow not getting what one is convinced one must have. Just as "sadness tends to come up at times because of the deprivations of one's desires," so too vainglory stirs up in its apprentices a desperate craving "to make their struggles known publicly, to hunt after the praise of men."[23] What makes these observations so telling is that they are not simply the automatic disdain of a stoic for any desire whatsoever. Rather, they reflect a sense that there is an enormous abundance that is real and available, yet hidden from minds in the grip of this mentality of deprivation.[24]

---

19. Very helpful surveys of Evagrius's life and thought may be found in Andrew Louth, *The Origins of the Christian Mystical Tradition* (Oxford: Oxford University Press, 1981), 100–113; and also in Bernard McGinn, *The Foundations of Mysticism*, vol. 1 of *The Presence of God: A History of Western Christian Mysticism* (New York: Crossroad, 1991), 144–57.
20. Evagrius, *Praktikos* §6, p. 17.
21. Ibid., §7, p. 17.
22. Ibid., §10, pp. 17–18.
23. Ibid., §§12, 13, pp. 18–19.
24. Perhaps the most penetrating and systematic analyses of noetic vice are offered by Augustine and Aquinas, whose views are insightfully examined in Paul J. Griffiths, "How Reasoning Goes Wrong: A Quasi-Augustinian Account of Error and Its Implications"; and Reinhard Hütter, "The Directedness of Reasoning and the Metaphysics of Creation," both in this volume.

Such painful dissonance between a mind constricted and itching and a mind awake to divine mercy is most poignantly evident in another story from the desert. It concerns a monk and a virgin who visited an elder and during the night had carnal relations. After they left the old man's cell the next day, they were overcome again but this time by a kind of malign curiosity, wondering how the elder could have failed to notice what they had done. So they returned to his cell and learned that he had in fact been aware of everything: "They said to him, 'What were you thinking at that time?' He said to them, 'At that time my thoughts were standing where Christ was crucified, and weeping.'" And the two, profoundly shaken by the elder's compassionate grief, are converted.[25]

The elder's mind, fixed on Christ crucified for sinners, is free from the need to assert his own virtue in an act of angry condemnation, free from the fear of losing his own reputation; the cross in this narrative represents God's powerful mercy breaking into the itching, pusillanimous needs of the fallen world, holding open the possibility of a wholly other disposition grounded in the generosity of divine action.

Discernment and Paschal Mystery

How does the cross work to uncover the mechanism of these thoughts and set the mind free from them? If Evagrius is right, a persistent fear of lack and scarcity is what drives the eight deadly thoughts. Perhaps we could say that for Evagrius the noetic effect of sin is not felt directly in the reason of humanity but in the will; a heart alienated from God grows blind to divine generosity, trust atrophies, love grows cold, and the mind succumbs to a fearful need to compensate itself. In such circumstances, reality comes to be interpreted as a realm of scarcity in which the hungry self must extract goods from others that it no longer knows how to receive freely from God.[26] One might well expect people in the grip of such thoughts to pursue an antidote to this fear through a wonderful elevating of the mind to bliss, and indeed it seems to have been just such an escapist mentality of pseudospiritual accomplishment that Paul critiques at Corinth. Alexandra Brown argues that for Paul these spiritual seekers were only practicing a more refined form of running away, a form that left them all the more subtly but deeply controlled by fear and the need to boast of superior social status:

The *psychikos*, whose intent is to rise *above* the world actually remains enslaved to it. Having received *gnosis* without *pneuma*, the psychics remain ignorant in the clutches of the world and its wisdom. Because they fail to receive the Spirit, they do not perceive *what is revealed* (2:9–10) by the Spirit, namely, the crucified Christ. They therefore

---

25. Greek Anonymous Series, *Apothegmata Patrum*, N 13. Quoted in Gould, *Desert Fathers on Monastic Community*, 126.

26. For clarity on the relation between desire and understanding in the process of knowing, see the essays of Griffiths and Hütter.

misperceive the critical interpretive power of the cross for eschatological life in the present.[27]

The paradox Paul has been able to discern because of the cross is this: The
more the pseudospiritual seek to evade their fears by assuming a higher status and comparing themselves with others, the more they remain enmeshed
in the idolatry to which fear and rivalry subjects them.

The word of the cross, however, is a word that brings to nothing this mentality because it is news about God's action to *embrace* the very status (slavery, humiliation, and death) that the pseudospiritual most fear. Jesus accepts
this status and, by his death, destroys the power of death to frighten and
dominate those who place their whole trust in God. Or as Heb 2:14 puts it:
"Since, therefore, the children share flesh and blood, he himself likewise
shared the same things, so that through death he might destroy the one who
has the power of death, that is, the devil, and free those who all their lives
were held in slavery by the fear of death."

At the risk of oversimplification, what I am suggesting here is this: The
cross becomes the basis of discernment because it grounds the mind in reality *free* from the distortions of fear, envy, and anger—all of which have as
their ultimate bogey-totem the shame and humiliation of death itself. To suggest, as Gooch does, that Paul's preaching of the cross encourages a proper
epistemological modesty is perhaps something of an understatement, but it is,
I think, nonetheless correct. It will be helpful, however, to see a little more
clearly how this new noetic environment that Jesus creates might be able to
reshape the minds of those who come to share it.

Perhaps the simplest way to put it is like this: Jesus' entire personal identity, Christians believe, is the immediate expression of his loving relationship
with the one he calls "Abba," and therefore his personhood and his way of
thinking are not distorted by the envious fears of the world. Jesus creates a
community in which persons whose thinking *is* so distorted, who suffer from
an undiscerning mind (*adokimon noun*, Rom 1:28), find themselves called
out of their old personhood by sharing in Jesus' loving relationship with the
Father: "For you did not receive a spirit of slavery to fall back into fear, but
you have received a spirit of adoption" (Rom 8:15). As minds are renewed
by confidence in God's loving generosity, it becomes possible again to discern
(*dokimazein*) truly "what is good and acceptable and perfect" (Rom 12:2).
This transformation from a mind possessed by fear and envy to a mind alive
to the immensity of divine love is, Paul believes, only possible by way of the
cross: ". . . joint heirs with Christ—if, in fact, we suffer with him so that we
may also be glorified with him" (Rom 8:17). Believers who suffer with Christ
lose all status, all claims to cultural, biological, moral, or spiritual superiority. Their minds are freed from the paralyzing magic of a self-esteem plucked
from the envying approbation of the world. They rest their sole confidence in
the resurrection of Jesus, that is, in the glory or recognition that comes from

27. Alexandra R. Brown, *The Cross and Human Transformation: Paul's Apocalyptic Word in 1
Corinthians* (Minneapolis: Fortress, 1995), 138. On the *psychikos/pneumatikos* distinction, see n. 7 above.

the Father. James Alison, developing the perspective of René Girard, has described all this with remarkable clarity. Commenting on John 5:41ff. ("I do not accept glory from human beings. . . . How can you believe when you accept glory from one another and do not seek the glory that comes from the one who alone is God?"), Alison writes:

> That is what Jesus was suggesting: in order to receive your reputation, your being noticed and recognized, by God, you have to be prepared to lose the reputation which comes from the mutually reinforcing opinion and high regard of those who are bulwarks of public morality and goodness and find it among those who are held as nothing, of no worth. . . . The order of this world has its own glory, which depends on mutually rivalistic imitation, and is a glory or reputation that is grasped and held onto with difficulty. Being enveloped in the order of this world prevents us from beginning to act in solidarity with those of poor repute, because if we do so we lose our reputation. But those whose minds are fixed on the things that are above, that is, who have begun to receive their "I" from their non-rivalistic imitation of Jesus, already begin to derive their reputation from the Father and not from their peers. This they learn to do in the degree to which, doubtless with much difficulty, they learn to give little importance to the reputation which people give them and thus become free to associate with those who have no reputation, just like the one who was numbered among the transgressors.[28]

So the new mind that is thus freed into the infinite resource of God is, paradoxically, not preoccupied with spiritual achievement. It has no boast except the cross, but in fact a truly discerning mind is free to understand all the dimensions of reality, including those the world despises and rejects.

Interruption: The Noetic Transition of the Cross

A painful transition is unavoidable here, and not only because, as Alison points out, those who have begun to derive their self-worth from God will likely not fit in well with the world's schemes of approval, and hence come to seem to others and perhaps to themselves like dismal failures. But beyond this, as the mind shares more deeply in the mind of Christ, there is the painfully growing awareness of how broken the world is and how immense is the divine compassion and justice in the face of this. Diadochus remarks that "at the outset, the soul in pursuit of theology is troubled by many passions, above all by anger and hatred." This happens not because the demons are arousing evil thoughts but precisely because the soul "is making progress":

---

28. James Alison, *Raising Abel: The Recovery of the Eschatological Imagination* (New York: Crossroad Herder, 1996), 181–82. See also the same author's excellent work, *The Joy of Being Wrong: Original Sin through Easter Eyes* (New York: Crossroad Herder, 1998). I am indebted to Alison throughout this essay.

So long as the soul is worldly-minded, it remains unmoved and untroubled however much it sees people trampling justice under foot. Preoccupied with its own desires, it pays no attention to the justice of God. When, however, because of its disdain for this world and its love for God, it begins to rise above its passions, it cannot bear, even in its dreams, to see justice set at nought. It becomes infuriated with evildoers and remains angry until it sees the violators of justice forced to make amends. . . . Nevertheless, it is much better to lament the insensitivity of the unjust than to hate them; for even should they deserve our hatred, it is senseless for a soul which loves God to be disturbed by hatred, since when hatred is present in the soul spiritual knowledge (*gnosis*) is paralysed.[29]

There is a noetic blindness caused by self-preoccupation, says Diadochus, but there is another more subtle form of mental constriction that can only be healed by an even more radical abandonment and handing over of all into the purposes of God. It is relieved, says Diadochus, not by an impatient insistence on one's own rectitude of judgment but by a steady holding of all things up into the plenitude of God's grace.[30] But in the initial stages of this transformation, such perception of plenitude may be almost entirely eclipsed by the perception of injustice and consequent anger.

Evagrius had prescribed for this period a time of patience, stillness, waiting, attention to the other—to use his term, *apatheia*. It is an ascetical process of self-stripping that, paradoxically, does not annihilate but rather liberates the self from its compulsions, from the "higher" temptations to attack violence with more violence, to combat injustice with an insidiously self-approving indignation. Part of the problem is that the self's survival instincts train us to think in very purposeful, utilitarian ways about what surrounds us. As Paul had warned the Corinthians, however, the real is not reducible to something we can use or appropriate for ourselves—even perhaps in the service of righteous indignation. Rather, the divine strength is likely to appear in our newly impatient frame of mind as mere foolishness, a painfully enigmatic cross. For Evagrius, this means that often we may not be able to experience much of reality at all. The real may accost us only in an experience of futility and darkness. Origen had suggested that ascesis and moral discipline would lead one to a clearer vision in which we begin to sense the true heart of things in themselves (rather than as fantasized by us). But this clarity is a difficult vision in which most of the world of our striving appears as pointless, as vain: "When a person has progressed in discernment and behaviour he may pass on thence to train his natural intelligence and, by distinguishing the causes and natures of things, may recognize the vanity of vanities that he must forsake, and the lasting and eternal things that he ought to pursue."[31]

---

29. Diadochus, *On Spiritual Knowledge*, §71, p. 277.
30. Ibid., §68, p. 275.
31. Origen, *Song of Songs Commentary*, 43–44.

So in addition to the possibility of anger and hatred being stirred up, there is a danger that in reaction to its frustration with the world's wrongs and its own inability to right the world perfectly, the soul may sour into what Evagrius calls *akedia*, a depressing sense of futility. Diadochus comments:

> When the soul begins to lose its appetite for earthly beauties, a spirit of listlessness (*akedia*) is apt to steal into it. This prevents us from taking pleasure in study and teaching, and from feeling any strong desire for the blessings prepared for us in the life to come; it also leads us to disparage this transient life excessively, as not possessing anything of value. It even depreciates spiritual knowledge itself, either on the grounds that many others have already acquired it or because it cannot teach us anything perfect.[32]

It is important to see that these twin problems of impatience and dryness are set loose because believers have begun to enter into the paschal mystery and have caught a glimpse of what the world looks like through the eyes of Christ. The convenient older noetic is no longer accessible, but a new vision is not yet at work either.

As J. Louis Martyn puts it, the cross remains an epistemological crisis. Paul's criticism of the Corinthians is that instead of abiding there with Christ on the cross, trusting in the unimaginable hope of the Father's love, they seek a perfectly graspable, religious wisdom of their own. But the only authentic

> new way of knowing is not in some ethereal sense a spiritual way of knowing. It is not effected in a mystic trance, as the pseudo-apostles had claimed, but rather right in the midst of rough-and-tumble life . . . [,] life in the midst of the new-creation community, in which to know by the power of the cross is precisely to know and to serve the neighbor who is in need.[33]

Martyn's point here would seem to confirm the views of Alison I considered above, namely, that if believers place their sole confidence with Christ in the Father's love, the new vision that begins to open before them can no longer fit within the confines of their own grasp. They will not be able to enter into the paschal mystery *and* retain a perspective or judgment that somehow relies on their own sense of self-worth, or status, or moral accomplishment. Any attempt to do so will only turn the mystery of Christ's dying and rising into a new datum to possess, rather than the noetic framework within which one now exists. As one New Testament scholar puts it, "The epistemological point is inseparable from the eschatological one and therefore epistemology cannot be reduced to a matter of individual subjectivity."[34] Paul seems to understand the death of Jesus as opening up a new order of reality in which

---

32. Diadochus, *On Spiritual Knowledge*, §58, p. 270.
33. Martyn, "Epistemology at the Turn of the Ages," 109.
34. Pickett, *Cross in Corinth*, 155–56.

everything is charged with a different polarity, a new meaning. "It is a way of knowing granted not to the natural person, but to those who are able to discern the eschatological significance of Christ's death and who view reality in terms of its consequences."[35] As I have suggested, such a conversion would transform both one's identity and derivation of self-worth, but also one's relations to others. Being drawn into the paschal mystery will take the form of a difficult and fumbling new way of seeing one another and of living for the sake of one another: "We are convinced [*krinantas*] that one has died for all; therefore all have died. And he died for all, so that those who live might live no longer for themselves, but for him who died and was raised for them" (2 Cor 5:14–15).

This loving holding of the other into the rescuing love of God may, therefore, be the foundational practice needed to ground a truly eschatological noetic. Perhaps that is something of what we find in the nonanxious humility and patience of the desert fathers in the face of many faults and weaknesses. Again and again we see them learning, almost like a new skill or language, how to interpret and understand the neighbor against the horizon of Jesus' self-giving on the cross. Somehow the fabric of reality, in this new state of being, can best be touched and sensed in the delicate practice of relationship with the other; the possibility of gradually coming to discern the fullness of the new reality and entering into it hangs upon the experiment of this new way of relating to the other. Anthony the Great is recorded as saying, "Our life and our death is with our neighbour. If we gain our brother, we have gained God, but if we scandalise our brother, we have sinned against Christ."[36] The neighbor here is revealed as a test, a discernment of the degree to which one is beginning to live into the new reality opened up by the cross. And this new reality marked so utterly by relationship with the other becomes a crucible in which old patterns of relationship are undone and new ones learned, grown almost, from the organic self-giving of Jesus. Abba Poemen comments on how this new relational pattern of life may begin to unfurl among the disciples of Jesus:

> "Greater love hath no man than this that a man lay down his life for his friends" (John 15:13). In truth if someone hears an evil saying, that is, one which harms him, and in his turn, he wants to repeat it, he must fight in order not to say it. Or if someone is taken advantage of and he bears it, without retaliating at all, then he is giving his life for his neighbor.[37]

One can see very frequently in these stories the struggle between the old order in which the truth of one's rectitude and of justice must be asserted and the new order unfolding in the working of Jesus' death and resurrection, in which vindication and moral worth and righteousness are not achieved by blotting out the other but by resurrection, by the Father's infinite loving of the

---

35. Ibid., 157.
36. Anthony the Great 9, in *Sayings of the Desert Fathers*, 3.
37. Poemen 116, in *Sayings of the Desert Fathers*, 184.

other into the new state of being—a state barely discernible by those whose minds are not yet filled with a sense of the divine plenitude.

So, for instance, when some righteous brethren come to Abba Poemen with complaints about others who irritatingly nod off during the liturgy, they expect him to provide a judicious correction of the slumberers and certainly the admonition to wake them up. But Poemen replies, "For my part when I see a brother who is dozing, I put his head on my knees and let him rest."[38] Here the new reality begins to dawn, one suspects, in a very confused way upon the minds of the righteous brothers, who must feel both chastened and yet perhaps attracted by this gentle care. Likewise, there must be a peculiar shift out of the polarities of self-condemnation and self-justification for the brother who startles awake in embarrassed exhaustion but finds his head cradled consolingly in the lap of the abba. The attractive and converting dimensions of this divine generosity are limned even more explicitly in the stories of thieves who find more than they had bargained for among the elders. Having been plundered, one of these old men took up a little bag the thieves had missed and struggled after them, crying, "'My sons, take this, you forgot it in the cell!' Amazed at the patience of the elder, they brought everything back into his cell and did penance, saying, 'This one really is a man of God!'"[39] In all these stories the old order of reality marked by need, condemnation, and rapacity is overtaken by an endless resource that not only grounds everything in mercy and forgiveness but makes an outpouring gift of the very thing that before could be perceived only as a scarce commodity to be grasped and possessed as one's own.

Discerning the Fullness of Reality

As this new order of reality begins to unfold, what noetic shifts and epistemological possibilities begin to appear? In the previous section I considered some of the ascetical yet exhilarating experiences likely to develop in the transition from the old order mentality to one marked by the paschal mystery. Now we want to consider what might legitimately be called the mystical dimensions of the new noetic, as minds awaken (like sleeping brothers cradled in the arms of Abba Poemen) to the hidden presence of the divine abundance.

The Apostle Paul asks the Corinthians to notice something that God is doing within and among them. Indeed, we could even say that throughout the letters he consistently points to God as the prime noetic agent, the one who calls and knows the Corinthians and thus engenders knowing in them. He seeks to awaken them to the ways in which God's life is reconfiguring the noetic possibilities of the believing community. He helps them open themselves to this new process of perception, a process in which God the Holy Spirit translates the loving generosity of God in Christ into the very patterns

---

38. Poemen 92, in *Sayings of the Desert Fathers*, 179–80.
39. An anonymous saying from one of the Latin collections, in *The Wisdom of the Desert: Sayings from the Desert Fathers of the Fourth Century*, trans. Thomas Merton (New York: New Directions, 1970), 59.

of the community's thought. To "have the mind of Christ" means, I will argue, to think within the framework of Jesus' own fidelity and joy with respect to the Father's abundant life; it also means, therefore, to be drawn into God's own humanly incarnate form of knowing.

The Mind of Christ

Part of the problem facing Paul is that while the Corinthians were committed to the gospel, they also, perhaps unconsciously, tended to transpose the status ideals of their society into the framework of the church. So Paul is working hard to "resocialize" the members of church, recalling to their minds their ecclesial formation and identity "in terms of their response to the 'word of the cross.'"[40] Paul's talk of God's wisdom, "secret and hidden" (1 Cor 2:7), seems to fit well with "the contemporary Jewish terms used to speak of God's eschatological design for the salvation of his people."[41] It is this wisdom in a mystery that is at work reconciling the world in Christ, but, as Paul deliberately emphasizes to the Corinthians, it is precisely this hidden dimension or depth of reality that the "rulers of this age" fail to discern. They have not been re-created by sharing in Jesus' dying and rising. By contrast, says Paul, "We have received not the spirit of the world, but the Spirit that is from God, so that we may understand [eidōmen] the gifts bestowed on us by God" (1 Cor 2:12).

Putting this all together with the joyful climax in 2:16—"But we have the mind [nous] of Christ"—we can see Paul holding before the Corinthians a vision of the divine generosity. This vision is what most crucially marks the Spirit-filled mind of Christ. It is a vision utterly free from fearful grasping, and in its confidence in the Father's love it is the outpouring (Spirit) of that divine generosity within the constraints of the broken world. This seems indeed to be what Paul is getting at in his parallel use of nous in the famous passage from Phil 2: "Let the same mind be in you that was in Christ Jesus, who though he was in the form of God, did not regard equality with God as something to be exploited, but emptied himself. . . . Therefore God also highly exalted him." Paul calls the Philippians, like the Corinthians, to let themselves be sharers in a common mind, that is, the mind of Christ. He urges them to immerse themselves in Jesus' nonanxious confidence in the divine resource that makes him free to live as the perfect embodiment of that giving life; in the context of the present world order, this giving can only be seen as folly, humiliation, and death. Yet the true power and boundlessness of the divine generativity is manifest in the resurrection of Jesus, whose life beyond the power of death redounds "to the glory of God the Father" (Phil 2:11).

Clearly, then, the "mind of Christ" is not some kind of alien rationality that displaces native human reason, but is rather a pattern of rationality that is constantly held open by faith to the wideness of God's mercy. In an

---

40. Picket, *Cross in Corinth*, 61.
41. Markus N. A. Bockmuehl, *Revelation and Mystery in Ancient Judaism and Pauline Christianity* (Tübingen: J. C. B. Mohr, 1990), 161.

important discussion of Paul's use of *nous* in 1 Cor 2:16, Robert Jewett summarizes his results as follows:

> If it [i.e., the mind of Christ] is the basis on which the church is to be united (1 Cor 1:10) and if it is the plan of salvation revealed in Christ, then it must be more than an individual rational capacity. . . . I would say that *nous* is a complex of thoughts and assumptions which can make up the consciousness of a person. It is quite different from a purely rational capacity, from the power of judgment and decision which the Greek idea presupposes. . . . It is a constellation of thoughts which is given in the gospel and as such it provides the basis for unity in the church.[42]

This particular pattern, or "constellation of thoughts," gives access to a new way of discerning reality. It seems that these thoughts also are too large, as it were, to be thought individually; the mind of Christ seems irreducibly relational in its constitution. Indeed, we have seen reason to think that participation in the mind of Christ is fundamentally a relational activity, a noetic event that transpires in the communion of love.

Diadochus explicates this relational framework by teasing out the new role of compunction in those who are growing spiritually. Their knowledge, he says, is contingent on their sensitivity to those around them and their consequent readiness to seek out in loving humility those who are alienated from them. "For spiritual knowledge, consisting wholly of love, does not allow the mind [*nous*] to expand and embrace the vision of the divine, unless we first win back to love even one who has become angry with us for no reason."[43] Perhaps we might understand this view by considering that this noetic relational matrix of reconciling love instantiates within the world something of the divine communion that is the very basis of reality. And so when one begins to think about everything in this profoundly reconciling way, one is intuitively more capable of perceiving the truth of life. This is, I believe, what Diadochus is saying when he comments:

> The qualities of a pure soul are intelligence devoid of envy, ambition [lit., "zeal"] free from malice, and unceasing love for the Lord of glory [note the direct contrast with the powers of the age who do not love and cannot understand the Lord of glory, 1 Cor 2:8]. When the soul has these qualities, then the intellect (*nous*) can accurately assess how it will be judged.[44]

The noetic significance of love cannot be overestimated here. For Diadochus, faith and hope help the soul to find freedom from worldly compulsions, "but love unites the soul with the excellence of God, searching out the Invisible by

---

42. Robert Jewett, *Paul's Anthropological Terms: A Study of Their Use in Conflict Settings* (Leiden: E. J. Brill, 1971), 378.
43. Diadochus, *On Spiritual Knowledge*, §92, p. 290.
44. Ibid., §19, p. 258.

means of intellectual perception (*aisthēsei noera*)."[45] Again, I want to suggest that this not be taken solely in an individualistic sense, but that we instead see Diadochus's social and relational concern operative here; in that case, the knowledge that love makes possible is a discernment of the relational ground of all things, their existence in and through and for communion with God and by means of participation in God's triune life.

What Kind of Knowledge?

Does this mean that we have worked our way back into a purely spiritual "faith-knowledge" that has no relevance outside the idiomatically religious sphere? There are two important preliminary points to be made here, I think. First, if the universe is constituted in Trinitarian form, then thinking with the mind of Christ will, as I have suggested, make possible a perception of reality in its truest depths. This need not mean that a Christian scientist, for example, will discover something other than quarks or whatever subatomic particles are discoverable; rather, a Christian scientist would discern such particles in their true identity as expressive events, outpourings, in the infinite exchange of love that is the divine life. Even the apparent necessities of nature are ultimately gratuitous, luminous with freely given love of the Trinity.

Second, the fact that Paul applies the mind of Christ principally to ecclesial life and the overcoming of its mutually divisive misperceptions need *not* mean that the mind of Christ is preoccupied, as it were, with church in an exclusive sense. For the church is simply those bits of the whole creation called up into a new pattern of relationship in which, however faintly and fitfully, something of the divine pattern of relationship can be recognized and sought. The church exists in the process of undergoing new creation not instead of the rest of the universe, but only as a sign to the whole creation of what God has in store for everything. And that means that the particular pattern of communal thinking identified as the mind of Christ is the pattern of knowing and loving in which all creatures are called to share. Practicing it in its provisional ecclesial form is meant to draw more and more of the creation into this mind. So when Paul or others talk about the mind of Christ in terms of the church's life or its decision making, we ought to think of this as a kind of dry run for the rest of the creation, not as a peculiar tribal activity of a coterie.

Knowledge as Communion

Let me now attempt to bring the points I have been making to their conclusion. Throughout this essay, I have highlighted in various ways the old-fashioned and quaintly unmodern point that moral and intellectual virtues are integrally related. Paul, Origen, Evagrius, and Diadochus have all maintained that vicious minds are not capable of perceiving much beyond the anxious and

---

45. Ibid., §1, p. 253.

manipulative grasp of their own fears and desires—and whatever they do espy of such greater reality they soon misperceive as either a potential object of possession or a bitter obstacle and focus of aggression. As the Letter to Titus describes such a state, folly or incomprehension is its very first characteristic: "For we ourselves were once foolish, disobedient, led astray, slaves to various passions and pleasures, passing our days in malice and envy, despicable, hating one another" (3:3).

I have suggested how the process of conversion away from such a state leads to ascesis and to a clearer vision of one's "evil thoughts," to use Evagrius's term, and how such a recognition goes hand in hand with an opening of the mind to the boundless gratuity of God in Christ. But as we have moved through the noetic significance of sharing in the paschal mystery, the communal dimension of graceful knowing has become more and more apparent. The mind of Christ is an irreducibly relational and communally knowing "subject."

So when Diadochus explores the growing transparency of the mind to God, we ought not to read this apart from the communal context he certainly presupposes. Take this beautiful mystical passage:

> He who loves God consciously in his heart [lit., "who perceives God in the heart by love," *aisthēsei kardias agapōn*] is known by God, for to the degree that he receives the love of God consciously in his soul, he truly enters into God's love. From that time on, such a man never loses an intense longing for the illumination of spiritual knowledge (*gnōseōs*), until he senses its strength in his bones and no longer knows himself, but is completely transformed by the love of God. He is both present in this life and not present in it; still dwelling in the body, he yet departs from it, as through love he ceaselessly journeys towards God in his soul.[46]

This dilation of the human being in love with God ceaselessly whets the appetite for a truth that itself becomes the knower ("until he senses its strength in his bones"), realizing this truth in a love that sets the knower free from self-preoccupation and makes him available to the other ("no longer knows himself"). Because the reality in which the knower participates is itself a radically self-sharing and freely loving existence, this mystical journey toward God in the soul cannot be solipsistic. Indeed, the self-forgetting desire for the other that characterizes this state of spiritual knowing finds its real embodiment in the neighbor; this relational pattern of existence is the framework for true knowledge. Not surprisingly, Diadochus immediately follows the passage just quoted with this one:

> When a man begins to perceive (*aisthanesthai*) the love of God in all its richness, he begins also to love his neighbour with spiritual perception (*aisthēsei pneumatos*). This is the love of which all the scriptures speak. Friendship after the flesh is very easily destroyed on some slight pretext,

---

46. Ibid., §14, p. 256.

since it is not held firm by spiritual perception. But when a person is spiritually awakened, even if something irritates him, the bond of love is not dissolved; rekindling himself with the warmth of the love of God, he quickly recovers himself and with great joy seeks his neighbour's love, even though he has been gravely wronged or insulted by him. For the sweetness of God completely consumes the bitterness of the quarrel.[47]

I note here the importantly intimate conjunction between spiritual perception or discernment and the divine love. This love is the ground of the deepening steadfast knowledge of the neighbor, and sets flowing a renewable understanding of the other. We could even say that the divine loving inhabits the human relationship, making it possible and bringing to light within it the amiable truth of the other that God alone (sometimes!) can know. It is precisely this feasting of the perception upon "the love of God in all its richness" that sets the mind free from fearful self-preoccupations and enmities, filling it with the divine abundance and so preparing it to risk the truth of the other— rather than merely the fantasized objectification of the other.

This kind of knowledge is one with the discernment shown among the desert fathers. It is an acute insight into the shape of God's loving design for the other. It is an awareness of the right patterns of activity by which to embrace the destiny of oneself with another, by which to allow God's call to self and neighbor to take flesh and come to life in the world. The test of this knowledge is found, therefore, in its unity with the relational life within which it can alone come to perception. If it builds up the body (cf. 1 Thess 5:11), then it is authentic and not spurious knowledge. Commenting on Paul's critique of false knowledge in 1 Corinthians, Luke Timothy Johnson observes:

> Any knowledge claiming to provide a liberty that can proceed in action heedless of the consequences to others only "puffs up"(1 Cor 8:1) the individual while running the risk of destroying the community. . . . Paul therefore speaks of edification as that expression of the "mind of Christ" (1 Cor 2:16) in which each person looks not to his or her own interests but to the interests of others.[48]

This freely self-giving love of Christ becomes, by the power of the Holy Spirit, the very structure of a new kind of talking and thinking and being with one another. The whole thrust of Paul's address to the Corinthians is to submit their divided and factionalized communal life to the unifying relationality let loose upon the world in Christ.

Alexandra Brown joins Johnson and others in noting the close association in Paul's writings between the cross event and a particular state of mind. To share with one another in the "mind of Christ" or to "let the same mind be in you that was in Christ Jesus" is, for Paul, to perceive reality within a

---

47. Ibid., §15, pp. 256–57.
48. Luke Timothy Johnson, *Scripture and Discernment: Decision Making in the Church* (Nashville: Abingdon, 1996), 115–16.

matrix of reconciliation, service, unity, and humility.[49] My most basic conviction about all this is that the reason this sharing in Christ's mind so frees the community to live for one another is because sharing in Christ's mind is knowing, in the provisional form possible in this life, something of the glory of the Father's love as the very foundation of one's existence. And when Diadochus dilates on the gift of contemplation, or, as he calls it, *theologia*, I think it is really the church's sharing in Christ's relationship with the Father that he is describing.[50]

Again, we might see something like this in Paul's reference to the building up of the church as the temple of the Holy Spirit (Eph 2:19–22), the earthly locus and form of the heavenly exchange of love that is God's life. And as that exchange takes place, the new act of knowing occurs, a knowing that is of course a being known, a lifting of the world, even in fragments, up into the life by which God knows and loves God. Such a relational ground of knowing is not without analogies. A rose, for instance, has a vast number of specifiable data about it that one can know, and yet all these are understood anew and differently when the rose is given by someone to a friend. When it is taken up into their mutual life, it indeed becomes a cherishable dimension of their life; it is knowable in a new way. Jesus has taken up the believing community into his life with the Father. This community, in the Gospel of John, becomes by Jesus' sending of the Spirit the dwelling place of God. Here the truth of the creation (that it is the beloved of God) may begin to radiate through the world. Because Jesus lives from the Father in a way that destroys death, he makes possible a communal life that is not driven by the fear of death. Because Jesus lives, the disciples live also: "On that day you will know that I am in my Father, and you in me, and I in you" (John 14:19–20). In the words of James Alison:

> His life will be seen in their capacity to live beyond (rather than live toward, i.e., moved by) death. It is by their coming to live beyond death . . . that they will know the complete mutual implication of the Son and the Father, because they will themselves be caught up in the making real and visible of that mutual implication. . . . By the disciples' loving imitation of Jesus' self-giving, they will creatively make present Jesus' sonship, and thus the divine paternity, in the world that does not know it.[51]

So knowing with the mind of Christ is not simply an acquisition of truths but "an expanding possession of the believer by the Father and the Son creating eternal life in the midst of this world through the creation of an imitative

---

49. Brown, *Cross and Human Transformation*, 139–48, esp. 146.

50. Diadochus, *On Spiritual Knowledge*, §67, p. 275: "The gift which enflames our heart and moves it to love His goodness more than any other is theology. It is the early offspring of God's grace and bestows on the soul the greatest gifts. First of all, it leads us gladly to disregard all love of this life, since in the place of perishable desires we possess inexpressible riches, the oracles of God. Then it embraces our intellect with the light of a transforming fire, and so makes it a partner of the angels in their liturgy. . . . It nourishes the intellect with divine truth in the radiance of inexpressible light."

51. Alison, *Joy of Being Wrong*, 189.

adhesion" by the believing community to the practices that identify Jesus' relationship with the Father.[52] "Those who love me will keep my word, and my Father will love them, and we will come to them and make our home with them." "This is my commandment, that you love one another as I have loved you" (John 14:23; 15:12).

This has three crucial implications. First, the faith, in the sense of the ideas by which the mind knows and seeks to understand what God has accomplished in Christ, becomes a new cognitive framework by means of which the Holy Spirit "will guide you into all truth" (John 16:13), restructuring the mind and prying it open to the infinite, deathless reality of God. This sets the believing community free to enact a new pattern of relationship, free from the fear, envy, and enmity that are death's instruments in controlling the mind.

Second, because of the nature of the reality in question—namely, the divine life—the "ideas" by which the mind apprehends such a reality are not purely conceptual. That is to say, they of course have a conceptual form by means of which they are present in the mind of someone trying to think about them, but the forms by which this divine reality makes itself known seem to be primarily relational events, acts of mercy and love. So, for instance, the truth of the incarnation is actually something one cannot grasp within the bounds of an individual mind but that unfolds its reality within the new practices of communal life that the incarnation establishes within the network of the world's life.

Third, the effect of this new communal pattern, the mind of Christ, continuously woven into the fabric of the world, is that the world begins to know everything differently. Indeed, as the world is drawn into the new life that Jesus is establishing in its midst, the world does not simply think differently but finds that its thoughts are not solely its own at all but God's, that the pattern of relational activity by which it has come to think everything, bringing everything eucharistically into this communal event, is the Trinitarian event of God's knowing and loving.

Admittedly, this beatific epistemology is painfully eschatological; for the present it is purely a matter of hope. Nonetheless, I think theology might legitimately claim that this is the direction in which knowing is headed. Herbert McCabe remarks regarding the relationship in Aquinas of epistemology to the beatific vision:

> It is an important theme of Question 12 [of the *Prima Pars*] that when, in beatitude, a man understands the essence of God, the mind is not realized by a form which is a likeness of God, but by God himself. God will not simply be an object of our minds, but the actual life by which our minds are what they will have become.[53]

---

52. Ibid., 191.
53. Herbert McCabe, appendix 1, "Knowledge," in Thomas Aquinas, *Summa theologiae*, vol. 3, *Knowing and Naming God*, trans. Herbert McCabe (London: Eyre & Spottiswoode, 1964), 100.

Or as the same author puts it in respect of the social dimensions of knowing all things in God:

> Christ is, indeed, to be found in the present but precisely as what is rejected by the present world, in the poor and despised and oppressed, he is to be found in those who *unmask* the present world, those in whom the meaninglessness and inhumanity and contradictions of our society are exposed. Christ will only be, so to say, at home in the world, in the kingdom of the future: it will then be possible to express the exchange of love which is God directly with our bodily lives, simply as our human existence, in the language of what will then be the present. Until then the exchange of love, the Holy Spirit, between men is expressed in the language of the future: and this is what the sacraments are.[54]

In these two passages the crucial points for our purposes are the same: that the ultimate state of knowing is one in which God is the primal knowing subject in whose act we participate, and that this divine act by which God is God, knows and loves God, is an exchange of love that can only take place in human terms by means of the loving interactions of communal life. My contention throughout this essay has been that such an event of knowing could never be legitimately understood as a human *possession*. But I have also argued that this need no longer bother us, either in terms of the accuracy or certainty of what we know, for we know by participating in another, in Christ, who has entirely desired to share on earth the beatific knowing that is the very life of heaven.

All of this suggests to me that faith is perhaps not, in the end, best understood by being set over against reason, or vice versa. Faith is human reason paying attention to God. But attending to God is, as we have seen, likely to mean a transformation of the understanding, a renewal, as Paul says, of the mind, and an expansion of mind beyond the bounds of the reason we know from our experience of individual existence. For the reasoning of faith is a coming to share in the reasoning of the one who knows and is known, loves and is loved by the Father. Faith and reason cannot be held over against one another, but only with each other against the fear, envy, and aversion to real life that mark the counterfeit cunning of sin.

---

54. Herbert McCabe, *God Matters* (London: Geoffrey Chapman, 1987), 175.

PART TWO

Assessing Reason Theologically:
Errancy—Directedness—Perplexity

CHAPTER SIX

How Reasoning Goes Wrong:
A Quasi-Augustinian Account of Error and Its Implications

— PAUL J. GRIFFITHS —

I want to raise here the question of a properly Christian account of reasoning's errors—of how and why reasoning goes wrong—and to do so with Augustine as interlocutor. My interest in this is not principally exegetical but normative: I intend that what I say about Augustine should be defensible as an incomplete and preliminary reading of him on this topic, but my main concern is to sketch a properly Christian account of how and why reasoning goes wrong, and my exegesis of Augustine is intended as aid to and illustration of this rather than as an enterprise of independent interest.

Accounting for reasoning's errors is a proper part of accounting for reasoning as such, and therefore must be addressed by Christians who want to think—to reason, indeed—about reasoning. But this kind of response to the question of what interest an account of reasoning's failures has for Christians only indicates the usual academic desire for completeness and closure, a desire that should be resisted and that certainly cannot be used to justify any particular intellectual enterprise. Better answers to the question of why a particular topic ought to be addressed are local and indexical. They point to a current and lively problem and explain the enterprise in question as a response to or engagement with that problem. The problem motivating this essay, then, is a contemporary (not just contemporary, I think, but at least that) overestimate on the part of many Christian thinkers (including perhaps Pope John Paul II himself) of the persuasive possibilities of reasoning with respect to theoretical questions, and a concomitant tendency to engage in contextually inappropriate and rhetorically sub-Christian acts of reasoning as a result.[1]

---

1. This tendency toward excessive optimism about reason's persuasiveness is certainly not the only salient feature of evaluations of reason popular in early postmodernity. Other contributors to this volume, notably Carver Yu, have identified an excessive suspicion of reason as the pressing problem of our time. A similar point is made in *Fides et Ratio*. However, both modernist and postmodernist suspicions tend to be made in full flight from or profound ignorance of fully Christian theological anthropology. From the standpoint of such an anthropology, Spinozistic rationalism, Humean skepticism, Kantian transcendental

Let us call those who have a high estimate of the persuasive powers of argument in matters of theory reason's optimists. They are likely to be puzzled by the fact of argument's unpersuasiveness. They are looking for the kind of argument that will immediately convince all who come across it, and since all arguments also deploy judgments, they will typically also expect the judgments deployed in the ideal argument to seem luminously correct to all who understand them. There is, reason's optimists may think, something about all human beings—their rationality, perhaps—that ought to make nonfallacious and misapprehension-free arguments immediately convincing to all.[2] But when faced with the starkly obvious fact that there are few judgments whose luminosity is of the required intensity and even fewer arguments whose validity is as obvious as it ought to be (and certainly none of either about anything remotely interesting, theoretically speaking), reason's optimists usually add a list of qualifications. I don't mean, such a person will say, that the judgments I'm making and the arguments I'm offering will—or ought to be expected to—convince everyone; no, they'll convince only adult, properly equipped, well-intentioned, well-educated, and attentive people.[3] But then the optimists' expectations have been severely constrained, for the set of people who meet these qualifications is vastly smaller than the set of all human beings. Its members may not extend beyond the optimists' friends and families.

Contemporary Christians, especially those who like to talk about natural law in an epistemic as well as an ontological sense, often act as if they are among reason's optimists. Arguments are offered in the public sphere, for example, about such highly theoretical matters as the legality and desirability of abortion, or the propriety of international debt-forgiveness, with the apparent hope that the previously unconvinced will hear them and be swayed by the luminosity of the judgments deployed in them and the irresistibly persuasive power of the argument in which the judgments are arrayed. And, in an attempt to make this result more likely (so it seems often to be thought), explicitly Christian talk is occluded in such arguments, even when they are offered by Christians. Such occlusion is thought desirable, usually, because it is expected that the presence of explicitly Christian judgment in an argument will make the persuasion of the non-Christian interlocutor less likely than it would be were such judgments explicitly present.[4]

---

rationalism, and Foucauldian genealogical suspicion are all variations upon the same theme. Yu is right to offer a covenantal view of reason as a response to both Hume and Kant. See Carver T. Yu, "Covenantal Rationality and the Healing of Reason," in this volume.

2. Spinoza's view of the status of the axiomata of the *Ethica* provides a paradigm of how an optimist about reason is likely to think about the possibility of arriving at judgments whose adequacy is obvious. His subsequent use of these axioms in argument shows, too, that he has an optimistic view of the persuasive capacities of argument. It is no accident that these views are expressed by someone who stands at the beginning of an explicitly and self-consciously anti-Christian (and, of course, anti-Jewish as well) mode of philosophizing. No Christian ought to have Spinozist views about reason; too many, unfortunately, do.

3. A splendid example of this rather desperate strategy is to be found in John F. X. Knasas, "Whither the Neo-Thomist Revival?" *Logos* 3, no. 4 (Fall 2000): 142–43. Knasas is a passionate and precise defender of the neo-Thomism of such thinkers as Étienne Gilson against the transcendental Thomism of such thinkers as Joseph Maréchal. When faced with the difficulty that few understand and fewer assent to arguments supposed to be comprehensible and convincing in principle (as they always say) to all, he can only wearily say that this is because metaphysics is difficult.

4. It may be the case that the nihilism of modern metaphysics—evident most fundamentally in its forgetting of the distinction between Being and beings (a distinction best not called "ontico-ontological" by those who wish to write in English), as analyzed winsomely and compellingly by David Hart in this

This is the immediate context that makes addressing the question of how theoretical reasoning goes wrong important. The adoption of the kind of rationalist optimism just mentioned encourages Christians to speak a language from which explicitly Christian talk has been expunged, and to do so with the vain hope of increasing agreement about theoretical matters. These are not merely errors; they are errors demeaning to the intellectual tradition they claim to represent, errors that lead to a misrepresentation of that tradition in public argument, and errors that can be corrected by the adoption of a just and moderate pessimism about the capacities of theoretical reason, a pessimism required by a proper theoretical account of why reasoning goes wrong.

I suspect, though I shall not here attempt to show, that the optimism about the capacities of reason in matters theoretical all-too-evident among some contemporary users of natural-law theory[5] stems from a confusion of the claim that there is natural law with the claim that the content of that law is knowable to all.[6] These are quite separate claims; it is perfectly possible to affirm the former without the latter, and the tendency to think that if you want one you must have the other ought to be resisted. I suspect, too, that a close look at the history of debate among Catholic Christians (and at magisterial teaching) in the last three centuries or so about the knowability of the natural law would show that the tendency to confuse these claims is a product of the polemical demands of the Counter-Reformation, first, and of the Enlightenment, second.[7] If you have to argue first with Luther and then with Spinoza and Locke, it is all too possible that unnuanced affirmations of the *duplex ordo cognitionis* will result. This is no longer our polemical situation, though, and so perhaps a fully Christian and properly nuanced moderate pessimism about theoretical reason can now be recovered. It is just such a moderate pessimism that I should like to state and advocate.

Moderate pessimists about reason, by contrast with optimists, have the advantage of thinking it normal that valid arguments with true premises in the theoretical realm do not persuade those who do not already assent to their conclusions.[8] Perhaps more precisely, they expect that the persuasiveness of arguments is closely linked to the luminosity of their premises' truth and of

---

volume—is compatible with both excessive optimism and excessive pessimism about reason's capacities. If this is so, it requires more attention of at least a taxonomic sort. See David Bentley Hart, "The Offering of Names: Metaphysics, Nihilism, and Analogy," in this volume.

5. I have in mind here the work of thinkers such as John Finnis, Robert George, and Ralph McInerny.

6. The qualifier "in principle," or "other things being equal" is usually entered at this point. But then it becomes very difficult to know what is meant by the knowability claim. Is to say that a pagan can know the content of the natural law "in principle" like saying that I can do cube roots in my head "in principle"? Both claims are probably true but almost completely vacuous.

7. But I must note here that some of what I will argue may sit uneasily with some magisterial teaching—for example, with Vatican I's *Dei Filius* and Leo XIII's *Aeterni Patris*—and that to the extent to which this is so I both am and should be concerned. I have further work to do here. But I am comforted by the fact that what follows is, in my judgment, entirely concordant with *Fides et Ratio*, even if not with all currently popular interpretations of that encyclical.

8. The following analysis of reason's failures is largely epistemological in focus, which may mean that it is subject to Janet Soskice's strictures upon epistemology-as-first-philosophy. (See Janet Martin Soskice, "Naming God: A Study in Faith and Reason," in this volume.) In any case, what is said in what follows should be understood to assume and endorse the analysis of the perplexities intrinsic and proper to reason as such that are given in the first part of Ernstpeter Maurer's essay, "The Perplexity and Complexity of Sinful and Redeemed Reason," in this volume.

their own validity. They will also—and reasonably, so far as I can see—doubt that many arguments have premises or validity high on the scale of luminosity, and that certainly none in the theoretical sphere do. It remains now to ask why this is so. Why, that is, do arguments in the theoretical sphere so rarely carry conviction? Why do they so rarely persuade those who do not already (and on other grounds) assent to their conclusions?

There are, I suggest, two fundamental causes for the typical failure of a valid theoretical argument with true premises to persuade those who are faced with it. The first is inadequate catechesis, the second is volitional depravity, and neither can be cured by argument. I will return to these categories in a moment. But before doing so it will help to have some examples before us.

Consider, first, Fermat's last theorem: $x^n + y^n = z^n$ *has no nonzero integer solution for x, y, and z when n is greater than 2.* Pierre de Fermat, a French lawyer and amateur mathematician who died in 1665, commented (probably in 1630) on this theorem in a marginal note to his edition of Diophantus's *Arithmetica*: "I have discovered a truly remarkable proof which this margin is too small to contain." He never offered the proof. Mathematicians have attempted to prove the theorem since, and it is possible that the proof offered by the English mathematician Andrew Wiles (together with Richard Taylor) in the mid-1990s is valid. Most of those who ought to understand it claim that it is. The claim made in Fermat's last theorem is one that, if true, is necessarily so. Its proof, if valid, is (like all mathematical proofs) one each stage of which is entailed by the stage preceding.

Consider, second, Anselm's claim, made in a work composed sometime in the 1070s: "Existit ergo procul dubio aliquid quo maius cogitari non valet, et in intellectu et in re"[9]—which may be translated, "Therefore, it is beyond doubt that something than which a greater cannot be thought exists both in the understanding and in reality." This is a claim that, on its face, attributes indubitability (to some? all? Anselm alone?) to the embedded claim that that-than-which-a-greater-cannot-be-thought exists both as idea and as reality. The argument underlying this claim makes it clear that Anselm thinks of the claim as necessarily true.

Consider, third, the following claim made by Robert P. George in 1999: "The wrongness of abortion follows from the truth—fully accessible even to unaided reason—that the life of a human being is intrinsically, and not merely instrumentally, good."[10] This is a bit more complicated. The truth of a particular claim, *the life of a human being is intrinsically good*, is said to be fully accessible to unaided reason, and from this embedded claim is said to follow another, namely, *abortion is wrong*. The argument that underlies all three claims, given in the essay from which the quotation is taken, makes it clear that George understands "unaided reason" to mean at least reason unaided by special revelation (he may also, mysteriously, mean reason unaided by

---

9. Anselm, *Proslogion*, Cap. II.
10. Robert P. George, "A Clash of Orthodoxies," *First Things* 95 (August/September 1999): 33–40.

anything except itself), and that he thinks all reasonable people ought to be convinced by the arguments he offers.[11]

That nothing much follows from a judgment's truth about the number of those who will or should accept it, nor from an argument's validity about the number of those who will or should be persuaded by it can be illustrated from my own responses to these three claims. I take Fermat's last theorem to be true and the Wiles proof to be valid, and I do so entirely on the basis of authoritative testimony. While I understand the theorem I do not understand the proof, and can therefore only judge its validity by appealing to those who do (or should) understand it. This I happily do. I take Anselm's embedded claim to be true, and the argument he offers for it to be valid, and I do both on the basis of having studied and (I think) understood both. As to Anselm's further assertion that the embedded claim is beyond doubt, I endorse this if it is a signal merely of the logical status of the embedded claim (i.e., that it is necessarily true), but not if it is an assertion about the epistemic duty of those faced with his argument.[12] And in the case of George, I take his embedded claim about the intrinsic goodness of human life to be false, his claim about the wrongness of abortion to be true, and his further assertion about the accessibility of the truth of both these claims to unaided reason to be dramatically (even ludicrously) false.

I do not intend to defend or even to elucidate these reactions to Fermat, Anselm, and George. I mention them only to illustrate the complexity of the question and the range of reactions possible to being faced with putatively true judgments and putatively valid claims. It is obvious, I take it, that none of the three claims mentioned—not Fermat's, not Anselm's, not George's— seems true to most who come across them. And, concomitantly, it is true that the arguments offered in their support usually do not persuade. But if the claims are true and the arguments valid, an explanation seems required, for something has clearly gone wrong. Reason's uses outside the church have a fragile or accidental quality, a lack, and that lack, I suggest again, is either inadequate catechesis or volitional depravity on the part of those faced with the arguments. And I now turn to these categories in more detail, in an attempt to explain why a just appreciation of their significance should call into question optimism about reason.

Inadequacies and Improprieties in Catechesis

Catechesis may be understood narrowly, as instruction in revealed truth as found in Scripture and in the tradition of the church. This is certainly part of

---

11. It is worth noting that many Christian thinkers would not assent to George's claim that the life of a human being is intrinsically good. Augustine, for example, famously distinguishes between use (*uti*) and enjoyment (*frui*) in the first book of the De doctrina christiana on the ground that what is enjoyed must be loved for its own sake (*propter seipsam*), while what is used is loved, finally, for the sake of something other than itself. Using these definitions, Augustine claims that only God may be enjoyed; our loves for other humans occur under the sign of use. This contradicts George (though not Kant, which is probably no accident).

12. In fact, I think it is pretty clearly the former, and I endorse Alvin Plantinga's view that while Anselm's argument is valid and its conclusion necessarily true, one may be violating no epistemic duties in not being persuaded by it. See Plantinga, *The Nature of Necessity* (Oxford: Clarendon, 1974), 196–221.

its meaning; the catechist, taking her stand upon 1 Tim 6:20, understands herself as having been entrusted with a *parathēkē*, a *depositum*, that she must hand on by teaching it to others. In this sense, catechesis' primary function is to hand on information. But the act of catechizing may and should also be understood to include the transmitting of skills, among them skills of reading and responding to Scripture (skills not derivable from Scripture alone), and skills of worship. Catechesis, to use Gilbert Ryle's terms, transmits not only knowing-that (information), but also know-how, the capacity to engage in a form of activity, what Wittgenstein would call "knowing how to go on." It is a species of apprenticeship as well as a course of instruction, and one of the ways in which the church recognizes this is to include mystagogy as an element intrinsic and proper to catechesis.

Now a general truth. Inadequate or improper catechesis is among the principal causes of inability to recognize a true judgment as true, a false judgment as false, a valid argument as valid, and an invalid argument as invalid. If, when faced with a judgment or an argument, you lack access to the relevant information, or skills essential to its or their assessment, you will typically be unable to come to any conclusion about the judgment's truth or the argument's validity. Recall the case of the proof of Fermat's last theorem. I cannot assess the truth of the theorem or the validity of its proof because I lack essential information and skill: I don't know the theorems deployed and assumed in the proof, and I lack the skill to follow and respond to arguments of the technicality and subtlety of those given in the proof. My catechesis in mathematics ceased at the age of sixteen, which is a partial explanation for this lack. (A fuller explanation would include my lack of capacity for the subject, a lack I suspect not remediable by catechesis.)

That adequate catechesis is needed for the assessment of judgments and arguments is clear. But when the judgment or the argument is highly theoretical, as it was in each of the three examples taken above, adequate catechesis is difficult to come by and controversial at every step of the way. Theoretical questions—questions in ethics, say, or axiology, or epistemology—are difficult. Arriving at useful substantive conclusions in any of these spheres typically requires at least mastery of a technical vocabulary and training in reading and interpreting a particular body of authoritative texts. Understanding Anselm, for instance, requires substantial scriptural knowledge and a certain ease with the modalities of possibility and necessity in argument. None of this comes easily, and none of it comes to "unaided" reason, if by that is meant reason without benefit of catechesis. The same is true of the arguments offered by George against his pro-abortion opponents. Further, and more significantly, being effectively catechized always requires submission to authority.[13] The catechumen must take on faith what the

---

13. On this, see Augustine's *De catechizandis rudibus* and *De magistro*. A more contemporary (and more Thomist) defense of the necessity of submission to authority in many spheres of life can be found in Yves Simon's work. See especially his 1940 Aquinas Lecture, published as *The Nature and Functions of Authority* (Milwaukee: Marquette University Press, 1940).

teacher says (this is as true in mathematics or chemistry as it is in religion); if she does not, she will be unable to make progress. And taking on faith the commitments that make possible, say, progress as an exegete and disciple of Nietzsche will predispose and equip those who do so precisely to be inadequately or improperly catechized sufficiently to understand or respond to arguments like those offered by George or Anselm. The converse is also true: Catechetical formation as a Thomist will not predispose or equip you properly to comprehend or assess what is said by Nietzscheans.

I became aware of the importance of proper catechesis for the ability to assess and respond to theoretical judgment and argument by studying Buddhism. A Buddhist scholastic has been thoroughly catechized in a way very different from a scholastic Christian: The technical vocabulary is different, the body of authoritative texts is different, and what is assumed as obvious is significantly different. Buddhist knowledge and skill scarcely overlap with Christian. My Buddhist interlocutors were not interested in assessing or responding to Christian thought, and would have been scarcely capable of doing so without years of effort even if they had been. I was in the same case with respect to Buddhism. Could I assess the validity of the arguments offered by the eleventh-century Buddhist scholastic Ratnakirti for his judgment *Everything that exists is momentary* when I first began to read him? With about as much confidence as I can now assess the Wiles proof for Fermat's last theorem, which is to say with almost none. I had not been adequately catechized, just as Ratnakirti's epigones were not adequately catechized to respond to Augustine's Trinitarian arguments.

Lack of proper catechesis is especially problematic with respect to theoretical questions. It matters less in practical or technical matters. If, for example, my Buddhist interlocutors and I want to argue about how many chairs there are in the room, we can easily do so and come to agreement. But if we want to argue about the proper ontology to deploy in giving an account of what a chair is, we cannot easily do so, and we are unlikely to come to agreement.

And now for a second general truth, drawn from these remarks about the significance of adequate catechesis. It is that the nature and extent of the catechetically produced convictions that inform a particular judgment about a matter of theory (about, say, the nature of human beings and their proper ends, or about the nature of knowledge and the methods by which it ought to be constituted) ought not to be systematically and deliberately obscured in argument for the truth of that judgment. The extent to which this is done is precisely the extent to which argument will fail and the tradition in the service of which such argument is offered will be brought into disrepute. Arguments such as George's in the essay mentioned above—for such truths as that *Abortion is wrong* and *Human life is intrinsically valuable*—fail in just this way, and they also bring the tradition they claim to represent into disrepute by doing so. It is notable, by contrast, that so far as I can tell the Wiles proof does not so fail. It is shamelessly open about the extent of the catechetical preparation one is going to need in order to be able to understand it. Is Christian ethics so much easier than mathematics?

A third and final general truth based upon these remarks about catechesis is that decisions about what to say to a particular interlocutor or group of interlocutors ought always to be made with an eye upon the kind of catechesis they appear already to have had.[14] This too is obvious, but one aspect of our current situation is the tendency to ignore it, and to adopt a single mode of argumentative engagement no matter the interlocutor. In many cases, awareness of the catechetical formation of the interlocutor will make argument of any sort entirely inappropriate. I would not offer to a five-year-old the kinds of argument about whether God's existence is self-evident that Aquinas offers in *Summa theologiae* 1a,2, but neither would I offer those arguments to a follower of Michel Foucault or a Sakya Buddhist, for different reasons. The mistake to worry about here—and it is a mistake everywhere evident in George's work—is to read the natural law tradition to mean that identical argumentative strategies ought to be adopted no matter what the catechetical preparation of the audience, or, worse, to think that some audience may have had no catechetical preparation.

Inadequate or improper catechesis is, then, an important cause of inability to assess properly the truth of a judgment or the validity of an argument. It goes far to explain why arguments in matters of theory are so rarely persuasive. That catechetical preparation is important in developing the capacity for such assessment is supportive of the thesis (for which there are other grounds) that the principal purpose of argument in such matters is not persuasive, but rather is to provide discursive meditation upon what is independently known to be the case. This, in my reading, is what Anselm is doing with his arguments for God in the second and third chapters of the *Proslogion*, and this is chief among the reasons why they do not and are not intended to persuade the unbeliever.[15]

Volitional Depravity

But catechetical inadequacy is not the only cause for reasoning's failure to persuade or be comprehensible in theoretical matters. Another is volitional depravity on the part of those being argued with. Augustine will be helpful in explaining this, and I will begin with what he says about error (*error*), and interpret his comments on that with some elucidation of what he thinks about judgment (*iudicium/notitia*).

Here is a programmatic Augustinian definition of error (he writes here about mistaking material objects [*corpora*] for their images in the mind [*similitudines*], but the definition of error given here is applicable more generally): "For when we endorse those things [i.e., material objects] as these things [i.e., mental images], we err; for error is precisely to endorse one thing as another."[16] The idea is that the judgment *This is a material object* made

---

14. Augustine's remarks (*De catechizandis rudibus*, 8.12–9.13) on the different kinds of catechesis appropriate to the *rhetor* and the *philosophus* are helpful and apposite here.
15. In this respect, though not in all, I endorse Karl Barth's exegesis of Anselm.
16. "Itaque cum eas [sc. corpora] pro illis [sc. similitudines] approbamus, erramus; error namque est pro alio alterius approbatio," *De trinitate* 9.11.16. Cf. *Enchiridion* 17. All renderings from Augustine's Latin are the author's translation.

with respect to a mental image is not in error about what material objects are; it is in error only in applying the predicate *is a material object* to the particular in question. This view is generalizable for Augustine because, as we shall see, his account of judgment sees it as the act of identifying a particular as belonging to a kind. Making a mistake in such an act, then, is to misplace the particular by allocating it to the wrong kind.

What then is Augustine's causal story about the occurrence of error in this sense? Here is a good instance:

> Violent crimes are committed when the motive force that impels the soul is defective and asserts itself in a disturbed and insolent way. Shameful acts occur when the passionate desires of the soul are immoderate in their thirst for fleshly delights. In just the same way, errors and false opinions contaminate life when the rational mind is itself defective.[17]

This, from the fourth book of the *Confessions*, is written as a description of Augustine's own state before he had seen his way through the errors of the Manichees (it continues, in plangent lament, *Qualis in me tunc erat . . .*). But it too is generalizable as an account of the conditions that must be in place in order that errors of judgment issuing in *falsa opiniones* may occur. The passage implicitly appeals to one of Augustine's favorite scriptural texts, 1 John 2:16, in which a threefold analysis of concupiscence is given. Augustine links the fleshly concupiscence of that text to the immoderately passionate desires of the soul; the "concupiscence of the eyes" (otherwise usually simply curiosity for Augustine)[18] to the corruption of the rational mind; and the "pride of life" to the disturbances in the motive force of the soul. The only point I want to emphasize here is that Augustine thinks that defect or lack (*vitium*) in reason (more precisely of the *rationalis mens*, the rational mind) is both necessary and sufficient for errors in judgment to occur. Intellectual error is inseparable from such lack.

This is not an isolated text. Consider the opening of *On The Trinity*, which contains a diatribe against "the calumnies of those who condemn faith as a starting-point, and are deceived through an immature and misguided love of reason."[19] Augustine is interested here in those who make false judgments about God's nature, and he identifies three kinds of error on that topic. First, there are those who apply to God concepts they have learned from their senses; this is to make of God a material object—for example, to think of God as white or red or extended in space.[20] Second, there are those who apply to God concepts that in fact apply only to humans. This is to make of God a

---

17. "Sicut enim facinora sunt, si vitiosus est ille animi motus, in quo est impetus, et se iactat insolenter ac turbide, et flagitia, si est immoderata illa animae affectio, qua carnales hauriuntur voluptates, ita errores et falsa opiniones vitam contaminant si rationalis mens ipsa vitiosa est," *Confessiones* 4.15.25; cf. 3.8.16.

18. See the treatment of Aquinas on *curiositas* by Reinhard Hütter in "The Directedness of Reasoning and the Metaphysics of Creation," in this volume.

19. "[E]orum . . . calumnias, qui fidei contemnentes initium, immaturo et perverso rationis amore falluntur," *De trinitate* 1.1.1.

20. This was Augustine's own error under the influence of the Manichees, explored at length in books 3–5 of *Confessiones*. See esp. 3.6.11; 4.1.1; 5.5.8.

human person—for example, to think of God as forgetful. Third, there are those who know that God is neither material object nor human person, but who confusedly apply to him incoherent concepts such as that of having begotten himself.

Each of the three kinds of errors is made by people whose minds have not been purified. This lack of purification is most evident, says Augustine, in the dogmatism of those who make these errors: "They are so loaded with the burden of their mortality that they want to seem to know what they don't know and they can't know what they want to know. And because they arrogantly affirm their presumptuous opinions, they close to themselves the path to true understanding."[21] Here the *mortalitatis onus* is the problem, the chief cause of the origin and defense of intellectual error with respect to theoretical matters. This burden can be lifted, thinks Augustine, only by a purification of the will. The errors about God's nature that he identifies are not simple intellectual mistakes, correctable by argument; they are, rather, produced by desire, most fundamentally the desire to be right without being instructed.[22] Such people have "more conceit than capacity" (*elatior quam capacior*),[23] and what Augustine hopes to do for them is to return them "to the beginning and right order of faith, realizing at least what health-giving medicine is provided for the faithful in holy church, wherein the observance of piety heals the feeble mind for the perception of unchanging truth."[24] Piety, then, is the principal instrument of purification, the best medicine; it is a necessary condition for coming to be in a condition such that the right judgments about God can be made.[25] The function of argument, then, is to return the impious to piety, not to convince them of the truth.

These points can be further developed by looking at what Augustine says about the act of judgment. In the ninth book of *On the Trinity*, he provides an analysis of judgment in the context of a discussion of the relations that connect the mind (*mens*) with its self-knowledge (*notitia sui*) and self-love (*amor sui*). He begins by making a distinction between coming to know transient particulars by way of empirical investigation, and coming to know changeless universals by way of rational contemplation. The act of judgment, strictly speaking, belongs only to the former. If, for example, I tell you what

---

21. "[S]ed mortalitatis onere praegravati, cum et videri volunt scire quod nesciunt, et quod volunt scire non possunt; praesumptiones opinionum suarum audacius affirmando, intercludunt sibimet intelligentiae vias," *De trinitate* 1.1.1.

22. This desire could well be called the fundamental desire evident in European philosophy from Spinoza to Kant.

23. *De trinitate* 1.2.4.

24. "[A]d initium fidei et ordinem redeant, iam sentientes quam salubriter in sancta ecclesia medicina fidelium constituta sit, ut at perceptionem incommutabilis veritatis imbecillem mentem observata pietas sanet," *De trinitate* 1.2.4.

25. The theme that faith has a necessary priority over knowledge because only faith can effectively purge the mind of its impurities is everywhere in Augustine. A locus classicus is *De civitate dei* 11.2: "Sed quia ipsa mens, cui ratio et intellegentia naturaliter inest [yes, these capacities are natural, in the sense that they belong definitionally to the mind], vitiis quibusdam tenebrosis et veteribus invalida est [but they are unavailable, corrupted and sickened by shadows] non solum ad inhaerendum fruendo verum etiam ad perferendum incommutabile lumen [the shadows are so dark and deep, the sickness so bad, that we cannot even endure, much less enjoy, God's light], donec de die in diem renovata atque sanata fiat tantae felicitatis capax fide primum fuerat inbuenda atque purganda [to be imbued with faith is the only way to be restored to cognitive health]."

I am thinking or feeling at a particular time, I am making and stating a judgment about a transient particular (I will soon be thinking or feeling something else, after all), and I do this by paying attention to what is going on in my mind (*quid in se ipso agatur attendens*, as Augustine puts it). If, by contrast, I tell you something about mind in general or as such, I am intuiting a changeless truth (*intuemur inviolabilem veritatem*). Error in judgment, then, belongs to those acts in which I improperly attribute a property to a particular. Error in this sense cannot belong to rational contemplation. There I can only fail to conform my mind to the changeless, which is not, *stricto sensu*, an error; rather, it is an absence.[26]

To illustrate this, Augustine considers the case of forming a judgment that a particular person is virtuous solely upon the basis of testimony: You hear good reports, and thus come to make the judgment that *S is a virtuous person*. Then you meet the person and discover that in fact he is not virtuous. Your judgment about him changes: The love that had been kindled in you toward what you had thought was his virtue is now brought up short, repelled, and then removed by the fact of that virtue's absence[27]—but what your love had really always been directed to was not this man's supposed virtue, but rather a "form of unmoved and stable truth . . . which continues in serene eternity to bathe my mind's eye with the selfsame light of the most pure and incorruptible reason."[28] The making of a judgment about a particular is, in this view, always the application of a universal truth to that particular. It is a judgment of the form *S is k*, where *S* is some particular (a supposedly virtuous man), and *k* is some universal, a "form of unshakable and stable truth" (*forma inconcussae ac stabilis veritatis*). Such a judgment is true when the particular of which it is made really does have the property in question; it is false when it does not.

Augustine's concern in offering this account of forming judgments about particulars is to emphasize that every such act involves appeal to universal truths grasped by an intuitive act of reason (*rationalis mentis intuitu*). You make a false judgment about a particular by incorrectly judging that the particular has a specific property it lacks or lacks a specific property it has. For example, you think, *This man is virtuous*, when he is not, or you think, *This man isn't virtuous*, when he is.

---

26. Augustine's account of error belongs in this respect with his account of evil as *privatio boni*. The mind whose loves are rightly ordered cannot fail properly (though not fully) to understand what it contemplates; the *rationalis mens* whose loves are not rightly ordered simply cannot contemplate what it should. There is, I think, a deep similarity between the Augustinian understanding of the act of judgment (here inadequately summarized) and the varieties of criterial immanentism analyzed and excoriated by Alan Torrance in this volume. (See Alan J. Torrance, "*Auditus Fidei*: Where and How Does God Speak? Faith, Reason, and the Question of Criteria.") Since the Augustinian version of Platonist epistemology is so deeply rooted in Christian (not just Augustinian—versions of it are present implicitly or explicitly in at least the contributions to this volume by David Bentley Hart, Mark McIntosh, and Martin Bieler, in addition to this one) thought, this may indicate a rent of genuine and enduring importance in the fabric of Christian thought. (See Hart, "The Offering of Names"; McIntosh, "Faith, Reason, and the Mind of Christ"; and Bieler, "The Theological Importance of a Philosophy of Being.")

27. "[S]tatim amor ille, quo in eum [sc., the man who has been reported virtuous] ferebar, offensus, et quasi repercussus, atque ab indigno homine ablatus," *De trinitate* 9.6.11.

28. ". . . forma inconcussae ac stabilis veritatis . . . eadem luce incorruptibilis sinceríssimaeque rationis et meae mentis aspectum . . . imperturbabili aeternitate perfundit," *De trinitate* 9.6.11.

Augustine further describes the formation of a judgment by saying that it is a kind of internal utterance (*verbum*), conceived in the mind by love. Internal utterances (judgments) are all *notititiae cum amore*. All such judgments are necessarily conceived (Augustine here plays with the meanings of conception) in response to the changeless form of truth (which is God). There is nothing else to which they could respond, but the love that brings the internal utterance into being may not be directed to God. It may, instead, be directed toward a creature rather than the Creator, and Augustine makes the distinction terminologically by saying that *amor* is always involved in making a judgment but that the *amor* may be *caritas* (when responsive to the Creator) or *cupiditas* (when responsive to the creature). A judgment conceived in *cupiditas* will, when it comes to birth—which means when it is actively applied to some particular—result in sin.[29] Indeed, the distinction between the conception (formation) and birth (active application) of a judgment can, according to Augustine, only be made when sin is involved. When the will does not rest in the act of knowing but in addition wishes to gain what is known, there is a separation between knowing and getting the good, and this separation makes sense only when *cupiditas* is in play. The just man forms an accurate judgment about the nature of justice and wants nothing more; he is already just, and so "his will rests content in that very judgment."[30] The unjust man forms a judgment about the nature of political honor and fame, but he cannot rest there; he must act in such a way as to obtain these things, but in so acting he is committing himself to a misapprehension of what they are, falsely thinking of them as things that might satisfy.

The upshot of this discussion is that for Augustine theoretical error is typically (perhaps always) a product of the will.[31] A judgment brought to birth along with covetous desire requires that what is known, though known accurately insofar as it is known at all, is, because of the weight of cupidity, placed under the sign of self-interested desire, and as a result misconstrued, increasingly and with passionate depth, as something of independent interest and worth. As that mistake occurs, it perpetuates and deepens itself until the object of desire becomes increasingly obscured by misjudgments produced by disordered love. Finally, the mist of error is all that remains, but it is a mist stirred by the will, ontologically empty but capable nonetheless of diverting attention from the eternal truths, and as a result producing cognitive error, misjudgment.

For Augustine, then, an erroneous judgment such as *Some swans are black* (he assumes that none are) is produced by the will leading thought (*cogitatio*) by the nose, as it were, through the things hidden away in the memory (*per*

---

29. "Nascitur autem verbum cum excogitatum placet aut ad peccandum aut ad recte faciendum," *De trinitate* 9.8.13.

30. "[V]oluntas in ipsa notitia conquiescit," *De trinitate* 9.9.14.

31. For precisely the same point, see Martin Bieler's discussion of Aquinas on the importance of the will in assent to the truth of faith, and especially his quotation of *Summa theologiae* 1,111,1 ad 1, which follows slightly more fully than he gave it: "[I]ntellectus enim assentit veritati fidei, non quasi convictus ratione, sed quasi imperatus a voluntate; nullus enim credit nisi volens ut Augustinus dicit" (the quotation is from Augustine's exegesis of John 6:44). See Bieler, "Theological Importance of a Philosophy of Being," p. 304 in this volume.

abscondita memoriae), and prompting it to take something from here and something from there (the idea of a black thing and the idea of a swan, for instance), and then to combine them into "something we call false" (*aliquid quod ideo falsum dicatur*), which is to say something found neither in the external world nor in the storehouses of the memory.[32] Will (*voluntas*), as Augustine says again and again, provides weight (*pondus*);[33] it directs or guides or forces (all tropes he likes) *cogitatio* to assemble a falsehood, to bring together truths in such a way as to paint a picture of a nonexistent.

One of the chief tasks of Augustine's entire corpus is to elaborate this view of the will as the principal producer of intellectual error. Here is one beautiful passage, the full exposition of which would require many pages:

> For it [*mens*, the mind] sees internally some beauties belonging to God's excellent nature, but instead of standing still in the enjoyment of these things [*eis fruatur*], as it should, it wants to award them to itself [*volens ea sibi tribuere*] and to become like him in its own right [*ex se ipsa quod ille est*] instead of being like him because of him [*ex illo similis illius*]. And so the mind turns away from God, becoming unstable and sliding downward into what is less and less but seems more and more [*moveturque et labitur in minus et minus, quod putat amplius et amplius*]. The result is that neither itself nor anything else suffices for it as it recedes from the one who alone suffices. And so, in its poverty and difficulty, the mind becomes excessively concerned with its own actions, and with the troubling delights [*inquietas delectationes*] which it gathers from them; and as a result of its compulsive desire for the acquisition of knowledge from things external to itself [*cupiditate acquirendi notitias ex iis quae foris sunt*] . . . it loses its security.[34]

This is an account of the fall transposed into psychological and epistemological key.[35] The mind ends by being mistaken about the nature of the delights it sees, but this mistake is produced by an act of the will: *volens ea* [sc. *pulchra*] *sibi tribuere*. Without that continuing act of the will, there is no conceptual mistake; with it, acts of reasoning in every theoretical sphere will be deeply and inextricably connected with error, even though not always erroneous.[36]

---

32. I paraphrase fairly freely here from *De trinitate* 9.10.17.

33. For *voluntas* as *pondus* see, strikingly, *De trinitate* 11.11.18, in allusive exegesis of Wis 11:21 (Vulgate enumeration), one of Augustine's favorite texts: ". . . sed omnia mensura et numero et pondere disposuisti."

34. *De trinitate* 10.5.7.

35. A much more detailed account is given in the twelfth book of *De trinitate*, and 12.14 is especially tropically rich. The *anima* slips and slides (*prolabitur*) away from what is common to what is private; it wants (*appetens*) something more than everything, and so is subject to concupiscence (*avaritia, cupiditas*); as a result, it spends its life fornicating with phantasms. See Paul Agaësse's discussion of this passage and the tropes associated with it in *La Trinité: Livres VIII–XV*, Oeuvres de Saint Augustin 16 (Paris, 1997), 620–24.

36. Lois Malcolm's discussion in this volume of the theology of the cross's implications for understanding human reason is relevant here. Crucifixion of the *cupiditas acquirendi notitias* is just what Augustine would have wanted. See Malcolm, "The Wisdom of the Cross."

Volitional Depravity and Inadequate Catechesis

The application of Augustine's account of reasoning's theoretical errors is clear. Theoretical reasoning goes wrong for him not in a technical fashion but because of disordered love. Our capacity for accurate reasoning (in the theoretical sphere, at least) is, therefore, indexed closely to the order of our loves.[37] Offering argument to those in error will therefore usually be an attempt to correct an affective and cognitive disorder with a technical device: The device will have no purchase. What those in cognitive error then need is encouragement to piety rather than argument.[38]

There is a difficulty at this point. Augustine seems at times to want to make volitional depravity not only sufficient but also necessary for reasoning's theoretical errors. If that is the correct view, then all I have said above about the importance of catechesis requires modification or abandonment, for what those comments amount to is the claim that inadequate or improper catechesis may also suffice for reasoning's theoretical failures. How then may these two views be reconciled?[39]

In brief, I suggest that catechetical inadequacy and volitional depravity each suffice for the occurrence of certain kinds of error in theoretical reason, most especially for inability to recognize a true judgment as true and a valid argument as valid. But neither is necessary. This means that catechetical inadequacies of various kinds may occur without volitional depravity, and that deep volitional depravity may go hand in hand with good catechesis (an anti-Donatist view of the nature of the church suggests this latter position). Diagnosis of the nature and extent of the presence of both in particular interlocutors will be required if productive argument is to be had.

But whatever is the case about the relative weight of each in predisposing people to err in their use of theoretical reason, they together account for the vast majority of cases of such error. If I am faced with a valid argument whose premises are true and I cannot recognize it as such, the cure for this condition will almost never be found in the offer of further argument. I will need either appropriate catechesis or increase of piety, and I am unlikely to be persuaded to either by argument. It follows from this position, I think, that the position here argued about how reasoning goes wrong will, if correct, be persuasive only to those rightly catechized and volitionally not too depraved. It does not, as a position, avoid its own strictures, and it can meet its own desiderata.

The position argued here is also compatible with (and has been illuminated by) Bruce Marshall's view, argued in his contribution to this volume,[40] that the world requires of those who inhabit it neither Trinitarian theism nor

---

37. Mark McIntosh's contribution to this volume is to be understood in significant part as an analysis of how love comes to be reordered and of what it is (cognitively) like to think and judge and know with love thus reordered. See McIntosh, "Faith, Reason, and the Mind of Christ."

38. For a much fuller account of what reasoning informed by piety would be like, refer to Ernstpeter Maurer's account of redeemed reason and Carver Yu's of covenantal reason, both in this volume. See Maurer, "Perplexity and Complexity," and Yu, "Covenantal Rationality."

39. In the remarks that follow, I depart from (and perhaps contradict) what Augustine thinks, but further exegetical work would be required in order to show this.

40. Bruce D. Marshall, "Putting Shadows to Flight: The Trinity, Faith, and Reason."

nihilism. Trinitarian theism is of course true, but recognizing this will typically require about as much catechesis as assenting to some variety of nihilism. That this is so is among the truths entailed by any properly nuanced Christian theological anthropology. Such an anthropology requires a decent epistemology, after all.

The position briefly set forth in this essay calls into question, as it is meant to and among other things, the dream of appealing to natural law in order to provide a broadly persuasive ordering of common life in a late-modern democracy, for there, if anywhere, we move in the sphere of theory. That dream is impossible and should be abandoned forthwith. The position argued also suggests—and this I take to be among its principal advantages and blessings—that when we Christians attempt to speak reasonably to non-Christians (or indeed to one another) we should speak from the full depth of our knowledge and without the procrustean *epoche* so often forced upon us by having to pretend that what we know is known by the exercise of reason alone. When Christians begin to argue as John Locke (in *The Reasonableness of Christianity*) or Immanuel Kant (in *Die Religion innerhalb der Grenzen der blossen Vernunft*) did,[41] the gospel has been abandoned.

---

41. Locke and Kant, of course, both called themselves Christians. But neither was remotely orthodox, and among the principal reasons for their lack of orthodoxy is precisely their understanding of the relations between specifically Christian commitments and public argument. Janet Soskice's essay in this volume on the difference between attribution of properties to God (à la Locke) and naming God (à la Pseudo-Dionysus and Aquinas) makes it abundantly clear wherein Locke's abandonment of Christian orthodoxy lies. (See Soskice, "Naming God.") One of the deep ironies and oddities of contemporary Christian intellectual life is that among the most conservative Christian intellectuals, Catholic and Protestant, is to be found adherence to a view of reason and argument that is functionally indistinguishable from that of eighteenth-century Europe's cultured despisers of religion.

CHAPTER SEVEN

The Directedness of Reasoning and the Metaphysics of Creation

— Reinhard Hütter —

The Directedness of Reasoning and the Crisis of Metaphysics—Why It Matters Theologically

It is hard to imagine a gulf deeper than the one that currently exists between those who regard human reason[1] in terms of utmost triumph and those who regard it in terms of utmost despair. Mathematically disciplined and technologically executed, human reason has transformed the globe in unprecedented ways. The academic disciplines based on reason's mathematical and technological acumen hold a robust trust—if not faith—in reason's capacity to grasp reality and, precisely because of this grasp, successfully to conform the world to human interests and needs.

Ironically, there is simultaneously a widespread sense of despair about reason's superior status and role. Instead of sovereignly guiding human affairs to their clearly defined and well-considered ends, human reason seems to be little more than a coping mechanism or a regulative fiction driven and directed by instincts and desires it can hardly perceive, much less rule. The academic disciplines that traditionally draw upon reason's reflexive, integrative, and directive capacities—as exercised by humanity in the act of understanding and interpreting both world and self—have fallen into a state of internal disarray

---

1. In the following, I refer to "reason" and "intellect" as fundamentally the same faculty. However, each stands for a particular aspect, insofar as reasoning is the discursive movement of the intellect. That is, "reason" carries the active connotation of the verbal form "to reason." The one implication of this internal differentiation that matters most in the following is that the faculty of the will has a larger effect on the discursive movement of reasoning than on the most basic act of apprehending intelligible truth. Similarly, I regard speculative and practical reasoning as particular aspects of the same faculty. As will become clear later, I follow in this Thomas Aquinas. Cf. esp. his *Summa theologiae* I.79.8–11. (For consistency's sake, all citations from the *Summa theologiae* [ST] in English are taken from the translation of the Fathers of the English Dominican Province, *St. Thomas Aquinas Summa Theologica* [New York: Benziger Brothers, 1948]. The Latin original offered in the footnotes is taken from Sancti Thomae de Aquino, *Summa Theologiae*, 3rd ed. [Turin: Edizioni San Paolo, 1999], which offers an improved version of the Leonine edition.)

while finding themselves exiled into what by all accounts seems to be a state of permanent marginalization within the late modern university. Reason triumphing in the form of instrumental rationality has produced its own demise as famously analyzed in Max Horkheimer and Theodor Adorno's *Dialectic of Enlightenment*.[2]

This arguable state of affairs is obviously not just an ivory-tower phenomenon, remote from and largely irrelevant to human society at large. Rather, the simultaneous triumph of and despair about reason mirrors late modern society as such: We encounter breathtaking developments in artificial intelligence and biotechnology together with atmospheric epistemological skepticism and ontological nihilism. The very triumph of instrumental rationality seems to invite simultaneously the most radical questioning of reason itself: What drives reason relentlessly and breathlessly from success to success? Is it propelled by something situated "behind" its very gaze? If so, is reason's gaze directed in ways it can neither account for nor alter? Moreover, if reason were directed and driven in such a way, what actually would allow us to assume a sovereign—and, for that matter, first of all, coherent—self?

Precisely at the time when instrumental rationality came fully into its own, no one raised this suspicion more forcefully than Friedrich Nietzsche.[3] In many ways contemporary scientific reductionism is doing nothing other than still catching up with Nietzsche's radical vision. Consider the following three samplings from Nietzsche's sprawling *oeuvre*:

> What then is truth? A movable host of metaphors, metonymies, and anthropomorphisms: in short, a sum of human relations which have been poetically and rhetorically intensified, transferred, and embellished, and which, after long usage, seem to a people to be fixed, canonical, and binding. Truths are illusions which we have forgotten are illusions; they are metaphors that have become worn out and have been drained of sensuous force, coins which have lost their embossing and are now considered as metal and no longer as coins.[4]

> There exists neither "spirit," nor reason, nor thinking, nor consciousness, nor soul, nor will, nor truth: all are fictions that are of no use. There is no question of the "subject and the object," but of a particular species of animal that can prosper only through a certain relative rightness; above all, regularity of its perceptions (so that it can accumulate

---

2. Max Horkheimer and Theodor W. Adorno, *Dialectic of Enlightenment: Philosophical Fragments*, ed. Gunzelin Schmid Noerr, trans. Edmund Jephcott (Stanford, CA: Stanford University Press, 2002).

3. Cf. Jürgen Habermas's way of situating Nietzsche's thought as the entrance into postmodernity in his *Philosophical Discourse of Modernity: Twelve Lectures*, trans. Frederick G. Lawrence (Cambridge, MA: MIT Press, 1987). Habermas's lecture on Nietzsche is especially instructive, because he rightly understands Nietzsche to be the catalyst both of *the critique of metaphysics* as developed by Heidegger and more recently by Derrida and of *skeptical science*, a science of suspicion based on the pervasiveness of the will to power in and behind all "knowing" as it was worked out in anthropological, psychological, and historical ways by Bataille, Lacan, and Foucault.

4. Friedrich Nietzsche, "On Truth and Lies in a Nonmoral Sense," in *Philosophy and Truth: Selections from Nietzsche's Notebooks of the Early 1870's*, trans. and ed. Daniel Breazeale (Atlantic Highlands, NJ: Humanities Press, 1979), 84.

experience). Knowledge works as a tool of power. Hence it is plain that it increases with every increase of power. The meaning of "knowledge": here, as in the case of "good" or "beautiful," the concept is to be regarded in a strict and narrow anthropocentric and biological sense. In order for a particular species to maintain itself and increase its power, its conception of reality must comprehend enough of the calculable and constant for it to base a scheme of behavior on it. The utility of preservation—not some abstract-theoretical need not to be deceived—stands as the motive behind the development of the organs of knowledge—they develop in such a way that their observations suffice for our preservation. In other words: the measure of the desire for knowledge depends upon the measure to which the will to power grows in a species: a species grasps a certain amount of reality in order to become master of it, in order to press it into service.[5]

If the morality of "thou shalt not lie" is rejected, the "sense for truth" will have to legitimize itself before another tribunal:—as a means of the preservation of man, as *will to power*.

Likewise our love of the beautiful: it also is our shaping will. The two senses stand side-by-side; the sense for the real is the means of acquiring the power to shape things according to our wish. The joy in shaping and reshaping—as primeval joy! We can comprehend only a world that we ourselves have made.[6]

Nietzsche's aphorisms press the matter in a radicalness that goes well beyond the soft reductionism of contemporary science. Yet before we get locked into the question whether Nietzsche is right or wrong, it is of foremost importance to acknowledge the degree to which both the epistemological skepticism and the ontological nihilism implicit in his rigorous exercise of suspicion have become the unexamined conventional wisdom of the intellectual class that occupies the so-called humanities in countless college and university faculties.[7] Arguably, Nietzsche represents the end of a road that a relentless voluntarism, first theological and later philosophical, engendered.[8] One of the disturbing characteristics of this by now widely accepted voluntarism is the ease with which it is capable of accelerating the triumphs of instrumental reason while at the same time holding truth to be a by-product of this very

---

5. Friedrich Nietzsche, *The Will to Power*, trans. Walter Kaufmann and R. J. Hollingdale (New York: Vintage Books, 1968), aphorism 480.

6. Ibid., aphorism 495.

7. The unexamined horizon is normatively Nietzschean in its fundamentally anti-metaphysical (that is, both anti-epistemological and anti-ontological) stance of celebrating "difference" for its own sake and of assuming "perspectivism" as an unquestioned first principle. Precisely because the intellect is driven and ruled by powers it can neither fully understand nor control, identity politics (being the uncritical acknowledgment of the ontological primacy of the will to power) has to replace discourse, reasoned argumentation, and the possibility of genuine insight. It does not much matter whether one favors Zizek's Lacanian reading of Schelling's *Ages of the World*, Vattimo's kenotic ontology, Rorty's neopragmatism, Foucault's archaeology of knowledge as a genealogy of power—for when hard-pressed, they all ultimately presuppose and rely upon an unexamined yet normatively assumed Nietzschean horizon.

8. Cf. Michael Allen Gillespie, *Nihilism before Nietzsche* (Chicago: University of Chicago Press, 1995), for a compelling account of the rise of modern nihilism from the seedbed of Ockham's voluntaristic theology.

process—a process that is meaningless in and of itself or, better put, simply self-referential, thereby tacitly affirming another tenet of Nietzsche's nihilism: the eternal return of things. Under the name of the god Dionysus, Nietzsche conceives being as a totality enfolded by the circularity of the eternal return. The very point of the eternal return is to negate the goal-oriented striving of the human, in short, to cancel out intentionality as well as teleology as the decisive parameters of human distinctiveness.

Yet while the question whether Nietzsche is right or wrong can be postponed, it cannot be avoided. If it is indeed the case that reason is ultimately directed by something that can at best only partially become the object of its gaze but that nevertheless actually *makes* humans by their reason able to negotiate reality by ceaselessly creating coping mechanisms, does then human life not simply become identical with coping with reality and, ultimately, coping as such? If reason indeed is nothing other than the extremely complex neural coping mechanism of a highly developed mammal, not only is reason then driven and directed by forces largely out of its control, but even more so, human reality becomes indistinguishable from the rest of the world, with the result that the intellectual procedure of scientifically penetrating reality must itself be understood as just a particularly effective moment of human coping. At the end of this road of scientifically objectifying human beings stands utter self-estrangement. As Robert Spaemann aptly put it, "The human being becomes an anthropomorphism to itself."[9] It seems quite obvious that, while the referents of such anthropomorphism can very well constitute the proper subject matter of scientific inquiry, a sheer anthropomorphism itself can hardly qualify as the proper subject and agent of such an inquiry. Yet because of scientism's determined avoidance of genuine philosophical reflection, this contradiction remains hidden to most, if not all, contemporary reductionist trends. However, as soon as reflection arises, it is hard to miss the fact that the very conditions of the possibility of science and scientific truth are of a metaphysical quality. That is, they are of immediate relevance to any scientific enterprise, yet at the same time, they antecede the particular set of subject matters of each individual science.

The assumption that there exists an investigation that is capable of exploring the principles of reality as they antecede and thus make possible the particular sciences is what has fallen into a deep crisis, a crisis intensely experienced since Nietzsche. To offer just one useful contemporary example, from the tradition of analytic philosophy, of what currently is in crisis: "We need to stand firm on the idea that the structure of elements that constitutes a thought, and the structure of elements that constitutes something that is the case, can be the very same thing."[10] The very fact that this idea needs to be articulated, that it calls for a philosophical defense in light of its pervasive questioning, that ultimately it might need to be held as a conviction instead

9. Robert Spaemann, "Ende der Modernität?" in *Philosophische Essays*, 2nd ed. (Stuttgart: Reclam, 1994), 240: "So wird der Mensch selbst sich zum Anthropomorphismus."

10. John McDowell, quoted in Fergus Kerr, *After Aquinas: Versions of Thomism* (Oxford: Blackwell, 2002), 29.

of simply constituting the unstated horizon of philosophical investigation precisely reflects what some lament as the "crisis of metaphysics" and most laud as the "end of metaphysics."[11]

Theology is deeply affected by the crisis of metaphysics, and this not only because theologians have drawn upon and transformed the tradition of metaphysics for at least fifteen hundred years.[12] Rather, the reason theology is affected by the crisis of metaphysics is of a genuinely *theological* nature. If the logos that elicits faith and legitimates theology is a contingent word spoken, a willful positing, such that it can in no way be related to the way things are and vice versa, and, more importantly, such that the way things are cannot be disclosed by this logos, such a "logos" only intensifies the specter of the will by placing one willful positing over against others, so that the last ground of reality is nothing but the agonism of warring wills and their contingent positings. Yet precisely because Christian theology is bound to the God whose Logos is from all eternity God, properly Christian theology will always have a metaphysical moment, in that it rightly expects that the structure of the world and the structure of the human mind should indeed correspond because they were *made* to correspond.[13]

The crisis of metaphysics is by now well established in the form of moments of "postmetaphysical thought," characterized by the familiar agonistic strategies of "situating," "outbidding," "unmasking," and "overcoming." It is quite difficult for theology not to fall into this trap of contending discursive strategies and their agonistic positings. For, indeed, Nietzsche's challenge cuts to the very core of the human being; indeed, his is a quasi-theological challenge that he wants to be understood as such. Would it not be most natural to face this challenge with a counterchallenge, that is, to posit theology's own normative horizon with the same apodicticity with which Nietzsche is eager to presuppose quite a different horizon? Yet it is theology's normative horizon itself that disallows it to succumb to this agonistic temptation, precisely because of the very nature of the horizon. For the following three fundamental

---

11. Readings of this "crisis" or "end" abound. For an accessible and representative reading, see Jürgen Habermas, *The Philosophical Discourse of Modernity* and his *Postmetaphysical Thinking: Philosophical Essays*, trans. William Mark Hohengarten (Cambridge, MA: MIT Press, 1992). Part of modern philosophy itself can be read as the crisis of metaphysics in the mode of its reflection, while other parts represent conscious efforts to overcome the crisis or to disprove the end of metaphysics. For the former, see Walter Schulz, *Philosophie in der veränderten Welt* (Pfullingen: Neske, 1972), and *Ich und Welt: Philosophie der Subjektivität* (Pfullingen: Neske, 1979). For the latter, see the remarkable intellectual heritage of Catholic philosophy in the nineteenth and twentieth centuries documented in *Christliche Philosophie im katholischen Denken des 19. und 20. Jahrhunderts*, ed. Emerich Coreth, SJ, Walter M. Neidl, Georg Pfligersdorffer, 3 vols. (Graz: Styra, 1987–1990). Currently, one can observe a surprising return to metaphysical themes in analytic philosophy. See esp. John McDowell, *Mind and World*, and Robert Brandom, *Making It Explicit: Reasoning, Representing, and Discursive Commitment* (Cambridge, MA: Harvard University Press, 1994). See also Philip Clayton, *The Problem of God in Modern Thought* (Grand Rapids: Eerdmans, 2000), 3–49.

12. David Bentley Hart's essay in this volume, "The Offering of Names: Metaphysics, Nihilism, and Analogy," offers a penetrating theological meditation of the problems that arise when metaphysics emancipates itself from its theological roots.

13. Cf. Josef Pieper, *Philosophia Negativa: Zwei Versuche über Thomas von Aquin* (Munich: Kösel, 1953), 20ff. For a way to rigorously unfold such an account of theology's "logos" being enabled by, accountable to, and responsive to the Logos, God's Word, who is Jesus, yet to let this theology of the Word itself do all the metaphysical work possible by construing it as a christological metaphysics, see Colin Gunton and Robert W. Jenson's essay in this volume, "The *Logos Ensarkos* and Reason."

beliefs constitute the horizon of theology: First, the world is created, that is, it is in its nature completely different from, and in its existence completely dependent upon, God. Second, the human being is created in the image of God. Third, the human being is called to a communion of vision and love with the God who is love. An important entailment of these three beliefs is the further belief that in this communion human beings receive a fulfillment that consumes and infinitely surpasses its created capacity so that truth, freedom, and love are seen and experienced as one and the same reality. The epistemic key and ontological cornerstone to these three fundamental beliefs are the person and work of Jesus Christ. While the following remarks do not unfold an explicit Christology, they are possible only in light of the Chalcedonian convictions of Christian orthodoxy. To put it more strongly, it is precisely Chalcedonian Christology in conjunction with a doctrine of creation that must conceptually unfold *creatio ex nihilo* and that suggests, if not entails, what I will call a "metaphysics of creation."

Under postmetaphysical conditions, these three fundamental beliefs, constituting the horizon of theology, seem very much like a willful positing, yet they are not. Rather, they convey a truth that is first of all suffered, like all genuine truth, and therefore is in no way a product of theology and therefore at its disposal.[14] Precisely in order to resist the temptation of agonism, theology has to be attentive to the metaphysical moment that simply is entailed in the belief that the world is created.[15] Thus, while it can be argued on the basis of the truth of the Christian faith that epistemological skepticism and ontological nihilism are false, it is equally important to press the criterion of internal consistency by showing that they involve a significant moment of performative self-contradiction.[16] Again, the reason for the latter's importance is not to propagate a philosophy "pure" of theological commitments but rather to avoid the agonism of willful positing by allowing theology to show on grounds other than its own substantive commitments that epistemological skepticism and ontological nihilism are untenable positions. This way of unfolding its metaphysical moment does not weaken Christian theology. Nor is this metaphysical moment to be confused with the modern apologetic strategy of defending the truth of the Christian faith on terms alien to its

---

14. See my *Suffering Divine Things: Theology as Church Practice* (Grand Rapids: Eerdmans, 2000); and Bruce D. Marshall, "*Quod Scit Una Uetula*: Aquinas on the Nature of Theology," *The Theology of Thomas Aquinas*, ed. Rik Van Niuewenhove and Joseph P. Wawrykow (Notre Dame, IN: University of Notre Dame Press, 2005), 1–35; 14, where he quotes Aquinas: "The name for this sort of knowledge is 'wisdom, a kind of knowledge by taste'—a wisdom which comes not first from learning, but from 'suffering divine things' (*patiens divina*)" (quoting ST I.43.5 ad 2 and referring also to ST II-II.45.2, II-II.97.2, ad 2 and I.1.6 ad 3).

15. Cf. Hans Urs von Balthasar, *Theo-Logic: Theological Logical Theory*, vol 1, *Truth of the World*, trans. Adrian J. Walker (San Francisco: Ignatius, 2000).

16. While it usually does not amount to a conclusive argument, such a demonstration can, next to relentlessly uncovering the performative self-contraction embedded in the positions criticized, address their unresolved problems and the paucity of the conceptual resources employed to answer those problems. For such ways of discursive demonstration, see Alasdair MacIntyre, *Three Rival Versions of Moral Inquiry* (Notre Dame, IN: University of Notre Dame Press, 1990), esp. ch. 9, "Tradition against Genealogy: Who Speaks to Whom?"; and Robert Spaemann, *Personen: Versuche über den Unterschied zwischen "etwas" und "jemand"* (Stuttgart: Klett-Cotta, 1996), as well as in many of his essays collected in his *Grenzen: Zur ethischen Dimension des Handelns* (Stuttgart: Klett-Cotta, 2001).

substance. On the contrary, its very metaphysical moment strengthens Christian theology simply by putting the fundamental belief to work that creation makes sense and communicates this sense to the intellect. It is thus especially in the middle of the crisis of metaphysics that theology cannot afford to embrace the postmetaphysical Zeitgeist.

Indeed, Christian theology cannot remain indifferent to the challenge posed by epistemological skepticism and ontological nihilism, for at least two reasons. First, the very practice of theology as faith seeking understanding depends on the assumption that rational inquiry is not simply a function of sub- and preconscious drives, be they directed to human survival or to the expression of an allegedly omnipresent and omni-efficient will to power. Second, it is only Christian theology that has achieved a full conceptual recognition and analysis of the will by developing profound accounts of the epistemological effects of sin.[17] In multiple ways, the postmetaphysical privileging of the will's rule over reason is to be best appreciated as simply parasitic on the Christian intellectual tradition. Yet deprived of their crucial hamartiological, christological, and ultimately soteriological contexts, these postmetaphysical accounts necessarily become distorted and wreak epistemological and ethical havoc. Ironically, because of their broad cultural diffusion, tacit Nietzschean assumptions have become the normal, if not normative, intellectual and ethical horizon for numerous Christians who are culturally literate but catechetically illiterate.

It is this confused and confusing mixture of cultural literacy and catechetical illiteracy that we find forcefully addressed in Pope John Paul II's encyclical, *Fides et Ratio* (1998). After critically assessing the various problems implied in contemporary philosophical eclecticism, scientism, and pragmatism, the encyclical touches upon the central feature of modern reductionism:

> The positions we have examined lead in turn to a more general conception which appears today as the common framework of many philosophies which have rejected the meaningfulness of being. I am referring to the nihilist interpretation, which is at once the denial of all foundations and the negation of all objective truth. Quite apart from the fact that it conflicts with the demands and the content of the word of God, nihilism is a denial of the humanity and of the very identity of the human being. It should never be forgotten that the neglect of being inevitably leads to losing touch with objective truth and therefore with the very ground of human dignity. This in turn makes it possible to erase from the countenance of man and woman the marks of their likeness to God, and thus to lead them little by little either to a destructive will to power or to a solitude without hope. Once the truth is denied by human beings, it is pure illusion to try to set them free. Truth and freedom either go hand in hand or together they perish in misery. (no. 90)

---

17. See most recently Merold Westphal, "Taking St. Paul Seriously: Sin as an Epistemological Category," in *Christian Philosophy*, ed. Thomas P. Flint (Notre Dame, IN: University of Notre Dame Press, 1990), 201–26.

While a theology engulfed by the crisis of metaphysics may laud postmeta-physical thought as a welcome moment of relief, such celebrations are as shortsighted as they are short-lived. Rather, by attending to the question of how reason and will relate, contemporary theology acknowledges the crisis of metaphysics and with it the dominating specter of the will. Yet how might we go about this task under present circumstances? Alasdair MacIntyre once said to me in a personal conversation that if one does not know anymore how to go forward, it is helpful to trace one's steps backward in order to find another way forward. Heeding this recommendation, I will proceed in the following argument largely by moving backward.

First, I will offer a sketch of the grammar of Christian thought of how faith, reason, and will interrelate in multiple and complex ways. While pri-marily a delineation of the constraints upon properly Christian thought about *ratio* and *fides*, what is said in this section is in principle also open to being found illuminating and possibly convincing to non-Christians. (The latter is crucial if the agonism of willful positing is to be avoided.) In the course of this preliminary meditation, the fundamental reality of judgment comes into view so as to offer a path on which to retrace our steps concerning the question of reasoning's directedness.

Second, I will turn to Thomas Aquinas in order to explore his complex yet rewarding way of analyzing the relationship between intellect and will. I have chosen Aquinas as my main interlocutor for more than one reason. First, I have been convinced by MacIntyre's argument in *Three Rival Versions of Moral Inquiry* that Aquinas is the most promising point to which to retrace our steps from the swampy regions of late modern discourse we currently find ourselves in. Moreover, I have chosen Aquinas for ecumenical reasons. He is the one theologian of the common tradition whose work still has to endure the most withering attacks by unwarranted Protestant prejudice: an Aristotelian distorting and obfuscating of the kerygma; a facile theology of glory oblivious to the centrality of Christ and his cross; an intellectualism that falls short of appreciating human depravity and especially the bondage of the will; and finally, a theology that harmfully privileges Pseudo-Dionysius and Aristotle over against the witness of Scripture. While recently both Catholic and Protestant scholarship has addressed and refuted most, if not all, of these false assumptions, the arguments fall on deaf ears for those eager to hold on to prejudices that help cement the walls between divided Christian communi-ties. Hoping against hope, I have returned to Aquinas in order to invite Protestants to take, next to Augustine, this arguably most important theolo-gian of the common Western tradition with a renewed seriousness.[18] Finally, I have chosen Aquinas because I think he offers the most fruitful answer to the problem I have sketched above. If there is a way forward, it is a way with

---

18. Ideally, I should have brought Aquinas and Luther into a direct conversation on the directedness of reasoning. Yet this would have surpassed the scope and format of this essay and will have to wait for a later time. For an account of sinful and redeemed reason that follows in Luther's footsteps, albeit in a Wittgensteinian manner, see Ernstpeter Maurer's essay in this volume, "The Perplexity and Complexity of Sinful and Redeemed Reason."

and from Aquinas, a way that I will intimate toward the end of the essay. My engagement of Aquinas will simply follow the way the central activity of judgment—involving both the act of the intellect and that of the will—is affected by the great disturbance of and offense to all self-sufficient wisdom: the reality of sin and the centrality of Christ. It thus will take the following form: judgment of *esse*—judgment in crisis—redeemed judgment—the conflict of judgments.

An account of the judgment of *esse* will provide the necessary backdrop for exploring how Aquinas relates intellect and will. An all-too-facile intellectualist reading of Aquinas will be called into question by considering his treatment of the intellectual vice of curiosity, which paradigmatically displays the reality of judgment in crisis. Aquinas's penetrating analysis of curiosity offers surprisingly fresh insight into why a "philosophy of genuinely metaphysical range" (*Fides et Ratio*) is a necessary component of his overall theological project and why it takes the form of a metaphysics of being. When transfigured by the normative horizon of the Christian faith, that is, by a redeemed judgment, the metaphysics of being is open to being elevated and assumed into the metaphysics of creation.[19] Finally, I will address with and from Aquinas the ongoing conflict of judgments we will encounter as long as reason remains for many "a prisoner to itself."[20] It is a metaphysics of creation that in the very conflict of judgments prevents theology itself from becoming just a willful positing and from thus becoming trapped by that agonism that flourishes wherever the specter of the will looms large.

Reason, Faith, and the Centrality of Judgment

Fides and *ratio* are highly complex force fields that constantly overlap and presuppose each other, although not in strictly reciprocal ways. Faith reasons in order to explore the reasons of faith (*fidei ratio*).[21] Yet reason in its own comprehensive reaching toward truth constantly anticipates—in a kind of faith, *rationis fides*—an antecedent coherence that is already presupposed in any process of inquiry.[22] As an inherently teleological activity, rational inquiry

---

19. See Martin Bieler's essay in this volume, "The Theological Importance of a Philosophy of Being," for a penetrating analysis of Aquinas's metaphysics of *esse* and its theological relevance.

20. *Fides et Ratio*, no. 23, referring to Rom 1:21–22. The full quote reads in the English translation: "The eyes of the mind were no longer able to see clearly: reason became more and more a prisoner to itself. The coming of Christ was the saving event which redeemed reason from its weakness, setting it free from the shackles in which it had imprisoned itself." For an inquiry into the tension between the encyclical's insistence on reason's self-imprisonment and its concomitant insistence on the possibility of a "philosophy of a full metaphysical range," see the chapter "Freedom, Truth, and the Will," in my *Bound to Be Free: Evangelical Catholic Engagements in Ecclesiology, Ethics, and Ecumenism* (Grand Rapids: Eerdmans, 2004), 194–208.

21. See Karl Barth, *Anselm: Fides Quaerens Intellectum. Anselm's Proof of the Existence of God in the Context of His Theological Scheme*, trans. Ian W. Robertson (London: SCM Press, 1960).

22. See esp. Michael Polanyi, *Personal Knowledge: Towards a Post-Critical Philosophy* (Chicago: University of Chicago Press, 1962). One of the key problems of modernity is the erosion of the faith that grounds reason, that is, the *rationis fides* that reason has to have in the teleological coherence of both reality and its own "intelligere" of reality. This is a problem that is acutely reflected in Kant's "Critique of Teleological Judgment" (*Critique of Judgment*, §§61–91). For a pertinent critique of modern rationality and a constructive way forward, see Carver T. Yu's essay in this volume, "Covenantal Rationality and the Healing of Reason."

needs to anticipate the existence of the goal for which it aims (this goal being not a particular object but an insight in which the inquiry's investigative motion comes to rest).[23] The *rationis fides* differs substantively from the *fides* that ultimately is the gift of the Spirit and the beginning of participation in God's life. How is this so? Let us first consider *rationis fides*, which is constituted in a twofold manner.

First, *rationis fides* is constituted by *being ordered toward truth*. Let me formulate this claim in the form of a thesis: *Rationis fides* is the anticipation of the unity of the truth that is the *telos* of any ordered inquiry. This thesis is not uncontroversial. Some might concede that philosophy is in some sense an "ordered inquiry." Yet based on an argument like the following, they would deny that this makes it teleological: "Order" can be used to designate only formal relations among concepts, for example, in mathematics or predicate calculus. Yet here, I think, we need to distinguish between purely logical investigations based on analytic judgments that bracket any consideration of reality, on the one hand, and inquiries directed to aspects of what is, on the other. In the case of the former, truth is contained in the logic of the terms themselves; in the case of the latter, truth of being itself is the end that the inquiry anticipates in its investigative intention.

On a deeper level, we need to maintain that truth is the end of *ratio*, that toward which *ratio* is always directed and ordered and in which *ratio* finds its fulfillment. While this is unquestionably a reasonable assumption, it is difficult to demonstrate. It seems that there are at least two ways of arguing for this claim. The first is negative: We say that everyone who argues against this claim commits a performative contradiction (i.e., in the very act of reasoned argumentation, reasoning displays its directedness toward truth—otherwise, why argue in the first place?). The second is positive: We interpret the phenomenon of *ratio* as something whose reception we cannot antecede—in short, as a given. Givenness, in turn, must be understood either as emergence or as gift. The strategy of explaining reason as an emergent phenomenon has to face the problems inherent in reductionism; it needs to think about reason in ways that contradict the very act of thinking itself, an act that has ontological and teleological implications that defy any reductive strategies. Therefore, we need to understand *ratio* as a gift integrally given in the comprehensive giftedness of creation. As an integral element of the gifted matrix of creation, *ratio* can rightly be assumed to have an end (*telos*) that is capable of being fulfilled. Yet every end is the end of a potentiality. The recognition of truth is the end of *ratio*'s potentiality.

Thus, Christian theologians should be committed to the view that *ratio* is teleologically ordered toward truth, with rational inquiry being reason's proper pursuit of its actuality and *rationis fides* being the confidence in *ratio*'s directedness toward truth.

Second, *rationis fides* is constituted by *being informed and directed by the will*. *Rationis fides* contains the tacit assumption of the *liberum arbitrium*, a

---

23. Since the insight gained will not be exhaustive but will raise new questions, there will never be a final rest to the intellect's motion of inquiry.

will that is free in that it is reason's own capacity to choose not only the goal of inquiry but also all the means necessary to pursue it. In critical reflection we are free to relate to the way we do things. However, we are unable to relate freely to our critical relating—unless we are liberated by being drawn into a freedom that allows us to relate to our relating by being shaped, rectified, and transformed in ways we could not have even anticipated without this liberation.[24] Thus, the *rationis fides* rests on something that transcends its capacity of anticipation: the quality of its willing. Yet reason in being ordered toward truth does not seem to have the capacity to determine or transform the quality of that will that directs it.

At this point the fundamental problematic of our inquiry arises: As long as the will remains unthematized, *rationis fides* remains untroubled. But as soon as the will is thematized, the question of reason's directedness by the will (and consequently reason's liberation from the will's incurvature) emerges with full force.

After having considered *rationis fides*, we need now to turn to faith itself. In its strict theological sense, *fides* must be clearly differentiated from *rationis fides*, for *fides* is the *active reception* of an inexhaustible yet concrete personal truth, a reception in and through which the believer begins to participate in the divine freedom. By desiring communion with God as the highest good, the believer's will is rectified and thus is conformed to the *telos* of God's own will in Christ. Thus, faith is inseparably both reception and actualization of this truth, which is characterized by the following constitutive elements: (a) *existentially, fiducia* as the comprehensive existential relying on the gift and its giver in the gift; (b) *intellectually*, the intellect receiving a new formal object—revealed truth as its first truth; (c) *volitionally*, the will being directed to communion with God as its highest good; and (d) *intentionally*, the will being conformed to God's own will in Christ. Thus, both intellect and will become part of the actualization of the gift.

Fidei ratio signifies the conceptual as well as substantive exploration (*fides quaerens intellectum*) of this received truth as *ratio* is guided and informed by faith. This exploration occurs through reason's participation in the freedom that *is* the will's conformation to the *telos* of God's will. Yet at the same time, this exploration continuously draws upon concepts forged by a reason that enacts its faith in the prolepsis of the unity of truth (*rationis fides*). Because of the nature of *fides*, *fidei ratio* brings to the fore what remains hidden to the inquiring process of *ratio* as such, being essential to its gaze: the constitution of the human as a self (the human's *concrete existence* and his/her relationship to himself/herself)[25] and the central role of the will in it.

In order to conclude our preliminary considerations, we need to consider *judgment*. The "red thread" between faith and reason seems to be *iudicium*,

24. I am drawing here on the work of Robert W. Jenson, esp. his "Ontology of Freedom," *Modern Theology* 10 (1994): 247–52, and his *Systematic Theology*, vol. 2 (New York: Oxford University Press, 1999), 105ff.

25. Søren Kierkegaard remains the most important analyst of this complex and ultimately unfathomable reality. See esp. his *Sickness unto Death*, ed. and trans. Howard V. Hong and Edna H. Hong (Princeton, NJ: Princeton University Press, 1980).

"judgment." There can be no sustained process of rational inquiry without continuous judgments regarding the subject matter at hand and the arguments advanced so far. In the course of any rational inquiry, the *rationis fides* is enacted in and through the act of judging. Similarly, there can be no *fidei ratio* without continuous judgments regarding the subject matter at hand and the arguments advanced. The decisive question seems to be, Is "judgment" simply a matter of the intellect as such, or does it somehow involve the will's operation—not just concerning the obvious case of external action but concerning the less obvious case of what one might call the mind's activity of judging? The "will" here addressed might better be described as reasoning's directedness—that which constitutes the horizon of the gaze in which judgments are made. This gaze is not just conceptual but volitional. Not only does the intellect move the will in light of particular judgments, but the will also exacts a constant impact on the intellect by directing it in light of the good to which the will is drawn. "Rectitude of mind" indicates an intellect directed by the will that is drawn to the ultimate good. Yet rather than remaining an abstraction, the ultimate good, the triune God, through efficacious grace, heals and redirects the will so that a fundamentally renewed mind "may discern what is the will of God—what is good and acceptable and perfect" (Rom 12:2). And for "discern" we could as well say "judge," since a renewal of discernment always issues in a renewal of judgment.[26] Thus, discerning or judging what the will of God is presupposes the renewal of our mind. Yet this renewal of our mind, which we cannot "will" but can only receive, presupposes an antecedent misdirectedness of our will. By implication, therefore, our mind is directed in ways we de facto intend (and thus our judgments are always the uncompelled and, in this sense, "free" enactment of our reasoning) but are neither able to perceive nor free to change.[27] (Willfully changing our reasoning's directedness would have to assume a will^y that would redirect our will^x.)

We have reached the appropriate point for formulating the guiding thesis of this inquiry. If what has been posited above obtains, we can meaningfully raise the question of reasoning's directedness only from within a horizon in which the problem, at least in principle, is already overcome. *Only within the horizon of faith, reason now being informed by a renewed will that is beginning to be redirected toward communion with God as its highest good, can the will as such become a sufficient object of reason's inquiry and can* fidei ratio *therefore consider the will's incurvature and thus appreciate what was and is at stake in its own directedness to proper ends.*

Before we turn to Aquinas, it is important to register three central assertions that are constitutive of *fidei ratio*. First, *credere* must always be conceived as

---

26. On the intricate relationship between discernment and judgment, see Lois Malcolm's exegesis of Paul in her essay, "The Wisdom of the Cross," and for the way the Eastern fathers drew upon this crucial link in order to give an account of "the mind of Christ," see Mark McIntosh's essay, "Faith, Reason, and the Mind of Christ," both in this volume.

27. This relationship between willing and thinking (here *phronein*) can also be observed in Phil 2:5 and 13. In Phil 2:13 it is emphasized that God effects the willing and the doing, and it is precisely on this basis that the exhortation in Phil 2:5 ("Let the same mind be in you that was in Christ Jesus") gains real momentum. The redirection of the mind implies a changing of the will that must be effected by God.

the act of grace in which we are liberated to participate freely and thus "decide" not *for* grace but *on the basis* of grace. Second, the cross stands for the ultimate and most radical establishment of wisdom received in faith. And the reception of this wisdom entails the reception of a freedom in which the will is absorbed in its ultimate good, that is, conformed to God's will.[28] *This is the genuine freedom in which reason can confidently develop again its genuine and original metaphysical range of inquiry.* Third, *iudicium* is central. If grace either perfects or recreates human nature (and the one must be conceived of in ways as radical and fundamental as the other), we will need to assume that *iudicium*, "judgment"—standing at the very core of the human's interaction with everything else, including himself/herself—is most centrally affected by this perfection or re-creation.[29]

We have finally reached the point of turning our attention to Aquinas. What will an engagement of Aquinas bequeath? It will open the possibility of a theological reading of the will that avoids the trap of an unrestrained voluntarism. At the same time, such an engagement will open up the space for a metaphysics of creation. More than just a particular philosophy, it is a necessary location for being able to think on the basis of creation and to expect conceptual and substantive guidance from creation—even and especially when judgment is in crisis.

Thomas Aquinas on the Directedness of Reasoning

Judgment of *Esse*

The concept of judgment is the central pillar of Aquinas's metaphysics of creation. This concept secures the realism fundamental to the whole, that is, it preserves the inherent coherence and integrity of creation by starting with the central assumption of the intellect's essential fittingness and thus unfathomable connectedness to reality.[30] Because the world, being creation, must be conceived antecedently as thought (*gedacht*)—or, better, as thought out (*erdacht*)—by God, the intellect grasps the simple essence of things and thus arrives at true judgments about them.[31]

Despite the strengths of this concept, one must wonder whether "judgment," conceived as fitting *in rebus naturalibus*, is nevertheless abstracting from a fundamental aspect of reality and thus remaining an abstract ideal in problematic ways. Why? This concept of judgment does not reflect on the

---

28. For a detailed exegetical and theological exposition of the "wisdom of the cross" and its epistemological implications, see the essay by Malcolm.

29. For an account of how the spirituality and theology of the East was profoundly informed by this recreated *iudicium*, that is, by the "mind of Christ," see McIntosh, "Faith, Reason, and the Mind of Christ."

30. For a detailed historical account of Aquinas's metaphysics, see John F. Wippel, *The Metaphysical Thought of Thomas Aquinas* (Washington, DC: Catholic University of America Press, 2000); and for a more systematically constructive interpretation, W. Norris Clarke, SJ, *Explorations in Metaphysics: Being—God—Person* (Notre Dame, IN: University of Notre Dame Press, 1994), 45–64, 102–22. In his essay "Theological Importance," Bieler offers a pertinent critique of Wippel's account of Aquinas's alleged use of "acts of being."

31. I am drawing here on the section "Wahrheit als Erdachtsein," in Josef Pieper, *Philosophia Negativa*, 20–23.

concrete existence under the condition of sin of the one who judges, an existence that raises the pressing question of reasoning's directedness. While correct judgments about pencils, dogs, roses, rectangles, and black holes are not endangered and called into question in principle by this reservation,[32] at least all judgments that appertain to the existence of the ones who judge—that is, persons—are fundamentally affected by it. And insofar as reflection upon the previously listed kinds of largely unproblematic judgments (whether implicitly or explicitly, but always inherently) involves the concrete *existence* of the one who reflects upon them, reasoning's directedness under the condition of sin unavoidably comes into play.

Is our excursion into Aquinas's thought on this matter already over before it really begins? It simply depends on whether we attempt to read his metaphysical account of the judgment of *esse* in an implicitly modern sense, that is, as an epistemology that is isolated from the concrete existence of the person who thinks, wills, and judges, or whether we understand Aquinas's account of judgment in the wider encompassing horizon of his theology. Crucially, Aquinas's wider, theologically informed horizon addresses the interrelationship between intellect and will that underlies the act of judgment. Aquinas addresses this interrelationship, first, by identifying intellect and will as distinct powers of the soul (ST I) and, second, by inquiring into their concrete enactment under the condition of sin (ST I-II and ST II-II). As will become sufficiently clear in the course of my argument, in order to be able to address both, Aquinas's account presupposes the very horizon of a redeemed judgment in which theology's discursive knowledge is informed by *sacra doctrina* increasingly bearing the stamp of the *scientia Dei* itself (ST I.1.3. ad 2).

The Human Being—Made in God's Image
Before plunging into the deep waters of Aquinas's account of the complex interaction between intellect and will, we need to acknowledge the warning that a noted Aquinas scholar recently expressed: "No one can do justice to Aquinas's theory of the will in a few pages. It is rich, complicated, and controversial, and a thorough treatment of it would require a book-length study."[33] Moreover, it is important to realize that in his *Summa theologiae*, Aquinas places his inquiry into the nature of the human being squarely into an explicitly *theological* horizon. He does so by drawing upon Augustine's *imago*-doctrine, which he received by way of Peter Lombard's *Sentences*. Yet this dependence upon Augustine is not simply a matter of the history of ideas. It is, rather, a matter of substance. Aquinas's anthropology represents nothing less than a philosophically argued yet theologically motivated and driven line of reasoning about the human being as created in the image of God. And

---

32. However, as Martin Bieler rightly pointed out to me, the psychiatric syndrome of "depersonalization" teaches us that the despair that arises from a fundamentally disoriented reasoning can even endanger correct judgments about matters of everyday life.

33. Eleonore Stump, "Intellect, Will, and the Principle of Alternate Possibilities," in *Christian Theism and the Problems of Philosophy*, ed. Michael D. Beaty (Notre Dame, IN: University of Notre Dame Press, 1990), 266. I have profited greatly from Stump's concise account of Aquinas's complex theory of the will, esp. as she unfolds it in her most recent magisterial account, *Aquinas* (London: Routledge, 2003).

if it indeed obtains that the human being is created in God's image, this quality must constitute the first formal principle of any subsequent claims about human nature. Aquinas locates this first formal principle in the form of the human, that is, the soul. He does so by distinguishing between, on the one hand, the end, or terminus, of God's act of creation and, on the other, perfection of this image through grace and the light of glory, that is, the gratuitous gift of communion with the triune God.[34] In short, Aquinas's anthropology is governed by a multilayered, complex structure: the human created in the image of God yet deeply wounded by the reality of sin and gratuitously directed toward restoration and perfection of the image, which reaches its completion only as human beings find themselves in personal communion with God, a communion gratuitously granted by the triune God through the Spirit in Christ and enacted as a communion of knowing and loving.[35]

Intellect and Will

In order accurately to appreciate Aquinas's analysis of the intricate interrelationship between intellect and will, we need to distinguish between his earlier, intellectualist leaning, up to the completion of ST I, and a later, more voluntarist leaning that comes to the fore with the inception of ST I-II and especially in *De malo* 6.[36] We need to gain first a solid appreciation of the earlier, intellectualist emphasis[37] in order to appreciate the nature of the specific shift to the later, nuanced voluntarism.

Aquinas understands intellect and will as two distinct yet mutually interrelated powers of the soul, the intellect naturally and of necessity adhering to the first principles[38] and the will adhering to the universal good as its proper object (ST I.82.1). Thus, perceived in abstraction from the concrete enactment of these two potencies, that is, simply according to their proper nature,

---

34. Cf. D. Juvenal Merriell, *To the Image of the Trinity: A Study in the Development of Aquinas' Teaching* (Toronto: Pontifical Institute of Medieval Studies, 1990), 153–235, esp. 168–69.

35. ST I.93, esp. articles 5 and 8; but see also ST I.45.7 and 43.3. The subsequent 114 questions of the *Prima secundae* and 189 questions of the *Secunda secundae* need to be read as an interpretation of this dynamic *imago Dei* or, better, as an investigation of all those aspects through which the human being already is the image of God and still—gratuitously—is to be restored and perfected in that image. Cf. Otto Hermann Pesch, *Die Theologie der Rechtfertigung bei Martin Luther und Thomas von Aquin* (Mainz: Matthias Grünewald, 1967), 401ff.; and Yves Congar, "Le sens de l'économie' salutaire dans la 'théologie' de S. Thomas d'Aquin (Somme theologique)," in *Festgabe Joseph Lortz*, vol. 2, ed. Erwin Iserloh and Peter Manns (Baden-Baden: Bruno Grimm, 1958), 73–122, esp. 105.

36. Rather than a radical change of mind, I want to interpret this shift as a change of emphasis and as a final clarification of the will as a power of the soul that is fully independent from the intellect. My account of Aquinas's later, voluntarist emphasis depends on Otto H. Pesch's detailed study "Philosophie und Theologie der Freiheit bei Thomas von Aquin in quaest. Disp. 6 De malo," *Münchener theologische Zeitschrift* 13 (1962): 1–25. I find convincing Pesch's chronological arguments that suggest that *De malo* was written shortly after ST I-II.1–21 (i.e., between 1270 and 1272, during Aquinas's second stay in Paris) and thus represents the latest phase of Aquinas's reflections on the relationship between intellect and will. On the particular historical cause for Aquinas's change of emphasis, see Pesch, "Philosophic und Theologic der Freiheit," 4–5.

37. For the sake of economy, I will draw exclusively upon ST I in order to establish Aquinas's earlier account in its most accomplished and concise form.

38. That is, *prima intelligibilium principia*. These principles are the first concepts formed by the intellect when a human being comes into contact with the sensible. On the historical context of Aquinas's discussion of sense and intellect, see the instructive account by Edward P. Mahoney, "Sense, Intellect, and Imagination in Albert, Thomas, and Siger," in *The Cambridge History of Later Medieval Philosophy*, ed. Norman Kretzmann, Anthony Kenny, Jan Pinborg, and Eleonore Stump (Cambridge: Cambridge University Press, 1982), 602–22.

Aquinas regards the will as the striving that emerges from the intellect's power of cognition. The movement of the will is the inclination toward something. Yet being a property inherent in the intellect's potency, the will is an essentially intellectual capacity and therefore an inclination to a good that is recognized as such. Thus, the will inheres in the intellect as that unique ground that moves it toward the good that the intellect has perceived as such.

Despite the clear distinction between intellect and will insofar as they are considered in principle, there obtains an intricate interrelationship between the two, which Aquinas discusses first under the question of "Whether the Will Is a Higher Power Than the Intellect" (ST I.82.3). The upshot of Aquinas's complex analysis in this article is that both powers include one another in accordance with their proper natures. For this reason the will itself can be the proper object of the intellect's inquiry.[39] Moreover, for the same reason, the will moves the intellect—but only in one particular way. On the one hand, Aquinas draws upon the distinction between the intellect's inherent relationship to the first principles and the will's orientation toward the universal good, and on the other hand, upon their particular interrelationship in the interplay of all the powers of the soul. This distinction allows for the following relationship: "But if we consider the will as regards the common nature of its object, which is good, and the intellect as a thing and a special power, then the intellect itself, and its act, and its object, which is truth, each of which is some species of good, are contained under the common notion of good. And in this way, the will is higher than the intellect, and can move it" (ST I.82.4 ad 1). Thus, insofar as the intellect's act and its object—that is, truth—are subsumed under the common notion of good, both of them fall under the common nature of the will's object, that is, that toward which the will is unfailingly bent: the good. In other words, because the will moves all faculties of the soul to their proper end, the will moves the operation of the intellect[40] to its proper end. And so Aquinas concludes his reflection upon the

---

39. ST I.82.4 ad 1: "If, however, we take the intellect as regards the common nature of its object and the will as a determinative power, then again the intellect is higher and nobler than the will, because under the notion of being and truth is contained both the will itself, and its act, and its object. Wherefore the intellect understands the will, and its act, and its object, just as it understands other species of things, as stone or wood, which are contained in the common notion of being and truth." If, supposedly, the will were superior or prior to the intellect, an investigation of the will would be a futile enterprise, since in this case the will would be both the agent and the object of the investigation, the result of which consequently would be only a play of forces contingent upon the will's particular whims. Interestingly, these "whims," by sleight of hand, assume a certain intellectual capacity of the will itself, yet a capacity clearly in service of desires that have no intellectual ground but rather form a preintellectual vortex of forces.

40. Following Aristotle's De anima, Aquinas distinguishes between the capacity of abstraction, that is, the agent intellect (intellectus agens) that abstracts from sense experience of particular things to form (confused) ideas, and the capacity of understanding, that is, the possible intellect (intellectus possibilis) that receives those ideas and develops them via the process of discursive reasoning into concepts. Underlying the agent intellect and the possible intellect is a more fundamental receptive act of the intellect that earlier Aristotelian commentators called nous pathetikos. Aquinas gestures to this primal intellective act of undergoing or suffering reality in ST I.79.2 ("Et sic intelligere nostrum est pati") and in De malo 3 a4 corp., where he refers to the intellect as "cuius actus consistit in recipiendo ab exteriori: unde dicitur quod intelligere est pati quoddam." For detailed accounts of Aquinas's complex way of relating active and possible intellect, see Robert E. Brennan, OP, Thomistic Psychology: A Philosophic Analysis of Man (New York: Macmillan, 1941), esp. ch. 6; and most recently, Robert Pasnau, Thomas Aquinas on Human Nature: A Philosophical Study of Summa theologiae 1a, 75–89 (Cambridge: Cambridge University Press, 2002), ch. 10.

interrelationship between intellect and will with the following summary: "From this we can easily understand why these powers include one another in their acts, because the intellect understands that the will wills and the will wills the intellect to understand. In the same way, good is contained in truth, inasmuch as it is an understood truth, and truth in good, inasmuch as it is a desired good" (ST I.82.4 ad 1).[41] In short, the will moves the intellect as an efficient cause, while the intellect moves the will as a final cause—that is, the will wills the intellect to understand, and therefore the will itself can be a proper object of the intellect's inquiry, while the intellect's understanding offers the will those goods toward which it inclines itself.[42]

As stated above, we can observe a remarkable shift in emphasis between Aquinas's teaching in ST I, which reflects and systematizes his earlier thought, and his later work in ST I-II and especially in *De malo* 6. Instead of moving the will, as a final cause, the intellect's operation is reduced to that of a formal cause, that is, to the role of presenting the object to the will and thereby offering a specification of the will's act.[43] In other words, the intellect as the will's formal cause does not suffice anymore to activate the will. Rather, lest the origin of the will's movement be thought to rest solely in the will itself— the will thus becoming its own prime mover, which would entail denying the will to be part and parcel of creation—God must be understood as the first mover of the will.[44] This change of emphasis, however, does not at all affect the intellect's distinct and proper mode of operation. Rather, now the will's unique character as completely independent of the intellect's operation comes into much sharper relief. Hence, while most emphatically not being its own first cause, the will is the proximate cause of its own motion: "The will when moved by God contributes something, since the will itself acts even though God moves it. And so the will's movement, although from an external source as the first source, is nevertheless not coerced."[45]

Judgment in Crisis

How are intellect and will now affected by sin? Aquinas approaches this question with a fundamental Augustinian commitment, quoting in the *sed contra* of ST I-II.74.1 Augustine's statement that "it is by the will that we sin, and live righteously."[46] On the basis of his previous discussion of the nature of will and intellect as powers of the soul, Aquinas identifies the will, being

---

41. "Ex his ergo apparet ratio quare hae potentiae suis actibus invicem se includunt: quia intellectus intelligit voluntatem velle, et voluntas vult intellectum intelligere. Et simili ratione bonum continetur sub vero, inquantum est quoddam verum intellectum; et verum continetur sub bono, inquantum est quoddam bonum desideratum" (82.4 ad 1).

42. The intellect also comprehends its own operation as intellect (ST I.87.3 ad 1).

43. ST I-II.9.1.

44. Cf. ST I-II.10.4 and *The De Malo of Thomas Aquinas*, trans. Richard Regan, ed. Brian Davies (Oxford: Oxford University Press, 2001), 463 (*De malo* 6 ad 4). On the once hotly debated question of the "praemotio physica," see the concise discussion in Gallus M. Manser, OP, *Das Wesen des Thomismus*, 3rd enlarged ed. (Freiburg: Paulusverlag, 1949), 603–25.

45. *De Malo of Thomas Aquinas*, 461(*De malo* 6 corp.).

46. "Voluntas est qua peccatur, et recte vivitur" (*Retractationes* I.9; PL 32, 596).

the principle of voluntary acts, as the principle of sins.[47] This fundamental insight gains crucial importance as Aquinas turns to original sin and asks "Whether Original Sin Infects the Will before the Other Powers" (ST I-II.83.3). In full consequence of his Augustinian position, he claims that original sin regards first of all the will. Recall Aquinas's earlier claim that the will moves the intellect as its efficient cause and his later claim that the intellect does not move the will, that is, as its final cause, but rather operates merely as its formal cause, presenting the object to the will. Both claims now bear surprising fruit in the specification of original sin. Consider Aquinas's remarks in ST I-II.83.3 ad 3: "The intellect precedes the will, in one way, by proposing its object to it. In another way, the will precedes the intellect, in the order of motion to act, which motion pertains to sin."[48] Here it is very important to remember Aquinas's earlier distinction between external acts (falling under the category of *poiesis*, "making") and internal acts (falling under the category of *praxis*, "doing"), that is, desire and knowledge (ST I-II.74.1). The one internal act we are most interested in here is the act of the speculative intellect (*iudicium speculativum*), or, in its Aristotelian rendition, *theoria*.[49] However, Aquinas does not ask explicitly how *theoria* might be affected by the will's sinfully misdirecting the intellect. Rather, because of the particular thrust of ST I-II, where the intellective and volitional movement of humans is perfected by grace and led toward their gratuitous ultimate end, Aquinas focuses on a particular class of internal moral acts, namely, those "acts which do not pass into external matter, but remain in the agent, e.g. to desire and to know: and such are all moral acts, whether virtuous or sinful" (ST I-II.74.1). Does this mean that *theoria*, the act of knowing that is directed to that which is solely and properly the intellect's object, can never be affected by the will and therefore by sin? In short, are we, according to Aquinas, at least epistemologically free from the effects of original sin?

One of the strengths of Aquinas's way of relating intellect and will is his ability to account for how the intellect's proper capacity has not been destroyed by human sin. The intellect is able to come to knowledge and judge properly (yet not inerrantly) in highly complex and nontrivial ways. Might therefore the question of reasoning's directedness, in its very own domain as *theoria*, be a moot one from Aquinas's point of view? Would one, therefore, in order to approach this question at all, have to descend the slippery slope of voluntarism?[50] Is this the very problematic where the late Augustine and

---

47. "Et ideo sequitur quod peccatum sit in voluntate sicut in subiecto" (ST I-II.74.1). Already in ST I.17.1 ("Whether Falsity Exists in Things") Aquinas establishes the will as the principle of sin: "In things that depend on God, falseness cannot be found, in so far as they are compared with the divine intellect; since whatever takes place in things proceeds from the ordinance of that intellect, unless perhaps in the case of voluntary agents only, who have it in their power to withdraw themselves from what is ordained; wherein consists the evil of sin. Thus sins themselves are called untruths and lies in the Scriptures."

48. "[I]ntellectus quoddam modo praecedit voluntatem, inquantum proponit ei suum obiectum. Alio vero modo voluntas praecedit intellectum, secundum ordinem motionis ad actum: quae quidem motio pertinet ad peccatum."

49. On Aristotle's *bios theoretikos*, see Joseph Dunne, *Back to the Rough Ground: 'Phronesis' and 'Techne' in Modern Philosophy and in Aristotle* (Notre Dame, IN: University of Notre Dame Press, 1993), 237–44.

50. J. B. M. Wissink puts the question the following way: "[W]hat would happen theologically, if we were to give priority to the good over truth? Then there could be goodness that remained unknown (even

the late Aquinas might part ways and companionship, the first allegedly calling forth Ockham and Luther, Pascal and Jansenius, the latter the rationalistic self-confidence of nineteenth-century neo-scholasticism?

When we turn to Aquinas's discussion of the vice of curiosity (indeed, a very Augustinian theme), we will realize that Aquinas allows for *theoria*, while not being cognitively defective, to be nevertheless deeply affected by a will sinfully turned away from the ultimate good. Aquinas's late and quite restrained voluntarism, still checked by a robust intellectualism, allows for a nuanced account of reasoning's directedness without falling into the trap of voluntarist skepticism.

The Virtue of Studiousness and the Vice of Curiosity— A Paradigmatic Test Case

Aquinas's treatment of the vice of curiosity is in the *Secunda secundae* of his *Summa theologiae*, an extensive treatment of the virtues, the vices, and the gifts, beatitudes, and fruits of the Holy Spirit that he discussed in the *Prima secundae* in briefer and more formal ways. Curiosity and the respective virtue of studiousness pertain to the cardinal virtue of temperance, that is, the moral excellence that rightly restrains and channels the bodily and intellectual passions that sustain but also endanger human flourishing.[51] In slightly more technical language, Aquinas would regard studiousness as "a subordinate virtue annexed to a principal virtue," that is, temperance, and "to be comprised under modesty" (ST II-II.166.2 corp.), a virtue that in turn is "annexed to temperance as its principal" (ST II-II.160.1 corp.).

It strikes me as important to register early on that seriously discussing studiousness as well as curiosity may look to many contemporary readers like indulging in a most irrelevant intellectual exercise. Yet nothing could be further from the truth than precisely this prejudice. Late modern societies that are fundamentally shaped by the overwhelming presence of electronic media and the obscene inundation of every aspect of human life by pictures and sounds have turned the vice of curiosity into a prescribed way of life. In a world in which curiosity rules, unmasking curiosity as a destructive and offensive vice therefore amounts to nothing less than a most radical critique of a culture of systemic superficiality and constant distraction.[52]

STUDIOUSNESS

Because it provides the crucial backdrop for fully appreciating the deeply problematic nature of curiosity, I will attend first to Aquinas's discussion of

---

for the divine intellect?); the will would become a reality independent of the intellect; ethical positivism would have the last word. Would that be a truly good world?" Wissink, "Aquinas: The Theologian of Negative Theology: A Reading of *ST* I, qq. 14–26," in *Jaarboek Thomas Institute te Utrecht* (1993): 52.

51. "[I]t belongs to temperance to moderate the movement of the appetite, lest it tend excessively to that which is desired naturally" (ST II-II.166.2 corp.).

52. For fundamentally different thinkers converging in their critique of a culture that breeds curiosity and an ensuing superficiality, see Herbert Marcuse's decrying the "tyranny of tolerance" in his *One Dimensional Man: Studies in the Ideology of Advanced Industrial Society* (Boston: Beacon, 1966), and Josef Pieper offering a biting critique of a culture of multimedial distraction in the section "Disciplining the Eye," in his *Four Cardinal Virtues* (Notre Dame, IN: University of Notre Dame Press, 1966), 198–202.

the virtue of studiousness. After establishing that the appropriate matter of studiousness is knowledge, Aquinas turns to the question "Whether Studiousness Is a Part of Temperance" (ST II-II.166.2). In a striking way, a quote from Augustine in the *sed contra* contrasts the three arguments that deny the question and, more importantly, anticipates Aquinas's telling answer: "'We are forbidden to be curious: and this is a great gift that temperance bestows.'[53] Now curiosity is prevented by moderate studiousness. Therefore studiousness is a part of temperance." Precisely because the human being is not just a body but a body informed by an individual intellective soul,[54] the human naturally desires what is appropriate to his soul: *cognoscere aliquid*, "to know something."[55] Unsurprisingly, "the moderation of this desire pertains to the virtue of studiousness." The real and exciting complexity of this seemingly straightforward position only emerges in Aquinas's responses to the objections, two responses in which the problematic of reasoning's directedness is immediately and dramatically relevant.

One of the objections raises the problem that knowledge has no connection with the moral virtues of which temperance and therefore also modesty and studiousness are a part. This is because they root in the appetitive part of the soul, that is, in the will. Knowledge, consequently, seems to pertain only to the intellectual virtues (prudence and its subordinate virtues), which arise from the soul's cognitive part, that is, the intellect. In his response, by implicit reference to ST I-II.9.1, Aquinas first restates the way in which the will directs the intellect: "The act of a cognitive power is commanded by the appetitive power, which moves all the powers." This fundamental insight into the way the will moves all the powers of the soul to their appropriate ends, as discussed above, allows Aquinas to make a critical differentiation. It is the differentiation between the twofold good with respect to knowledge. There is, first, the one that is connected with the act of knowledge itself: "[T]his good pertains to the intellectual virtues, and consists in man having a true estimate about each thing." There is, second, the one that belongs to the act of the appetitive power, that is, the will. And this good "consists in man's appetite being directed aright in applying the cognitive power in this or that way to this or that thing" (ST II-II.166 ad 2). Being able to form the appetite aright in order that this power of the will might rightly apply the cognitive power is what makes studiousness a virtue in the first place. To turn Aquinas's point around: Only because the will indeed does have a specific effect on the intellect does a particular moral virtue pertain to the cognitive power.

Let us turn to the other pertinent objection. Studiousness cannot be a subordinate virtue of temperance because the former does not resemble the latter

---

53. "Curiosi esse prohibemur: quod magnae temperantiae munus est" (*De Moribus Ecclesiae*, Cap. 21: PL 32, 1327).

54. That is, the substance of the human being is determined comprehensively by the intellect (*mens*, or *intellectus*). The *anima intellectiva* is the sole substantial form of the human being; it also governs all of the body's functions. Cf. ST I.76.1–4.

55. It should come as no surprise when Aquinas quotes in this very instance the familiar opening line from Aristotle's *Metaphysics*: Πάντες ἄνθρωποι τοῦ εἰδέναι ὀρέγονται φύσει (All human beings naturally desire knowledge).

in the mode of its operation. While temperance is a kind of restraint that opposes the vice of excess, studiousness seems to be first of all the application of the mind to something that opposes the vice of neglect. Aquinas again responds with a distinction, now between contrary inclinations. He prepares this distinction by drawing upon Aristotle's teaching that in order to be virtuous, one must avoid all that to which one is most naturally inclined. The virtue of studiousness has two seemingly contrary aspects because of the contrary inclination the human being displays regarding knowledge: "For on the part of the soul, he is inclined to desire knowledge of things; and so it behooves him to exercise a praiseworthy restraint on this desire, lest he seek knowledge immoderately: whereas on the part of the bodily nature, man is inclined to avoid the trouble of seeking knowledge" (ST II-II.166 ad 3). Consequently, as it pertains to the first inclination, studiousness constitutes a kind of restraint, but insofar as it pertains to the second inclination, "this virtue derives its praise from a certain keenness of interest in seeking knowledge of things; and from this it takes its name." Thus, studiousness restrains, channels, directs, and applies the cognitive power in a concentrated, sustained, and keenly interested way to the arduous task of gaining knowledge that is appropriate as well as profound.

CURIOSITY

With the virtue of studiousness as necessary backdrop, we are now able finally to turn to the vice of curiosity. How does Aquinas treat the vice of curiosity, and how might the intellect's speculative power, *theoria*, be affected by it? In ST II-II.167.1, Aquinas goes right to the core of the matter by asking "Whether Curiosity Can Be about Intellective Knowledge." First, he reports three objections, a not untypical assemblage of some of the ways strict intellectualists would want to defend the intellect's supremacy from any incursions from the side of the will. Yet again, Aquinas's choice of the *sed contra*, this time not from Augustine but from Jerome, is quite a foreboding of the kind of response that is about to come: "'Is it not evident that a man who day and night wrestles with the dialectic art, the student of natural science whose gaze pierces the heavens, walks in vanity of understanding and darkness of mind?' Now vanity of understanding and darkness of mind are sinful. Therefore curiosity about intellective sciences may be sinful."[56]

Fully consistent with what he has previously established, Aquinas maintains that while knowledge as such is always good, the desire for and study in pursuit of knowledge of the truth may be right or wrong. First, acquiring a particular knowledge may be accidentally linked to evil. Second, the appetite and study that is directed at the knowledge of truth may itself be inordinate. This can be the case in four ways: First, in turning from one's

---

56. "Nonne vobis videtur in vanitate sensus et obscuritate mentis ingredi qui diebus ac noctibus in dialectica arte torquetur, qui physicus perscrutator oculos trans caelum levat?" (*In Ephes.*, Lib. II, super IV[17]; PL 26, 536).

primary obligation to a less useful occupation (as the pastor who, instead of persistently studying the Scriptures and continuing to develop the linguistic and conceptual tools necessary for this task, turns to other, more "interesting" intellectual pursuits such as computer programs or Web sites with ready-to-go sermons, liturgies, and other aids). Second, in seeking knowledge from persons by whom it is illicit to be taught (as the medical student who wants to study the human response to extreme cold with a Nazi physician who gained his knowledge by systematically freezing concentration camp inmates to death). Since I will dwell longer on the third way, I will immediately move to the fourth: in studying "to know the truth above the capacity of [one's] own intelligence, since by so doing men easily fall into error." Aquinas's concern at this point has a striking similarity to the way Paul Griffiths analyzes the nature of error and the respective need for instruction.[57] Because, as already pointed out above, for Aquinas, reasoning is the discursive activity of the intellect, and because any extended and complex argument about the truth of something that transcends epistemic obviousness (*This is a chair; this is a pencil*) easily brings the uninstructed person to the limit of his/her own intellectual possibilities, error becomes increasingly likely, and instruction prior to the informed engagement of one's discursive powers in complex inquiries and their discursive disciplines increasingly necessary. Curiosity in these matters can only amount to dangerous dabbling, while studiousness implies the modesty to acknowledge the necessity of prior instruction.

Finally, we turn to the way most pertinent to our purposes in which the appetite to know can itself be inordinate: in desiring "to know the truth about creatures, without referring [one's] knowledge to its due end, namely, the knowledge of God."[58] Here we finally have Aquinas identifying an inherently restricted—and in this precise sense, misdirected—act of the speculative intellect, or *theoria*. A knowledge of creatures that is not directed to its dutiful end, namely, the knowledge of God, is a distorted, sinful knowledge not because it is faulty in and of itself (that is, there need not be any cognitive defect in this knowledge). Rather, this knowledge becomes distorted, sinful knowledge by its lack of reference to and reverence for the One who grants being in the first place. Knowing "the truth about creatures" unquestionably refers to *theoria*, the speculative act of the intellect directed to everything that is not God or one of God's operations—in short, the full scope of the *ens inquantum ens*. It is Aquinas's response in the *ad primum* that offers additional warrant for this assumption: "Hence there may be sin in the knowledge of certain truths, in so far as the desire of such knowledge is not directed in due manner to the knowledge of the sovereign truth, wherein supreme happiness consists."[59] What a sweeping anticipatory indictment of

---

57. See Paul J. Griffiths, "How Reasoning Goes Wrong: A Quasi-Augustinian Account of Error and Its Implications," in this volume.
58. "Tertio, quando homo appetit cognoscere veritatem circa creaturas non referendo ad debitum finem, scilicet ad cognitionem Dei."
59. "Et ideo potest esse vitium in cognitione aliquorum verorum, secundum quod talis appetitus non debito modo ordinatur ad cognitionem summae veritatis, in qua consistit summa felicitas."

the whole range of modern immanentism this is, be it in philosophy, natural science, or the so-called humanities.[60]

Thus, Aquinas assumes also *theoria* to be affected by sin in that the intellect in its concrete operation is moved in a way that restricts or distracts it from considering its proper end, the knowledge of the ultimate truth and the supreme good, and in this sense misdirects it without necessarily causing a cognitive defect in what is known. Aquinas's nuanced and epistemically restrained voluntarism undercuts the kind of voluntarist skepticism that would arise from the assumption that the will rules unaccountably and irresistibly over the intellect.

Knowing and Reasoning

It is here that Aquinas's subtle distinction between intellect and reason—and hence between knowing and reasoning—to which I alluded earlier does some surprisingly helpful work. It allows us to gain a clearer grasp of the way reasoning can be profoundly misdirected while the intellect's epistemic capacity per se remains unaffected.[61] The latter is actually the very presupposition necessary for reasoning to be misdirected in the first place. Even while being discursively misguided, the intellect always continues to perceive some truth, since this is precisely what allows it to remain in error and not in a state of undifferentiated delusion. Therefore, "the intellect cannot be false in its knowledge of simple essences; but is either true, or it understands nothing at all" (ST I.17.3 corp.). Hence, it is not in the primal intellective act but in the discursive process of reasoning, of linking intellective judgments in one or another way into complex arguments and theories, that the will, and hence the agent, comes into play.[62]

It is useful to remember at this point Aquinas's insight that similar to the intellect, the will is moved in two ways: first, so far as concerns the exercise of its act and, second, so far as concerns what seems to be—or indeed is—a particular good, that is, "the specification of the act, derived from the object" (ST I-II 10.2 corp.).[63] While the will is not able to influence the intellect's basic operation, it is quite able to will that the intellect not continue thinking about

---

60. For a penetrating critique of criterial immanentism and its hegemonic grasp on liberal Protestant theology, see Alan J. Torrance's essay, "*Auditus Fidei:* Where and How Does God Speak? Faith, Reason, and the Question of Criteria," in this volume.

61. Cf. ST I.17.3 corp. ("Whether Falsity Is in the Intellect"): "Now as the sense is directly informed by the likeness of its proper object, so is the intellect by the likeness of the essence of a thing. Hence the intellect is not deceived about the essence of a thing, as neither the sense about its proper object. But in affirming and denying, the intellect may be deceived, by attributing to the thing of which it understands the essence, something which is not consequent upon it, or is opposed to it. For the intellect is in the same position as regards *judging* of such things, as sense is as to judging of common, or accidental, sensible objects. *There is, however, this difference, as before mentioned regarding truth (Q. 16, A. 2), that falsity can exist in the intellect not only because the knowledge of the intellect is false, but because the intellect is conscious of that knowledge, as it is conscious of truth*; whereas in sense falsity does not exist as known, as stated above (A. 2)" (my emphasis).

62. Thomists therefore distinguish between the "order of specification" arising from the object of the (intellective) act, and the "order of exercise" arising from how the agent exists. I am indebted to Romanus Cessario, OP, for this insight.

63. Eleonore Stump rightly points out that according to Aquinas, "If the will is presented by the intellect with an object which can be considered good under some descriptions and not good under others, then the will is not necessarily moved by that object either. . . . It is open to the will not to will that object by willing that the intellect not think about it" (Stump, "Intellect, Will, and the Principle of Alternate Possibilities," 268; cf. ST I.82.2).

something particular and to direct the intellect instead to consider something else. This accounts for the easy distractibility of reasoning in practical as well as theoretical matters.[64]

Instead of considering complex large-scale examples of misdirected reasoning from the history of science, such as "Aryan physics" (opposing Einstein's theory of relativity), or from dialectical-materialist sociology, economy, and history (acknowledged core disciplines of all the bygone Communist regimes), consider the simple case suggested by Eleonore Stump and applicable by family resemblance:

> Suppose that Anna has just won some money in a contest and that she plans to use the money to buy a frilly pink canopy bed for her daughter, something she has been coveting but unable to afford. As she sits reading a magazine, she comes across an advertisement urging readers to give money to support children in third-world countries and showing a picture of a ragged, emaciated child. Anna no sooner glances at the ad than she turns the page. Why does she do so? The answer to the question will, of course, involve the will's issuing commands which result in Anna's turning the page; *but underlying these commands is something like the will's directive to the intellect not to think about the ad and the needy children it describes.* The will makes this directive in virtue of a hasty calculation on the part of the intellect that looking at the ad is not good. . . . Informing or influencing this calculation will be Anna's coveting of the frilly pink canopy bed for her daughter, a passion in Aquinas's sense. Perhaps without the influence of that coveting Anna's calculation about the ad might have been different.[65]

Aquinas's analysis of the vice of curiosity makes it plain why Stump's example, while pertaining to a matter of practical reasoning, can easily be applied to the act of speculative reasoning as well.[66]

---

64. Aquinas offers a complex discussion of this matter in ST I-II.17 ("Of the Acts Commanded by the Will"), in which he applies and extends the highly complex feedback system between intellect and will. Command is an act of reason, yet the very fact that reason moves by commanding is due to the power of the will: "Consequently it follows that command is an act of reason, presupposing an act of the will, in virtue of which the reason, by its command, moves (the power) to the execution of the act" (ST I-II.17.1 corp.). However, the aspect most pertinent to our concern is found in article 6 ("Whether the Act of Reason Is Commanded"), where Aquinas distinguishes between the exercise of the act (which is always commanded "as when one is told to be attentive, and to use one's reason") and the object of the exercise of reason. Here we encounter the crucial distinction between the uncommanded aspect and the aspect that is open to command: "One is the act whereby it apprehends the truth about something. This act is not in our power: because it happens in virtue of a natural or supernatural light. Consequently the act of reason is not in our power, and cannot be commanded. The other act of the reason is that whereby it assents to what it apprehends. If, therefore, that which the reason apprehends is such that it naturally assents thereto, e.g., the first principles, it is not in our power to assent or to dissent to the like. . . . But some things which are apprehended do not convince the intellect to such an extent as not to leave it free to assent or dissent, or at least suspend its assent or dissent, on account of some cause or other; and in such things assent or dissent is in our power, and is subject to our command" (ST I-II.17.6 corp.). Cf. also *De malo* 3 a3 corp.

65. Eleonore Stump, "Intellect, Will, and the Principle of Alternate Possibilities," 269 (italics mine).

66. See Aquinas's discussion of "Whether Falsity Is in the Intellect" in ST I.17.3 and the concise summary he offers in *De malo* 3 a3 corp. of the ways the intellect and the will are moved and not moved. Here again, "regarding the intellect, things necessarily linked to naturally known first principles necessarily move the intellect. . . . But the intellect is not compelled to assent to conclusions if they be not necessarily linked

Toward the Redemption of Judgment

Curiosity's Horizon of Discovery (Metaphysics of Creation) and Its Cure (Grace)

If it is the case that curiosity is the vice that affects *theoria* by restricting and distracting the intellect and by misdirecting the discursive process of reasoning, we need now to ask, What constitutes the horizon from which the vice of curiosity can be identified in the first place? And how can a redirected gaze of *theoria* be suggested at all? Aquinas's third argument in ST II-II.167.1 corp., and especially his response to the first objection, implies that this horizon is nothing less than a theologically motivated and informed metaphysics of creation.[67] How so? Let us recall both passages. First, the pursuit of knowledge may be wrong "when a man desires to know the truth about creatures, without referring his knowledge to its due end, namely, the knowledge of God. Hence Augustine says that 'in studying creatures, we must not be moved by empty and perishable curiosity; but we should ever mount towards immortal and abiding things'" (ST II-II.167.1 corp.). Second, since the sovereign good of humanity consists in the knowledge of the sovereign truth, Aquinas avers, "there may be sin in the knowledge of certain truths, in so far as the desire of such knowledge is not directed in due manner to the knowledge of the sovereign truth, wherein supreme happiness consists" (ST II-II.167.1 ad 1).

What happens in both cases is that in order to specify curiosity as an intellectual vice, as sinfully misdirected reasoning, Aquinas consistently presumes what Robert Sokolowski calls "the Christian distinction" between the Creator and everything (*ta panta*).[68] However, it is precisely this distinction that constitutes the defining mark of the metaphysics of creation over against any other form of metaphysics.

To put it in the form of a thesis: A metaphysics of creation is the necessary horizon (a) to understand why curiosity is a vice and (b) to direct the intellect's gaze to its proper object, the ultimate truth. Yet what do I mean by a *theologically* motivated and informed metaphysics of creation? What differentiates it from other versions of metaphysics, especially an Aristotelian metaphysics, as the science of being as being (*ens inquantum est ens*)? To put it in terms that are possibly too condensed, while a metaphysics of being presupposes the ontological difference between being and beings, a metaphysics of creation admits its dependence "from above" by presuming a second, and ultimately more fundamental, difference. It is the difference between *esse*

---

to naturally known first principles, as is the case with contingent and probable things. Likewise, neither does the intellect necessarily assent to necessary things necessarily linked to first principles before it knows there is such a necessary connection" (*De Malo of Thomas Aquinas*, 245, 247).

67. The following section is relatively brief, since I can happily rely upon Bieler's nuanced and profound treatment of this matter in his essay in this volume, "Theological Importance."

68. Robert Sokolowski, *The God of Faith and Reason: Foundations of Christian Theology* (Notre Dame, IN: University of Notre Dame Press, 1982), 32–33. For the far-reaching implications of this distinction for the question of naming God and for the way modern univocal strategies of attribution differ fundamentally from analogical ways of naming God, see Janet Martin Soskice's essay in this volume, "Naming God: A Study in Faith and Reason."

commune/esse ipsum—an absolute abundant *actus essendi* that is open to both participation (creation) and subsistence (God) and, while abstracting from both, is to be found in both—and *ipsum esse subsistens*, that is, God.[69] Hence, while remaining implicit in the metaphysics of *esse*, the dependence upon *sacra doctrina* and its normative distinction between the Creator and everything else becomes explicit in the metaphysics of creation.[70]

Yet why does the metaphysics of creation antecedently depend upon the metaphysics of being? I cannot improve upon the answer given by Martin Bieler: Precisely because it is "the way of being." Aquinas shows "that creation consists in the gift of being (*esse*): '*Creare autem est dare esse.*' The 'way of being' is the '*dare esse*' by which God in his care is present in all things."[71] Because it allows for the best conceptual expression of the *dare esse*, of the gift of creation, the metaphysics of being is open to being elevated and assumed by the second difference into the metaphysics of creation.[72] And because the metaphysics of creation is an extension of *sacra doctrina* into the metaphysics of being, that is, an expression of *fides quaerens intellectum* that reads the world as God's creation, this move makes the metaphysics of creation vulnerable, dependent upon the conceptual and substantive veracity of the metaphysics of being that it assumes.

A theologically informed metaphysics of creation is constituted by the second, onto-theological, difference because the first, or ontological, difference is dramatically insufficient for understanding the world as *creatio ex nihilo* and, moreover, fundamentally incapable of establishing the horizon that enables us to appreciate the true nature of curiosity in the first place. Rather, only the onto-theological difference between *esse ipsum* and *ipsum esse subsistens*, in which *esse* itself is analogically conceived, fulfills the theological requirement to understand the world as creation.[73]

A metaphysics of creation (a) is able analogically to consider and interrelate all of reality, all of what is, thereby reflecting the intelligible unity in the difference of creation; (b) is inherently directed to and participationally dependent upon divine transcendence because of the centrality of the second difference; and (c) is therefore able intellectively to present to the will the ultimate object of desire, its due end. However, the intellect cannot reform or redirect the will so that the good of the second difference becomes the will's definitive end of desire. Thus, the metaphysics of creation begs the question of the will's primal mover and especially its renewal or healing through grace, so

---

69. For a short and accessible account, see Josef Stallmach, "Der actus essendi und die Frage nach dem Sinn von 'Sein,'" in *Actus omnium actuum: Festschrift für Heinrich Beck zum 60. Geburtstag,* ed. Erwin Schadel (Frankfurt: Lang, 1989), 47–58.

70. Cf., in greater detail, Bieler's section "Aquinas's Philosophy of Being," in his essay "Theological Importance."

71. Bieler, "Theological Importance," p. 311 in this volume.

72. For an extraordinary account of the openness of the metaphysics of *esse* to the metaphysics of creation, see Heinrich Beck, *Der Akt-Charakter des Seins* (Munich: Max Hueber, 1965).

73. Aquinas draws in his metaphysics of creation upon both Aristotle and Plato, yet in the form of a superior synthesis that is made possible by the antecedent assumption of the intellect's due end as also desired by a rectified will, namely, the supreme truth and good. It is precisely the second difference that accounts for why the supreme truth and good do not need to become operative (as knowledge *simpliciter*) in the process of intellectual inquiry.

that, as the intellect is being informed by faith, the will may be informed by charity.[74] In short, a genuine metaphysics of creation always begs Christology and can only achieve its purpose ultimately "after Christ."

Aquinas's discussion of the relationship between intellect and will, assuming reasoning's directedness under the condition of sin, yields at least three crucial insights: First, the metaphysics of creation is a necessary implication of *fides quaerens intellectum*, lest creation remain a closed book to the *fidei ratio*. Second, the metaphysics of creation becomes a criterion for a critical Christian engagement of the philosophies of the day.[75] Third, Aquinas's short remark amounts to a profound indictment of all forms of modern "unbiased" and supposedly strictly empirical research.[76] There is, though, one question that still needs to be addressed: If the metaphysics of creation here identified is understood to be informed by theology, how do the metaphysics of creation and theology relate to each other?[77]

The Explicit Dependence of a Metaphysics of Creation on Theology

The metaphysics of creation explicitly depends on a theological a priori.[78] This is the case, first, because it is ordered by the second difference and, second, because its proper operation presupposes a rectified will that indeed desires what the intellect points to in posing the second difference. Thus, a volitionally sustained and, only therein, successful metaphysics of creation depends on an intervention of grace that is by definition beyond its intellective scope. It is this dependence on a reality it can gesture toward yet cannot account for in the horizon of its proper object of inquiry that makes the metaphysics of creation a disreputable discipline in the modern, post-Enlightenment academy. For the second difference introduces analogicity and, with it, a moment of corrective negativity that will prevent the construction of a conceptually closed "system" or of a dialectical machinery bent on the comprehensive conceptual penetration of reality.[79] While its arguments are in principle universally accessible (assuming the absence of error), a metaphysics of creation will be less

---

74. Assuming that from the root of original sin there unceasingly arises in humanity the incurvature of the will and thus desire bent to inferior ends, directing reasoning in a way that isolates the knowledge achieved from the supreme truth, Aquinas shows himself sufficiently Augustinian to be brought into a fruitful conversation with the other Augustinian: Martin Luther. For two strong, albeit diverging, readings of reasoning's fallenness that privilege the Augustinian moment more strongly than does Aquinas, see the essays by Griffiths ("How Reasoning Goes Wrong") and Maurer ("Perplexity and Complexity") in this volume.

75. For some programmatic reflections in this direction, see Hans Urs von Balthasar, *Von den Aufgaben der katholischen Philosophie in der Zeit*, 2nd ed. (Freiburg: Einsiedeln, 1998).

76. Moreover, in light of Aquinas's perspective, Heidegger's critique of modern metaphysics and science under the category "forgetfulness of being" needs to be understood as a weaker version of Aquinas's own indictment. Heidegger's "forgetfulness of being" is ultimately fated, especially since Heidegger's "last god" remains playfully and painfully hidden in and under being's withdrawal and granting. Thus, Heidegger's way of rendering the issue allows skeptical and nihilistic consequences impossible in Aquinas's thought. For a penetrating critique of Heidegger, see Hart, "Offering of Names."

77. For another way to put the matter, cf. the section "*Analogia Entis* versus *Analogia Fidei*?" in Bieler's essay, "Theological Importance," in this volume.

78. This dependence does not, however, entail that a metaphysics of being (supposing the will's rectification) is in itself unable to grasp the ontological difference between *esse commune* and *esse subsistens*!

79. Therefore, a metaphysics of creation in the spirit of Aquinas would fall neither under the by now quite fashionable *Metaphysikkritik* developed in various forms by Heidegger and Derrida nor under the anti-Hegelian *Systemkritik* of Adorno and his students. On the fundamental difference between a metaphysics of the concept in which dialectic rules (Hegel) and a metaphysics grounded in the second difference

than universally acceptable, not just because philosophy is an intrinsically controversial phenomenon,[80] but more importantly because it requires a see-ing and willing, informed by a particular practice of judgment, that is shared only in historically contingent ways. In other words, a metaphysics of creation presupposes a tradition of discourse with a certain formation of thought and character as well as a will restored to its original destination, namely, desire for the ultimate good. Therefore, the *duplex ordo cognitionis*[81] (as it is implied in a genuine metaphysics of creation) obtains—to use Aquinas's own terms—*simpliciter*; yet under the condition of sin, it obtains only *secundum quid*. Differently put, precisely because the *duplex ordo cognitionis* is the result not of a primal intellective act but, to the contrary, of discursive reasoning, it is in need of magisterial affirmation (Vatican I).[82]

The metaphysics of creation cannot afford to obscure its own dependence upon the appropriate directedness of reasoning, lest the proper activity of judgment be bent by the vice of curiosity. Moreover, it has to reflect upon the fundamental requirement of the formation of thought and character; a will restored to its original destination, necessary for a full judgment of *esse*, becomes vulnerable to the argument from history—a quite strong yet, in and of itself, inconclusive argument.[83] It is a truism and borders on the banal that no tradition and/or school of philosophical inquiry has put forth a set of arguments that has resisted being thoroughly critiqued and eventually under-mined by competing schools (yet not necessarily in conclusive ways).[84] And this vulnerability also is true of the metaphysics of creation. Yet by hamarti-ologically qualifying its concept of judgment by attending to reasoning's directedness in the concrete existence of the one who judges, the metaphysics of creation would be able to offer an account for the reason that it is just a school of thought. At the same time, however, this kind of theologically schooled metaphysics of creation would have the tools necessary to under-stand itself as a tradition of discourse and inquiry not matched by any other philosophical school. This is the case precisely because of its dependence upon a rectification it cannot produce on its own but can only gesture toward in its concrete discursive activity. Hence, hamartiologically humble and his-torically reflective, the metaphysics of creation could interpret the veritable collection of dead—that is, "overcome"—theories that litter the battlefields

and hence ruled by analogy, see Bernhard Lakebrink, "Analektik und Dialektik: Zur Methode des Thomistischen und Hegelschen Denkens," in *Perfectio Omnium Perfectionum: Studien zur Seinskonzeption bei Thomas von Aquin und Hegel*, ed. C. Günzler et al. (Città del Vaticano: Libreria Editrice Vaticana, 1984), 9–37.

80. Cf. Robert Spaemann, "Die kontroverse Natur der Philosophie," in *Philosophische Essays* (Stuttant: Reclam, 1994), 104–29.

81. On this central concern of neo-Thomist philosophy, its magisterial definition at Vatican I, and its relevance for theological formation, see Romanus Cessario's essay in this volume, "*Duplex Ordo Cognitionis.*"

82. Cf. Marshall, "*Quod Scit Una Uetula*," 23ff., with whom I agree about the way theology and philosophy relate for Aquinas. Only regarding the metaphysics of creation, that is, the theological assumption of the metaphysics of being, do I wish he were not as analytically abstaining as, alas, he is.

83. Similarly, Aquinas's proofs of God's existence might hold argumentative force as long as the judg-ment of *esse* is fully in place, as long as we know how to "see," while they lose this force as soon as this formation is lost. Cf. Gustav Siewerth, *Das Schicksal der Metaphysik von Thomas zu Heidegger* (Einsiedeln: Johannes Verlag, 1959), 52–62.

84. Cf. Spaemann, "Die kontroverse Natur der Philosophie."

of philosophical argument as philosophy caught in the incurvature of human existence under the condition of sin and thus fated to exist in the form of the eternal return of its conceptual possibilities.[85] In other words, the metaphysics that draws upon its own history as a tradition of discourse in the horizon of the Christian faith can constructively face the challenge of the coming and going of philosophical schools and trends.[86] Yet at the same time, the metaphysics of creation operates *argumentatively*, like any other rational discourse, very well aware that, as Leibniz once put it, ultimately every argument is an argument *ad personam*, but aware as well that some arguments are coherently and comprehensively better than others.[87]

The Implicit Dependence of Theology on a Metaphysics of Creation

Theology intends the reliability and veracity of its central concepts and their rootedness in the way things are. Only this reliability and veracity open the possibility of a genuine analogical discourse in theology, without which there is neither doctrine nor dogma. Scripture either suggests these concepts explicitly or begs them implicitly. Yet because of their rootedness in the way things are, it should be possible to unfold them, so to speak, on their own—that is, it should be possible for them to make sense on their own. Thus, the metaphysics of creation is ultimately normed by Scripture insofar as it is the latter's fundamental witness that constitutes the horizon that ultimately informs it. Yet insofar as the metaphysics of creation shapes the concepts with which theology operates, it also has a norming effect. But what is this norming effect all about?[88]

Metaphysics of Creation—Metaphysics of *Esse*

As I averred at the beginning of this inquiry, Christian theology is bound to the God whose Logos is from all eternity God, and therefore Christian theology

---

85. For quite a different way of accounting theologically for the comings and goings of philosophical schools and trends, see Paul Tillich, "Philosophy and Fate," in *The Protestant Era* (Chicago: University of Chicago Press, 1948), 3–15.

86. It might be conceivable to read the work of the later MacIntyre in this very way, especially his Gifford Lectures, *Three Rival Versions of Moral Inquiry*. I should hasten to emphasize that the disputability and vulnerability characteristic of a theologically—or, better, hamartiologically—reflective metaphysics of creation is by no means a necessarily unique advantage. Of course, genealogical accounts (Nietzschean, Foucaultian) of philosophy's nature and history might very well be able also to offer reasons for their own contingency and disputability. In other words, this advantage does not decisively separate a (Christian) metaphysics of creation from other meta-accounts of philosophy's nature—and this again is a good thing, precisely because of the very vulnerability and disputability of a metaphysics of creation.

87. Yet what if such a metaphysics of creation does not seem to be conceptually available or affordable? What if metaphysics has turned into a mask of intellectual pride and curiosity behind which the sinner can hide as a philosopher whose univocal concept of being submits God to the rule of the concept, that is, to onto-theology that thereby obliterates the Creator/creature distinction and that finally lets the speculative mind rule triumphantly in the system (finding its most consistent instantiation in Hegel's *Science of Logic* that by speculatively sublating the Creator/creature difference in the absolute Idea amounts to nothing less than a theo-logic under the universal rule of the concept)? What if philosophy as such thus becomes the speculative enactment of curiosity? By thinking radically from within the crisis of judgment, theology will have to take a different route, the route taken by Martin Luther.

88. I am indebted to Romanus Cessario, OP, for his strong Thomistic insistence on accounting for the full implications of what I dub theology's "metaphysical moment." I am quite aware that my way of addressing his concern will in his eyes still fail to explain how the natural order is an inherent part of the divine order, or how only the theory of physical premotion will properly account for the way all being, insofar as it constitutes the natural order, is governed by and ordered to God.

will always have a "metaphysical moment" in that it expects the structure of the world and the structure of the human mind to correspond because they were *made* to correspond; hence the metaphysics of creation. Yet Aquinas teaches us to take this moment a step further by following the implication of "creation" to its very end. If the theocentric character of being obtains all the way down, if *ta panta* is creation all the way down, Christians should not be surprised to encounter fragments of a philosophical path or to be able to reconstruct such a path that argues this truth from the structure of being itself. Aquinas's creation of a philosophy of being, drawing upon the fragments of this path encountered in Plato, Aristotle, and neo-Platonism, constitutes his own full reconstruction of the kind of metaphysics that must hypothetically be possible if indeed being is theocentric all the way down.[89] In other words, theology must at least hypothetically be able to encounter its own metaphysical moment as external to itself—"external" because the economy of salvation relies upon the prior gift of creation, and "its own" because the gift of creation is in no way alien to the economy of salvation. It is this externality that has an appropriate norming effect on theology, since indeed all of being is governed by and ordered to God. Yet, ironically, this externality of a pure metaphysics of *esse* remains hypothetical unless it is concretely assumed into the metaphysics of creation. It is precisely here that—as governed by God's providence—the norming externality of creation is met by reasoning redirected to its ultimate good.

Redeemed Judgment

We can raise the question of the directedness of reasoning meaningfully only in a horizon in which the problem is, at least in principle, already overcome. To put it in stark theological terms, only in the horizon of redemption can the fall be understood—that is, only retrospectively.[90] Similarly, Aquinas's account of curiosity presupposes a horizon in light of which the problem under discussion is, at least inchoately, overcome. In other words, being able to inquire into the directedness of reasoning under the condition of sin presupposes a redirected reasoning and thus a redeemed capacity of judgment. Here Aquinas assumes the epistemic and volitional reality of what Paul called the eschatological existence "in Christ," which begins inchoately in and through faith.

Let us first consider the end, the beatific vision. In contrast to human existence under the condition of sin, in the beatific vision God's goodness is clearly beheld "through the certitude of the Divine Vision." Beholding the divine essence, that is, the infinity of God's goodness, means to adhere to God of necessity: "[T]he will of the man who sees God in His essence of necessity adheres to God, just as now we desire of necessity to be happy" (ST I.82.2 corp.). It is important to understand, however, that this necessity, far from

---

89. Bieler, "Theological Importance," p. 311, in this volume: "Aquinas created a *new* philosophy of being that cannot be reduced to its sources."

90. To put it in exegetical terms, only in light of Rom 1:16–17 and 3:21ff. can the Apostle Paul thematize Rom 1:18–3:20.

destroying human freedom, constitutes the very fulfillment of freedom. For it is God's goodness that inexhaustibly fulfills the intellect's as well as the will's specific desires of truth and happiness.

Yet short of the beatific vision, where "the essence of God itself becomes the intelligible form of the intellect" (ST I.12.5 corp.), we have to settle for faith. And it is fascinating to realize how, according to Aquinas, faith needs to be understood as a fundamentally redirected reasoning, a dynamic in which the will commands the intellect to assent to God's revelation. Here is Aquinas's succinct definition of faith, as found in ST II-II.2.9 corp.: "Now the act of believing is an act of the intellect assenting to the Divine truth at the command of the will moved by the grace of God."[91] The line of movement is from grace to will to intellect. Hence, it is grace that reorients the will to command the intellect to believe. In other words, the whole operation in which the human's will and intellect are active according to their proper created function nevertheless fully pertains to grace, that is, God's operation.[92] Bruce Marshall puts the whole matter in a beautifully clear way:

> The will, Aquinas argues, elicits the mind's assent to the teaching of scripture and creed. Even though the mind can "see" neither that the content of this teaching must be true, nor that its status compels assent, the will clings to the good which is held out in this teaching, and induces the intellect to hold it true. . . . Lit by grace, the heart (as we might now say) finds in the triune God of whom this teaching speaks its true desire, and so cleaves to this teaching not only as true, but as the first truth, "which is the goal of all our desires and actions."[93]

The reorientation of the will, caused by grace, is the source of redeemed judgment. It establishes now with faith's unique certainty (a) God's triune identity and Christ as the truth per se, and (b) the Creator/creature distinction, that is, the condition of the possibility of assuming the metaphysics of being into the metaphysics of creation. Redeemed judgment shows immediately forth in the fact that theology's genuine task, according to Aquinas, is not to prove but to judge, to exercise and apply the judgment of faith in a sustained, comprehensive, and rigorous way. Marshall puts it thus: "The epistemic primacy of sacred doctrine is of a negative or limiting kind (i.e., *sacra doctrina* does not prove, but judges). No true statement can be inconsistent with the contents of Christian teaching."[94] Yet since one central entailment of *sacra doctrina* is the Creator/creature distinction, the second difference, theology applies its

---

91. On the ecumenically problematic issue of merit, while the assent of faith does not merit grace, it is important to realize that insofar as Aquinas regards faith as "meritorious" at all, he emphasizes that it is through the power of grace that faith merits eternal life. Cf. ST I-II.112.2 ad 1; and Pesch, *Theologie der Rechtfertigung*, 669.

92. Aquinas states this point in especially clear ways when it comes to justification: "God does not justify us without ourselves, because whilst we are being justified we consent to God's justification (*justitiae*) by a movement of our free-will. Nevertheless, this movement is not the cause of grace, but the effect; hence the whole operation pertains to grace" (ST I-II.111.2 ad 2).

93. Marshall, "*Quod Scit Una Uetula*," 13.

94. Ibid., 16.

practice of redeemed judgment most consistently and comprehensively by assuming the metaphysics of being into a metaphysics of creation, that is, by realizing the Creator/creature distinction conceptually.[95] Redeemed judgment realizes being's beckoning.

The Gaze of Faith and the Wisdom of the Cross— With Aquinas beyond Aquinas

Faith has nothing less than an iconic effect. For the baptismal dynamic of faith (dying and rising) is not metaphorical but eschatological, and thus, thanks to the will's restoration by grace, it provides a reconstituted gaze, the gaze of faith, as through a glass darkly. The human capacity to reason does not have to be destroyed and reinvented in this dying and rising. Rather, the will's orientation is now constantly informed in a substantive, albeit inchoate, way by its ultimate good, God. Yet this fundamental reorientation, this eschatological restoration of our gaze, is experienced under the condition of sin as an encounter with a Logos contra to our "logos" and its particular (mis)directedness, in other words, as an encounter with the Counter-Logos, the wisdom of the cross.[96] What has to die and rise is not our reasoning capacity as such but rather the fundamental orientation of our reasoning under the condition of sin, the will that, instead of being fulfilled by participating in God's will and being thus genuinely freed, is locked *incurvatus in se* after having forfeited its ultimate good.[97]

Reasoning's directedness now participates through faith, inchoately, in the directedness of the Logos to the Father that *is* the Spirit, the triune identity that is the eternal law of triune love.[98] This participation in the Spirit, caused by the Spirit through faith, elicits a redeemed capacity of judgment that originates in a horizon constituted by *Gelassenheit* (the human will resigning to and thus participating in God's will) and by the complete release of any *Machtförmigkeit* of our epistemic gaze (the "let it be" that is the root of a metaphysics of creation in contrast to an onto-theology). Thus, a complex cotemporality of all three realities of judgment—redeemed judgment, judgment of *esse*,

---

95. Martin Bieler puts it succinctly in his significant yet sadly neglected book *Freiheit als Gabe: Ein schöpfungstheologischer Entwurf* (Freiburg: Herder, 1991): "There is no Christian tradition without metaphysics lest it be ready to abandon the difference between Creator and creature and with it renounce itself. The question is not *whether* metaphysics but only *which* metaphysics is appropriate to the biblical tradition" (78; my translation).

96. For a detailed exegetical and systematic account, see Malcolm's essay, "Wisdom of the Cross."

97. In an interesting essay, Jean Porter has shown that Aquinas's account of the virtues is able to answer for the surprising possibility that infused cardinal virtues might cause significant tensions in the justified person. Infused cardinal virtues "can exist in the presence of contrary habits, that is, vices, which render their operation difficult and unpleasant (I-II. 65.3 ad 2). . . . Indeed, the infused cardinal virtues can and do exist, at least potentially, in those who lack the use of reason altogether, as well as those who have some capacities for moral action but lack the maturity necessary to the full development of the acquired virtues." Porter, "The Subversion of Virtue: Acquired and Infused Virtues in the *Summa Theologiae*," in *Annual of the Society of Christian Ethics* (1992); 32.

98. See Bruce D. Marshall, *Trinity and Truth* (Cambridge: Cambridge University Press, 2000), on the epistemic role of the Spirit: "The action whereby the Spirit induces us to love God by sharing in the mutual love of the Father and the Son is epistemically decisive: from it ultimately stems our willingness to hold true the narratives which identify Jesus and the triune God, and to order the rest of our beliefs accordingly" (209).

and judgment in crisis—reflects the struggle over reasoning's directedness and thereby substantiates the conflictual relationship between theology and philosophy (with the exception of a metaphysics of creation). Philosophy, *ex sua natura*, is equally blind for the fall as for Christ and, as post-Christian, that is, modern, tends either to integrate and subsume from theology what it might regard as speculatively relevant (Hegel) or to fundamentally distance itself from the theological horizon, thus becoming crypto-theological by reclaiming and recasting central theological topoi (as with Kant, Nietzsche, and Heidegger).[99]

The Metaphysics of Creation in the Conflict of Judgments

Yet even the metaphysics of creation will remain an exercise of thinking *in peregrinatione*, "on the way"—that is, an exercise in the middle of the conflict of judgments. For epistemological skepticism and ontological nihilism on the one side and the triumphalism of instrumental reason on the other, while conceivably capable of being analyzed and criticized argumentatively, cannot be overcome by the force of argument alone. Thus, foundationalist strategies that breed the next round of skeptical rejoinders in their attempt to overcome the last round, as well as reductive strategies that commit performative contradictions in their very act of reduction, while predictably finding their disciples, will lead nowhere, because they obscure the concrete existence of the person who judges. Only if the very fact of existence comes into view, and, with it, the problem of existence as one essentially already overcome, can the crisis of reason as well as its instrumentalization be overcome. Yet this ultimately is a matter of conversion from the created things to the Creator, and of a corresponding catechesis. And the latter is nothing less than the initiation into a whole tradition of discourse and an exercise in the renewal of judgment.[100] Therefore, only the conflict of judgments, including the conflict between a metaphysics of creation and other versions of philosophical discourse or style, points to a problem that otherwise would not even be perceptible. It is the offense of the wisdom of the cross, the offense of *Fides et Ratio*'s optimism about reason's full metaphysical range as it is informed by wisdom (*philosophari in Maria*),[101] and the offense of a metaphysics of the second difference that lead into the conflict of judgments. This conflict is by no means to be avoided. On the contrary, it is a reflection of freedom, because only here in the difference between redeemed and unredeemed judgment—between reasoning directed to the creature alone, thereby precisely obscuring it as creature, and reasoning redirected to the Creator—shines forth the status of a

---

99. Most recently, John Milbank and some of his students have pressed this problematic, and, to their merit, it is now broadly acknowledged in the present English-speaking discussion on the relationship between theology and philosophy.

100. Hence, I concur with Paul Griffiths' conclusions at the end of his essay, "How Reasoning Goes Wrong."

101. Cf. Ferdinand Ulrich, *Homo Abyssus: Das Wagnis der Seinsfrage*, with an introduction by Martin Bieler, 2nd ed. (Freiburg: Johannes Verlag Einsiedeln, 1998), 275–76, and especially the way Martin Bieler unfolds this notion in the final section, "*Philosophari in Maria*," of his essay, "Theological Importance," pp. 317–326 in this volume.

world and existence over which the spiritual battle, the Spirit's battle, has not yet come to an end.

The drama of misdirected reasoning is not that it simply fails and knows nothing. On the contrary, misdirected reasoning is distressingly and shockingly successful in its reductive focus on the creature. Here a metaphysics of creation offers a discursive witness and argumentative pressure by creating a coherently argued difference in judgment and thus provoking the kind of intellectual conflict and crisis that is necessary in order fully to appreciate what only grace followed by catechesis can give. This conflict might best be provoked by assuming, from the implicit perspective of redeemed judgment, the *duplex ordo cognitionis—simpliciter*—and thus expecting rightly what de facto cannot be achieved, mirroring in this way Paul's argumentative strategy in Rom 1:20.

Yet the metaphysics of creation does more than that. In the form of an admittedly indirect *catechesis*, it would analogically unfold the very "grain of the universe"[102] that reasoning properly directed is called audaciously to explore. This ideal setting of a most rigorous and advanced catechesis in the horizon of redeemed judgment is the source as well as the *Sitz im Leben* of Aquinas's inexhaustible trust in the intellect's capacity for truth, a trust deeply foreign to most late moderns, but one shared by and mirrored in the encyclical *Fides et Ratio*.

To the degree that we are able to recapture *catechesis* as the ultimate horizon for our efforts at reasoning rigorously, we have good reason to trust in reasoning's capacity, properly directed and exercised in the horizon of redeemed judgment, to develop a genuine and original metaphysical range of inquiry.

---

102. An important concept of John H. Yoder used constructively by Stanley Hauerwas in his recent Gifford Lectures in order to show how a rigorously argued, christologically centered, and unfolded theology of witness is "natural theology" rightly understood. Yet, I would submit, precisely in order not to remain trapped in the nominalism of incommensurable language-games between which we switch back and forth, thereby ultimately enacting equivocation, catechesis would be ill-advised to forfeit the analogicity that a metaphysics of creation affords.

CHAPTER EIGHT

The Perplexity and Complexity of Sinful and Redeemed Reason

— ERNSTPETER MAURER —

In this essay I will explicate the distinction between sinful and redeemed reason in a perspective inspired by Martin Luther and his *Disputatio de homine*
(1536).[1] Furthermore, I will concentrate on structural problems of reason that
went undiscovered until the twentieth century (although they may have been
implicit in much philosophical reflection). My fundamental thesis may be
summarized as follows: Reason is unable to define itself and at the same time
is always in the temptation to define itself, with far-reaching consequences.
Redemption changes not the structure but rather the perspective. The limits
of reason are discovered as creative potential; reason is liberated from self-
definition and defined by faith—a peculiar definition that provokes the proliferation of *fides quaerens intellectum*, of faith seeking understanding,
exactly by avoiding clear-cut criteria.

The conflict between faith and reason is a Pauline motif, explicit in such
difficult passages as Rom 1:18ff. and 1 Cor 1:18–2:16. The passages are difficult because there is no simple confrontation. Human wisdom may be stul-
tified by divine wisdom (1 Cor 1:20), but there is a story in the background.
The stultification is a reaction (a creative reaction, of course!) to the human
presumption of knowledge, including knowledge of divine reality. And God's
creative reaction liberates the human person, including reason. That is why
we can talk about such a liberation. We should not forget, however, that this
is deeply mysterious. Given the fact that human persons are fallen, even the
use of language must be impregnated by sin. Granted that the divine Spirit
has liberated us and revealed the divine mystery to us—the depths of God (1
Cor 2:10ff.)—it is nevertheless not self-evident that we communicate this to
anybody else. The communication of faith is mysterious, although the forms

---

1. Martin Luther, *The Disputation Concerning Man*, trans. Lewis W. Spitz, in *Luther's Works*, vol.
34, *Career of the Reformer IV*, 2nd ed. (Philadelphia: Muhlenberg Press, 1976), 135–44.

of language and thought remain human. Indeed, Paul uses argumentative patterns, Stoic insights, and the like in order to communicate the mystery of divine grace. The conclusion must be that language and reason are ambiguous, since there are no clear criteria for the difference between sinful reason and reason informed by faith.

The situation seems to be even more complicated because the term "reason" is not clear even from a philosophical point of view. Recent philosophy of science has intensified some fundamental conflicts implied in the traditional account of human reason. On the one hand, there has been a tendency toward conceptual precision that would have been unimaginable in former centuries. Such precision has to do with the consequent and exclusive application of mathematical tools. Early analytical philosophy played this off against "merely" metaphorical and ultimately senseless philosophical discourse—in the name of an "ideal language," the isomorphic picture of the ultimate structure of the world. But the same Ludwig Wittgenstein who proclaimed this self-purification of language was finally attracted by the self-evidence of ordinary language and its open-ended variety of language games. The criteria for "ideal language" are too narrow—but the variety of language games may be too wide. What is valid for language (and language is certainly an important aspect of *ratio*) seems to be true for the definition of reason in general. Science monopolizes the definition of reason at the expense of neglecting all non-mathematical precision—which has to do with the inflationary technical applicability of mathematically designed theoretical structures. But there are spheres of reality that resist quantification. Is it impossible, then, to articulate theories concerning these spheres? Is it impossible to talk about art or feelings or values reasonably—that is, in more than subjective or downright irrational utterances? Once more, the modern self-clarification of reason seems to be caught between "not enough" and "too much." Such an unsatisfactory situation follows mainly from reason's modern usurpation of ultimate authority. Finally, the reflexive move whereby clarification of reason can be expected *only* by pure reason leads to antinomies that corrode, or at least threaten, the foundations of modern scientific rationality. I will sketch this rather ambivalent result of recent philosophy of science in the first part of this essay.

Interestingly, *self*-clarification of reason is the point in Luther's dialectical assessment of *ratio*. Reason is almost divine, at least within creation, but is unable to know adequately its own exceptional position. Consequently, there is no reliable human self-knowledge available to philosophy.[2] This strong conclusion results from the philosophical definition: If the human person is essentially *animal rationale*, a living being endowed with reason, reason and humanity are not simply the same but are closely connected. Reason's self-assessment is—or rather, should be—a necessary condition for human self-knowledge. And the disastrous tendency to confuse a necessary condition

---

2. Ibid., 137 (theses 8.10f.): Reason "is a sun and a kind of god appointed to administer these things in this life. . . . In spite of the fact that it is of such majesty, it does not know itself a priori, but only a posteriori. Therefore, if philosophy or reason itself is compared with theology, it will appear that we know almost nothing about man."

with a sufficient condition narrows the horizon. Such a negative balance, however, is not the last word. What about the positive aspect that reason is indeed almost divine? The *theological* assessment of reason must take into account that *ratio* is excellent only within the context of creation and in strict relation to divine wisdom. Reason must reflect that it has been *given* to human persons. *Ratio* is not simply at our disposal—which is certainly a limitation, because we cannot fathom our own essential capacity. But if reason turns out to be inexhaustible by reasonable thought, this might indicate the depth of human personality—a reflection that we have been created in the image of God. Surprisingly, the limitations of reasonable self-clarification become transparent for the dramatic story going on between God and human persons. However, there is no simple harmony. Human wisdom is deeply involved in the divine struggle with human presumption. Therefore, the perplexities of reasonable self-clarification are symptomatic of human arrogance—but the same perplexities may be transfigured as soon as they are seen in the light of divine wisdom. Perplexity is transformed into complexity. This "change of aspects" is demonstrated in the second part of this essay. Such a change implies that there is no subtractive distinction between sinful and redeemed (aspects of) reason. Rather, reason as a fundamental and essential feature of human personality as a whole participates in sinful and redeemed existence. *Tertium non datur*—if there is no neutral position in the divine struggle with human presumption, it is not convincing to exempt just *ratio* as *differentia essentialis* from this struggle.

Perplexity

Reason is unable to define itself and at the same time is always in the temptation to define itself, with far-reaching consequences. This is what I call "perplexity." There are some fundamental structures of reason in which the intellectual grasp of the truth seemingly reaches its peak—and collapses. I use the phrase "fundamental structures" in a quite innocent way. Any analysis of human rationality has to cope with the foundations of mathematics, regardless of ontological decisions. Sometimes the structures of reason seem to correspond to equally fundamental structures of reality. If my desk is gray, I can easily distinguish the desk from its color by imagining it painted orange with dark brown stripes. The statement "This desk is gray" corresponds structurally to my gray desk. But this will not be the case with a lot of other statements, including physical laws. What about "Force equals mass multiplied by acceleration"? Or, still more difficult, "Acceleration equals distance divided by the square of time"? What is "the reality" that corresponds to "t^2"? However, the idea of an ideal language that corresponds precisely to "what is the case" cannot be discussed in the present context. In my view, Wittgenstein's *Tractatus logico-philosophicus* produces more problems than it solves. (And here I am in perfect agreement with Wittgenstein himself.) Nevertheless, there is one interesting point. Reason—at least since Kant, and certainly in the twentieth century—tends to identify the ontological structure of reality with mathematical regularities. Reality is reduced to what may be reconstructed mathematically. But in that case, the structural problems in the foundations of mathematics gain some ontological weight.[3]

Infinity

There are at least two concepts of infinity, and possibly more. The most important distinction has been discovered by Georg Cantor: Given any set of elements, we can take certain elements from such a set in order to define partial sets (*Teilmengen*). The set of these partial sets will always contain more elements than the original set. A set with three elements contains eight partial sets. A simple example would be the set of three elements {1, 2, 3}. The set of partial sets (*Potenzmenge*) contains the following sets: {1}, {2}, {3}, {1, 2}, {1, 3}, {2, 3}, {1, 2, 3}, and {} (*leere Menge*). It is intuitively clear that every set containing n elements at the same time contains pairs, triples, . . . , $(n–1)$-tuples of elements, and one n-tuple (the set itself).

Cantor's proof demonstrates that this relation is generally true; consequently, it is valid for sets with an infinite number of elements, *which may be counted by a progressus ad infinitum*. The common example is the set of natural numbers {1, 2, 3, 4, . . .}. By *reductio ad absurdum*, we can assume a set that contains the same number of elements as the set of its partial sets. In this case, there will be a "mapping," or "projection," between the elements of the set S and the elements of the *Potenzmenge*. There will be a special set S_0 of all the elements of S that are mapped to certain partial sets that do not contain those elements. In our simple set {1, 2, 3} above, one such mapping would be {1} ← → {2, 3}. We will soon discover that it is impossible to count all the elements of the *Potenzmenge* with only the elements 1, 2, 3. We can count the pairs of elements and get the special set S_0: {1} ← → {2, 3}, {2} ← → {1, 3}, {3} ← → {1, 2}. But there are simply not enough elements to count all the partial sets. Nevertheless, *in the case of an infinite set, there should be no problem*. We may assume that the stock is big enough. There should always be a natural number mapped to any partial set. Consequently, we may assume that there are natural numbers mapped to partial sets that do not contain those natural numbers, and other natural numbers mapped to partial sets that do contain those numbers (which is no problem). The former set S_0 is one of the partial sets. But what about the number of S_0? Does it belong to S_0? In this case, the number is *per definition* mapped to a partial set that does *not* contain the number. In other words, it does not belong to S_0. But that is the definition of S_0! The number is an element of S_0 *just because* it does not belong to S_0. This inconsistency demonstrates that it is principally impossible to count the partial sets of a set containing an infinite number of elements by mapping the partial sets to the elements. In such cases, the number of partial sets must be "more than infinite" or, more precisely, *infinite in a noncountable*

---

3. I use the term "ontology" in the rather technical sense suggested by Willard V. O. Quine. See, e.g., Willard V. O. Quine, *Ontological Relativity and Other Essays* (New York: Columbia University Press, 1969).

way. This is already counterintuitive: There are different levels of infinity. But then a severe argument arises, which is not only counterintuitive but, again, simply inconsistent. The *set of all sets* must contain all its partial sets. This set of all the partial sets of the set of all sets must contain more elements than the set of all sets. This statement is inconsistent.[4]

It is notable that this problem arises not in the context of philosophical reasoning but on purely mathematical grounds. Set theory is one of the most fundamental structures in mathematics. Obviously, the fundamental mathematical structure is open to logical consequences that are quite undesirable. Moreover, there have been more discoveries of that kind, especially the famous *set of all sets that are not self-containing*, which contains itself precisely because it does not contain itself, and vice versa. The discovery of that set by Bertrand Russell was shocking, because it destroyed all attempts to lay a foundation of mathematics by reduction to logical and set-theoretical axioms.[5]

The reaction to those undesired discoveries was mainly characterized by reductionist decisions. Usually, infinity is reduced to the *progressus* or *regressus ad infinitum* in order to avoid antinomies. I call this a decision because there is no strict mathematical reason for such a reduction. On the other hand, this decision has not been freely taken but rather dictated by *anxiety.* For most mathematicians and scientists, mathematics is fascinating because of its crystalline hardness and reliability. The crystalline structure has to be preserved in any case, even if there are philosophically and theologically more interesting alternatives. The relation between antinomies and contradiction is quite fascinating in a peculiar perspective. An antinomy is not the same as a contradiction; rather, it is a very precise argumentation. Why should we avoid it? The reduction of mathematical structures to countable (and computable) patterns may expose a perverse self-definition of reason, even a self-determination to mere technical rationality. The question is, rather, are there significant antinomies, and are they representative of just those features of reason that cannot be simulated by a computer? Interestingly, the logical and set-theoretical antinomies are mocking our *aseitas,* our aseity! Most of them have to do with self-reference and with the attempt to achieve a certain closure or conclusiveness. They have not been intended as—and they disturb mathematical and logical attempts to establish—an ultimate foundation of precise thought.

The fascinating point is that the ultimate foundation of precise thought is closely linked to antinomies that prevent such a closure. There are different conclusions from this insight. We may conclude that it is absurd to talk about any ultimate foundation of thought. We may also conclude that there must be something beyond thought that cannot be explicated. And we may conclude that any explication of the "beyond" will require more than just logically

---

4. Cf. Wolfgang Stegmüller and Matthias Varga von Kibéd, *Probleme und Resultate der Wissenschaftstheorie und Analytischen Philosophie III: Strukturtypen der Logik* (Berlin: Springer, 1984), 40ff.

5. Cf. Alan J. Torrance, "*Auditus Fidei*: Where and How Does God Speak? Faith, Reason, and the Question of Criteria," in this volume, p. 48.

structured language, that is, *significant* antinomies. (Note that all these "conclusions" are not conclusions in a strong sense of the word, because this
would already require an ultimate calculus that cannot be established because
of the antinomies.)

In a theological perspective, there emerges a description of sinful reason
that refuses the confrontation with surprising features of its own reasoning.
This is perverse because reason follows an idea of consequence that narrows
(or strangulates) its own possibilities.

Unity

Scientific unity tends to reductionism in the sense of physicalism: Since all
processes we can observe presuppose physical change, there is nothing more
than physical change, and all other reality is only emergent. Hilary Putnam
has demonstrated the self-refuting structure of such a reductionism: There is
always a cut between the observer and the system observed. This cut forces
us to give up "the dream of a description of physical reality as it is apart from
observers, a description which is objective in the sense of being 'from no particular point of view.'"[6] Putnam ironically characterizes this (absurd) point of
view as the "God's Eye View." Of course, no scientist expects to reach the
ideal of impersonal knowledge in practice. "But that there should be *principled difficulties* with the ideal itself—that it should turn out that we can no
longer visualize what it would *mean* to attain the ideal—this is a fact which
constitutes for us, constituted as we are, the most profound of paradoxes."[7]

The God's Eye View is inconsistent, because it must include the relation
between observer and physical reality. This relation must be analyzed as physical structure, for example, reduced to neural patterns. As ideal theory, the
final theory must at the same time describe the structure of the world and give
an epistemological analysis of that description. This may be difficult, but possible, as long as we accept different theories that may be related to one
another in a metatheoretical way. But the final theory must be *unified* in the
sense that it is identical with its own metatheory. This may be possible if all
the propositions can be read in at least a double way (note that this is a piece
of science fiction theory). But then the theory describes more than reality. In
a certain way, we have repeated Cantor's argument and presupposed a theory
that contains more than itself. If the supposition of an all-encompassing, consistent, and objective theory is inconsistent, we may conclude that "objectivity" and "consistency" are not objective in a way that may be operationalized
mechanically. Objectivity and consistency are values, and exactly as values,
they are not specifiable in nonpersonal terms.

Scientific rationality, then, is self-consuming as soon as it is reduced to nonpersonal structures. At the same time, such a reduction of rationality tends to

---

6. Hilary Putnam, *Realism with a Human Face*, ed. James Conant (Cambridge, MA: Harvard
University Press, 1990), 11.
7. Ibid., 17–18.

be a rational denial of rationality. A merely physical description of intellectual "functions" will of course deny all nonphysical features of reason in a trivial way. Such reductionism as rational denial of rationality is a genuine antinomy. Again, we may ask for a certain philosophical or theological—at any rate, existential—dimension of such a decision. Again, there may be a certain anxiety, because value-talk will never be as precise as any physical theory. The interesting question, however, is whether such a lack of precision in the mathematical sense is necessarily a disadvantage. Why should personal talk be unambiguous? We come to a point comparable to the one before: It might be possible to enjoy certain lacks of precision as soon as we discover that such "imprecision" is creative and fruitful. There may be significant antinomies and there may be significant ambiguities (*Doppeldeutigkeiten*) in semantics (and, of course, nonsignificant inconsistencies due to our failure to do better). There are at least two possible reactions: anxiety or pleasure.

With words such as "anxiety" and "pleasure," I do not intend any existential interpretation. Nevertheless, such words can be helpful in underscoring that at the core of rationality there are decisions that are not the result of rational operations. None of the options is compelling or necessary. There are fundamental decisions, but we do not "make" these decisions, although we may identify ourselves with one of the options. This has to do with the affective orientation of the mind. What transcends mere rationality is marked by terms such as "intuition" or "disposition," but both surprisingly converge with our affective life (see below). Therefore, the decision is not a deliberative choice. There are no striking arguments for taking one way or the other. One way is too narrow; the other way seems too wide. (Note that the theological description is exactly the reverse, because few scientists choose the wide way.) There is an inclination rather to accept the narrow way of reductionism.[8] And this is symptomatic of sinful reason: Both problems—"bad infinity" in the rather boring sense of *progressus ad infinitum* and reductive unity in the shape of physicalism—emerge from reason's attempt at ultimate self-constitution. To be precise, the sinful feature is closely connected with claiming *ultimacy*, replacing the Creator with a created faculty.

Reason's attempt at ultimate self-constitution is provoked by the seemingly embarrassing complexity of the human person that has always been observed: Even if we manage to give a clear definition of "soul" over against "body," the soul as principle of life "contains" emotions and other capacities

---

8. For a more detailed account, see Paul J. Griffiths's essay, "How Reasoning Goes Wrong: A Quasi-Augustinian Account of Error and Its Implications," in this volume. Griffiths argues that the foundations of reasoning are not as self-evident as we tend to assume. This is valid especially for the ontological framework of our arguments, which has to be learned and therefore is a result of adequate catechesis. There is an additional complication, because "the nature and extent of the catechetically produced convictions that inform a particular judgment about a matter of theory . . . ought not to be systematically and deliberately obscured in argument for the truth of that judgment" (p. 151). But reason's seemingly self-disciplined restriction to a mathematically clear ontology exactly obscures its own status as a conviction by claiming self-evidence that even gives conviction-independent criteria for evidence. See Torrance, "*Auditus Fidei*," p. 48: "Even in the most exact sciences, reason necessarily assumes a series of suppositions and assumptions taken on faith, as these include memory, testimony, the collective testimony of the scientific community—and we might also include nondemonstrable heuristic intuitions, . . . subliminal awareness, and the like."

(*Seelenvermögen*). We share some of these emotions with animals. But there may be "higher" emotions, for example, courage. In any case, they have to be governed by *ratio*. But even *ratio* is a manifold structure. According to Kant's distinctions, *Verstand* is the capacity of logical operations and clear-cut concepts that give structure to the stream of sense-data. This stream has already been ordered by the "pure forms of intuition" (*Anschauungsformen*), which are not dependent on sense-data: space and time. Mathematical forms and logically connected concepts structured by the pattern of the categories are described as software that processes the sensual input. This function perhaps summarizes the genuine meaning of *ratio* (mathematical reasoning as a characteristic feature of human persons) and clearly exposes the limitations of mere rationality in comparison with *Vernunft*. For Kant, this term implies more, especially the ability to anticipate a synthesis by intuition. Again, the ultimate foundations of reasoning—the fundamental unity of my thought as well as the last level of independent reality—escape from the structure of *ratio*. On the other hand, it is the *same mind* that is able to impose mathematical structures on the sense-data and that transcends such operations, possibly transcending human existence as spirit. Therefore, all these distinctions are possible and even plausible, but they are not clear-cut.

The problematic difference between *Verstand* and *Vernunft* anticipates the modern problems with infinity and unity. Axioms have to be grasped by the mind (*Vernunft*). This would then lead to an integration of the *anima rationalis* "top-down." But mathematical and logical operations as characteristic features of *ratio* have a tendency to "run away." At the same time, there must be an integration of scientific knowledge "bottom-up." Interestingly, scientific rationality (*Verstand*) stresses the material substrate of knowledge, thus undermining personal unity top-down. The problems are complementary, and both have to do with reflection and self-reference in a strong sense: *Reason seeks to determine itself and to overcome its own internal complexity*. In order to create a clear arrangement, there must be an integration *either* top-down *or* bottom-up. In a more recent staging, we would have to decide whether we want to be compared to computer programs ("artificial intelligence") or to natural but nonpersonal phenomena like clouds and tornados. As I mentioned before, the problem has to do with the claim for ultimate foundations, which of course must be unequivocal, because otherwise they are not rational. But then the problem might—in a theological perspective—be solved by simply accepting the difference-in-unity between *Verstand* and *Vernunft* as well as between body and soul. Why should we expect the ultimate synthesis? Reason may accept its own unfathomableness and enjoy the possibility of ever new discoveries between logical discipline and "bodily" sensitivity. There is no strict argument to refute such a relaxed attitude that receives one's own personal unity rather than actively constituting such a unity by reduction. And yet there emerges a strong tendency to establish personal unity once and for all.

Both models of unequivocal integration, however, ironically produce patterns of argument that are undesirable. Reason *either* mechanizes reasoning to the effect that antinomies surprisingly "personalize" the mathematical framework, *or* its quest for controlling reality turns out to be a quite strong decision that tends to negate the possibility of decisions. The two strategies seem to be complementary, but there is no perspective *within* reason that discloses a synthesis. Self-defining reason reaches its peak—and unwillingly produces an abundance of antinomies. This may already be a hint to the second part of my fundamental thesis: Redemption of reason will change not the structure of reason but rather the estimation of the collapse. Redeemed reason will appreciate and even enjoy its own complexity and unfathomableness as *creature*. However, there are still two more aspects of sinful reasoning that exclude human persons from this joy.

Abstraction

One of the fundamental features of sinful reasoning is omnipresent comparison. Why does the intellect always compare? It has to do with abstraction, which is possible only by comparison and intuition. *Prima vista*, there are no concepts without abstraction, because clear-cut concepts presuppose genus-species relationships in the strict (set-theoretical) sense. The simplest sets are defined by common attributes for all elements of a special set. Of course, scientific concepts are much more complicated. But they are complicated because they try to avoid intuition. Therefore, all qualities are reduced to comparable quantities. This is another version of reductionism (see above). The new aspect is the quest for general, or universal, features. The price for generalization by way of abstraction is an *impoverishment of language*.

This will be evident as soon as we try to analyze metaphorical language. Traditionally, the metaphor is just a rhetorical variation that can in principle be eliminated by propositional language. (In the background there is the ideal of a unified propositional description of all reality.) But there are theories of metaphorical language that stress the *semantic surplus* as the most interesting feature of metaphorical language. My *locus classicus* may be found in a theological text in which Luther discusses the impossible reduction of successful metaphors to ordinary propositional talk. This passage in the *Antilatomus* (1521)[9] ends with a heavy christological accent: According to 2 Cor 5, our sins are transferred to Christ, who is without sin and was made sin for us. This *translatio* as *metapherein* is the fundamental metaphor. However, I will not discuss the christological significance of this passage but rather will concentrate on the philosophical content of Luther's argument, which may be read as a piece of linguistic reflection done by a matchless translator.

An instructive example is the Hebrew word *shinnantam* in Deut 6:7. The Hebrew root *shnn* has to do with sharpening. A very literal translation reads as follows: "You shall sharpen [these words] to your children." "You shall impress these words upon your children" certainly sounds better. Interestingly,

---

9. Martin Luther, *Against Latomus*, trans. George Lindbeck, in *Luther's Works*, vol. 32, *Career of the Reformer II* (Philadelphia: Muhlenberg Press, 1958), 195ff. (Weimarer Ausgabe 8, 83ff.).

we have to replace one metaphor with another. This is not necessary in German, where the word *einschärfen* is as adequate as the Latin *acuere*. Of course, such a phrase is metaphorical, because words cannot be sharpened in any literal sense as can a sword or a knife. Moreover, we cannot sharpen words *to* someone or even *into* someone's mind. If we try to explain the metaphor in nonmetaphorical language, we must say, "You shall speak these words to your children again and again, so that they will internalize the meaning of these words and become obedient and wise." (Note that at least "internalize" is still a metaphor.) In this version, the analogy between sharpening a sword by repeating a certain action and sharpening the mind by repeating a certain exercise has been eliminated. Luther's point is that this elimination is a loss. The nonmetaphorical version is by no means more precise. Therefore, Luther has greater confidence in the metaphor, which is more gracious and perhaps the *only* adequate expression.[10] The metaphor provides a collection and concentration of several aspects that may be explicated— "narration," "repetition," "insight," "judgment"—but understanding the metaphor requires a kind of multidimensional perception, comparable to a three- or four-part composition in which the polyphony cannot be reduced to the single parts. Luther concludes that it is inadequate to split up the different aspects and translate the same word differently in different contexts. This may be unavoidable in some cases, but it is preferable to collect the different aspects in a single word, so that the different contexts provide semantic variety and at the same time are connected with each other.[11] The task is to find the starting point for variation: a "simple signification" that must not be confounded with a nonmetaphorical meaning but rather will be the most vivid and expressive paradigm for the use of the word. Irreducible metaphors may be interpreted by a chain of analogies that starts with the most simple use of the word (*significatio simplex*).

This consideration reminds me of Wittgenstein's famous "family resemblances."[12] There are words that cannot be defined but nevertheless work well in ordinary language. Actually, most words in ordinary language cannot be defined in a precise way. They get their semantic profiles exactly from chains of overlapping applications to similar situations, starting with self-evident paradigms. Analogy is thus omnipresent in ordinary language. Luther's point is that many biblical texts would lose their significance if metaphors were replaced by the "adequate" word with a "proper" meaning, precisely because the analogical relations *are* (part of) the meaning. He seems to interpret metaphorical language as a special and rather creative case of analogical application of words that discloses surprising horizons of comparison. Such surprise

---

10. Ibid., 197: ". . . that the first meaning is the more agreeable, and perhaps the only one." (WA 8, 85: ". . . ut gratiori significationi et fortasse soli.")

11. Ibid., 199: "Is it right to make so many terms out of one when you can combine all, or most, into a single meaning and simply vary the figurative uses?" (WA 8, 86: ". . . iustum autemne est tot vocabula ex uno multiplicare, cum possis vel omnia vel plurima in unum significatum colligere et figuris solis variare?")

12. See Ludwig Wittgenstein, *Philosophical Investigations*, trans. G. E. M. Anscombe, 3rd ed. (New York: Macmillan, 1968), §66–67.

may exhibit essential features of reality. Luther's insight has inspired Eberhard Jüngel, who supposes that metaphors are genuine language, whereas precise concepts are secondary—an inversion of the traditional view.[13]

Of course, it is quite difficult to explicate the semantic content of a metaphor, but it is equally difficult to deny that there is such a content if we presuppose that there are parts of reality that must be "seen as . . ." or "seen in comparison with . . ." in order to be seen adequately. This may not be true for pencils and keys, but it is certainly true for our "inner life." If a human person is *successfully* characterized metaphorically, such a metaphor *will* have a semantic content that, of course, cannot be grasped intentionally. But is it necessary to restrict "semantic content" to a kind of language that maps reality or to a linguistic structure of oppositions? It is quite interesting to compare Luther's account with Donald Davidson's denial of a semantic content, because they are *almost* in agreement.[14] Davidson distinguishes between the semantic content and the point of a metaphor. He does not neglect but rather highlights the peculiar use of words with a simple meaning; such use may disclose surprising and subtle analogies. Metaphors have a hidden force; they beautifully hit the point. But the words do not change their "normal" semantic content.[15] This is exactly what Luther wants to say when he insists on the *significatio simplex* and resists any multiplication, because the metaphor would be eliminated, or at least trivialized, by such a pedantic distinction between the original and second and third (and so on) meanings. Metaphorical language cannot be reduced to a cognitive content that in principle may be paraphrased by simple propositions. But there is a quite significant difference: Davidson *identifies* the semantic content with something that can be said directly. This is begging the question, since Davidson's sharp distinction between semantic content and use is at least debatable.[16] Davidson admits and even underscores that metaphors lead to discoveries. Why is it difficult to call this "content"? He contrasts limited semantic content with possibly (indeed, in most cases) inexhaustible analogies and refinements in the use of a word.[17] Perhaps this contrast of limitation and unlimited semiosis results from a naive concept of infinity.

---

13. See Eberhard Jüngel, "Metaphorical Truth. Reflections on Theological Metaphor as a Contribution to a Hermeneutics of Narrative Theology," in *Theological Essays*, trans. John B. Webster (Edinburgh: T & T Clark, 1989), 16–71.

14. Donald Davidson, "What Metaphors Mean" (1978), in *Inquiries into Truth and Interpretation*, 2nd ed. (Oxford: Clarendon, 2001), 245–64.

15. Ibid., 256–57: "[T]he unexpected or subtle parallels and analogies it is the business of metaphor to promote need not depend, for their promotion, on more than the literal meanings of words. . . . [A]s much of metaphor as can be explained in terms of meaning may, and indeed must, be explained by appeal to the literal meanings of words. A consequence is that the sentences in which metaphors occur are true or false in a normal, literal way, for if the words in them don't have special meanings, sentences don't have special truth. This is not to deny that there is such a thing as metaphorical truth, only to deny it of sentences. Metaphor does lead us to notice what might not otherwise be noticed, and there is no reason, I suppose, not to say these visions, thoughts, and feelings inspired by the metaphor are true or false."

16. Ibid., 259: "What distinguishes metaphor is not meaning but use. . . . And the special use to which we put language in metaphor is not—cannot be—to 'say something' special, no matter how indirectly." Cf. Wittgenstein's extreme suggestion that the meaning of a word is nothing other than its use in language (*Philosophical Investigations*, §43).

17. Davidson, "What Metaphors Mean," 263: "When we try to say what a metaphor 'means,' we soon realize there is no end to what we want to mention."

The most striking example for words that cannot be reduced to precise concepts is the expression of feelings. But how can we express feelings? Do we "describe" our "inner" reality? Note that already this distinction between "external" and "internal" reality is metaphorical and, moreover, *unsurpassable*. The metaphor "internal" cannot be eliminated by nonmetaphorical concepts. One of the most interesting features of this metaphorical context is that language and reality are interwoven and, in certain situations, even result in a feedback. In most cases, there is no inner reality independent of language that may be described more or less adequately. Certainly, there is a difference between inner life and language, because sometimes we do not find the right word, and the feelings may have changed in the process of looking for adequate expression. But this should at once demonstrate the difficulty: There is no adequate "truth-as-correspondence" as soon as our inner life is concerned. Again this difficulty has to do with self-reference (albeit in a less formal structure): Inner reality is *my* reality, and a very deep level of reality. On the other hand, Wittgenstein has deconstructed the idea of "private language": There are words in our common language that may be adequate. We are able to express feelings and even to understand each other. Moreover, we are able to enrich each other's self-understanding by reflecting what we have understood—even without interpreting the other's self-understanding.

My point is that language will become more and more metaphorical the more we approach humanity and personality. Consequently, the task of conceptual talk—claiming any general validity—gets more difficult. Abstraction is not the same as generalization, and we must look for *nonabstractive universals*. Any work of art—as a very special unity or whole (*Ganzheit*)—is the result of details growing together. Of course, the Latin version of "growing together" is *concrescere*. This is the limit of abstractive concepts. They are not excluded in aesthetics: We must compare different works of art by the same artist or by different contemporary artists or by artists in different contexts and so forth in order to find the right accents. But the function of abstraction is limited. Any universal "concept of art" is threatened by high generality and insignificance. The comparison aims not at common attributes but at *subtle differences*, which may indeed connect two works of art much more intensely than common stylistic features.

Against this background, the success of quantitative concepts in science—together with the concentration on mechanical causality (in the modern sense of cause-effect succession)—is dangerous as soon as it becomes paradigmatic for universal insights in general. There may be universal contexts constituted by difference, by encounter—including surprise and ambiguity—and by teleology, that is, anticipation of a whole that is not the sum of its parts. This is valid especially for the universality of human nature: Is a human person characterized by qualities, or by a story? Is the definition *animal rationale* possibly wrong in the beginning by comparing us to animals instead of concentrating on divine-human encounter? This is the point in the first part of Luther's *Disputatio de homine*, which concentrates on the possibilities and the tragedy of *ratio* as *differentia essentialis* of human being.

Atomism

The reverse of abstraction is a concept—or rather, a metaphor—of personal unity comparable with a zero-point "I." If the essential feature of human beings is just the difference over against other animals, there is nothing left besides the concept "reason." But the meaning of this concept must remain unclear. In former times, it may have been unproblematic, because *ratio* was the human ability to think logically. Now, however, this concentration on logical capacities of the mind as peak of humanity raises the question whether logical capacities restricted to computability reduce the intellect to a computer program. Reason must be more than the ability to think logically. But all attempts to say exactly what this "more" may mean are trapped by a certain paradox: If the difference between the mind and a computer program is articulated in precise terms, it will be exactly that precision that allows the computer scientist to simulate the specific difference. The meaning of "I" seems to fade away; self-transcendence becomes the subject's attempt to get at a distance from all different reality. This distance implies that no nonpersonal reality can be understood in other than mechanical terms. But at the same time, the term "subject" has become empty. The correct intuition that the "I" is different in principle from all objective reality is distorted by the sharp distinction. There may be interaction, but it is restricted to physical causality. The possibility of interaction *sui generis* between subjects (including physical reality) has been ruled out.

There is even one more paradox: Interestingly and ironically, relations are omnipresent in scientific description but excluded from the realm of the personal. Relations—of course, in the sense of mathematical functions and quantified throughout—are characteristic of scientific theories. But the sharp distinction makes it necessary to describe the inner life in an atomistic manner: I "have" a will and certain feelings. And relations are reduced to reversible connections that will never be encounters in the strong sense. This leads back to the problem of abstraction. As long as all the human "I's" have nothing in common other than their sharp difference over against physical reality—which is described in relations—the thoughts, wishes, and feelings of such an "I" can always be reduced to physical and neurophysiological patterns. Interpersonal language as language *sui generis* counts as merely an imprecise and preliminary attempt to express the inner life that might better be replaced by behaviorist descriptions (which in my opinion would be a misreading of the late Wittgenstein).

I fully agree with Carver Yu's analysis that there is a dramatic interplay between an overvaluation of reason and an utter devaluation of it. I would even add that there are already theological dimensions in such a drama: It is the story of the interplay between arrogance and despair. Carver Yu's analysis of strong empiricism is quite instructive, since there is no consistent empiricism; if consistent at all, "it will eventually explode."[18] Interestingly,

---

18. Carver T. Yu, "Covenantal Rationality and the Healing of Reason," p. 227 in this volume.

there are the Kantian (imploding) antinomies that show in a complementary way that reason cannot be reduced to the field of experience, because such a reduction is inconsistent; there is always "more" than we can explain rationally and theoretically. I would even argue more strongly for an antireductionism, because *any* truth relation will immediately transcend the reduction to sense impression, and that may be true for *any* interesting distinction-in-connection, for example, between the external world and me. The first person is not replaceable. Carver Yu underlines the role of "the complex whole,"[19] which is *prior to any atomistic abstraction.* Consequently, the intuition of the world as a complex whole precedes any analysis, and this complex whole integrates the world and me. This is one of the final loops in Wittgenstein's seemingly reductive *Tractatus.*[20] Obviously, we have met a fundamental structure in the aporetic story of reason.

Complexity

Redemption changes not the structure but rather the perspective. This difference in perspective may be compared to the difference between a malignant caricature and a kind of sketch or a musical theme and its retrograde inversion.[21] The limits of reason are discovered as creative potential; reason is liberated from self-definition and defined by faith—a peculiar definition that provokes the proliferation of *fides quaerens intellectum* exactly by avoiding clear-cut criteria. Anselm coined the formula in the context of very strict patterns of argument used to clarify fundamental assertions of Christian faith. My considerations follow a slightly different direction, because the term "reason" is not clear at all and is open to clarification within the confrontation between faith and reason. Therefore, we must distinguish at least two aspects: (1) It is not possible even to start without language and, consequently, without reasonable chains of thought, and (2) it is always possible that our explication of faith leads to counterintuitive patterns of thought, which have to be clarified; otherwise, we might confuse mere absurdity with divine mystery. The clarification, however, may in turn change the character of reason. The two aspects do not necessarily contradict each other—as long as we do not impose rational restrictions on reasonable God-talk that are not consistent even within the realm of scientific argumentation (as shown in the first part). But the relation of the two aspects, "reasonable explication of faith" and "reason questioned by faith," remains intricate. The analysis of *ratio* in the perspective of faith will perhaps discover aspects that may be discovered as well by secular philosophy. But are these aspects really the same? *Are there context-independent aspects?* Aspects without a certain perspective are a self-refuting idea. But then the whole game may be played again one level higher.

---

19. Ibid., 229.

20. See Ludwig Wittgenstein, *Tractatus Logico-Philosophicus*, trans. D. F. Pears and B. F. McGuinness (London: Routledge & Kegan Paul, 1961), 6.45.

21. The term "structure" is not decisive in this context, but it is helpful to underline that all the elements and their characteristic connections remain the same and yet may be radically transformed by a change of perspective and nuance.

Subtle philosophical reflection knows that there are no context-independent aspects, and theology may say that the search for such independent insights is a typical feature of sin—striving for the God's Eye View. Obviously, these insights are not identical but convergent. The whole debate is at least reasonable, not just absurd. But "reasonable" in what sense? The *story* of the concept "reason" refutes any attempt to get a crisp and short definition. *Ratio* is what emerges in the debate. At the same time, there will emerge some constant features (cf. Luther's *significatio simplex*). These are elementary, but they are not neutral; rather, they are ambiguous in relation to sin or faith. From a theological point of view, *reason is fulfilled by the conflict*, deepening the self-understanding of *ratio*. This is what I mean by "proliferation."

Martin Luther took up such intricate relations in a twofold line of discussion. On the one hand, Paul's remarks on human and divine wisdom look like an intellectual version of the Pauline "doctrine"—or rather, "story"—of justification developed in Romans and Galatians. Already at a very early stage in the development of his theological paradigm change, Luther connects this doctrine of the conflict between human and divine justice—between human misunderstanding of the divine law and God's scandalous presence on the cross—with a discussion of limits and possibilities of philosophy. "He who wishes to philosophize by using Aristotle without danger to his soul must first become thoroughly foolish in Christ."[22] Theological speculation (*theologia gloriae*) is the intellectual form of self-justification, destroyed by God's action *sub contrario*. The critique of presumptive reason follows from the Pauline *theologia crucis*. On the other hand, Luther always connects his distrust of reason with a high assessment and quite refined use of logical structures. This may be a result of Luther's nominalist training, but this account is too simple, because Luther refutes *any* philosophical patronizing in theology. The radical dimension in Luther's remarks on reason is not the confrontation but the highly complex dialectical movement between radical criticism *and* a surprising apotheosis of *ratio*—a movement concentrated in the *Disputatio de homine*. This movement indicates that there is no way of formal or subtractive distinction between neutral capacities and their sinful perversion, which is valid especially for the distinction between sinful and redeemed reason.[23] A careful analysis of the disputation's first part demonstrates that the same argument has two different readings. Reason is almost divine but is unable to assess its own exceptional position adequately—and as soon as reason insists on self-clarification, there will emerge structural problems that cannot be solved, above all, the question of personal unity integrating *anima* and *ratio*.[24] This suggests the picture of a rather slippery slope, because *ratio* that avoids any self-reference will be nothing more than

---

22. Martin Luther, *Heidelberg Disputation* (1518), trans. Harold J. Grimm, in *Luther's Works*, vol. 31, *Career of the Reformer I*, 2nd ed. (Philadelphia: Mühlenberg Press, 1958), 41. The phrase "to his soul" has been added by the translator.

23. Luther, *Disputation Concerning Man*, 139 (thesis 26): "[T]hose who say that natural things have remained untainted after the fall philosophize impiously in opposition to theology."

24. Ibid., 138 (thesis 15): "Indeed, concerning the formal cause which they call soul, there is not and never will be agreement among the philosophers."

a computer program, contributing nothing to human self-knowledge. Evidently, such a limitation is absurd.

But there is a different reading: Reason may "simply" *do without* ultimate claims at self-clarification. Such a *relaxed* reason presupposes the encounter with divine reality. In this widening horizon, reason is liberated from the exertion to control reality (including rationality), but exactly such a relaxed reason reflects the story going on between God and human persons. In such a narrative context, *ratio* is embraced by *fides* in the theological definition of humanity according to Rom 3:28: "A person is justified by faith apart from works prescribed by the law."[25] This rather peculiar "definition" by reference to the divine action of justification is a summary of the biblical drama. Since the human person as a whole—and certainly not as an isolated individual—is involved in the story, human reason will be affected by this dramatic struggle. It will be involved too, and therefore the difference between presumptive and relaxed reason reflects fundamental decisions—which are not free, however, since they are certainly no result of considerations from a distance. The bondage of the will—the most famous theory articulated by Luther—implies that reason is not able to inform the will but rather vice versa, which of course implies that the will's fundamental direction mysteriously transcends rationality. At this point we are led back to 1 Cor 2:6ff. God's Spirit penetrates our hearts, so that we participate in the mind of Christ (v. 16). But it is not a question of human decision to be penetrated by God's Spirit, because such an event has never emerged in any person's mind (v. 9). Nevertheless, Paul envisions a renewed *mind* (Rom 12:2)—reason illuminated by faith. This renewal makes it possible to describe "the old mind" retrospectively as sinful reason.

Sinful Reason

I assume that the core of sin is *superbia*, "prideful presumption." The presumption of divinity leads to various forms of anthropological theories in which the human person illegitimately claims divine predicates.[26] There are two fundamental possibilities for a specific role of human reason within a phenomenology of sin.

Self-substantiation
If *ratio* tries to define itself, such self-substantiation exhibits patterns of *incurvatio*, of being curved in upon oneself. There is the presumption of aseity. Such an imitation of divine existence leads on the one hand to desperation and on the other hand to arrogance. Both aspects may be traced throughout the exposition of perplexity: Strict reasoning shrinks back from the surprising

---

25. Ibid., 139 (thesis 32): "Paul in Romans 3[:28], 'We hold that a man is justified by faith apart from works,' briefly sums up the definition of man, saying, 'Man is justified by faith.'"

26. Paul J. Griffiths discusses Augustine's remarks on the mind that wants to become like God in its own right instead of simply receiving its God-like status: "This is an account of the fall transposed into psychological and epistemological key" ("How Reasoning Goes Wrong," 157). The second part of my essay tries to work out this transposition.

consequences of mathematical structures; reason gives its assent to self-sacrifice over against physical reductionism; human persons are just thinking animals; and the transcendence of the self, finally, is nothing but emptiness (*psychologia negativa*). These *angustiae*, these anxieties, however, correspond to intellectual arrogance, since they all presuppose the superiority of *ratio* in a nonpersonal sense. This is a radical inconsistency, because there is no impersonal reason.

There emerges the following irony: Reason seems to have made a decision—the decision to eliminate all decisions theoretically. Paradoxically, consequent behaviorism is a decision. In Luther's theological perspective, such a decision is not free, however, but a sign of human bondage. *Reductionism is obsessive.* The intellect must be liberated from such an obsession. Any attempt at self-liberation will repeat or even tighten the vicious circle; new and fresh perspectives must therefore come from outside. My theological suspicion is that faith illuminating reason is a sufficient condition for such a liberation. I will not argue for the stronger version—that faith is the necessary condition—but since there is no self-liberation, any alternative must have redemptive features. Within the theological framework, I suggest that it is exactly the irony that effects such a liberation. The strictness of reductionism would then be comparable to the *usus elenchticus legis*, the unmasking and convicting function of God's law. The self-strangulating reductionism leads to the self-sacrifice of the mind or to redeemed reason.

Universalism

If *ratio* tries to control *all* reality, such universalism exhibits patterns of *concupiscentia*: There is the presumption of *infinitas*. Freedom and infinite self-transcendence are confused and thereby reduced. Of course, this corresponds to arrogance and anxiety, since *ratio* must establish itself by theoretical success unlimited. Again, we may trace the confusion throughout the exposition of perplexity: The intellect claims a perfect intuition of reality by logical and mathematical regularities. Universal truth is attained by artificial concepts that exclude metaphorical language. These *universalia*, however, destroy human freedom exactly by a merely *rationalist* self-transcendence. The perversion lies in the self-identification with a (pseudo)universal structure, suddenly and surprisingly confronted with the mockery of antinomies. In a certain sense, the structures emancipate themselves from reason's control.

Again, there emerges an irony. Reason in its idolatrous search for regularity, including the computability of *ratio* itself, is forced to a cautious use of infinity in order to avoid any discovery of personality in nonpersonal reality. This is a rather strange picture: Within the logical and mathematical structure there emerge structures of personality—and reason refuses to accept them. They are surprising, and surprise has to do with encounter. Of course, antinomies must not be confused with freedom, but perhaps they are the trace of freedom in language. They *encourage* intuition over against step-by-step argumentation.

Redeemed Reason

Created and fallen reason cannot be neatly distinguished. Especially the last point demonstrates the difficulty. Reason just as self-transcending faculty is not neutral in relation to sin and is perhaps the most significant feature in the perverse presumption of divinity. Luther's position assumes that *all* elements of reason have been preserved, but in a perverse arrangement. The person as a whole is a caricature of the *imago Dei*. The characteristic feature of this caricature is the denial and refusal of slight transitions within human reasoning that cannot be controlled by sharp criteria. Therefore, redemption has to liberate the mind by melting these sharp criteria. Since there are no neutral "elements" of *ratio* (and possibly no "elements" at all but rather complex relations of aspects), the transitions are important and even pleasant. The ironic perplexities of reason push the person toward the *hilaritas* of faith. They heighten the tension, however. On the one hand, they entice reason to give up its overall control with pleasure rather than with resignation. On the other hand, they may provoke even more humorless and possibly desperate attempts at restrictive self-clarification and self-purification. This is not a question of "free" decision; rather, it is comparable to laughing at or feeling offended by a joke.

Passivity

Personal unity and (nonatomistic) individuality emerge from encounter, interaction, relation. This is a decisive insight in Luther's *Disputatio de homine*: There is no chance for human self-recognition until persons recognize themselves in their origin, which is God.[27] The false assumption that reason is the supreme authority can be shattered only by the encounter with divine reality. We have to *receive* the faculties and possibilities of reason; we do not control our own reasoning. But this has to do with the fact that we experience creation—including our *ratio*—as a gift, in order to enjoy it. To experience the rational capacities of human persons as something given is one aspect of faith seeking understanding. This implies not only the reception of natural capacities at the beginning of personal life but also a constant growth of intellectual capacities by experiences of nonrational encounter.

We receive the balance of different and various levels and layers of personality from other persons and we pass it on. There is such a thing as an "I," but it is not a substance; rather, it is a process, but it is not reducible to neural processes. There is such a thing as will, but it is not something we possess. The subject is not at anyone's disposal (*unverfügbar*), but that does not imply unqualified transcendence; rather, it presupposes a mixture of hilarity and imperturbability (*Gelassenheit*). The person is not even at his or her own disposal (*selbstentzogen*). The positive feature of surprise presupposes the concept of story, which needs some specifications in order to become a concept

---

27. Luther, *Disputation Concerning Man*, 138 (thesis 17): "Nor is there any hope that man in this principal part can himself know what he is until he sees himself in his origin which is God."

at all. Interestingly, some of these essential conditions remind us of the confusing discoveries in mathematics: The tension necessary for any story in a significant sense combines consequence with complication. The persons act in a certain way that results from their character. But at a certain point there emerges a tendency that may confuse the protagonists: Conflict may arise exactly from their attempts to avoid it. The persons may even be created anew by such conflict (even if it is not solved). Another characteristic feature of story is irreversibility. Certain structures may be repeated, but no two occurrences are ever the same, nor are they even comparable. The same qualities may result in different individual characters, depending on their arrangement. Human persons are unfathomable just *because*—not *although*—persons are interwoven in a texture with feedbacks.[28]

All these aspects have to do with passivity in the positive sense of receiving ourselves but also in the less positive sense of being acted upon (which in certain situations may be very positive—e.g., being liberated or simply being hugged by our children) and possibly in the negative sense of suffering. I may discover my own self in the course of a dialogue with a "Thou." This may be a surprise, and it will not just *reveal* some internal quality but also *create* that quality. It will create that quality because such a quality is a relation that emerges in the dialogue. (I cannot rule out the possibility that this quality was "hidden" somewhere in my heart, but who knows? In any case, I do not!) Since something similar may be true for my "Thou," the situation is a very precious balance. All these personal qualities, including personal language, will not result from abstraction, and the semantics of this language depends on a network of encounters growing together. But then it is simply impossible to reduce the "I" to some neural pattern. Quite apart from Putnam's arguments, such a reduction would have to compare stable self-experiences with recurrent neural configurations. But there is nothing like stable self-experience. There may be a certain continuity and certain analogies ("I'm in love again"), but those depend on situations that are not repeatable. They are not repeatable in a trivial way, because I can only *once* fall in love with one and the same woman *for the first time*. The semantics of personal language will not be unambiguous; perhaps it will even insist on antinomies as soon as they are condensations of the inner tensions that distinguish a single human person from stones, dogs, and computers. Is there anything more liberating than a situation that confronts me with a tension in my own personality—and confronts me in a way *that I may laugh*? Laughter

28. Cf. Carver T. Yu's remarks on preestablished harmony in "Covenantal Rationality": Neither objectivism nor subjectivism can be argued for with the strength of a logical proof. Knowledge is located in the fullness of life (235). Knowledge is a form of communion and a web of relation prior to reasoning. Assuming this picture—an assumption that is at least not trivial, since there is no proof, but also not arbitrary—we get to the preestablished harmony. *The structure of self-forgetfulness (236) will be one of the most fascinating features in this picture.* The interpenetration of inside-outside differences may transcend the self-centeredness of sinful reason. My question, then, might be whether self-transcendence is active or passive. In order to avoid a repetition of the modern story, the mind's transcendence must be understood as a gift. The most basic intuitive trust is indeed a certain form of faith, but this is not the same as Christian faith. The interesting question will be whether both the connection and the difference between these two perspectives or levels of faith can be properly described.

is already a strange combination of passivity (I am *brought* to laugh; I never decide to laugh) and a high grade of rationality (I must *understand* the joke).

Limitation

Created limits are not limitations in the sense of restriction or coercion. Rather, they belong to the beauty of creation, and it is important to rediscover this. Limitation does not contradict infinity; indeed, there is no intensive infinity without limitation. Therefore, universalism will be limited not by clear-cut borders but by transversality and pluralism. By "pluralism" I do not mean arbitrariness in the "postmodern" sense. Rather, this pluralism follows from the insight that *relations* are the fundamental ontological level of description.

Of course, this is a theological insight.[29] Indeed, I use not the Aristotelian but the Augustinian concept of "relation" (and possibly not even the latter). In any case, it is a Trinitarian concept of relation that prepares the framework for a fresh ontological discussion. One aspect of the Trinitarian mystery is the insight that the divine persons are not connected by the relations but are almost identical with the relations; at any rate, there are no independent *relata*. To be more precise—and more cautious—the divine persons are not simply identical with the relations. But the fascination of the Trinitarian relations has to do with the strange continuity and transitions mentioned by Basil the Great (or Gregory of Nyssa—philology has not come to a decision): "[H]e who has conceived the Father, and conceived of Him apart by Himself, has at the same time mentally accepted the Son also; and he who lays hold of the Son does not dismember the Spirit from the Son, but in due sequence, so far as their order is concerned, yet unitedly, as regards their natures, forms within himself an image of the faith that is a blending of the three in the same way."[30] The continuous transitions seem to express exactly the divine mystery and infinity. Another argument leads to a similar point: Augustine underlines the difference between substance and accidental features. But in the case of God-talk—in which the accidental determinations have to be eliminated, because there is no accident in God—there is one of the Aristotelian accidental categories left: relation that seems to be "substantialized."[31] Substance and relation must not be confused, but it is necessary to get an intuition of their convergence.

One of the "psychological analogies" for this divine mystery is the inexplicable depth of human self-recognition. There we are confronted with the structural problem of self-reference, that is, the irreducible difference between me as someone *referring* and me as someone *referred to*.[32] Part of the solution is the threefold self-reference characteristic of the human mind: Insight, memory, and will integrate and penetrate the whole human mind in a threefold

29. Cf. Colin Gunton and Robert W. Jenson, "The *Logos Ensarkos* and Reason," p. 84 in this volume, where "relationality" is introduced as a key notion: "The being of the triune God is constituted in the relations of the in-fact embodied Son to his Father in the Spirit. Must not then the creation have a relational structure that is appropriate to its being created by such a God?"

30. Saint Basil, *The Letters* XXXVIII.4, trans. Roy J. Deferrari, vol. 1 (Cambridge, MA: Harvard University Press, 1961), 209.211.

31. Cf. Augustine, *De trinitate* V.6.

32. Cf. *De trinitate* X.6.

way, because each of the three represents *me* and at the same time is related to the other two.[33] If this argument is interpreted in a strict way (and I am not sure whether this is an overinterpretation), each of the three represents me *just because* it is related to the other two. The true meaning of "me" is disclosed in the transition. The solution may be characterized as a strange concept of relation in which each of the *relata* contains or encompasses the essence, but in an irreducibly distinctive way, so that the essence realizes itself in the relations. This structure may be found in Anselm's argument concerning the *filioque* (possibly independent from this question): The divine mystery has to do with *God proceeding from God alone*. If this process is an implication of divine aseity, the divine persons are not identical with, but are an implication of, divine essence.[34]

Of course, it would be an example of *superbia* to give an outline of Trinitarian relations worked out in the history of theology. I want only to give some hints of the *ontological puzzles* associated with the category "relation." The Trinitarian explication of Christian God-talk forces us to admit the limits of fundamental logical and ontological patterns. And vice versa: The logically odd movements of biblical and biblically formed language may be the linguistic trace of divine presence. But there is one important further step. If there are ontological puzzles implied in Christian God-talk, we may ask whether this has implications for ontology in general. And at least in the context of Luther's anthropology and his concept of a person there emerges a *relational ontology*.[35] Biblical texts such as Gal 2:20—"It is no longer I who live, but it is Christ who lives in me"—seem to imply the external constitution of the human person as a fundamental event connected with redemption by faith: "The life I now live in the flesh I live by faith in the Son of God, who loved me and gave himself for me." The person is not only liberated by a personal encounter but also driven away from self-constitution and drawn into a miraculous communication with Christ. It may be controversial among Luther's interpreters whether this is "just" or "irreducibly" metaphorical— and Luther's anthropology and "ontology of the person"[36] will certainly be controversial between Wittenberg and Rome—but these metaphors are recurrent in Luther's writing and thinking. If we take them as irreducible metaphors, we get the impression that Luther describes the redeemed person in general, and redeemed reason in particular, in terms of at least mysterious relations. That does not mean that the divine mystery is drawn into

---

33. Cf. *De trinitate* X.18.

34. Cf. Sancti Anselmi de processione spiritus sancti contra Graecos liber (Patrologia Latina 158, 285–326), 287: "praedictis duobus modis est Deus de Deo."

35. In an early unpublished communication, Gunton and Jenson stated that the prohibition of contradiction is "the self-constraint of discourse, by which it is to be something other than babble. But why would it otherwise be babble? Because then it would not be analogous to the discourse God is. The self-constraint of our discourse . . . is an analogue of the fundamental condition of the discourse that God is: that the Son is not the Father and the Father is not the Son." This argument changes the assessment of the prohibited contradictions, since personal difference in the Trinity must be closely connected with relation and transition. Both cannot be articulated if *p* and not-*p* are simply the same. But the difference between p and not-p is grounded in a relation, not vice versa.

36. The allusion refers to Wilfred Joest's concise analysis of Luther's anthropology, *Ontologie der Person bei Luther* (Göttingen: Vandenhoeck & Ruprecht, 1967).

anthropological patterns; indeed, it means the opposite. The human person becomes mysterious in the light of Christ. We no longer claim any full understanding of human reality—but we now understand why such a complete self-understanding is not necessary and not even desirable. This experience is both discouraging and enriching.

Recall my example of self-discovery-in-dialogue. If it is true that certain qualities are created in this encounter, and that both persons involved in the dialogue experience this, then the persons are, to a certain degree, constituted by the relation. As I said, there is a precious balance between the persons and, moreover, between the persons and their relation. It is important that the relation is not something neutral "between" the persons. Rather, each person includes the whole relation, and the persons are distinguished not by qualities but by the different direction of the relation. Perhaps the *turning points* in the dialogical movement are the most significant points of self-recognition. What interests me in this context is the combination of limitation and infinity, of concreteness and universality. A personal relation is certainly limited, but a successful relation of that kind will never make the persons computable. It is perfectly possible—and in a certain sense desirable—that two persons know each other better and better and yet may constantly surprise one another. Personal interaction creates human subjects in the sense that they are *unverfügbar*: not at anyone's disposal. There emerges a certain depth or infinity within a limited situation, infinitely free from *concupiscentia* but oriented toward the abundance of love.

Since such a relation is interwoven with further comparable relations, there are manifold interactions that multiply the combination of limitation and infinity. There may emerge nonabstractive universals. It is not necessary to find a common language for all situations and for all contexts, although it is highly desirable to find a style of intercontextual dialogue in order to engage all human persons in the liberating dialogical movement started by the divine Word incarnate. I would even say that this ongoing movement is liberating precisely *because* it does not aim at one universal language but aims at a texture of many limited dialogues growing together (*con-crescendo*). However, there are precise conditions for adequate terms, which I call "spongy." This is a metaphor that describes the characteristic features of theological (and most philosophical) terms from the perspective of computer science, in which each term has to be well defined in an unambiguous way. The metaphor is not depreciatory, however. The semantic structure of spongy terms—for example, "person"—may be the trace of a movement in human self-discovery. The ambiguities and tensions within the term "person" are adequate, reflecting the human *Unverfügbarkeit*, which must not be eliminated. There may be other structural aspects in the "evolution" of the term, for example, distinctions that are not clear-cut. For the term "person," the distinction between "inner life" and "surface" is constitutive. This distinction is not drawn by a hard line but evolves in a fractal way. The finer distinctions are dependent on the way human persons communicate and articulate the term "person." This may even imply antinomies ("the depth of the surface") and reflection, since language and reality, word and object, are necessarily entwined. The sponginess of terms results from the manifold perspectives concentrated in one term. A spongy term is not vague, then, but ambiguous in a precise and significant way.

Thus, set theory is not the fundamental structure of the universe. This will be true in all cases of personal knowledge, where intersubjective levels emerge from intersection and interweaving rather than generalization. Ambiguity will become constitutive because the incommensurability of perspective must not be eliminated. Such incommensurability not only may concentrate in antinomies but also will certainly limit any unity of science. There are (at least) sciences and humanities, which concentrate on regularity (*intellectus*) and history (*voluntas*) in a very complex balance. The person is embedded in various patterns of action and reaction. And these patterns concern the body as well as the soul: That we are organisms is a very important point for epistemology—we do not simply construct a picture of a reality that is completely different from ourselves. Rather, this picture is part of that reality. On the other hand, our intellect will in principle never completely submerge in reality. This is the root of the self-distinction that is concentrated in the term "will." Is it a power, a potential, or simply the auxiliary verb hypostatized? There is no subtractive distinction between "subject" and "object." It is not at all clear where the subject "ends" and where reality "begins," because the subject is part of reality, a very peculiar and strange reality.[37]

There are even more theories with intersections and theoretical exchange, but without final integration. In this model, reason will be able to develop manifold perspectives on the human person within creation. This is what I mean by the new definition of reason provoking the proliferation of *fides quaerens intellectum* exactly by avoiding clear-cut criteria. The complexity of the spongy term "reason" may be sketched as follows: On the one hand, the *anima rationalis* is distinctive and essential for human persons. But the content of the term vanishes as soon as we try to give a precise definition. The difficulty has to do with the tension between *anima* and *ratio*—and it is neither possible nor desirable to eliminate this essential tension. The "definition" necessarily oscillates between the spheres of the animal and of the formal, only touching the extreme positions, following certain trajectories. Reason is different from passion and emotion and is perhaps in control of both, at least sometimes. Reason's self-discipline leads to logical and mathematical purification, so that precision is optimized by replacing qualitative with quantitative (computable!) concepts. But as soon as "reasonable" becomes synonymous with "computable," something must have gone wrong. If reality is nothing more than what remains comparable to our artifacts, "artificial intelligence" will give the ultimate definition of "reason." My alternative takes a turn that discloses essential features: The intellect is embraced by and embedded in processes of human life that are not only complementary but also in tension with formal or mathematical structures of thought. Moreover,

---

37. Of course, the intellect is able to imagine things that may happen in the future and to give its assent.

these processes cannot be neatly distinguished from reasoning because they are closely connected with *intuition*. Interestingly, intuition seems to surpass mere reasoning and at the same time may be described as sensitivity, taste, feeling, and timing—in short, *Fingerspitzengefühl*. But this movement implies that reason is fulfilled and perfected by quite bodily and even instinctive— which implies an animal dimension—(re)actions. The trajectory takes another turn because sensitivity and taste, feeling and timing, are operative in our holistic intuitions, which are the creative starting point for reasonable analysis and precise conceptual work. From the merely rational—or rather, logical and technical—point of view, these intuitions may only be described negatively, as *in*commensurable with standards of precision and unambiguity. They resist quantification and conceptual unification. But exactly such a resistance may become a productive challenge for analytical and theoretical work. From another point of view, these irrational ramifications may even emerge from theoretical concentration. The word "intuition" denotes a dimension inherent in reason that essentially remains out of control by reason— and exactly so keeps reason alive and reasonable.

Redemption and Story

In the first part of the essay, I have tried to give an analysis of reason's structural limitations, whereas in the second part of the essay, I have sketched a theological interpretation of this analysis in the categories of sin and redemption. The connection between the two parts is rather complex. The theological interpretation does not simply complete or refute the analysis of *ratio*, nor does this analysis confirm the theological insight. One of the models for such a connection, as already mentioned, is Luther's distinction between law and gospel. But this distinction is only the outline of a confrontation or a dramatic development that includes catastrophe and catharsis. In short, although the divine law is designed to lead the human person and this person's acts by explicating the will of God, the sinful person is actually led astray and provoked by the same law to look for his or her own self-righteousness. Finally, confronted with the law, the same person may experience a desperate self-recognition— the last step before the liberation by the gospel (Rom 7:14ff.). It is the *law as letter* that leads to desperation and spiritual death, until Christ's Spirit enables us to reread the letter in a *spiritual* way (2 Cor 3) in order to discover the gospel between the letters, to understand the divine word as God's declaration of love.

The important structure is that *one and the same text may be law or gospel*, depending on the reading. The text may be read as letter. In the Spirit, however, the letters will be transformed into a living word. *But the letters remain the same.* This is the important analogy: The narrative order must not be neglected. If we start with the human mind, and with human possibilities in general, the explication may lead to desperation as far as the human mind seeks to constitute itself. This is even more dangerous if we keep in mind that human reason is something divine—as Luther underlines in the *Disputatio de homine*—comparable to the law, which may be even more destructive if understood as divine law. In the perspective of faith, this desperation of sinful reason is the last step before reason's liberation. This step, however, is contingent, *unverfügbar*. There are no compelling arguments for the human mind to leave behind the obviously fascinating attempts of structural self-constitution by surrender to calculus. Of course, Cantor's and Putnam's arguments against logical and physicalist reduction may be seen as conclusive within human reasoning. But there is room for different reactions, and one possible reaction will always be the anxious self-restriction to logical patterns and scientific theories. Consequently, all other dimensions of human personality belong to the suspicious realm of poetry. *The human mind fears its own mystery.*

Earlier I alluded to the *usus elenchticus legis*. In the confrontation with the law, we discover our own sinful perversion, especially that we prefer a divine-human contract—a "deal"—to simple love of God. Our attempts to fulfill the law *only as letter* expose our unwillingness simply to respond to the divine declaration of love. In Luther's interpretation, the law is deeply ambiguous. Similarly, the immense possibilities of human reason may provoke our rebellion against God but at the same time expose the limits of the human attempt to control the creation. These limits are exposed exactly within the story of human persons seduced by their own possibilities. This story has its center in the Christ story. According to 1 Cor 1:18–2:16, the cross is a scandal for the Jews and simple stupidity for the Greeks. However, Christ crucified has exposed the limitations of all the powers in the world who did not recognize the Lord of glory (1 Cor 2:8). God's wisdom exposes the world's wisdom as something deeply ridiculous. This confrontation includes the ontological structures—the "elements" (cf. Col 2:8)—that may be grasped by human reason in order to be worshiped in a perverse way.

Admittedly, the situation addressed in 1 Cor 1:18ff. is not connected immediately to problems of scientific rationality. Paul is concerned with counterproductive diversity in the community, and his argument aims at reconciliation. But exactly in this context it is clear that the sinful disposition closes the sinner's mind to the immensity of God's reconciling love. On the other hand, says Mark McIntosh, to have the mind of Christ (1 Cor 2:16) means "to think within the framework of Jesus' own fidelity and joy with respect to the Father's abundant life; it also means, therefore, to be drawn into God's own humanly incarnate form of knowing."[38] Such a conversion results in a new pattern of mind, directed by love. The sinful disposition is characterized by envy and fear of scarcity, leading to diversions. Conversely, there emerges "a vision of the divine generosity . . . utterly free from fearful grasping."[39] The new pattern of mind is open to abundance exactly by a sense of dependence. Such a combination points to a new assessment of relations; moreover, it does not give up logical precision but relaxes it by "delegating" it to an irreducible plurality of persons and perspectives: "It seems that these

---

38. Mark McIntosh, "Faith, Reason, and the Mind of Christ," p. 135 in this volume.
39. Ibid.

thoughts . . . are too large, as it were, to be thought individually; the mind of Christ seems irreducibly relational in its constitution. . . . [P]articipation in the mind of Christ is fundamentally a relational activity, a noetic event that transpires in the communion of love."[40] Against this background, scientific reason may be transformed without simply losing its characteristic features. But it makes a difference whether the renunciation of a unified theory is *nolens volens* dictated by the insight that ultimate theories are inaccessible to us, or whether the certainty that precise plurality is beautiful is reflective of the joy that is found in divine abundance. If the universe is "constituted in Trinitarian form, then thinking with the mind of Christ will . . . make possible a perception of reality in its truest depths." A Christian scientist exploring quarks, quasars, and the like may at the same time "discern such particles in their true identity as expressive events, outpourings, in the infinite exchange of love that is the divine life. Even the apparent necessities of nature are ultimately gratuitous, luminous with freely giving love of the Trinity."[41]

As I said above, the distinction is difficult because all elements of created reason have "survived" the fall, but in a perverse arrangement. The perversion is comparable to obsessive compulsions: As long as human persons insist on human self-constitution over against being constituted by divine creativity, all elements of the human mind have to serve this ultimate goal. And the more the human mind succeeds in eliminating perspectives incommensurable with a certain type of rationality as sketched in the first part of the essay, the more it will be unable to recognize creative and liberating alternatives. (This is the story of the Enlightenment, which in fact was the enthronement of technical rationality rather than the human mind's liberation.) The relecture of this destructive dynamics in the development of the modern mind will expose the hidden irony in this development. But this is already an interpretation from a distance and a sign of liberation. From such a distance, it is possible to rediscover the complexity of reason. We should give thanks to God for the gift of reason—and by the same token, we should not take reason too seriously. The human mind should not try to grasp ultimate insights—and perhaps exactly in this way it may come close to them.

The second part of the essay may be read in analogy to the *tertius usus legis*, the "third use" of the law. As members of the body of Christ, we are able to reread the law in a spiritual way and to discover the liberating potential of certain limitations. Similarly, reason's limitations may reflect the created beauty of the human mind. There is no beauty without limitation—and the question is, rather, whether the limits are the trace of divine creation and creativity or just the result of human blindness and stupidity, which may reflect the human rebellion against God.

There is one last level in understanding the combination "redemption and story." One major aspect of redeemed reason may be the concentration on living language rather than logically structured concepts. This is clear in the

---

40. Ibid., 136.
41. Ibid., 137.

context of metaphorical language and spongy terms. Moreover, such strange terms and words have their *Sitz im Leben* in narrative or dramatic contexts. As Alan Torrance rightly argues in his essay, theological perception (*noein*) requires the transformation (*metanoia*) by the Spirit of our perception.[42] Of course, this implies "a profound transformation of the epistemic orientation of the whole person. . . . There is a radical discontinuity between the old and new paradigms, and there is nothing that can be done from within the old paradigm that may constitute a propaedeutic for the new."[43] But there *will* be criteria developed from "within" and a posteriori. Or rather, there will be a more sensitive judgment, which distrusts criteria that can be applied mechanically. One of the features of narratives is irreversibility—and this must be opposed to repeatable processes and structures. One and the same sentence may have very different meanings in different situations. Sometimes such a difference in meaning may be surprising. Against this background, the conceptual analysis of reason's limitations may change its meaning simply because the second reading follows the surprising discovery of the ironies in the mind's self-constitution. What before was meant to prepare the ultimate foundation of knowledge is disclosed as a highly interesting part of the picture, interesting because of the creative failure to prepare the ultimate foundation of knowledge.[44] That is why the relation between internal conceptual analysis and its fresh and fruitful use in theological contexts is so complex.

---

42. He rendered it very helpfully the following way in an unpublished communication: Adequate theological perception "involves an element of discontinuity, (a shift) which means that *prospectively* such a perception is unanticipatable. At the same time, however, it denotes *retrospectively* an event which constitutes a radical fulfillment by way of this transformation. Thus, there is a profound *continuity*."

43. Torrance, "*Auditus Fidei,*" p. 36–37.

44. Such a pattern may account for the fact that there *is* a Christian metaphysics. A sound mind will indeed describe ontological structures of the world—or better, of creation—adequately, and there is no reason why such a (redeemed) description should *necessarily* differ from classical metaphysics on the *propositional* level. There may be a sacramental analogy: As the elements are transformed in the context of worship rather than magically, metaphysical propositions are transformed by the widening horizon of human experience in relation to God's action rather than by falsification or other modifications of their propositional content (see n. 35 on the principle of noncontradiction). In *this* respect I agree with one of the basic tendencies in Romanus Cessario's essay, "*Duplex Ordo Cognitionis,*" p. 330 in this volume, namely, the rejection of fideist irrationalism. In any case, there must be some continuity between a metaphysics of creation and a metaphysics of being, as suggested by Reinhard Hütter in his essay, "The Directedness of Reasoning and the Metaphysics of Creation," in this volume. However, the picture may be less harmonious. The criterion for the "unity of truth" (Hütter, p. 170) must be relationality, not vice versa. This will indeed lead to a *transfiguration* of metaphysics: "When transfigured by the normative horizon of the Christian faith, that is, by a redeemed judgment, the metaphysics of being is open to being elevated and assumed into the metaphysics of creation," p. 168. But then, I am not sure whether a metaphysics of creation is vulnerable because of its dependence on a metaphysics of being (cf. 186). If a metaphysics of creation concentrates on life, relation, irreversibility, etc., there is room for productive debate with metaphysical positions. I assume that there is no metaphysical structure that does not refer to the foundations of mathematics, but it is exactly the question whether logical strictness—a kind of *Zwanghaftigkeit*—conflicts with redeemed *Gelassenheit* and the release of *Machtförmigkeit* (p. 191). This conflict demonstrates, however, that the difference is not necessarily on the propositional level but on the level of sinful and liberated will—and on this point, I agree with Reinhard Hütter.

PART THREE

Situating Reason Theologically:
Reason in the Passage of Modernity

CHAPTER NINE

Covenantal Rationality and the Healing of Reason

— CARVER T. YU —

As I see it, the context for the following discussion on faith and reason is one in which reason has been severely undermined. It has been variously reduced to the epiphenomenon of biochemical reactions, a psychological process that negotiates among various hidden vital forces, something that reflects the structure of consciousness in its processing of sense impressions into experience, something that reflects certain structures intrinsic to the use of language, or simply a sociocultural tool for creating consensus. The philosophical conviction in regard to the correspondence between thought and reality, or the identity between logos in human thought and Logos of Being, is gone. Cut off from any objective mooring, reason becomes nothing more than a self-affirming device in the solipsistic process of self-consciousness or social construction and may thus be regarded as indistinguishable from fancy; scientific truth is likewise no different from myth. How should theologians respond to such modern/postmodern deconstruction of reason? Should we celebrate the downfall of reason for the fact that faith need no longer fear its challenge? Or should we lament the downfall of reason for the corollary demise of truth? The task for a theologian in this time of cultural crisis is to redirect the human spirit from the path that leads to nihilism with spiritual resources from the Christian faith. To put it another way, it is our task to restore reason to its proper place, so that it might be neither utterly devalued nor overvalued (to use the expression of *Fides et Ratio*).

Contextual Analysis: Obsession with Immanence and the Myth of Autonomy

How has reason come to such a state, and how may we find the way back to its true nature? To find the way back, we have to retrace the path along which reason has become distorted. There have been various attempts to get to the ontological root of the crisis of European humanity so as to find a starting point for reconstruction. In these attempts we can see signs of the root of the problem in modern philosophy.

Husserl, in his *Crisis of European Sciences*, points to the distortion of universal science (*theoria*) into objectivistic-naturalistic science as the root of the crisis of European humanity. His transcendental phenomenology aims on the one hand to expose such a distortion and on the other hand to establish the absolute irreducibility of the ego as the sure foundation for universal science. In such a move, however, the ego is "purified" to such an extent that it may be conceived as existing without the world. In Husserl's own words, "Consciousness, considered in its 'purity,' must be reckoned as a *self-contained system of Being*, as a system of *Absolute Being*, into which nothing can penetrate, and from which nothing can escape; which has no spatio-temporal exterior, and can be inside no spatio-temporal system; which cannot experience causality from anything nor exert causality upon anything."[1] In *Cartesian Meditations*, Husserl conceives of the ego as a monad of pure consciousness.[2] From such a starting point, Husserl has to struggle against the self-absorbing pure identity, and therefore absolute immanence, of the ego. In what sense is transcendence meaningful and possible? His phenomenology takes on the task of awakening the ego from the illusion of self-sufficiency, unveiling the intrinsic connection between the self and others, and elaborating "the idea of a subjectivity incapable of shutting itself up."[3] Whether or not the project has been successful is not our concern here. Husserl's struggle does indicate a problem in modern philosophy, namely, the problem of transcendence in immanence.

Heidegger identifies the same problem from another direction. If to Husserl objectivism is the defining characteristic of the problematic European sciences, then to Heidegger subjectivism is the essence of the modern age. The modern age began, according to Heidegger, when "the very essence of man itself changes, in that man becomes subject."[4] Descartes defines the human subject as "thinking substance." Substance in both Aristotle and Descartes is the "ultimate *hypokeimenon*," which by definition is absolutely self-subsistent. Thus, the human subject is an isolated entity, which needs no other entity in order to be. As "pure subject," the human person stands over against the world and represents the world to himself/herself. "That the world becomes picture is one and the same event with the event of man's becoming *subjectum* in the midst of that which is."[5] At the same time, through Descartes, the concept of truth as certainty also characterizes the modern age. It demands absolute assurance, absolute safety, and thus calls for

---

    1. Edmund Husserl, *Ideas*, trans. W. R. Boyce Gibson (London: Collier-Macmillan, 1972), 139.
    2. "The Ego, taken in full concreteness, we propose to call by the Leibnizian name: *monad*." Edmund Husserl, *Cartesian Meditations*, trans. Dorion Cairns (The Hague: Martinus Nijhoff, 1960), 67–68.
    3. Emmanuel Lévinas, *Collected Philosophical Papers*, trans. Alphonso Lingis (The Hague: Matinus Nijhoff, 1987), 151.
    4. Martin Heidegger, "The Age of the World Picture," in *The Question Concerning Technology and Other Essays*, trans. William Lovitt (New York: Harper & Row, 1977), 127.
    5. Ibid., 132.

absolute dominance as well as a stabilizing constancy.[6] This stabilizing constancy can be found only in the *ego cogitans*. "This constancy is the permanence of that which can never be doubted in any representing, even if this representing is a kind of doubting. . . . Reality is characterized as constancy by permanence (the persistence of representational thinking)."[7] *Hypokeimenon*, or *subiectum*, which originally means "that endures of itself" and "that lies constantly present" as the thing itself, is now used for the constantly representing subject. The subject, and the subject alone, acquires the status of "that endures of itself" and "that lies constantly present." The subject "subjects" and "enframes" the world into "world-picture."[8] The world as such, instead of being the horizon in and through which *Dasein* "exists" so that *Dasein* may become truly the "there" (*Da-*) for Being, becomes a "standing-reserve" or "enframed something" (*Ge-stell*) at the disposal of man.[9] The world thus becomes opaque. The subject is confronted with nothing other than itself. The total horizon of the self consists of nothing that does not come out of and is not identical with itself. Transcendence is completely obliterated. What characterizes the spirit of modernity is therefore its obsession with immanence. Knowledge in the modern age, as Lévinas observes, becomes "a relationship of the Same to the Other in which the Other is reduced to the Same and stripped of its foreignness."[10]

As the subject sees itself as the only horizon as well as the ground of itself, it also perceives itself as the only source of its acts and representations, the sole creator of its norms or laws. In this sense, the subject is a law unto itself. It is autonomous in the sense that it imposes laws not only on itself but also on the totality of reality. Reason cast within such a framework is inevitably directed toward self-grounding as well as rationalization of self-created laws. *Rationality becomes synonymous with the ideology of autonomy and the abolition of transcendence.*

Reason within such self-absorbing immanence is reason estranged from its true nature. Yet reason takes revenge by driving autonomous reason to epistemological despair, by demanding reasons even for the belief in reason, thus showing the groundlessness of autonomous reason, taking it to nihilism as its logical conclusion. Nihilism in the present age stands at the end of the history of this particular path of metaphysical endeavor. Its coming was long anticipated. In fact, right after Descartes, we have Hume's "destruction" of the Cartesian ego. Even for Kant, despite his seeming success in tying Hume's "bundle" with his transcendental "string," the certainty of the external world remains elusive. At the same time, reason carries the critique right to the heart

---

6. Martin Heidegger, "Metaphysics as History of Being," in *The End of Philosophy*, trans. Joan Stambaugh (New York: Harper & Row, 1973), 22–23.
7. Ibid., 29.
8. See Heidegger, "Age of the World Picture," 127–30.
9. Martin Heidegger, "The Question Concerning Technology," in *The Question Concerning Technology and Other Essays*, 17–21.
10. Emmanuel Lévinas, *Transcendence et Intelligibilité* (Geneva: Labor et Fides, 1984), 12ff., cited in Alain Renault, *The Era of the Individual*, trans. M. B. DeBevoise and Franklin Philip (Princeton, NJ: Princeton University Press, 1997), 144.

of his transcendental scheme, questioning the analyticity of analytic judgment and therefore what is a priori in understanding (as posed in Quine's "Two Dogmas"). The question concerning the universality of the structure of understanding indicates how fragile his transcendental scheme is.

In such an act of self-critique, we see reason rising above the metaphysics of immanence. In this act we see precisely the true nature of reason—reason rising above self-grounding, transcending itself, and orienting itself to that which is other than itself. Whenever the metaphysics of immanence prevails, reason continues to question its inner logic until openness for transcendence finally emerges. In both Hume and Kant, we see such a metaphysics holding sway. In Hume, it is immanence of the consciousness in the form of sense impressions. In Kant, it is the lawmaking a priori structure of consciousness. A respective critique of the two will endeavor to break open the metaphysics of immanence as a preparation for understanding reason within the covenantal structure of reality.

Obsession with Immanence in the Form of Sense Impressions and Reason's Critique

Hume's "destruction" of the self-grounding subject in Descartes' rationalistic scheme is powerful. However, he has not carried the critique far enough. The root of the matter is the metaphysics of immanence. Without addressing the issue, Hume's critique is deficient right from the start. Instead of autonomous reason standing on its own ground, we have in exchange sense impression affirmed as the ground of certainty and ultimate reference by an act of animal faith. Yet the question concerning the origin of sense impression has not been raised; it is just accepted as a given in the consciousness. Sense impression in Hume allows no opening to that which is exterior to consciousness. Any perspective that transcends sense impression is regarded as a violation. Once sense impression is taken as the ultimate ground of certainty, reason becomes unsure of its own ground, for obviously sense impression cannot be the ground of reason.

In the hands of the empiricists, reason is reduced to a tool for connecting ideas, a critical tool for examining whether certain ideas are reducible to sense impressions, or a metacritical tool for showing the self-contradictions of reason itself so as to affirm sense impression as the only sure foundation. Reason operating within the strict confines of sense impression is reason robbed of its transcendent perspective. To restore reason to its proper position, we must ask some tough foundational questions about the empiricist faith.

Empiricism from the Enlightenment onward makes a strong claim that experience is the only source of knowledge, "experience" being narrowly defined in terms of sense impressions and ideas derived from them. As a result, certain experiences are in principle precluded as experience in the empiricist sense. The experience of the interrelatedness of things in the world, which evokes a sense of wonder, is immediately dismissed as something that belongs to the personal and poetic, or is regarded as nothing but the product of the mind in its act of relating ideas. Nor is the experience of ourselves as distinct from the world counted as genuine experience, for the experience of ourselves as distinct from the world cannot be reduced ultimately to sense impressions. Likewise, the intuitive experience of the inseparability of our being with the world (our being-in-the-world) is regarded as philosophical fancy. However, by defining experience in such a way, empiricism—if it is to be consistent at all—will eventually explode by itself. Even Hume's skepticism can hardly be sustained.

Hume's first proposition is that "all our ideas, or weak perceptions, are derived from our impressions, or strong perceptions; and that we can never think of anything we have not seen without us or felt in our own minds."[11] With this simple proposition, all those ideas not reducible to sense impressions are to be held suspect. Based on the assumption that sense impression is the ultimate criterion for knowledge, critical reason can call almost anything into question, as I shall try to show. The idea of causal connection, for example, since it cannot be reduced to sense impressions, is called into question. Likewise, the idea of the external world is exposed to be groundless as soon as critical reason asks,

> By what argument can it be proved that the perceptions of the mind must be caused by external objects entirely different from them though resembling them (if that be possible) and could not arise either from the energy of mind itself, or from the suggestion of some invisible and unknown spirit or from some other cause still more unknown to us?[12]

Critical reason demands that the argument be substantiated only "by experience surely, as all other questions of a like nature." But as Hume himself puts it, "Here experience is and must be entirely silent. The mind has never anything present to it but perceptions and cannot possibly reach any experience of their connection with objects. The supposition of such a connection is therefore without any foundation in reasoning."[13] Solipsism seems inevitable, yet, ironically, even solipsism is impossible here, for the "I" as the subject of sense impressions is eventually exploded by critical reason exercised within the confines of sense impression. What is solipsism without the "I"? It is well known that Hume renders the "I" as nothing but "a bundle or collection of different perceptions":

> For my part, when I enter most intimately into what I call *myself*, I always stumble on some particular perception or other, of heat or cold, light or shade, love or hatred, pain or pleasure. I never can catch *myself* at any time without a perception and never can observe anything but the

---

11. David Hume, *A Treatise of Human Nature*, cited in Antony Flew, *David Hume—Philosopher of Moral Science* (Oxford: Blackwell, 1986), 19.

12. David Hume, *Enquiries Concerning Human Understanding and Concerning the Principles of Morals*, ed. L. A. Selby-Bigge (Oxford: Oxford University Press, 1962), 152–53.

13. Ibid., 153.

perception. . . . I may venture to affirm of the rest of mankind that they are nothing but a bundle or collection of different perceptions, which succeed each other with an inconceivable rapidity, and are in a perpetual flux and movement.[14]

However, as soon as we substitute "a bundle of perceptions" for the "I" in the very passage, the whole argument sounds rather strange, and a fundamental problem reveals itself. With the substitution, Hume's original argument sounds like this:

> When *the bundle of perceptions* enters most intimately into what it calls itself, the bundle always stumbles on some particular perception or other, of heat or cold, light or shade, love or hatred, pain or pleasure. *The bundle* never can catch *itself* at any time without a perception and never can observe anything but the perception. . . . *It* may venture to affirm of the rest of mankind that they are nothing but a bundle or collection of different perceptions.

Here it seems that if Hume's argument is to make sense at all, the bundle, which is mistakenly identified as "I," has to be something more than just a summation of perceptions. The bundle reflects on itself as well as all the perceptions that constitute the very bundle itself. What exactly is this reflective activity? To what reality does it point? If the reflection is one of the perceptions, then to what category of perception does it belong? If, however, it cannot be categorized as one of the perceptions, then the bundle has within itself something more than mere perceptions, and the "I" must then be more than just a bundle of perceptions. Thus, critical reason, if it is to be consistent at all, has to call into question Hume's reduction of the "I" to a collection of perceptions.

If critical reason were to take Hume's empiricist assumption and push it to its logical conclusion, would not his empiricism likewise be called into question?

Critical reason has to ask yet another fundamental question: What exactly is sense impression, or perception? We have taken it for granted that we have a clear and distinct idea of what perception is—but do we? At the same time, on the ground of sensation alone, how has Hume managed to establish the fact that ideas are the weakened form of sense impressions? What category of sense impression informs him about the connections between sense impressions and ideas? The concept of "derivation" (i.e., ideas being *derived* from impressions) should immediately be held suspect, for it reminds us of "causal connection." If skeptical reason is to be applied, is it not conceivable that impressions and ideas have actually no derivative relation—that they are separate and independent entities, which happen to coincide in a certain manner?

Hume insists on the fact that "all our distinct perceptions are distinct existences." In no uncertain terms, he states, "All these [i.e., our perceptions] are

---

14. David Hume, *A Treatise of Human Nature* I.4.6, ed. A. D. Lindsay (London: J. M. Dent & Son, 1934), 239.

different, and distinguishable, and separable from each other, and may be separately considered, and may exist separately, and have no need of anything to support their existence."[15]

How has Hume managed to derive such a wealth of ideas concerning perceptions from mere sense impressions? How does he come to know so much and to be so certain about the nature of perceptions, that they are "distinguishable, and separable . . . , and have no need of anything to support their existence"? All of these are metaphysical statements with no support from sense impressions. Based on what sense impressions may we derive the separability of perceptions, or their having no need for support? The fact that the sensation of color is always distinct from the sensation of taste and they are not necessarily connected does not therefore render each of these sensations separable and independent. In fact, insofar as experience is concerned, we have never stumbled on a separable sense impression such as "red" or "sweet" or "hot." Whenever we experience "red," it is never an abstract "redness" without a "red thing." It is always experienced as a part of a complex whole. That is, it is inseparable from the complex whole if it is to be experienced at all. To resolve the whole of complex sense impressions into atomic separable impressions, we need abstract thinking rather than sheer experience. The complex whole is immediately experienced, while the atomic impression is always the result of analytic reflection. The fact is, sensations always come as a "bundle." Whenever we experience sensations, we always experience the "bundledness" of these sensations at the same time. Is not this "bundledness" as real as the sensations themselves? Why does the "connectedness" of sensations have to be explained by the "habit" of mind, something that is completely outside experience?

If we can assume that individual sense impressions can be taken to be immediate and self-evident, then why not the presence of the world as it is presented to us in our everyday experience? Likewise the "I," which is even more immediate than the atomic perceptions abstracted out of the dissolution of the "I"? The experience of the world as a complex whole is certainly more immediate than the atomic perceptions as the building blocks of the complex perception we call the world.

Equally problematic is the idea of consciousness. Hume talks about the mind and consciousness as if we know what they are as ideas, which again are supposed to be reducible to sense impressions. As Hume states, "For since all actions and sensations of the mind are known to us by consciousness,"[16] it is vital that we ask, What exactly is consciousness? Do we have sense impressions of our consciousness? To what category of sense impression can the idea of consciousness be reduced? We have sense impressions, and we have ideas out of those sense impressions. We therefore have knowledge out of sense impressions and knowledge out of the relations of ideas. But how do we come to know that there is such a thing as consciousness? To put the question in a slightly different way, can we ever catch consciousness as such

---

15. Ibid.
16. Ibid., I.4.2, 190.

without the consciousness of something other than consciousness itself? Can consciousness be consciousness at all without that "something" that it is conscious of? Since whenever we stumble on consciousness we always stumble on the consciousness of something, and in no circumstance have we not stumbled on a consciousness without something, it is quite conceivable to conclude that without that "something," consciousness may not be. To make it more explicit, we may even say that *consciousness is world-dependent, as in no circumstance does consciousness appear without the world.* Even in transcendental consciousness, even as the self is reflecting on itself, on its own structure of consciousness, we can never have consciousness of the self without the world. No matter where we turn, the world is always there. Even as we talk about the structure of consciousness, we cannot but talk about it as structure for the perception of the world. Without the world, the structure of consciousness is empty. We may even turn Kant's Copernican Revolution around to affirm the world as the center around which consciousness revolves. *Instead of consciousness constituting the world, it is the world that makes consciousness real and concrete.*

Our questioning of the logic of immanence in Hume's empiricism opens up the possibility of a Copernican revolution in reverse. We must carry the questioning further, into Kant's scheme of grounding reason on itself.

Copernican Turn in Reverse—
Nature Questioning the Structure of Consciousness

Our dialogue with Kant to open up the horizon of transcendence will take a slightly different approach. We shall take up a theme—that of reason as a self-appointed judge interrogating nature. We shall attempt to turn the tables and have reason interrogated by nature, hoping that reason may see the need to take the guiding hand of nature in order to have knowledge. In so doing, again, we hope to break open the metaphysics of immanence so that reason may regain the transcendent perspective.

To assert the authority of reason, Kant's strategy is to show that reason is as immediate as sense impressions. Again, immediacy in self-consciousness is the measure of certainty. To establish the fact that reason is as immediate as sense impressions, Kant takes reason to the very heart of consciousness. His Copernican turn is from the objective order to the innate order of the consciousness. Reason is secure as the "eternal laws," the a priori necessary conditions of experience. As a priori necessary conditions of experience, reason is therefore autonomous, being independent of whatever sense impressions there are, and independent even of whether there is any objective order. Reason may therefore establish itself as an autonomous judge, as Kant demands in the preface of the second edition of *Critique of Pure Reason*:

> [Reason] *must not allow itself to be kept, as it were, in nature's leading-strings*, but must itself show the way with principles of judgment based upon fixed laws, constraining nature to give answer to questions of

reason's own determining. Accidental observations, made in obedience to no previously thought-out plan, can never be made to yield a necessary law, which alone reason is concerned to discover. Reason . . . must approach nature in order to be taught by it. *It must not, however, do so in the character of a pupil who listens to everything that the teacher chooses to say, but of an appointed judge who compels the witnesses to answer questions which he has himself formulated.*[17]

"Reason . . . must approach nature in order to be taught by it." By this Kant means that the science of nature must be solidly grounded on observations. But reason is the ultimate judge insofar as how these observations may be organized into a rational structure. According to Kant's demand, reason should formulate questions to nature, and reason even determines the way nature may answer.

However, Kant knows full well that as reason formulates questions to nature, it does so "as if" there is such a thing as nature responding to reason's questions in accordance with its own inner laws. What if there is no such nature? In fact, to Kant, there is no such thing as nature in itself; there is only nature as it has been presented to the mind, "framed" in a certain way by the innate structure of the mind. But then, if the self-appointed judge is the source that determines how nature is to appear to the mind, or if, as Kant has said, "we know a priori only what we ourselves put into things," then what is there for the judge to learn from nature through interrogating it? If, however, the self-appointed judge does have something to learn, does it mean that there is an ontological and cognitive distance between nature and the self-appointed judge? If this is the case, we may continue to ask, what if the self-appointed judge asks a question that implicitly violates the integrity of nature? Can nature "refuse" to answer? Can there be constraints from nature as to the kinds of questions reason may ask? Is it not possible to conceive of a certain stubbornness in nature, which may object to the way it is being "framed" into the structure of the mind? Again, Kant and his followers would regard these questions as misguided, for it is nature that must conform to the structure of consciousness. If, however, they allow their position to be taken to its logical conclusion, then nature becomes nothing but an objectified complex of our presentations; the objective world may even be regarded as nothing more than a stable illusion common to all human beings.

However, in the subject's attempt to subject nature in the image of reason, nature does not seem always to conform. In fact, the trouble is, nature is full of surprises to the Kantians and constructionists of all kinds. They have a lot to answer for when they attempt to subject nature to a subjectivist constructionist scheme. I would like, then, to turn the tables and have the self-appointed judge interrogated by nature, which continues to puzzle me in a profound way.

---

17. Immanuel Kant, *Critique of Pure Reason*, trans. Norman Kemp Smith (London: Macmillan, 1929), 20 (Bxiii). Italics mine.

How, for example, can Kantians show that it is the structure of the mind that leads us to construct a world in which only electric monopoles, and not magnetic monopoles, are allowed? And what about the various physical constants in nature? Are they merely part of the structural constants of the mind? If so, then Kantians would have to show us where they are to be located and identified in the consciousness and how they may be derived through an explication of the structure of understanding. Is it not possible that nature too has some fundamental structure presented to human consciousness as something given, something irreducible? For example, insofar as symmetry can be perceived everywhere in laws of nature, Kantians would of course see symmetrical structure as intrinsic to the way the mind works. But then, why occasionally do we see the breaking of symmetry in nature? Does the mind break symmetry occasionally to achieve architectural beauty? Could this not be "the cunning of nature," which from time to time exposes to us our own unwarranted arrogance?

Kant claims to have shown us the forms of sensibility and categories of understanding, and we cannot think of things in the world except as things that exist in space and time, causally connected with one another. Indeed, using these forms and categories isolated by Kant, we can deduce some basic physical laws. Armed with the fundamental concept of substance, we can deduce the law of conservation. We can also show that Newton's laws of motion are all intrinsic to our understanding of the world in terms of space, time, and causality. In fact, the first law is nothing but a statement of the principle of causality. That is, there can be no change of the state of a body without a cause. The second law relates cause and effect in a quantitative way. That is, the strength of cause (force) is proportional to the strength of effect (change of motion). The third law is about the symmetry of causality, that cause and effect may be related reciprocally. We may therefore argue that we can arrive at these laws by conceptual explication.

However, the three laws of motion are quite different from the law of gravitation. Armed with the second law of motion, together with careful observations, Kantians can work out a *description* of gravitational force by the equation $F = GMm/r^2$. But the magnitudes involved have to be explained. The "inverse square" relation can of course be explained in terms of the spherical area sweeping across the gravitational field. The larger the area, the weaker will be the field strength. That is, the field strength is inversely proportional to the area. And as the area is proportional to the square of the radius, the inverse square law can thus be understood purely in terms of geometry. But in order to do that, homogeneity of gravitational field has to be assumed. Kantians have to explain more clearly from what categories of understanding the homogeneity of gravitational field is to be derived. Perhaps more significantly, the law points to the fact that gravitational force depends on the product of inertial masses. We have to ask them how this may be derived from forms of sensibility or categories of understanding. Is the gravitational density of matter real or fictitious? Is the inertial mass real or fictitious, as something concocted by the mind? Why does gravitational force have to depend on mass? Is this dependence something given in nature? Here we may ask, *Can this not be an indication that there is something irreducible in nature, that our forms of sensibility and categories of understanding are informed and determined by it?*

As for the explication of the law of gravity in terms of forms of sensibility and categories of understanding, Kant would find Einstein's general theory of relativity highly useful, for he would be able to explain gravitation in terms of space-time geometry, which exactly is synthetic a priori according to him. But unfortunately, it also would deal a heavy blow to his scheme. First, his unwavering affirmation of Euclidean geometry would have to be completely revised. Even more serious than that is the question of how he would be able to deduce from the concept of space and the concept of mass the curving of space by mass in the way described in the general theory of relativity. This would have serious implications, and he would have to rethink his transcendental scheme, for now space and mass would be a continuum; the two would "grip on" each other. Thus, we may ask, Is the curving of space by mass something given and therefore anticipated by the mind? And what about the gravitational constant? Would he be able to show that all these are part of the given structure of consciousness? Or is it possible that all these are in fact something given in the way things are, revealing to us the stubbornness of a certain definite structure in nature?[18] F. S. C. Northrop, in drawing implications from the law of gravitation in light of general relativity, points out most aptly:

> This ultimate basis of space-time in the public, contingent, physical object of knowledge, rather than in the necessary constitution of the epistemological knower, follows from the tensor equation of gravitation in Einstein's general theory of relativity. Its ten potentials defining the gravitational field at the same time prescribe the metrical structure of space-time. Thus space-time has all the contingent character that the field strengths, determined by the *contingent distribution of matter* throughout nature, possess. Not even Kant would have referred these contingently distributed field strengths to the necessary constitution of the scientist as knower.[19]

Perhaps even more fundamentally, the theory of relativity brings to Kant the whole problem of the nature of space, for if space can only be conceived in terms of relation, then the subject has to be placed within a structure of relation, and the transcendental ego can no longer be the center of reference.

---

18. Richard Feynman describes the fundamental difference in attitude between the scientist, who is involved in discovering physical laws, and the transcendental philosopher, who contemplates the structure of the mind: "I am interested not so much in the human mind as in the marvel of a nature which can obey such an elegant and simple law as this law of gravitation. Therefore our main concentration will not be on how clever we are to have found it all out, but on how clever nature is to pay attention to it." Feynman, *The Character of Physical Law* (Cambridge, MA: MIT Press, 1989), 14.

19. F. S. C. Northrop, "Einstein's Conception of Science," in *Albert Einstein: Philosopher-Scientist*, ed. Paul Arthur Schilpp (Evanston, IL: Library of Living Philosophers, 1949), 396 (italics mine).

"The way is now open to regard the knower as a relational part of, and continuous with, physical nature."[20]

Intuitively we know, though we may not be able to refute definitively the determined doubt of skeptics, that we are confronted with something irreducible, something much greater than what can be derived from the mind. Here we may draw an analogy from Popper's heuristic argument for the existence of other minds:

> I know that I have not created Bach's music, or Mozart's; that I have not created Rembrandt's pictures, or Botticelli's. I am quite certain that I never could do anything like it: I just do not have it in me. . . . But on the solipsistic hypothesis, all these creations would be those of my own dreams. They would be creatures of my own imagination. For there would be no other minds: there would be nothing but my mind. I know that this cannot be true.[21]

By the same token, the immensity of the cosmos overwhelms me; its complexity yet simplicity gives me an endless sense of wonder. I also know that I could never imagine the vastness and intricate relatedness of things if they were not thrust before me. To think that it is I who concoct in my own mind the structure of all that there is appears to me to be the utmost form of arrogance.

Such arrogance is possible when we are locked in epistemological discussions purely in logico-linguistic terms, without paying close attention to how actual scientific discovery has been achieved. Of course, a reflective theoretical physicist, as Einstein points out, is keenly aware of the fact that the "axiomatic basis of theoretical physics cannot be abstracted from experience but must be *freely invented*,"[22] yet at the same time, he is equally aware of the fact that "nobody who has really gone deeply into the matter will deny that in practice the world of phenomena uniquely determines the theoretical system, in spite of the fact that there is no logical bridge between phenomena and their theoretical principles."[23] To him, the ideal of merely connecting the facts of experience for instrumental purpose could not have kindled his passion "from which really great achievements have arisen," but "*behind the tireless efforts of the investigator there lurks a stronger, more mysterious drive: it is the existence and reality that one wishes to comprehend.*"[24]

The Covenantal Nature of Reason

Reason questioning its own attempts at self-grounding points to something beyond itself. Such self-transcending orientation of reason, when taken into consideration, will point to a more holistic understanding of reason.

---

20. F. S. C. Northrop, "Natural Science and the Critical Philosophy of Kant," in *The Heritage of Kant*, ed. G. T. Whitney and D. F. Bowers (Princeton, NJ: Princeton University Press, 1939), 60.
21. Karl Popper, *Realism and the Aim of Science* (Totowa, NJ: Rowman & Littlefield, 1983), 83–84.
22. Albert Einstein, *The World as I See It*, cited in F. S. C. Northrop, "Einstein's Conception," 394–95 (italics mine).
23. Ibid., 401.
24. Ibid., 400 (italics mine).

What is reason? To answer this, we first must ask, What is knowledge? Putting reason in such a proper context is highly important. The problem with philosophers such as Kant is that they treat reason as a faculty in abstraction from all the life activities of human existence, enthroned as a detached judge before whom all life experiences are to be paraded and put in the dock for questioning. Reason has to be located in life for the fullness of life. Knowledge (understanding, wisdom) is a way through which such fullness is to be attained.

What is knowledge? When I say, "I know X," I am referring to a state of affairs in which "I" and "X," two distinct entities, are related by the word "know." I am speaking of a cognitive event through which "X," something that is cognitively distant from "I," is brought into cognitive union with "I." Knowledge refers to a state of relation in which communion has been attained. It is well known that the Old Testament term *yada'* has the connotation of sexual intercourse, an intimate form of relation. To know something is to enter into communion with that something in accordance with its nature. In the communion, the object of knowledge becomes "mediatedly immediate" to the knower. The character, the boundary, and the possibilities of relation of the object with others are acknowledged in such a way that the knower is constrained to relate to or interact with it in accordance with all these. To know something is thus to know how it is possible to relate with the thing and to enter into the web of relation that the thing opens up to the knower. To come into communion with the thing is also to come into communion with all those implicated by the relation. Insofar as human persons seek knowledge, we manifest our desire for communion and actively bring it to actualization. The seeking for knowledge and understanding betrays in us the desire or impulse to come into union, to some degree of immediacy of relation, with that which is other than ourselves. In this sense, we agree with Augustine that knowledge is motivated by love. To a certain extent, the intensity of the subject's desire to know is proportional to the intensity of the subject's love for the object of knowledge.

From the theological perspective, this is not difficult to understand. The created world is a world of vast variety among beings, a kingdom of unique individuals destined for unity in Christ (Eph 1:10), for all things are "from him and through him and to him" (Rom 11:36). It is therefore a world of distinctive realities in communion, communion in which the distinctiveness of each and every individual is preserved. As that which is part of those consisting in Christ (Col 1:17), there is in each and every created thing a natural inclination, intrinsic to its being, toward communion with the rest of the created order. A thing can be said to be true to its being, that is, to exist in truth, only when it participates in the communion of being and becomes unified in Christ, the Logos of creation. A thing exists in truth when its covenantal character (i.e., its charitable nature) is realized. In this sense, truth and charity, or truth and love, cannot be separated. From this perspective, the pursuit of knowledge is nothing but a pursuit of communion. To know something is to actuate communion with it. To know it is to put it within a world of interconnectedness, of mutual participation, interpenetration, engagement, and resonance. Such knowledge is motivated by love and fulfilled in love. To know something without a love for it is a distortion of knowledge right from the start.

To love something in the knowing of it, the subject transcends its self-centeredness and submits itself under the truth and integrity of the thing to be known. An act of knowing therefore involves a certain degree of self-forgetfulness, with the ego lost in wonder for the thing being known. An act of knowing is an act of response; it stems not purely from an inner urge but is "called" (or attracted) into action by that which is other than the self. It is a covenantal act of responsibility and mutuality.

Skeptics do not understand the charity in knowing. To them, knowing is an act that is centered in the self. They comprehend the world from the center of their consciousness and refuse to make one single step out of the center because that is their absolute security. They are secure with themselves, for they know themselves in the self and through the self. The self is the totality of secure knowing. They know the world as an objectified image of themselves. Knowing is self-objectification. In such a maneuver of knowing, they lose the real world meant for their "possession" (apprehension). What they "possess" is a phantom of their own making. They know full well that it is nothing but a phantom, and so is their skepticism. Their skepticism reveals the falsehood in which they are being involved in knowing. Their rejection of such "reality" as the really real reflects the truthfulness endowed in them as beings meant for truth and charity.

Kant calls it "a scandal to philosophy and to human reason in general" that there is still no satisfactory proof for the existence of things outside of us.[25] But as Heidegger rightly points out:

> The "scandal of philosophy" is not that this proof has yet to be given, but that *such proofs are expected and attempted again and again.* Such expectations, aims, and demands arise from an ontologically inadequate way of starting with *something* of such a character that independently *of it* and "outside" *of it* a "world" is to be proved as present-at-hand.[26]

The world is given not merely as something "outside" but much more as something on which the very being of the subject depends. Even the very act of doubting the existence of the world would not be possible without the sustenance of the world. The world is in this sense intrinsic to the very act of doubting. Thus, the world "outside" is also "inside"—through and through— the being of the subject. To the Chinese mind, whether in the Confucian or Daoist tradition, this is easy to understand. The Confucian tradition regards *Ren* as the ideal state of humanity. It is a state in which human persons become truly human. To attain this state, persons have to begin with *Jing*—an attitude of respect or awe in the face of the reality of the world. All knowledge

---

25. Kant, *Critique of Pure Reason*, 34 (Bxl), cited in Martin Heidegger, *Being and Time*, trans. John Macquarrie and Edward Robinson (Oxford: Blackwell, 1962), 247.
26. Heidegger, *Being and Time*, 249.

begins with a deep respect for Dao, which speaks through the world in general and humanity in particular. Doubt about the existence of the world is to the Chinese the outcome of the distortion of reason. It becomes therefore irrational even to prove the existence of the world. To the Chinese mind, it is necessary to trust in the world before it is possible to know it. *Knowledge thus begins with trust in the integrity and knowability of the world.*

Reason, which becomes real only in functioning in the act of knowing as an act of covenantal response, is very different from the autonomous reason idealized by the Enlightenment philosophers.

Reason is a capability endowed in human persons for the making of covenant. It enables us to transcend precisely our self-centeredness, to remain individual selves without being locked within those selves. To put it another way, it enables us to maintain the integrity of our own being while being truthful to the true nature of that which is other than ourselves. Reason is integral to the act of response in accordance with the reality of the covenantal partner. Reason is the power for truthful response in order to achieve communion. Thus, reason acts in order that the subject may be faithful in following the object into the various modalities of its being so as to interact with it, eventually "apprehending"("possessing") its true being and entering into communion with it accordingly. Insofar as "creation is the external basis of covenant, and covenant is the internal basis of creation" (Karl Barth), reason is the natural endowment for the articulation of the covenantal nature of all that is.

Reason as it should be has its focus fixed on the attainment of communion and unity in the Logos. It regards itself as no more than an instrument of self-transcendence in a covenantal mode of existence. To function properly, reason cannot direct its focus merely on itself. It has to direct its focus toward the covenantal reality of things and their unity in the Logos. Thus, the transcendent perspective is vital to the proper function of reason. Once the transcendent perspective is lost, reason becomes imprisoned in self-love and self-grounding; it becomes lost in endless self-reflection, leading to the critical negation of itself. Such a self-love is hardly true love for itself. As the mind seeks to know itself with great zeal, it is quite clear that the mind loves. However, as Augustine aptly asks, "What does it love? Is it itself? . . . Perhaps, then, it does not love itself, but loves that which it imagines of itself, which is perhaps widely different from what itself is."[27] *Reason that turns narcissistic is sick. It needs healing.*

To use Augustine's analogy, reason is "that in the mind, which the act of looking is in the eyes. For to have eyes is not the same as to look; nor again to look the same as to see."[28] That is to say, even as reason has the power to look, if it indulges in itself and does not care to look, there is no possibility for it to see anything beyond itself. Even as it looks, if it does not look in the

---

27. Augustine, *On the Trinity*, trans. Arthur W. Haddan (*Nicene and Post-Nicene Fathers*; Peabody, MA: Hendrickson, 1994), 3:136.
28. Augustine, *Soliloquies* I,12, trans. Charles C. Starbuck (*Nicene and Post-Nicene Fathers*; Peabody, MA: Hendrickson, 1994), 7:541.

direction of the light, it will likewise fail to see. Reason needs to be directed by the light to look beyond itself toward the source of the light. That which incites reason to look in the direction of truth—giving it orientation and a sense of assurance—is faith, and that which can heal reason of its despair in seeking is hope.[29] As Augustine puts it,

> [A] right and perfect act of looking, that is, one followed by vision, is called Virtue; for Virtue is either right or perfect Reason. But even the power of vision, though the eyes be now healed, has not force to turn them to the light, unless these three things abide. Faith, whereby the soul believes that thing, to which she is asked to turn her gaze, is of such sort, that being seen it will give blessedness; Hope, whereby the mind judges that if she looks attentively, she will see; Charity, whereby she desires to see and be filled with the enjoyment of the sight.[30]

Faith is not, as some would take it to be, a willfulness to believe without, or even in contradiction to, reason. Rather, faith and reason do not operate one without the other. Faith is never exercised without reason, and reason cannot sustain itself without faith. The two sustain and affect each other. Faith is an intuitive acknowledgment of the indubitable, which cannot be rejected without putting reason at stake. Even the most radical skeptics who doubt everything cannot have doubt about the fact that they doubt. Their radical doubt tacitly acknowledges something indubitable. Augustine pushes doubt to the edge where skeptics cannot but admit the reality of something indubitable. His argument does not seem to rely on the principle of noncontradiction like Descartes' *cogito ergo sum*; rather, it relies on an intuitive grasp:

> Seeing that even if he doubts, he lives; . . . if he doubts, he understands that he doubts; if he doubts, he wishes to be certain; if he doubts, he thinks; if he doubts, he knows that he does not know; if he doubts, he judges that he ought not to assent rashly. Whosoever therefore doubts about anything else, ought not to doubt about all these things; which if they were not, he would not be able to doubt of anything.[31]

It is quite clear that without such tacit acknowledgment, skeptics' radical doubt would be rendered absurd or irrational. Such acknowledgment is in consonance with reason, though it is not a conclusion by rational proof. Reason is therefore not the ground for such an intuitive grasp. The ground is reality itself, which confronts the skeptics as irreducible and irrefutable. The fact that they move, think, doubt, and live depends on this ground, which they doubt, or seek to comprehend, but admit being uncertain of what they are able to comprehend. In this light, faith may be regarded as humans' endowed capability to have "ontological resonance" with reality, so that even

---

29. Ibid.
30. Ibid., I.6.13.
31. Augustine, *On the Trinity* X.10.14.

in doubting we cannot but affirm certain things to be true. Reality is the ulti-mate reason for any claim of certainty; it is the ground for reason to be gen-uine reason; it "compels" us to recognize it in and through our own being "as if" there is a resonance between the two. To put it another way, faith may be understood as the endowed disposition and capability in humans to be responsive to reality in a faithful way. *Fides* means in the primary sense "fidelity," or "faithfulness." Humans are created in such a way that we are answerable to reality, to be faithful to it so as to be true to our own being as well. To be faithful to the integrity of reality also means to be obedient to the inner logic with which reality unfolds itself. Obedience is a fundamental dis-position in the seeking of understanding of reality. In obedience, seeking is thinking after reality rather than presuming or even prefabricating what real-ity might be.

To put it yet another way, faith is intuitive trust, without which no human action, including the exercise of reason, would be possible. The most basic trust is the fact that there is something rather than nothing, that at least there is the instance of doubting or thinking, if not the subject who doubts or thinks. As soon as the question arises, What is the ground for affirming that there is something and not nothing? or Why is there something and not noth-ing? there is the intuitive trust for reason. As soon as reason starts the process of skeptical critique in order to get to the truth "that there is no truth," there is the intuitive trust that "truth" can be attained through the exercise of rea-son. Faith in this sense is trust with compelling "reason" that is much more fundamental than the rationality established by reason alone. The "reason" that cannot be articulated by the exercise of rational thinking is the ground that makes reason real and functionable. To use Tillich's metaphor, what we call "reason" here is the "depth of reason" that precedes reason but is insep-arable from the exercise of reason.

On the level of human existence, faith as trust is essential. Trust as judg-ment without indubitable rational proof but not without reason is tacit in human action and the conduct of life. For example, I have no indubitable proof that my mother is truly my mother. However, I trust that she is my mother, not in an arbitrary way without reason. The trust comes from an inner assurance through countless affirmations in the way my mother loves me. Those affirmations are not justifications of the category of indubitable rational proof. Yet taken together, they are compelling enough for me to make the judgment that my mother is truly my mother. The exercise of criti-cal reason demanding and looking for indubitable rational proof in this life situation would be an abuse of reason. Another example is the trust tacit in a rational discourse between two individuals concerning the nature of reason. To conduct the discourse, there has to be a tacit trust of the reality of the other as well as the fact that what the other says represents his/her thought so that there is a common basis for the discourse to be possible.

Reason confronts the reality of mystery and thus the reality of revelation when it confronts another human person. The subjectivity of another human person presents a certain degree of hiddenness, which poses a limit to the way reason may operate. Entering into the realm of the personal, reason can only operate with a sense of trust, following the lead of the other person in the unveiling of himself/herself. Here faith opens the possibility of dialogue in which reason may function in the mode of dialogical rationality. Reason in this context is the capability of truthful or faithful following. Autonomous reason becomes an illusion. Thus, it is in interpersonal encounters that the arrogance of autonomous reason is exposed. In the mode of faithful following, reason is sustained by trust so as to press forward toward a true understanding of the other person. To achieve such an understanding, reason and faith work together.

To confront the mystery of another person is to confront something that transcends rational grasp. The other person opens up the transcendent horizon of the wholly Other. To enter into the mystery of the Absolute Subject, reason has to be healed of its self-absolutization and purified of its autonomous inclination in order to function properly. Reason is therefore rational response to the divine reality unfolded in revelation. Insofar as the image of God is a unique endowment for human persons to be responsive to God, reason may be perceived as an essential part of the image of God. It is the capability to be "informed" by the divine reality and to direct our response in accordance with it. In the act of response, the center of determination is in the Absolute Subject. Reason is therefore continually challenged to transcend itself. Reason as an endowed capability of self-transcendence becomes realized in such a responsive act of seeking understanding. The correlation of reason with faith, hope, and love becomes most clearly manifested in such a dialogical understanding.

CHAPTER TEN

Naming God:
A Study in Faith and Reason

— JANET MARTIN SOSKICE —

The earliest Christian theologians wrestled their pagan or heretical foes with confident intellectualism. Think of Justin Martyr's *Apologies* or Gregory of Nyssa's *Contra Eunomium*. Paul himself was no mean rhetorician. Later and in a different literary genre we have Dante's *Commedia* with its confident harmony of faith and reason, despite Dante's acknowledgment of human guile and culpability. But for us moderns faith, it seems, must seek shelter from reason's assaults or else stoutly assert the primacy of faith over the claims of reason. Either way, the two are in conflict.

We know that human beings, and therefore human thoughts and actions, were as subject to disorder and sin for Paul and Gregory of Nyssa and Dante as for us, but reason was still for them a useful friend. It is reason, in the personified form of the pagan Virgil, who guides the Christian Dante through Inferno and Purgatory to the very steps of Paradise; Virgil indeed has initially more insight into willful self-delusion than does Dante. Virgil seems to know that there is a God who orders the world. He understands that in our greed and ignorance we wound each other, the natural world, and ourselves. He can explain to Dante that "soothsayers" are condemned by their presumption to follow each other, endlessly, in a circular ditch, their heads on backward so they can only see what is behind. Yet Virgil cannot, for all that he is reason personified, follow Dante into the Paradise toward which he has been the guide.

We might suppose that Virgil should either enter heaven with Dante or else not possess such insight into the human condition and the life of virtue, but Dante keeps him outside. Virgil does not know Christ. Dante's Virgil seems to have heard that there is such a one, but he never utters the name of Christ. In *Purgatorio* canto 9, St. Lucy (perhaps a figure of enlightening grace) comes to Dante in a dream. He knows penance—contrition, confession, and works of love, and is wounded by the sword of the Word. Virgil can read the Book of Nature, but he does not know the Word. The things of faith are for him, literally, a closed book, and he cannot make the final journey. For this journey we need to know not everything, but simply Christ. In Dante there is no tension between faith and reason: God has made us to find our true fulfillment, and even the fulfillment of our reason, but it is grace that takes us there. Reason can guide, but in the end only penance, the cross, and relationship with the Savior will bring us the *salus* that is delight and flourishing and our true end. This is an end that is "supernatural," not because it is contrary or outside of nature, but because it is our nature by grace perfected.

In all this Dante is the pupil of Thomas Aquinas: God is our origin and end. We are made for fellowship with God, and our nature is such that it is capable of perfection by grace. The Creator is the beginning and true end of all creatures. Within Thomas's scheme of things, reason, however burnished and dazzling, is ancillary to faith, or holy teaching. In the ancient and medieval Christian world reason, itself a creature, is the God-given human reception of the world's intelligibility. Today reason is a capacity of human animals, a precision technique of the mind, and has little about it of a metaphysical alliance with reality.

The past twenty years have seen unprecedented interest in Aquinas's writings from philosophers and theologians outside the seminaries, and many of them are not Roman Catholics. There are good reasons why Aquinas should be attractive, especially to those whose background is in analytic philosophy. We find in his thought features philosophers admire: precision of expression, rigor in argument, and an interest in what we would today regard as questions of philosophy of language. We find in Aquinas an empiricism that insists that *we are the kind of creature who knows through experience.* Yet modern religious apologetics has antecedents unknown to Thomas—for instance Newton and all the physico-theologians in his wake concerned with what we can know from evidence, and, in a different but overlapping trajectory, a string of philosophers troubled about certainty, including Montaigne, Descartes, Hobbes, Locke, Hume, and Kant. Modern philosophy is informed by skepticism, and even when not skeptic itself it tends to gravitate around questions put by skepticism.[1]

The early modern crisis of knowledge was such that philosophy in many quarters became *epistemology*—the problem of knowledge. In retrospect, the anxieties about salvation that shook the late medieval church, although doubtlessly provoked by clerical corruption, indulgences, failed conciliar movements and so forth, had a good deal to do with uncertainty about everything. It is not clear that we are beyond the trauma of *knowing* yet.[2]

When we consider "faith and reason," we have behind us the seventeenth- and eighteenth-century projects of natural theology—projects that find some

---

1. David Bentley Hart, "The Offering of Names: Metaphysics, Nihilism, and Analogy," which begins on page 255 in this volume.
2. Nor, despite postmodern efforts, have we freed ourselves from that last philosophical redoubt, "the citadel of the self," which, as David Hart points out, looks as much a prison as a sanctuary. See Hart, p. 280.

parallel in Aquinas but that are, in other respects, quite different. Modern philosophical terminology such as "justified belief," "warranted assertibility," "epistemic rights," and "epistemic duties" sits oddly with the texts of Aquinas. These are the terms of art of a primarily epistemological discussion that has dominated religious apologetics in the English-speaking world since Locke, Hume, and Kant. Whereas for Aquinas and for Dante "faith and reason" were bound together in a marvelous economy where grace perfects nature, we must repeat the endless argument over "arid rationalism" and "mere credulity."

Between Dante's time and our own a sea change has taken place. Some credit to the rise of modern science the fact that we no longer conclude with Dante that it is "love which moves the sun and the other stars" (*Paradiso*, canto 33). It is not obvious why this should be. The most fundamental shift in belief has not been in cosmology but in metaphysics, although some have argued, in ways that disregard the metaphysical commitments of contemporary astrophysics, that modern science itself makes metaphysics impossible. What can be said in retrospect is that after at least a millennium of settled alignment to belief in the Creator God as delineated in Judaism, Christianity, and Islam, the philosophy of the early modern period, including the philosophy of God, set off in directions of its own. This was not initially the work of skeptics or agnostics—on the contrary, it was done largely in the defense of faith. Theologians and Christian philosophers alike, excited by the bright promise of reason, endeavored to show that truths which were once held on the fragile testimony of ancient books could now be more solidly based on reason alone. This project, insofar as it sought to deliver the biblical God on the basis of reason, failed. We might say that it should never have been embarked upon, for the idea that the particularity of the revelation to Moses or in Christ could be, without loss, replaced by the findings of reason is heretical. One unintended result of this pious if misguided modernist project was a diminution of the radical transcendence brought into Western thought—not by the Greeks—but by a distinctively Christian and Jewish belief in creation *ex nihilo*. With this came a loss of the radical distinction between Creator and creature, and accordingly a collapse of religious language into effective "univocity," but this is to anticipate.

By way of drawing out what changed I would like to compare two thinkers, John Locke and Thomas Aquinas, on a topic of interest to them both and one of perennial interest in the philosophy of religion: the names, or attributes, of God. Bringing these two together is useful not least because they had much in common. Both were devout men. They were interested in the coherence of theism and shared a high view of reason. Neither accepted the ontological argument or that the idea of God was innate,[3] but both thought that reason unassisted by revelation could make evident that there is

---

3. Aquinas, *Summa theologiae* (hereafter ST) Ia2–11 and John Locke, *Essay Concerning Human Understanding*, ed. Peter H. Nidditch (Oxford: Oxford University Press, 1975), book I, ch. 4.

a God.[4] Furthermore, in the writings of both we see a structural link between the proofs, or demonstrations, of God's existence and the divine attributes—"that God is" is bound up with "what God is." The names cannot be separated from our means of naming.[5]

For both Aquinas and Locke, it is a matter of piety that reason should be able to make evident that there is a God and on this basis say some things about the God thus made evident. They take their lead, as did Augustine and John Calvin before them, from Paul: "Ever since God created the world his everlasting power and deity—however invisible—have been there for the mind to see in the things he has made" (Rom 1:20 JB). This demonstrability is an instance of God's kindness to us, his rational creatures.[6]

These similarities make the differences more striking, and in the matter of naming a change has taken place somewhere between the thirteenth and the seventeenth centuries, a change that we describe in shorthand by noting that omnipotence, omniscience, and eternity are, for Locke, *divine attributes*, whereas for Aquinas they are *divine names*.

Here is Locke on the name of God in the *Essay Concerning Human Understanding*. The context is his dismissal of innate ideas. The "idea of God" comes in because some of Locke's predecessors who argued for innate ideas maintained that the idea of God would be one of these. Locke disagreed, and his argument here is couched in terms of the philosophy of language. In his version of the description theory of meaning, every term (or name) has an associated idea that determines its application; thus, to call something gold is to have a conception of gold and to apply it in particular circumstances. He says this concerning the name "God":

> The name of God being once mentioned in any part of the world, to express a superior, powerful, wise, invisible being, the suitableness of such a notion to the principles of common reason, and the interest men will always have to mention it often, must necessarily spread far and wide, and continue it down to all generations.

Men do not need this idea "stamped on the Mind,"

> since he has furnished Man with those Faculties, which will serve for the sufficient discovery of all things requisite to the end of such a Being.

And Locke tells us that he will show

---

4. Aquinas, ST Ia 2; compare Locke, *Essay*, book IV, ch. 10, and book I, ch. 4, 94–95. There is some debate as to whether Aquinas believed his "Five Ways" worked as proofs for the existence of God, but he seemed to feel each demonstrated the existence of that which all people call God.

5. In the *Summa theologiae*, Aquinas famously follows his succinct presentation of the Five Ways with an account of what we can and cannot know of God, and of how we describe God. These questions treat of God's simpleness, perfection, goodness, limitlessness, existence in all things, unchangeableness, and eternity. Locke gives his account of the "divine attributes" in the *Essay*, book IV, ch. 10, and variously throughout. See also book II, ch. 23.

6. See Locke, *Essay*, book I, ch. 4.

that a Man by the right use of his natural Abilities, may, without any innate Principles, attain the Knowledge of God, and many other things that concern him.[7]

"Knowledge of God" includes knowledge that there is a God and certain things about him, that is, his qualities. Locke in general thinks we can know (as opposed to believe) very little, not only about God but also about anything at all, so his claim about religious knowledge is uncharacteristically strong.

For Locke, the idea of God is a compilation of various simple ideas. He makes clear that not any idea will do. Many persons and tribes have grossly imperfect ideas on this matter, but they are misguided—probably by their acceptance of mere fashion or tradition. The idea of God that Locke offers is superior, he believes, because it is the fruit of reason and therefore will carry all before it:

[T]hey, who made the Discovery [of God as a superior, powerful, wise, invisible being], had made a right use of their reason, thought maturely of the Causes of things, and traced them to their original; from whom other less considering people, having once received so important a notion, it could not easily be lost again.[8]

All those who reflect seriously upon the "Constitution and Causes of things" can arrive at this knowledge that there is a Being superior, powerful, wise, and invisible:

[O]ur Reason leads us to the knowledge of the certain and evident Truth— That there is an eternal, most powerful, and most knowing Being; which whether any one will please to call God, it matters not. This thing is evident, and from this Idea duly considered, will easily be deduced all those other attributes which we ought to ascribe to this eternal Being.[9]

We get then not only "God" but a clutch of positive predicates—the divine attributes, or "qualities" as Locke sometimes terms them. By use of God-given reason, anyone may know not only that there is a God but also that God is a knowing and providential Being.[10]

For Locke, philosophical reflection is not just one way but the best way to the knowledge that there is a God and also to some understanding, limited but sufficient, of the divine nature. Indeed, Scripture is not only dispensable for this purpose, but it is also confusing. Locke does not doubt the truth of revelation nor deny that we should believe in it, but he fears we may be confused

---

7. Locke, *Essay*, book I, ch. 4, 90–91.
8. Ibid., book I, ch. 4, 90.
9. Ibid., book 4, ch. 10.
10. When Locke says that this idea of God is "natural," he does not mean that it is spontaneous or even an idea likely to be held by many, but rather that it is appropriate. I am grateful to Dr. Ian Harris for this formulation.

as to just what revelation is and how it should be understood. Biblical commentaries, he notes, multiply conflicting interpretations, and even "though every thing said in the text be infallibly true, yet the reader may be, nay cannot chuse but be very fallible in the understanding of it."[11]

This surprising combination of biblical piety and skepticism prompts us to recall that Locke was writing when the English Civil War was still recent. Old certainties—religious, social, and political—had been contested. Even Scripture was contested, if not in its overall authority then at least by variant and sectarian readings that led to bloodshed. Locke wanted to establish means by which right-thinking people may come to agreement on matters of importance, and palpable as any desire to answer skepticism and avoid chaos is his distrust of the stranglehold of religious authority and tradition. He is opposed, in his own terms, to Romanists as well as to Enthusiasts. He wants authority without authoritarianism, and the best way to have knowledge on matters of such great moment as the existence and nature of God— and to have it without dogmatism—is to have it on the basis of reason alone. As for Scripture, we simply cannot, he believes, attain the same certainty from texts subject to the vagaries of interpretation as we do from the right use of reason—reflecting upon things evident to us.[12] Employing a bold analogy, Locke says that even as the Son of God "when cloathed in flesh" was subject to human frailty (except for sin), the "will of God, when cloathed in words" will always be liable to doubt and uncertainty.[13] We arrive at this decidedly eighteenth-century conclusion,

> Since then the Precepts of Natural Religion are plain, and very intelligible to all Mankind, and seldom come to be controverted; and other revealed Truths, which are conveyed to us by Books and Languages are liable to the common and natural obscurities and difficulties incident to Words, methinks it would become us to be more careful and diligent in observing the former, and less magisterial, positive, and imperious, in imposing our own sense and interpretations of the latter.[14]

When Aquinas dealt with such predicates as "eternal," "One," and "simple," he stood in a tradition of reflections *de nominibus dei* going back to Denys the Areopagite and beyond—a theological and mystical as well as a philosophical tradition. Locke's confidence that not only God's existence but

---

11. Locke, *Essay*, book III, ch. 9, 490.
12. "The History of the Deluge is conveyed to us by Writings, which had their Original from Revelation: And yet no Body, I think, will say, he has as certain and clear a Knowledge of the Flood, as *Noah*, that saw it; or that he himself would have had, had he then been alive, and seen it" (Locke, *Essay*, book IV, ch. 18, 691). It is worth remarking briefly that Locke displays a modern (post–sixteenth century) attitude to the Bible as text, one that presumes it will be read by solitary readers rather than within a community.
13. Note that while Locke is clear that words are open to more than one interpretation and thus, that the words of Scripture may lead to confusion, he does not seem to sense the same problem with the words that, of necessity, make up any philosophical argument. The only way to achieve the hermeneutic clarity to which he aspires would be if God conveyed his truths directly to each one of us by means of angels, with no linguistic intermediary at all.
14. Locke, *Essay*, book III, ch. 9, 490.

also God's qualities could be spelled out apart from revelation and through rational reflection alone is new, or rather was new in Descartes, whom Locke follows here. Apellations that had been distinctively theological became with Descartes the terminology of rational analysis and metaphysics alone.[15] With Descartes the "divine names" have become the "classical attributes."

Aquinas would have been baffled by Locke's need to forswear the assistance of Scripture or of tradition, as would his predecessors in the "divine names" tradition. But why? Is it because Aquinas lived, compared to Locke, in times of relative stability? Apparently not, for his world was as restless as that of Locke. Does it mean that Aquinas is not genuinely philosophical, falling at the last hurdle by giving precedence to faith over reason? No doubt it appeared so to the eighteenth-century defenders of rational religion.[16] From their perspective, the years from the sack of Rome to the late sixteenth century were "Dark Ages," a deliberate contrast to their own self-designation as "the Enlightenment." They supposed that patristic and medieval philosophers either knew little of philosophy or else uncritically mixed philosophical with Scriptural teaching.

But natural theology was not the invention of the seventeenth century. Aquinas, Dionysius, and Augustine knew the natural theology of the Greeks as a noble philosophical project that antedated Christianity by some centuries. While both Aquinas and Locke thought reason might demonstrate that God exists, Aquinas believed that knowledge gained this way would always be minimal, fragmentary, and confused, in need of the supplement of revelation, or "holy teaching" at every juncture. Aquinas would have been amazed by Locke's ambitious claims for reason, and this was not from an unquestioning obedience to religious authority; he had *reasons* for putting constraints on *reason* in the matter of knowing and naming God.

Let us recall the relationship of patristic and medieval theology to the natural theology of antiquity. Greek natural theology was an adjunct of Greek natural science, especially of its cosmology. The early Christian theologians mined this natural theology when it suited them ("spoiling the Egyptians"), but recognized its inadequacies for Christian purposes. Most important for this essay, the Christian writers of the patristic and the medieval periods saw clearly in a way the physico-theologians of the eighteenth century did not that philosophy would not yield a Creator in the Jewish or Christian sense. It might allow for a world-former or a first cause but not a Creator *ex nihilo* who *freely* chooses to create all that is. Indeed, far from unwittingly baptizing the god of

---

15. Jean-Luc Marion does not hesitate to blame Descartes' *Meditations* for this: "The problematic of the divine names—originally a theological issue—is transposed *here*, perhaps for the first time, into the strictly metaphysical domain." Marion, "The Essential Incoherence of Descartes' Definition of Divinity," in *Essays on Descartes' Meditations*, ed. Amélie Oksenberg Rorty (Berkeley: University of California Press, 1986), 297.

16. Locke was not a deist. He did not doubt the importance of revealed religion, for all his hesitancy as to how we could be sure to have received it. He accepted Jesus as the Messiah, and his "acceptance of grace and forgiveness was repugnant to the Deist sensibility." W. M. Spellman, *John Locke* (London: Macmillan, 1997), 77. See Spellman's chapter, "The Heterodoxy of a Simple Faith," for an account of Locke's religion, and the book throughout for insisting that, however he may have come down to us, Locke himself was a man of deep Christian convictions whose thoughts were never far from these matters.

Greek philosophy, the patristic theologians and rabbis hammered out the doctrine of *creatio ex nihilo* in critical response to Greek natural theology. "God creates a beautiful world but does so using beautiful colors," suggests the philosopher. "No, God creates even the colors," says the Rabbi.[17] *Creatio ex nihilo* is not a Hellenistic notion; indeed, the Greek philosophers thought it incoherent.

Between the third century and the thirteenth some changes took place. The philosophy by which the early theologians both defined themselves and from which they also distanced themselves was Platonism, or more precisely a Neoplatonism into which Stoic and Aristotelian ideas had been woven. Aquinas, as is well known, wrote just at the time of the recovery of Aristotle to the Christian West, mediated by Islamic and Jewish sources.

The authority of Aristotle was, for medievals such as Maimonides and Aquinas, immense but not boundless. One of the sharpest points of disagreement for Maimonides concerned creation. We are now accustomed, however little we may understand it, to the idea that the universe results from an "initial singularity" or a big bang—a kind of secular *creatio ex nihilo*. But this is, in Aristotelian terms, absurd. The idea of such a beginning was contradictory, for a beginning is already a change, and to have a change one needs time in which that change can occur. This line of reasoning leads ineluctably to an idea of everlasting time and matter, and such was Aristotle's position.

Despite his deference to Aristotle in matters sublunary, Maimonides could not agree that the universe is eternal. In Jewish understanding, but not in Aristotle's, one could have God without any universe. Furthermore, given Aristotle's views about the eternity of the universe, no questions can be asked about the purpose of the universe or the final cause of the heavens; there is no question of "purpose" at that level in Aristotle's system. But these are questions that Maimonides thought the followers of Moses must ask. Aristotle's prime mover is as much a part of the cosmic order as that which is moved, and that which is moved is governed by the laws that govern everything, including the movements of the prime mover. In this quasi-mathematical scheme of things there is no room for divine freedom and, since the system is fixed and without beginning or end, no room for miracles. Maimonides thought the barren formalism of Aristotle's "eternal universe" must be rejected on religious grounds and *creatio ex nihilo* defended as a fundamental principle of the Jewish religion. It is, as he puts it, "a high rampart erected around the Law."[18]

---

17. My rephrasing of an exchange between Rabbi Gamaliel and a philosopher in the Genesis rabba. See Gerhard May, *Creatio ex Nihilo: The Doctrine of 'Creation out of Nothing' in Early Christian Thought* (Edinburgh: T&T Clark, 1994), 23.

18. Moses Maimonides, *The Guide for the Perplexed*, trans. M. Friedländer (New York: Dover Publications, 1956), 181. José Faur sets out Maimonides' views in the following way: "The only possible relation between absolute monotheism and a world brimming with diversity is Creation ex nihilo, repudiating an ontological relation between God and the Universe. . . . 'Belief in the creation of the world,' wrote Maimonides, 'necessarily requires that all the miracles are possible.' Consequently, 'Whoever believes in the eternity (of the world) does not belong at all to the congregation of Moses and Abraham.'" José Faur, *Homo Mysticus: A Guide to Maimonides's Guide for the Perplexed* (Syracuse: Syracuse University Press, 1999), 89. Faur is citing Maimonides' *Treatise on Resurrection*.

"According to our theory, taught in Scripture, the existence and non-existence of things depends solely on the will of God and not on fixed laws."[19] By reason of this teaching on creation, Maimonides' God is altogether more personal than Aristotle's, who is not "personal" at all. Yet at the same time, Maimonides' God is also more unknowable and unnameable, at least philosophically. For whereas the lineaments of Aristotle's god are deducible from the universe of which it is prime mover and with which it is a causal whole, the God of Maimonides and of Aquinas is entirely "other" than creation.[20]

The main objection to Greek natural theology made by Aquinas and Maimonides is the same: The God of the Bible creates freely all that is. Aquinas emphasizes that what is essential to *creatio ex nihilo* is not temporal beginning but rather the autonomy of Creator vis-à-vis creation. God need not have created *at all* and so can never in any sense be a "part" of the system. The dependence is one way: The created order is completely dependent upon God, but God is not dependent upon the created order. This Creator God is not only an "uncaused cause" (an ascription that could be predicated as well of Aristotle's god), but as Creator *ex nihilo* stands entirely outside the realm of creaturely causality and is entirely responsible for it.

There are significant implications for religious language and thus for the divine names. All our creaturely predication is flawed when it comes to speaking of God. Even if we say that "God is the source and cause of all that is" in a Maimonidean or Thomistic account, this "causing" cannot be of the same order as finite causings. In terms of the Jewish and Christian idea of *creatio ex nihilo*, God is the cause of everything *including* space and time. Yet we cannot form a sentence such as "Prior to space and time God *causes* space and time to come into being" without being aware that we are speaking of "cause" here in a distended sense.[21] Indeed, Aristotle's god could literally be a "first cause" (albeit not in a temporal sense), as could the Neoplatonic god in a scheme of emanation because both gods are part of worldly continuum. But the God who creates *ex nihilo* can only be said to be "first cause" by distortion of language.[22]

---

19. Moses Maimonides, *Guide for the Perplexed*, 202.

20. Maimonides seems to presume, as does al Ghazali, that *creatio ex nihilo* entails a beginning in time, that is, they seem to disallow the possibility that the Creator may have freely created an everlasting universe. Aquinas allows this last possibility, although he believes that, as a matter of fact, the universe is not everlasting. David Burrell puts it nicely: "Maimonides simply presumes (as did Ghazali) that an everlasting universe leaves no room for free creation; in this he conflates *creatio ex nihilo* with *creatio de novo*—that is, not simply that nothing is presupposed to creation but that it takes place such that there is an initial moment of time. Aquinas declares his indebtedness to both by concurring with Maimonides that neither position—everlasting or temporal creation—admits of proof, and yet he refuses to foreclose the conceptual possibility of a free creator (in the biblical or Qur'anic sense) creating everlastingly. . . . He does concede that postulating an initial moment would make the case more evident . . . but, strictly speaking, the case for creation *de novo* rests solely with revelation. . . . (There is no conceptual difficulty with an eternal God creating an everlasting universe, precisely because one can distinguish the *eternity* which characterises God alone from a temporality without beginning.)" David B. Burrell, CSC, "Freedom and Creation in the Abrahamic Traditions," *International Philosophical Quarterly*, 40, no. 2 (June 2000): 168–69.

21. Maimonides saw clearly the implications of *creatio ex nihilo* for religious language, but it seems to me that Aquinas went beyond him in developing a theory that explains why our speaking of God does not collapse into equivocation.

22. That is, "Causality is a relation linking two things in the same category, hence God cannot be the cause of the world." Kenneth Seeskin, *Search for a Distant God: The Legacy of Maimonides* (New York: Oxford University Press, 2000), 87.

Among those with mistaken and partial notions of God, Aquinas would list, as did Locke, those polytheists and anthropomorphites who believe God has a body or sits in chairs. Aquinas, but perhaps not Locke, would also list the natural theologians, among them Aristotle. Aristotle has not made a mistake of *reason*. He is by no means muddled or confused, nor is there anything wrong with his philosophy; it just does not take us far enough.

For Aristotle, as for Greek philosophy generally, the idea of creation from nothing involves self-contradiction, for *out of nothing, nothing comes*. Coming into being is a *change*, and change occurs within an existing order.[23] Therefore, the universe must be as eternal as God. Furthermore, it makes as little sense, in Aristotelian natural theology, to posit the prime mover without the universe as it would to posit the universe without the prime mover. *Creatio ex nihilo* comes not from the Greeks or from philosophy but from Jewish and Christian reflection on the sovereignty and freedom of the God of the Bible, as well as on God's grace. *Creatio ex nihilo* defends the Jewish understanding of God as free and volitional and as having knowledge of individuals. As such, it is necessary for the Jewish and Christian view of providence.

Maimonides did not think *creatio ex nihilo* could be demonstrated by reason alone (if so, his beloved Aristotle would have hit upon it), but neither could philosophy actually show it to be false. It cannot be demonstrated by Aristotelian philosophy because one cannot, as Aristotle rightly observed, argue from facts about the world to something altogether outside the world order. We might argue from what we see about us to a prime mover, but we could never, on the basis of philosophy alone, deduce that the prime mover created space and time. Reason might give us a first cause, an unmoved mover, and intelligence of some sort, but it will not provide the idea of the free, loving, and provident Creator of whom Scripture speaks. This is no fault of Aristotle's; his system did not require a loving God, but the Jewish and Christian faiths did. *Creatio ex nihilo* is thus a datum of faith, yet once in place it compels philosophical attention—especially since it has repercussions for our speaking of God.

Locke and other early modern exponents of natural theology thought we could establish far more on the basis of reason alone than Aristotle did. In this they were undoubtedly optimistic and, for all that they held themselves to be working with reason alone, governed by implicit Christian premises that philosophy on its own could not provide.[24] While placing stricter limitations on what we could *know* than would other philosophers or scientists of his time, Locke nonetheless thought we could know by demonstration quite a lot about God—not just that God exists but also that God is powerful, knowing, wise, and providential (book IV, ch. 10). He imports, without sufficient justification, qualities of the Christian God into his God of reason,

---

23. Aquinas also notes that creation can only be termed a "change" in a distended sense.

24. It has been pointed out that Locke's formulation of the cosmological argument is weak and that he makes moves that are either fallacious or dependent on unstated or dubious premises. Nicholas Wolterstorff, "Locke's Philosophy of Religion," in *The Cambridge Companion to Locke*, ed. Vere Chappell (Cambridge: Cambridge University Press, 1994), 189.

and in this he seems to follow Newton. Just as Newton did not want "merely a 'philosophical' God, the impersonal and uninterested First Cause of Aristotle,"[25] so Locke wants more; he wants a providential God and a moral lawgiver. Locke wants reason to deliver the Christian God, but it cannot. The natural theology of the ancient Greeks was more chaste and more realistic in its ambitions.

What then of Aquinas? The *Summa theologiae*, while rigorous philosophically, from the outset deals with the God of scriptural revelation—a feature that is concealed by our forgetfulness of the extent to which a Dominican of his time inhabited a world saturated by Scripture. Natural theology, insofar as it appears, is by way of enhancement of this purpose. Even in the question "Is there a God?" where Aquinas sketches the Five Ways (his proofs for the existence of God),[26] the *sed contra* is not only a quotation from Scripture but one that quotes precisely the passage held by both Greek and Latin fathers to be of supreme importance for the revelation of the divine name. This biblical citation should give us the clue, as it would have done for Aquinas's medieval readers, that what follows is an exposition of the divine names parallel to those we might find in Dionysius or Bonaventure: "ON THE OTHER HAND, the Book of *Exodus* represents God as saying, *I am who am.*"

This name is the truest name for God in Aquinas's view; it names God as the very plenitude of Being. As it develops, this means not simply that "there is a God" but that God is Being itself and the source of all being. The discussions of the divine "names" of God that follow (questions 3–11) are all in their various ways reflections upon the fact that the Creator is not a creature. This radical rupture is both the reason why God is not "nameable" by us, and at the same time the basis of all our speaking and praise of the God from which our very being and speaking flows. So at this juncture where he might appear most dryly philosophical, Aquinas is also closest to the tradition of mystical theology, as his citations disclose: Dionysius, John Damascene, Augustine.[27]

While the divine names of ST 2–11 resemble the "divine attributes" of Aristotle (or for that matter those of Newton and Locke), they are not the same. Aquinas is speaking of the God revealed to faith, that is, the Creator. We see this readily in question 8 (God's existence in things) where, in response to the questions "Does God exist in everything?" and "Is God everywhere?" Aquinas replies that God exists in everything and everywhere as Creator in the Christian sense.

But perhaps the contrast with Aristotle's natural theology is clearest (although Aquinas does not criticize the philosopher directly) in question 10 (the eternity of God). In Ia 10, article 3, Aquinas addresses the question "Does eternity belong to God alone?" and he answers, "Yes." Aristotle's answer to this question, as Aquinas would have known, is "No." Matter is

---

25. Alexander Koyré, *From the Closed World to the Infinite Universe* (Baltimore: Johns Hopkins University Press, 1957), 225.

26. Aquinas, ST Ia2.3.

27. See Anna Williams, "Mystical Theology Redux: The Pattern of Aquinas' *Summa Theologiae*," *Modern Theology* 13, no. 1 (January 1997): 53–74.

also "eternal" in Aristotle's natural theology as it is in Plato's. But in Thomas's terms, Aristotle's god and Aristotle's universe might better be called *everlasting*, and not *eternal*.[28] The *eternal* God of Aquinas, or the fathers, is not one who exists backward and forward forever, but one who creates time itself.

This should prompt us to reflect that the same term may serve different functions in different theologies (and especially when speaking of different gods). To say that God is "creator" may mean, depending on one's scheme of things: that God creates from preexistent matter; that God creates matter but not space and time; that God creates matter, space, and time; or that God creates "volitionally," and so on.

The meaning of all the attributes found in Greek natural theology changes when applied to one who is Creator *ex nihilo*. It is significant that the discussion of the "names" that follows the Five Ways (questions 3–11) is all, as Thomas tells us, by way of saying how God *does not exist*.[29] Divine eternity, for example, is discussed under those ways in which God does not exist because it is by means of this notion that we recall that God, as Creator of time, cannot be a creature of time in just the way we are. (This does not mean God is "timeless," or that God cannot understand that we are temporal creatures.) That God is eternal we can know; what God's eternity is in itself we cannot, anymore than we can know the divine essence. The inadequacy of our speaking is a point Augustine never tires of making. He writes in *De trinitate*:

> [W]e should understand God, if we can and as far as we can, to be good without quality, great without quantity, creative without need or necessity, presiding without position, holding all things together without possession, wholly everywhere without place, everlasting without time, without any change in himself making changeable things, and undergoing nothing. Whoever thinks of God like that may not yet be able to discover altogether what he is, but is at least piously on his guard against thinking about him anything that he is not.[30]

But *creatio ex nihilo* is not only the curb on careless speaking; it is also our ground—as creatures made by and for the Creator—of any speaking at all. Gregory Nazianzen explains:

> God always was, and always is, and always will be. Or rather, God always Is. For Was and Will be are fragments of our time, and of changeable nature, but He is Eternal Being. And this is the Name that He gives to Himself when giving the Oracle to Moses in the Mount. For in Himself He sums up and contains all Being, having neither beginning

28. This means a difference in what the two will mean by "divine immutability" as well.

29. See the prologue to question 3. He will go on in questions 12 and 13 to discuss how we know and describe God.

30. Augustine, *De Trinitate*, trans. Edmund Hill (Brooklyn: New City Press, 1991), book V, prologue, 190.

in the past nor end in the future; like some great Sea of Being, limitless and unbounded, transcending all conception of time and nature, only adumbrated by the mind, and that very dimly and scantily . . . not by his Essentials.[31]

Although it is impossible to speak adequately, it is our created destiny to speak of God and to praise God. In this revealed economy, creation is pure gift, the product of no metaphysical necessity. We have our very being as an excess of Being itself. The self-gifting that is the eternal life of the Trinity flows, not by a compelled or inevitable emanation as with the Neoplatonists, but by grace and love. God is the beginning and end of all creation, and our speaking of the great "Sea of Being" is based on this participation in the divine life. We speak to praise.

Newton, more than a millennium later, shows no such caution or joy. His Supreme God is "a Being eternal, infinite, absolutely perfect," but "patently, not above time and space: His eternity is of sempiternal duration, His omnipresence is infinite extension."[32] Newton's God is akin to that of Aristotle, but more robustly anthropomorphic—a master and ruler of the world that he inhabits as supreme being.

Locke, while rigorous to a fault on what we can know of God, also lacks the caution that informs patristic and medieval theology on the question of naming God. We hear none of the echoes of Augustine, John Damascene, and Dionysius that inform Aquinas. Locke's God is not "unnameable" but rather like us in his qualities, only infinitely more so:

If we examine the *Idea* we have of the incomprehensible supreme Being, we shall find, that we come by it the same way; and that the complex *Ideas* we have both of God, and separate Spirits, are made up of the simple *Ideas* we receive from *Reflection; v.g.* having from what we experiment in our selves, got the *Ideas* of Existence and Duration; of Knowledge and Power; of Pleasure and Happiness; and of several other Qualities and Powers, which it is better to have, than to be without; when we would frame an *Idea* the most suitable we can to the supreme Being, we enlarge every one of these with our *Idea* of Infinity; and so putting them together, make our complex *Idea of God.*[33]

We get no breakdown, as we do in the *Summa*, of the different ways in which we may know and name God: negatively, with metaphor, from creatures, by analogy. Locke's divine "Qualities and Powers, which it is better to have, than to be without" seem to be predicated univocally of God and human beings. Furthermore, by making them qualities, certain "names" drop out of Locke's list altogether—for instance, that God is "simple" or, in the

---

31. Gregory Nazianzen, "On the Theophany, or Birthday of Christ," *Nicene and Post-Nicene Fathers*, Series 2, vol. 7, ch. 7, 346.
32. Koyré, *From the Closed World*, 226.
33. Locke, *Essay*, book II, ch. 23, 314 (italics mine).

strict sense (where this does not mean as first in a cardinal series), "One." These can scarcely be seen as qualities "which it is better to have, than to be without." The taut sense of speaking before a God who is wholly Other yet wholly Given, which informs the early questions of the *Summa*, is absent from Locke. Locke's deity is not a crucified but a calcified God.

The question "How can we name God?" (or, if one prefers a more modern formulation, "What can we say of God?") is susceptible of two readings: one that takes the question to be fundamentally epistemological and the other ontological. For Locke, it is a question in his broader project of epistemology—but knowledge of God is not fundamentally different from knowledge of anything else. For Locke, the question asks, "What is it that can we know about God on the basis of reason alone?" and the answer is that we can know that God exists and we can know certain of his positive qualities, enough to provide the basis of Christian understanding. For Aquinas, the question "How do we name God?" points to a mystery. In the first questions of the *Summa theologiae*, the problem is best expressed not as "What can be said of God?" but as "How can *anything* be said of God?"— a problem that should surely be addressed at the start of a *Summa* of hundreds of pages.

What can be said of God? Nothing adequately, but then almost everything. From Scripture, church teaching, the fathers, from delight in creation, we know what we can say. We can say that God is rock, fountain, cause, ruler, lawgiver, eternal, One, living, existent.

This essay has concentrated on one premise given by faith to reason, but one with profound consequences, that of *creatio ex nihilo*. Once in place it restructures pagan thought entirely, however similar the terminology remains. It releases the world from the impossible burden of being eternal when everything it consists of is temporal. It frees thought from treating God as metaphysically continuous with the world, as in Greek philosophy, or as epistemically continuous with knowledge of persons and of material objects, as in Locke's univocal scheme. Both kinds of natural theology obliterate the transcendence of God as delivered by Scripture. Once given the knowledge that God is Creator *ex nihilo* (and revelation is above all a gift), then our reason comes into its own.

CHAPTER ELEVEN

The Offering of Names: Metaphysics, Nihilism, and Analogy

— DAVID BENTLEY HART —

As the cause of all and transcendent of all, God is truly without name, and yet he bears the names of all the things that are. Truly he reigns over all things, and all things revolve around him who is their cause, their source, and their final end. He is all in all.

—Denys the Areopagite

How is Λόγος the fateful . . . which sends each thing into its own? The gathering laying-out assembles all destining in itself, by bringing beings to us and letting them lie before us, keeping each being, whether absent or present, in its place and on its way, and by its assembling it secures all things in the all.

—Martin Heidegger

Attributes and Names

In what follows,[1] I want to ruminate on the principal issue Janet Soskice raises in her essay in this volume: that is, her elegant distinction between the theological enunciation of the "divine names" and the philosophical enumeration of the "attributes of deity." The difference between the two practices, it seems clear, is nothing less than the difference between two ontologies:

---

1. Much of this essay, especially in the second, third, and fourth sections, is very close—in substance and manner of exposition—to arguments made at various junctures within my *The Beauty of the Infinite: The Aesthetics of Christian Truth* (Grand Rapids: Eerdmans, 2003). This is not surprising, since the initial draft of this essay and the final draft of that book were written at the same time, as fruits of the same research and meditation. While this essay has, for me, the virtue of concentrating those arguments into a single stream of ontological reflection, some may perhaps wonder—not without some understandable impatience—how I would situate my claims here in a broader theological frame, subject to scriptural and dogmatic constraints and imperatives. To answer such concerns, I would refer the curious to the book, where these claims are so situated.

between a metaphysics of participation, according to which all things are embraced in being as in the supereminent source of all their transcendental perfections, and a "univocal" ontology, which understands being as nothing but the bare category of existence, under which all substances (God no less than creatures) are severally placed. The former permits practices of theological nomination—in liturgy, metaphor, metaphysics, and so on—because, even in asserting that there is an infinite qualitative difference between the coincidence in God's simplicity and plenitude of all the transcendental moments that compose the creature (goodness, truth, beauty, unity, etc.) and the finite, multiplicit "prismation" of being's light in the creature, it allows for a continuity of eminence between those moments and the transcendent wellspring from which they flow. Thus, one may in some sense name God from creatures, even though the infinite disproportion between divine being and finite beings places the truth of those names infinitely beyond the capacity of finite reason properly to grasp. Naming God then always has the form of analogy, an irresoluble tension between the cataphatic and apophatic, a language of likeness chastened by the pious acknowledgment of an ever greater unlikeness. The problem this would seem to raise, though, is that of the immense epistemological caesura that one must of necessity tolerate between the attributive use of a word "here below" and its properly nominative use in regard to God—for how much is really said (or known) when one speaks "names" whose "truthfulness" is certified precisely by its transcendence of finite comprehension? The latter ontology, it would then certainly seem, offers thought a more obvious and substantial form of "analogy": a direct proportionate similitude between attributes inhering in discrete beings (albeit between finite and infinite instances). Thus, to say "God is good" is to say much the same thing as "Henry is good," but with far greater certainty, and with no ambiguity. The metaphysics of participation, one could argue, precisely insofar as it regards God not as a being but as the source and ultimate truth of all beings, places an abyss between God and creatures that neither thought nor language can traverse without losing its moorings in human understanding; but a univocal ontology allows the essences of our attributions to remain intact, even when they are modified by the addition of the further attribute "infinite."

The problem, though, with identifying the divine attributes univocally, as features of the divine substance in much the same way as they are features of created substances,[2] is that the God thus described is a logical nonsense. A God who is a being among beings, who possesses the properties of his nature

---

2. Soskice adduces perhaps the best example: Locke's formula for arriving at a rational understanding of God. We begin from various simple ideas derived from finite reality and appropriate to God, which we then multiply by infinity and combine to fashion for ourselves the complex idea of a supreme being (*An Essay Concerning Human Understanding*, book II.23, §33). A more guarded and austere example, though, would be that of Kant, who allowed (*Prolegomena to Any Future Metaphysics That Will Be Able to Present Itself as a Science*, trans. P. G. Lucas, [New York: Manchester University Press, 1962], 121–80) that analogy might be used of God, but only insofar as it remains rhetorical and quadratically proportional (a:b::c:d), and does not take the form of a simple comparison between two discrete things, or between two things in relation to a third thing held in common (which sounds quite reasonable till one grasps how utterly vacuous the knowledge of this proportion is if there is not an *ontological* participation of one of the two sets in the other).

in a composite way, as aspects of his nature rather than as names ultimately convertible with one another in the simplicity of his transcendent essence, is a myth, a mere supreme being, whose being and nature are in some sense distinct from one another, who receives his being from being as such and so is less than being, who (even if he is changeless and eternal) in some sense becomes the being he is by partaking of that prior unity (existence) that allows his nature to persist as the composite reality it is. He is a God whose being has nonexistence as its opposite; he is not, that is to say, the infinite *actus* of all things, *id quo maius cogitari nequit*, but only an "ontic" God. There simply is no such God. Atheism is not simply the mirror inversion of this sort of theism, but both its inmost secret and its most necessary corrective. If God is thought of in such terms—if his true transcendence as the being of all beings is forgotten, hidden behind the imposing spectacle of a more conformable "supreme being"—then the longing to know the truth of God cannot but lead to the rejection of God as truth; the inevitable terminus of "theism," so conceived, is nihilism.

In a sense, this is merely to repeat a claim that one school of modern continental philosophy (call it the "ontological-hermeneutical") regards as a truism: that nihilism is the hidden "vocation" of the Western intellectual tradition, that the will to "positive" truth that is the unique passion of Western thought must finally—in what Nietzsche called the inversion of the highest values—give birth to a discourse of absolute truthlessness, or the "truth" of innumerably many perspectives. Nihilism was first described by Jacobi in the course of his critique of Kant, and it was he who first discerned a necessary liaison between its spiritual pathos and the intellectual ambition embodied in metaphysical systems. But it was Nietzsche who first argued that the "death of God" has come about as the result of the Christian (which is to say the vulgar Platonic) will to power—that pitiless, ascetic, ultimately life-denying hunger for absolute possession of the "most high principle" that must pursue God till it has killed him.[3] For Gianni Vattimo, the prophet of "playful nihilism" or "weak thought," nihilism is not simply the destiny of all Western metaphysics, but its solution, inasmuch as metaphysics is itself (he says) violence: the wresting of first principles from the intractable multiplicity of experience, the construction of a "hierarchy within totality" meant to contain and control the unmasterable flow of "difference," a subordination of life to some supreme lifeless value (*ousia, kinesis, eidos, ego, Geist,* etc.).[4]

---

3. This, obviously, would not be a cause of grief for Nietzsche were Christianity not a particularly depraved collusion of inhuman desire and all-too-human pusillanimity, a product of the resentment of the spiritually and physically debile who do not possess the resources, in the wake of God's death, to affirm the whole of being in all its prodigality, creativity, and destructiveness (and so forth and so on, *in taedium maximum*).

4. See Gianni Vattimo, "Towards an Ontology of Decline," in *Recoding Metaphysics: The New Italian Philosophy*, ed. Giovanni Borradori (Evanston, IL: Northwestern University Press, 1988), 60. In recent work, I should note, Vattimo has come to claim that the peaceful annunciation of nihilism and the death of metaphysics is the result of the announcement of the *kenosis* of God in Christ. See, for instance, Vattimo, *Belief*, trans. Luca D'Isanto and David Webb (Stanford, CA: Stanford University Press, 1999); and idem, "The Trace of the Trace," in *Religion*, ed. Jacques Derrida and Gianni Vattimo (Stanford, CA: Stanford University Press, 1998).

But the most interesting (and infuriating) theorist of metaphysics' nihilistic vocation is Heidegger, and it is his treatment of the matter that, in an unexpected way perhaps, makes an explicit connection between the "question of being" and the question of naming God.

To formulate the argument I want to make very simply: the forgetfulness of the difference between naming God and describing his attributes, characteristic of Western thought since—let us say—at least the early modern period, is one and the same with the forgetfulness of the "ontico-ontological difference." Admittedly, there is a certain irony in resorting to Heidegger's rebarbative patois in order to argue (as I shall) that only classical Christian metaphysics escapes such forgetfulness; for Heidegger himself, Christian metaphysics is nothing but a strikingly intense form of *Seinsvergessenheit*, but my use of the term is appropriate. The event of modernity within philosophy, after all, consisted for Christian thought in the death of a certain vision of being: it was the disintegration of that radiant unity where the good, the true, and the beautiful coincided as infinite simplicity and fecundity, communicating themselves to a world whose only reality was its dynamic participation in their gratuity and so consisted also in the consequent divorce between this thought of being—the supereminent fullness of all perfection—and the thought of God. In this "moment" (which occurred over several centuries), "being" somehow became the name of what formerly would have been regarded almost as being's opposite: a veil or an absence, explicitly or implicitly invoked, but in either case impenetrable—the veil veiling itself, the empty category of sheer uniform existence that adds nothing to the essence of things, and whose only "determination" is an absolute privation of all determinacy. And God's transcendence, so long as philosophy suffered any nostalgia for "that hypothesis," came to be understood as God's absence, his hiddenness behind the veil of being, breaking through, if at all, only as an explanatory cause. However hostile, then, Heidegger's own diagnosis of the "oblivion of being" may be to Christian thought, it nevertheless proceeds from a sadness quite familiar to theology in the post-Christian era. Heidegger recognizes that the particular pathology of modernity lies—to some very large degree—in the loss of a certain kind of wonder or perplexity, a certain sense of the abiding strangeness of being within the very ordinariness of beings. Not, it must be said, that he really desires to reverse the course of this decline; for him the nihilistic dissolution of every transcendental structure of being—every metaphysics—is something both good and bad, both a promise and a risk, and something that must be followed to its end. Following Nietzsche, he reads the history of nihilism as the story of the Western will to positive truth, which must—before it can be transcended—exhaust itself, and so bring metaphysics to its ultimate collapse. And, in this account of things, the theological understanding of the transcendence of being over beings appears as merely a particularly acute instance of a duality intrinsic to every metaphysics: like every speculative "system," Christian philosophy is subordinate to that original forgetfulness that allows metaphysics its fruitful but erring reign over

Western thought, and so while theology possesses a kind of understanding of the ontological difference, it arrives at that understanding only by abstracting some general characteristic of beings and projecting it as the "ground" or "principle" or "truth" of beings—which it then identifies with God. This is what Heidegger calls the "double founding" of "onto-theology," the grounding of beings in being, and then the further grounding of being in some supreme being. Thus, Christian philosophy is, at the end of the day, merely "metaphysics" once more, oblivious of the utter qualitative distinction between being and beings; and while metaphysics may illuminate the ontological difference for thought in some measure, it does so necessarily by way of a more original obscurity, a withdrawal or hiding of being behind one or another ontic exemplar—behind one or another of the masks being wears in the drama of its passage through successive metaphysical epochs and regimes.

Thus, Heidegger's genealogy of nihilism is perfectly seamless: After that first lightning flash, that blissful dawn, when being originally manifested itself for thought in the West, in the naive but for that very reason pure language of the pre-Socratics, the West's initial moment of philosophical wakefulness necessarily began to harden into fixed and rigid forms. Whereas the pre-Socratics, immersed in the "lighting" of being, enjoying a "poetic" immediacy of language to event, understood being as *aletheia* or *physis* or *logos*—as, that is, the unveiling of being in beings, the temporal arising and passing away of beings, and the "gathering laying-together" of the event that grants beings and being to one another—thought could not long endure the mystery of these *names* for being, and soon had to begin to substitute for them the inert conceptual *properties* of being. This is the apostasy of Plato, for instance, in turning his gaze away from the silent mystery of being's "yielding hiddenness" and toward the visibility of original essences, *eide*, the frozen, eternalized "looks" of things. Here the search for truth as a positive possession of reason—a thing among the things of the world—takes hold of reason, and here the history of metaphysics is inaugurated in earnest, and—no matter what new concept will displace *eidos* (*ousia, actus, ego, Geist*)—the entire course of this epochal "destinal sending" is set in motion by this always more essential oblivion. Now, in the twilight of the metaphysical age, we find ourselves in the time of realized nihilism, of the technological *Ge-stell*, in which reality is understood as just so many quanta of power, the world as nothing but the representation of the self-established subject, and the things of earth as mere material, a "standing reserve" awaiting exploitation by the merciless rationality of technology. The ancient nuptial ecstasy of word and world—of poetic saying and ontological unveiling—has now become all but impossible. This is the moment of highest risk. But if in this moment we reclaim the more essential truth of this nihilistic destiny—that truth is not an object to be possessed, that the world is not reducible to the "sufficient reason" for its existence, that we should not press toward foundations and principles but should rather dwell in the "worlding of the world" and find the truth of things in their limpid *Anwesen*—we can perhaps heal ourselves of the positivist passion, await the world in a state of poetic and passive expectancy, look for a new dawning of the light of being, speak thoughtfully the names of that nameless mystery as it shows itself to us.

All of which has an undeniable charm about it; but it is at just this point that one should pause and ask whether the sweet, melancholy quietism in such language does not dissemble a certain kind of metaphysical ambition. For Heidegger's account of nihilism, and of what stands beyond nihilism, is dictated not simply by a scrupulous honesty regarding the history of Western thought, but much more by his own ontology—which itself could well be characterized as nihilistic. For Heidegger, whose earliest attempt at a "funda-mental ontology" transcribes into ontological terms Husserl's phenomeno-logical collapse of the distinction between "it is" and "it appears," being is so entirely pure of determination as to be convertible with nothing. It is simply the manifestation of the manifest, the inexhaustible movement of manifesta-tion itself, the silence whose self-effacement allows beings (in their absolute difference from being) to sound forth. Being's generosity—its *es gibt*, its with-drawal or "nothing-ing," which lets beings come to presence in the "junc-ture" of being and, in due order, give way to other beings—is merely its nothingness among beings, its "refusal" to appear as the absolute. Here, cer-tainly, the "metaphysics" of light (of being as the overflowing fullness of the transcendentals) has been overcome (or, more accurately, abandoned), but only in favor of a "metaphysics" of darkness. For being is, in a sense, dark-ness itself, the *dialectical* negation that indifferently grants all beings their finitude. Its every "mittence" is, as Heidegger says, an "errance"; it gives "light" only by being dark, by hiding and leading astray; as much as truth is a peaceful letting-be-manifest, it is also a struggle of obscurity and light, *Erde* and *Welt*, in which peace and strife are inseparably joined. *Logos* forces *physis* into a gathered containment. No less than the Stoic image of the cos-mos as a finite totality in which every form is continually displaced by another, the whole under the irresistible sway of ἀνάγκη, the later Heidegger's understanding of the destinal epochality of being's temporality ever more absolutely identifies the event of being not only with the "presencing" and "whiling" of beings but also with their annihilation. Like Hegel, Heidegger thinks of truth as also, intrinsically, destruction. *If* this is indeed how being must be conceived in order for the thinker to escape the oblivion of being that lies at the heart of "metaphysics," then indeed theology has no name for being—or, it would seem, for God.

This *if*, though, is precisely the question I want to raise: Is Heidegger's ontology genuinely an alternative—*the* alternative—to "onto-theology," or does Heidegger himself perhaps fail to think adequately the difference between being and beings, and so the difference between nomination and attribution? This is worth asking for many reasons. For one thing, Heidegger's thought gives powerful expression to the deepest impulse of mod-ern Continental philosophy in its interminable struggle to liberate itself from theology, and thus it is a particularly transparent instance of philosophy func-tioning as a theology evacuated of transcendence. In Heidegger's attempt to ask the question of being anew, free from the heritage of metaphysics, he presents us with an exquisitely poignant image of the descent of thought into an absolute and self-sealing discourse of immanence. This by itself makes it profitable to ask whether his understanding of the "oblivion of being" is one to which theology must pay heed; for the ontologist and the Christian metaphysician alike may concur that something has been forgotten, but it also remains the case that what each regards as forgotten is what the other regards as the most extreme form of forgetting. More to the point here, however, our question is worth asking simply because Heidegger's thought is very much concerned with naming (with the poetic *logos* in which the silence of being peals forth, veiled in its very unveiling, with the naming of the "gathering" of the "ring-dance" of the "fourfold," etc.), because he wants so desperately to free the discourse of truth from the morbid mythology of grounds and of sufficient reason, which finds the truth of the world only in the world's barest and meagerest possibility or featureless principles, and which must in some sense erase the event of the world to establish the ground of the world. For Heidegger, the truth of the apple lies not in the metaphysical principles that secure it within the rationality of being, but in the event of the apple in its appearing, in all the richness and poverty of its transient particularity, and the language of truth that alone can "correspond" to this truth is a "poetic speaking" that allows the event of the apple within the world to show itself within words. Such a view of things certainly attests to a quite earnest desire to free thought from the destructive passion of instrumental reason, in order to "return" philosophical reflection to a condition of peaceful dwelling in the givenness of the world; and there is, moreover, a clearly discernible theological pathos in Heidegger's longing to see a peaceful belonging together and intimacy between *res* and *signum*, sustained by their coincidence in the event (or act?) that embraces them both. But the most important reason for asking our question is that, in Heidegger's terms, the naming of being in beings is impossible: for if beings show forth being only in the occlusion of being, in being's "nihilation," then the names we speak are—at the end of the day—so many "opaque signifiers"; if being shows itself only through the immemorial event of its self-effacement, upon which thought (bound as it is to static representations) can then only supervene with a quaint anachrony, then being is silence itself, absolutely different from all saying, a nothingness against which all beings are "set off," and the "naming of being" (or the naming of the God who is not a being among beings) is an empty paradox. This is the Derridean "vocation" of Heideggerean ontology.

Happily, though, when it is disentangled from Heidegger's *Seinsgeschichte*, Christian philosophy proves to possess resources for understanding and overcoming the "nihilistic terminus" of modernity in a way that does not arrive at this hopeless impasse; and it can, moreover, provide an account of the ontological difference far more cogent than any Heidegger ever enunciated. For Heidegger was in error, and for the most surprising of reasons: because he, perhaps more than any other philosopher in Western thought, was oblivious of the difference between being and beings. In taking phenomenological "givenness" to a dialectical extreme, and abstracting from it an ontology, he hid from himself the true question of being—which was raised uniquely in theological tradition, and answered there in a way beyond every nihilism (nowhere more perfectly than in Denys's *Divine Names*). And in constructing his genealogy of metaphysics as one continuous decline from philosophy's first moment of ontological wakefulness to a final eclipse of being in the "age of the world-picture," Heidegger succeeded in concealing from himself the most remarkable aspect of the history of Western metaphysics: to wit, its Christian interruption.

Ereignis and *Actus*

I should note, I suppose, that Heidegger's purblindness was in some great degree willful, and even a little perverse. As I have said, his early journey from phenomenology to ontology was made possible by—and so was confined to—phenomenology's collapse of any meaningful distinction between "it is" and "it appears." At some level, perhaps, this represented a kind of transcendental restraint on his part, or critical sobriety, but it by no means purged his thinking of "metaphysical" presuppositions. How, after all, can one elect such a point of departure unless one has arrived in advance at a decision—a conjecture—that has foreclosed the very question of the relation between being and manifestation? More importantly, how much sense does it make to attempt to extract a fundamental ontology from a philosophical discipline from which the question of being has been scrupulously and necessarily "bracketed" out? Inasmuch as Heidegger was obliged, at the beginning of his project, to argue toward the legitimacy of any ontology at all, and then had to do so only in terms that the phenomenological realm of inference (the economy of appearance and hiddenness) permitted, there was no point in the early development of his thought at which it became possible to think of being outside of the closed circle of what appears and what does not appear. Not that Heidegger was in any way discomfited by the epistemological limits he thus imposed upon himself. In truth, the acceptance of such limits was, more than anything else, a decision taken in the service of a rather transparent play for power—one nowhere more evident than in his essay of 1927, "Phänomenologie und Theologie."[5] It was here that Heidegger attempted to seize away from theology the high ground of "metaphysics," discourse on being, by drawing an absolute distinction between philosophy's properly ontological sphere of inquiry and theology's "ontic science" of faith—the science, that is, of something called "Christianness" and of the special comportment of belief toward the cross of Christ (which, when all is said and done, reduces theology to a purely psychological and "local" pursuit). Heidegger could easily, it is true, have called upon a well-established tradition of Protestant dogmatics to defend the peremptory division of prerogatives for

---

5. In Martin Heidegger, *Wegmarken* (hereinafter *W*), in *Gesamtausgabe*, vol. 9 (Frankfurt: Vittorio Klosterman, 1976); in English, *Pathmarks* (hereinafter *P*) (Cambridge: Cambridge University Press, 1998).

which he argued, but to any attentive reader it should be clear that his only genuine concern was to secure for his philosophy an inviolably unique claim upon ontology, and to do so precisely by despoiling theology of the language of being and beings that—contrary to Heidegger's account of things—had become available to human reflection only when the Christian doctrine of creation assumed, but altered, antique metaphysics. Granted, Heidegger claims that he discriminates between the spheres of faith and philosophy not so as to accord one priority over the other (the ontic and the ontological, or the empirical and the theoretical, he argues, simply belong to different orders), but he no sooner makes this assertion than he demonstrates its duplicity: the philosopher, for example, is able to see that the theologian's special language of sin falls under the more original, ontological determination of *Dasein*'s guilt (*Schuld*), and thus the analysis of guilt can clarify and correct the concept of sin, but never the reverse.[6] "There is no such thing as a Christian philosophy,"[7] Heidegger helpfully informs us.

However—and there is a piquant irony in this—it is precisely Heidegger's assiduous struggle to begin his project from a vantage pure of theology that ultimately renders his project incoherent and in fact makes it impossible for him genuinely to contemplate being *in its difference* from all beings. This is obvious from the period of *Sein und Zeit* onward. By denying himself any stirring of reason's necessarily ecstatic movement toward a horizon continuous with and yet transcending the scope of experience, and by seeking to capture the truth of being (or meaning of being) entirely within the horizon of *Dasein*'s being-in-the-world, Heidegger condemns himself to circling interminably between the two poles of the ontic process of arising and perishing, within which ambit he can do no more than arbitrarily isolate certain "existentiell" structures of experience and treat them as existential openings upon the question of being. It scarcely matters, then, how comprehensive or thorough his phenomenology of this being-in-the-world may be, because any conclusions he may draw therefrom regarding being (or even regarding how *Sein* appears for *Dasein*) are little more than intuitive—indeed oracular. Nowhere does this essential mystification in the early Heidegger's thought disport itself more flagrantly than in 1929's "Was ist Metaphysik?" It is tempting to allow oneself to be carried away by this essay's beguiling treatment of the "nothing's" power to awaken us to beings *as* beings, or by its lovely meditation on boredom, or especially by its treatment of anxiety as a *Stimmung* possessed of a unique ontological probity;[8] but, if one succumbs, one will in all likelihood fail to note how many baseless assertions throng each of Heidegger's moves. To take the most striking example: It may be true that anxiety apprises us that all things are "set off" against the nothing, but to cross from what is after all a simple recognition of ontic contingency to any conclusion concerning being as such requires either that one abandon to some degree the ontic economy of existence and nonexistence (of finite determination), or that

6. W 64/P 51–52.
7. W 66/P 53.
8. W 110–12/P 87–88.

one treat this economy as the sole truth of being (which leaves the real question of being, as distinct from all beings, unaddressed). Heidegger chooses the latter course, but one should not be deceived that in doing so he is fleeing the "metaphysical" and embracing the "scientific." Simply said, it does not matter which fundamental mood—boredom or anxiety, happiness or wonder—reveals to us the uncanniness of existence; the only "nothing" made available within this experience is merely the opposite of existence. Thus, to do as Heidegger does, and argue for a kind of secret synonymy between the "nothing" and "being" (following a rather impressionistic logic: being discloses beings as beings, the nothing discloses to us that beings are beings, thus in the being of being the nothing nothings . . .), is simply to avoid the question actually at issue. That is to say, in this obviously dialectical scheme, the "nothing" can be taken as "ontological" only if being is to be conceived as the opposite of the existence of (ontic) things. But this is vacuous. If being is really, *ontologically* different from all beings—even if one grant that it is the ontic oscillation between existence and nonexistence that first wakens us to this difference—then being cannot be the opposite of anything;[9] it stands over against neither existence nor nonexistence within finite reality but is the "is" both of "it is" and of "it is not," and so the difference of one from the other is something utterly distinct from the difference of being from both. The simple opposition of "is" and "is not," understood as the simple functioning of noncontradiction within finite things, is not an ontological determination but is merely what raises the ontological question in the first place. To confuse being with the simple nonexistence that anxiety has the power to reveal is as much a species of *Seinsvergessenheit* as is to confuse being with simple existence; one has simply mistakenly identified being with one moment in the determination of finite "essences"—with, that is, the ontic "not this" rather than the ontic "this." It is true that the distance between beings and nonbeing reveals to us that being is not a being among beings. At the same time, however, if we resist lapsing into dialectic, it should also reveal to us that being is as mysteriously beyond nonbeing as beyond everything that is. After all, it is the synthesis within beings of *what* they are and *that* they are (and so of what they are not) that makes it impossible, within the grammar of ontic process, to speak properly of being *qua* being. The ghost of Leibniz still haunts us with his maddening question: How is it that there are beings at all, and not much rather nothing? And no obscure conflation of being and the nothing will suffice to dispel philosophical perplexity here, as the question might just as well be phrased thus: What permits beings and nonbeing to be distinct from one another, such that beings are the beings they are while nothing (*ex quo nihil fieri potest*) remains nothing? How can there be such a distinction and such a unity?

I think that at some level Heidegger can be accused of a very basic logical mistake. Granted, it is not always easy to follow Heidegger's logic well enough to identify either its strengths or its flaws, especially in his earlier

---

9. See Maximus the Confessor, *Chapters on Love* III.65.

period, where it is often annoyingly difficult to assign any clear meaning to his use of the word *Sein*. There it is even occasionally possible to read him as being concerned solely with something like *esse commune*—a general existence, which is nothing apart from what exists. In his mature work, however, after his so-called *Kehre*, Heidegger supposedly turns his eyes from *Dasein* to *Sein*, and then to the *es gibt* of the event that grants the "ontico-ontological difference" (albeit in the form of a forgetting) to every age of thought. Here we discover—so says John Caputo[10]—that the abstract "beingness" of beings is clearly not what Heidegger means by *Sein*.[11] At some level this is certainly so: When he speaks of being, Heidegger does indeed mean more than the "existence" of "existents"; he clearly means the possibility or event of such existence. That said, he confines the concept of being to a finite economy of "presencing" that is nothing but the process of "beingness," of becoming and passing away, and as a result his ontology remains a reflection only upon how beings appear within this economy. This is a problem, because properly speaking the question of being is: Why is there an economy of existence at all, and not much rather nothing? This would seem to mean that no moment within this economy, at the end of the day, can account for the economy as a whole. Nor does Heidegger escape the realm of the merely ontic by turning from the question of being to that of the *Ereignis*. As Caputo points out, Heidegger came to argue not that metaphysics is utterly oblivious of the ontological difference as such—philosophy has always known something of the difference, even where it reduces being to a being—but that metaphysics always fails to grasp the distance of the difference between being and beings:[12] being and beings are imagined as a circle of mutual grounding, between two separate kinds of "thing," which blinds the metaphysician to the mystery of being's purity from beings, and so to the mystery of the eventfulness of the passing over of being to beings and of beings to being. The mystery is hidden from view behind the splendid machinery and intricate hierarchies of rigid presence, substance, structure; the givenness of beings in their *Anwesen*—their arrival, their tremulous "whiling," their passing away again into concealment—goes unremarked in its self-effacing silence.

For this reason, Heidegger claims that he must begin the thinking of being anew, not merely from the vantage point of the difference, but from the vantage of the event of the difference. In 1959's *Identität und Differenz*, he takes two "steps back" from beings. The first is a step into the "ontico-ontological difference," of which metaphysics is conscious, but only according to some generalized model of a characteristic proper to beings; but the second is a step into the still more original *differing* of the difference, the *"Austrag"* (*auseinander-zueinander-tragen*) that grants being and beings to one another and opens for each epoch of thought the possibility of its forgetful thinking of the difference.[13] This appropriating event (*Ereignis*) must not be confused

---

10. John Caputo, *Heidegger and Aquinas: An Essay on Overcoming Metaphysics* (New York: Fordham University Press, 1982).
    11. Ibid., 143.
    12. Ibid., 155–56.
    13. Martin Heidegger, *Identität und Differenz* (Pfullingen: Gunther Neske, 1957), 65.

with "creation," according to Heidegger. It is a "letting-be-seen," not a kind of causality or *actus*; it is the giving that gives by withdrawing itself. What it gives is the process of ἀλήθεια or φύσις, the surging up and whiling of beings in the "juncture" of the event. In 1946's "Der Spruch des Anaximander," Heidegger had described this juncture as lying between two concealments—the future "to come" and the past "having been"[14]—a twofold absence that it holds apart so as to allow things to come to presence.[15] Nor is what the juncture makes present some kind of discrete perduring substance poised between these absences; the present "presences" only in allowing itself to belong also to the absent[16]—and here we glimpse something of the essence of tragedy.[17] In a footnote added to the text in 1950, Heidegger says that the discrimination (*Unter-Schied*) of which he is here speaking "is infinitely distinct [*unendlich verschieden*] from being, which remains the being *of* beings."[18] This event may also be called *Logos*, which Heidegger takes to mean, originally, a "laying-out before that gathers together":[19] *Logos* gathers all destining (*Schicken*) to itself, keeping each being, whether absent or present, "in its place and on its way," sending each into its own, and by its assembling *Logos* "secures all things in the all."[20] Heidegger's "temporalization of being" consists, then, simply in this: Being and beings are given to one another by an event that opens a finite juncture between the arrival of the concealed future and departure of the concealed past, where beings waver into presence, linger, and waver away into nothing. Time is being's passage from nothing to nothing, surmounted by a mysterious, noncausal event that assembles, limits, apportions, and sustains the economy of nihilation. This event, as *Logos*, occurs for us in language, and then in the thoughtful hearing of language's gathering saying of the world's "worlding"—as is nowhere more powerfully expressed than in the almost incantatory conclusion of "Brief über den Humanismus": As clouds are the clouds of the sky—making it visible, distinctly, as sky precisely by obscuring it—so language is the language of being; and, as the vast depths of the earth are barely scored by the inconspicuous furrows drawn by the farmer's plow, so thought is a humble laboring at the surface of language, whose immensity it scarcely touches.[21]

Again, I would not care to deny how seductive and impressive Heidegger's vision can be—so seductive and impressive, indeed, that only the most humorlessly pertinacious reader is likely to notice the little man hiding behind the screen, working the levers. Nevertheless, I reiterate my earlier charge: However much Heidegger may have succeeded at producing the appearance of a new kind of ontology, he never succeeded in understanding being as truly

---

14. In Martin Heidegger, *Holzwege* (hereinafter *H*), *Gesamtausgabe*, vol. 5 (Frankfurt: Vittorio Klosterman, 1977), 334–36.

15. *H 355.*

16. *H 357.*

17. *H 357–58.*

18. *H 364.*

19. Martin Heidegger, "Logos (Heraklit, Fragment 50)," in *Vorträge und Aufsätze* (hereinafter *VA*), *Gesamtausgabe*, vol. 7 (Frankfurt: Vittorio Klosterman, 2000).

20. *VA 226–27.*

21. *W 364/P 276.*

ontologically different from beings. Even his tortuous meditations upon the *Ereignis* serve only to confirm the event of the world in its own immanence, its ontic process, and all the while the real question of being fails to be posed. How is it that becoming is? This is never truly Heidegger's question; and one passage in "Anaximander" seems to me to express perfectly why it cannot be:

> Whatever has its essence in arrival and departure we would like to call becoming and perishing, which is to say, transience, and therefore not what has being [*das Seiende*]; for we have long been accustomed to opposing being [*Sein*] to becoming, as if becoming were a nothingness and did not even belong to being, which one habitually understands only as sheer perdurance. If, though, becoming *is*, then we must think being so essentially that it not only comprises becoming in some empty concept, but that, rather, being ontologically [*seinsmäßig*] supports and characterizes becoming (γένεσις—φθορά) in its essence.[22]

I must say, it seems to me that there is almost nothing in these sentences that is not obviously wrong. To begin with, to say that, in distinguishing between becoming and being, "metaphysics" customarily treats becoming as a kind of nothingness is to say something simply false; it sounds like one of those silly slanders of Platonism for which a serious scholar should have no patience. Surely it is more correct to say that the problem of philosophy has always been that of the synthesis of "nothingness" and "essence" within becoming, the persistence of unity within change, and so—quite logically— Western metaphysics has traditionally recognized that nothing that is (including becoming) is able to account for itself; hence, being and becoming are not to be accounted synonyms. But that is a mere cavil compared to what one should say regarding the far graver problem bedeviling Heidegger's central argument: "if becoming is . . ." it begins. Not to be too cavalier in dismissing his reasoning here, but I must observe that one could just as easily argue that being has always been characterized as altogether different from any number of things—lampshades, armchairs, clever ideas, lizards, passion fruit—but if these things are. . . . In every case, it is the "is" of the thing—whether it be becoming, a lampshade, a clever idea, or what have you—that proves irreducible to the thing. It would be convenient, of course, if one could dissolve the verb—the mysterious "to be"—into its subject, but one cannot. And "becoming" is no exception to this rule; it refers to the ontic "how" of finite existence, which means it cannot refer, of itself, to the ontological "that" of existence. Moreover, while it is an article of faith for Heideggereans that being has been understood, throughout metaphysical history, simply as sheer enduring presence, it is a belief gaily unencumbered by evidence.

---

22. *H* 343: "Was jedoch dergestalt in Ankunft und Abgang sein Wesen hat, möchten wir eher das Werdende und Vergehende, d.h. das Vergängliche nennen, nicht aber das Seiende; denn wir sind seit langem gewohnt, dem Werden das Sein entgegenzusetzen, gleich als ob Werden ein Nichts sei und nicht auch in das Sein gehöre, das man seit langem nur als das bloße Beharren versteht. Wenn jedoch das Werden *ist*, dann müssen wir Sein so wesentlich denken, daß es nicht nur im leeren begrifflichen Meinen das Werden umgreift, sondern daß das Sein das Werden (γένεσις—φθορά) seinsmäßig im Wesen erst trägt und prägt."

This is not to deny that eternity has traditionally, in Western thinking, been regarded as an aspect of that which is other than all beings, but certain things must be kept in mind. To begin with, the difference between timeless eternity and substantial perdurance is an absolute difference, a qualitative difference, rather like that between truth and truths, or between being and beings, and so it is no more correct to speak of eternity as sheer presence than to speak of it as sheer absence—which any garden-variety Neoplatonist could tell you. Moreover, even if the metaphysical certitude that becoming is not being might occasionally take the form of a crude distinction between changing things and a great changeless substance (though nowhere in Platonism or Christianity, as far as I know), it is a certitude that arises from the recognition that nothing in the ontic play of existence and nonexistence (not even becoming, or the process of "unhiddenness") is its own "is," and that the "is" cannot be something that becomes, that has an opposite, or that contains potential. And, perhaps most importantly, as a negation, "eternity" is an absolutely necessary and entirely benign moment in prescinding from beings to being, to which there is no alternative that is not nonsensical. For Heidegger, the incorrigible tendency of metaphysics is to isolate some general characteristic of beings, convert it into a concept of being *qua* being, and then treat beings as though they were mere instances or reflections of this supreme, changeless abstraction. Curiously enough, though, this is precisely what Heidegger himself does: He chooses to make the world of finitude the ground of the "truth" of being, and does so by taking the ontic characteristic of temporal change, of becoming and transiency, generalizing it as the process of hiddenness and unhiddenness, and abstracting from it various names for being; this process he then mistakes for the ontological difference itself, which means that he can conceive of being only as a reflection of our own "beingness." Then, over this entire dialectic of existence and nonexistence, he erects an arch of fate, of a "destining" that apportions finite things to their placement and displacement in a cycle of interminable immanence,[23] and so confirms beings in their potentiality (their nothingness) as the "ground" of being.[24] In scholastic terms, Heidegger has merely elevated possibility over actuality.[25] What he certainly

---

23. See Martin Heidegger, "Moira (Parmenides, Fragment VIII, 34–41)," in *VA* 235–61.

24. See Martin Heidegger, "Vom Wesen des Grundes," in *W* 123–75. This essay was originally published in the 1930s.

25. "Possibility is always higher than actuality, sicut Martinus dicit" (Caputo, *Heidegger and Aquinas*, 284). This touches upon an issue that requires more space than I can grant here. Heidegger claims that the language of *actus* and *actualitas* in Thomas reflects a "Roman" distortion of Aristotle's *energeia*, characteristic of the ancient Latin world's culture of force, fabrication, technology, and conquest, a culture whose governing motif was one of efficiency. I find this worse than unconvincing, however: Not only is it the case that Thomas carefully discriminates between a crudely univocal use of the language of cause or act and his properly analogical use (a fact that would not really make any difference against Heidegger's essentially intuitive argument here), but it is also the case that *actus* is neither philologically, semantically, nor historically bound to the connotations Heidegger assigns it (after all, one can *agere gratias, poenitentiam,* or *pacem,* and it is very important *se agere* well, but one must *aedificare* or *condere pontem*). It is true that Heidegger reportedly believed that earlier Greek patristic language might be more elusive of his critique, but I for one resist taking comfort from this, as I believe that Thomas's language is entirely continuous with the language of the Cappadocians, Dionysius, Maximus, etc. Perhaps it is interesting to ask whether Heidegger could have read Dionysius or Maximus, speaking of God as the fullness of being, "leading" (to use the Dionysian term) beings into being, or as the light shining in and on all beings, drawing them to himself, or as the infinite source of beauty that "excites" the "eros" of beings out of their nonbeing, and interpreted this simply as a discourse of double founding, a mere causal economy between a supreme thing and

has not done is address the essential mystery: How is it that either possibility or actuality *is*? Whence comes the "is" in "it is possible"?

Does it, after all, make any particular sense to grant possibility priority over actuality? Obviously, at the level of the ontic, the possible is always in excess of whatever is, in any moment, actual; but, once again, this merely restates the problem. It is precisely *because* this is the case at the level of the ontic that thought is obliged ultimately to seek, beyond the ontic supremacy of the possible, the ontological truth of the actual. For, in itself, an economy in which the possible is higher than the actual is manifestly impossible. What Heidegger calls *Anwesen* consists, necessarily, in a dialectic between "this" and "not this"—between what is and all that might be, that has been, that will be, all that is concealed, potential, and that is *not*. But this is precisely the dialectic that must remain an inert impossibility if the difference between possible and actual is not enfolded within a prior actuality. Not to sound too doctrinaire, but the nothing cannot magically pass from itself into something; *fieri* simply cannot precede *esse*. Heidegger obviously makes a vague gesture in the direction of this rather elementary impasse by distinguishing between the "ontico-ontological difference" and its event, but here too, unless this event is understood as the donation of being from a plenitude of actuality, such a distinction is little more than a revision of the problem it pretends to address. One must either be willing to speak of something like an *actus essendi subsistens*, or cease speaking of being altogether; and to misrepresent talk of this transcendent act, that infinitely and simply is all that the possible might possibly be, as simply "ontic" discourse, concerned with some efficient cause or power, is to trade in empty caricature. From the high patristic period onward, Christian thought had developed an ontology of the infinite, which Aquinas brought to its most lucid Latin expression: Being is not reducible either to essence or to finite existence; "infinity," which for Aristotle was to be ascribed only to the inchoate potentiality of matter, became now a name for the fullness of *esse*, which is the transcendent act in which essence and existence alike participate; and thus being differs from beings more or less as does goodness from anything good. *This* language of participation, however much one may wish to resist its logic, is no naive "essentialism" or "causalism," nor certainly is it the "reciprocal grounding" of "onto-theology." Nor is the concept of *actus* it presumes some pale reflection of one or another general characteristic of beings. Rather, indeed, it is this approach to ontology alone that makes it possible to conceive of the distinction between being and beings as something other than an ontic economy. Even if, in the realm of the ontic, the possible is in some sense the fountainhead of the actual, this obviously finite order still must be conceptually inverted (which involves an appeal

---

derivative things. Could Heidegger have read Dionysius's language of the divine ecstasy that calls forth and meets our ecstasy, and so gives being to beings, or of the Good's supereminent "no-thing-ness," and treated this too as a form of ontic causality infinitely magnified, without significant analogical ambiguity? Such questions are pointless, though, as Heidegger's commitment to his own metaphysics of process, epochality, language, and "thought" was irreconcilable with any discourse of transcendence, which is what—in any event—the patristic language is; and to ask such questions, moreover, is perhaps to have conceded that scholastic *actus* was indeed what Heidegger said it was—which it was not.

to the infinite) if one is to be able to think of being as such, for possibility—however one conceives of it—must first *be*.

This is, I readily confess, an argument for "necessary being." It may seem that, in turning away from Heidegger's ontology only to retreat to so antique and "metaphysical" a redoubt, I am behaving rather like a French soldier fleeing to the shelter of the Maginot line after the German armies have already circumvented it, but I can see no coherent alternative. In the defense of such a move, I can only observe that "necessary," in this context, cannot mean a first cause in any ontic sense (or, as Thomas would say, in any sense appropriate to the order of secondary causality); rather, it indicates the transcendent "possibility of possibility," which must be infinite actuality. This is a logic that no "ontologist" can really escape. Even Heidegger, by thinking of possibility as "higher" than actuality, is really only transposing his terms; he is thinking of the possible *as* the actual, as possessing greater (albeit indeterminate) "eminence," which must be forcibly distributed into temporal determinacy and definite manifestation by the apportioning hand of destiny. Heidegger sees the "no-thing-ness" of being not as an infinite purity from all limit, but as a mirror inversion of ontic presence in the ontic absence of past and future, and so he sees the withholding of being in beings not as the qualitative transcendence of the infinite, but (almost) as the restrained immensity of the "there," the absolute compresence of the totality deferred into temporality. Even, then, if we concede that Heidegger's *Sein* is not *esse commune* (which clearly it is not), we must also recognize that, in its complete dependence upon the dialectic of existence and nonexistence, Heidegger's "ontology" is a species of "double founding"—of, that is, metaphysics, and of the most causal variety. Heidegger's second step back from metaphysics is not a step into a more original distinction than the "ontico-ontological difference," but merely a stepping away from the infinite into the finite, so as to complete metaphysics' decline by a descent into a passive self-sealing immanentism, reflecting the world's transitoriness to itself in the fixed, anonymous mirror of the "event." Having thus failed to think his way toward being's real difference from beings, Heidegger accomplishes nothing by differentiating the *Ereignis* "infinitely" from all being but to confirm—through negation—the totality in its finitude. This, though, is the fate of every "metaphysics" (at least according to Heidegger): In that it considers the ontological difference from the vantage of the ontic, it can do no other than arrive at a (in the univocal sense) cause. Only the theological understanding of being's infinite act, neither determined in beings nor lacking anything in their absence, comprehends the difference as belonging first to being, not beings; which is to say, only theology views ontology from the place of a gift received.

None of which is to deny the brilliance of Heidegger's diagnosis of nihilism; no one else ever laid out with such compelling clarity the pathology of modernity. Nor would I even wish to reject entirely his suggestion that nihilism is a fate written in the history of metaphysics from its earliest dawn. And surely no theologian can take exception to Heidegger's desire to free philosophy from the arid and ultimately nihilistic reduction of "truth" to sufficient reason or positive ground. However, no less than Nietzsche, Heidegger was a creature of the history he sought to understand, to "retrieve," and in a sense to conclude. Coming when he did, in the dying twilight of Western philosophy's long, sedulous suppression of its memory of Christian philosophy, he was rather like a man standing on a vast level plain as night falls, gazing into the distance, entirely unaware that lying midway between him and the horizon to which he is turned is an immense chasm, veiled in shadows. He was able thus to look back to the birth of philosophy, construct a genealogy of nihilism that very plausibly (if not always convincingly) tells the story of thought's decline from its first glimpse of being's mystery, and even bring nihilism to its consummation, while all the time remaining abysmally oblivious of how deep theology's interruption of that genealogy was. It was possible, therefore, for Heidegger to ask the question of being anew, without any fear of his philosophy gravitating back into the environs of theology (thus forfeiting its precious and hard-won autonomy), because the forgetfulness of the question's meaning had by his time become so entirely complete. Hence, the philosopher whose idiom was the most robustly and indefatigably "ontological" ever was the philosopher who most signally failed to ask—or even grasp what it would mean to ask—the question of being.

Ad Nihilum and Ex Nihilo

If, as my argument implies, modern philosophy's forgetfulness of being is nothing other than a forgetfulness of Christian thought, and if Heidegger is the first philosopher in whose work this forgetfulness has become so forgetful even of itself as to mistake itself for the one thing it cannot possibly be— an ontology—then perhaps Heidegger's greatest significance as a philosopher lies in his value as a kind of cautionary epitome. What matters most is not what he rejects—say, an ontology of infinite actuality that he simply does not understand—but what he is moved, in consequence, to embrace. After all, the special genius—or, at any rate, special charm—of Heidegger's thought is its recovery of a genuinely pagan vision of being: the muscular naiveté of Heracleitos and Hesiod, but steeped in the lugubrious, effete, cosmopolitan fatalism of late antiquity and fringed with opulent Romantic embroideries; the languid "thinker," weary with the burden of history, discovers among Attic ruins the hidden traces of a truly tragic—which is to say, sacrificial— ontology. Within such an ontology, obviously, certain issues cannot be raised: the baffling truth that every "this" is "this" on account of that transfinite unity that shows itself in every thing, every part of every thing, and every series of things; or the clarity and intelligibility of discrete forms; or the persistence of things in themselves, in recognizable integrity, across time; or the way in which desire and knowledge each seem to precede the other; and so on. Such questions are, by definition, questions of the "transcendentals," and bespeak the Platonist's servile fascination with the "looks" of things. But being, for Heidegger, is an original alienation from form, the movement of an original "not." One might wish to ask how it is that all things are unities within change, how order and thought and beauty are one and yet distinct, how the world and perception are inseparably joined in a circle of love and knowledge, and so forth, but for Heidegger—absurdly enough—these are not properly ontological questions at all. The only answer he could provide would be that the world appears thus because it must so appear. For being to disclose itself in beings, it must be forced or "nihilated" into the limits of the ontic, its power must be wrested into the juncture as limited and transient forms of "presencing," *Welt* must be ripped from the depths of *Erde*, the thing must gather from the four regions in order to be set off against being's nothingness. The truth that a thing is, and is what it is, follows from the necessary reduction of the nothing to something, according to the determinations of an empty but irresistible "destining." One must rest content with the metaphysical dogma that what is must be, and cease to ask how it could be so. Actually, in treating questions regarding the transcendental moments in which all things subsist, and by which knowledge receives the world, as mere "ontic" questions, more or less on the same level as questions concerning causality, Heidegger makes all too obvious how very oblivious of the ontological difference he really is; but it is only by way of such an oblivion that he can make his pilgrimage back to the pre-Socratic immersion in φύσις with a pure heart. A vision of being as a closed finite order of placement and displacement, life and death, presided over by fate, is simply the aboriginal pagan vision of being as sacrifice: as order won through strife, as an economy of destruction and reviviscence, as the totality of beings sealed within itself. It is an ontology with no horizon but beings, which can do no more than abstract from nature, violence, and transience to a dark, inexhaustible reservoir of ontic possibility, and to an inescapable process of coming to pass and passing away.

In some sense, I want to endorse Vattimo's talk of the "violence of metaphysics" (though not in quite his apocalyptically dramatic terms). Western philosophy has never, insofar as it has functioned as a self-sufficient discipline distinct from theology, been able to think of the being of the world except in terms of a kind of strife between order and disorder, a certain set of tragic limits to being's expression of itself, and so an inescapable structure of deceit within the fabric of the finite. Every "metaphysical" ontology presumes that, in some way both primordial and ultimate, difference *is* violence, even (indeed, especially) when it is an ontology of the postmodern variety that thinks it has freed itself of the "totalizing" tendencies of "onto-theology." There is nothing startling or blameworthy in this, given that all nontheological philosophy is, by definition, a discourse concerning necessity—not, that is to say, *necessitas* in the theological sense, the utter fittingness with which divine freedom expresses the goodness of its nature in the generosity of its act (being itself the *actus* of all that is), but necessity in the sense of being's finitude, its absolute limitation to the condition of the world in its "worlding," its fatedness. However well a "pure" metaphysics may be able to conceive of ontological dependency, it can never, by its own lights, arrive at the thought of true contingency. Even a Heracleitean metaphysics of chance is anything but a philosophy of the freedom of either the ontic or of the ontological, but is—as Nietzsche so well understood—a doctrine of the absolute necessity of the being of this world; even the most etherealizing "idealism" can at best conceive of the ultimate as the apex or "absolute" of the totality of beings, the spiritual resolution of all the ambiguities of the immanent, but can never really think in terms of true transcendence. If the ambition of metaphysics is to deduce from the features of the existence of the world the principles of the world, then it must see all the characteristic conditions of the world as manifestations of its ground. Thus, metaphysics must embrace, not merely as elements but as principles of being, all the tragic and negative aspects of existence: pain, ignorance, strife, alienation, death, the recalcitrance of matter, the inevitability of corruption and dissolution, and so on. And it must respond to such sad necessities according to one or another wisdom of the immanent: joyous affirmation, tragic resignation, heroic resolve, Dionysian anarchy, the "rational love of God," the "negation of negation," or some form of nihilism, tender or demonic. Being, conceived in terms of the totality, is a pitiless economy, a structure of sacrifice in which beings suffer incompletion and destruction in order that being may "be." The world and its principles sustain one another in a dialectic of being and beings, a reciprocal movement of fulfillment and negation, the completion of finitude in the mystery of the absolute, and the display of the absolute in the violence of its alienation. The land of unlikeness is explicable only in the light of the forms; but where else can the forms shine forth? But it is just this—the tragedy of being in its dispensation—that is the wellspring of philosophy's power, for thought can move from the world to the world's principles only in such measure as what is, is what must be; only because being is constrained by necessity to these manifestations, and only because being *must* show itself in beings, is an autonomous metaphysics possible. Once necessity is presumed, every merely human philosophy is possible. Thereafter, it is not so much discernment as sensibility that draws any given thinker to the crystalline intricacies of the Platonic cosmos or to the delirious abandon of the Dionysiac, to the great epic of the Concept or to the tediously uniform debris of "difference," to the dry clarity of a logic of substance and accidents or to the poetic irrationality of a mysticism of the "event."

If this is so, though, then perhaps one could rewrite Heidegger's genealogy of nihilism, preserving many of its features intact but casting it anew as the story of the persistent, polymorphous myth of metaphysical necessity—its fabulous birth in the age of the pre-Socratics, its protean passage through innumerable schools and systems, its defeat at the hands of a powerful and seemingly victorious champion, and its rebirth in a new, more terrible, more invincible form. Such would be, obviously, a subversion of the Heideggerean tale, but not an absolute rejection; it might, in fact, make the story more coherent. According to Heidegger, again, being has reached its eschaton, the most extreme limit of its decline, its fated gathering to its ultimate essence,[26] in the time of the technological *Gestell*;[27] but, having achieved this the vantage of ultimate extremity, thought can now look back over the history of *Seinsvergessenheit*, understand what has brought us to this moment, glimpse that flash of light that illuminated being in thought's "first beginning," and prepare ourselves, with a certain pious *Gelassenheit*, for another beginning. In a sense he is right: "systematic" philosophy, as an independent enterprise of critical reason, has reached the point of collapse; Christian thought's interruption and rescue of Western metaphysics has been followed by a revolt of reason whose ultimate form cannot now be anything but nihilism made transparent to itself; so Heidegger, the last metaphysician (or the first of the last metaphysicians), who can see the shape of nihilism, but who—as that increasingly otiose thing, a philosopher—cannot step back from this destiny, instead attempts to press through it to a resignation that somehow anticipates and so overcomes nihilism, and that thus returns to metaphysics' origin. However, again because his move is the final reactive agitation of a revolt, the thought of being available to him is still nihilistic, still a finite ontic economy, stripped even of the soothing mirages of modern metaphysics: *Geist*, ego, positivity, and so forth. Ultimately, Heidegger succeeds only at returning to an oblivion of being as profound as his own, the pre-Socratic inability to separate wonder at being from brutish awe before nature and fate, part and whole, becoming and totality—that is, the pre-Platonic indistinction between being and sacrifice.

Western thought had attempted to rise from this superstitious subjugation to the world's mere event. Plato and Aristotle, however imperfectly, were both shaken by that effulgent moment of wonder that can free reflection from mere animal dread; perhaps the one could not quite transcend the dialectic of change and changeless essences, the other the dialectic of finite form and unrealized potency, nor either the still "sacrificial" economy of finitude, but both stood within an opening in Western thought that theology could transform into a genuine openness before the transcendent God. Still, Heidegger may be somewhat correct in seeing, even in this openness, the inauguration of Western reason's long journey toward technological mastery as the highest ideal, toward instrumental control as the governing model of all truth, toward—in short—nihilism. Perhaps there truly was, precisely in the birth of philosophy as a self-conscious enterprise of rising above the ephemerality of the phenomena to take hold of their immutable premises, a turning away from the light toward the things it illuminated, a forgetfulness of being within philosophy's very wakefulness to being. And perhaps in this fateful moment of inattention to the mystery of being's event, the relentless search for being's positive foundations commenced, and then proceeded along a path that, in the end, would arrive at the ruin of philosophic faith. All of this may be— indeed, in some obvious sense, is—quite true. But the Platonic *eros* for the

---

26. *H* 327.
27. See Martin Heidegger, "Die Kehre," in *Die Technik und die Kehre* (Pfullingen: Neske, 1962).

beautiful, good, and true was also a longing for something more than mere "grounds"; it was a desire for being's fullness, though one not yet able to understand being as gift. Other ancient schools of thought were generally less precocious in their advances toward Christian theology. Stoicism, for instance, however magnificent, humane, and sophisticated it was in its most developed forms, was still somewhat retrograde in this regard, and was bound to a vision of the cosmos as a fated economy of placement and displacement, and to a more transparently sacrificial cosmic mythology of eternally repeated *ekpyroses* (the universe as an eternal sacrificial pyre), but Stoicism too was profoundly marked by philosophical wonder before the goodness and loveliness of cosmic and divine order. The syncretism of late antiquity may often have produced monstrosities of occult "wisdom" and grotesque aberrations of philosophy and religion alike, but in the case of the Platonic tradition it also made it possible for a philosopher like Plotinus to reflect upon the generosity of the good and the convertibility of the good and being, and thus press against the boundaries of the totality. But it was only when Christian thought arrived, and with it the doctrine of creation, that the totality was broken open and, for the first time ever, philosophy was granted a glimpse of being's splendid strangeness within its very immediacy and gratuity.

With this "Christian interruption" of metaphysics, every principle of necessity was made subordinate to the higher principle of grace. Christian thought, then, in its long history of metaphysical speculation, far from constituting just another episode in the genealogy of nihilism, was in fact so profound a disruption of many of the most basic premises of philosophy, and so audacious a rescue of many of philosophy's truths from the impotent embrace of mere metaphysical ambition, that it is doubtful yet that philosophy can grasp what has happened to it, or why now it cannot be anything but an ever more indignant and self-tormenting flight from that interruption. The language of creation—however much it may be parodied as a language regarding efficient causality and metaphysical "founding"—actually introduced into Western thought the radically new idea that an infinite freedom is the "principle" of the world's being and so for the first time opened up the possibility of a genuine reflection upon the difference between being and beings. And the Christian understanding of God as Trinity, without need of the world even for his determination as difference, relatedness, or manifestation, for the first time confronted Western thought with a genuine discourse of transcendence, of an ontological truth whose "identity" is not completed by any ontic order. The event of being is, for beings, a pure gift, into whose mysteries no *scala naturae* by itself can lead us. And if the world is not a manifestation of necessity but of gratuity—even if it must *necessarily* reflect in its intrinsic orderliness and concinnity the goodness of its source—then philosophy may be able to grasp many things, but by its own power it can never attain to the source or end of things. If being is not bound to the dimensions prescribed for it by fate or the need for self-determination or the contumacy of a material substrate, then the misconstrual of the contingent for the necessary constitutes philosophy's original error.

It is for this reason also that theology's interruption of the "history of nihilism" was philosophy's redemption, immeasurably deepening its openness to being and increasing the intensity of its highest *eros*. Within Christianity's narrative, the world acquired a new glory. For all that it had been robbed of the imposing dignity of metaphysical necessity, it had been imbued with the still more extraordinary dignity of divine pleasure; the world had become an instance of what could only be called beauty—beauty of a kind more absolute and irreducible than any then known to pagan Greek culture. A God whose very being is love, delight in the glory of his infinite Image, seen in the boundlessly lovely light of his Spirit, and whose works are then unnecessary but perfectly expressive signs of this delight, fashioned for his pleasure and for the gracious sharing of his joy with creatures for whom he had no need—is a God of beauty in the fullest imaginable sense. In such a God, beauty and the infinite entirely coincide. The very life of God is one of, so to speak, infinite form, and when he creates, the difference between worldly beauty and the divine beauty it reflects subsists not in a dialectic between multiplicity and unity, composition and simplicity, shape and indeterminacy, but in the analogy between the determinate particularities of the world and that always greater, supereminent determinacy in which they participate. Thus it is that theology alone preserves and clarifies all of philosophy's most enchanting prospects upon being: precisely by detaching them from the mythology of "grounds" and by resituating them within the space of this peaceful analogical interval between divine and worldly being, within which space the sorrows of necessity enjoy no welcome. Thus, for Christian thought, knowledge of the world is something to be achieved not just through a reconstruction of its "sufficient reason," but through an obedience to glory, an orientation of the will toward the light of being and its gratuity; and so the most fully "adequate" discourse of truth is worship, prayer, and rejoicing. Phrased otherwise, the truth of being is "poetic" before it is "rational" (indeed, it is rational precisely because of its supreme poetic coherence and richness of detail) and thus cannot be known truly if this order is reversed. Beauty is the beginning and end of all true knowledge. Really to know, one must first love, and having known one must finally delight; only this "corresponds" to the Trinitarian love and delight that creates. The truth of being is the whole of being, in its event, groundless and so, in its every detail, revelatory of the light that grants it. In a strangely impoverished and negative way, Heidegger—the apostate from theology—almost understood this, but ultimately proved to be only a "metaphysician" after all. Then again, Heidegger, like Nietzsche, was unable to see that his own revolt against metaphysics was itself really nothing but a necessary moment in metaphysics' recovery of itself from theology. Philosophy could not, after all, accept the gift Christian thought extended to it and remain what it had been—a science of mastery, an interrogation of the "ground"—but neither could it ignore Christianity's transformation of its native terms. Once the splendor of truth had been assumed into the Christian love of beauty, its *philokalia*, once the light of the world had been taken into the discourse of ontological analogy and divine transcendence, and once the difference between being and beings had entered thought and disrupted every attempt to deduce from the world its metaphysical identity, philosophy could not simply reassert itself as an independent project but had to discover a new foundation. Philosophy, like a king in exile, would have to suffer the most extreme divestment and privation before it could reclaim its lost privileges. This is the true sense in which theology is part of the history of nihilism: It leaves nothing good behind in the philosopher's hands, it plunders all of philosophy's most powerful interpretive instruments for its own uses (despoiling the Egyptians, to use the classic metaphor), and so makes it necessary, in the aftermath of theology's cultural influence, that philosophy advance itself ever more openly as a struggle against the light, an ever more vehement refusal of the generosity of the given.[28] If nihilism is indeed the hidden core or secret vocation of metaphysics, in the post-Christian age nothing but that core, that vocation, remains: and so it must become ever less hidden, ever less secret.

Christian tradition, in making the eternal beauty of ancient philosophical longing so much more prodigal in its availability, and in urging philosophical *eros* toward a more transcendent end, deprived the world of any grounds within itself and so further gilded the world's glory with an additional aura of gratuity and fortuity. The shining forth, the *phainein*, of the phenomena now belonged to another story, and so no longer provided irrefragable evidence of reason's ability to gain possession of the world's principles. To free itself from theology, then, philosophy had to discover a new order of evidence, one not compromised by collaboration with Christianity's complex discourse of divine transcendence. This could be accomplished only by way of an initial refusal of the world's alluring and terrifying immediacy; through a simple but peremptory act of rejection, the order of truth could be inverted, moving truth from the world in its appearing to the subject in its perceiving. Thus, reason's "freedom" would be secured anew. At the same time, however, such a rejection could not but unveil, with unceremonious suddenness, the nihilistic terminus that Nietzsche and Heidegger saw as being inaugurated in the eidetic science of Platonism. Descartes phrases the matter with exquisite precision: "Now will I close my eyes, I will stop up my ears, I will avert my senses from their objects, I will even erase from my consciousness all images of things corporeal; or, at least . . . I will consider them to be empty and false."[29] If this austerely principled act of self-abnegation (or self-mutilation) was

---

28. This is not to deny that Christian theology had a part to play in the transition from the implicit nihilism of antiquity to the explicit nihilism of modernity: late mediaeval voluntarism; the rise of nominalism; a late scholastic tendency to insulate the spheres of theology and philosophy from one another; the occasional triumph in Catholic and Protestant discourse alike of a concern for God's sovereignty over a concern for God's goodness; flirtations with occasionalist epistemology and, simultaneously, univocal ontology; the ever more pronounced tendency to understand divine freedom as pure, unconstrained *arbitrium* (which an earlier theology would correctly have seen as a limitation on the liberty of God's *voluntas*), and the consequent tendency to understand human freedom as pure spontaneity of will and unpremised choice; and so on. But this is only to say that secularization begins in theology's apostasy from itself, and that Heidegger—the failed theologian—is the perfect emblematic figure of Western philosophy in its sad senescence.

29. René Descartes, *Meditations* III.

not modernity's founding gesture, it was at any rate the perfect crystallization of its untender logic. Thereafter, the verity of the world was something to be found only within the citadel of subjective certitude, through an act of will. Philosophy's transcendental turn made instrumental reason its own foundation; the truth of the world would no longer be certified by the *phainein* that gives things to thought, but only by the adjudications of the hidden artificer of rational order, the ego. Understanding, indiscerptible from the power of the will to establish and negate, could not now be understanding of a prior givenness, but only a reduction of the exterior to something conformable to and manipulable by reason. Philosophy may begin in wonder, the *thaumazein* of a gaze enraptured by the radiance of the world, striving to ascend to the source of that radiance, but it ends, it would seem, in an anxious retreat from world to self, from wonder to suspicion, from light to will. It was Christianity's rescue of the world's light from the myth of necessity that forced philosophy to take the transcendental turn; and Christianity's story of transcendent freedom made possible its own distorted reflection in a discourse of truth premised upon the subject's rational reconstruction of experience from its own freedom of will; but only a conscious project of immanent reason, not dependent on a transcendent source of truth, could decisively liberate philosophy from theology's narrative of being as gift. The phenomena had to be conformed to our gaze, rather than the reverse; indeed, in no genuine sense could they be taken as "phenomena" at all—the shining forth of being in beings, inviting vision to a movement beyond itself. Wakefulness to transcendence had to be replaced by the clear-eyed disenchantment of a controlling scrutiny. And when the wakened gaze was forsaken for a gaze that establishes its own truthfulness, thought could possess no world that was not its own artifact; and that world could be no more than the passive and indifferent realm of thought's investigations and scientific adventures.[30] Thereafter the phenomena, when again admitted into philosophy's calculations, could be no more than mensurable objects of curiosity or use. Natural light—impotent to produce propositions or "clear and distinct ideas," able only to offer the world to recognition or to illuminate it as mystery—could *prove* nothing, but was now seen as itself needing transcendental probation and authentication.

Descartes, admittedly, did not intend to confine thought within an inviolable interiority; indeed, he found the surest confirmation of the trustworthiness of his perceptions in the presence within his mind of the thought of the infinite, which must, he claimed, have been placed in him by God, inasmuch as it cannot in any way be abstracted from finite experience. But it is just this divorce between empirical knowledge and the concept of the infinite, as

---

30. This is not, let me be clear, a kind of primitivist protest against science and technology, with all their plenteous goods and plenteous ills (though I am quite sympathetic to such protests and read William Morris insatiably). My concern is the "ideology of knowledge" or "mythology of understanding," so to speak, and the question of whether some form of nominalist disenchantment, combined with some form of transcendental epistemology, was necessary for the advance of the sciences (which I do not believe) is not one I mean here to address.

Descartes understood them, that makes it obvious that, from the transcendental vantage, immanent and transcendent truth are dialectically rather than analogically related; the former concerns a world of substances that exhaust their meaning in their very finitude, while the latter can appear among these substances only in the form of a paradox—a "knowledge" whose only evidence and condition is itself. God's infinity thus conceived is not truly the infinite; it is not qualitatively other than every finite thing precisely by being "not other," but instead the possibility and "place" of all things, the unity and fullness of being in which all beings live and move and are; rather, it is merely the negation of finitude, the contrary of limit, found nowhere among my finite cognitions. This "modern" infinite is not only beyond finite vision; it is without any analogous mediation—any *via eminentiae*—within the visible. A world certified by my founding gaze, and then secondarily by God (the postulated *causa efficiens et causa sui*), can admit the infinite into its calculus only as the indivisible naught that embraces every finite quantity, the "not this" that secures every "this" in the poverty of its particularity. However, the power of such an "infinite" to disrupt the ordered internal universe of the ego, as Descartes thought it must, is an illusion. The distinction between God's featureless, superempirical infinity and the palpable limits of the perceiving ego functioned for Descartes as proof that the "I" does not constitute its experience in any original way, but rather is itself constituted by the creative will of an invisible God. It required only the next logical step of distinguishing the empirical ego from the transcendental ego to collapse the distinction between the infinite and subjectivity altogether. This was Kant's greatest triumph. The transcendental project in its inchoate, Cartesian, insufficiently "critical" form could escape the circularity of knowledge—the ceaseless oscillation of epistemic priority between understanding and experience, between subject and object—only by positing, beyond empirical ego and empirical data alike, a transcendent cause. But Kant clearly knew that this is simply to ground the uncertifiable in the unascertainable. Moreover, he certainly felt no impulse to retreat to an alternative anything like the premodern language of illumination, which would resolve the question of the correspondence between perception and the perceived by ascribing that correspondence to the supereminent unity in which the poles of experience—phenomena and gaze—participate. Now that every standard of validity had been definitively situated within the knowing subject, within the self's assurance of itself, such a metaphysics was a critical impossibility, as it could never be established by the autonomous agency of reason; indeed, it could be seriously entertained as a satisfactory answer only by a mind resigned to a certain degree of passivity, a trust in a transcendent source of truth that is, by definition, elusive of the scrutiny of the independent ego. And so Kant was more or less compelled to ground the circle of knowledge in a transcendental capacity behind empirical subjectivity, the "transcendental unity of apperception" that accompanies all the representations available to the empirical ego; this was, manifestly, a metaphysical conjecture, but it was one to which the limits of modernity's conjectural range permitted no alternative—not, of course, that an alternative would have been desirable. Kant thus gained for subjectivity not only a mastery over the realm of the "theoretical," but a "supersensible freedom" so profound that even the moral law—once the exclusive preserve of God, the gods, the good beyond being—could be regarded as its achievement. Bliss was it in that dawn to be alive, no doubt, when the Christian universe was inverted and philosophy knew the exhilaration of breaking free from dependency upon God—either the Christian God or his shadowy Cartesian surrogate—to claim for itself an autonomy greater than any it had ever yet possessed.

Yet when the first frisson of excitement subsided, it became obvious—to some, at least—that it was an autonomy curiously devoid of freedom. There was undeniably a kind of Promethean rebellion in philosophy's turn to the transcendental ego, but also a fate not unlike that of Prometheus bound to his pillar in the Caucasus. And while Hegel might seem an implausible Heracles, it was he more than anyone else (more even than Fichte) who saw that a liberty that consisted in resting secure in the impregnable citadel of the self, peering out through its machicolations at a landscape purged of all metaphysical mystery, never hoping to take possession of the lands beyond its walls, was scarcely distinguishable from incarceration. He understood that philosophy would always be in retreat if it could not actually overcome theology's metaphysical tradition, provide an account of theology that could cogently portray the Christian story as an unrefined foreshadowing of a story that only philosophy would be able to tell fully, and so assume theology into itself. Thus it was that he went about recovering the largely forgotten rationality of classical Trinitarian doctrine (modern theology's most irksome irony), so that he could rethink it, subvert it, and bring its disruptive force back under the governance of philosophical reflection. Hegel was willing to surrender some real measure of the isolated ego's independence because he was engaged in the near impossible task of bringing under speculative control the radical contingency that Christian theology had introduced into the "absolute," and—more—in an attempt to overcome a final irreducible difference that Christian thought had imagined within God; by "historicizing" Spirit, Hegel sought at once to "spiritualize" history and to "idealize" the Trinity, making God and history a mutually sustaining process. What Hegel could not tolerate was the notion either of a God who possesses in himself difference, determinacy, plenitude, and perfection independent of any world, or of a world thus left devoid of meaning in the ultimate speculative sense of "necessity" and so reduced to the status of something needless, something thoroughly aesthetic, not accomplishing—but merely expressing—a love God enjoys in utter self-sufficiency. Divine infinity, conceived as Trinitarian, always infinitely "determined" toward another, does not require time's tragic probations and determining negations; all created being is an unnecessary, *excessive* display of God's glory, and thus the world of things is set free in its "aimless" particularity. The Christian infinite is its own "exteriority," without need of another, negative exteriority to bring it to fruition. And without the majestic mythology of necessity governing the realm of the absolute, philosophy enjoys no sure authority over the contingent.

This is no less intolerable a state of affairs for "postmetaphysical" forms of philosophy than it is for Hegel. The most radically anti-idealist thinkers, from Nietzsche to Derrida, tend to possess an inflexible conviction that being is finite, that what is must be, that death is the possibility of life and absence the possibility of presence, and that the world's most terrible limits are being's indispensable conditions. Heidegger, especially, cannot do without a firm faith in the necessity of being's event, its necessary limitation within the dispensations of its epochal sending, its finitude. Being *must* be thus: manifestation as obscuration, truth as duplicity, mission as "errance." Here the ambiguous Platonic wakefulness to wonder is submerged again in brute passivity, the full Christian awakening is entirely purged from memory, and philosophy becomes a crepuscular and elegiac meditation upon its own death. And Heidegger's postmodern epigones are ontological fatalists of the purest water. For all of them, the event of world and thought can be understood only as an order of sacrifice, an original economy sustaining order over against (but in dependency on) chaos, absence, the invisible excess, the "unpresentable"—but it must not be conceived as gift, as the donation of form from an always more eminent splendor that *limits itself*, not out of necessity, but according to the kenotic and ecstatic love of the *summum bonum*. Thus, there can be no names for what exceeds the representable order; it is the dissimulation of this excess that gives us the illusory world of presence; and this unnamable sublimity, far from having any analogy among the phantasms that issue from it, is the terrible night into which all things are offered up by time as a perfect offering and in which all light has always been and always will be extinguished.

In any event, this is merely the barest sketch of a revised genealogy of nihilism, which could take a far fuller and more varied form. Here it is best simply to remark that, in the case of Heidegger, there is a peculiar poignancy in the impossibility of his position: he is animated by a theological hunger, in the service of which he pursues an entirely unsustainable, antitheological logic of immanence—which makes him, really, a very late Romantic. It makes perfect sense that his thought should then—as his late essays amply attest—dissolve into a kind of Arcadian nostalgia, an almost Rousseauvian yearning for the pure word that can speak the event in its immediacy, an innocent and pristine tongue, uncorrupted by duplicity or dead metaphor (a language to which, with an aching proximity, Greek and German alone are nearly transparent). The perpetual flight from metaphysical "attribution" to poetic "naming" is an interminable descent to the poverty of "simple saying."[31] Interminable because Heidegger's own ontology—which is clearly a univocal ontology—must frustrate such a yearning utterly; the *Ereignis* is always the same event, invariable and without metaphysical height or depth, and so all words equally manifest and dissemble it: say and "unsay" the same thing. In short, nothing is said, of being or of God. At most, one can sit on the bank of the Ister, alongside the shade of Hölderlin, attempting to speak the world's

---

31. W 364/P 276.

"worlding" by naming beings in their momentariness: "river". . . "sky" . . . "grass" . . . "more river.". . . This is not, I make bold to assert, profound. If truth is to be understood as simply a more lyric species of tautology, what is this but the nihilism of modernity in its all but purest form? And would it not be wise then at least to *seek* another kind of speaking, one that is neither simple metaphysical attribution nor "simple saying," but a language that can name the difference between being and beings in a movement of simultaneous disjunction and union, of names at once descending and ascending—the language, that is, of analogy?

The *Oculus Simplex* and the *Analogia Entis*

I do not believe in Heidegger's famous *Kehre*. There may be the appearance of a more "objective" tone in his later writing, but Heidegger himself (contrary to his assertions) remained to the last a prisoner of the transcendental perspective, refusing—not from critical scruple, really, but from a sober calculation regarding over what territory thought can now plausibly assert its sovereignty—to look beyond his gaze, toward his vision's natural horizon or toward the more original (or more transcendent) distance that makes that horizon possible. The "turn" of his idiom from "authenticity" and "resolve" to talk of "destinal" historical epochs probably had more to do with his political degeneracy than anything else; the later language has an exculpatory impersonality about it that might provide a decrepit and impenitent Nazi, hiding in the *Schwarzwald*, some small shelter. Hence, it is perfectly legitimate for us to return to his earlier point of departure and ask whether phenomenological rigor really ever required of him that he abandon a transcendent ontology, or that he remain fixed in the difference between existents and nothingness, or even that he step away from this opposition to circle back to it from the vantage of the "event."

Why, for instance, should the "correct" *Stimmung* prompting our investigations, and opening them to being, be that of anxiety, rather than of wonder, or even *eros*? Anxiety enjoys no better claim to ontological probity simply because of the vacuity with which it regards particular objects than do moods that encompass and yet somehow exceed these objects, moods that perhaps "rise" toward a fullness that can account both for the splendid "thereness" of particular things and also for the hunger that they animate in us for their source. Why should the inward retreat of anxiety command our assent more forcefully than the outward abandon of desire? It may be that love's appetite, excited by the beauty, sublimity, or simple existence of things, is uniquely able to press on to their wellspring, the supereminent plenitude of the transcendentals, where unity, beauty, goodness, truth, knowledge, and desire are convertible with one another. And it may also be that what discloses itself within this mood is being's inexhaustible self-outpouring in beings, an infinite act at once gathering all things together in transcendent peace and prismating its own infinite determinacy in the endless diversity, here below, of finite combinations of its transcendental moments. What one sees and the "more" that one sees within what one sees are always determined by prior intentions (both simple eidetic intentions and hermeneutically richer linguistic and cultural prejudices), and no mood escapes this necessity. It is simply false, therefore, that the nothingness disclosed by dread is less "metaphysical" or "onto-theological," or more immediately available to reflection, than the "no-thing-ness" of being—the transcendent fullness of determinacy disclosed by love. The "ontologically erotic" gaze that loves and desires being is more attentive to what constitutes or "en-acts" the seen than is an anxious awareness of the nothingness that shyly hides itself behind the seen. Love sees each thing's fortuity, its mystery, its constancy within a transfinite unity, its immediate particularity, its radiant inherence within its own "essence," its intelligibility, and its way of holding together in itself the diversity of its transcendental aspects as a realized unity amid, and in unity with, multiplicity and change. The gaze of love seeks the being of things in the abiding source in which they participate; it is a way of seeing that is acquainted with moments of enchantment, which awaken it, however briefly, to a recognition of the persistence of being's peaceful and sustaining light (which is utterly unlike either the violence of time and nature or the stillness of an ultimate ground) and of this light's "gratuitous necessity"; and these moments, however fleeting or imperfect, compel thought to risk a conjecture toward the infinite.

This gaze of love, that is to say, sees being as an infinite font of manifestation, showing itself in the existence and essences of things, kenotically allowing (and so without alienation from its own diffusive goodness) the arrival in itself of what is, in itself, nothing: the pure ontic ecstasy of contingent existence. It is a gaze that necessarily strives to pass beyond the ontic play of negativity and positivity, and so sees—or expects to see—how ontic negation must be inverted, so as to reveal that it is the effect of a prior plenitude. Heidegger calls being "eschatological," but does so in a vein of etiolated Hegelianism, which leaves the word's meaning suspended between the historical-dialectical and the existential. There is, however, a genuinely ontological sense in which being can be called eschatological: For finite beings, every instant is eschaton, each moment is an arrival from nothing (not from the concealed, or the "ultimate ground," but from nothing at all) into the infinite, a birth into its uttermost end. Each moment is a call and a judgment, issued across the ontically impossible distance between nonexistence and existence (not just between possibility and actuality), by which beings receive a vocation and a verdict at once, and so are "adjudged" with an ontological justice, which brings them to their ultimate encounter with being. For finite beings, forever becoming, being is absolute futurity. Finite being is an eros in its very essence, an ecstasy out of itself and toward an infinity of beauty known both as concrete immediacy and as transcendent mystery.

It may seem that I am doing nothing here but recommending a mystifying relapse into a second philosophical naiveté, simply to cast off the burden of

sober critical reason. I would say, however, that what I want to urge is a theological reappropriation of what might be called the "covenant of light"[32]—
that is, a trust in the immediacy of the given, a view of knowledge as an effect
of the *eros* stirred by the gift of the world's truth—and so an emancipation of
theology from any superstitious credulity before the arid dogmatisms of
(modern or postmodern) transcendental logic. I can imagine no objection to
Heidegger's attempt to arrive at ontology by way of phenomenology (in a
sense, this is simply the path blazed by Platonism), but what I would like to
advocate is a phenomenology liberated from transcendental stricture. One
can begin from the phenomenological presuppositions that being is what
shows itself, and that the event of the phenomenon and the event of perception are inseparable, and still say that only a transcendental prejudice would
dictate in advance that, in the event of manifestation and in the indiscerptibil-
ity of phenomenon and perception, one may not and cannot see a light
exceeding them as an ever more eminent phenomenality—not merely an
object's hidden sides, or the interplication of the visible and the invisible in
one another, but the descending incandescence of the infinite simplicity that
grants world and knower one to the other. Not that one can merely deduce
Christian metaphysics from empirical perception, obviously; but such a metaphysics is certainly not a fabulous founding of the visible in the invisible, or
of the immanent in a merely posited transcendence. It is, rather, a way of seeing that refuses to see more or less than what is given (including givenness
itself). Even were it not my contention (which, quaintly enough, it is) that this
metaphysics is intrinsic to Christianity, and that without it neither theology
nor biblical hermeneutics can be fully prosecuted, still I would say that the
Christian philosopher should proceed in obedience to such a "transcending"
phenomenology: an initial trust in being's goodness and veracity, a surrender
of self to the testimony of creation (embraced, naturally, within and consum-
mated by an essential faith in God revealed in Christ). The experience of the
beautiful, for instance, is a sudden intimation of the fortuity of necessity and
of the contingency of a thing's integrity; it is an awe awakening one to the difference of being from beings, and of "existence" from "essence," allowing
one to see within the "nonnecessary" concord of a phenomenon and its event
a fittingness that is also, manifestly, grace. In this moment of agitation, one
discovers a surfeit of splendor that commands one's wonder. One then sees
that though the "what it is" of a thing is never commensurate to the surprising truth "that it is," it is always good that this is *this*, and that this *is* (however sin and death distort an object and our perception of it). This mysterious
coherence of the wholly fitting and utterly gratuitous then urges reflection
toward the proportion of their harmony, which is to say toward the infinity
where essence and existence coincide as the ontological peace of both a primordial belonging-together and an original gift; neither of these (neither the

---

32. There is an obvious affinity between what I say here and Carver T. Yu's treatment of "covenantal rationality." See his essay, "Covenantal Rationality and the Healing of Reason," in this volume.

belonging-together nor the gift) is nameless, but neither can be grasped according to the discrete properties of finite reality.

It has become common in some quarters to call the tradition of Christian metaphysics that evolved from the time of the New Testament through the patristic and medieval periods the *analogia entis*, and this term I shall adopt.[33] This tradition succeeded in understanding (in ever greater depth) the liaison between the biblical doctrine of creation and the metaphysics of participation that is announced obscurely by the New Testament, and in integrating it into Trinitarian dogma, and thus made it possible for the first time in Western thought to contemplate both the utter difference of being from beings and the nature of true transcendence. The general preference for the term *analogia entis* was sealed in the last century by the remarkable Erich Przywara, and by his compelling interpretation of patristic and medieval metaphysics as a systematic ontology.[34] His arguments defy any easy summary, and the various nuances that he and other authors have given the phrase "analogy of being" are far too complex and subtle to treat of here; but I can say that, at the most fundamental level, the term "*analogia entis*" means only that being can be neither univocal between God and creatures (which would reduce God to a being among beings, subject to a higher category) nor equivocal (which would, curiously enough, have precisely the same result), and so the only coherent understanding of the relation of created being to uncreated must be analogical. *In him* we live and move and have our being. Every creature exists in a state of tension (as Przywara likes to put it) between essence and existence, in a condition of absolute becoming, oscillating between what it is and that it is, striving toward its essence and existence alike, receiving both from the movement of God's grace while possessing nothing in itself, totally and dynamically dependent, sharing in the fullness of being that God enjoys in infinite simplicity, and so infinitely other than the source of its being. Thus, the analogy of being does not analogize God and creatures under the more general category of being, but is the analogization of being in the difference between God and creatures; for this reason, it is quite incompatible with any naive "natural theology." If being is univocal, then a direct analogy from essences to "God" (as the supreme substance) is possible, but if the primary analogy is that of being itself, then an infinite analogical interval has been introduced between God and creatures precisely because God is truly declared in the essence and existence of all things. Conversely, the rejection of analogy, far from preserving God's transcendence, can actually only objectify God idolatrously as an "over against." Such a duality inevitably makes God

---

33. For fuller treatments of the place of and necessity for a philosophy of being within theology, one should turn to the essays in this volume of Martin Bieler, "The Theological Importance of a Philosophy of Being," and Reinhard Hütter, "The Directedness of Reasoning and the Metaphysics of Creation," with both of which I am in agreement.

34. See Erich Przywara, *Analogia Entis: Metaphysik* (Einsiedeln: Johannes-Verlag, 1962). It is a term, admittedly, that some theologians have rejected—in the most notorious case, that of Karl Barth, with a vehemence bordering on the demented. But Barth's misunderstanding of the term and of Przywara's project, and the disastrous theological consequences of rejecting it render his complaints vacuous.

and creation balancing terms in a dialectical opposition, thus subordinating God to being after all.

In the *analogia entis*, however, the term above all terms is God, the full act of being, in whom all determinacy participates, but who is himself beyond all finite determination, negation, or dialectic—not one of two poles, not the infinite "naught" against which all things are set off (which would still be a "finite infinite"). And it is not possible to regard this transcendent act as a primordial convertibility of being and nothingness, requiring its tragic solution in the finite—by way of Hegel's "becoming," or Heidegger's "temporalization," or what have you—since such a convertibility would already comprise an ontic opposition, a finite indetermination subordinate to its own limits, and so would still be in need of an ontological explanation, some account of the prior act of simplicity in which its unresolved and essential contradiction would have to participate in order to constitute a unity (in order, that is, to be). Being can neither be reduced to beings nor negated by them; it is peacefully expressed and peacefully withheld in its prismation in the intricate interweaving of the transcendentals. Even the transcendental moments of "this" and "not this" have their source in God's triune simplicity, his coincidence within himself of determinacy (as Trinity) and "no-thing-ness" (as "the all" [Sir 43:27] in whom we live, move, and are). The analogy thus permits the very difference of creatures from God, their integrity as what they are, and their ontological "freedom" to be understood as manifestations of how the Trinitarian God is one God. The analogy allows one to see being as at once simplicity and yet always already difference, not as a result of alienation or diremption, but because the fullness of being is God's one movement of being, knowing, and loving his own essence; to be is to be manifest; to know and love, to be known and loved—all of this is the one act, wherein no "essence" is unexpressed and no contradiction awaits resolution. The analogy thus stands outside the twin poles of the metaphysics of the necessary: negation and identity. After all, purely dialectical and purely "identist" systems are ultimately the same; both confine God and world within an economy of the absolute, sharing a reciprocal identity. If God is thought either as total substance or total absence, foundation or negation, "ground of Being" or static "Wholly Other," God is available to thought merely as the world's highest principle rather than as its transcendent source and end.

For us, the analogy of being—the actual movement of our being's likeness to God within an always greater unlikeness—is the event of an endless becoming. This means that, for Christians, becoming is not to be understood according to the tragic wisdom of any metaphysical epoch (Platonism's melancholy distaste for time, change, distance, despite their necessity, or Hegel's dialectic, or Heidegger's resolve, or any other *Stimmung* that can grasp becoming only "backwards" from death). Our being and our essence alike perpetually exceed the moment of our existence, lying always before us as gratuity and futurity, mediated to us only in the *eros* and uncertainty of our life *in fieri*. Finite existence, far from being the dialectical labor of an original contradiction or an oblivion of the hyperouranian forms, is a pure gift, grounded in no original substance, rising from nothingness into God's infinity, absolute fragility, and fortuity, impossible in itself and so actual beyond itself. Becoming is a pure ecstasy *ex nihilo*, a constant and living tension between what a thing is and what it is not, between its past and its future, between what is interior to it and what exterior, and so on. It is nothing but the rapture of its own arrival, and while its contours are always necessarily defined by the shadows of what no longer is and what is not yet, it is only because of sin that these are sources of sadness or anxiety (mourning for the lost, lust for the unattained) rather than of faith, hope, and love ("remembrance" of our true end, *eros* for God's infinity, the love of all things in God). Creation is, in every moment, a liberation that sets us free either to love all things in the love of God or to turn toward things and away from God (the true *Seinsvergessenheit*),[35] and is, consequently, always a moment of judgment. The event of our being is already emancipation from metaphysical necessity; it is the ontic ecstasy of the *ex nihilo*, the primordial impulse of prayer and worship, an awakening, a displacement of nothingness by openness, a reflex of light; and our response to this original ontological vocation can be, in any moment, obedience or rebellion (in which we experience God's gift as either election or dereliction). In this sense, becoming must be a "crisis" for sinful creatures, but the original and ultimate truth of becoming is peace, birth, life. One is always called to "become what you are," to be born into one's end; as Maximus the Confessor says, our end is our beginning, our *logoi* are found in God's Logos, we come to be in God by participation.[36] That which is most interior to us, "essence," is the most exterior; we become what we are by entering ever more into the infinitely accomplished "exteriority" of God, the plenitude of his triune act of love and knowledge, appropriating what is "ours" only through an original surrender of every ground. Our very nature and essence exceed our grasp, and our hunger for the Good above us is our feasting upon being, our ontological delight (rather than a morbid embrace of our own substance or foundation). This primordial ecstasy never need fold back upon itself in a dialectical recovery of "self" from "other" or of *anamnesis* from the phenomena; our perpetual oscillation between actuality and possibility, our striving towards our "essence," is how we partake of God's love and knowledge of us in his Logos. This alone is our being, and is all of our being; for we belong to him, not to ourselves.

It is the analogy of being between God and creatures that alone liberates beings from the tragedy of identity, which is at the heart of any metaphysics or theology (whether dialectical and dualist or idealist and monist) that fails to think being analogically. As the analogy is situated not between discrete substances sheltered under the canopy of being—between "my" essence, to which existence is superadded, and God's essence, to which existence attaches simply as a necessary attribute—but between the entire act of my being and the transcendent act of being in which it participates, the event of

---

35. See Bonaventure, *Itinerarium Mentis in Deum*, V.3–4.
36. Maximus the Confessor, *Ambiguum VII*. See especially PG 91:1077C–1080C.

my existence, in its totality, is shown to be good and true and beautiful in its
very particularity. Being may be understood as at once the truth of essence
(the transcendental determinations that are imparted and mediated to us
throughout time in the event of our existence, as continuously we become
what we are) and of existence (the gratuitous event of our participation in
the triune dynamism of God's life as we are called, every moment, into
unmerited being). In God, being is one perfect act of self-manifesting love,
while in us it is always a dynamic synthesis of the incommensurable "what"
and "that" of our being. This is the difference that both divides and unites,
the distinction between infinite and finite that allows finite being to subsist in
infinite being's single act. Our likeness to God, which is our end and so calls
us into being, is embraced in an ever greater unlikeness—and this is the difference that truly lets us *be*. When the difference between being and beings is
truly forgotten, and with it the analogy between being and beings, it is this
interval that is forgotten. Then we think of the most eminent truth of our
being not as transcendent mystery, but as the ground of the "I," and from this
fatal inversion springs all the grandeur, melancholy, and cruel futility of metaphysics in its "nihilistic vocation." When metaphysics has its premise in an
analogy of identity, or in a continuity of identity between what one is and the
eternal "I am," "I know," "I see," or "I will," it does not matter whether
one's grammar is monist or dualist; all reality subsists in the interval between
two vanishing points: the supreme principle or substance, and the bare, featureless, changeless essence of "my" most proper "self." This is even true of
the most spiritually elevated achievement of Western metaphysics,
Neoplatonism, when left unredeemed by the doctrine of creation and by, in
consequence, the *analogia entis*. For if the truth of things is their pristine likeness in substance (in positive ground) to the ultimate ground, then all difference is not only accidental, but false (though perhaps probatively false): to
arrive at truth, one must suffer the annihilation of particularity, a pitiless
reduction of the exterior to an absolute interior without any outward con-
tour; the calculus of identity is absolute zero, destitute of form. The reduction
of truth to identity (no less than its currently more fashionable reduction to
absolute alterity) is nihilism from the first: the most high is the utterly deso-
late, truth is nothingness. And so, once again sounding the Nietzschean
alarm, one can say that the abolition of truth as a value was always already
secretly inaugurated in the search for truth as positive ground. The elations
of Neoplatonism are so very instructive here because they are still so obviously incapable of freeing themselves from the pathos of every epoch of
Western philosophy. The interval discriminating the most high from the here
below is the tragic moment of exteriority, alienation, probation, which is
nonetheless the necessary distance of reflection, *theoria*, *anamnesis*, and
return. But the movement from there to here is one of division, reduction,
contamination, and oblivion, and the converse movement, from here to there,
is a repetition (though inverted) of this same impoverishment: reduction,
decortication of the world, oblivion of the flesh, a flight of the alone to the
alone. Truth's dynamism is destruction, a laying waste of all of finite being's

ornate intricacies, erasing the world from the space between the vanishing point of the One and the vanishing point of the *nous* in their barren correspondence. This is why the tragic "dualism" haunting Platonism could give rise so naturally to the tragic "monism" of Plotinus—for dialectic and identism are finally the same. Which is also why, incidentally, the postmodern dread of eternity and recognition in no way escapes the melancholy of Platonism's dread of "dissemination": these are merely the two extremes of one ontological vision, fixed in the same interminable dialectic of Same and Other.

The doctrine of creation, however, escapes this dialectic altogether: it asserts that all things live, move, and are in God not because they add to God, or in any way determine his essence, but because they are gracious manifestations of his fullness. This alters metaphysical thought radically: it binds beings to being precisely by breaking the bond of necessity between them. The *maior dissimilitudo* of the ontological analogy means that the *similitudo* between God and creatures, rather than dwelling merely in a thing's flawed likeness to some higher essence, distorted in the mirror of space and time, consists rather in each thing's pluriform and dynamic synthesis of its transcendental moments and the particular event of its existence, which synthesis is what constitutes it as a being. Each actuality, in differing from God, testifies to the fullness of God's actuality. Indeed, the "ever greater unlikeness" of the proportion means that the "likeness" is itself ever greater the more fully anything is what it is, the more it grows into the measure of its difference, the more profoundly it drinks from the transcendent moments that compose it and allow all its modes of disclosure to speak of God's infinite goodness. All beings, inasmuch as they are intrinsically *ex nihilo*, become what they are by drawing on an infinite wellspring of determinacy, particularity, and actuality. Whereas an analogy of identity finds truth in the ever less particular emptiness of a simple and absolute singularity, the analogy of being finds truth in the ever greater particularity that each thing acquires as it enters ever more into the infinite that gives it being.[37] This means also, one should then note, that there is a far greater intimacy between God and creatures granted by the *analogia entis* than by identist thought: the most high principle does not stand over against us (if secretly within us) across the distance of a hierarchy of lesser metaphysical principles, but is present within the very act of each moment of the particular. The infinite nearness of the *interior intimo meo* is possible precisely because of the infinite transcendence of the *superior summo meo*.

It is a phenomenological (and, for Heidegger, ontological) maxim that, for anything to appear, there must indeed be a more general hiddenness: the unseen sides of an object that, in being hidden, allow a distinct form to emerge from "total" presence; the obscuration of everything the object shields from view; the hiddenness of past and future that allows the object to

---

37. Thomas Aquinas writes that "veritas fundatur in esse rei magis quam in ipsa quidditate." This means, he argues, that the "adequation" that truth is consists in an assimilation of the intellect to the *esse* of any given thing, whereby it accepts each thing as it is (*In I Sent.*, D. 19, q. 5, a. 1, *solutio*). This is an elegantly succinct formulation—truth is the fullness, not the impoverishment, of a thing's modes of being; judgments are true if one accepts beings as beings in the fullness of their determinations.

disclose itself in the exteriority of its temporal "ecstases"; and indeed the invisibility of being itself, the deferral of its absoluteness in its gracious giving way to the finite. However, it makes all the difference whether one sees this movement of hiddenness within manifestation in terms of an original negation or in terms of a self-outpouring that flows from the plenitude of full Trinitarian manifestation. The analogy allows one to see in the difference of being from beings and in the "withdrawal" of being that permits beings to stand forth—which involves a seeming "constriction," "occlusion," or "withholding" of being—not a negation or nihilation, but a *kenosis*. After all, if the continuity between being and beings is not univocal but truly analogical, then being need not be conceived as somehow ontic—as, say, an inexhaustible reservoir of possibility that must be apportioned by the nothing's "nothing-ing"—but can be understood entirely as the transcendent act of self-outpouring love, which is full in being utterly "exposed"; being can be understood as the immediate act of the entire circle of manifestation in the realm of the ontic, granting actuality at once to both visibility and invisibility, presence and absence, out of its own self-manifesting, self-knowing, self-loving abundance. Being is not negated by the "negative" because the entire economy of manifestation is its good gift. The concept of ontological analogy instructs the pure eye, the *oculus simplex*, to see the gracious *kenosis* of the supereminent in the finite, and the exaltation of the finite in the peaceful simplicity of the infinite. The analogy teaches vision to see the supereminent convertibility of the transcendentals not as the savage blaze of "total light," a substance rent apart in the diversity of existence, but the embracing unity that allows difference to be, by giving it space in which to differ. Apart from the analogy, the eye fails to see that in the very coherence of the moments of experience there is a prior act of grace in which unity and difference both subsist; one might not see that the great sea of possibility that is fitfully actualized as "world" is still infinitely distinct from the actuality—the unity—that allows even the possible to be. For all things—all the words of being—speak of God because they shine within his eternal Word. One may name God from beings.

Every metaphysics, simply said, that does not grasp the analogy of being is a Tower of Babel, attempting to mount up to the supreme principle rather than dwelling in and giving voice to the prodigality of the gift. It is the simple, infinite movement of analogy that constitutes everything that is as a being, oscillating between essence and existence and receiving both from beyond itself; and it is the movement of analogy that makes everything that is already the return of the gift thus given, the offering of all things by the Spirit up into the Father's plenitude of being, in the Son. *Ex nihilo in Deum*— and there is no other "place." By this movement, each thing comes to be as pure event, owning no substance, made free from nothingness by the unmerited grace of *being* other than God, participating in the mystery of God's power to receive all in giving all away—the mystery, that is, of the truth that God is love. If indeed there is a sacrificial logic to metaphysics, as Vattimo and others say (the world and its highest principle sustaining one another in an economy of mutual founding, each in some sense both affirming and negating the other, each bound to the other by the logic of necessity), then the analogy of being that first appears in Western thought in the doctrine of creation is the only true "overcoming of metaphysics," the end of the myth of sacrifice: Creation and salvation are gifts adding nothing to the being of God, and so nothing of the world needs to be destroyed to give glory and sustenance to the ultimate principle. Instead, our piety is one of rational worship, bloodless sacrifice, thanksgiving for a gift, liturgy, the offering of names.

PART FOUR

Readings of Reason
after *Fides et Ratio*:
Why Philosophy Matters for
Theology

CHAPTER TWELVE

The Theological Importance of a Philosophy of Being

— MARTIN BIELER —

The Philosophy of Being in *Fides et Ratio*

The encyclical *Fides et Ratio* is an impressive document of the Catholic Church's esteem of philosophy (57ff.).[1] It observes with sorrow the continuing drama of a "growing separation between faith and philosophical reason" (48), which leads to the abandonment of metaphysical inquiry based on philosophy's "own principles and methods" (49). This development not only results in an impoverishment of theological reasoning (53, 62, 66, 77) but also leads to a distrust in reason (45ff.) and to a profound "'crisis of meaning'" (81) in general.[2] The basic concern the encyclical forwards in its emphasis on the importance of a "philosophy of genuinely metaphysical range" (83) is the *protection and support of human freedom and dignity* (90), of the living human being, who is, according to Irenaeus of Lyons, the glory of God:[3] "I ask everyone to look more deeply at man, whom Christ has saved in the mystery of his love, and at the human being's unceasing search for truth and meaning. . . . Only within this horizon of truth will people understand their freedom in its fullness and their call to know and love God as the supreme realization of their true self" (107). Or more succinctly: "Truth and freedom either go together hand in hand or together they perish in misery" (90). *The horizon of human freedom liberated by God in Christ has to be the*

---

1. I am citing the English text of the encyclical according to *Origins* 28 (October 22, 1998): 317–47. For the Latin version, see the home page of the Vatican: http://www.vatican.va. Translations of other works are mine if not otherwise indicated.

2. For the broader context of the modern discussion about the possibility and the character of metaphysics, I gladly refer to the profound and enlightening essays of David Bentley Hart and Reinhard Hütter, whose concerns I fully share. See Hart, "The Offering of Names: Metaphysics, Nihilism, and Analogy," and Hütter, "The Directedness of Reasoning and the Metaphysics of Creation," in this volume.

3. Irenaeus of Lyons, *Adversus haereses* IV.20.7: "Gloria enim Dei vivens homo, vita autem hominis visio Dei."

hermeneutical key for the encyclical's view of philosophy. In this wider horizon, philosophy's dependence on faith is clearly stated (20ff., 67), a dependence that is in no way the expression of a competition between them (17) but rather of the "indissoluble unity between the knowledge of reason and the knowledge of faith" (16).

It is most noteworthy that the encyclical is exactly in its engagement for human dignity and freedom a strong plea for the importance of a philosophy of being[4] such as that realized in exemplary form in the work of Thomas Aquinas, who contributed decisively to a "unified and organic vision of knowledge" (85) as an "essential condition for sincere and authentic dialogue between persons" (92). The effort for a "unified and organic vision of knowledge" is directed not against pluralism but toward overcoming the disintegration of our cultural body of knowledge, which endangers human freedom: "The segmentation of knowledge, with its splintered approach to truth and consequent fragmentation of meaning, keeps people today from coming to an interior unity. How could the church not be concerned by this?" (85).

Although it is the declared intention of *Fides et Ratio* not to canonize any particular philosophy (49, 78), there can be no doubt about the fact that the encyclical moves along the lines of Thomas Aquinas's metaphysics when it outlines the future tasks of philosophical investigation. First of all, it strongly emphasizes the importance of a philosophy of being (5, 66, 90, 97), which meets the necessary requirements of a metaphysics that is indispensable for unfolding the truth revealed in Christ (82–83). Second, it seems to conceive a philosophy of being in the way Aquinas does by referring to the "act of being" (*actus essendi*): "Set within the Christian metaphysical tradition, the philosophy of being is a dynamic philosophy which views reality in its ontological, causal and communicative structures. It is strong and enduring because it is based upon the very act of being itself, which allows a full and comprehensive openness to reality as a whole, surpassing every limit in order to reach the One who brings all things to fulfillment" (97).[5] The philosophical path to a "unified and organic vision of knowledge" that does not eliminate pluralism apparently leads, according to the encyclical, to the Thomistic *esse*: All things in their own specific form are united by sharing the same *esse* (Thomas Aquinas, *Summa contra gentiles* I.26 [239]), in which they participate "not as a part, but by diffusion of its procession" (*Summa theologiae* I.75.5 ad 1).[6]

---

4. I am skeptical about the possibility of choosing just any basic thought to develop a philosophy. Why not a philosophy of relation or of structure instead of a philosophy of being? Because if we try to explain what we mean with these notions, we come back sooner or later—at least in a Christian context with its high esteem of the human person—to ontology and alas to a philosophy of being. Nicholas of Cusa, who has been regarded as one of the founding fathers of modern philosophy as opposed to the philosophy of being we find in Aquinas, presents with his thinking an excellent example of this necessity. See Hubert Benz, "Nikolaus von Kues: Initiator der Subjektivitätsphilosophie oder Seinsdenker?" *Theologie und Philosophie* 73 (1998): 196–224. See also Josef Stallmach, *Ineinsfall der Gegensätze und Weisheit des Nichtwissens: Grundzüge der Philosophie des Nikolaus von Kues* (Münster: Aschendorff, 1989), 92–99.

5. See also John Paul II, "Inter Munera Academiarum," *L'Osservatore Romano* (June 4, 1999), 11 (in German; for the Latin original, see the issue of March 25, 1999).

6. For further explanation, see the section, "Aquinas's Philosophy of Being," below. In the following, I will cite Aquinas's *Summa theologiae* only with numbers (e.g., *Summa theologiae* I.1 ad 1 = I.1 ad 1).

The encyclical further emphasizes the development of philosophy "within the horizon of personal self-consciousness" (1). Anthropology and metaphysics are from the start by their formal object in deep unity, "since it is metaphysics which makes it possible to ground the concept of personal dignity in virtue of their spiritual nature." At the same time, the encyclical states, "In a special way the person constitutes a privileged locus for the encounter with being, and hence with metaphysical inquiry" (83). In the end we understand what being (*esse*) is all about only if we consider it in the light of human freedom liberated by God's saving action in Christ. This leads to the idea of a christologically oriented "meta-anthropology"[7] that deals with "reality in its ontological, causal and communicative structures," grounded in God's gift of being.[8] Therefore, only in the "dynamic relationship of faithful self-giving with others" (32) do we have access to the mystery of being.[9] Human beings created in the image of God are the key for an adequate understanding of every kind of being, because they represent a form of being that in some way transcends this world by relating as freedom to God, and because they are— in this transcendence—for us in this world the one gift without which we would not have full access to our own freedom. It is in the encounter with the thou that the meaning of the world and of my own being is opened up for me. The other thou in loving freedom interprets for me the being I receive as a gift of love. Therefore, the starting point for metaphysics has to be the encounter with another loving human being, which also has to be the basic model for epistemology.[10]

With all of this, the encyclical confirms in an astonishing way the direction of a *deepened* interpretation of Thomistic metaphysics as it can be found in the writings of Gustav Siewerth, Ferdinand Ulrich, Hans Urs von Balthasar,[11] W. Norris Clarke, Kenneth L. Schmitz, and others. In my view, the approach taken by the encyclical is by no means an outdated way of dealing with the questions of the modern world. The purpose of this essay is to show why such an approach makes sense and in what direction a future philosophical investigation could go in order to take up the encyclical's justified concern. Because of lack of space I will not discuss the meaning of a philosophy of being for

---

7. See Martin Bieler, "Meta-anthropology and Christology: On the Philosophy of Hans Urs von Balthasar," *Communio: International Catholic Review* 20 (1993): 129–46.

8. For dealing with the arguments issued by Jacques Derrida and others against the use of the category of "gift" in Christianity (see John D. Caputo and Michael J. Scanlon, eds., *God, the Gift, and Postmodernism* [Bloomington: Indiana University Press, 1999]) important clarifications can be found in Hans Urs von Balthasar's biblical study *Herrlichkeit III.2.2: Neuer Bund* (Einsiedeln: Johannes Verlag, 1969). See also the helpful reflections by John Milbank, "Can a Gift Be Given? Prolegomena to a Future Trinitarian Metaphysics," *Modern Theology* 11 (1995): 119–61.

9. See Carver T. Yu's concept of covenantal rationality in "Covenantal Rationality and the Healing of Reason," in this volume.

10. See W. Norris Clarke, *Explorations in Metaphysics: Being-God-Person* (Notre Dame, IN: University of Notre Dame Press, 1994), 31–44; and esp. Ferdinand Ulrich, "Sein und Mitmensch," *Salzburger Jahrbuch für Philosophie* 19 (1974): 93–128. The point is that "meta-anthropology" in this way accesses creation as being right from the beginning "a divine call"; see Robert W. Jenson, *Systematic Theology II: The Works of God* (Oxford: Oxford University Press, 1999), 68.

11. See Martin Bieler, "The Future of the Philosophy of Being," *Communio: International Catholic Review* 26 (1999): 455–85.

Christology or the understanding of the Trinity,[12] although these questions are most important.[13]

A philosophy of being is interesting not primarily as a launching point for conversions. We may have serious doubts about such a role for philosophy[14] without underestimating the significance of sound philosophical teaching for a reorientation of human beings. Much more urgent is the question of how a philosophy of being can contribute to a better understanding of what we believe in and what consequences result from that belief. In my view, a philosophy of being that unfolds the gift-character of being will be crucial for a future theology in developing its own theological rationality because it is so closely connected with the reality of human freedom in its communicative character, origin, and aim.

The use of a philosophy of being in theologically relevant matters has met stern resistance, especially in the Protestant tradition. Therefore, I will take up in a first step some significant points of this critique and develop a preliminary model of the relationship between theology and philosophy—rooted in an understanding of revelation as a gift—in order to locate the competence of a philosophy of being with respect to theology.[15] In a second step, I will provide a meditation on the relationship between faith and reason according to Aquinas that further clarifies the wider theological setting of a philosophy of being. I will show how Aquinas's model of the relationship between faith and reason is structured by the *bonitas* of God's self-communication in Christ. In a next step, I will give an outline of Aquinas's philosophy of being that also deals with the *bonitas Dei*, but in a different way than theology. In a final step, I will fuse together the theological and philosophical ways of dealing with the *bonitas Dei* in taking up the central theme of the *philosophari in Maria*, with which the encyclical concludes (108). Mary is the model for receiving being as a gift because she receives Christ. But she also opens up in her suffering (Luke 2:34–35; John 19:25–27) a better understanding of the substitutionary atonement by Christ.[16] In this last section, I want to show what it means that by God's becoming a human being, living and dying for us, grace comes "on the way of being" (F. Ulrich) in order to absolutely affirm every individual human being in his or her specific (most difficult) situation. The result of these reflections will be that a renewed philosophy of being helps us unfold the core of Christian faith in unequaled depth for meeting the needs of our time.

---

12. See Martin Bieler, *Freiheit als Gabe: Ein schöpfungstheologischer Entwurf* (Freiburg: Herder, 1991), 139–209 (Trinity); and idem, *Die Befreiung der Freiheit: Zur Theologie der stellvertretenden Sühne* (Freiburg: Herder, 1995), 230–317 (Christology).

13. See, e.g., Michael Schulz, *Sein und Trinität: Systematische Erörterungen zur Religionsphilosophie G. W. F. Hegels im ontologiegeschichtlichen Rückblick auf J. Duns Scotus und I. Kant und die Hegel-Rezeption in der Seinsauslegung und Trinitätstheologie bei W. Pannenberg, E. Jüngel, K. Rahner und H. U. von Balthasar* (St. Ottilien: EOS Verlag, 1997), 508.

14. See Paul J. Griffiths's essay, "How Reasoning Goes Wrong: A Quasi-Augustinian Account of Error and Its Implications," in this volume.

15. For an extended discussion of the problem, see Bieler, *Freiheit als Gabe*, 77–95.

16. See Hans Urs von Balthasar, *Spiritus Creator* (Einsiedeln: Johannes Verlag, 1967), 202ff.; *Pneuma und Institution* (Einsiedeln: Johannes Verlag, 1974), 261–65; and *Theodramatik III: Die Handlung* (Einsiedeln: Johannes Verlag, 1980), 369ff.

Analogia Entis versus *Analogia Fidei*?

One of the major events in the history of Protestantism was the formulation and acceptance of the Barmen Declaration in May 1934 by the Confessing Church in Germany. The main point of the declaration is formulated in the first thesis, after the citations of John 14:6 and 10:1–9: "Jesus Christ, as he is testified by the Sacred Scripture, is the one Word of God we have to listen to, to trust in in living and dying, and to obey." This statement is followed by the rejection of the false teaching that the church may yet have other sources for preaching apart from and besides this one Word.[17] It is quite clear that Karl Barth, as the mastermind behind the formulation of this declaration, wanted to exclude every form of natural theology, be it the *Anknüpfungspunkt* of Emil Brunner or the *naturalis cognitio Dei* of Thomas Aquinas. For Barth this exclusion was of utmost practical relevance, for every attempt to weaken the exclusivity of Christ as God's revelation by other sources of revelation would inevitably lead to a "nostrification"[18] of God by our distorted views. We have to direct our attention to the one place where God speaks unsurpassably and in absolutely binding manner for himself: to the Son, who reveals the Father (John 1:18; 14:6–11). Barth could watch closely how much damage the denial of this basic principle of theological hermeneutics caused in the Germany of those days. The blindness of Christians to the horrors of the persecution of Jews is the most striking example of this damage.[19] It is quite understandable then that Barth considered the *analogia entis*—the way he conceived it at that time—*the* "invention of the anti-christ,"[20] against which he put the *analogia fidei*, anchored in Christ.

But with Barmen the issue of natural theology was not closed, not only because of the need to deal adequately with the questions and problems of our time[21] but also because of the need to clarify the christological starting point: Does the theological concentration on Christ imply or exclude philosophical knowledge of God? Catholic theologians especially have pointed out that Christology and philosophical knowledge of God are not necessarily opposed to each other—quite the contrary. If God speaks in Jesus of Nazareth as a human being to us, he takes up human thinking. As von Balthasar describes, that is already true for the history of Israel:

> The word of God takes hold of the nation of Israel in its place in history in the context of a universal evolution, not only in its political situation

---

17. "Theologische Erklärung zur gegenwärtigen Lage der Deutschen Evangelischen Kirche," in *Bekenntnisschriften und Kirchenordnungen der nach Gottes Wort reformierten Kirche*, ed. Wilhelm Niesel, 2nd ed. (Zurich: Evangelischer Verlag A. G. Zollikon, 1938), 335.

18. See Karl Barth, *Das christliche Leben: Die kirchliche Dogmatik* [KD] IV/4: *Fragmente aus dem Nachlass, Vorlesungen 1959–1961*, ed. Hans-Anton Drewes and Eberhard Jüngel (Zurich: Theologischer Verlag Zürich, 1976), 214–15.

19. Eberhard Busch showed in an excellent book how well-based, stringent, and firm Barth's position was in this matter: *Unter dem Bogen des einen Bundes: Karl Barth und die Juden 1933–1945* (Neukirchen-Vluyn: Neukirchener Verlag, 1996).

20. Barth, KD I/1, viii. But see also KD II/1, 90.

21. See Christof Gestrich, *Neuzeitliches Denken und die Spaltung der dialektischen Theologie: Zur Frage der natürlichen Theologie* (Tübingen: J. C. B. Mohr, 1977).

between the great powers of the Near East . . . , but throughout in those deeper structures, which can be called worldview, Weltanschauung, meaning of life, wisdom, philosophy, metaphysics and religion. . . . Every level of development of the whole evolution *may* (if God wants to use it) become the necessary presupposition for a further unfolding of revelation.[22]

Human thinking will not remain unchanged in this process: "Human wisdom, if God wants to use it in his revelation, will never be released from completely dying away from itself. The wisdom of this world proves to be folly in order to become God's wisdom."[23] But that again means neither a destruction nor a replacement of human wisdom; grace does not destroy but presupposes and perfects nature.[24] God is revealed in the gift of creation, but humankind does not hear and see the message, because it does not want to (Rom 1:18ff.).[25] So the problem is not how to get rid of philosophical truth claims[26] in order to secure the authority of revelation, but how to get back to a way of thinking—philosophically and theologically—that is open anew for the true mystery of creation.

It is not possible to have a "pure" theology, which uses philosophy only as a quarry for its terms and tries to make in the end all philosophical knowledge of God superfluous.[27] Theology is accompanied by philosophy all the way down, for the importance of philosophy for theology is not a matter of getting into theology by some *praeambula fidei*, which can finally be left behind. False philosophical concepts remain a constant threat to theology,[28] whereas a sound philosophy is an enormous help for the development of theology's own subject matter.[29] But it is also not possible to settle philosophical matters first, independent of any relation to revelation and theology.[30] We need Scripture, which—opened by the Holy Spirit—bears witness to Christ in his *unity* of divine and human nature and enables us in this way to read the meaning of creation again, in a depth never before known.[31] So theology and philosophy must *right from the beginning* be

---

22. Hans Urs von Balthasar, *Verbum Caro* (Einsiedeln: Johannes Verlag, 1960), 93.

23. Ibid., 96.

24. "Utitur tamen sacra doctrina etiam ratione humana. . . . Cum enim gratia non tollat naturam, sed perficiat, oportet quod naturalis ratio subserviat fidei" (I.1.8 ad 2).

25. Thomas Aquinas, *Super primam epistolam ad Corinthios lectura* 3.3 (179).

26. "Studium philosophiae secundum se est licitum et laudabile, propter veritatem quam philosophi perceperunt, Deo illis revelante, ut dicitur *Rom* 1,[19]" (II-II.167.1 ad 3).

27. When Aquinas says that philosophical contributions for theology are not necessary ("Non quod ex necessitate eis indigeat, sed ad maiorem manifestationem eorum quae in hac scientia [sc. sacra doctrina] traduntur" [I.1.5 ad 2]), he is not questioning the importance of philosophy ("Sic enim fides praesupponit cognitionem naturalem, sicut gratia naturam" [I.2.2 ad 1]) but rather pointing out that theology is a science in its own right, that it is even higher than every other science: "Non enim accipit sua principia ab aliis scientiis, sed immediate a Deo per revelationem. Et ideo non accipit ab aliis scientiis tamquam a superioribus, sed utitur eis tanquam inferioribus et ancillis" (I.1.5 ad 2).

28. "Nam error circa creaturas redundat in falsam de Deo sententiam" (Thomas Aquinas, *Summa contra gentiles* II.3 [869]).

29. I.1.5 ad 2.

30. There is, e.g., no philosophy of Aquinas that could be separated from his theology. See Josef Pieper, *Unaustrinkbares Licht: Das negative Element in der Weltansicht des Thomas von Aquin*, 2nd ed. (Munich: Kösel, 1963), 80.

31. Bieler, *Freiheit als Gabe*, 91ff.

developed *together*[32] in accordance with the unity of divine and human nature in Christ, who is God's self-giving move toward the world *in persona*[33] and hence, as Balthasar puts it, the *"concrete Analogia entis."*[34]

As soon as a human being is enabled by the grace of God to respond cognitively to the revelation in Christ, he or she is *at the same moment* basically enabled to see God's trace in his creation again by philosophical means: The book of nature becomes readable again for us by God's revelation in Christ. The necessary connection between theology and philosophy testifies that the gift (creation) *itself* is open toward the One who gives (creator) and makes himself present in his gift (creation).[35] This connection also testifies that the gift remains dependent on the giver who has yet unrevealed possibilities to give—as is apparent in Christ. Theology needs philosophy in order to listen to creation's own language, and philosophy needs theology in order to know the One who is the origin and aim of creation.[36] A theology indifferent to philosophy would ignore God's true givenness in creation, and a philosophy indifferent to theology would refuse the giver in his gift. Both possibilities destroy the gift-character of creation and with it the *oikonomia* of salvation in Christ. So the fact of a specific dependence of theology on philosophy (and vice versa) is not something foreign to the formal object of theology, because the gift-character of creation that philosophy deals with testifies to the One who reveals himself in Christ as love itself. In short, this relationship between theology and philosophy has a theological quality: "The fact that theology has a philosophical a priori is a theologically most significant finding. It is an assertion about the innermost [*Eigenste*] of God, the assertion that he is self-renunciation, self-giving, that he is love."[37]

The "and" of theology and philosophy corresponds to the "and" of divine and human nature in Christ, who fulfills in himself in the Trinitarian context the move of God toward creation and the move of creation toward God at the same time.[38] Every attempt to dissolve this unity of God and creation in the Trinitarian givenness of God for us in Christ, this "medium" we have to start with,[39] by a "pure" theological (God without human nature) or philosophical (human nature without God) starting point is actually a nostrification of God

---

32. Hans Urs von Balthasar, *Theodramatik II.1: Die Personen des Spiels: Der Mensch in Gott* (Einsiedeln: Johannes Verlag, 1976), 173. See also Hans Urs von Balthasar, *Theologik I: Wahrheit der Welt* (Einsiedeln: Johannes Verlag, 1985), vii–xvii.

33. Bieler, *Befreiung der Freiheit*, 297–306.

34. "In diesem Sinne kann Christus die *konkrete Analogia entis* genannt werden, da er in sich selbst, in der Einheit seiner göttlichen und menschlichen Natur das Massverhältnis für jeden Abstand zwischen Gott und Mensch bildet. Und diese Einheit ist seine Person in beiden Naturen." Hans Urs von Balthasar, *Theologie der Geschichte* (Einsiedeln: Johannes Verlag, 1959), 53.

35. See, e.g., E. L. Mascall, *The Openness of Being: Natural Theology Today* (London: Darton, Longman & Todd, 1971).

36. A clean-cut separation of the realms of theology and philosophy is not possible; see Bieler, *Freiheit als Gabe*, 88–90. Of course, creation is not only a philosophical but also a theological issue. But the approaches to creation in theology and philosophy are different. The question is exactly why we need also a philosophical approach to creation.

37. Klaus Hemmerle, "Das Verhältnis von Philosophie und Theologie aus theologischer Perspektive," *Herder Korrespondenz* 31 (1977): 35.

38. See Martin Bieler, "Karl Barths Auseinandersetzung mit der analogia entis und der Anfang der Theologie," *Catholica* 40 (1986): 241–45.

39. "Circa secundum nota, quod incipiendum est a medio, quod est Christus. Ipse enim mediator Dei et hominum (1 Tim 2,5) est, tenens medium in omnibus, ut patebit" (Bonaventura, *Hexaemeron* I.10).

in the Barthian sense. It suggests, like the snake in paradise, that God has not really given himself and that we have to secure his givenness by our own means from a seemingly firm standpoint (isolated theology or philosophy), which we suppose will allow us to control the right cognition and with it the access to what we need.

But what is the right order of the relationship between philosophy and theology? In the end it is God himself who decides about the nature of the relationship between nature (*natura*) and grace (*gratia*) by giving himself to the world as its creator and savior. So it is finally up to theology to clarify what kind of relationship theology and philosophy should have. This establishes a "form-primacy" of theology, which requires philosophy to hand itself over (but *not* to give itself up)—with its questions *and* its answers—to theology as the inner *telos* of metaphysics according to the principle that grace does not destroy but presupposes and perfects nature.[40] In my opinion, the thinking of Aquinas is an outstanding model for a correct and fruitful relationship between theology and philosophy in which theology has this form-primacy.

Faith and Reason: The Model of Aquinas

The form-primacy of theology clearly has the lead in the thinking of Thomas Aquinas.[41] It might seem that this is not the case, because he does not develop his Christology until the third part of his *Summa theologiae*.[42] Thus, his thinking might be seen as one of the major examples of how natural theology inevitably leads to an unfriendly takeover of dogmatics by philosophy. But Aquinas has good reasons for developing his Christology in the third part of the *Summa theologiae*: Christology must be embedded in a Trinitarian context, which explains the possibility of creation (*Prima pars*),[43] and it must show how the divine nature of the Son fits together with human nature and its modus operandi (anthropology and ethics: *Secunda pars*) in the unity of the person of Christ (*Tertia pars*).[44] In this cumulative way, Christ appears as the one who contains and explains everything.[45] That does not mean that

---

40. Erich Przywara, *Analogia entis: Metaphysik: Ur-Struktur und All-Rhythmus* (Einsiedeln: Johannes Verlag, 1962), 78ff.

41. For the following, see also Martin Bieler, "Gott und sein Ebenbild: Zur neueren Thomasforschung," *Theologische Literaturzeitung* 127 (2002): 1003–24.

42. See, e.g., the critical comment made by Gustav Martelet, "Theologie und Heilsökonomie in der Christologie der 'Tertia,'" in *Gott in Welt: Festgabe für Karl Rahner*, ed. J. B. Metz, W. Kern, A. Darlap, and H. Vorgrimler (Freiburg: Herder, 1964), 23–42.

43. "Mysterium Christi explicite credi non potest sine fide Trinitatis" (II-II.2.8 c).

44. Compare this with the structure of Barth's *Kirchliche Dogmatik*.

45. "La *Tertia* couronne la totalité de la Somme parce que et parce que seulement Jésus-Christ est le résumé de la Révélation: *c'est l'union des deux natures, humaine et divine, dans l'unique personne du Verbe qui effectue la médiation du Dieu-exemplaire et de l'homme-image, médiation réelle en tant qu'elle est la Révélation.*" Michel Corbin, *Le chemin de la théologie chez Thomas d'Aquin* (Paris: Beauchesne, 1974), 802. The exitus-reditus scheme corresponds to that, for it expresses the movement of creation, embraced, initiated, penetrated, and led by the movement of God's Trinitarian life, which becomes accessible to us by the mission of Christ and the Spirit. See Max Seckler, *Das Heil in der Geschichte: Geschichtstheologisches Denken bei Thomas von Aquin* (Munich: Kösel-Verlag, 1964). For a comprehensive draft of the problem, see Thomas F. O'Meara, *Thomas Aquinas, Theologian* (Notre Dame, IN: University of Notre Dame Press, 1997), 41–86.

Christology is not right from the beginning the basis and key for everything in the *Summa*.[46] According to Aquinas, we are not able to know that God is triune without revelation.[47] Without Christ, as he is attested by Scripture, there is no teaching of the Trinity.[48] And without Trinity and redemption in Christ, we will neither understand what creation is all about, nor will we know the nature of a human being,[49] because this requires the knowledge of that which fulfills this being, the *finis* for which the being strives and exists.[50]

It is theology that deals with God's revelation in Christ. But how does theology gain access to its subject matter? By faith. The act of faith aims at God himself and not only at propositions.[51] It is not only a *credere Deo* and a *credere Deum* but also a *credere in Deum*.[52] For Aquinas creation can be known by natural reason, by philosophy[53]—if it is enlightened by faith[54]—in

---

46. "From one point of view Christology is presupposed in the whole of his theological work, since revelation was fully given only with Christ. . . . In one sense, then, the whole of his theology is simply Christology." Per Erik Persson, *Sacra Doctrina: Reason and Revelation in Aquinas*, trans. Ross Mackenzie (Oxford: Basil Blackwell, 1970), 276. Accordingly, the Eucharist contains "totum mysterium nostrae salutis" (III.83.4 c). Compare also some of the testimonies in other writings of Aquinas: "Omnia in ipso [sc. Christ] condita sunt, sicut in quodam exemplari" (*Super epistolam ad Colossenes lectura* 1.4 [37]). "Et ideo non oportet sapientiam quaerere nisi in Christo . . . sicut qui haberet librum ubi esset tota scientia, non quaereret nisi ut sciret illum librum, sic et nos non oportet amplius quaerere nisi Christum" (ibid. 2.1 [82]). "Sapientia nostra non est ut sciamus naturas rerum et siderum cursus et huiusmodi, sed in solo Christo" (*Super epistolam ad Ephesios lectura* 1.3 [25]). "Principale autem in doctrina fidei Christianae est salus per crucem Christi facta" (*Super primam epistolam ad Corinthios lectura* 1.3 [45]). "Fides autem christiana principaliter consistit in confessione sanctae Trinitatis, et specialiter gloriatur in cruce Domini nostri Iesu Christi" (introduction to *De rationibus fidei contra Saracenos, Graecos et Armenos ad Cantorem Antiochenum*).

47. I.12.13 ad 1; 32.1 c; II-II.8.3 c; 171.3.

48. I.27.1 c. "Ante Christi adventum fides Trinitatis erat occulta in fide maiorum. Sed per Christum manifestata est mundo per Apostolos" (II-II.2.8 ad 2). "In nomine Christi tota Trinitas intelligitur" (III.66.6 ad 2).

49. "Cognitio divinarum Personarum fuit necessaria nobis dupliciter. Uno modo, ad recte sentiendum de creatione rerum. . . . Alio modo et principalius, ad recte sentiendum de salute generis humani, quae perficitur per Filium incarnatum, et per donum Spiritus Sancti" (I.32.1 ad 3).

50. "Cum *quaelibet res sit propter suam operationem*" (III.9.1 c). "Finem autem oportet esse praecognitum hominibus, qui suas intentiones et actiones debent ordinare ad finem. Unde necessarium fuit homini ad salutem, quod ei nota fierent quaedam per revelationem divinam, quae rationem humanam excedunt" (I.1.1 c). "Perfectio ergo rationalis creaturae non solum consistit in eo quod ei competit secundum suam naturam, sed etiam in eo quod ei attribuitur ex quadam supernaturali participatione divinae bonitatis" (II-II.2.3 c). I-II starts after the prologues with the quaestio of "De ultimo fine hominis." For the question of how the philosophical and theological perspectives are united in Aquinas's dealing with the problem of the ultimate aim of human existence, see Hermann Kleber, *Glück als Lebensziel: Untersuchungen zur Philosophie des Glücks bei Thomas von Aquin* (Münster: Aschendorffsche Verlagsbuchhandlung, 1988).

51. "Actus autem credentis non terminatur ad enuntiabile, sed ad rem" (II-II.1.2 ad 2). The formal object of faith is in the first place the *veritas prima* (*ipse Deus*) and then that which is set in order toward God (II-II.1.1 c). Aquinas points out that the "mysterium humanitatis Christi" is "*pietatis sacramentum*, ut dicutur *I ad Tim* 3,[16]" (II-II.1.8 c).

52. II-II.2.2 c.

53. 2 Sent 1.1.2 c; De potentia 3.5 c; I.12.12 c.

54. "Philosophi, de rebus humanis naturali investigatione perscrutantes, in multiis et sibi ipsis contraria senserunt. Ut ergo esset indubitata et certa cognitio apud homines de Deo, oportuit quod divina eis per modum fidei traderentur, quasi a Deo dicta, qui mentiri non potest" (II-II.2.4 c). See also Thomas Aquinas, *Super epistolam ad Romanos lectura* 1.7 (123–45); I.1.1 c; I-II.91.4 c; II-II.22.1 ad 1. For this, see Eugene F. Rogers Jr., *Thomas Aquinas and Karl Barth: Sacred Doctrine and the Natural Knowledge of God* (Notre Dame, IN: University of Notre Dame Press, 1999), 96–165. Arvin Vos is correct when he writes that for Aquinas preambles of faith are not preconditions of faith. "He holds that people may simply accept them on faith if they do not understand the demonstration that proves them." *Aquinas, Calvin, and Contemporary Protestant Thought: A Critique of Protestant Views on the Thought of Thomas Aquinas* (Grand Rapids: Eerdmans; Washington, DC: Christian University Press, 1985), 71. But it is another thing when we start *thinking* about the revelation in a *systematic manner*. Then even the *vetula* (Thomas Aquinas, *In Symbolum Apostolorum*, prologue) cannot do without *some* kind of more or less explicit philosophy.

such a way that we can have *scientia* about the fact of creation and the modes of being.[55] But about the Trinitarian life of God and the redemption in Christ we cannot know anything on our own. Nobody could know anything about the incarnation of the Son, because this was hidden in the will of God.[56] Therefore, we need God's special help to grasp the *scientia* possessed by God himself and those in heaven. This help is the gift of faith. The act of faith is a "cum assensu" *cogitare*.[57] Or, as Aquinas puts it in a more elaborate version: "To believe is an act of the intellect assenting to the divine truth by the order of the will that is moved by God through grace."[58] He emphasizes that even though we have in some way access to the *veritas divina*, we cannot see it in this life[59]—with rare exceptions.[60] So we do not have *scientia* of the revealed mysteries of God, which natural reason cannot grasp,[61] but we do have *certitudo*, because the *lumen fidei* renders that which we have to believe even more certain to us than anything else.[62]

It is astonishing to see how important for Aquinas is the will in grasping the revealed truth of God. According to Aquinas, the human intellect assents to the truth of faith not because it is convinced by *ratio* but because it is ordered to do so by will ("non quasi convictus ratione, sed quasi imperatus a voluntate").[63] The origin of revelation is God's will, and it aims at our freedom.[64] We are called to respond as loving beings to the love of God shown to us in revelation. This means in a first step that faith *as opposed to scientia*[65] (!) is necessary, for otherwise there would be no merit, no genuine involvement of human freedom,[66] because we would be forced to accept the truth by its undeniable evidence. So the hiddenness encountered by faith is one of the consequences of the *ratio boni* of God's self-communication. Here again Aquinas proves to be a "voluntarist."

If the will is so important for faith, it is necessary to ask how faith differs from arbitrariness. Aquinas posits two different ways of judging in order to explain the nature of theology: "per modum inclinationis" and "per modum cognitionis." The *modus inclinationis* is the way a virtuous man judges the

---

55. III.10.3 c. For an analysis of the notion of *scientia* in Aquinas, see John I. Jenkins, *Knowledge and Faith in Thomas Aquinas* (Cambridge: Cambridge University Press, 1997), 11–98.

56. "Ea enim quae ex sola Dei voluntate proveniunt, supra omne debitum creaturae, nobis innotescere non possunt nisi quatenus in sacra Scriptura traduntur, per quam divina voluntas innotescit" (III.1.3 c). See also *Super epistolam ad Ephesios lectura* 1.3 (25).

57. II-II.2.1 c.

58. "Ipsum autem credere est actus intellectus assentientis veritati divinae ex imperio voluntatis a Deo motae per gratiam" (II-II.2.9 c).

59. "Fides est habitus mentis, qua inchoatur vita aeterna in nobis, faciens intellectum assentire non apparantibus" (II-II.4.1 c). For the eschatological structure of *fides* in Aquinas, see Eberhard Schockenhoff, *Bonum hominis: Die anthropologischen und theologischen Grundlagen der Tugendethik des Thomas von Aquin* (Mainz: Matthias Grünewald, 1987), 376ff.

60. Moses and Paul (II-II.174.4 c; 180.5).

61. For the problem of how we can know God's nature here below, see John F. Wippel, *Metaphysical Themes in Thomas Aquinas* (Washington, DC: Catholic University of America Press, 1984), 215–41.

62. I.1.5 c.

63. I.111.1 ad 1.

64. "Licet ad credendum necessitate coactionis nullus arctetur, cum credere sit voluntarium" (II-II.1.6 ad 3).

65. "Fides et scientia non sunt de eodem" (II-II.1.5 c). In this respect, faith is related to hearing, not to seeing (II-II.1.4; III.41.2 ad 1).

66. I.1.8 ad 2; II-II.2.9.

things that are connected with the virtue he has.[67] This kind of judgment is a *cognitio per connaturalitatem*,[68] an affective cognition that produces love of God.[69] It is a judgment made possible by the move of an inner instinct, which is sufficient reason for believing because it attests God's loving presence to us.[70] The believing person is in this way urged by the authority of the Holy Spirit when he or she is confronted with the challenging content of Scripture. Therefore, faith is neither mere opinion nor the *visio* of *scientia*.[71] We might say that the inner instinct confirms that we deal in revelation with the reality and the quality of the One who is the root of all human obligation because he is the *bonum subsistens* itself. Hence, even though the principles of *sacra doctrina* remain hidden to us in the modus of *scientia*, we can know in this way "for sure" *that* we have to believe.[72]

Here at the core of his theological reflection on faith, Aquinas draws heavily upon his metaphysical insights in order to clarify the nature of faith. The deeper we delve into Aquinas, the stronger we sense the unity of philosophy of being and theology in his thinking. And the result of this unity is that he sees in every aspect of creation the *concrete* imprint of God's superabundance. An example of the significance of philosophical reflection inside theological reflection is Aquinas's dealing with the difficulty that arises with the question of exactly *what kind* of voluntary assent is involved in the act of faith. It is not astonishing that Aquinas had to struggle to find his way in the maze of intricate problems opened up by this question. In *De veritate* 14.2 ad 10,[73] Aquinas makes the statement that the beginning (*inchoatio*) of faith is in affection insofar as the will directs the intellect to assent to that which belongs to faith. But this act of will is an act neither of *caritas* nor of hope but of the (mere) appetite for a promised good. This clearly is yet an insufficient definition of the nature of the will's part in faith, because it actually lacks the necessary presupposition of the full *connaturalitas* linked to *caritas*, the *connaturalitas*

---

67. I.1.6 ad 3. See Rafael-Tomas Caldera, *Le jugement par inclination chez Saint Thomas d'Aquin* (Paris: Librairie Philosophique J. Vrin, 1980).

68. "Sic igitur circa res divinas ex rationis inquisitione rectum iudicium habere pertinet ad sapientiam, quae est virtus intellectualis: sed rectum iudicium habere de eis secundum quandam connaturalitatem ad ipsa pertinet ad sapientiam secundum quod donum est Spiritus Sancti: sicut Dionysius dicit, in 2 cap *de Div. Nom.*, quod Hierotheus est perfectus in divinis *non solum discens, sed et patiens divina.* Huiusmodi autem compassio sive connaturalitas ad res divinas fit per caritatem, quae quidem unit nos Deo. . . . Sic igitur sapientia quae est donum causam quidem habet in voluntate, scilicet caritatem: sed essentiam habet in intellectu" (II-II.45.2 c).

69. I.64.1 c.

70. "Ille qui credit habet sufficiens inductivum ad credendum: inducitur enim auctoritate divinae doctrinae miraculis confirmatae, et, quod plus est, interiori instinctu Dei invitantis. Unde non leviter credit" (II-II.2.9 ad 3). The development of Aquinas's teaching of the *interior instinctus* is outlined by Max Seckler, *Instinkt und Glaubenswille nach Thomas von Aquin* (Mainz: Matthias Grünewald, 1961).

71. II-II.2.1 c.

72. II-II.8.4 ad 2. "As Aquinas understands it, the *ratio* or idea under which the articles of faith are grasped is that of *being divinely revealed.*" Jenkins, *Knowledge and Faith*, 190. (Pages 185–97 in Jenkins's book are quite helpful for the subject matter.) Jenkins refers in this context to Alvin Plantinga's understanding of "warrant" (245) as a useful concept, even though he criticizes Plantinga's interpretation of Aquinas (173–76). It seems to me that the discussion of the "Aquinas/Calvin Model" in Plantinga's recent book *Warranted Christian Belief* (New York: Oxford University Press, 2000), 241–89, is not at odds with Jenkins's view. Plantinga is there as good a follower of a "supernatural externalist interpretation" of Aquinas as Jenkins claims to be (Jenkins, *Knowledge and Faith*, 185–97).

73. See Bruce D. Marshall's essay, "Putting Shadows to Flight: The Trinity, Faith, and Reason," in this volume.

without which there is no access to matters of faith. This seems also to be an insufficient description of the merit of faith, which does not exist without grace and *caritas*. The reason Aquinas teaches in this way is that in his view the *ultimus finis* has to be *first* in the intellect and *then* in the will (II-II.4.7 c). But at the same time he sees that faith without *caritas* cannot be a fundament (II-II.4.7 ad 5), because it simply would not be a virtue (I-II.23.7 c).

There is also another line of thought in Aquinas that says that the first act of will is not moved by the ordering of the intellect but "ex instinctu naturae, aut superioris causae" (I-II.17.5 ad 3). This means that we have here a movement of the will and hence a connaturality and coaptation (*coaptatio*) with the *bonum* for which we strive[74] that is not mediated by the intellect. The other necessary clarification we find along this line in the *Summa theologiae* beyond the explanations given in *De veritate* is that there has to take place in the will an elevation of human nature by grace for the assent of faith.[75] God moves from inside by grace (II-II.6.1 c). It is the inner instinct, which needs information, as Seckler emphasizes,[76] by which the Holy Spirit presents to us the matters of faith so that they can be grasped as such by the intellect. We can move only inside the change, the full *connaturalitas* already brought about by grace that affects the whole being of a person and enables *caritas*. This beginning movement, in which we move, is not our *caritas* with its merit or fruit but the beginning of faith as God's "first step" toward us, which results in an effective transformation of our person[77]—signaled by the *interior instinctus*—even before we respond to it.[78]

Because Aquinas has to keep the powers of the soul apart in order to describe their role in the unity of the act of faith, he is interested in not reducing one of them to the other. He assigns to the intellect what belongs to the intellect and to the will what belongs to the will, which gives the correct impression of a reciprocal priority of the powers toward each other. (The "one-sided" emphasis on the *ultimus finis* being first in the intellect particularly underlines the receptiveness of human beings.) But this reciprocity and mutual interdependence of the soul's powers, which is a trace of the rhythm of love determined by the communication of being,[79] works only in the unity

---

74. See H.-D. Simonin, "Autour de la solution thomiste du problème de l'amour," *Archives d'Histoire Doctrinale et Littéraire du Moyen Age* 6 (1931): 191ff. For the connection between *inclinatio* and *connaturalitas*, see I-II.23.4 c: "Bonum ergo primo quidem in potentia appetitiva causat quandam inclinationem, seu aptitudinem, seu connaturalitatem ad bonum: quod pertinet ad passionem amoris." See also I-II.27.1 c. (For the relationship between *amor* and *voluntas* in this context, see Albert Ilien, *Wesen und Funktion der Liebe im Denken des Thomas von Aquin* [Freiburg: Herder, 1975], 96–112.) The *connaturalitas* of the *interior instinctus* is not the *cognitio per connaturalitatem* of *sapientia* that presupposes *caritas*, but the change brought about by grace that is the precondition for *caritas*.
75. "C'est donc le désir de la fin dernière surnaturelle qui constitue pour S. Thomas le mobile de l'acte de foi. Ce désir n'implique pas nécessairement que la volonté soit sous l'influence de la charité, mais il ne s'expliquerait cependant pas sans une élévation surnaturelle des facultés humaines." Roger Aubert, *Le problème de l'acte de foi: Données traditionelles et résultats des controverses récentes*, 2nd ed. (Louvain: Publications universitaires de Louvain, 1950), 58. For the change in Aquinas's teaching with regard to this decisive necessity of grace for the inner instinct between *De veritate* and the *Summa theologiae*, see Henri Bouillard, *Conversion et grâce chez s. Thomas d'Aquin, Étude historique* (Paris: Aubier, 1944).
76. Seckler, *Instinkt und Glaubenswille*, 156ff.
77. "Dilectio Dei est causativa boni quod in nobis est" (*Summa contra gentiles* III.150 [3228]).
78. For the possibility of such a transformation, see Bieler, *Befreiung der Freiheit*, 387–407.
79. See Ferdinand Ulrich, *Homo abyssus: Das Wagnis der Seinsfrage*, 2nd ed. (Einsiedeln: Johannes Verlag, 1998), 382ff.

of the one being these powers share in the human person and therefore in the one act of freedom[80] in which the powers and, with them, their virtues enter the game *at the same time* (I-II.113.4), because only from the *essentia animae* as the subject (*subiectum*) of grace flow the virtues into the powers that result from the soul (I-II.110.4).[81] It is not the will that wants, but the person by the will.[82] So the deeper level that enables the interplay of the powers and virtues is the change brought about by the infusion of grace,[83] in which the whole person is moved.[84] This means that faith in the act of a concrete person, who never acts with only one power,[85] is incomplete without being formed by *caritas*, and the notion of an unformed faith signals that—because of the reality of *intellectus* and *voluntas* being two different powers of the soul—faith cannot be simply reduced to *caritas*. We have the intellect in the act of faith "in between," so to speak, the movement of the human will driven by the Holy Spirit in the inner instinct—the beginning of faith—and *caritas*, the mother and root of all virtues, rendering (unformed) faith into a movement toward God. Yet in the act of faith, we have not two separate kinds of human will (*instinctus* and *caritas*), but two aspects of the same power (will).

In its "middle position," the intellect attests the priority of God's move toward us. But we cannot tear apart these different aspects of faith in a temporal manner, because similar to creation, God's movement toward us in grace has the result that the human being capable of answering by faith is "already" there, corresponding to the logic of the perfect gift.[86] For this structure of simultaneousness we can refer also to Aquinas's notion of friendship constituted by God's special communication, and his understanding of justification and of creation. Looking at Aquinas's understanding of faith, we can say with Bernard of Clairvaux that the act of faith is as much totally an act of God as it is totally an act of a human being—but in different respects.[87]

Having said that we know *that* we have to believe, still necessary is a further identification of God by our intellect, one that does not add something new to the articles of faith[88] but ponders their inner logic, which is more than

---

80. See George P. Klubertanz, "The Unity of Human Activity," *Modern Schoolman* 27 (1950): 75–103.

81. See Pius Künzle, *Das Verhältnis der Seele zu ihren Potenzen: Problemgeschichtliche Untersuchungen von Augustin bis und mit Thomas von Aquin* (Freiburg, Switzerland: Universitätsverlag, 1956), 171–218. Künzle shows how the necessity of powers that naturally result from the soul is based on the difference between *esse* and *essentia* in the created being.

82. See Dorothée Welp, *Willensfreiheit bei Thomas von Aquin: Versuch einer Interpretation* (Freiburg, Switzerland: Universitätsverlag, 1979), 241–42.

83. "Ipsa igitur Dei moventis motio est gratiae infusio" (I-II.113.8 c).

84. "Alia vero vocatio est interior, quae nihil aliud est quam quidam mentis instinctus, quo cor hominis movetur a Deo ad assentiendum his quae sunt fidei vel virtutis" (*Super epistolam ad Romanos lectura* 8.6 [707]). See also the (critical) remarks made by Otto Hermann Pesch with regard to the unity of the human act in his *Die Theologie der Rechtfertigung bei Martin Luther und Thomas von Aquin: Versuch eines systematisch-theologischen Dialogs*, 2nd ed. (Mainz: Matthias Grünewald, 1985), 732ff.

85. "Voluntas et intellectus mutuo se includunt" (I.16.4 ad 1; cf. I.82.4; I-II.74.5 ad 2). See also Bénézet Bujo, *Die Begründung des Sittlichen: Zur Frage des Eudämonismus bei Thomas von Aquin* (Paderborn: Schöningh, 1984), 50ff.

86. See the books of Bouillard, *Conversion et grâce* and Seckler, *Instinkt und Glaubenswille*.

87. "Non partim gratia, partim liberum arbitrium, sed totum singula opere individuo peragunt: totum quidem hoc, et totum illa, sed ut totum in illo, sic totum ex illa." Bernard of Clairvaux, *De gratia et libero arbitrio* XIV.47, in *Sämtliche Werke* (Innsbruck: Tyrolia, 1990), 1:242. See also Thomas Aquinas, *Summa contra gentiles* III.70 (2466).

88. II-II.1.6–10.

just noncontradiction. We have to ask how it is actually God himself who is presented to us in revelation. Because the articles of faith are not available to us in the form of *scientia*, only those who have access to revelation by faith in the way described will be capable of reading the logic of love, which is the essence of *sacra doctrina*.[89]

This next step of asking for the inner logic of the articles of faith is necessary if we want to be involved as whole persons, with all our hearts.[90] Moved by love toward God, we are enflamed to see his beauty, as Aquinas says.[91] *Sapientia* as a gift of the Holy Spirit makes a correct judgment "secundum rationes divinas" possible.[92] It gives us the taste for these *rationes*,[93] in order to discover what the articles of faith contain.[94] The contemplation of God's beauty to which the gift of *sapientia* leads is followed by admiration,[95] joy about what is seen,[96] and love for God.[97] So theology takes on the form of prayer.[98] In this life there is no perfect contemplation but only a beginning of that which will be fulfilled in eternal life. Only through God's effects in his creation can we grasp something of his truth at the present time.[99] Scripture itself points back to nature by its use of metaphors.[100] This reference to that which is natural to us explains why theology relies on *cognitio naturalis* for a deeper understanding of revelation.[101]

Besides refuting arguments that speak against the articles of faith, theology has to deal with the articles' positive implications. It cannot prove the articles, but it can show what is implied in them, what they are talking about.[102] For Aquinas there are two basic articles, in which everything else is included: that God exists and that he provides for our salvation.[103] This is further elaborated in II-II.1.8: The 14 articles of faith enumerated by Aquinas concern the

---

89. II-II.1.5 ad 2. "Ex his autem principiis ita probatur aliquid apud fideles sicut etiam ex principiis naturaliter notis probatur aliquid apud omnes. Unde etiam theologia scientia est" (ibid.).

90. "Ita negligentia mihi videtur, si, postquam confirmati sumus in fide, non studemus quod credimus intelligere" (Anselm of Canterbury, *Cur Deus homo* I.1).

91. II-II.180.1 c.

92. II-II.45.2 c.

93. II-II.45.2 ad 1. "Est enim sapiens, cui quaeque res sapiunt prout sunt." Bernard of Clairvaux, *Sermones diversi, Sermo 18*, in *Sämtliche Werke* (Innsbruck: Tyrolia, 1998), 9:334–36.

94. I.1.8 c.

95. II-II.180.3 ad 3.

96. II-II.180.1 c; 7 ad 1.

97. "Et haec est ultima perfectio contemplativae vitae: ut scilicet non solum divina veritas videatur, sed etiam ut ametur" (II-II.180.7 ad 1).

98. Lydia Maidl, *Desiderii interpres: Genese und Grundstruktur der Gebetstheologie des Thomas von Aquin* (Paderborn: F. Schönigh, 1994).

99. "Sed quia per divinos effectus in Dei contemplationem manuducimur" (II-II.180.4 c).

100. I.1.9. See also Markus Gumann, *Vom Ursprung der Erkenntnis des Menschen bei Thomas von Aquin: Konsequenzen für das Verhältnis von Philosophie und Theologie* (Regensburg: Friedrich Pustet, 1999), 71–81. Furthermore, Aquinas reminds us of the following fact: "Fides non potest universaliter praecedere intellectum: non enim posset homo assentire credendo aliquibus propositis nisi ea aliqualiter intelligeret" (II-II.8.8 ad 2). In this, I go along with Romanus Cessario, OP. See his *"Duplex Ordo Cognitionis,"* in this volume.

101. Mark F. Johnson, "God's Knowledge in Our Frail Mind: The Thomistic Model of Theology," *Angelicum* 76 (1999): 26–45.

102. I.1.8 c. "Il y a un lien des mystères de la foi, lien qui n'est accessible que dans la foi mais n'en constitue pas moins un contenu intelligible et l'objet propre de la théologie est le déploiement discursif de ce lien, dans le plein respect du mystère qui en est le centre." Michel Corbin, "La fonction et les principes de la théologie selon la Somme théologique de saint Thomas d'Aquin," *Recherches de science religieuse* 55 (1967): 341.

103. II-II.1.7 c.

majesty of divinity and the mystery of the *humanitas Christi*—the principles established in the two basic articles. Thus, the Trinity and Christ are the two basic principles of *sacra doctrina*. How they are the root of any kind of *caritas* becomes apparent in the first article of III.1. The importance of this article cannot be overestimated. There Aquinas says that something is fitting for something if it is in accordance with its nature. For example, it is fitting for a human being to think, because the human is by nature an *animal rationale*. The nature of God is his goodness, as Aquinas confirms in referring to Dionysius Areopagita.[104] To the *ratio boni* belongs the communication of self toward others. Thus, to the *ratio summi boni* belongs the highest form of communication of self. From this follows for Aquinas: "Hence to the essence of the highest good belongs the communication of itself to the creature in the highest way" ("Unde ad rationem summi boni pertinet quod summo modo se creaturae communicet"). Therefore, the incarnation is fitting for God.

But Aquinas carefully avoids stating that God *had* to act in a certain manner. For God, the incarnation was not necessary in any cogent way, but *rebus sic stantibus* we can see that the incarnation was the *better* way for saving mankind. In this latter way the incarnation of the Son was necessary and fitting,[105] because God wanted it that way, as Anselm of Canterbury says.[106] How God is the *summum bonum* we know only from Scripture, where God's will in Christ is accessible to us. This means that the criterion of the *bonum* as communication of self is not taken from outside revelation but is integral to the articles of faith that express God's triune freedom toward the world (first basic article), a freedom that makes a genuine loving involvement of God in this world (creation and incarnation) both possible and—as we know from Scripture and by the testimony of the Holy Spirit—real (second basic article).[107] Everything else in *sacra doctrina* follows from there.[108] We are reminded of Anselm's finding of the *unum argumentum*, which identifies God as "aliquid quo nihil maius cogitari possit."[109] This "aliquid quo nihil maius . . ." is at the same time "quiddam maius quam cogitari possit."[110] Anselm's formulas are nothing but the two basic expressions of God's self-giving: God reaches us even in our thinking (*quo nihil maius*: prevalent the *mysterium humanitatis Christi*) and remains at the same time free and independent in his love (*quiddam maius*: prevalent the *maiestas divinitatis*).[111] All

---

104. See also Thomas Aquinas, *In Librum Beati Dionysii De Divinis Nominibus* 1.1 (36).

105. III.1.2 c.

106. "Et si vis omnium quae fecit et quae passus est veram scire necessitatem, scito omnia ex necessitate fuisse, *quia ipse voluit*" (*Cur Deus homo* II.17).

107. How this is the case is shown very well by Wilhelm Thüsing, *Die neutestamentlichen Theologien und Jesus Christus: Grundlegung einer Theologie des Neuen Testaments*, 2nd ed., vols. 1–3 (Münster: Aschendorff, 1996–1999).

108. "Parce que la raison ne s'ajoute plus de l'extérieur à la foi et lui est en quelque sorte intérieure, le discours théologique est devenu, à travers cette nouvelle formulation, le déploiement de l'intelligibilité et de la cohérence internes de la foi, la manifestation, selon les raisons de la foi, d'une totalité cohérente qui doit son intelligibilité non pas à l'homme, mais à Dieu et à Lui seul." Corbin, *Le chemin de la théologie*, 828.

109. Anselm, *Proslogion* 2.

110. Ibid., 15.

111. Ferdinand Ulrich, "Cur non video praesentem? Zur Implikation der 'griechischen' und 'lateinischen' Denkform bei Anselm und Scotus Erigena," *Freiburger Zeitschrift für Philosophie und Theologie* 22 (1975): 70–170.

of this shows that the *Summa theologiae* is an extensive development of the logic of God's self-giving. The notion of *convenientia*,[112] which is all-present in III, is Aquinas's main tool for sketching the logic of self-giving, which is first of all founded in God's triune accordance with himself in the life of the processions. That life is finally "extended" toward the creation, most of all toward us, who are supposed to become friends of God,[113] that is, beings who receive the gift of God's inner life to the full extent. This explains why *processio* and *bonitas* mark the center and the organizing principle of the *Summa theologiae.*[114]

Aquinas's Philosophy of Being

Aquinas's theology is saturated with his philosophy of being. That is the first impression that comes from reading him. And we may well ask if there is not some tension between his understanding of the status of faith and the philosophy he is using to develop his theology.[115] Aquinas is very often referred to as Aristotelian, and the suspicion that here we have more Aristotle than gospel usually arises quickly. It is well known that Luther was especially sensitive to that, but he was not the only one to criticize the use of Aristotle in theology.[116] As we know today, the view that Aquinas simply betrayed the biblical tradition in favor of Aristotle is not correct.[117] It has even been observed that Aquinas was Aristotelian in order to *defend* Christian positions.[118] But in addition, it is important to say—also from the point of view of Aquinas's philosophy—that Aquinas was not just an Aristotelian in Christian disguise. There can be no doubt that Aquinas owes much to Aristotle, but the Aristotelian heritage is only one element of Aquinas's philosophy. The Platonic aspect of participation in Aquinas is as important as the Aristotelian aspect.[119]

---

112. Gilbert Narcisse, *Les raisons de Dieu: Argument de convenance et Esthétique théologique selon saint Thomas d'Aquin et Hans Urs von Balthasar* (Fribourg: Éditions Universitaires, 1997).

113. Holger Dörnemann, *Freundschaft als Paradigma der Erlösung* (Würzburg: Echter Verlag, 1997).

114. "La notion sur laquelle repose toute la construction de la *Somme*: la procession." Ghislain Lafont, *Structure et méthode dans la 'Somme théologique' de saint Thomas d'Aquin*, 2nd ed. (Paris: Cerf, 1996), 80. "L'ensemble de la construction est certainement dominé par le thème de la *Bonté de Dieu*" (ibid., 169). See also Wilhelm Metz, *Die Architektonik der Summa Theologiae des Thomas von Aquin: Zur Gesamtsicht des thomasischen Gedankens* (Hamburg: Felix Meiner, 1998), 101, 196.

115. See, e.g., the critical remarks made by Persson, *Sacra doctrina*. Critical questions *must* be asked; see Kari Elisabeth Børresen, *Subordination and Equivalence: The Nature and Role of Woman in Augustine and Thomas Aquinas* (Kampen: Kok Pharos, 1995).

116. Denis R. Janz, *Luther on Thomas Aquinas: The Angelic Doctor in the Thought of the Reformer* (Stuttgart: Franz Steiner, 1989), 17–24.

117. See, e.g., Pesch, *Theologie der Rechtfertigung*; and Ulrich Kühn, *Via Caritatis: Theologie des Gesetzes bei Thomas von Aquin* (Berlin: Evangelische Verlagsanstalt, 1964).

118. John Milbank and Catherine Pickstock, *Truth in Aquinas* (London: Routledge, 2001), 41.

119. R. J. Henle, *Saint Thomas and Platonism: A Study of the Plato and Platonic Texts in the Writings of Saint Thomas* (The Hague: Martinus Nijhoff, 1970); and Fran O'Rourke, *Pseudo-Dionysius and the Metaphysics of Aquinas* (Leiden: E. J. Brill, 1992). Anthony Kenny's talk of "the official anti-Platonic position that St Thomas commonly defends" in his latest book, *Aquinas on Being* (Oxford: Oxford University Press, 2002), 72, shows how little he has understood of Aquinas's conception of being (*esse*). Kenny's book is actually more about his treatment of Thomistic notions than about issues of Aquinas's metaphysics. In addition, Kenny's use of the secondary literature is completely insufficient. He writes, e.g., as if Etienne Gilson had never written a book called *Being and Some Philosophers* (2nd ed.; Toronto: Pontifical Institute of Mediaeval Studies, 1952). The comment made by Brian J. Shanley may also be applied to Kenny: "To use the language of Gilson, Frege-friendly readings of Aquinas end up as some form

Aquinas created a *new* philosophy of being that cannot be reduced to its sources.[120] What was apparently needed for Aquinas was a fresh look at creation. Grace does not urge us to deduce a particular philosophy directly from theology; rather, it opens our eyes to discover the world as God's creation anew. Furthermore, it fosters an openness of theology and philosophy for each other, because grace and nature (creation) *never* reach us in a separate way. Hans Urs von Balthasar echoes basic insights of Aquinas: "The formal object of theology . . . lies at the very heart of the formal object of philosophy (along with the mythology which belongs to it). Out of these mysterious depths the formal object of theology breaks forth as the self-revelation of the mysterious depths of being [*Sein*] itself; such a revelation cannot be derived from what the creature's understanding, working by itself, can read of the mystery of being."[121] Ferdinand Ulrich uses an even denser formula by saying that grace comes "on the way of being [*Sein*]."[122]

What is meant by the "way of being"? Aquinas wants to show that creation consists in the gift of being (*esse*): "To create is to give being."[123] The "way of being" is the "*dare esse*" by which God in his care is present in all things.[124] It is not possible to develop here the metaphysics of Aquinas at great length.[125] I can only mention major points of it. The starting point for our discovery of the *dare esse* is the meeting with a concrete being (*ens*).[126] In this meeting, the human mind at once grasps the first principles,[127] which converge with the transcendentals *ens, res, unum, aliquid, verum et bonum.*[128] In this first act of knowing we have an *implicit* cognition of God,[129] because in the cognition *that* a concrete being *is*, we touch the source of all beings. There are two major aspects in every being: the essence (*essentia, res*) of a thing, which defines its limits,[130]

---

of essentialism. Aquinas's authentic doctrine of being—with its emphasis on *esse* as the *actus essendi*, the act of all acts and the perfection of all perfections—simply cannot be harmonized with post-Frege analytical dogmas. It is rather the case that Aquinas challenges those dogmas." Shanley, "Analytical Thomism," *The Thomist* 63 (1999): 132. (That is not all Shanley has to say about analytical Thomism.) For a further critique of Kenny's notion of being, see Barry Miller, *The Fullness of Being: A New Paradigm for Existence* (Notre Dame, IN: University of Notre Dame Press, 2002).

120. Fernand Van Steenberghen, *Die Philosophie im 13. Jahrhundert* (Munich: Schöningh, 1977), 310ff.

121. Hans Urs von Balthasar, *Herrlichkeit I: Schau der Gestalt* (Einsiedeln: Johannes Verlag, 1961), 137. The translation of this text, by Adrian Walker, is taken from Bieler, "The Future of the Philosophy of Being," *Communio: International Catholic Review* 26 (1999): 481.

122. "Da die Gnade auf dem Weg des Seins kommt." Ulrich, *Homo abyssus*, 333.

123. "Creare autem est dare esse" (1 Sent 37.1.1 c).

124. The *dare esse* is a *constant* act: "Non enim aliter eas in esse conservat, quam semper eis esse dando, unde si suam actionem eis subtraheret, omnia in nihilum redigerentur" (I.9.2 c).

125. For a more extensive discussion of the topic, see Bieler, *Freiheit als Gabe*, 226–44.

126. Michael Tavuzzi, "The Preliminary Grasp of Being," *The Thomist* 51 (1987): 555–74. Over against a Kantian view, Aquinas is clearly a "realist" when he says that our intellect reaches the "intima rei" (*De veritate* 1.12 c). He would agree with Thomas Nagel, who writes, "Kant's claim that empirical reasoning tells us only about the phenomenal world is empirically incredible, given the evidence—and what is empirically incredible is incredible, period." *The Last Word* (New York: Oxford University Press, 1997), 99. (On the primacy of the external in a Thomistic context, see Joseph Owens, *Cognition: An Epistemological Inquiry* [Houston: Center for Thomistic Studies, 1992], 33–54.) But Aquinas would still say, "Veritas principaliter est in intellectu" (I.16.1 c).

127. Bieler, *Freiheit als Gabe*, 326ff.

128. *De veritate* 1.1. Jan A. Aertsen, *Medieval Philosophy and the Transcendentals: The Case of Thomas Aquinas* (Leiden: E. J. Brill, 1996).

129. "Omnia cognoscentia cognoscunt implicite Deum in quolibet cognito" (*De veritate* 22.2 ad 2).

130. "Omnis creatura est finita simpliciter, inquantum esse eius non est absolutum subsistens, sed limitatur ad naturam aliquam cui advenit" (I.50.2 ad 4).

and the being (*esse*) of a thing (*ens*), which transcends the limits that separate one thing from another (*aliquid*).

The substance in its unity (*unum*) does not know a "more or less," as Aquinas says; it either exists or not.[131] Of course, there are reduced forms and ways to be (e.g., sickness), but that does not question the fact that concrete beings by being participate in the *esse* that is not participated in by parts (which would mean a "more or less").[132] Thus, we have in every concrete being by its very participation in being (*esse*) a moment of absoluteness[133] that contrasts its limitations. This contrast makes it necessary to differentiate between *esse* and the *essentia*, in whose limits the *esse* is received. The difference shows that no concrete being *is* its own being (*esse*);[134] otherwise, it could not undergo any destruction and it would not have started to be. If a being is not its own *esse*, it participates in *esse*,[135] in which all others participate as well.[136] But that is only one side of the matter. The difference between *esse* and *essentia* also shows that being as *esse commune* does not subsist apart from the limited beings.[137] Otherwise, it would not rely on *essentia*, by which[138] *esse* is received in the concrete substance (*ens*).[139] If being (*esse*) does not subsist in itself, it seems to be in some way less than the concrete being. But then how can it be the reason for our subsistence? Apparently we must ask for the source, in which *esse* and *essentia* are one, in order to be able to communicate the being (*esse*) by which we and everything else in this world exist.[140]

But then what is *esse*, by which we exist? The understanding of *esse* is the core of Aquinas's philosophy.[141] Aquinas rarely speaks in the first person singular. But in *De potentia*, which is a turning point in the development of his philosophy,[142] he does: "It is apparent that what I call *esse*. . . ."[143] He knows

---

131. I.93.3 ad 3.

132. I.75.5 ad 1.

133. "Esse absolute praeintelligitur causae" (I.13.11 ad 2). "Esse autem ab alio causatum non competit enti inquantum est ens" (*Summa contra gentiles* II.52 [1277]). "Esse causatum non est de ratione entis simpliciter" (I.44.1 ad 1).

134. "Nullum igitur ens causatum est suum esse" (*Summa contra gentiles* II.52 [1277]).

135. "Ens autem dicitur id quod finite participat esse" (Thomas Aquinas, *Super librum De causis expositio* 6).

136. Thomas Aquinas, *De potentia* 7.2 c; I.4.3 c.

137. *De potentia* 7.2 ad 7; Thomas Aquinas, *Quodlibeta* 10.2 ad 4.

138. Thomas Aquinas, *De spiritualibus creaturis* 1c and ad 15; *Summa contra gentiles* II.55 (1298); I.7.2; 50.2 ad 4.

139. Does it make any sense to speak of "substance" in a world of quantum physics? If we understand substance not as a closed entity, which is not open from inside (a "res incurvata in se"), then it makes much sense. See Richard J. Connell, *Substance and Modern Science* (Houston: Center for Thomistic Studies, 1988); Wolfgang Smith, *The Quantum Enigma: Finding the Hidden Key* (Peru, IL: Sherwood Sugden & Co., 1995); and William A. Wallace, *The Modeling of Nature: Philosophy of Science and Philosophy of Nature in Synthesis* (Washington, DC: Catholic University of America Press, 1996).

140. According to Aquinas, God is *not* the *esse commune*: "Esse divinum, quod est eius substantia, non est esse commune, sed est esse distinctum a quolibet alio esse. Unde per ipsum suum esse Deus differt a quolibet alio ente" (*De potentia* 7.2 ad 4). As nonsubsistent, *esse* is not a *principium quod* but a *principium quo*. This distinction goes back to Boethius and Marius Victorinus. See David Bradshaw, "Neoplatonic Origins of the Act of Being," *Review of Metaphysics* 53 (1999): 383–401.

141. "Toute la métaphysique thomiste de la participation est basée sur cette notion simple et inépuisable de l'esse: l'esse est l'acte premier intensif qui embrasse et contient tout." Cornelio Fabro, *Participation et causalité selon S. Thomas d'Aquin* (Louvain: Publications Universitaires de Louvain; Paris: Éditions Béatrice-Nauwelaerts, 1961), 508.

142. Fernando Inciarte, *Forma formarum: Strukturmomente der thomistischen Seinslehre im Rückgriff auf Aristoteles* (Freiburg: Karl Alber, 1979), 130ff.; Leo Elders, *Die Metaphysik des Thomas von Aquin in historischer Perspektive 1: Das ens commune* (Salzburg: A. Pustet, 1985), 160.

143. *De potentia* 7.2 ad 9.

that he has something special to say; in his view, *esse* is a "completum et simplex, sed non subsistens."[144] According to Ferdinand Ulrich, who deeply influenced Hans Urs von Balthasar, this sentence marks the center of Aquinas's philosophy of being. *Esse* is not *subsistens* but *inhaerens*.[145] By *esse*, every being is actualized, and the *"non subsistens"* of *esse* testifies that *esse* is poured out into beings without withholding anything. It is the pure "actuality of all acts and, because of this, the perfection of all perfections" ("actualitas omnium actuum, et propter hoc est perfectio omnium perfectionum").[146] It is first of all a gift[147] for us by which we receive ourselves *and* our "being connected" with all other beings. The *completum et simplex* appears in the subsistence of beings, because that which receives being (*esse*) already is.[148] Every being participates in the *completum et simplex* of the *esse* that is already poured out. So it is not the *essentia*, nothing incomplete,[149] that receives the *esse* but the full-fledged substance as *ens*.[150] The *terminus ad quem* of creation, the "tota substantia rei,"[151] is reached at once by *dare esse*, because creation is a *perfect* giving. This philosophical contemplation of the constitution of substance by the communication of *esse* provides a better understanding of how human freedom is structured by the gift-character of created being.[152] In the end, *esse* is another word for freedom, first of all with respect to God: "The divine being, on which the meaning of divine power is based, is infinite, not limited to any kind of being, but precontaining in itself all perfection of being."[153]

In its unity of fullness (*completum et simplex*) and emptiness (*non subsistens*), being (*esse*) really is "similitudo divinae bonitatis,"[154] the gift by which everything in this world is constituted. This notion of *bonitas* indicates that we have here a similarity to the Trinitarian life, which consists not in some far-fetched triad but in a genuine "connaturality" that arises from the phenomenon itself. The way Aquinas gains his insights into *esse* is completely philosophical, even though it presupposes in fact explicit or implicit faith in

---

144. *De potentia* 1.1 c. See also the enlightening text in *In Librum Beati Dionysii De Divinis Nominibus* 13.3 (989): "Nam ipsum esse creatum non est finitum si comparetur ad creaturas, quia ad omnia se extendit; si tamen comparetur ad esse increatum, invenitur deficiens et ex praecogitatione divinae mentis propriae rationis determinationem habens."

145. *De potentia* 7.2 ad 7.

146. *De potentia* 7.2 ad 9.

147. Being (*esse*) is a very special kind of gift, as Fabro reminds us: "Toutefois, dire que l'être est un 'donné,' signifie quelque chose de spécial et d'original. L'être n'est pas un 'donné' dans le sens qu'on dit d'un objet de perception externe. . . . L'être constitue donc pour la conscience la possibilité de tous les objets et contenus d'être 'donnés'" (Fabro, *Participation et causalité*, 540). In every gift we receive, *esse* goes with it—although *not* participated in by parts.

148. "Die Dinge werden ins Sein gerufen, und sie sind *schon*. D.h.: Dem *Schon*-Sein geht kein Prozess der Verwirklichung voraus, sie sind augenblicklich, wobei dieses 'Augenblicklich' zeitlich gleich Null ist. 'In his quae fiunt sine motu, simul est fieri et factum esse' (I, 45, 2 ad 3)." Inciarte, *Forma formarum*, 116. "Cum creatio sit sine motu, simul aliquid creatur et creatum est" (I.45.2 ad 3).

149. The principles of a being are "concreata" rather than "creata" (I.45.4 c). "Creatio non dicit constitutionem rei compositae ex principiis praeexistentibus: sed compositum sic dicitur creari, quod simul cum omnibus suis principiis in esse producitur" (I.45.4 ad 2).

150. "Substantia fit proprium susceptivum eius quod est esse" (*Summa contra gentiles* II.55 [1298]). "Illi enim proprie convenit esse, quod habet esse; et hoc est subsistens in suo esse" (I.45.4 c).

151. I.45.1 ad 2.

152. See Bieler, *Freiheit als Gabe*, 245–376.

153. "Esse autem divinum super quod ratio divinae potentiae fundatur, est esse infinitum, non limitatum ad aliquod genus entis, sed praehabens in se totius esse perfectionem" (I.25.3 c).

154. *De veritate* 22.2 ad 2.

the Trinity.[155] That makes it all the more interesting for theology, because it shows how everything speaks *from its innermost being* of the Trinitarian creator. Balthasar even asked if there is not in the *nonsubsistent esse* a glimpse of the *kenosis* of the eternal Son, who gave himself to the world.[156] This is not utterly surprising if the world was created in the Son.[157] But the connection between the nonsubsistence of *esse* and the *kenosis* is of course a statement that is not possible for any philosophy on its own.

But again, what does being as *esse commune* mean? In his recent book, John F. Wippel points out the importance of the difference between *esse* and *essentia* for the metaphysics of Aquinas. He regards the difference between a thing and its "distinct act of being (*actus essendi*)" as "extremely important."[158] But in the overall account he presents of Aquinas's metaphysics, Wippel does not clarify the exact meaning of the *actus essendi*—even though he furnishes the reader with valuable insights into the development of Aquinas's metaphysics. He seems to limit the importance of the difference between *esse* and *essentia* in the end to the dependence of the creatures on their creator, who is *ipsum esse subsistens*. This dependence is a fact, but how can this dependence *as such* be understood as something positive, and in what way is "ipsum esse creatum" "similitudo divinae bonitatis"? Wippel admits that Aquinas "on some occasions at least" means by speaking of "participation of beings in being" "that they participate in the act of being in general or in *esse commune*."[159] Further on, he rightly refuses (against Klaus Kremer and Josef de Vries) an identification of *esse commune* with God.[160] The motion of discovery Wippel describes is also correct: "In the order of discovery one may move from one's discovery of individual beings as participating in *esse commune* to the caused character of such beings, and then on to the existence of their unparticipated source (*esse subsistens*). Once this is established, one can then speak of them as actually participating in *esse subsistens* as well."[161] So far so good, but then Wippel's argumentation makes us wonder whether he views the *esse commune* as a ladder that can be thrown away after reaching the goal: "*Esse commune* does not exist as such apart from individual existents, except in the order of thought."[162] This may have a good

---

155. "Das rechte Aushalten der Phasen der Verendlichungsbewegung des Seins . . . hat seine letzte Bedingung der Möglichkeit in der im Glauben erfahrenen abgründigen Einheit und Verschiedenheit von Person und Natur in Gott." Ulrich, *Homo abyssus*, 168.

156. "And may it not be the case (as Ferdinand Ulrich tries to show) that the final mystery of the kenosis of God in Christ has an analogous structure in the metaphysical mystery of being, which shines forth as it destroys, which mediates the radiance of the divine only by pointing forward to the utter humility of the Cross?" Hans Urs von Balthasar, *The Glory of the Lord: A Theological Aesthetics*, vol 4, *The Realm of Metaphysics in Antiquity*, trans. Brian McNeil et al. (San Francisco: Ignatius, 1989), 38.

157. "Nam esse rerum fluit a Verbo sicut a quodam primordiali principio" (I.58.6 c). For the broader context, see Bruce D. Marshall's important remarks on "Jesus' universal primacy" in *Trinity and Truth* (Cambridge: Cambridge University Press, 2000), 108–13.

158. John F. Wippel, *The Metaphysical Thought of Thomas Aquinas: From Finite Being to Uncreated Being* (Washington, DC: Catholic University of America Press, 2000), 31.

159. Ibid., 103. We might like to read in Wippel *how* "La participation *est* la diffusion même de la bonté divine." Louis-Bertrand Geiger, *La participation dans la philosophie de S. Thomas d'Aquin* (Paris: Librairie Philosophique J. Vrin, 1942), 239.

160. Wippel, *Metaphysical Thought*, 111ff.

161. Ibid., 117; see also 114–17.

162. Ibid., 121. For "except in the order of thought," see *Summa contra gentiles* I.26 (241): "Multo igitur minus et ipsum esse commune est aliquid praeter omnes res existentes nisi in intellectu solum." It should

Thomistic meaning, but Wippel seems to favor a solution that has the *esse subsistens* on the one hand and entities with "their particular acts of being (*actus essendi*)" on the other. With respect to these "acts of being," Wippel remarks that "this usage may strike Aquinas's reader as unusual."[163] Indeed it does. With the help of the *Opera Omnia* on CD-ROM edited by R. Busa, I could not verify a single instance of this kind of pluralistic use of *actus essendi* or *actus entis* in Aquinas,[164] and I am afraid that this pluralistic use of *actus essendi* is a severe distortion of Aquinas's view, which leads to the danger of missing the point of Aquinas's metaphysics altogether. Aquinas certainly affirms that every being has its own *esse*. That is exactly the meaning of the expression *ens*.[165] But this meaning of *ens* is taken from the *one actus essendi*,[166] in which it participates because it (*ens*) is not its own *esse*.[167] So it is misleading to simply dissolve *esse commune* into the plurality of beings and therefore reduce it in fact to "*ens commune.*" By this reduction of *ipsum esse* as the one act of being, which extends to everything,[168] to an empty communality, the *esse* as *completum et simplex*—and with it the presence of the creator in his gift[169]—is destroyed. The creatures are then like isolated pieces cut from the creator, who no longer dwells in them as their innermost reality.[170] In opposition to that, Aquinas proposes with his seemingly strange concept of being (*esse*) as *completum et simplex sed non subsistens* the true givenness of the creator in his creation, by which creatures are more than just neutral facts without dignity. At the same time, he achieves a genuine understanding of the real difference between creator and creation as determined by God's communication of *esse*.

---

be noted that Aquinas speaks here from *ipsum esse*, as on many other occasions. The *esse commune* is not just simply nothing but "non subsistens" *as* "completum et simplex" (*De potentia* 1.1 c). Therefore, it is *inhaerens* in beings. For the interpretation of *Summa contra gentiles* I.26 (241), see Ludger Oeing-Hanhoff, *Ens et unum convertuntur: Stellung und Gehalt des Grundsatzes in der Philosophie des hl. Thomas von Aquin* (Münster: Aschendorffsche Verlagsbuchhandlung, 1953), 85–86; Johannes Baptist Lotz, *Der Mensch im Sein: Versuche zur Geschichte und Sache der Philosophie* (Freiburg: Herder, 1967), 63–64.; and O'Rourke, *Pseudo-Dionysius*, 144ff.

163. Wippel, *Metaphysical Thought*, 121. Already Gustav Siewerth used the unfortunate term "die einzelnen Seinsakte," but at least with the remark that they are "vom Sein selbst durchwaltet." *Gesammelte Werke II: Der Thomismus als Identitätssystem*, ed. Franz-Anton Schwarz (Düsseldorf: Patmos, 1979), 313.

164. For the meaning of the notion *actus essentiae* in this context, see Fabro, *Participation et causalité*, 260ff.

165. "Unde per suum esse substantiale dicitur unumquodque ens simpliciter" (I.5.1 ad 1). "Nam ens dicitur quasi esse habens, hoc autem solum est substantia, quae subsistit" (Thomas Aquinas, *In duodecim libros Metaphysicorum Aristotelis expositio* 12.1 [2419]). "Esse autem est aliquid fixum et quietum in ente" (*Summa contra gentiles* I.20 [179]).

166. *De veritate* 1.1 ad 3 in contrarium.

167. "Quia nulla creatura est suum esse, sed habet esse participatum" (I.12.4 c).

168. "Nam ipsum esse creatum non est finitum si comparetur ad creaturas, quia ad omnia se extendit" (*In Librum Beati Dionysii De Divinis Nominibus* 13.3 [989]).

169. For this topic, see Ferdinand Ulrich, *Leben in der Einheit von Leben und Tod* (Einsiedeln: Johannes Verlag, 1999), 3–143.

170. ". . . Oportet igitur Deum adesse omnibus rebus inquantum esse habent. Esse autem est id quod rebus omnibus intimius adest. Igitur oportet Deum in omnibus esse" (Thomas Aquinas, *Compendium theologiae* 1.130). ". . . Unde oportet quod Deus sit in omnibus rebus, et intime" (I.8.1 c). The far-reaching philosophical and theological consequences of a misunderstanding of being (*esse*) have been sketched by Marie-Joseph Le Guillou, *Das Mysterium des Vaters* (Einsiedeln: Johannes Verlag, 1974); Gustav Siewerth, *Das Schicksal der Metaphysik von Thomas zu Heidegger* (Einsiedeln: Johannes Verlag, 1959); and (first of all) Ulrich, *Homo abyssus*.

Aquinas sums all of this up in the metaphor of light. He compares *esse* with the light that shines through the multiple things of this creation. Even if we do not see the light directly, we can still see it within the colors of this world.[171] As the light comes from the sun, so *esse* flows from the ultimate source of all beings. As long as this flow continues, the beings remain.[172] And it is quite clear to Aquinas that the creatures do not receive the light in the same way as it exists in the sun.[173] But theirs is nevertheless a genuine participation.[174] Aquinas says that God causes created things *in one single flow, because he himself acts in accordance with the unity of his own being*, but this flow is received in different ways, according to the specific nature of each being. Here he uses the metaphor of the one light in different colors and interprets it—well noteworthy—as a communication "secundum rationem boni."[175] Aquinas confirms that difference comes not from *esse* but rather from the substance that receives *esse*.[176] With this statement he does not downgrade the importance of difference in any way but links it to God himself, who is the ultimate source of *forma* and *materia*. He also does not rule out the fact that the principles of *essentia* are part of *esse* itself, because nothing created can be outside *esse*.[177] But *essentia* presupposes intelligence, which means that *essentia* cannot be explained by nonsubsisting *esse* alone. The form is "sigillatio divinae scientiae in rebus,"[178] because God is the one who thought out the plurality of forms[179] in order to pour out his life into creation by the transmission of *esse*,[180] not in a Neoplatonic or Hegelian way, but in a gracious act of his Trinitarian freedom, which is not bound by any preset ideas.[181] He puts up and enacts the real difference between *esse* as received in substance and *essentia* by communicating *nonsubsisting* being (*esse*). The *essentia* in the concrete being proceeds from God *through* the nonsubsisting *esse*, which *as such* is flowed out into the concrete beings that are constituted by this flow.[182] In this flow, being (*esse rei*) results (!), so to speak, *from*

---

171. Thomas Aquinas, *Super Boetium De Trinitate* 1.3 ad 1.

172. "Sicut lumen causatur in aere a sole quandiu aer illuminatus manet. Quandiu igitur res habet esse, tandiu oportet quod Deus adsit ei, secundum modum quo habet esse" (I.8.1 c). *Compendium theologiae* 1.130.

173. "Sic autem se habet omnis creatura ad Deum, sicut aer ad solem illuminantem. Sicut enim sol est lucens per suam naturam, aer autem fit luminosus participando lumen a sole, non tamen participando naturem solis; ita solus Deus est ens per essentiam suam, quia eius essentia est suum esse; omnis autem creatura est ens participative" (I.104.1 c).

174. "Ipsa actualitas rei est quoddam lumen ipsius" (*Super librum De causis expositio* 6).

175. Ibid., 20.

176. "Non enim ab ipso esse sumitur differentia, sed magis ex habitudine ipsius substantiae ad esse" (Thomas Aquinas, *Qaestiones quodlibetales* 9.4.1 ad 4). See also *Summa contra gentiles* I.26; II.52.

177. "Nihil autem potest addi ad esse quod sit extraneum ab ipso, cum ab eo nihil sit extraneum nisi nonens, quod non potest esse nec forma nec materia" (*De potentia* 7.2 ad 9).

178. *De veritate* 2.1 ad 6.

179. For this plurality and the question of "possibilities" in God, see Martin Bieler, introduction to *Homo abyssus: Das Wagnis der Seinsfrage*, 2nd ed., by Ferdinand Ulrich (Einsiedeln: Johannes Verlag, 1998), xxviii–xxix (with further literature).

180. *In Librum Beati Dionysii De Divinis Nominibus* 2.3 (158).

181. "Et ideo magis ordo rerum refertur in voluntatem divinam quam in potentiam vel scientiam" (*De veritate* 23.2 ad 3).

182. Rudi A. te Velde rightly emphasizes that there is no double participation, "one according to which the essence has actual being, and another which accounts for the formal determination of the created essence in itself as a partial likeness of the divine essence." Velde, *Participation and Substantiality in Thomas Aquinas* (Paris: Beauchesne, 1945), 90. See Joseph de Finance, *Être et agir dans la philosophie de saint Thomas* (Paris: Beauchesne, 1945), 150: "L'esse est l'effet propre de Dieu, non sans doute en ce

below, "by the principles of the essence" ("*per principia essentiae*").[183] So *esse* is in itself the unity of oneness and multitude, unity and difference, richness (*completum et simplex*) and poverty (*non subsistens*), which represents as gift the fullness of God's *bonitas*.[184] In this unity, *esse* is not only the most common but also the most individual and intimate for all beings.[185] (It would be interesting to compare this with the Chinese Dao.) How should we explain this unity? Thank God it cannot be explained, but it can be discovered and "touched," as Plato would say. It is the "nothingness" of the fruitful love of God reflected in this unity that is totally unfavorable to any enclosure of the mystery of being and freedom into a Procrustes' bed. So genuine language (not split from silence), respecting this, catches a glimpse of the mirth of the One in whom our (seemingly) conflicting concepts with their limitations are redeemed.[186]

Philosophari in Maria

It is crucial to understand the nonsubsistence of being (*esse*) as an *aspect of perfection*, not just as a phase that has to be overcome in the subsistence of a concrete being.[187] In order to understand the full meaning of the communication of *esse*, it is important to view God not only as the *terminus a quo* of creation but also as its *terminus ad quem*. When Aquinas views the *tota substantia rei* as *terminus ad quem* of creation, he knows at the same time that every being is *for the sake of its action (propter suam operationem)*. In human beings this action takes on the form of a free response, and with this response as move toward God, a being is not only good in a certain sense (*bonum secundum quid*) but is understood to become just simply good (*bonum simpliciter*),[188] which of course is possible only by grace. Concrete subsistence is the pursuit

---

sens absurde que Dieu infuserait l'existence à des natures déjà réelles, mais en ce que l'essence est par lui posée dans l'être avec et par l'être qui l'actue"; and Ulrich, "Sein und Mitmensch," 116–17: "Hervorgang des Wesens aus dem Sein und Voraussetzung des Wesens für das Sein in seiner Verendlichung dürfen nicht geschieden werden."

183. "Esse enim rei quamvis sit aliud ab eius essentia, non tamen est intelligendum quod sit aliquod superadditum ad modum accidentis, sed quasi constituitur per principia essentiae. Et ideo hoc nomen Ens quod imponitur ab ipso esse, significat idem cum nomine quod imponitur ab ipsa essentia" (*In duodecim libros Metaphysicorum Aristotelis expositio* 4.2 [558]). "Et est actus entis resultans ex principiis rei" (Thomas Aquinas, *Scriptum super libros Sententiarum* III.6.2.2 c). This opens up the possibility for a philosophical understanding of evolution. See Bieler, *Freiheit als Gabe*, 307–17.

184. "There was multitude rerum et distinctio ab intellectu divino excogitata et instituta in rebus ad hoc quod diversimode divina bonitas a rebus creatis representetur" (*Compendium theologiae* 1.102). "Oportuit igitur esse multiplicitatem et varietatem in rebus creatis, ad hoc quod inveniretur in eis Dei similitudo perfecta secundum modum suum" (*Summa contra gentiles* II.45 [1220]).

185. "Cum ergo esse inveniatur omnibus rebus commune, quae secundum illud quod sunt, ad invicem distinctae sunt" (*De potentia* 3.5 c). "Ipsum enim esse est communissimus effectus primus et intimior omnibus aliis effectibus" (ibid., 3.7 c). "Das so verstandene Sein ist nicht mehr nur das esse commune, sondern es ist *als solches zugleich* auch das esse proprium." Inciarte, *Forma formarum*, 130.

186. "There was something that He covered constantly by abrupt silence or impetuous isolation. There was some one thing that was too great for God to show us when He walked upon our earth; and I have sometimes fancied that it was His mirth." Gilbert Keith Chesterton, *Orthodoxy* (New York: Image Books, 1959), 160. I read Ernstpeter Maurer's essay in this volume, "The Perplexity and Complexity of Sinful and Redeemed Reason," as a precise testimonial for this mirth.

187. See Martin Bieler, "Freiheit und Schöpfung bei Gustav Siewerth," in *Gott für die Welt: Henri de Lubac, Gustav Siewerth, und Hans Urs von Balthasar in ihren Grundanliegen: Festschrift für Walter Seidel*, ed. Peter Reifenberg and Anton von Hooff (Mainz: Matthias Grünewald, 2001), 231–45.

188. *De veritate* 21.5.

of the source of all *esse* and therefore a process of perfection in the sense of *bonum simpliciter.*[189] The communication of *esse* aims at the free loving response of human beings, not only toward God but also toward each other. Aquinas takes up this subject matter with the term *convenientia*. The central article *De veritate* 1.1 states that the human soul, which is in a certain way everything ("quae quodammodo est omnia, sicut dicitur in III de Anima"), is that which is apt to come together with every being ("convenire cum omni ente"). But all other things are also fit for *convenientia* rather than for repulsion of others.[190] The term *convenientia* in *De veritate* 1.1 c refers to *verum* and *bonum*, that is, to *ratio* and *voluntas*, the two pillars of human freedom.[191] Successful *convenientia* on the level of human beings is conscious love carried by the power of divine peace that lets human beings grow together with others and—by the same token—be themselves.[192] Here again we have the unity between unity and difference. The *convenientia* of free loving persons is the essence of beauty in our world.[193]

The human being who truly loves represents explicitly the meaning of *esse*, the *similitudo divinae bonitatis*, because in him or her the intention of the communication of *esse* breaks through. As a "completum et per se subsistens in natura rationali,"[194] something unlimited in a limited nature, the human person bears witness to the meaning of the "completum et simplex sed non subsistens" as a gift of the love of the "ipsum esse subsistens."[195]

Creation is an act of love that aims at love. It is God's love that keeps creatures moving,[196] for the continual communication of *esse* makes history possible but also necessary. God's intent in creating the world is the friendship between God and human beings. It is inside this relationship that the communication of *esse* and the meaning of *esse* has to be understood. This shows that the ontological difference between *esse* and *ens* is a *dialogical* difference with far-reaching consequences for anthropology.[197] The recipient of *esse* ("proprium susceptivum eius quod est esse") that makes the meaning of *esse* apparent for us is another loving human being accepting us—in accepting the gift of God.

Mary is the figure of the church by receiving the gift of God par excellence: Christ. Therefore, the encyclical emphasizes the *philosophari in Maria*. Mary is the model for the reception of grace by nature, a model that owes itself to

---

189. "Omnia, inquantum sunt, tendunt in Dei similitudinem, qui est ipsum esse" (II-II.34.1 ad 3).

190. "Ens, inquantum ens, non habet rationem repugnantis, sed magis convenientis: quia omnia conveniunt in ente" (I-II.29.1 ad 1).

191. "Radix libertatis est voluntas sicut subiectum: sed sicut causa, est ratio" (I-II.17.1 ad 2).

192. "Divina pax facit omnia ad se invicem concreta: nihil enim est in rebus quod non habeat cum aliquo alio unionem, vel per convenientiam in specie, vel in genere, vel in aliquo quocumque ordine. Sed quia haec unitio, distinctiones rerum non tollit, ideo dicit quod est inconfusa" (*In Librum Beati Dionysii De Divinis Nominibus* 11.2 [901]).

193. Günther Pöltner, *Schönheit: Eine Untersuchung zum Ursprung des Denkens bei Thomas von Aquin* (Freiburg: Herder, 1978).

194. III.16.12 ad 3.

195. I.4.2 ad 3.

196. See Jan Aertsen, *Nature and Creature: Thomas Aquinas's Way of Thought* (Leiden: E. J. Brill, 1988).

197. See esp. Ulrich, *Homo abyssus*.

the prototype of every kind of reception.[198] The mystical tradition has seen Mary in her receptive role (which has a most fruitful result) as the unity of poverty and wealth by meditating upon her being at the same time virgin (poverty) and woman (wealth).[199] In this unity, in which poverty is a *rich* poverty, she represents the unity of the *completum et simplex* (wealth) and the *non subsistens* (poverty) of *esse*. As figure of the church, who receives God's gift, she stands for the *uterus spiritualis*[200] every growing child needs in order to fully realize the meaning of the gift of being.

Philosophari in Maria can mean in a first step to understand everything in this world to be in its innermost structure a gift of God that carries Christ himself. The whole world as creation appears then as structured by the logic of God's self-giving. Philosophy is then in the service of seeking and finding God in all things (Meister Eckhart, Ignatius of Loyola). In a further step, *philosophari in Maria* can mean that we are drawn with Mary into following the suffering Christ. Philosophy participates then in a theology of substitutionary atonement,[201] which seeks the reconciliation of human freedom living in alienation. In this endeavor the forms of alienation, which go along with sin, are criticized not from the outside but in exercising a "metaphysics in repetition,"[202] which is ready to get in touch with the fears and hopes of the other and to listen for an answer *from there*. That act is the philosophical carrying of the other's burdens by not forgetting our own burdens (Gal 6:2–5), a special kind of learning that leads to unexpected horizons. It is an act in which not a theory but the philosophical *aletheuein en agape* (Eph 4:15) itself is the critique of ideology.[203]

I would like to show with an example in what direction the contribution of the above outlined philosophy of being for a theology of substitutionary atonement could go. (Other case studies of, for example, sociological nature would be possible.) I mentioned the necessity of a *uterus spiritualis* for the child in order to receive his or her own being as a gift. The science that has dealt most with the difficulties associated with this reception, which remains the task of our life,[204] is psychology. From the core of Aquinas's metaphysics could arise a new dialogue between theology, philosophy, and psychology.

---

198. "*Accipere* dicitur esse commune creaturae et Filio, non secundum univocationem, sed secundum similitudinem quandam remotam, ratione cuius dicitur *primogenitus creaturae*" (I.33.3 ad 2).

199. Meister Eckhart, *Deutsche Predigten und Traktate*, ed. and trans. Josef Quint (Munich: Carl Hanser, 1963), 159ff.

200. II-II.10.12 c.

201. Recent literature for the biblical background of substitutionary atonement includes Martin Hengel, *The Atonement: The Origins of the Doctrine in the New Testament* (London: SCM Press, 1981); Bernd Janowski, *Stellvertretung: Alttestamentliche Studien zu einem theologischen Grundbegriff* (Stuttgart: Katholisches Bibelwerk, 1997); Martin Gaukesbrink, *Die Sühnetradition bei Paulus: Rezeption und theologischer Stellenwert* (Würzburg: Echter, 1999); Thomas Knöppler, *Sühne im Neuen Testament: Studien zum urchristlichen Verständnis der Heilsbedeutung des Todes Jesu* (Neukirchen-Vluyn: Neukirchener Verlag, 2001); and Günter Röhser, *Stellvertretung im Neuen Testament* (Stuttgart: Katholisches Bibelwerk, 2002).

202. Ferdinand Ulrich, "Das Problem einer 'Metaphysik in der Wiederholung,'" *Salzburger Jahrbuch für Philosophie 5/6* (1961/62): 263–98.

203. Ferdinand Ulrich, "Der philosophische Akt als Ideologiekritik," in *Ideologia e filosofia* (Brescia: Morcelliana, 1967), 328–58.

204. Ferdinand Ulrich, *Der Mensch als Anfang: Zur philosophischen Anthropologie der Kindheit* (Einsiedeln: Johannes Verlag, 1970).

First steps in this direction have already been made by Ferdinand Ulrich, who refers several times to the provocative yet thoughtful book *Life against Death* by Norman O. Brown (1959). Brown offers in his book a critical relecture of Sigmund Freud that shows that much of what Freud discovered makes more sense than even Freud himself realized.[205] Ulrich for his part offers with his relecture of Brown in *Leben in der Einheit von Leben und Tod* an instructive example of what such a renewed dialogue could look like.

Brown starts his presentation of psychoanalysis with a discussion of the notion of repression. The unconscious that Freud addressed stems from repression.[206] Our pursuit of pleasure meets the resistance of reality. In order to avoid the consequences of an unbroken pursuit of pleasure, the reality principle leads the pleasure principle on a detour that may end from the side of the reality principle in a permanent dead end (repression). But the unstopped pursuit of pleasure leads to the search for further fulfillment. According to Brown, that is how history, with its tremendous dynamics of cultural developments and its insatiability, starts.[207] At the beginning stands the pursuit of pleasure carried by the sexual instinct in the broad sense Freud understands it:

> Freud's definition of the sexual instinct shows that he means something very general. It is the energy or desire with which the human being pursues pleasure, with the further specification that the pleasure sought is the pleasurable activity of an organ of the human body. He attributed the capacity of yielding such pleasure (an erotogenic quality, he calls it) to all parts of the surface of the human body and also to the internal organs.[208]

In children this energy is at first equally distributed to all parts of the body. We may say that children in this state of being "polymorphously perverse" (in the sense of being perverted from the fixation to the genital)[209] are completely one with their own bodies as well as with the world.[210] They are, so to speak, flowed out into their bodies and with that into the world. According to Brown, Freud views this as "the pattern of our deepest desires."[211] The

---

205. "But even Freud is not enough. . . . Rigorous probing reveals that the entire metapsychological foundations of psychoanalysis need reinterpretation." Norman O. Brown, *Life against Death: The Psychoanalytical Meaning of History* (New York: Vintage Books, 1959), xii. I am well aware of the critique brought forward against Freud by Frederick Crews, *The Memory Wars: Freud's Legacy in Dispute* (New York: New York Review of Books, 1995), pointed out to me by David Hart; Malcolm Macmillan, *Freud Evaluated: The Completed Arc* (Cambridge, MA: MIT Press, 1997); and Richard Webster, *Why Freud Was Wrong: Sin, Science, and Psychoanalysis* (New York: Basic Books, 1995). Especially Macmillan shows that Freud erred in too many cases. But even though Freud's answers do not satisfy, the field of exploration he opened and the stimulus he gave still make him an outstanding pioneer in psychology.

206. Brown, *Life against Death*, 5. The fundamental importance of repression for Freud's psychology is best viewed in his *Studienausgabe II: Die Traumdeutung*, ed. Alexander Mitscherlich, Angela Richards, and James Strachey, (Frankfurt: Fischer, 2000). For a critical and constructive discussion of Freud's dream theory, see Dieter Wyss, *Traumbewusstsein? Grundzüge einer Ontologie des Traumbewusstseins* (Göttingen: Vandenhoeck & Ruprecht, 1988).

207. Brown, *Life against Death*, 9–19, 92ff.

208. Ibid., 25–26.

209. Ibid., 27.

210. Ibid., 42ff.

211. Ibid., 30. That this state should not be confined to egocentrism has been shown by Augustinus Karl Wucherer-Huldenfeld, "Schwierigkeiten mit der narzisstischen Selbstliebe in Freuds Metapsychologie,"

character of activity that corresponds to this state is play, in which the child experiences the surrounding powers as supportive, not as constraining.[212] Brown wants to understand all of this in further developing Freud also in Christian terms—referring for this purpose to Martin Luther.[213] And he sees this "pre-ambivalent stage in infancy" standing in opposition to Freud's dualistic instinct theory, which posits a life and a death instinct.[214] For Brown the possibility of redemption of human existence "lies in the reunification of the instinctual opposites." Thus, he asks the decisive question: "How can Life and Death be unified?"[215] But why should they be unified?

According to Freud, death is an innate part of life. If this is true, then flight from death is the root of the basic problem of human existence.[216] "At the human level, the repressed death instinct cannot affirm life by affirming death; life, being repressed, cannot affirm death and therefore must fly from death."[217] Death belongs to life because birth means separation: "And explicitly Freud's theory of anxiety brings birth and death together as separation crises. Freud is thus moving toward a structural analysis of organic life as being constituted by a dialectic between unification or interdependence and separation or independence."[218] Death and birth are so closely related because birth not only sets an organism on the road to death but also means for the child "a biological separation from the mother conferring biological individuality on the child."[219] The response to the "experiences of separateness, individuality, and death" is anxiety. The child growing up in the *uterus spiritualis* of the family experiences a further necessity for separation and again wants to avoid the pain associated with it.[220] For Brown the development of the different stages of the child's bodily organization (oral, anal, phallic) that Freud described in his groundbreaking "Drei Abhandlungen zur Sexualtheorie" (1905)[221] are driven by the wish to revoke the child's birth by gaining control *over* the body instead of being this finite body.[222] It is basically oriented toward the past and initiates at the same time a restless run into the future. The *presence* of freedom is lost and with it the possibility of *Gelassenheit*.[223]

---

in *Theologie im Dialog mit Freud und seiner Wirkungsgeschichte*, ed. Kurt Lüthi and Koloman N. Micskey (Vienna: Böhlau, 1991), 129–67.

212. Brown, *Life against Death*, 32ff.
213. Ibid., 49.
214. Ibid., 84–85.
215. Ibid., 86.
216. Ibid., 100.
217. Ibid., 103.
218. Ibid., 105.
219. Ibid., 114.
220. Ibid., 115–16.
221. Sigmund Freud, *Studienausgabe V: Sexualleben*, ed. Alexander Mitscherlich, Angela Richards, and James Strachey (Frankfurt: Fischer, 2000), 37–145. For a recent adaptation of this theory, see Günter H. Seidler, *Der Blick des Anderen: Eine Analyse der Scham: Mit einem Geleitwort von Léon Wurmser und einem Vorwort von Otto F. Kernberg*, 2nd ed. (Stuttgart: Klett-Cotta, 2001), 126–228.
222. Brown, *Life against Death*, 116ff. A different reading of this development is given by Erich Neumann, who emphasizes justly: "Eine der wesentlichen Entwicklungs-Schwierigkeiten und-Notwendigkeiten des Kindes besteht darin, dass es als Ich erst allmählich in die abgeschlossene individuelle Einmaligkeit seines eigenen Körpers hineinwandern muss." *Das Kind: Struktur und Dynamik der werdenden Persönlichkeit* (Frankfurt: Fischer, 1999), 29–30. That is part of the birth, too, and therefore inevitable! Yet it does not exclude Brown's observation of a connection between the bodily development of the child and the attempt to reject death.
223. Ferdinand Ulrich, *Gegenwart der Freiheit* (Einsiedeln: Johannes Verlag, 1974).

The "Oedipal project," which was so essential to Freud, is in this perspective "not, as Freud's earlier formulations suggest, a natural love of the mother" but "the project of becoming God . . . , the fantasy of becoming father of oneself," the attempt to create paradise by oneself.[224] So the Oedipus complex implies aggressiveness against the parents on whom the child depends, "irrespective of how the parents behave," because the parents stand as such in the way of the child's project.[225] This aggressive nature of the complex explains the guilt and the fear (castration as loss of the means to cope with the original state of pleasure) attached to it.[226] Furthermore, the basic character of the complex shows that it is in principle independent of a concrete father figure.[227]

The rejected death comes back in the form of the death instinct Freud described, which now shows in its separation from life an aggressive and destructive face. But also the pleasure principle is in this separation a form of alienation: "The destruction of the biological unity of life and death transforms the Nirvana-principle into the pleasure-principle, transforms the repetition-compulsion into a fixation to the infantile past, and transforms the death instinct into an aggressive principle of negativity."[228] The unity of life and death is broken by the *refusal to be born and to be separated from the mother.* The child does not want to bear the risk of separation and therefore excludes the death of separation from life, which turns into boredom and dullness.[229] The succession of the child's primordial being flowed out in the body by a next stage of positive renunciation is hindered by this refusal, and the child pays for it with the inability to live the authentic responsible life that Kierkegaard meant when he spoke of the particular existing human being. Apparently the development of the child is not just a disaster. It certainly has positive aspects, but it is infected by the destruction of the unity of life and death, by what appears from a Christian perspective to be original sin.

The unity of life and death described by Brown is transparent to the unity of the *completum et simplex* ("life") and the *non subsistens* ("death") of being (*esse*) as *similitudo divinae bonitatis*, which is represented in the *convenientia* of loving human beings,[230] but also to the biblical theme of the unity

---

224. Brown, *Life against Death*, 118.
225. Ibid., 120.
226. Ibid., 122ff.
227. Ibid., 122.
228. Ibid., 104.
229. Ulrich, *Leben in der Einheit von Leben und Tod*, 7ff., 80ff.
230. "Durch die Dialektik von Lebenstrieb und Todestrieb hat Freud (wenn auch entstellt) den Austrag dessen, was wir die 'Verendlichung des Seins als Liebe' nennen, gleichsam 'somatisiert,' als Grundgestalt alles Lebendigen aufgedeckt. Eros fasst das Organische zu immer grösserer Einheit zusammen und entbirgt dadurch das in der Vielfalt des materiell Seienden entäusserte, aber *in seiner* Kenosis als überwesenhafte Fülle des *Lebens jenseits* seiner Kenosis erreichbar wird, sondern nur dort bejaht und als 'Leben' enthüllt ist, wo der Mensch in seine Verendlichung, d.h. in seinen Tod einstimmt; nicht an-sich-hält und in 'ungetrübter Einfachheit' verharrt, vielmehr den Anderen, das Du und die Welt, aufgrund seines *Seins* als weggeschenkte *Gabe*, sich zum Schicksal werden lässt, in der gesteigerten 'Spannung gegen' den Tod zugleich selbst-'los' entspannt ist." Ulrich, *Leben in der Einheit von Leben und Tod*, 254–55. For similarities and differences between Aquinas and Freud, see Stephan H. Pfürtner, *Triebleben*

of cross and resurrection. By receiving being as a gift, a person receives with it the intact unity of life and death. This unity of life and death is an imprint of the logic of gift; the one who gives separates the gift from himself or herself toward the other, and the other accepts this separation gratefully. This is the positive "death" of separation, viewed from two sides (giver and receiver). But this separation is positive only because exactly *through* this separation the giver becomes *present* in the gift, gives his or her life in and with the gift. And the receiver in return accepts the presence of this life *in* the gift. This is the positive "life" of presence, also viewed from two sides.[231] These four aspects of the unity of life and death correspond to basic traits of Aquinas's metaphysics[232] and—from the negative side of brokenness—to the four forms of despair Kierkegaard described in *The Sickness unto Death*.[233]

In the "necessary" (original sin)[234] refusal to receive one's own being, this unity is broken. But because this unity corresponds to the innermost nature of a human being, everyone who "loses" it is forced to get it back and to build it anew by gaining control over it. As Kierkegaard formulated it, this is then the attempt "to begin a little earlier than do other men, not at and with the beginning, but 'in the beginning.'" Instead of seeing "his given self as his task—he himself wants to compose his self."[235] This stabilizes the refusal to receive and makes the case even worse. In this state of despair the original unity of life and death is imitated by artificially reintroducing the missing pieces of the lost unity (e.g., the infinity broken away from finity, as Kierkegaard described it, or the rejected death described by Brown) into the damaged self. But that means, for example, mixing resignation (perverted poverty) with hubris (perverted wealth), because the original unity, in which the "pieces" are friendly aspects of the whole, is lost. The self is not healed in this way but further damaged because it stays basically on the same track and makes just another turn in the refusal to receive itself. In this turmoil the self appears less and less as something good, which can be received and accepted. So one attempt to create the self prepares the next breakdown, which in turn necessitates another attempt.

Reaching a human being in his or her loneliness and isolation caused by such continued damage of the self is possible only if another being understands—in some way or another[236]—how this damage takes place and carries the despair associated with it by "becoming" the other in acceptance.[237] The core

---

und sittliche Vollendung: Eine moralpsychologische Untersuchung nach Thomas von Aquin (Freiburg, Switzerland: Universitätsverlag, 1958); and M. G. Cottier, "'Libido' bei Freud und 'appetitus' bei Thomas von Aquin," in Norbert A. Luyten, *Das Menschenverständnis nach Thomas von Aquin* (Freiburg, Switzerland: Universitätsverlag, 1976), 59–82.

231. Ulrich, *Leben in der Einheit von Leben und Tod*, 70–72.

232. Bieler, *Freiheit als Gabe*, 271ff.

233. Søren Kierkegaard, *The Sickness unto Death: A Christian Psychological Exposition for Upbuilding and Awakening*, ed. and trans. Howard V. Hong and Edna H. Hong (Princeton, NJ: Princeton University Press, 1980), 29–42.

234. See Bieler, *Freiheit als Gabe*, 222–25, 321–23; and *Befreiung der Freiheit*, 76–90.

235. Kierkegaard, *Sickness unto Death*, 68.

236. This has much to do with the atmospherical in relationships. See Hubertus Tellenbach, *Geschmack und Atmosphäre: Medien menschlichen Elementarkontaktes* (Salzburg: Otto Müller, 1968).

237. "Amor dicitur transformare amantem in amatum, in quantum per amorem movetur amans ad ipsam rem amatam" (Thomas Aquinas, *De malo* 6.1 ad 13).

of substitutionary atonement is Christ's accepting identification with us (which sets *in* that a positive *difference* between him and us)[238] in an unsurpassable manner. Therefore, our life is hidden with Christ in God (Col 3:3)—*extra nos*—and at the same time it is *in* us, for Christ lives in us (Gal 2:20). By carrying the other's burden we help each other find out about this *foreign* truth of ourselves, which is closer to us than our innermost selves.[239] The service rendered to each other in this way is the mutual support in reconnecting with our original-new true selves and in being taken out of the vicious circle of freedom's captivity into a unity in which the splintered pieces of our existence fit together "by themselves."[240]

It is the one decision of receiving or not receiving one's being as a gift that forms the concrete worldview of a human being, which deals in principle with everything affected by the unity of the *completum et simplex* and the *non subsistens* of being (*esse*)—with the whole realm of creation. Ulrich has shown in detail how this very simple decision and the temptations associated with it shape all kinds of most difficult worldviews. Every human being repeats (in the sense Kierkegaard used the term repetition) in a very personal way the communication of being (*esse*) by dealing with his or her own being in relation to others and the world. The way we receive our being shapes the way we "put it in action" toward others. If, for example, someone experiences his *esse* being handed over to him as something powerful yet not respected, he will produce a tremendous impact on the world in order to find acceptance for himself and others—with all the opportunities and dangers implied in that. If we want to understand how another person exists in this world, what worries her, what interests him, we have to ask how that person experiences and lives the communication of being. Grace coming "on the way of being" means in this respect more than just God becoming a human being. It means God coming—incarnate—into the communication of being and its repetition that every one of us experiences and lives in his or her special way. It means God becoming involved in our stories by standing on our side. In this way happens the *re-creatio*, the reconciliation that Christ himself is.

It is very instructive to see how from this point of view seemingly abstract Thomistic themes such as the relationship between *esse* and *essentia* become transparent to the personal-dialogical event of communication and are in this way apt to enlighten psychological problems that would remain otherwise inaccessible in their deeper meaning. By treating this theme in different contexts, Ulrich offers impressive means for a better understanding of suffering freedom.[241] The question may be asked whether it would not be fruitful for

---

238. Bieler, *Befreiung der Freiheit*, 398ff.

239. See the essays in this volume of Lois Malcolm, "The Wisdom of the Cross," and Mark McIntosh, "Faith, Reason, and the Mind of Christ."

240. See Ferdinand Ulrich, "Sprache der Begierde und Zeitgestalten des Idols," in *Phänomenologie des Idols*, ed. Bernhard Casper (Freiburg: Karl Alber, 1981), 133–269.

241. See, e.g., Ulrich's interpretations of fairy tales as narratives of the becoming self by philosophical means. Ulrich, *Erzählter Sinn: Ontologie der Selbstwerdung in der Bilderwelt des Märchens*, 2nd ed. (Freiburg: Johannes Verlag Einsiedeln, 2002).

psychology to take notice of this approach. Ludwig Binswanger developed his psychology by taking up thoughts of Husserl and Heidegger—with respectable results.[242] Why not try something similar with a renewed metaphysics inspired by Aquinas and Kierkegaard (who is also mentioned in the encyclical [76])?[243] The results would be even more promising.

Ulrich's approach helps clarify what decisions are at stake in particular human situations. It also helps clarify how the "directedness of reasoning"

---

242. For Binswanger's philosophical background, see Ludwig Binswanger, *Ausgewählte Werke II: Grundformen und Erkenntnis menschlichen Daseins*, ed. Max Herzog and Hans-Jürg Braun (Heidelberg: Roland Asanger, 1993).

243. See Bieler, *Freiheit als Gabe*, 106–38, 276–97. It may seem awkward to link Kierkegaard with Aquinas, but a closer look at both shows how justified is a dialogue between them. To stimulate such a dialogue is the merit of John J. Davenport, even though his view of Aquinas needs further clarification: "Towards an Existential Virtue Ethics: Kierkegaard and MacIntyre," in *Kierkegaard after MacIntyre: Essays on Freedom, Narrative, and Virtue*, ed. John J. Davenport and Anthony Rudd (Chicago: Open Court, 2001), 265–323.

What brings Aquinas and Kierkegaard together is their emphasis on the givenness of human freedom, which leads to a specific kind of ontology. (Taking into consideration not only Kierkegaard's decisive theological background but also his preoccupation with the Aristotelian Adolf Trendelenburg and with Plato, it should not be too surprising that Aquinas and Kierkegaard are in their basic convictions compatible. Maybe also Franz Xaver von Baader with his emphasis on "gift" is [in a hidden way] a link between Aquinas and Kierkegaard.) Kierkegaard also has an ontology centered in the givenness of the human self: "The focal point of his ontology is a single phenomenon: the 'givenness' of my total existence and of my potentiality as human self in particular." Arnold B. Come, "Kierkegaard's Ontology of Love," *International Kierkegaard Commentary XVI: Works of Love*, ed. Robert L. Perkins (Macon, GA: Mercer University Press, 1999), 89. His ontology culminates in the assertion that a human being cannot find himself without relating to God. "It is Kierkegaard's clear meaning that the two acts of relating, 'to itself' and 'to another,' are inseparable. One cannot do the one without doing the other simultaneously. In other words, his anthropological ontology integrally includes a 'religious' dimension." Arnold B. Come, *Kierkegaard as Humanist: Discovering My Self* (Montreal: McGill-Queen's University Press, 1995), 11–12. (See Kierkegaard, *Sickness unto Death*, 13–14.) Come sees from there three mysteries set by the givenness (creation) of the human self: "Firstly, givenness posits my own being as a unique-identity of eternal validity and dignity. I must love my self. Secondly, this identity is grounded in and flows from a connection (unity, kinship) with an eternal, unfathomable, inexhaustible, and continuing source. I must love God. Thirdly, this eternal source is present in me in such a way that it demands that I recognize and affirm this same validity and dignity in every other human being. I must love my neighbor." Come, "Kierkegaard's Ontology of Love," 91–92. Hans Urs von Balthasar mentions in other words and in slightly different orientation the same three points as the core of an ontology of finite freedom that is in accordance with Aquinas and modern personalism: Balthasar, *Theodramatik II.2: Die Personen des Spiels: Die Personen in Christus* (Einsiedeln: Johannes Verlag, 1978), 421–22.

But how is this ontology of Kierkegaard grounded in metaphysics? In his splendid book *Kierkegaard as Humanist*, Come gives a convincing account of Kierkegaard's view of the "religiousness A" that is in many ways parallel to what, according to Aquinas, a philosopher enlightened by God's grace can know by philosophical means. But Kierkegaard also unfolds the "religiousness B" (Christianity) that heals and fulfills human freedom. (For Kierkegaard as theologian, see the fine discussion of Kierkegaard in Alan J. Torrance's essay in this volume, "*Auditus Fidei*: Where and How Does God Speak? Faith, Reason, and the Question of Criteria.") On these common grounds Aquinas and Kierkegaard could contribute to a new kind of metaphysics in a complementary way. Whereas Aquinas is certainly much more extensive and comprehensive in his development of basic ontological categories, Kierkegaard helps us ponder the psychological, ethical, and existential relevance of these categories. When, e.g., Robert Pasnau grants Aquinas the honor of having developed a theory that solves (his word) the body-mind problem (*Thomas Aquinas on Human Nature: A Philosophical Study of Summa theologiae 1a, 75–89* [Cambridge: Cambridge University Press, 2002], 140), we would search in vain for a similar achievement in Kierkegaard's writings. But we can learn a lot from him about what it means for us to exist as a synthesis of the psychical and the physical. With Aquinas can be shown how the whole creation is structured by the gift-character of being (*esse*); with Kierkegaard, how this becomes relevant in the concrete act of freedom of the individual. Both help make transparent traditional metaphysical themes to the phenomenon of self-giving love.

That Kierkegaard was much more of a dialogical and social thinker than much of the secondary literature on him concedes has been shown (besides Come) by Bruce H. Kirmmse, *Kierkegaard in Golden-Age Denmark* (Bloomington: Indiana University Press, 1990]); and Bruce H. Kirmmse, ed., *Encounters with Kierkegaard: A Life as Seen by His Contemporaries* (Princeton, NJ: Princeton University Press, 1996). See also the important remarks made by Joachim Ringleben, *Die Krankheit zum Tode von Sören Kierkegaard: Erklärung und Kommentar* (Göttingen: Vandenhoeck & Ruprecht, 1995), 280.

(Reinhard Hütter) is involved in philosophical questions. If we want to communicate as theologians how the liberation of freedom means for every human being a different story, because every one of us is wanted by God as this particular being, and how it is at the same time a story that unites all of us, we can count on the practice as well as the insights related to a renewed philosophy of being.

CHAPTER THIRTEEN

Duplex Ordo Cognitionis

— Romanus Cessario, OP —

General Principles

Let me remark first on the general philosophical instruction that many students receive in theological courses of study. Pope John Paul II has called philosophy one of the noblest of human tasks, and reminds us that its study is fundamental and indispensable to the structure of theological studies and to the formation of ministers of religion and, especially, of priests. It has been my experience, however, that many theological students in seminaries and elsewhere come to their theology lessons without a firm grasp of the basic philosophical categories that remain indispensable for the study of Catholic doctrine. Indeed, the almost exclusive employment of the historical method impedes the students from recognizing how "logic, the philosophy of language, epistemology, the philosophy of nature, anthropology," and metaphysics are vital to the various branches of theology (see *Fides et Ratio*, no. 91). The need for philosophy within theology is not merely historical, but genuinely systematic and methodic, implying that authentic philosophy in the Catholic tradition ought to be a constitutive element of all theological formation.

Too frequently philosophy is treated in one of two ways. The first is as a mere generic category fillable by any "credits" in the field whatsoever, irrespective of the tradition of thought that is represented by the instruction received. This obviously implies a view of philosophy as naturally either syncretistic or agnostic. Alternately, the Catholic tradition of philosophizing often is reductively interpreted in a merely historical way—as though what were important about the Catholic philosophical tradition were merely its material role in the developments of the past, and not its formal and essential mediative function within life and theology as a whole. The point is not that historical engagement is harmful per se, but that it neither is nor can be a substitute for the speculative integrity required in philosophy and theology.

Realist philosophy and metaphysics provide an absolutely indispensable foundation for the appropriation of sacred truth and in the development of both systematic and moral theology. Yet often theologians lack a basic philosophical formation, even about what would be required to attain a thorough and accurate knowledge of the *Catechism of the Catholic Church*. The main philosophical concepts of nature, person, being, substance, matter and form, cause, end or finality, relation, soul, wisdom, virtue, vice, and so forth remain, I surmise, foreign to the majority of Christian theologians.

In order to supply theologians with the kind of formation required for the work of evangelization, professors of philosophy must offer a complete formation in the Catholic tradition. Among them should not be found those who, because they want to explore new paths for scholarship, "simply deny the universal value of the Church's philosophical heritage" (*Fides et Ratio*, no. 69). Indeed, it would not seem too much to ask that the professors of philosophy who teach theological students exemplify what Pope John Paul II recalls as characteristic of the best tradition in Catholic intellectual life: *philosophari in Maria*.

Three quotations of Pope John Paul II from *Fides et Ratio* help to underscore the proper role of philosophy within theological instruction, and so help us better understand the *duplex ordo cognitionis*. *Fides et Ratio* affirms

> the need for a philosophy of genuinely metaphysical range, capable, that is, of transcending empirical data in order to attain something absolute, ultimate and foundational in its search for truth. This requirement is implicit in sapiential and analytical knowledge alike; and in particular it is a requirement for knowing the moral good, which has its ultimate foundation in the Supreme Good, God himself. (no. 83)

The importance of metaphysics for moral theology is clearly underscored here. The classical formulation for this insight is that in order for practical truth to be conformed to right appetite, right appetite must first be engendered through knowledge of the end.[1] Such knowledge is in essence speculative while through extension becoming practical. Lacking the transcendent metaphysical dimensions of human knowledge, the truth that the natural law participates the eternal law itself ceases to be knowable. Pope John Paul II teaches further that

> the word of God refers constantly to things which transcend human experience and even human thought; but this "mystery" could not be revealed, nor could theology render it in some way intelligible, were human knowledge limited strictly to the world of sense experience. Metaphysics thus plays an essential role of mediation in theological

---

1. Of course, the end is known both through nature and by grace, as the order of nature is further ordered to the beatific end. But precisely for this reason, because grace works through nature, the natural order of ends must be known, and the mode of access to the order of ends is not solely through revelation but necessarily through natural reason.

research. A theology without a metaphysical horizon could not move beyond an analysis of religious experience, nor would it allow the *intellectus fidei* to give a coherent account of the universal and transcendent value of revealed truth.

If I insist so strongly on the metaphysical element, it is because I am convinced that it is the path to be taken in order to move beyond the crisis pervading large sectors of philosophy at the moment, and thus to correct certain mistaken modes of behaviour now widespread in our society. (no. 83)

The mediative role of philosophy within theology is irreplaceable. The basic principles, structure, and transcendent origin of created being are philosophical elements presupposed by the message of the gospel. These "preambles of faith" are essential to the intelligibility and communicability of the deposit of faith as such. For this reason, fideism or indifference to philosophical education does integral harm to the theological project. The tendency either to reduce the Catholic philosophical tradition to mere historical appreciation of medieval thought or to deny it any normative systematic role within theology implicitly relegates the act of faith to the sphere of a merely contingent "religious experience" too easily relativized and treated according to naturalistic methods. It was precisely to counter these tendencies that *Dominus Iesus* was issued, and one may see the same essential problematic formally presented in the teachings of *Fides et Ratio* here cited, as also in *Evangelium vitae* and *Veritatis splendor*.

The third point specifically insisted upon in *Fides et Ratio* stresses the need for *realist* philosophy:

> . . . that philosophy verify the human capacity to know the truth, to come to a knowledge which can reach objective truth by means of that *adaequatio rei et intellectus* to which the Scholastic Doctors referred. This requirement, proper to faith, was explicitly reaffirmed by the Second Vatican Council: "Intelligence is not confined to observable data alone. It can with genuine certitude attain to reality itself as knowable, though in consequence of sin that certitude is partially obscured and weakened." (no. 82)

The need for realism, for an account of the human person's primal intellectual contact with reality, is paramount. Especially given the widespread and various forms of postmodern nihilism, deconstruction, and relativism, it is important to vindicate the authentically first principles of being and knowledge.[2] This is an essential dimension of the position of the church in the world at the beginning of Christianity's third millennium. If nothing can be known

---

2. By vindicating the authentic principles of being, of course, one intends two things: negatively, the reduction to absurdity of the denial of these normative principles and the manifestation of the disorder which their loss causes to ensue; positively and primarily, the development of these principles and the progressive synthesis of these principles with all that the evidence of being, and of the lesser sciences, provide.

of reality, then neither moral responsibility nor the reality of God nor the testimony of the apostles will or can be credited. This is an issue of vindicating the knowledge of being as such, and hence of exposing students to the nature and importance of metaphysical objectivity. As the Holy Father suggests, this is a privileged moment for anthropology itself, in which the natural rudiments of the dignity of the person become apparent.

The negation of metaphysical objectivity that is fashionable today defines and implies certain "mistaken modes of behaviour now widespread in our society." Only metaphysical truth and the vindication of metaphysical objectivity[3] implicit therein are adequate to correct these errors. It follows that this must constitute an essential element in theological formation. Yet skepticism about the reliability and importance of metaphysical knowledge is widespread not only in contemporary secular society, but it also at times permeates theological method itself. Often it is proposed that the fall has so undermined the epistemic reliability of human reason as to vitiate the capacity to know absolutely. It is thought that one may somehow "bracket" the issue of metaphysical objectivity and then continue to use reason within theological discourse as though truth and logic were sufficiently addressed merely by pointing at the data of revelation and subsequently interpreting it according to any given categories whatsoever. One cannot avoid the realization that this utterly undermines and is contrary to the very nature of the doctrine of the faith, because it implies that the Word spoken by God and revealed to us in the person of Jesus Christ is one whose transcendent truth is not meant to be affirmed by the human mind. Frankly, what is it that the Second Person of the Trinity assumed if not human nature? And if human nature is unintelligible in its own right, what possible sense can be given to the doctrine of the incarnation of the Word? If being is unintelligible, then the revelation of God—who is perfect being—will be perfectly unintelligible.

Thomas Aquinas employs a masterful principle, which may be summarized in this way: that every negation presupposes a prior affirmation. In *De potentia* q. 7, a. 5, he writes, "The understanding of negations is always based on affirmations, as is manifest by the rule of proving one by the other." The negation of the mind's primal openness to and contact with reality is a negation for which no proportionate affirmative evidence either exists or ever could be found. Any proportionate evidence, whether physical, conceptual, or even mystical would, in some way, *be,* and as such constitute a knowable reality. But one must proceed further to reach the actual roots of such fideist irrationalism. If it is said that the mind's contact with reality is prohibited by a priori categories of the mind, or by its cultural prejudices, or by its historical

---

3. The intelligibility is not merely *ad hoc*, but *per se*. That is to say that it is not merely a matter of what some person or persons may fail to understand, but a normative function of the *adequatio* of intellect to reality. Hence, while the term "intelligibility" is relational, it pertains to the relation of the human intellect as such to reality. This is, of course, discomfiting to those for whom nominalism defines the contours of epistemology. Hence, to distinguish totally and simply between predicates that relate claims to knowers and predicates that relate claims to reality is implicitly to presuppose that there is no real "middle term" of knowledge. It is to deny what Thomas Aquinas so clearly teaches in *De ente et essentia*, that the selfsame essence exists in two distinct ways: in the thing, and in the mind.

limitations, or most radically by the damage done to the human person as a result of original sin, one must point out the following: One's knowledge must extend beyond any given boundary as a condition for identifying it as such. How is it *known* that there are such categories, prejudices, and limits? This issue ought to be brought to light as a proposition regarding *truth*.

The doctrine of the faith is true; that is to say that it corresponds with what actually is the case. But the very idea of truth requires us to affirm that the human intellect is not defined by some given material content or structure of its own, for were it so defined it could not conform itself to whatever is the case so as to know it. If the claim is made that the human intellect is possessed of some material content, structure, or category, which blocks its immediate contact with reality so as to render the idea of truth inapplicable to human knowing, one must ask how it is known that this material content, structure, or category actually obtains? The situation of the person who denies that metaphysical objectivity that is essential to the very idea of truth is not only one of self-contradiction, but of permanent agnosis. It is as though one were to say to someone who did not know one's mother, "Is this photograph a good likeness of my mother?" The interlocutor, having no direct knowledge of or access to the "original" on which the photograph is based, has no possible way of confirming whether the photograph is a good likeness or not. But the one who claims that the human mind is limited by its material content or structure so that being is unintelligible is making a real claim about the mind in a context in which there is no reason to affirm that the real nature of the mind is available to knowledge. On such a hypothesis there is no way for the person to know that the material structure and content of his mind *permits* self-knowledge, for such self-knowledge would require that the mind be fundamentally capable of knowing what is the case. If it is not capable of knowing what is the case, it may be conditioned contrary to what is the case even in its own regard; on such a hypothesis this would be impossible to know. This is to indicate that by the very nature of the claim it cannot be supported by any reason or affirmative evidence.

One can only obtain in any conclusion that which has already been given in the premises. Therefore, one who claims to draw inferences about reality from premises that contain no real evidence is guilty of the most manifest sophistry. But the situation is far worse than this. With the idea of truth destroyed, some will suggest that a "pragmatic" conception of "truth" suffices, which is defined by "enrichment of life" or "human fulfillment" rather than the adequacy of the mind to reality. Yet one who denies metaphysical objectivity implies also that the mind cannot know in what these consist. Accordingly, cultural and ideological prejudice may then assume a canonic and normative status as the basis for the interpretation of revelation. Different, arbitrarily assumed interpretative postures then generate a succession of "theologies du jour," whose only normativity consists in their temporary prominence in the consciousness of some individual or group. Since arbitrary preference is indefinitely variable, divine revelation is essentially beclouded and obscured, reduced to any trope placed upon it under the guiding influence of a metaphysically invertebrate pluralism. While real pluralism occurs within the analogical community of discourse that proceeds from divine revelation and natural *truth*, false pluralism constitutes a species of solipsism, in which the truth, far from measuring the mind, is measured by it. Just as Humean agnosis about nature leads logically to the denial of the conceivability of miracles (for knowledge of the miraculous implies sufficient knowledge of nature to determine that some event or act—e.g., raising Lazarus from the dead—exceeds natural capacity), so agnosis regarding being and nature implies the impossibility of affirming the supernatural as such.

The very doctrine of the incarnation implies a twofold order of being, truth, and knowledge: that of created nature (assumed by the Word) and that of the uncreated God and his grace. As Athanasius teaches, what is not assumed cannot be redeemed. If we know nothing of human nature, we can say neither what it is, nor whether it is, nor whether it has been assumed. As Henri de Lubac puts it, "In my view, which is that of every Catholic, any idea of a claim of created nature in relation to the supernatural should be absolutely excluded." (De Lubac is treating the subject of Michael Baius.)[4] This avowal is all the more arresting and impressive coming from an author who did not concur with Aquinas's teaching in *De malo*, q. 1, art. 5, ad 15 that the deprivation of the beatific vision in a hypothetical state of pure nature would not be a punishment. Hence, even an author who is associated with denial of the claim that human nature could in a different order of providence be ordered to a lesser felicity apart from grace here affirms that the order of nature is distinct from and has no claim upon the supernatural.[5] Thus, clearly so long as one's feet are solidly within the Catholic tradition, the twofold order of nature and grace is defining. If the truth of human nature is wholly inaccessible to the mind, then the continuity between the one who is created and the one who is redeemed becomes unknowable. Yet if the one who is created is *not* the one who is redeemed, then Christianity is not a doctrine of salvation but of complete transmutation of nature. Moreover, the natural law is nothing other than a rational participation in the eternal law, and hence is itself a mode of the divine government of the world. But this means that denial of natural truth is a derogation of God's creation and providence.

---

4. Henri de Lubac, *Augustinianism and Modern Theology*, trans. Geoffrey Chapman (New York: Herder, 1969), 33. For example, consider an error of Baius cited by Pope Pius V, "Ex omnibus afflictionibus" (1 October 1567): "Vita aeterna homini integro et angelo promissa fuit intuitu bonorum operum, et bona opera ex lege naturae ad illam consequendam per se sufficiunt" (*DS* 1904).

5. From the vantage point of the radicalization of de Lubac's arguments regarding the natural desire for God undertaken later by certain members of the *Communio* circle, it can be difficult for some scholars to see the degree to which he himself constrained the radicality of his own thesis by this prior affirmation of Catholic faith that "any idea of a claim of created nature in relation to the supernatural should be absolutely excluded." On this matter, as well as regarding de Lubac's adjustment of his thesis on natural desire, and also on the discrepancy between either version of this thesis and the teaching of Thomas Aquinas, see the recent and sterling scholarship of Lawrence Feingold, *The Natural Desire to See God according to St. Thomas Aquinas and His Interpreters* (Rome: Apollinare Studi, 2001). This work has the great virtue of outlining the consensus of Thomistic commentators of many schools (including even Suarez) on the question of obediential potency by contrast with the accounts given by de Lubac and LaPorta. It also offers at the end a "Conclusion: Summary of the Arguments Showing that there is no innate Appetite for the Vision of God, but only an Elicited and Imperfect Natural Desire," which should be required reading for anyone who wishes to affirm that for Aquinas there is properly speaking a natural desire for intrinsically supernatural beatitude.

When we thank God in prayer for the creation, for what are we thanking God? Clearly, we must have experience and knowledge of being, nature, and natural perfection as the condition for appreciating the doctrine of the creation, for reading Scripture (written in human language), and for understanding what redemption or elevating grace or the supernatural are. For all these reasons and more, metaphysical objectivity is essential to Christian doctrine and anthropology. A theological formation that fails in its metaphysical component is a theological formation predicated upon an error that vitiates the whole theological life and that disorders our natural understanding of creation.

Prototypical Errors

At this juncture it may help to identify certain prototypical errors regarding nature and grace that ensue when the metaphysical objectivity essential to Christian theology is negated. By blocking the role of natural judgment within theology, such errors dislodge the mind from revelation and thus considerably complicate the task of the theologian.

Denial That It Is Human Nature That Is Redeemed

One prototypical error is the suggestion that divine glory regenerates humanity into something different in essence from our previous nature. Under the influence of this conviction that grace radically alters nature, intellectual engagement and philosophical reasoning may be construed as idle or even as distractions with respect to the requirements of the Christian life. Yet it does not require much effort to see that were these sentiments literally true that man would not be redeemed by God, for to redeem man is to redeem the creature endowed with human nature. Clearly, if the creature who is redeemed is not man but is literally another species of being, then no human being has hope of heaven, for only beings other than human would then be able to enjoy the divine friendship. The role of grace within such an account would literally be to terminate the human so that a new being could thrive. This plainly contradicts the Christian belief that the nature that is redeemed and ordered by grace to supernatural beatitude truly is the same nature that suffered the fall.

In fact, it is precisely because of this persistence of the natural principle that Aquinas holds that even the souls in hell retain rational nature together with the motion of natural desire for the good, which motion is the cause of the incessant remorse that they suffer (cf. *Summa theologiae*, I-II, q. 85, a. 1, resp.). This strong separation between salvation and nature brings to mind the efforts of some authors of the *Communio* school, who propound a strong theoretical separation of the person from nature. This is especially true in the latter's effort to separate Aquinas's metaphysics from his ontology and theory of knowledge.[6] Rather than affirming that everything belonging to the nature

---

6. See Steven A. Long, "Personal Receptivity and Act: A Thomistic Critique," *The Thomist* 61 (January 1997): 1–31; and also his "Reply" to the criticism of Dr. Kenneth Schmitz, in *The Thomist* 61 (July 1997): 373–76.

is predicated of the person (a point insisted upon by Aquinas at the height of theological import, regarding the mystery of the incarnation [cf. *Summa theologiae* III, q. 3, ad 3: "In the mystery of the Incarnation, there results a communication of the properties belonging to the nature, because whatever belongs to the nature can be predicated of the Person subsisting in that nature, no matter to which of the natures it may apply"]), the person is treated as emancipated from natural structure—in the one instance (when salvation and nature are separated) by a mutative account of grace, and in the other (the personalist tendencies of the *Communio* school) by denying the pertinence of natural categories.[7] These tendencies do not cohere with the Athanasian teaching that that which is not assumed is not redeemed.

A Mutative View of the Action of Grace on the Soul

While the beatific end transcends either temporal measure or comprehension (for the finite intellect never measures God but always is measured *by* God), there is a dangerous ambiguity in the idea that the life of grace entirely changes life and language, or that it is itself beyond comprehension.

Of course, "entire" may denote an accidental rather than substantial change. For instance, in Aquinas's teaching, even the addition of the *lumen gloriae*—the quasi-formal disposition that emends the created intellect's ontological deficiencies and renders it able to know God—could qualify as "entirely" changing the intellect. But when such formulations regarding the newness of the life of grace are given to justify a refusal to acknowledge the philosophical element within theological contemplation, it appears that what is really being affirmed is a change of species. A rational consideration of nature cannot be granted on such a view, because nature is itself wholly changed without remainder. The criticism once made by Scotus against Aquinas's account of the *lumen gloriae*—the light of glory that emends and perfects the finite intellect so as to render it capable of receiving the beatific vision—would indeed be true of such an account.

Scotus (erroneously) thought that the quasi-formal disposition described by Aquinas would change the species of the intellect (cf. *Ordinatio* I [Vatican ed.], distinction 3, 113–14; III, pp. 70–71). Yet Aquinas anticipates and denies this objection, since for him there is never doubt that the First Intelligible and principle of all knowledge is not beyond the intellect "as sound is to sight, or as an immaterial substance is to the senses" but solely exceeds the finite power of the intellect. Hence, he argues that the intellect is accidentally perfected rather than substantively changed in species (see *Summa contra gentiles*, book III, chapter 54). If Aquinas had maintained that the *lumen gloriae* were an essential rather than an accidental modification of the human intellect, then Scotus's criticism—that man would be *mutated* by

---

7. The idea that rescuing the human person from nature and from natural categories such as act and potency is necessary for philosophical anthropology at various moments unites Continental rationalists, fideists, reductively phenomenological personalists (as opposed to those for whom phenomenological method is no substitute for metaphysics), and theorists radicalizing certain aspects of what was once called *la nouvelle théologie*.

the *lumen gloriae* rather than merely illumined by it as by a superior princi- ple received in the manner of an accident—would be true. Such are the cav- ernous depths concealed in the dark equivocacy of the expression that grace "totally" or "wholly" alters human nature, the essence of man: the depths of an implied *change of species* such that the one who is created *is not the one redeemed*. Clearly, such a reading of the relation of nature and grace is incom- patible with the truth of the Christian faith.

To the contrary, it is the profound depth of the spiritual soul with which man is created that enables humanity to receive the divine aid, whereby one becomes a cosharer in the divine nature through the participation of grace. If God can raise up sons of Abraham from the very rocks, this can only be by rendering them no longer rocks. For only a knowing and loving being may, through the active agency of God, be brought to graced knowledge and love of God.[8] On this account, the writing of sacred Scripture in human language, and the redemption rather than discarding of human nature within the higher life of grace, retain their intelligibility.

Denial of Man's Rational Participation in the Eternal Law, and of the Role of Speculative Wisdom in the Christian Life

The views criticized above give rise to a way of speaking that suggests that theory, conceptual knowledge, and abstraction are incapable of conveying truths about God and revelation. Whether the proposed space for Christian life is depicted as mystagogic or wholly praxic, one finds that this life is opposed to merely theoretical or conceptual inquiry.[9] This is not, of course, far removed

---

8. Steven Long pursues these points extensively in his essay, "Obediential Potency, Human Knowledge, and the Natural Desire for God," *International Philosophical Quarterly* 37 (1997): 45–63. See also, by the same author, "On the Possibility of a Purely Natural End for Man," *The Thomist* 64 (April 2000): 211–37. Speaking of the specific obediential potency of man with respect to grace (as opposed to those obediential potencies which merely respect miraculous transmutation), he writes: "The similitude of the stained-glass window illumined by the sun's rays well bespeaks the character of the doctrine of obe- diential potency as applied to the relation of nature and grace. The stained-glass window, were it cog- nizant, could not 'know what it was missing' were it never to irradiate its bright colors under the influence of the sun. It would be a window, still, and function as part of the structure—though it would, in a given respect, not be fulfilled. It would be what it is, not fail to be part of the whole structure of which it would form an integral part, nor lack its own participation in the good of the whole as a specific perfection. Yet its nature stands properly revealed only under the extrinsic causality of the sun's illumination: seeing it so illumined, we know what stained glass truly is for" (p. 236).

9. Clearly, there is a distinction to be made between what Newman once called "real" discourse and "notional" discourse, as likewise Aquinas distinguishes more adequately between connatural (or lived) knowledge and speculative knowledge. Nonetheless, this is not to deny the importance of speculative intelligence but to point out the poverty of the human creature in whom such knowledge may at times be found disjunct from a lived appreciation of its object. Similarly, there are concerns about the curvature of the will under the fall of man as this affects knowledge. But clearly some acts hit their natural mark after the fall, however insufficient this mark may be vis-à-vis salvation, for man does not disappear into noth- ingness but retains substantial nature—the same nature that will be redeemed from its fallen condition. Further, the will is only an appetite *sequens formam intellectam*, and so it must implicitly be informed with the metaphysical truths pertaining to Christianity inasmuch as it comes to live in the light of the Christian gospel. Finally, given that grace is not the mutation of nature, *grace must work through and perfect nature*, rendering the role of purely natural considerations of maximal importance for Christian theology. There is the state of integral nature before the fall, of fallen nature, and of redeemed nature. But all of this presupposes nature, and so the role of natural contemplation within Christian life is necessar- ily definitive. That is, God assumes *human* nature in Christ. But then one must have some conception as to what this *is*, as well as an understanding of how the true glory of nature is revealed only in the life of grace—that is, an account of obediential potency—and, correlatively, an understanding of what the pro- portionate ends of nature would be in distinction from the fall and from the supernatural life.

from the language of truth as conforming not to reality but to "life," a language associated with Maurice Blondel's *L'Action: essai d'une critique de la vie et d'une science de la pratique*,[10] with both fundamentalist and purely praxic approaches to the living of the Christian life, and with those accounts—prolific within theory whose presuppositions are formatively analytic—that superordinate the practical to the speculative.[11] Yet this is a throwing out of the baby with the bath water—one might almost say, of the Christ Child, whose human nature subsists in the Word. The *kenosis* is a truth of the speculative and ontological order (we do not *make* or *do* the incarnation, and *essence* or *nature* and the *mode in which essence exists* are objects whose intelligibility is *ontological* such that they delineate and circumscribe the mystery).

Further, the derogation of speculative intelligence implies that the natural law—which is nothing but the rational participation of the eternal law—does not make up part of the perennial inheritance of Christianity. Indeed, it places the divine immutability in question, for the immutability of the natural law is wholly a function of its participation of the eternal law. The eternal law is promulgated from the instant of creation and participated in rationally by man. But the dignity of this rational participation retreats to the vanishing point in accounts that fail to affirm the very nature of natural law as nothing other than a participation in the eternal law. Such derogation of the dignity of speculative intelligence by default engenders irrationalist and gnostic rejection of the rational form of human experience, as also it engenders the cognate rejection of human rational participation in the suprarational life of the theological virtues.

Implicit Denial of Ontological Truth in the Name of Ontological Transformation

The foregoing points, of course, lead to the foyer of the gnostic affirmation that catechesis need involve no rational appropriation of doctrinal propositional truth—or rather, that such appropriation while required is wholly non-definitive and secondary. Such a view reduces the objects of revelation to praxic recombinants whose law is not distinct from the lives that instantiate them. Yet if the doctrine of the church is taught not via intellective means but rather "learned" from "example," one wonders by what power or faculty this learning takes place.

Sacred Scripture and sacred tradition are articulated in human language and entrusted to the humblest of laws, the ontological and logical laws of identity and noncontradiction. Revealed truth cannot simultaneously and in the same respect be and not be, nor be in like manner simultaneously true and false. Christ cannot both *be* God and *not be* God. The truths regarding man's transformation in grace are indeed *truths* that call for assent of mind and will.

---

10. Maurice Blondel, *L'Action: essai d'une critique de la vie et d'une science de la pratique* (Paris: Alcan and Presses Universitaires de France, 1893).
11. See, e.g., the new natural law theory associated with John Finnis, *Natural Rights and Natural Law* (Oxford: Clarendon, 1980).

While essentially supernatural mysteries transcend human nature and its finite understanding, this does not negate the dignity of man's rational nature, nor alter the datum that grace works through nature (*Summa theologiae* I, q. 62, resp.). Indeed, this divine transcendence does not preclude analogical insight into such mysteries (cf. Augustine's account of the Trinity). One might respond to the gnostic inflection of the derogation of the speculative simply in terms of the lived spiritual experience of the church, which has enjoyed two millennia of experience of union with its risen Savior, and has raised up spiritual sons and daughters whose experience has intimately ratified the intellective contemplation of the divine mysteries.

The claim that rational contemplation of the divine is otiose in Christian life is vain, inasmuch as man comes forth from his Creator seeking out the deeper reasons of things, a tendency all the more vital and true where the greatest friendship and the most profound truth resides. Theoretical discussion of the meaning of life and dogma is only as necessary to man as is the nobility of his spiritual vocation and the inner truth of his own identity as created by God and redeemed in Christ. Clearly not every Christian is called to the same degree of speculative insight into divine matters, but such insight nonetheless retains the dignity of its consecration to God and is necessary to the common good of the church. Denial of the essential role of such speculative contemplation negates the *minima natura* of dogmatic intelligibility, as also the *praeambula fidei*, or preambles of faith (natural knowledge that God is, that God is immutable, simple, etc.). Whereas sacred Scripture includes the natural theology of Rom 1, as well as lines urging Christians to "be transformed by the renewal of your mind" (Rom 12:2), Christianity minus the natural speculative exigencies of rational human nature and the intelligibility of being would yield a creed not of authentic transformation in Christ but of mutative impoverishment, the impenetrable darkness of being, and the derogation of the *imago Dei*.

False Dichotomy between Experience and Knowledge

A note may here be inserted regarding the danger of construing the relation between experience and knowledge on the pattern of Cartesian or otherwise misleading or erroneous accounts of the intellect. For the intelligence of man is nourished by sense experience, and is not of itself necessarily constituted by an alienation from experience. The false construal of abstraction as deformative of nature, and of speculative wisdom as somehow necessarily opposed to connatural knowledge, is liable to corrupt one's understanding of the relation between human intelligence and dogma.

Distortion Regarding the Nature of Dogma

The idea of dogma as life, and of life as the expression of dogma, bears resemblances already suggested above with the writing of Blondel. Yet life and dogma are convertible only in Christ, in whom sovereign truth and life coincide. Even in the saints, the difference obtains between sovereign truth and the need for conformity to that sovereign truth. Dogma articulates divine truth that *ought* to be the foundation for holy lives. Clearly, dogma does not articulate simply any life whatsoever but rather the divine life. To say otherwise is to promulgate a new religion of veneration for the world in which any life whatsoever is equally revelatory of the divine truth—as though the incarnation of the Word and the nature and mission of his church could be supplanted by human nature alone. Dogma announces the transcendent truth; to deny to this its intelligible structure and then christen this negation "ontological" would indeed be a triumph of nominalism cloaked in gnosis.

Conclusion: A Superset of Fideist Errors

Christ possesses both divine and human nature; this is truly an ontological affirmation. It, and everything implied by it, is true. The errors briefly discussed above constitute a sort of superset of fideist errors according to which the intelligibility of being and nature, and man's rational nature itself, are thought to constitute an impediment to grace rather than the very essential conditions for receiving it. Alternately, the intelligible preconditions for the elevation of man into the supernatural life of the Trinity are treated as of secondary importance, as though the true were a sublunary issue of little import—a view that hardly befits those for whom God is infinitely perfect being, goodness, and truth.[12]

---

12. The author acknowledges the invaluable assistance of Professor Steven A. Long, Department of Philosophy, University of St. Thomas, St. Paul, Minnesota, and sometimes lecturer in the Catholic Studies Program at the same university.

A Philosopher's Postscript:
Engaging the Citadel of Secular Reason

— CHARLES TAYLOR —

I

A strongly defended position within Latin Christendom about the relation of faith and reason has been this: Some truths are evident to unaided reason, and other further truths can only be made evident to us by revelation. This way of thinking distinguishes two domains.

This solution has, of course, been hotly contested, principally by those who have mistrusted unaided reason, like Luther. Those who do not want to follow this far-reaching denigration of reason nevertheless find it hard to defend the original distinction of domains. One major reason for this is that matters that were placed in the first domain, accessible to reason, by, for example, Aquinas, no longer unproblematically appear so. The proofs for the existence of God are an example. For a long time it was thought evident that we demonstrate the existence of a good Creator; that this Creator was triune was thought beyond the scope of unaided reason, and could only come by revelation.

In cultures deeply convinced of the existence of God, woven around such a belief-commitment (as was our civilization until recently), it seems clear that demonstrations of this kind go through. But today we see that this is not so. It depends where you are "coming from," to use the California dialect. We are forced to accept that people can "come from" very different places, and that very few truths in the domain of first or last things seem obvious from all of these vantage points.

But, it might be objected, that does not impugn reason. People can "come from" very bad places; bad in two senses: (1) perspectives very unsuited to descry fundamental truths from; and (2) perspectives shaped by "volitional depravity," to quote Paul Griffiths.[1] So conclusions that are (in some sense) *an*

---

1. See Paul J. Griffiths, "How Reasoning Goes Wrong: A Quasi-Augustinian Account of Error and Its Implications," in this volume, p. 152.

sich valid in reason can be very far from universal acceptance. (In fact, Griffiths's two reasons for our failing to understand proofs, namely, inadequate catechesis and volitional depravity, seem to correspond to my [1] and [2] above, respectively.)

"But hold on," an unbelieving interlocutor might say. "You people are making things easy for yourselves. Anyone who can't see that it is clear that God exists is ipso facto coming from a 'bad' place. But what makes it a bad place? Simply that people there don't agree with you."

This objection assumes that we all have our unthought background—that for some certain things are obvious, and for others not—and that there is no non–question-begging way of adjudicating which are better and which worse. So there is no "bad" place *simpliciter*, but just "bad from a Christian stand-point," "bad from an atheist standpoint," and so on.

The way to overcome this hurdle is to point to the nature of argument in this domain. The case of natural science can be a good starting point. Science, following the influential language of Thomas Kuhn, operates within "para-digms." A shift in these can alter the terms of the enquiry, even the questions one asks. One conclusion from this would be that there is no rationally moti-vated transition from one to another paradigm. Kuhn himself seemed at times to draw this conclusion. But if one looks closely at certain cases, as, for exam-ple, Alasdair MacIntyre has done for the move from Aristotelian to Galilean-Newtonian mechanics, one can see quite well that the shift is rationally determined. Whereas the Paduan Aristotelians were left with the insoluble anomalies of projectiles and cannon balls, these anomalies disappear, and a whole range of phenomena begin to be tractable, once you shift to the iner-tial perspective.[2] Later, MacIntyre showed that something like this mode of argument can serve to show the superiority of one tradition of moral think-ing over another.[3] This kind of argument, which I have called "supersession" argument, has the basic feature of defining asymmetrical positions. You move from A to B via the overcoming of some error-inducing factor, such as a con-fusion, an elision, a too-simple palette of possibilities, and the like. It is clear from the standpoint of B that outlook A was conditioned by this error. The way of A to B was in fact mediated by the recognition of this error, as one is confident that now we are waking and before we were dreaming, because get-ting from there to here involved waking up. There is an asymmetry here, because, to use Ernst Tugendhat's term, an *Erfahrungsweg* of this (error-reducing) kind leads from A to B, but there is no such way of going in the reverse direction.[4]

---

2. Alasdair MacIntyre, "Epistemological Crises, Dramatic Narrative, and the Philosophy of Science," in *Why Narrative? Readings in Narrative Theology*, ed. Stanley Hauerwas and L. Gregory Jones (Grand Rapids: Eerdmans, 1989), 138–57.

3. Alasdair MacIntyre, *Three Rival Versions of Moral Enquiry* (Notre Dame, IN: University of Notre Dame Press, 1990).

4. See Ernst Tugendhat, *Selbstbewusstsein und Selbstbestimmung* (Frankfurt: Suhrkamp STW, 1979). I have discussed this kind of supersession argument in Charles Taylor, "Explanation and Practical Reason," in *Philosophical Arguments* (Cambridge, MA: Harvard University Press, 1995). See also Reinhard Hütter's essay, "The Directedness of Reasoning and the Metaphysics of Creation," in this volume.

I have tried to develop elsewhere the logic of such supersession arguments.[5] Perhaps it might help to go through it in greater detail here. First, these arguments establish not a single proposition as being true and incorrigible, but rather a comparative: Whatever else is right, moving from A to B involves an epistemic gain. From B, one may move on further, but there cannot be cause to move back to A. Whatever the ultimate epistemic ranking of B, it beats A. Second, our ordinary understanding of an argument showing B to be superior to A operates through some third feature, a "criterion," C. So we usually argue that B has C, and A does not (or B has C to a greater degree than A); therefore B beats A. By contrast, a supersession argument convinces us in the first instance, not by some criterion (although we can sometimes dress it up in this form after), but by the fact that we see that the shift from A to B comes about through some error-reducing move. We see that underlying our earlier acceptance of A lay a confusion between two distinct things, or an ignoring of considerations that are clearly relevant; correcting for this error brings us to B. The superiority of B lies in the fact that it is what A becomes once this error is corrected for. The argument does not pass through applying some criterion to A and B, but through a recognition of error.

Third, the appeal to a criterion frequently makes sense when we can hope that the proponents of both A and B can accept it as decisive. We then have a way to resolve the dispute between them: Let's see which claim meets the criterion, and may the best claim win. But the fundamental asymmetry of transitions through supersession arguments means that the really convincing consideration is normally invisible from A, for it involves the perception of an error, or at least restriction of view, which once seen makes A incredible. The normal way of proceeding is that (1) I get you to accept the criterion, then (2) we apply the criterion (test A and B against the criterion), then (3) one of us loses and goes over to the other side. This stepwise procedure is impossible in the supersession cases; to get the A-supporters to accept the criterion (e.g., that their position involves some confusion) is to get them to abandon A. There is no independent step here.

Fourth, for many people formed in the culture of mediational epistemology, this makes supersession arguments of no epistemic value. If I can't convince you through a criterion that you can accept from your point of view, then there is no objectively convincing reason to move from A to B, only subjectively convincing reasons from the standpoint of B; hence the rejoinder I put in the mouth of the unbelieving interlocutor above. But this inference does not follow. There *are* good reasons; it is just that they are only available from standpoint B.

It seems clear to me that acquiring or deepening faith frequently involves such superseding transitions—that is, it moves from an A to a B where things look very different from B than they did from A, but where at the same time one can see very clearly from B that one has broken through previous errors,

---

5. See Taylor, "Explanation and Practical Reason," in *Philosophical Arguments*.

obstacles, periods of blindness. We have a very good example, I believe, in Mark McIntosh's essay in this volume, where the movement from our ordinary fearful, envious perspective (A) to that of the desert fathers (B), first changes our perspective very radically (things appear utterly different) while at the same time, making this transition brings out very clearly how much we were formerly bedeviled (*c'est le cas de le dire*) and bemused by fear, worry about how we are perceived, ego-gratifying fabulations, and the like.[6]

Once some have gone through such a transition, others of us who have not can get an inkling of it, and in the light of how these trailblazers act and radiate what they see from their new perspective, as well as our general awareness of the possibility of this kind of transition, we can come to a reasoned faith that there is that higher perspective and that it gives a truer view than the one we are stuck at now. (Indeed, in virtue of this act of faith, we are not as fully "stuck at" the lower perspective as we were before.)

But what does this say about faith and reason? For the desert fathers, it was reason all the way down (or better, all the way up). Not that they had nothing to receive, but rather that from where they stood, the need to receive was so obvious that one turned fully toward God. Faith itself seemed overwhelmingly the only reasonable response. But from other, less good places, the relationship is more fraught and complicated. Moved by an obscure sense that there is something greater, higher, some healing power, some fullness of love, or whatever, we throw ourselves onto this track: We become baptized, pray, take the sacraments, try to live agape. There is really a leap of faith, and it has to be from here.

But this seems to render hopeless the idea of drawing a line between matters of faith and those that are accessible to reason, irrespective of starting point. Unless one wants to select some place as the normative starting point—below this, one is really depraved, above only moderately—what is accessible from this place by reason is what we define as "accessible to reason," what is not is a matter of faith. Or else we can try to draw the line historically: Where would we be if there had never been revelation? Neither of these seem to me to be promising paths to pursue.

(It might be worthwhile making another kind of distinction. Perhaps this is already current in theology; I apologize if it is. This distinction is between revelation, as defined by the officially recognized events in our tradition [e.g., Sinai and the incarnation], on one hand, and all the other ways in which we are "taught by God" or informed by the Spirit, on the other. Thus, Hamann objected to Herder's dismissal of the idea that God first taught humans language—not that Hamann accepted the story in Süssmilch's simple, "Just So Story" version, but rather that he wanted to keep a place open for a conjecture that is harder to define [for instance, that in some way human language evolves partly through interlocution with God]. Something like this seems to me highly probable; I am far from being in a good enough "place" to demonstrate it, but I can imagine what such a place would look like.)

---

6. Mark McIntosh, "Faith, Reason, and the Mind of Christ."

One thing emerges from the above, a kind of rehabilitation of reason. Starting at the right place, reason takes us all the way up. But this does not tell us a lot about the power of "unaided" reason because getting to the right place needs a lot of nudging, pushing, pulling, and other works of the Spirit. Indeed, totally unaided reason probably does not get you farther than your nose.

It also tells us that we need new understandings of reason. In some ways, we should return to Plato's *logos*, particularly in the expression *logon didonai*, to "give an account." Giving an account needs two things. Of course, we have to reason consequently, according to whatever counts as rigorous steps in this argument. But we also have to have the language to articulate what we want to reason about. Logos has an argumentative face, but also an articulative one, finding the words to unlock the secrets of what we are studying, like Newtonian "mass," or a mind *aphantaston*, free from fantasy, as a gift of God.

But does this mean that we can make no principled distinction between theology and philosophy? This conclusion, it seems to me, does not follow. Certainly what does is that the boundaries of philosophy will vary a great deal in history and from culture to culture; this is hardly news. But we may still be able to identify a realm of argument called philosophical, distinct from the theological.

This does not at all mean that they are isolated from each other. On the contrary, they are in one way inextricably intertwined. Theology tries to articulate the "deposit of faith" as this has come down to us (and we do not entirely agree on what this is, with different views of how we relate the Bible to the tradition of the church, etc., but we can leave this aside for the moment). This theology can perhaps consist of more than one position about the nature of human beings, language, history, the evolution of the cosmos, and so on, but certainly not with all. For instance, a certain kind of materialist reductionism, à la Hobbes, where everything is reduced to "matter in motion," is surely incompatible with the Christian revelation.

Anyone who wants to work out more fully what the deposit of faith entails will eventually want to work out some philosophical anthropology, philosophy of history, of natural science, and so on. She will find herself doing philosophy, as we normally describe it. Right away we can see a connection between the two domains. Our theologian, and indeed, any person of faith, will approach, say, philosophical anthropology from the standpoint of faith. She will find incredible, for instance, reductive materialist accounts. She will look for other ways of understanding human beings. In this way, faith informs her work, and she will not be building artificial barriers.

It is obvious from this standpoint that philosophy, or for that matter, the different sciences, can never be totally enclosed domains, where one checks one's deepest metaphysical and faith convictions at the door. People who speak of the need for, say, "methodological atheism" in history or social science do not know what they are talking about.

This still does not mean that we cannot mark a boundary: theology/philosophy, or theology/science. We can, because however one arrives at the approach one takes to, say, philosophical anthropology, it still needs to be worked and argued out. There are two facets to this, corresponding to the two verbs I have just used. Let's say I am working out a philosophy of history. My whole understanding of history will be informed by the historical nature of the Jewish and Christian revelations (as Augustine's was, for instance). But in a philosophy of history this still has to be worked out, taking account of the whole sweep of history, the forms of historical development, an adequate theory of historical causation, and so on. In working this out, I bring in considerations that go way beyond the deposit of faith as usually conceived, and at the same time these considerations will be available to many others in the field who do not share my faith position. Indeed, working out my position will inseparably involve arguing with these other, largely unbelieving, practitioners. The working out will never be as effective if I do not engage in argument with them, and my arguments will be ineffective if I am not working out my fundamental, faith-driven insights.

This field of working and arguing out can define a discipline, which here we might call "philosophy of history," in which scholars and other thinkers engage with certain considerations that they all recognize as relevant (or at least where their respective senses of relevance heavily overlap). It is in a certain sense "autonomous" from theology, not because the insights are not frequently faith driven (and we believing Christians hold that the best, most fruitful insights are faith driven), but because it incorporates a domain of considerations (historical development, causation, etc.) that is the site of arguments addressed to all participants, irrespective of what drives their insights. This defines the integrity of this philosophical field.

II

The view I have offered above suggests that distinctions such as faith and reason, or reason and revelation, need to be historically situated. What will be considered within the scope of rational demonstration can vary from epoch to epoch; and of course, in an intellectually and ideologically fractured age like our own, there will be important differences on this score between different schools.

The idea that there must be one sempiternally fixed scope for reason, even though this may not be fully evident in benighted ages, plays too easily into the prejudices of the contemporary age. We see this in an idea such as "criticism." In a widely held view, being "critical" involves submitting our beliefs to rational examination. The progress of Enlightenment consists simply in applying this operation to beliefs formerly held sacrosanct and unquestionable. Thus, at a certain moment in history, biblical criticism starts, and people begin to subject the stories in the Bible to various tests of consistency, of plausibility in view of the known laws of nature, of interpretation in the light of the outlook of the time, and so on. This daring step removes the (illegitimate) immunity that certain beliefs and texts enjoyed before.[7]

---

7. See Paul Hazard, *La crise de la conscience européenne (1680–1715)* (Paris: Boivin, 1935), and his idea that Descartes' provisional exclusion of theology and morality from his method of doubt was rescinded later in the century, and these fundamental questions were made subject to the same tests.

This view also comforts another central prejudice of Enlightenment, connected to the idea of criticism. Reason, to be true to its nature, must accept nothing from outside that it has not itself checked. That is what it means to be fully critical in a thoroughgoing way. The Kantian distinction critical/dogmatic relies on this picture. But in the first section, we envisaged situations in which it would be "rational" to take what we have received in some sense from "outside" as criterial, and not just as a dubious entrant that must have its papers checked. The predicament of the desert fathers was our example.

Enlightenment ideology, while fixing the procedures of reason and criticism once and for all, does this in a form that identifies the rational with what has been checked through the proper procedures by the subject, whether these are conceived in the original Cartesian form, or in some later variant, like the immensely influential Kantian form. Reason must be, in Husserl's word, "self-responsible."[8] Normative revelation on this view must be, by its very nature, subrational. Reason becomes intrinsically connected with an inside/outside distinction, which is almost impossible to question, because it seems consubstantial with rationality itself.

It might be helpful to look more closely at this ideology and the use it makes of the image of light. Enlightenment has to do with possessing knowledge. The enlightened are capable of acquiring knowledge because they have overcome or set aside the obstacles, the factors, that darken counsel and mislead the mind: superstition, unchallenged traditional beliefs, and irrational frameworks of representation. The enlightened can see the world straight, without these screening factors, and therefore are capable of valid learning. In order to see straight, they have to want to see straight, which means that they are no longer attached to the old traditions or frameworks. But becoming detached from these is not easy because they draw us very powerfully.

The draw is twofold. These traditions have authority; they come across as making a claim on our allegiance because they purport to come from some higher source: God, or some higher beings, or the cosmos. And they also comfort us because they make sense of our world, or give us a secure place within it, or promise some kind of deliverance from it. Overawed by authority, lured by the comfort it seemed to offer, our earlier predicament was rather reminiscent of that of children in relation to their parents or guardians. Becoming enlightened is like growing up; we become responsible for our own lives and the framing of our own beliefs. We finally leave what Kant describes as a "selbstverschuldete Unmündigkeit."[9]

Something like this seems to be the framework story. To get closer to the image of light here, I want to look at various modes of the valid knowledge that Enlightenment enables. The first is the one foregrounded by Descartes, whose paradigm is mathematics. This offers the certainty of self-evidence. Clear and distinct perception yields something undeniable. With clarity, the

---

8. Edmund Husserl, *Die Krisis der europäischen Wissenschaften und die transzendentale Phänomenologie*, 3rd ed. (Hamburg: Felix Meiner, 1996), §27, p. 110.

9. Immanuel Kant, "Beantwortung der Frage: Was ist Aufklärung?" in *Immanuel Kant: Werke in zehn Bänden*, ed. Wilhelm Weischedel, vol. 9, *Schriften zur Anthropologie, Geschichtsphilosophie, Politik und Pädagogik* (Darmstadt: Wissenschaftliche Buchgesellschaft, 1964), 53–61; 53.

thing is in full view; there is nothing obscure in it, no facet not revealed. With distinctness, the object is sharply bounded; there is no possibility of confusion with anything else. This way of knowing draws its images heavily from vision and implicitly brings into play the metaphor of light: The clear and distinct object is in full view and well illuminated. Knowledge cannot get better or surer than this.

The second paradigm mode is that dominating post-Baconian science. Scheler coined the term "Leistungswissen" for this.[10] This is defined in contrast to the mode of knowing central to the tradition that started with Plato and Aristotle. This consisted in discerning the underlying, continuing, determining patterns that give their shape to the ever changing and imperfect objects that surround us. This kind of science had no essential connection with gaining greater control over these objects.

Bacon wanted to turn his back on this kind of science, which he saw as inspired by pride and prone to illusion. Instead, he proposed to track just those efficient causal connections that allow us to effect our purposes more completely. This kind of knowledge could be checked through success in practice, and thus was not prone to illusion. In addition, its principal motivation was not pride but charity; it aimed to "improve the condition of mankind."[11] Bacon proposed a kind of egalitarian revolution. In place of the older science that was typically practiced by leisured elites, aiming at the satisfaction of contemplating the order of things, the new science would build on the work of the despised "mechanics"—miners, metallurgists, and tinkerers of all sorts—and would make the lives of ordinary people better.

The science that emerged from the seventeenth-century revolution was a sort of fusion of Bacon's and Descartes' aspirations, systematic and mathematical as the latter had projected, but mapping a disenchanted world, no longer shaped by ideas or forms, the domain of efficient causation, and offering purchase for more and more effective interventions. This kind of knowledge was in principle, if not always in practice, essentially related to new possibilities of control, of getting things done; hence the Schelerian title. It also required, as Descartes saw, a disengagement of the agent from a cosmos whose different levels of being were understood in terms of spiritual or moral meaning, such as is portrayed in the different versions of the Great Chain of Being. In this sense the world was objectified. This became one of the defining paradigms of the Enlightenment.

Already we can see some common features between these two paradigms. Before I examine a third one, I would like to bring some of these features out. One is atomism: The method involved in these two kinds of knowledge involves breaking the field to be examined down into its smallest parts. This is explicitly stated by Descartes in his *Regulae ad directionem ingenii*. Always break a problem down into its constituent parts, grasp it piecemeal, and build

10. Max Scheler, *Die Wissensformen und die Gesellschaft, Gesammelte Werke*, Vol. VIII (Bern: Francke, 1960).

11. F. Bacon, *Novum Organum*, I. 73, translation from *Francis Bacon: A Selection of His Works*, ed. Sidney Warhaft (Toronto: Macmillan, 1965), 350–51.

up to the global solution. Something like this atomism was also a common idea in the first phases of the scientific revolution of that century, as we see in the resolutive-compositive method of Galileo, and in the "corpuscularian" philosophy of the founders of modern physics.

Second, the method here involved a kind of control. This was true of the new science, as we have just seen: Successful scientific discovery was internally linked in principle with greater control over things. But control operated at another level. Applying the proper method for either rationalist or empiricist science required that we grasp the objects in a certain way. Thus for Descartes, getting a clear and distinct grasp on things required in the first stage isolating the particular idea. It needed to be first of all grasped on its own in order to be clear and distinct. Later, one built up connections between particular ideas, focusing now on the (clear and distinct) connections between them, until finally one had a view of the whole. One had to exercise a tight control over the representations (ideas) in order to bring out their connections, and the larger picture had some of the character of a construction.

Much of this character carries over when we move from the "rationalist" formulations of Descartes to the "empiricist" ones of Locke. Once more, we start from simple ideas and then connect them by tracing their (empirically verified) correlations. Once more, the edifice of science is seen as a construction out of basic parts. The connections are meant to follow correlations found in experience; in this respect we are far from the "constructivism" of much of today's "postmodernism." The operation is in that sense guided, but Locke himself applies this metaphor of building in several places.[12]

Thus, the emphasis on control, the high place accorded to artifice, applies not only at the level of the world, where knowledge increases power, but also in the realm of thought; scientific thinking is also the object of a strict control, and our thoughts are correspondingly objectified or reified as "ideas," quasi-objects susceptible of manipulation. Ideas are likened to building materials.[13]

This form of control contrasts with the procedure that is dominant in the science derived from the great ancients, for instance, Aristotle. There the ultimate success comes in the discerning of the underlying pattern, the third common feature in our two paradigms. For Aristotle, it comes in our grasping the *eidos* of a particular kind of thing. The path toward this knowledge, which Aristotle speaks of as "induction" (*epagogê*), may involve some analysis, focusing on particular organs of an animal, for instance. But all this serves the end of grasping the overall shape, which is not simply a compound of these partial takes, but arises as a fresh insight and goes beyond them. In a parallel way, Platonic dialectic may require that we analyze the features of some property (e.g., justice, piety). We do this by batting around definitions. But this serves to liberate us so that we are capable of a new insight into the unchanging form.[14] In neither case is the metaphor of construction apposite

---

12. John Locke, *An Essay Concerning Human Understanding*, ed. P. H. Nidditch (Oxford: Clarendon, 1975); see, e.g., "Epistle to the *Essay*," 14, where Locke speaks of himself (with perhaps a forced modesty) as an "under-labourer"; see also book 2, ch. 2, sec. 2; and book 2, ch. 12, sec. 1.

13. Locke, *Essay*, 2.2.2; and 2.12.1.

14. Plato, *Republic*, 532B–C. See also Plato's *Seventh Letter*.

here. Construction as artifice requires that we keep control throughout, up to and including the final assembly of the theory. Method guides all. For Plato or Aristotle, the overall shape of things comes from beyond any construction, as a fresh insight, which makes sense of all the detailed analytic work that precedes it. Because it is a fresh insight into an encompassing order, it has no necessary connection with increased control, which is exactly why Bacon saw it as vain and possibly illusion. In the post-Baconian world, control over the object realm is closely linked with control over the process of thought whereby we grasp this object realm.

With this in mind, I will try to focus more clearly the image of light under-lying the Enlightenment. True knowledge involves uncovering the nature of things free of the distorting or irrational frameworks that have hitherto been imposed by authority. We can see better now how these frameworks are fre-quently identified with some larger notion of encompassing pattern or order, such as the Aristotelian notion of a cosmos shaped by forms, or an order of hierarchical complementarity. Proper understanding has the courage and maturity to free itself of these and focuses on an atomistic, constructivist (but not in the contemporary, postmodern sense, where this is opposed to corre-sponding to reality), objectifying take on reality. Here things fall fully in the light; the earlier darkness was the shadow cast by the false hegemonic ideas of encompassing order. In its crudest variant: in the old days, kings and priests connived to make ordinary people believe that their subordination was part of the natural, cosmic, God-given order. Then we tore apart the veil of superstitious illusion, and now we see just human beings in full light. We are now painfully aware that the social arrangements they live in are unjust and irrational and must be changed.

The light here is focused light. And it is cast by us. The power to cast this light arises in us. We make things clear by centering on one clear and distinct idea, or by singling out the human beings who used to be just role-fillers in this supposedly more real entity, the kingdom. We can now see very clearly the contrast with earlier uses of the image of light, say, in Plato. Here the light is not cast by us; it is ambient, it surrounds us. It is cast not by us but by some source (e.g., the idea of the good, likened to the sun in the *Republic*[15]). What we have to do is look in the direction of the light, instead of focusing on the dark side of the universe, among the changing, imperfect copies of the ideas.[16]

Something similar can be said about the light image in John's gospel. The source of the light is God. We flee it into the darkness because we do not want our deeds known. Plainly we do not cast this light; our choice is rather whether to stand in it or flee from it.

Modern talk about the light of reason refers to this light we cast as reason-ing beings. This now seems to many people the only sense this phrase can bear. This is the upshot of a long development, away from outlooks in which the notion of a self-manifesting reality, either on the model of the Platonic

---

15. Plato, *Republic*, book VI.
16. Ibid., book VI, 518C.

ideas, or on God conceived as a source of revelation. This long and complex development involved an interiorization of the light of reason, which passed an important stage with (or perhaps slightly before) Augustine and his turn inward. But this was not yet the crucial stage, because for Augustine the turn inward led us upward to the self-revealing God. What was needed to complete the move was the modern idea of a constructive method or procedure under our control, which could suffice to generate the light of reason, and along with this the three features mentioned above.[17]

This goes along with an important shift in the understanding of reason, from a substantive to a procedural view. A substantive view of reason is one which holds that to be fully rational or in conformity with reason, you have to get reality substantively right. This is plainly built into Plato's idea of *to logistikon*, which is the power in us to see the ideas. By contrast, a procedural view identifies reason with certain modes of operating. Here the perfection of their operation may not coincide with the correct result (e.g., if the premises are false, the perfect deduction will yield a falsehood). Thus Descartes, in outlining his method, has to add an additional argument in order to ensure that it will yield substantive truth. This is the role played by the proof of a veracious God.[18]

Enlightenment, understood against the background of these images, constitutes what Wittgenstein called a "Bild," a picture that can "hold us captive,"[19] because we are unaware of the way in which this construal, which is after all one among other possible ones, has become for us the only conceivable meaning of the term. We can see also how, on this reading, normative revelation must be intrinsically counter-Enlightenment.

We can also see now why this Enlightenment is hostile to mystery. This can be understood negatively, as what resists understanding. In this sense, there is certainly an incompatibility between mystery and the hopes and ambitions of the Enlightenment to understand everything through proper, light-casting method. But in another sense, mystery can be understood positively, as what can perhaps at some stage be understood, but has to be understood "mystically," that is, by one being inducted or initiated into it. In this sense, the contrast to mystery is what can be understood by disengaged objectification, that is, all the things that are the proper objects of Enlightenment method. But there are certain kinds of encompassing order that can only be grasped by opening yourself to them, allowing them to shape you, that is, the very opposite of the stance of disengaged objectification. These include such banal things as taking in the atmosphere at a party, or more importantly, trying to sense the full range of what your interlocutor is trying to communicate, not just the "propositional content" but, say, the kind of distress underlying it.

---

17. See Louis Dupré, *Religious Mystery and Rational Reflection* (Grand Rapids: Eerdmans, 1998), chs. 1 and 2.
18. See Charles Taylor, *Sources of the Self* (Cambridge, MA: Harvard University Press 1989), chs. 6 and 8.
19. "Ein Bild hielt uns gefangen," *Philosophische Untersuchungen*, pt. 1, para. 115. Cited in Ludwig Wittgenstein, *Schriften* (Frankfurt am Main: Suhrkamp, 1960), 343.

And the gamut runs to the kind of openness that is the aim of some kinds of prayer to realize. On the standard Enlightenment image, what you are opening to here has to be counted as darkness, because you have to suspend your own light-casting powers to receive the object.

It is obvious why one should want to avoid giving gratuitous concessions to this idea of Enlightenment rationality. Clearly, the expanded notion of reason I offered above, including an articulative and not only an argumentative dimension, is meant to challenge and extend it. For we can recognize that the exercise of articulation may frequently require an openness to what is outside or beyond us, which fits ill with the master image of light cast from within.

III

Another important conclusion that seems to flow from this recalibration of our notion of reason is this: The most useful thing to do may not be to run through the old proofs but to acquire an in-depth and sympathetic (and you do not have the first without the second) grasp of the kinds of places occupied in our day from which people have trouble emerging into faith. In this connection, I have been trying in recent years to make a study of certain facets of the modern secularist worldview.

The trouble is that what people say is not necessarily the best guide. For instance, many secularists say things like "Science has disproved God, or proved that everything is made of matter, and so the whole Christian story can't be true." This kind of remark seems bristling with fallacies to someone like me. But instead of blowing one's philosophical top, a more instructive thing is to try to see what underpins this position.

Thus, it seems utterly absurd to say, "Science has proved . . . ," and then complete the sentence with any proposition about first or last things, whether it be that God exists or does not exist. But let's try to probe deeper. Why define reality as "matter," in the meaning of the act? What is "the meaning of the act" here? This goes back to the Baconian-Cartesian-Newtonian revolution I invoked above, what Scheler called "Leistungswissen"—knowledge where the criterion of advance is (at least notionally) control and what one can do with it. Bacon tried to justify this theologically: As against the Aristotelian mapping of forms, the knowledge of cause and effect can enable you to "improve the condition of mankind"; as against being actuated by pride (Aristotelians), moderns will be actuated in their scientific work by charity.

Sciences that can obviously make a difference like this have acquired a unique prestige in our culture; even when they are sometimes pursued in a purely "theoretical" interest, everyone knows that all this can suddenly acquire impressive technological use. To be adept at this is to have a sense of power ("knowledge is power" for Bacon), as well as a sense that this power can be for good ("improve the condition of mankind"). So it is easy to slip into feeling that the kind of stuff you deal with here (matter) is all that matters (pun intended). People who are struggling with the kind of objects that you can never really get a grip on, that you can never really demonstrate something about (e.g., the number of Persons in God), are lost in a fog, concerned with their own conceit of supposed wisdom, not down there making things better for flesh-and-blood human beings. The next step is easy: All there is, is matter and the things that can be reduced to matter. This "must" include human beings. (How could it not? We have already proved that that is all there is, and we are part of what is). Here begins, of course, the sorry, ludicrous, and tortuous story of attempted reductive explanations.

That is one way into the secularist citadel. Once you have traveled that route, you find other high barriers to getting out, or if you like, other routes down and in that are easy to travel. The second is a story, really a master narrative. Getting through to the natural science perspective involved a big fight. We do not need to repeat the Galileo story; we can also talk about Copernicus, who had the courage to displace the earth from the center of the universe; then Darwin, who took humans down a peg; then Freud, who showed that even the high citadel of the mind was mired in the mud of libidinous instinct. I am repeating here the kind of cheerleading one can find in a book such as Ernest Jones's biography of Freud. It took courage to face down our fears, our illusions, our delusions of grandeur and get to the truth, to face the reality of a meaningless universe.

There is a coding of history here in terms of a master trope of maturation. As children we are afraid of the dark and need to be tucked in; as adults we come gradually to be able to face the rough facts about the world. Belief belongs to the childhood of the human race. Mature, philanthropic, scientific materialism is the truly adult form. That is a powerful barrier because it cannot but resonate in everyone; we are all living still our childish fears at some level. Moreover, there is probably not one of us who believes who does not also feel that his or her faith is in some important respects childish.

The third main wall, or main access gate of the citadel, is the moral one, the one that has been the staple of Enlightenment writers since Voltaire. Turning to spiritual matters is turning away from the urgent tasks of improving the human condition; indeed, it can lead us to act directly against this goal, as we see in events all the way from the eighteenth-century persecution of French Protestant Jean Calas[20] to the 9/11 terrorist attacks.

These are the main sides of the citadel, but there are others: The belief in a virtually measureless universe of indifferent matter, from which in some way we emerge, can awaken a sense of awe, even a sense mystery, something eighteenth-century thinkers tried to capture with their notion of the sublime. This has also been a powerful draw toward unbelief. Think of Hardy, or certain passages of Nietzsche, or Dawkins in his poetic moments.

Then there is the subsection of the third wall that codes religion as authority, beyond reason, and an enemy of freedom. This is an important part of the story of religion as misanthropy.[21]

---

20. After his adult son committed suicide, Calas was falsely charged with strangling his son to keep him from converting to Catholicism. The conviction was overturned after Voltaire argued the family's case before the king and council of state at Versailles, but not before Calas was tortured and executed.

21. Luc Ferry, *L'Homme-Dieu ou le sens de la vie* (Paris: Grasset, 1996).

Here is a pencil sketch of a many-sided position where a number of different considerations draw us together to a central stance—one big "bad" place,
from the standpoint of faith. One is nudged one way rather than another in
a series of crucial turning points: to materialism, to the master narrative of
Enlightenment as maturity, to religion as misanthropy; and then one is locked
in. Of course there are motivational cruxes at each of these turns. What if
one responded to the accusation that faith betokens immaturity (a deadly
one, as I argued above, because autobiographically, you know that it has a
lot of truth to it), by following the injunction to "be like little children"?
More precisely, one might sense that this kind of "maturity" wanted to foreclose the kind of transformation of heart and being that the gospel lays
before us; and one puts fidelity to this transformation first. It is clear that the
allures of the citadel would look terribly flat and uninteresting to the desert
fathers. But situated as we are, we hesitate, have second thoughts, feel the
weight of scorn. Indeed, the desert fathers would see how much the fear of
that scorn weighs with us.

What does this tell us about faith and reason? We can see that the turns
into the citadel have a volitional component. Indeed, the whole position inter-
weaves judgment and desire. Do we want to speak here of "volitional depravity"? In one sense, this is obviously right since anything that turns us from
God must take us from our right path. But rhetorically, in our culture, where
we usually reserve the term for serial killers, we may just be throwing sand in
our own eyes when we use the term.

That is because there is a lot of good in the citadel. Once embarked on the
wrong turn of seeing the service of God as inimical to the human race, one
can be moved by great generosity to act for human good. Of course, the generosity is inwardly poisoned by the sense of one's superiority over those
benighted believers, but Christians are hardly free from sentiments of this
order. If we are thinking not of what we can prove, in some context-free
sense, but rather of how to help people out of a citadel that is really a prison,
then we will need to speak to what is best in it, rather than simply polemiciz-
ing against what is worst.

One of the obvious bad features of the materialist citadel is that it makes
people inarticulate about what really moves them to the good: for instance,
the sense that human beings have an exalted status, in virtue of which they
cannot be treated as things or animals, that they should be succored, that they
should be given the chance to flourish, and so on. Very often secularists have
trouble saying what it is about human beings that constitutes this status. This
can become an urgently relevant matter when it is a question of discussing
issues of medical life and death, or human and animal rights, and so on. But
I am not raising it here in order to aliment a polemic on this kind of issue.

Rather, my point is this: The positive answers about what gives human
beings dignity (*Würde*, in Kant's sense) can be surprisingly thin and unsatisfactory in the mouths of many secularists, just because the citadel will not
allow them to say certain things. So people talk about the dignity that
attaches to thinking beings, reasoning beings, beings capable of choice. Or

else driven by tough-minded utilitarian considerations, they may try to confine the relevant features to the capacity to feel pleasure and pain. But even at the highest, "Kantian," end of these descriptions, there is so much missing, which you can see if you look at a work such as Jean Vanier's L'Arche, where handicapped people are housed and cared for. The miracle is that this care is devoid of the kind of objectifying look *de haut en bas* that recurs so often in the caring professions in relation to people who are in various ways incapacitated or helpless.[22] When people speak about this with Vanier and those who work there, they say things such as "the handicapped are also our teachers; we learn so much from them." Anyone can say this; the "miracle" is that they mean it. And they can mean it because they see something beyond the standard human faculties conferring "dignity" in the Kantian perspective. They are seeing their charges as beings capable of love, very often in forms that are rare among the independent, fully functioning adults in the world around us.

No one who is moved by a sense of human dignity can help being touched at some level by this concrete demonstration that dignity has a wider and deeper base than our standard philosophy accepts. Touched, one will be. Whether one goes along with this insight, or shuts it out to protect the citadel, is of course another question. But this is an example of what I mean by speaking to what is good in the fortress; a point where its philanthropy, in the original sense of this term, can meet something fuller and deeper in the same genre, an appeal to go beyond in the same direction, inviting a transition to a better place.

---

22. See Richard Sennett, *Respect in a World of Inequality* (New York: W. W. Norton, 2003).

Contributors

Martin Bieler, *Privatdozent* in systematic theology at the University of Berne (Switzerland), is an ordained pastor of the Swiss Reformed Church. He is the author of *Freiheit als Gabe: Ein schöpfungstheologischer Entwurf* (Freiburg: Herder, 1991) and *Befreiung der Freiheit: Zur Theologie der stellvertretenden Sühne* (Freiburg: Herder, 1996).

Romanus Cessario, OP, professor of moral theology at St. John's Seminary, Brighton, Massachusetts, is a priest of the Roman Catholic Church. His most recent books include *The Moral Virtues and Theological Ethics* (Notre Dame, IN: University of Notre Dame Press, 1991), *Introduction to Moral Theology* (Washington, DC: Catholic University of America Press, 2001), *The Virtues, or the Examined Life* (New York: Continuum, 1994, 2002), and *A Short History of Thomism* (Washington, DC: Catholic University of America Press, 2004).

Paul J. Griffiths, Schmitt Chair of Catholic Studies at the University of Illinois at Chicago, is a member of the Roman Catholic Church. His most recent books include *Religious Reading: The Place of Reading in the Practice of Religion* (New York: Oxford University Press, 1999), *Problems of Religious Diversity* (Oxford: Blackwell, 2001), and *Lying: An Augustinian Theology of Duplicity* (Grand Rapids: Brazos, 2004).

Colin Gunton (1941–2003) was professor of systematic theology at King's College, London, and an ordained minister of the United Reformed Church, England. Among his numerous books are *The One, the Three, and the Many: God, Creation, and the Culture of Modernity* (Cambridge: Cambridge University Press, 1993), *The Triune Creator: A Historical and Systematic Study* (Grand Rapids: Eerdmans, 1998), *The Christian Faith: An Introduction to Christian Doctrine* (Oxford: Blackwell, 2002), *Act and Being: Towards a*

Theology of the Divine Attributes (Grand Rapids: Eerdmans, 2002), and *The Theology of Reconciliation* (London: T & T Clark, 2003).

David Bentley Hart has taught historical and systematic theology at the University of Virginia; the University of St. Thomas, St. Paul; Duke University Divinity School; and Loyola College, Baltimore. He is Eastern Orthodox and the author of *The Beauty of the Infinite: The Aesthetics of Christian Truth* (Grand Rapids: Eerdmans, 2003).

Reinhard Hütter, associate professor of Christian theology at Duke University Divinity School, is a member of the Roman Catholic Church. His most recent books include *Suffering Divine Things: Theology as Church Practice* (Grand Rapids: Eerdmans, 2000), and *Bound to Be Free: Evangelical Catholic Engagements in Ecclesiology, Ethics, and Ecumenism* (Grand Rapids: Eerdmans, 2004).

Robert W. Jenson, senior research fellow at the Center of Theological Inquiry in Princeton, New Jersey, is an ordained pastor of the Evangelical Lutheran Church in America. Among his numerous books are *Unbaptized God: The Basic Flaw in Ecumenical Theology* (Minneapolis: Fortress, 1992), *Systematic Theology*, 2 vols. (New York: Oxford University Press, 1997–1999), and *On Thinking the Human: Resolutions of Difficult Notions* (Grand Rapids: Eerdmans, 2003).

Lois Malcolm, associate professor of systematic theology at Luther Seminary, St. Paul, is a member of the Evangelical Lutheran Church in America. She is the author of *Kenotic Abundance: The Wisdom and Power of the Cross* (Grand Rapids: Eerdmans, forthcoming).

Bruce D. Marshall, professor of systematic and historical theology at Perkins School of Theology, Southern Methodist University, Dallas, is a member of the Evangelical Lutheran Church in America. He is the author of *Christology in Conflict: The Identity of a Saviour in Rahner and Barth* (Oxford: Blackwell, 1987), and *Trinity and Truth* (Cambridge: Cambridge University Press, 2000).

Ernstpeter Maurer is professor of systematic theology at the University of Dortmund, Germany, and a member of the Evangelical Church of Westphalia, Germany. His most recent books include *Der Mensch im Geist: Untersuchungen zur Anthropologie bei Hegel und Luther* (Gütersloh: Kaiser, Gütersloher Verlagshaus, 1996), *Rechtfertigung: konfessionstrennend oder konfessionsverbindend?* (Göttingen: Vandenhoeck & Ruprecht, 1998), and *Luther* (Freiburg: Herder, 1999).

Mark McIntosh, associate professor of theology, Loyola University, Chicago, is a priest of the Episcopal Church. He is the author of *Christology from Within: Spirituality and the Incarnation in Hans Urs von Balthasar* (Notre Dame, IN: University of Notre Dame Press, 1996), *Mystical Theology: The Integrity of Spirituality and Theology* (Oxford: Blackwell, 1998), and *Mysteries of Faith* (Cambridge, MA: Cowley Publications, 2000).

Janet Martin Soskice, reader in modern theology and philosophical theology, University of Cambridge, is a member of the Roman Catholic Church. She is the author of *Metaphor and Religious Language* (Oxford: Clarendon, 1985) and of the forthcoming *Naming God*.

Charles Taylor, emeritus professor of philosophy at McGill University, Montreal, is a member of the Roman Catholic Church. Among his numerous books are *Hegel* (Cambridge: Cambridge University Press, 1975), *Sources of the Self: The Making of Modern Identity* (Cambridge, MA: Harvard University Press, 1989), *The Ethics of Authenticity* (Cambridge, MA: Harvard University Press, 1991), *Philosophical Arguments* (Cambridge, MA: Harvard University Press, 1995), and *Varieties of Religion Today: William James Revisited* (Cambridge, MA: Harvard University Press, 2002).

Alan J. Torrance, professor of systematic theology at the University of St. Andrews, Scotland, is an ordained minister of the Church of Scotland. He is the author of *Persons in Communion: An Essay on Trinitarian Description and Human Participation* (Edinburgh: T & T Clark, 1996).

Carver T. Yu, vice president and professor of systematic theology at China Graduate School of Theology, Hong Kong, is an ordained minister of the Hong Kong Presbytery of the Cumberland Presbyterian Church. His most recent books include *Being and Relation: A Theological Critique of Western Dualism and Individualism* (Edinburgh: Scottish Academic, 1987), *History of Christianity from a New Perspective* (Taipei: Reformation Translation Fellowship, 1994), *Freedom and Commitment* (Hong Kong: Chinese Christian Literature Council, 2001), and *Life Is Beautiful: The Glory of Being Human in Literature* (Hong Kong: Chinese Christian Literature Council, 2004).

Index of Authors

Index of Subjects